HINDENBURG
AND THE
WEIMAR REPUBLIC

PAUL VON HINDENBURG

1847-1934

HINDENBURG

AND THE

WEIMAR REPUBLIC

ANDREAS DORPALEN

PRINCETON, NEW JERSEY

PRINCETON UNIVERSITY PRESS

1964

Publication of this book has been aided by the
Ford Foundation program to support publication,
through university presses, of works in the humani-
ties and social sciences

Printed in the United States of America
by THE WILLIAM BYRD PRESS, INC.

TO THE MEMORY OF

LUDWIG DORPALEN

1876 · 1942

PREFACE

ESPITE the vital role he played during the declining years of the Weimar Republic, Field Marshal-President Paul von Hindenburg has received comparatively little scholarly attention. Stolid and inarticulate, he seemed to lack that human appeal that arouses the historian's interest, and as a maker of history he left his imprint on the course of events by inaction rather than action. Yet for this very reason a study of the Weimar Republic centered on him offers a particularly fruitful approach to that state's tragic story. As a man without political interests and initiative, Hindenburg had few political views of his own and while he had strong emotional attachments, he was always ready to adjust to the predominant trends and pressures of his time. His attitudes and decisions thus provide not only a key to his personality, but can serve also as a sensitive barometer of the prevailing political climate of which they were an effect much more than a cause.

At the same time, the fact that Hindenburg could emerge as the central figure during those years of crisis, in spite of his marked personal limitations, constitutes in itself a significant facet of the Weimar tragedy. The qualities of detached wisdom and determination with which the "Hindenburg myth" had endowed him since the early days of World War I were those the country needed most, and the varying fortunes of that myth, the changing attitudes of his countrymen toward him during the years of his presidency are also an integral and revealing part of Weimar history.

Closely interwoven, the stories of Hindenburg and of the Weimar Republic thus confront the historian with challenging political, social, and psychological problems; they are deepened by the human drama overshadowing Hindenburg's life throughout his presidency. The victim as much as the beneficiary of the "Hindenburg myth," he found himself drawn into politics which he detested, called upon to make decisions he would have liked to avoid, and forever torn between the dictates of common sense and his emotional preferences. To evade these conflicts, Hindenburg preferred to remain in the background rather than occupy the center of the political stage and let others assume the lead and responsibility for actions and policies. Thus, once again, his story and that of the Weimar era easily blend

vii

into one, and the present study is as much that of the Weimar Republic as it is that of the man who headed it for the greater part of its fretful existence.

In writing this book I have had help from a great many sources. I am especially indebted to Dr. Heinrich Doehle, a member of Hindenburg's secretariat; Dr. Hermann Pünder, *Staatssekretär* to Chancellors Marx, Müller, and Brüning; and Dr. Walter Zechlin, *Reichspressechef* during the larger part of Hindenburg's presidency, who have answered innumerable questions, both orally and in writing. I have also had valuable help from Dr. Heinrich Brüning, the former chancellor, and from Dorothea Groener-Geyer. Adelgunde Gräfin von Westarp, Dr. Friedrich Freiherr Hiller von Gaertringen, *Landgerichtsdirektor* Josef Marx, Ruth Groener, Maria Freifrau von Gayl, and Otto Schmidt-Hannover have given me access to documentary sources in their possession. I need hardly add that the conclusions drawn from the information and materials provided to me are solely my own.

I am also most grateful for the help I have had from the staffs of the Bundesarchiv, Koblenz; the Hoover Institute and Library, Stanford, California; the Institute for Social History, Amsterdam; the Institut für Zeitgeschichte, Munich; the German Social Democratic Party, Bonn; the Stadtarchiv, Cologne; and the U. S. Document Center, Berlin. The librarians at St. Lawrence University and Ohio State University were indefatigable in tracking down books and periodicals, and Colette M. Armstrong, Ann E. Liston, and Jean E. McConnell typed and retyped the manuscript with painstaking care. Professor Harold J. Grimm, chairman of the department of history at Ohio State University, furthered the progress of this book in many ways, and my former colleague, Professor William D. Mallam, of St. Lawrence University, patiently guided me with his editorial advice. Gerald L. Soliday, one of my graduate students, helped gather some of the materials.

This book, finally, could not have been written without the generous financial support I received from the Social Science Research Council, the American Philosophical Society, and the Mershon Program for the Study of National Security at Ohio State University. Ohio State University also facilitated my work by relieving me of my teaching duties during the winter quarter 1961.

My family bore with me during what must have seemed an interminable time of research and writing, patiently going wherever the search for materials took me. My wife spent long hours copying documents, while my son Peter came to my help when I could not cope with the mechanical intricacies of the microfilm projector. Bruce eased many a wearisome task by interested questions. I am very grateful to them for their forbearance.

Andreas Dorpalen

Ohio State University
Columbus, Ohio

CONTENTS

ABBREVIATIONS

BdRPr.	*Büro des Reichspräsidenten*
cab. mtg.	cabinet meeting
Dt.	*Deutsche (r)*
DBFP.	*Documents on British Foreign Policy*
DGFP.	*Documents on German Foreign Policy*
Egelhaaf	Gotthold Egelhaaf, *Politische Jahresübersichten*
Gesch. in Wiss. u. Unterr.	*Geschichte in Wissenschaft und Unterricht*
Gesch.-Kal.	*Geschichts-Kalender*
I.M.T.	International Military Tribunal
Jahrb. d. öff. Rechts	*Jahrbuch des öffentlichen Rechts*
Kl. Erw.	Kleine Erwerbungen
Nazi Conspiracy	Office of U.S. Chief Counsel for Prosecution of Axis Criminality, *Nazi Conspiracy and Aggression*
RKz.	*Reichskanzlei*
Schulthess	Schulthess' *Europäischer Geschichtskalender*
U.D.Z.	*Die Ursachen des Deutschen Zusammenbruchs*
Verhandlungen	*Stenographische Berichte der Verhandlungen des Deutschen Reichstags*
Z. f. GeschWiss.	*Zeitschrift für Geschichtswissenschaft*
ZS.	*Zeugenschrifttum*

HINDENBURG
AND THE
WEIMAR REPUBLIC

CHAPTER 1

EARLY SERVICE IN THE REPUBLIC

IELD Marshal Paul von Hindenburg, second and last president of the Weimar Republic, left his imprint on the earliest beginnings of the republic. The fate of the new state hung uneasily in the balance after its painful birth on November 9, 1918, when the Marshal agreed to join forces with it. A new government, the so-called Council of People's Commissars, struggled desperately to assert its authority in the midst of military defeat and political chaos. Based on a tenuous alliance between the moderate or Majority Socialists and the more radical Independent Socialists, it was at once threatened by Communist Spartacists and extremist Independents in Berlin who called on the starving, embittered masses to overthrow the "traitors of the revolution" and establish a Soviet Republic. The chairman of the Council of People's Commissars, Friedrich Ebert, knew how easily the Bolsheviks had seized power in Russia thanks to their control of the capital; if he were to defeat the Spartacists and their allies, he had to obtain military support. Such support, however, could be provided only by the old monarchist army, but he could not but wonder whether the supreme command of the army would be willing to give it to him.

Fortunately for Ebert, the army command found itself in a dilemma not unlike his own. Deprived of its once unassailable authority, it needed the political support of the government as much as the government needed its military assistance. Its most pressing task was to lead the troops home from enemy territory; beyond this immediate assignment, it was anxious to salvage the officer corps as the nucleus of the future army.[1] Neither mission, however, could be accomplished without the help of a stable, moderate government that enjoyed the confidence of the masses. The interest of the army demanded therefore that it lend its support to the Council of People's Commissars.

The supreme command was headed by Hindenburg, but it was not the marshal who approached Ebert, but his second-in-command, General Wilhelm Groener. The septuagenarian field mar-

[1] Wilhelm Groener, *Lebenserinnerungen: Jugend, Generalstab, Weltkrieg*, Friedrich Freiherr Hiller von Gaertringen, ed. (Göttingen, 1957), p. 467.

3

shal, scion of an old Prussian family, whose life and career were closely interwoven with the rise of the Prusso-German monarchy, would hardly have entered into negotiations with a Socialist, who, as he saw it, had arrogated to himself the place that rightfully belonged to the Kaiser. Quite apart from these emotional inhibitions, Hindenburg was not the man to take on his own such a decisive step as a rapprochement with Ebert. Groener, on the other hand, was a South German of middle-class background and as such more flexible in his outlook and attitude. He had had contact with Socialists in various posts he had held in the war; as director of the War Food Office he had come to know and respect Ebert. It was he who saw the imperative need for an understanding with Ebert, and since he knew that Hindenburg would not want to have any direct dealings with the Socialist leader, he decided to establish the initial contacts by himself, in the name of the marshal. He was confident that Hindenburg would approve of a collaboration with the Socialists once the advantages of such an arrangement had been explained to him.

On the morning of November 10, Groener sent Ebert a telegram in which he informed him of Hindenburg's willingness to supervise the return of the troops. On his part, the marshal "expected" the government to provide transportation and food and full support in the maintenance of military discipline. When he received no answer, he called Ebert on the direct line that connected army headquarters in Spa with Ebert's office in the Reich chancellery. The two men quickly came to an understanding. Once more Groener expressed the willingness of the supreme command to supervise the withdrawal of the field armies; in return, he demanded, in Hindenburg's name, a promise that the government would support the marshal and officer corps in the maintenance of order and discipline in the army. The officer corps, he declared, expected the government to take up the fight against Bolshevism; for this purpose it was putting itself at the disposal of the government. Ebert readily accepted these terms. "Convey the thanks of the government to the Field Marshal," he said with heartfelt relief.[2]

Before Groener could report Ebert's thanks, Hindenburg had to be informed of the agreement that had been reached in his name. As expected, Hindenburg approved of the general's action

2 Groener to Ebert, Nov. 10, 1918, in Lothar Berthold and Helmut Neef, *Militarismus und Opportunismus gegen die November-Revolution: Das Bündnis der rechten SPD-Führung mit der Obersten Heeresleitung, November und Dezember 1918* ([East] Berlin, 1958), pp. 102–03; Groener, *Lebenserinnerungen*, p. 467.

since he too understood that cooperation with the new government offered the only means of ensuring stable conditions. At the same time he was glad to see Groener take the initiative in these unpleasant dealings with the new authorities. Hindenburg continued to maintain this attitude of utter passivity throughout the following weeks and months, never giving a firm commitment or a clear-cut decision. Groener recalls in his memoirs that, "He took hardly ever an active part in the decisions which had to be made. He was informed about everything—and waited to see how things would turn out." For Groener, however, his tacit approval was sufficient. It assured him of the support of his own subordinates, many of whom were reluctant to serve the new republican government. They did, however, accept this necessity when they saw their venerable commander in chief bow to the new reality.[3]

The agreement concluded between Ebert and Groener on that fateful November 10 was concluded between equals and implied no subordination of the supreme command to the government. Each partner derived his authority from a different source, Ebert considering himself the trustee of the nation, while Hindenburg, on whose behalf Groener negotiated, had been entrusted with his post by the Emperor. As in the days of the monarchy, the army and the government faced each other as independent equals, but now there was no monarch to link them together.

From their respective viewpoints the pact involved serious risks for both sides. Ebert was striving for a Germany in which each citizen would enjoy the opportunities of democratic freedom and self-development and in which the army would have its necessary but subordinate military function as a defense force. Now he was lending the precarious prestige of his newly formed government to an army command about whose monarchist and anti-parliamentarian inclinations he could have no doubts. Hindenburg and Groener, in turn, were giving their support to a republican, socialist, and antimilitarist government to which as devout monarchists and professional soldiers they were strongly opposed. They could not envisage a state in which the army was merely an instrument of power and did not also serve as the spiritual backbone of an essentially undisciplined citizenry. They were not willing therefore to content themselves with the secondary role that Ebert wished to assign to the army. As Groener states in his memoirs, "We hoped to secure, through our contribution, part of the power in the new state for army and officer corps. If we

[3] *Ibid.*, p. 468.

succeeded, we would be able to preserve in the new Germany the best and strongest element of our old Prussian values in spite of the Revolution." [4] Yet, whatever the risks, neither side thought it had any choice but to work with the other.

The supreme command derived some evident benefits from the agreement. The pact enabled the generals to lead their troops back in good order, and by protecting the officer corps against social revolution and mutiny, it made possible its survival as a self-centered, homogeneous body with its own goals and values. The advantages the government reaped from the understanding were less obvious. It is true that the Ebert-Groener agreement assured the orderly return of the army, but given its war weariness and demoralization it could not be kept together for further duty once it had reached its home bases. Thus it was unable to provide any effective military help against Spartacists and other insurgents. Its major contribution to the survival of the republic was to associate Hindenburg's name in a sort of silent partnership with the new regime. The fact that the marshal was willing to work with the new government made it easier for most officers to remain at their posts or accept new assignments. Thus, when the office of the Prussian minister of war fell vacant in December 1918, Colonel Walther Reinhardt to whom it was offered accepted it only after he had received the marshal's consent.[5] Similarly, other officers put themselves readily at the disposal of the government when new military formations were organized, knowing that they could count on the approval of Hindenburg.[6]

The existence of a dual authority in the new state had its lasting effect on its power structure. It also helped to keep alive those social and political cleavages that were to plague the republic throughout its short-lived existence. And by some ineluctable historical logic these very problems so closely connected with Hindenburg's shadowy association with the beginnings of the republic catapulted the marshal into the presidency of the Weimar Republic some years later.

ᔕᑎ

The man who helped the Weimar Republic survive in its earliest stages and who was destined to play so significant a role

[4] *Ibid.*, pp. 448–49.

[5] Fritz Ernst, *Aus dem Nachlass des Generals Walther Reinhardt* (Stuttgart, 1958), p. 13.

[6] Karl Dietrich Bracher, *Die Auflösung der Weimarer Republik: Eine Studie zum Problem des Machtverfalls in der Demokratie* (Stuttgart and Düsseldorf, 1955), p. 243; Groener, *Lebenserinnerungen*, p. 468.

during the last years of its existence seemed a rather unlikely candidate for these tasks during the greater part of his life.

Paul (Ludwig Hans Anton) von Beneckendorff und von Hindenburg came from old Prussian Junker stock.[7] Born on October 2, 1847, in the Prussian fortress of Posen, where his father served as an aide to the fortress commander, he was trained in the Prussian cadet corps, and participated in the Prusso-Austrian War of 1866 and the Franco-Prussian War of 1870–71. After the latter campaign he was assigned to the War Academy, and upon his graduation, with high honors, there followed tours of duty in various staff posts, interrupted by brief periods of field service. In 1879, while stationed at Stettin, he married Gertrud von Sperling, the daughter of a Prussian general; she bore him three children, two girls and a son.

Although Hindenburg attracted the attention of his superiors— Count Schlieffen, then a colonel on the general staff and later its famous chief, had words of high praise for his ability[8]—his advancement was not especially rapid, and his assignments were strictly routine. In 1911, after having commanded an army corps for several years, he retired from active service. Sixty-three years old, he was ready to pass on the burden of his duties to younger shoulders. He was not advanced to the rank of colonel general at his retirement, as were others in his position, nor was he appointed *Inspekteur* of any army which would have assured him of a command post in time of war.[9] It was the appropriate ending to an honorable but not especially distinguished career.

The fact, however, remains that of the hundreds of colonels of his generation he was one of the two dozen who had reached the top steps of the military ladder. He had, in fact, been proposed by Schlieffen for chief of the general staff and was mentioned

---

[7] On his mother's side Hindenburg, like Bismarck, was descended from a middle-class family, but he preferred to ignore the *bürgerlich* element in his background. In his memoirs he reports in some detail the history of his paternal ancestors, but is curiously reticent about the family of his mother. Generalfeldmarschall von Hindenburg, *Aus meinem Leben* (Leipzig, 1920), pp. 3–6.

[8] Walter Görlitz, *Hindenburg: Ein Lebensbild* (Bonn, 1953), pp. 35–36. Both Field Marshal von Moltke and Count Waldersee, the Quartermaster General, agreed with Schlieffen's judgment. *Ibid.* Later Schlieffen seems to have changed his mind, however. Discussing Hindenburg's proposed appointment as chief of staff of an army corps in 1896, he felt that Hindenburg had not distinguished himself as a staff officer and had not been entirely satisfactory in the field either. Schlieffen to Gossler, June 20, 1896. Copy in Foerster Papers. Hindenburg did, however, receive an appointment as chief of staff at the time, although not with the corps to which he was to be assigned originally.

[9] Information from Col. Hermann Teske, head of the *Militärarchiv* at the *Bundesarchiv*, Koblenz.

for war minister in 1909.[10] While his family belonged to the old *Militäradel,* it was not especially well connected, nor was the taciturn, stolid Hindenburg the man to cultivate social contacts in order to further his career. Obviously, then, his advancement was due to personal qualifications rather than any favoritism, although his assignment to a guards regiment at the outset of his career gave him a headstart over less fortunate classmates.

Hindenburg's special qualities did not primarily pertain to the military sphere. What his superiors valued in him were personal attributes of appearance and temperament. Huge even by army standards, the tall, slow-moving man had an imposing presence; his imperturbable calm conveyed the impression of determined strength and endowed him with unquestioned authority. "I remember a number of people from the nineteen-thirties who were not exactly shy or easily flustered," one observer wrote recently, "yet who had something like stage fright and felt quite unsure of themselves when they were to face Hindenburg. This was not merely a matter of the authority of the office, even less that of military rank or glory or old age; rather there was at work here a personal fluidum to which few who met him remained immune." Hindenburg was aware of this personal impact; he was not, the observer points out, an actor who carefully chose, trained, and rehearsed his voice and his gestures, but he sensed that this effect required a disciplined bearing, and this he consciously cultivated. "He always faced people outside [his immediate family] circle with evident self-control, concerned with his dignity, even when he sought to be jovial. To display such dignified bearing, he considered his duty. . . , but without this personal substance this conscious display could hardly have had the strong effect to which so many have testified."[11]

To his superiors these qualities must have seemed important enough to compensate for his lack of initiative and imagination. When Schlieffen proposed him as his successor, he may have looked on Hindenburg as a faithful executor of his (Schlieffen's) plans rather than as a resourceful planner. By his authoritative and yet conciliatory nature he could be expected to preserve the general staff as a smoothly functioning machine. But the terms of

10 Görlitz, *Hindenburg,* pp. 42, 44–45; Fürst Bernhard von Bülow, *Denkwürdigkeiten,* Franz von Stockhammern, ed. (Berlin, 1930–31), II, 203–04; Friedrich von Boetticher, *Schlieffen* (Göttingen, 1957), p. 71.

11 Theodor Eschenburg, "Die Rolle der Persönlichkeit in der Krise der Weimarer Republik: Hindenburg, Brüning, Groener, Schleicher," *Vierteljahrshefte für Zeitgeschichte,* IX (1961), 3–4.

his retirement suggest also that these gifts were not considered sufficient to entrust him with a major wartime appointment.

Nevertheless shortly after World War I broke out in 1914, Hindenburg was given the command of an army in East Prussia. His appointment, however, was made only after his chief of staff, Major General Erich Ludendorff, had been selected, and was meant to provide that able but headstrong and temperamental officer with a nominal superior who could be trusted not to interfere with decisions.[12]

The genesis of their collaboration set the tone for their subsequent relationship. Throughout the war Ludendorff seems to have been the initiator of their plans and policies, while Hindenburg, as he put it in his memoirs, considered it as his foremost task to allow and, if necessary, secure Ludendorff as much leeway as possible in his planning.[13] Hindenburg, however, was not merely a figurehead, and the impact of his personality gave their partnership its distinct character. In Hindenburg's composure, Ludendorff found a counterpoise and on more than one occasion was steadied by it.[14] Hindenburg's conciliatory ways also helped to ease the strain created by Ludendorff's domineering ways at headquarters.[15]

Soon the impact of Hindenburg's personality began to extend beyond the men under his command. Within days after the victory of Tannenberg over the Russians in August 1914, he became a national hero and his name a household word. The nation, terrified at the thought of further Russian advances, felt immensely relieved at the news of the crushing defeat which had

---

[12] For the details of Hindenburg's selection see Groener's account to Schnee in *Deutsche Rundschau*, LXXVII (1951), 793–94.

[13] Hindenburg, *Aus meinem Leben*, p. 78.

[14] Hoffman to his wife, Oct. 21, 1914, Jan. 7, 1916, Hoffmann Papers/1; Elard von Oldenburg-Januschau, *Erinnerungen* (Berlin, 1936), pp. 133–34; Eugen Schiffer, *Ein Leben für den Liberalismus* (Berlin-Grunewald, 1951), p. 45. Hindenburg's calm may have saved the day at a critical point in the famous battle of Tannenberg, in August 1914, although Ludendorff has denied ever having considered a withdrawal. See Walter Elze, *Tannenberg* (Breslau, 1928), pp. 131–33, 368–70; Erich Ludendorff, *Vom Feldherrn zum Weltrevolutionär und Wegbereiter deutscher Volksschöpfung: Meine Lebenserinnerungen* (Munich, 1940–51), II, 365. Hindenburg himself is vague on this point in his memoirs, *Aus meinem Leben*, p. 87. Extensive materials on this question in the files of the *Büro des Reichspräsidenten* contain conflicting accounts. A statement for the *Reichsarchiv*, approved by the Marshal on February 9, 1933, does not clarify the issue completely either. *BdRPr.*, R 54/269.

[15] General Wetzell, quoted in Hans von Haeften, *Hindenburg und Ludendorff als Feldherrn* (Berlin, 1937), pp. 49–50; General Count von der Schulenburg, in *Die Ursachen des deutschen Zusammenbruchs. Das Werk des Untersuchungsausschusses* (Berlin, 1925) (hereafter cited as *U.D.Z.*), iv, iii, 368.

been inflicted on the Tsar's forces. Hindenburg was hailed as a brilliant strategist, a great general and leader of men—a belief that official propaganda agencies carefully fostered to divert attention from the difficulties on the western front. It soon became clear, however, that the nation saw in him more than a victorious army leader. Hindenburg became in the popular mind the symbol of the state's might and the guarantor of victory: he inspired the reassurance needed in this hour of crisis that no one else had been able to give. His massive figure with its square head, his calm composed features, the impression of authority which his pictures conveyed, inspired new confidence in a people that had just felt the first twinges of uncertainty about the war's outcome. Hindenburg seemed like a rock, steadfast and imperturbable, that no enemy could defeat.

While the emergence of the Hindenburg "myth" had its mass psychological advantages, it tended to complicate matters on a higher level. The Kaiser had shared the nation's relief at the news of the victory at Tannenberg; he had duly honored Hindenburg and had raised him, successively, to the rank of colonel general and field marshal. But the volatile highstrung monarch had never had any liking for this stolid old man, and he found it exasperating to see Hindenburg acquire a prestige that was beginning to overshadow his own. With the passing of time the problem of the relationship between the Kaiser and Hindenburg grew more acute. As the war wore on, month after month, there was a growing demand that the victor of Tannenberg be entrusted with the over-all command of the German forces. Frustrated and uneasy, the country came to believe that only Hindenburg and Ludendorff could give it the victory that eluded the Kaiser and his chief of staff, General Erich von Falkenhayn. As long as he could, the Emperor refused to give in to the nation's wishes. He thought that Falkenhayn's qualifications were superior to those of Hindenburg-Ludendorff, and he sensed that by entrusting the supreme command to these two men, he would be yielding new ground to the marshal to the detriment of his own standing; in the end, he feared, he might be pushed entirely into the background and become a mere figurehead. Events, however, forced his hand. After a series of setbacks on both the eastern and western fronts in the spring of 1916, the clamor for the immediate appointment of Hindenburg and Ludendorff to the supreme command grew into an irrepressible furor.[16]

[16] Andreas Dorpalen, "Empress Auguste Victoria and the Fall of the German Monarchy," *American Historical Review*, LVIII (1952), 26.

It is indicative of Hindenburg's tremendous prestige that among the most active supporters of this demand were some who wished Hindenburg to replace Falkenhayn, not because his leadership would assure victory, but because victory had become unattainable and only he could convey this fact to the nation without plunging it into a revolution. Bethmann Hollweg, the chancellor, and other government leaders of both the Reich and the states had reached the conclusion that the war could no longer be won militarily (and in a fleeting moment of weakness Hindenburg himself had voiced the same view to Bethmann). A negotiated peace, on the other hand, was bound to disappoint many popular expectations; it could be made acceptable to the country only if Hindenburg as supreme commander lent it his full authority as the best possible solution. Erzberger, one of the leaders of the Catholic Center Party, trying to make Hindenburg's appointment palatable to the Emperor, went so far as to suggest to one of the monarch's aides that with Hindenburg in Falkenhayn's post the Kaiser could even afford to lose the war, for with the marshal's appointment he had done everything possible. To lose the war without Hindenburg, on the other hand, would mean the end of the dynasty.[17]

William still hesitated, but the voice of the people was growing too strong and too desperate to be ignored any longer. Falkenhayn's position had become untenable, and Hindenburg was the only possible successor to his post. In the end, urged by his family as well as his staff, the monarch gave in. On August 29, 1916, Hindenburg became chief of the general staff and Ludendorff was made his co-responsible first quartermaster general.

In contrast to Falkenhayn Hindenburg became not only the chief of the general staff, acting as the Emperor's top military adviser, but was also put in charge of the supreme war command, the monarch's special prerogative. This position Hindenburg exercised largely himself, in the name of the Kaiser; nominally he remained subordinate to the Emperor, and personally he continued to accept this status of subordination.

His indispensability to the country gave Hindenburg powers that William did not dare challenge. To Hindenburg, the tradi-

[17] Karl Heinz Janssen, "Der Wechsel in der Obersten Heeresleitung 1916," *Vierteljahrshefte für Zeitgeschichte*, VII (1959), 337–71 (Hindenburg's view on p. 341); Erzberger, quoted in Georg Alexander von Müller, *Regierte der Kaiser? Kriegstagebücher, Aufzeichnungen und Briefe des Chefs des Marine-Kabinetts Admiral G. A. von Müller*, Walter Görlitz, ed. (Göttingen, 1959), pp. 183–84; also Max Weber, in Marianne Weber, *Max Weber: Ein Lebensbild* (Tübingen, 1926), p. 584.

tional monarchist, they meant little. Ludendorff, however, lost no time in using his newly gained powers and insisted on the adoption of a stepped-up production plan, significantly called the "Hindenburg-Programm," rather than the "Kaiser-Wilhelm-Programm," and on the enactment of an auxiliary labor service law in complete disregard of the needs and realities of the home front. The demand for unrestricted submarine warfare soon followed— over Bethmann Hollweg's objections that without proper diplomatic preparation this might bring the United States into the war. When the Emperor's approval of an unlimited U-boat campaign had been obtained, Ludendorff set out to engineer Bethmann Hollweg's dismissal. The generals considered the chancellor too weak and too ready to compromise,[18] and bitterly opposed his attempts to improve civilian morale by electoral reforms that they claimed would weaken both the army and the home front. They launched their final assault on Bethmann Hollweg in July 1917 when he failed to prevent the Reichstag from demanding the early conclusion of a peace without annexations; they felt such a demand could only strengthen the enemy's determination to destroy Germany. Aided by a growing opposition to Bethmann in the Reichstag, the generals threatened to resign should Bethmann remain in office. The chancellor knew that he had no choice but to submit his own resignation, and the Kaiser felt compelled to accept it. Acceptance of the generals' resignation had become inconceivable, but so had a denial of their request, for it was not even considered.[19]

Hindenburg alone would never have insisted on the removal of Bethmann Hollweg though he had no great liking for him. In fact, the great fear of Ludendorff and his closest collaborators was that should the Emperor insist on retaining Bethmann, Hindenburg would bow to the Kaiser's wishes.[20] Carefully timed, Ludendorff's final attack on Bethmann was launched in July 1917 at the height of the Reichstag crisis when the Emperor could be

[18] On Bethmann Hollweg's actual views and the pressures to which he was subjected, see the informative book by Fritz Fischer, *Griff nach der Weltmacht: Die Kriegszielpolitik des kaiserlichen Deutschlands 1914/18* (Düsseldorf, 1962).

[19] Th[eobald] von Bethmann Hollweg, *Betrachtungen zum Weltkrieg* (Berlin, 1920–21), II, 169–238; Bernhard Schwertfeger, *Kaiser und Kabinettschef: Nach eigenen Aufzeichnungen und dem Briefwechsel des Wirklichen Geheimen Rates Rudolf von Valentini* (Oldenburg, 1930), pp. 146–67; same, in *U.D.Z.*, IV, iv, 28–31; Oberst [Max] Bauer, *Der grosse Krieg in Feld und Heimat: Erinnerungen und Betrachtungen* (Tübingen, 1921), pp. 123–24; Dorpalen, "Empress Auguste Victoria," pp. 27–28.

[20] Bauer, *Der grosse Krieg*, pp. 123–24, 141; same to Frank, May 5, 1926, Bauer Papers/34; Ludendorff, in Erich Eyck, *Geschichte der Weimarer Republik* (Erlenbach/Zurich and Stuttgart, 1954–56), I, 32.

expected to give in: General Ludendorff submitted his resignation, and the marshal, as Ludendorff put it in his memoirs, thereupon joined him in submitting his. To make his position unmistakably clear, Ludendorff allowed the statement to leak out that this time, he, for one, would not make any further concessions. His threat had the desired effect.

After the removal of Bethmann Hollweg there remained few limits to the dominant power of the supreme command. Bethmann's successor, Michaelis, was appointed only after he had been approved by Hindenburg and Ludendorff, and Count Hertling, who replaced Michaelis a few months later, owed his appointment in turn to the fact that he was known as an enthusiastic supporter of the generals. Those found unacceptable were relieved of their posts. Among the victims was Herr von Valentini, the chief of the Emperor's civil cabinet, who had tried to salvage a few of the Kaiser's diminishing prerogatives; in January 1918 he was replaced by Friedrich von Berg, a staunch admirer of Hindenburg. Richard von Kühlmann, Hertling's foreign secretary, whose realism the army leaders considered defeatist, was also forced to resign. The generals interceded with similar lack of restraint in the formulation of policies: during the peace negotiations with Russia, they forced the Emperor and the government, under new threats of resignation, to insist on much larger territorial acquisitions than the latter considered advisable. William made one more half-hearted effort to relegate the generals once more to the military sphere, but did not pursue it because he knew that he was powerless to do so. Everyone else seemed to know this too, with the possible exception of Hindenburg; having no personal interest in power he continued dutifully to make himself Ludendorff's mouthpiece and supported the latter's demands. Yet he remained as respectful as ever of the Emperor and carefully toned down the letters addressed to the Kaiser which his aggressive associate drafted for him—as always he considered himself his Emperor's loyal servant.[21] He does not seem to have realized that, following Ludendorff's counsel, he was constantly impinging on the rights and prerogatives of the monarch and thus weakening the latter's position.

The full extent of Hindenburg's public stature was revealed in the hour of Germany's defeat. On September 29, 1918, the gen-

21 When at the height of the military crisis on September 29, 1918, Foreign Secretary von Hintze urged him to hurry at once to the Emperor to request the immediate initiation of armistice talks, the Marshal demurred since it was only 11 a.m. and he had his daily audience with the Kaiser only at noon. Hintze, in *U.D.Z.*, IV, ii, 401.

erals demanded the immediate conclusion of an armistice to avert a military catastrophe. Some days later, however, they became more confident again of the army's ability to withstand further enemy attacks and chided the government for submitting to the terms which President Wilson was stipulating in the armistice negotiations. On October 24, the supreme command issued an order to be read to all troops denouncing Wilson's latest message and demanding the immediate evacuation of all occupied territory as "unacceptable to us soldiers." This answer, the statement continued, "can mean but one thing for us—to carry on the fight with all the strength at our disposal. If our enemies realize that they cannot break through the German lines despite all sacrifices, they will be ready to grant us a peace which will safeguard Germany's future and especially that of the broad masses of our people." The order was believed to express the government's views and was meant to strengthen the latter's hand in the armistice negotiations. It was perhaps the only army order signed by Hindenburg before it had been submitted to Ludendorff for approval. Whatever its purpose, it virtually decreed that the armistice negotiations be broken off. It caused a furor in government circles and was sharply attacked in the Reichstag. Yet although it had gone out over Hindenburg's signature, the attacks were directed at Ludendorff. The newly appointed Chancellor Prince Max von Baden asked the Emperor to dismiss Ludendorff, but insisted that Hindenburg remain since the departure of the marshal would plunge the army and nation into despair. On the following day the Kaiser met with the generals, and after a heated exchange with Ludendorff relieved the latter of his post. Hindenburg witnessed the scene in silence, and said no word in defense of his long-time associate; he offered his own resignation, on the grounds that he did not wish to part with his trusted collaborator. His request was rejected, and he bowed to the Emperor's decision.[22]

The news of Ludendorff's dismissal caused little excitement since Hindenburg remained at his post. The nation greeted his staying with genuine relief. When told of Ludendorff's resignation Prince

[22] Prinz Max von Baden, *Erinnerungen und Dokumente* (Stuttgart, 1927), pp. 492–506; Ludendorff, *Kriegserinnerungen*, pp. 614–17; Albrecht von Thaer, *Generalstabsdienst an der Front und in der O.H.L.: Aus den Briefen und Tagebuchaufzeichnungen 1915–1919*, ed. by Siegfried A. Kaehler and Helmuth K.G. Rönnefarth (Göttingen, 1958), pp. 247–48. Hindenburg covers the incident in one vague paragraph, *Aus meinem Leben*, p. 396. See also Alexander Griebel, "Das Jahr 1918 im Lichte neuer Publikationen," *Vierteljahrshefte für Zeitgeschichte*, VI (1958), 373–76.

Max was in conference with some cabinet members. "And Hindenburg?" he asked. "He stays." The ministers, he recalls, jumped up from their chairs and expressed their relief with a heartfelt "Thank God." That same day, Gustav Stresemann, the leader of the National Liberals, wrote to a party friend: "I trust you will agree with me when I ask you to do everything in your power to prevent Hindenburg's departure from his post. Under no circumstances must we allow ourselves to be burdened with the responsibility, in the judgment of history, of having overthrown Hindenburg. I believe that we could bear more easily the abdication of the Emperor than Hindenburg's leaving." A press survey made by the army found that except for those of the extreme left all papers agreed that Hindenburg was rendering the country a great service by remaining at his post. Even Socialist papers were glad to see him stay on, "since, ever the soldier, he had kept from meddling in politics and could be expected to observe this same restraint in the future." There was general agreement, too, that though he would not return as the victor, his name would always be held in the highest esteem by the nation.[23]

Hindenburg's survival of the defeat with his military fame unimpaired was the more remarkable since he had always emphasized that the responsibility for any failure was ultimately his. To Ludendorff's dismay he had readily accepted the chief credit for the victories their armies had won on the grounds that he, as Ludendorff's superior, would also have had to bear the onus of any defeat.[24] Yet there was no mention now, in the face of defeat, of Hindenburg's responsibility, and his prestige remained undiminished.

ᔐ

Though the military defeat did not affect Hindenburg's popular standing, the role he played in connection with the Emperor's abdication in November 1918 was to be a source of continued difficulties for him.

In one of the notes with which Wilson had answered the German request for an armistice and a peace treaty, he had hinted

---

[23] Max von Baden, *Erinnerungen*, pp. 504, 512; Stresemann to Friedberg, Oct. 26, 1918, in Gustav Stresemann, *Vermächtnis: Der Nachlass in drei Bänden*, Harry Bernhard, Wolfgang Goetz, and Paul Wiegler, eds. (Berlin, 1932–33), I, 12–13; Schallehn, "Die deutsche Presse zum Rücktritt des Generals Ludendorff," MS., Groener Papers/26/237.

[24] Hindenburg, quoted by Johannes Haller, in *Die Welt als Geschichte*, XIX (1959), 124; also Oldenburg-Januschau, *Erinnerungen*, p. 221; Franz von Papen, *Der Wahrheit eine Gasse* (Munich, 1952), p. 142.

that the Emperor's abdication might secure more favorable peace terms for Germany. Wilson left no doubt, moreover, that he could not be fully convinced of the sincerity of Germany's constitutional reforms as long as the Kaiser remained on the throne. The feeling gained ground among the war-weary masses that only the person of the monarch prevented the conclusion of an early armistice. By the end of October 1918 there was a widespread demand for the abdication of the Emperor to bring hostilities to an end.

If Hindenburg paid any attention to these demands, he brushed them off as fantastic and frivolous; there was no room for such thoughts in his world of monarchist loyalty. Such demands were merely the work of contemptible radical schemers, and at first the abdication request seemed unreal to him. It lost its remoteness, however, when on October 30 William appeared at supreme headquarters at the Belgian resort town of Spa, explaining that he wished to be with his troops in their hour of crisis. He had in fact left Berlin at the urging of his wife and one or two confidants who feared that he might give in to the growing demand for his abdication. The Empress had always had great admiration for Hindenburg, who appealed to her in his stolid simplicity, and she was certain he would protect her husband from all pernicious influences and reject any suggestion of abdication.[25]

The hope that the abdication problems could be ignored at headquarters was futile. Prince Max was convinced by now that William's abdication was imperative. If the monarchy was to be saved, both the Kaiser and the Crown Prince would have to give up the throne at once. He dispatched an envoy to Spa to acquaint William with the domestic situation and the widespread demand for his abdication; but supported by Hindenburg and Groener, who had taken Ludendorff's place, the Kaiser rejected all thought of abdication. During a brief stay in Berlin, however, on November 5 and 6, Groener became convinced that William's abdication had become unavoidable.[26] A mutiny had broken out at the naval base at Kiel, and there had been alarming reports of disobedience in other parts of the country. Yet it was not until the evening of November 8 that he convinced Hindenburg that the army no longer stood by the Emperor. By then most garrisons in the Reich had gone over to the revolutionaries, large-scale desertions were

25 Dorpalen, "Empress Auguste Victoria," p. 36.
26 By this time the retention of William on the throne was actually no longer an issue in the pre-armistice negotiations. On November 5 the Western Powers had informed Germany of their willingness to negotiate an armistice with Germany even though William was still Emperor.

being reported from Liège and Namur, and the flow of supplies was reduced to a trickle. The moderate Socialists, who had been willing to preserve the monarchy provided both Emperor and Crown Prince withdrew, showed signs of increasing restiveness as the days passed without any move by the Kaiser. Their leaders had frantically warned before November 8 that they could not restrain their followers any longer—the rank-and-file of the party was ready to join forces with the more radical Independent Socialists and overthrow the monarchy altogether. There was still a slim chance of saving the monarchy if William abdicated at once, but the generals could not bring themselves to acquaint the monarch with the gravity of the crisis.[27]

In the early morning of November 9 another emissary of the chancellor, Admiral von Hintze, appeared at Hindenburg's office. Prince Max's liaison man at army headquarters brought with him the latest messages from the capital—all of them warned that unless the Emperor abdicated at once, a revolution would sweep him and the monarchy away. Hintze persuaded the marshal that the Kaiser must be informed at once of the hopelessness of his position. With a heavy heart the marshal set out to call on the monarch; on his way Groener joined him, and the two men presented themselves to the Kaiser.

The marshal began by asking to be allowed to resign. He found it unbearable, he lamented, to have to confess to his war lord that he could no longer carry out the Emperor's wishes. William said nothing and turned to Groener. The general could only confirm Hindenburg's views. Colonel General von Plessen, a member of the Emperor's entourage, objected and he was seconded by Count von der Schulenburg, chief of staff of the Crown Prince. Schulenburg was certain that an attack on some of the rebellious garrisons would quickly lead to the restoration of order; reliable troops were available and would be willing after a short rest to march back to Germany under the Emperor's command.[28] Hinden-

27 Max von Baden, *Erinnerungen*, p. 627; Groener's subsequent justification is refuted by a contemporary letter of Thaer; Groener, *Lebenserinnerungen*, p. 456; Thaer, letter of Nov. 15, 1918, in *Generalstabsdienst*, p. 270.

28 Yet some months earlier Schulenburg had already predicted that Emperor and monarchy were probably doomed. General Ludwig Beck, German chief of staff in 1933–38 and one of the leading participants in the anti-Nazi resistance movement, recalled later that on the eve of Ludendorff's great spring offensive of 1918 Schulenburg had warned him: "Mark my words. We'll be very successful in tomorrow's battle; perhaps we'll take as many as 100,000 prisoners and capture 1,000 guns. But in the end our position is going to be worse than before . . . and the chances of winning the war will be even slimmer!" And on July 16, 1918, after it had become clear that the third offensive which had been launched the day before would not succeed, Schulenburg told Beck: "Yesterday we definitely lost the war,

burg and Groener, however, insisted that Schulenburg was mistaken and after some hesitation William accepted their views.

Groener's judgment was confirmed by a report that his aide, Colonel Heye, submitted later that morning on talks he had had with a group of frontline commanders on the morale of their troops: their men were weary and anxious for peace; they did not want to fight any more, and the Emperor would not be able to lead them against the revolutionaries. "All they want is an armistice—the sooner the better." The troops would march back in good order under their generals, Heye added, provided there would be no more fighting. One implication ran through everything that was said to the Kaiser that morning: a monarch who can no longer count on the support of his army and who is faced with revolution at home cannot remain on his throne. Groener was the only one present willing to draw this inevitable conclusion, but he was unwilling to say so; being himself a Wuerttemberger, he felt that it was up to the Prussian generals to impress this necessity on their monarch. Hindenburg, on the other hand, still rejected all thought of abdication and maintained that neither the chancellor nor the Reichstag had the right to make such a request. But try as he would, he too could not close his eyes to the gravity of the crisis. He admitted, out of range of the Kaiser's hearing, that the monarch might have to find a temporary refuge abroad if his safety could no longer be assured at army headquarters. Personally he favored Holland, partly because of its proximity, but primarily because as a monarchy it was likely to receive the Emperor with greater cordiality. He envisaged only a temporary stay until the Emperor's safety was no longer in question.[29]

If the army leaders failed to face reality, the government could not afford to do so. During the morning of November 9 the chancellor kept sending pleas to the Kaiser, urging him to abdicate without further delay in order to preserve the monarchy. One emissary felt that William was about to give in when suddenly Count Schulenburg suggested that the monarch resign merely

---

and probably we lost also, not only the Emperor, but the monarchy as well." Ludwig Beck, *Studien*, Hans Speidel, ed. (Stuttgart, 1955), pp. 217–18. Yet on November 9, 1918, Schulenburg blandly suggested: "Our men will readily accept the thesis that their sister weapon, the Navy, with its Jewish war profiteers and goldbrickers, stabbed them in the back." Quoted in Alfred Niemann, *Revolution von oben, Umsturz von unten* (Berlin, 1928), pp. 322, 349.

[29] Kuno Graf von Westarp, *Das Ende der Monarchie am 9. November 1918*, Werner Conze, ed. (Stollhamm [Oldbg.] and Berlin, 1952), pp. 42–48, 95; Joachim von Stülpnagel, "Ereignisse vom 30. 10. bis 11. 11. 1918, MS., Depot Stülpnagel, H 08–5/17, *Militärarchiv* at *Bundesarchiv*.

as German Emperor and remain King of Prussia since he could then provide a unifying symbol for the Prussian forces and prevent their disintegration.

Demands for immediate abdication had meanwhile come from Berlin with ever-increasing urgency. If the monarchy was to be saved, Prince Max implored William, he would have to act right away. The capital was in turmoil; radical elements might proclaim the establishment of a republic at almost any moment—it was a matter of minutes, not hours. Faced with these appeals, William seized on Schulenburg's suggestion and announced his readiness to give up the imperial throne and remain King of Prussia. In his place Hindenburg would be entrusted, in name as well as in fact, with the supreme command over all German forces. No one except Groener seems to have questioned this plan though it was utterly unrealistic, both politically and constitutionally.[30] When he called again, the chancellor was informed that an abdication statement was being drafted and would shortly be transmitted to him. This message was inevitably misunderstood in Berlin since nothing was said of a partial abdication. Prince Max assumed that the monarch was surrendering both his German and Prussian crowns and, fearful lest developments in Berlin would get entirely out of control, hurriedly issued a communiqué announcing William's abdication both as German Emperor and King of Prussia. He added on his own responsibility that the Crown Prince too had renounced his succession rights to both thrones. This news came too late to save the monarchy. Less than an hour later, Philipp Scheidemann, a Socialist leader, proclaimed the establishment of a democratic republic to prevent the creation of a Soviet dictatorship by leftist extremists.

Hindenburg and Groener had meanwhile returned to their offices. On hearing about both the chancellor's and Scheidemann's proclamations, they met hurriedly with some of the Emperor's aides. Since they were powerless to defend William's rights with armed force, it was agreed that the monarch would have to content himself with a formal protest against these lawless procedures. In order to avoid further confusion, however, it was decided that the protest was not to be published for the time being, but deposited in a safe place. This in effect meant acceptance of what had happened. The question of where the Emperor ought to go arose

---

[30] William took it so seriously that when he wrote a letter to his wife that evening he addressed it to "Her Majesty the Queen of Prussia." Information from Privy Councillor Gottfried von Dryander, a member of the Emperor's civil cabinet, who delivered the letter to the Empress.

again; once more Hindenburg stated his preference for the Netherlands, and all those present agreed with him. Admiral Hintze apparently was instructed to make the necessary arrangements with the Dutch authorities.

Around 4 o'clock that afternoon there was another conference at the Emperor's villa. William protested vehemently against the chancellor's unauthorized move and insisted on remaining with the army. Hindenburg summed up the conclusions of the earlier meeting. In agreement with all those present, he suggested to the Kaiser that he might have to consider seeking refuge in the Netherlands due to the growing unreliability of the troops. The Emperor turned over to the marshal the supreme command of all forces, but reserved his decision as to whether he would leave for Holland. He authorized Hintze, however, to take all preparatory steps for such a departure, and for security reasons decided to spend the night on his train.

Shortly after the conference broke up, there were new alarming reports of an immediate revolutionary rising at Spa. The monarch was urged by some of his aides to leave at once for safety in the Netherlands. They had not consulted Hindenburg but claimed, and doubtless believed, that they expressed his wishes. William agreed, then changed his mind, and decided to postpone his departure until the next morning. Later that evening he was urged once more, at Hintze's request, to leave Spa at once. Although Hintze had not discussed this new plea with Hindenburg either, he too claimed that the marshal shared his concern. William was warned that the situation had become untenable; rebel detachments were advancing on Spa. The fact that Hintze appeared to be speaking in Hindenburg's name was decisive for William, as he wrote that same night to the Crown Prince. He ordered his departure for 5 o'clock the next morning and at the appointed hour left for the border.

Hindenburg knew very little about these developments. He was told on the evening of November 9 that the monarch had decided to leave at once and asked whether he could bid his sovereign goodbye; he was advised, however, that a call at this moment might be inopportune. Hindenburg did not suggest that the Emperor postpone his departure. Shortly afterwards he was informed of the Emperor's change of plans. When his aides were appraised of the monarch's renewed change of plans, Hindenburg had retired for the night and he was not awakened. Evidently they felt that the marshal would have no objection, and there was no reason therefore to disturb his sleep. The next morning when Hindenburg was told of the departure, the Emperor was already at the Dutch border.[31] The marshal took the news calmly, unaware that it would haunt him to the end of his life.

∽

With the Emperor gone, Hindenburg had become, in name as well as fact, the commander in chief of the army. In the existing confusion and disintegration it was his authority alone that held the officer corps together, and the army's chief contribution to the survival of the newborn republic was the association of Hindenburg's name with the new state.

This very fact, however, confronted Groener with a delicate problem. The general was determined to safeguard at all costs the one great asset he felt the supreme command and indeed Germany still had—the person and the prestige of Hindenburg. Groener was frank to admit in later years that he was fully aware of the marshal's personal limitations, but he was also convinced that the nation needed more than ever the authority that issued from this last almost legendary representative of the old traditional Prussia. Hindenburg's standing had to be preserved also for possible future missions; if he remained untouched by the present troubles, he might some day provide the bridge to a better and stronger Germany. It was therefore imperative that he should not be tainted by too close an identification with the new republican era.

For this reason Groener was willing to conduct all negotiations with the government while Hindenburg stayed in the background. For the same reason Groener proposed that they direct the return of the troops from army headquarters and not return to Berlin. There was always the danger that in the capital the marshal might be drawn into the political turmoil of those troubled days. Groener also took pains to dissociate Hindenburg and the supreme command from the Armistice which was signed on November 11, 1918, at Compiègne, near Paris, in the now famous diningcar of Marshal Foch's special train. Erzberger, the leader of the German armistice delegation, had been instructed by both the army and the government to accept the severe armistice terms since further military resistance was out of the question. Against all expectations, he was able to secure some minor alleviations, and on his return to Spa both Hindenburg and Groener acknowledged gratefully that he had rendered the Fatherland an invaluable service.

[31] Westarp, *Ende der Monarchie*, pp. 54–129; Groener, *Lebenserinnerungen*, pp. 459–64; Max von Baden, *Erinnerungen*, pp. 628 n. 1, 630–47; Niemann, *Revolution*, pp. 308–13; Hindenburg to William II, July 28, 1922, *ibid.*, p. 472.

Yet what they conceded in the privacy of their office, they were not willing to acknowledge in public. Groener kept quiet lest he burden the marshal and the supreme command with the responsibility for a decision that was bound to be highly unpopular. Hindenburg doubtless was motivated by similar considerations, but more than one observer felt that he was also unwilling to speak up for Erzberger, a man already detested by the conservative-nationalist groups the marshal felt closest to in both background and outlook.[32]

To establish Hindenburg's special position and mission beyond any doubt, Groener decided to issue an order that defined the marshal's exceptional status and in the same vein claimed for the army complete independence from both the government and the constituent assembly which was shortly to be elected:

"Field Marshal von Hindenburg [it ran] considers it his duty to safeguard as long as possible the existence of the Supreme Command by backing it with the full strength of his personality; the continued existence of the Supreme Command is imperative since the Ministry of War in Berlin is unable, under the pressure of developments there, to take the measures required by the reorganization of the Army. As an agency outside of Government and Constituent Assembly the Supreme Command is in a favorable position to exert its influence wherever necessary during the deliberations of the Assembly, especially on the Government. The need to protect the name and person of the Field Marshal as a unifying symbol for the entire nation is the greater since it is impossible to tell at this moment what new elements of disintegration may try to assail Army and people."

To keep Hindenburg out of politics, Groener discouraged also all efforts of antirepublican groups to claim the marshal as their man. Two attempts were made by the rightist German National People's Party to persuade him to run as its candidate in the forthcoming elections for the constituent assembly. Hindenburg declined on the grounds that as head of the armed forces he ought not to be associated with any one party (but most likely he would have rejected the requests even if he had been a private citizen). Groener, however, was anxious to prevent any similar approaches in the future and his order warned:

"The Field Marshal must not be used as a propagandist attrac-

[32] Matthias Erzberger, *Erlebnisse im Weltkrieg* (Stuttgart and Berlin, 1920), pp. 335-39; Schiffer, *Leben für Liberalismus*, pp. 43-44; Groener, quoted in Thilo Vogelsang, *Reichswehr, Staat und NSDAP: Beiträge zur deutschen Geschichte 1930–1932* (Munich, 1932), p. 15 n. 6.

tion by any one party. If the Marshal were drawn into the party struggle, his historical name would acquire a reputation which might estrange him from part of the nation. This must be avoided; after the military outcome of the war which has affected the *entire* nation, the Field Marshal has a moral and historical obligation to serve the entire nation, not a single party, as long as he is in the service of the Fatherland." [33]

While Groener made every effort to remove Hindenburg from the political arena, he could not insulate the army from politics completely. In fact one of his first measures after the Emperor's departure acknowledged the strength of the revolutionary forces by giving them official standing with the army. Skillfully handled by him and enjoined by the government to enforce strict obedience in service, the soldiers councils which were springing up at all military units in imitation of the Russian soviets proved much more moderate in their demands than the workers and soldiers councils in the towns and cities of the homeland, and discipline could thus be maintained without serious difficulty.

Inevitably Groener made enemies by tolerating the soldiers councils. It is a measure of his skill and discretion that the critics directed their attacks solely against him and left Hindenburg untouched. In his determination to preserve the marshal as a symbol of strength and unity for the nation, he willingly endured these attacks. Hindenburg, on the other hand, was less ready to come to Groener's defense. He supported him with some spirit in personal letters and conversations and was also willing to grant in private that his own experiences with the soldiers council at army headquarters had not been unfavorable, but even years later he was still reluctant to defend Groener's actions in public. [34]

On November 14 Hindenburg and Groener left Spa to establish their headquarters on German soil. They intended to go to Homburg, a resort in the foothills of the Taunus Mountains, not far from Frankfurt-on-the-Main, which had been one of the Emperor's headquarters during the war. Plans had to be changed, however, when Homburg's workers and soldiers council insisted that except for Hindenburg, whom even this group would not touch, all

[33] Groener, *Lebenserinnerungen*, pp. 468–69, 476–77; Hindenburg to Westarp, Dec. 28, 1918, in Kuno Graf von Westarp, *Konservative Politik in der Weimarer Republik*, I, 38, MS., Westarp Papers.

[34] Groener, *Lebenserinnerungen*, pp. 469–70; Gordon A. Craig, *The Politics of the Prussian Army* (New York and Oxford, 1955), pp. 349–50; Georg Maercker, *Vom Kaiserheer zur Reichswehr* (Leipzig, 1921), pp. 20–21; Westarp, *Ende der Monarchie*, pp. 158–59; Hindenburg to Philipp, chairman of the Reichstag committee investigating the causes of Germany's defeat, Mar. 23, 1924, Bundesarchiv, Kl. Erw./223.

members of the supreme command would have to divest themselves of arms and epaulettes. The council in Kassel, an industrial center, proved more hospitable and readily welcomed the marshal and his staff. To honor and please him, the traditional black-and-white Prussian colors were displayed on his arrival and the council members wore black-and-white arm bands instead of the usual red ones. A proclamation, issued by the chairman, Albert Grzesinski, a leading Social Democrat and later Prussian minister of the interior, urged the population to show Hindenburg all due respect: "Hindenburg belongs to the German people and the German army. He has led his army to glorious victories and did not desert his people in its hour of crisis. Never has he been closer to us in the greatness of his dutiful service than he is today. He is under our protection. We know that both the civilian and military population of Kassel respects and admires him and that he is safe here from any disturbance. The Field Marshal bears arms as do all officers and enlisted men when they accompany him."

Perhaps the most interesting aspect of the proclamation was the comparison it drew, by implication, between Hindenburg and the Emperor who *had* left his people. Presumably the council thus hoped to impress diehard monarchists, but whether it did so is doubtful. The statement proved helpful, however, to those who, like Groener, sought to focus the hope of the country on Hindenburg. Soon a continuous stream of visitors was calling at army headquarters to pay their respects; Hindenburg saw them all, gratified that his popular standing had not suffered from the military collapse, and gladly allowed himself to be hailed as a symbol of national unity. But if he let his admirers pay him homage, he also insisted that nothing had changed in his relationship to his monarch—he was still his Emperor's loyal servant. He refused to set up his headquarters in the castle of Wilhelmshöhe, outside of Kassel, since the castle belonged to the Kaiser and he would not use it without permission. At his insistence the supreme command had to establish its offices in an uncomfortable, unheated nearby hotel.[35]

There, in the heart of the Hessian *Bergland,* remote from the turmoil he had had to endure at Spa, Hindenburg found peace. With the faithful Groener attending to everything, he set up a

[35] Groener, *Lebenserinnerungen,* p. 471; Richard Merton, *Erinnerungswertes aus meinem Leben, das über das Persönliche herausgeht* (Frankfurt/M., 1955), p. 53; Görlitz, *Hindenburg,* pp. 209, 211; Otto-Ernst Schüddekopf, *Das Heer und die Republik: Quellen zur Politik der Reichswehrführung 1918 bis 1933* (Hanover and Frankfurt/M., 1955), p. 34 n. 101.

comfortable routine that left ample time for long daily walks in the castle grounds. After the physical and mental strain of the last two months, at last he could once more relax.

Occasionally, however, Groener required his help. One of the most pressing tasks facing the army was to secure control of Berlin for the moderate Majority Socialists. Berlin's soldiers and workers councils insisted, however, that the troops assigned to the capital enter it without ammunition. Ebert, anxious to avoid a clash between the army and the councils, procrastinated. Groener, however, could not wait. If his forces were to restore order in the capital, they would have to do so at once; he knew that he could not keep them together much longer. Immediate action was so imperative that he asked Hindenburg to abandon his customary aloofness and approach Ebert himself, and the marshal agreed.

The letter which Hindenburg sent to Ebert was drafted with great care by Groener. Given the antirepublican attitude of the officer corps, its tenor presented a difficult problem. It was to ask Ebert's consent to the entry of fully armed and equipped divisions into Berlin; at the same time it had be worded in such a way as to shield the marshal against any charges of humbling himself before the Socialist leader. With customary skill Groener accomplished both tasks. He had Hindenburg explain condescendingly that he was addressing himself to Ebert, "because I am told that you too as a loyal German love your Fatherland above all and are ready to forget all personal thoughts and wishes, just as I did in order to deal with the crisis of our Fatherland. I have therefore joined forces with you in order to save our people from the threatening catastrophe." The officer corps, the message continued, had put itself at the disposal of the new government to supervise the orderly retreat and demobilization of the army, but its dedicated service had earned it harassment and insults rather than gratitude and recognition. The decree by which the government had relegated the soldiers councils to a purely advisory role was being ignored. Hindenburg's letter continued, "Obviously we can change these conditions only if the Government has at its disposal an organ which is able to enforce its decrees. Under the circumstances only the Army can fulfill this task—that is, an Army based on rigorous discipline." The government would have to reaffirm therefore by a new decree that all power of command rested exclusively with the military authorities. The soldiers councils would have to be dissolved, though they might appoint some individual spokesmen to serve as liaison between officers and enlisted men and perform purely informational functions. Finally, measures would have to be taken to assure officers of due respect on and off duty.

Going beyond the military sphere, Hindenburg (and Groener) also called for a national assembly to be convened in December. Groener had tried earlier to have the Reichstag recalled in the hope that its bourgeois elements could be mobilized to check the ascendancy of the Socialists. He had failed, but he now hoped to turn the Socialist tide by way of a national assembly. Hindenburg's letter ended in the same condescending tone it began:

"The destiny of the German people is in your hands. Whether the German people will once more rise to new greatness will depend on your decision. I am ready, and with me the entire Army, to assist you unreservedly. We all know that after the deplorable outcome of the war the Reich must be built up on new foundations and in new forms. What we want is not to delay the rehabilitation of the state for a generation by permitting blindness and folly to destroy all foundations of our social and economic life.

"I know that the radicals attack me for allegedly interfering with politics. However, I felt in my heart that I should talk to you about these matters. I wish you the strength of determined action."

Ebert's reply was evasive, but when Groener threatened to proceed on his own, the troops assigned to Berlin were permitted to enter the capital fully armed.[36] New difficulties arose, however, almost at once. A few days after the entry of the troops, there assembled in Berlin the first national congress of workers and soldiers councils. The bulk of the delegates were moderate Majority Socialists; the Independents controlled no more than 20 per cent of the votes, and the Spartacists were represented by only a handful of members. There were some turbulent scenes, but the majority, anxious to restore lawful conditions, decided to hold elections within a month for a constituent national assembly. A newly elected central council was authorized to supervise the government's policies, but was told not to interfere with their implementation.

While the congress proved moderate in political matters, the opposition carried the day when the meeting turned to the military situation. Old hatreds against the officer corps broke through; bitter memories of abuses, humiliations, and maltreatment were

[36] Groener, *Lebenserinnerungen*, pp. 471–74; Hindenburg to Ebert, Dec. 8, 1918, in Schüddekopf, *Heer und Republik*, pp. 35–36; E[rich] O[tto] Volkmann, *Revolution über Deutschland* (Oldenburg, 1930), pp. 124–31; John W. Wheeler-Bennett, *The Nemesis of Power: The German Army in Politics 1918–1945* (New York and London, 1953), pp. 28–31.

revived, and opponents in the political debates now found themselves united in their common distrust of the military caste. Speaker after speaker expressed his alarm over the collaboration between government and supreme command; their words reflected a deep-seated fear that such collaboration would lead to the eventual suppression of the new democratic state by the military. A resolution was passed calling for the dismissal of the supreme command. The meeting followed this up by adopting an eight-point program to safeguard the ascendancy of the republic over the military: under the supervision of the central council, the government was to have full command over the army and the navy; the authority of the soldiers councils was to be recognized by officers and men alike "to ensure the achievement of the goals of the socialist revolution"; all rank insignia were abolished and soldiers forbidden to carry arms when off duty; and finally, the standing army was to be replaced as quickly as possible by a people's militia. Ebert, confronted by a solid majority of the congress, watched helplessly as it tore up his precious agreement with Groener.

The reaction of the supreme command was quick and furious. Ebert was notified that neither Hindenburg nor Groener would accept the resolutions of the congress and that they would fight them "to the last ditch." If the government were to identify itself with the policies of the councils, they both would hand in their resignation. Hindenburg also informed all commands that he did not accept the program adopted by the congress. Pledging continued support to the Ebert government, he announced that he was asking it to shield the military against all further interference by the councils. Shortly afterwards Groener and one of his aides, Major Kurt von Schleicher, met with the government and representatives of the councils. Hindenburg's threat of resignation had its desired effect. Groener received every assurance that the resolutions would not be carried out, and the program of the congress was quietly shelved.[37]

Groener had in fact scored a decisive success; the incident marked the beginning of the decline of the councils and reaffirmed the special status of the army. At the moment, however, his victory seemed to have little significance. Four days after his meeting with the republican leaders Groener ordered his troops, at Ebert's request, to free Berlin of the radical units that had been terroriz-

[37] *Ibid.*, pp. 31–34; Volkmann, *Revolution*, pp. 143, 149–51; Groener, *Lebenserinnerungen*, pp. 474–77; Schüddekopf, *Heer und Republik*, pp. 30, 37–39; Arthur Rosenberg, *Geschichte der deutschen Republik*, (Karlsbad, 1935), pp. 53–56.

ing the capital. The attempt failed miserably. Of the original ten divisions that had entered Berlin on December 11, the bulk had melted away and only 800 men could be mustered to carry out this assignment on December 24. After some initial success these forces found themselves surrounded by hostile crowds that were quickly assembled by the Independents and Spartacists; thoroughly confused and demoralized, they decided to give up the fight. Many went over to the opposition and others threw down their arms and ran away. In its first encounter with its opponents, the army had suffered a humiliating defeat.

Fortunately for both army and government, the victors were unprepared to follow up their success. Torn by internecine quarrels, they let the one moment pass when they might successfully have seized power. By their passivity they allowed the government and the army to recover from their first setback. A few days later the Independents gave further ground when they resigned from the government in protest against Ebert's request that the army suppress the activities of the radical military units. The Majority Socialists were now in full control of the government and filled all vacancies with men from their own party.

Among the new members was Gustave Noske, long the Socialists' military expert, who was put in charge of the nation's defense. Noske was convinced that ruthless measures would have to be taken to put an end to the spreading chaos, and he was ready to take them. It was he rather than Hindenburg and Groener who during the following weeks rescued the government and nation from the convulsive disorders engulfing Germany. This he was able to do with the help of newly organized volunteer units, the so-called "Free Corps" that put themselves at his disposal and that he equipped and expanded.

This arrangement suited Groener perfectly. Since he did not want to involve the supreme command in these domestic conflicts in order "to save [it] for more important future tasks," he welcomed the appointment of Noske, who was willing to assume full responsibility for his actions. "All measures, now and later, were taken in close consultation with the Supreme Command," Groener recalled twenty years later in his memoirs, with gratification, "but it was Noske, soon to become Reichswehr Minister, who took over the direction and assumed the responsibility before Government and people."

Noske did his job well and by mid-January 1919 his forces had restored the government to full control in the capital. Then, in rapid succession, the radicals were removed from wherever else they had established themselves or were trying to seize control. The troops proceeded with great ruthlessness, often completely unwarranted in view of the weakness of the opposing forces. In the Ruhr Valley, in fact, large-scale violence was touched off solely because of their brutal actions. By May 1919, the power of leftist radicalism had been broken, but at the price of much bloodshed and a deepening of the nation's social cleavages.[38]

With Noske restoring order at home, the supreme command could devote itself to a task of equal urgency, but domestically less explosive—the defense of Germany's eastern frontiers against Polish forays. In late November 1918, Hindenburg had issued an appeal urging the organization of volunteer corps in defense of the eastern territories. He did so in open defiance of the government since an attempt to come to a peaceful settlement with the Poles was in progress. Hindenburg felt directly involved in the issue because the struggle centered in his native town, Posen, where the Poles were rising against the Germans. Large numbers of volunteers answered Hindenburg's call, but they came too late to save Posen; the Polish risings spread, and soon the entire province was under Polish control.

Undismayed, the supreme command proceeded to draw up plans for the reconquest of the lost territories. The withdrawal of the German armies from France and Belgium had by then been completed; since there was no longer any need to stay in West Germany, Hindenburg and Groener moved their headquarters to Kolberg, a seaside resort on the Baltic coast, to be close to the scene of the new operations. Hindenburg arrived in Kolberg on February 14 and on the following day issued another appeal calling for the establishment of additional military units in East Prussia and Silesia. But once more he failed in his efforts to recapture Posen. The Poles appealed for help to the Allies, and on February 16, two days after Hindenburg's move to Kolberg, Marshal Foch issued an ultimatum to the German Government, demanding an immediate cessation of all military operations against Posen. The government had no alternative but to bow to Foch's orders, since the supreme command felt unable to risk a resumption of hostilities. All it could do now was to organize units to defend the eastern territories still under German control.

[38] Groener, *Lebenserinnerungen*, pp. 478–81; Robert G. L. Waite, *Vanguard of Nazism: The Free Corps Movement in Postwar Germany, 1918–1923* (Cambridge, 1952), pp. 13–16; Harold J. Gordon, *The Reichswehr and the German Republic: 1919–1926* (Princeton, 1957), pp. 26–52; Peter von Oertzen, "Die grossen Streiks der Ruhrbergarbeiterschaft im Frühjahr 1919," *Vierteljahrshefte für Zeitgeschichte*, VI (1958), 231–62; Rosenberg, *Geschichte*, pp. 72–82.

Groener applied himself to this task with his customary drive and organizational skill. He also had a hand, for a time, in the operations of some of the German Free Corps in the Baltic states. Under the pretext of fighting off the Russians these forces hoped to obtain land there for settlement. But Groener soon became disillusioned with this dubious enterprise and halfheartedly cast about for a way to liquidate the ill-starred venture.[39]

∽

Outwardly Hindenburg's personal life continued in its calm regularity throughout that turbulent winter of 1918–19. There was the daily walk in the morning, conferences with Groener, the reception of visitors, some correspondence, the signing of official documents. Behind this outward placidity, however, Hindenburg was wrestling with personal problems that seemed no less grave to him than those of the nation. The decision to stay with the army had been difficult, but he had felt himself bound by the Emperor's orders. Moreover, when the Emperor formally abdicated on November 28, 1918, he expressly urged all officials and soldiers to assist the new regime in its efforts to shield the German people "against the threatening dangers of anarchy, famine, and foreign domination." He was still obeying the command of his sovereign, then, when he kept working with Ebert. Many of his fellow generals ignored the ex-monarch's wishes and retired from active service; they soon turned into open enemies of the hated republic which he was still serving. He felt that they were taking the easy way out while he was doing his duty, and he was pained to see those to whom he felt closest, socially and professionally, beginning to look askance at him.

His uneasiness increased when the *Kreuzzeitung*, the monarchists' leading daily, launched a direct attack on Groener in January 1919 and charged him with revolutionary sympathies and opportunism. Such charges, Hindenburg felt, were directed as much at him, Groener's superior, as they were at his trusted aide. Some days after this attack, Count Kuno Westarp, the one-time leader of the Conservatives in the Reichstag, raised the question with Hindenburg whether the supreme command had shown sufficient energy in protecting the army and the officer corps against revolutionary influences. Hindenburg rejected Westarp's reproaches and pointed out that he had remained at his post only on the express orders of "His Majesty, my King and Master." He added that he

<hr>

[39] Groener, *Lebenserinnerungen*, pp. 478–81; Waite, *Vanguard*, pp. 101–07, 132; Volkmann, *Revolution*, pp. 92–96, 237–39, 243–45, 306–11.

had done so at a great personal sacrifice and quoted proudly from a telegram that the monarch had sent him a few days before which concluded: "God bless you, my dear Field Marshal, for your steadfast loyal work on behalf of our German Fatherland." Such an acknowledgment, he maintained, was his best reward, and while he believed that he was right in remaining at his post, he was ready to leave as soon as there was someone "who could assume the responsibility before history and my king." But even the Kaiser's approbation could not fully calm his doubts about the role he was playing. Years later he would still refer to those winter and spring months of 1918–19 as the days of his "martyrdom," and he remained always at pains to explain that he stayed at the head of the army only "on the order of His Majesty and from love of the Fatherland."[40]

Two other problems added to his discomfort. His relations with Ludendorff had been seriously strained since that October day when the two men had parted ways. Ludendorff had deeply resented Hindenburg's failure to come to his defense at their last conference with the Kaiser. His resentment increased when the marshal refused once again, in late November, to defend him against attacks in the press for the role he had played during the pre-armistice negotiations. In mid-November 1918, in fear of his life, General Ludendorff left Germany and spent some three months in Sweden. During this period of exile he wrote his war memoirs in which he gave full vent to his anger; his friends persuaded him with great difficulty to delete a searing indictment of Hindenburg's mental sloth and lack of perception. In February 1919, Ludendorff came under public attack again: during a debate in the national assembly, Scheidemann, now minister-president of the newly created Reich government, accused him of being an ingenious gambler. Hindenburg sent Scheidemann a letter of protest against this attack on his "loyal collaborator," and called Ludendorff a "fervent patriot who in his dynamic way had always had the best interests of the nation at heart" and for whose actions he, Hindenburg, shared the responsibility. Scheidemann reiterated his charges against Ludendorff in another assembly debate, but in a personal letter assured the marshal of his profound respect and expressed his regret that Hindenburg considered an attack on Ludendorff an attack on himself. When an aide of Ludendorff called on Hindenburg to refute Scheidemann's charges publicly, the mar-

---

[40] Hindenburg to Army, Nov. 10, 1918, in Schüddekopf, *Heer und Republik,* p. 19; *Kreuzzeitung,* Jan. 27, 1919, quoted in Westarp, *Ende der Monarchie,* p. 15; Hindenburg-Westarp exchange, Feb. 2–7, 1919, *ibid.,* pp. 15–18; personal information.

shal, however, demurred. The moment was inopportune, he claimed, and would only permit the publication of his correspondence with Scheidemann. He justified his reticence with the need for maintaining the nonpartisan role that Groener wished him to play.

Some weeks later a reconciliation was arranged between the two men. Ludendorff insisted that Hindenburg make the first move and suggested that a note on the occasion of his forthcoming birthday would be a suitable gesture. Anxious to settle the dispute, Hindenburg wrote asking him to forget the "misunderstanding" that had separated them, and Ludendorff took the proffered hand of the marshal. Later in 1919, after he had retired from active service, Hindenburg issued a brief public statement in which he assumed full responsibility for all the decisions of the supreme command: "General Ludendorff has always acted in full agreement with me." And conscious of his special niche in the hearts of his countrymen, he added a warning that must have been of little comfort to Ludendorff, "An attack on General Ludendorff is actually an attack on me."[41]

While his differences with Ludendorff could be mended with relative ease, the problem of his relationship with the ex-Emperor was not as easily solved. From his Dutch exile William had followed the public debate that had risen over his role on the fateful November 9 and over the motives leading him to take refuge in Holland. He had noticed with growing concern the widespread acceptance of the assertion that he had deserted the army and nation in their hour of crisis; these charges disturbed him deeply, not only because he thought them untrue and insulting, but also because unless refuted at once, they might bar his return to the throne for all time. It was essential therefore that those who had advised him to go to Holland should openly assume responsibility for their counsel. He was particularly anxious for Hindenburg to state publicly that he had urged the Emperor to leave for Holland. Hindenburg's prestige would lend such a statement special weight and might go far to exonerate him. William resented the marshal's silence; if anyone explained to him the reasons for Hindenburg's reticence, he apparently failed to appreciate them. Perhaps there was also an element of jealousy in his recurrent requests since he

41 Eduard Heilfron, ed., *Die deutsche Nationalversammlung im Jahre 1919–1920* (Berlin, n.d.), I, 101 (Feb. 13, 1919), 372–73 (Feb. 18, 1919); Hindenburg-Scheidemann exchange, Feb. 16–19, 1919, in Schulthess' *Europäischer Geschichtskalender* (hereafter cited as Schulthess), 1919, I, 71; Görlitz, *Hindenburg*, pp. 217–19; Wilhelm Breucker, *Die Tragik Ludendorffs*, pp. 77–93; Ludendorff, *Vom Feldherrn*, I, 50–51, II, 362–63 (where the deleted passage about Hindenburg is reprinted).

had doubtless heard of the innumerable delegations making their pilgrimage to the marshal's headquarters—William may well have seen Hindenburg again as a threatening rival whose popularity must be checked.

In mid-March, Hindenburg, evidently in reply to the Emperor's pleas, abandoned the reserve he had so far observed. He issued a statement "to prevent misconceptions," and explained "why the Emperor went to Holland." In a few words he outlined the political and military situation as it presented itself on that fateful November 9, and after stating briefly why the Kaiser could not return to Germany or seek death in the front-lines, he continued: "Finally, the Emperor could leave the country. He chose this way in agreement with his advisers, after infinitely hard struggles, simply in the hope of thus rendering the Fatherland the best service, sparing Germany further losses, hardships and misery, giving her back peace, quiet, and order. That the Emperor was mistaken in this belief is not His Majesty's fault."

Clearly, the document understated the role of the Kaiser's advisers; but the fact that it had nothing to say on Hindenburg's views during those fateful deliberations was even more disappointing to the ex-monarch. It also failed to satisfy those who, like Count Schulenburg, had taken a different stand on November 9. Immediately after that fateful day Schulenburg had drafted a memorandum in which he pictured Hindenburg and Groener as having urged abdication on the Emperor since early morning as against his own very different attitude. The statement found its way into the press, and Hindenburg issued a sharp reply in which he challenged General Schulenburg's competence as a witness since he "was not sufficiently informed about the actual situation." Since Hindenburg did not wish to be drawn into a press battle, he attempted no detailed public refutation of Schulenburg. Privately, however, he circulated a statement in which he took issue with Schulenburg's assertions "in order to eliminate, in justified self-defense, errors which were understandable in the excitement of the moment, but which may also lead to an undesirable and inaccurate judgment of my person and my entourage."

After some further exchanges in which Schulenburg was joined by Plessen, Hintze, and General von Marschall, the chief of the Emperor's military cabinet, an agreement was reached to draw up a joint protocol with Count Westarp's assistance. The drafting of the new memorandum took several months and was not completed until July, after extensive correspondence and many conferences. On almost all points this protocol was closer to

Hindenburg's version of the events than to that of his opponents: he succeeded in obtaining the deletion of any assertion that he had advised William to abdicate and to leave for the Netherlands. Nor did he assume sole responsibility for the advice he did give; the statement which he accepted, after prolonged negotiations, said merely that at the conference with the Emperor in the afternoon of November 9 "the Field Marshal, on the basis of earlier deliberations and in agreement with the representative of the Foreign Office, Herr von Hintze, as well as the other advisers present, suggested as a last resort the move to a neutral country and mentioned Holland as the most suitable one. As yet no final decision was reached."

Hindenburg's victory was short-lived. Schulenburg and Plessen issued additional statements in which they upheld their version of Hindenburg's role and by implication questioned the marshal's veracity. And the Kaiser on his part kept insisting that the marshal had not yet satisfied his demand for a forthright public acknowledgment of the decisive role he had played on November 9. Three more years were to pass before Hindenburg wrote the ex-monarch a letter in July 1922, immediately published in all accessible papers, in which he stated that during the afternoon of November 9 he had "recommended in the name of all of us and as a last resort the departure for Holland which I considered then merely a temporary one." He added that he had no doubt that the Emperor would not have left if he had not thought that he, Hindenburg, in his capacity as chief of the general staff, considered this move imperative in the interest of monarch and Fatherland.[42]

The controversy placed a heavy strain on Hindenburg. Westarp, on a visit to Kolberg, noticed how deeply he was affected by the dispute, and Hindenburg complained later to Plessen that the conflict had ruined his health. Torn between the officer's honor code and his strong sense of realism, he felt weak and uncertain. He was still convinced, and always remained so, that the Kaiser's departure was the only possible way out of a hopeless impasse, but he would not state publicly this conviction. Nor could he bring himself, out of loyalty to his sovereign, to shoulder on his behalf, regardless of what he had said, the full responsibility for the Emperor's departure to shield the ex-monarch against charges of cowardice and desertion.

In actual fact it was of course Hindenburg's attitude that had tipped the scales. William had come to army headquarters on

[42] This account is based on Westarp's *Ende der Monarchie;* Schulenburg's memorandum, in Niemann, *Revolution,* pp. 325–31.

October 30 in search of protection against the revolutionary forces, and he left when Hindenburg and Groener could no longer offer that protection. If others too advised him to leave, their suggestions carried weight only in the light of what the two generals said. Rightly the Kaiser considered Hindenburg's counsel as decisive, and so did his entourage.

Granted that the marshal's views caused the Emperor to depart, the question remains, however, whether the monarch could ask him to assume responsibility for the decision to leave for the Netherlands. William insisted that Hindenburg had forced him to leave by stating that only his departure would spare the country the horrors of a civil war. Strickly speaking, this was not correct. The Emperor had other alternatives: he could have stayed, possibly risking death or capture and trial before a revolutionary tribunal, or he could have ended his life. If he decided to leave, the decision was his and his alone.[43]

If that thought ever crossed Hindenburg's mind as it must have, he never seems to have spoken about it. Hindenburg's sense of propriety prevented him from drawing the monarch personally into the dispute about the events of November 9. Perhaps, in a moment of candor, he also admitted to himself that he might have acted exactly as William did, had he been in the latter's place. For in trying to shift the responsibility to him, was not the ex-Kaiser doing to him exactly what he himself had done to Ludendorff, and was now doing to Groener?

☙

While the past was making its claim on the marshal, he could not ignore the present completely. On January 19, 1919, elections had been held for a national assembly which was to draft a constitution for the new republic. The election results were in many ways inconclusive: most workers supported the moderate Majority Social Democratic Party which obtained 163 seats; the more radical Independent Socialists got a mere 22; and the Spartacists, now renamed Communists, did not participate in the elections. With 185 (out of 421) the socialist parties failed, however, to secure a majority in the assembly. The *Bürgertum*, on the other hand, had a majority with a total of 236, but it was deeply split, with its representation divided among four major parties: left-of-center Democrats, Catholic Center, right-of-center German People's Party, and the reactionary German National People's Party. The Democrats and the larger part of the Center were

[43] Westarp, *Ende der Monarchie*, pp. 175–78; Niemann, *Revolution*, p. 313.

supporters of the republic; the two last named groups favored the restoration of the monarchy.

However unclear the preferences of the electorate were in other respects, the bulk of the voters upheld the republic. The government that was established in February 1919 consisted in consequence of a coalition of Social Democrats, Democrats, and Centrists. Its members differed on basic questions of social, cultural, and economic policy, but they believed in the principles of political democracy and were determined to make it work.

How far Hindenburg followed these developments it is impossible to determine, but it is unlikely that he had more than a perfunctory interest in the proceedings at Weimar. His aversion to politics and his distrust of parliamentary activities kept him from following the debates; besides his preoccupation with the problem of the Emperor's departure for Holland claimed a large share of his attention. When he studied the constitution after his nomination as presidential candidate in 1925, he stated frankly that he was quite unfamiliar with the document.[44]

Whatever he did learn about the activities of the assembly gathered at Weimar must have caused him misgivings. The strong vote in support of the republican form of government boded ill for the restoration of the monarchy. The demand of large numbers of the deputies for the adoption of black-red-and-gold, the colors of the old liberal movement and of the Revolution of 1848, as the national colors of the new Germany, in the place of the Imperial black-white-and-red, doubtless shocked him profoundly. And there were also some perturbing attacks on the old army and German militarism which must have been brought to his attention. On the other hand, developments took a more reassuring turn in matters of immediate concern to him. Ebert was elected president of the new republic on the basis of a provisional constitution passed in an early session of the assembly, and Noske became minister of defense in the new government that superseded the Council of People's Representatives. In their respective posts these two men would ensure continued cooperation between the supreme command and the government. (Hindenburg himself had been mentioned as a possible candidate for the presidency, but the reaction of the assembly had been so overwhelmingly negative that the idea was dropped at once.) [45]

Late in February the Assembly discussed the establishment of a

[44] Rudolf Olden, *Hindenburg oder der Geist der preussischen Armee* (Paris, 1935), p. 188.
[45] *Ibid.*, p. 213; Görlitz, *Hindenburg*, p. 229.

new regulár army. A "Law for the Creation of a Provisional Reichswehr" was quickly passed since, except for the Independents, everyone was agreed on the need for speed. It provided for the establishment of an army "on a democratic basis," but since a subsequent executive decree reserved as before the right of appointments, promotions, transfers, and dismissals of officers up to the rank of colonel to the military authorities, the prospects for genuinely democratic selections appeared rather doubtful. Except for the Independents, however, no one worried about this problem. Special arrangements were made for Hindenburg and the forces under his command: his staff retained the designation, by now rather anachronistic, of supreme command and was to receive orders directly from Reich President Ebert, with Noske serving merely as an intermediary. By a further decree Ebert turned over to Hindenburg full power of command over all units under his jurisdiction. The gentlemen's agreement between Ebert and Groener was thus maintained in its original form, and Hindenburg was spared the embarrassment of accepting orders from a parliamentary government. The arrangement was clearly unconstitutional since the provisional constitution, in Article 8, expressly subordinated the supreme command to the Reich government. But Groener, ever anxious to shield the marshal from too close identification with the new regime, insisted on this solution, and he had his way.[46]

He succeeded because the republic was still in great need of Hindenburg's name and support. Behind all plans and programs for the future the threatening question of the peace terms that Germany would have to accept loomed large. The government had learned through press reports and other intelligence that the treaty that was being drafted at Paris would be much harsher than had been expected in view of the agreement, in the pre-armistice negotiations, on Wilson's Fourteen Points as the basis for the peace treaty. Once more, then, Hindenburg's backing might ease the task of reconciling the nation to this new shock.

The terms presented to Germany at Versailles on May 7, 1919, came indeed as a shattering blow to most Germans, and the fact that they were not negotiable was taken as an additional humiliation. Yet if the material terms seemed overly harsh to them, the crowning indignity was seen in the so called *Schmachparagraphen* (articles of shame). These called for the extradition of William II

---

[46] Heilfron, *Nationalversammlung*, II, 733–844, 909–11; Gustav Noske, *Von Kiel bis Kapp: Zur Geschichte der deutschen Revolution* (Berlin, 1920), p. 168.

and his military advisers to be tried as war criminals before an international tribunal, and they included above all the "war guilt clause." That clause stated that the Germans had caused all the loss and damage that Germany's enemies suffered as a consequence of the war "imposed upon them by the aggression of Germany and her allies." More than anything else, the "guilt clause" turned the question of acceptance or nonacceptance of the treaty into a political issue.

The immediate German reaction was to reject the treaty, but soon cooler counsels prevailed. Rejection, it was felt, could serve a purpose only if it were backed by military resistance, for few were willing to accept passively the Allied occupation of all of Germany that was expected to follow upon refusal to sign the treaty. The government turned therefore to the supreme command to get its advice. The outlook was bleak; the nation seemed incapable, both materially and mentally, of offering any further resistance. Arms and ammunition had been surrendered in accordance with the armistice agreement, and the lack of materiel precluded the adequate equipment of any forces beyond those already under arms. An inquiry circulated by Groener among the corps commanders showed that few Germans were prepared to take up arms again; only in the eastern provinces was there some readiness to fight off the Poles. While military resistance might be temporarily successful in the east, it was out of the question in the west. Groener was forced to conclude that the resumption of hostilities could only lead to the destruction of Germany's unity and to the breakup of the country into separate territories. This he was determined to prevent, for such disintegration would bar forever Germany's rise to new greatness.

In this sense, Groener reported to Hindenburg: "It would of course be easiest to take the position that an officer can't compromise in questions touching on our military and national honor. I am personally convinced, however, that there are moments in the life of a people when it becomes impermissible to sacrifice yourself for a point of honor, when self-preservation becomes the overruling historical necessity. I am determined to draw all consequences from this conviction." Since he was about to confer with the government at Weimar, Groener asked Hindenburg for a statement of his views.

Hindenburg knew that large parts of the officer corps insisted as a matter of honor that at least eastern Germany be defended by force of arms. Yet the marshal understood also that Groener was right and that a resumption of hostilities was hopeless and could only end in the breakup of Germany. But what would his friends and his officers think, and above all the Emperor, if he were to acquiesce in a treaty that demanded the admission of Germany's war guilt and the extradition of the monarch as a common criminal? He was trying to repudiate at that very moment the charges of Schulenburg, Plessen, and others who claimed that he had not upheld the army's honor on the day of the Emperor's abdication. Would not his acceptance of Groener's views expose him to new charges of un-Prussian behavior? The country, moreover, seemed to expect him to resume the fight as thousands of letters and telegrams pouring into his office suggested.

There was no escaping Groener's sober realism, however, and once more common sense won out, but the marshal's acceptance of Groener's proposal was hedged with reservations: "In point of fact I agree with you and I don't mind saying so openly. But I cannot and will not give up those views which have guided me all my life. If the government wishes to know my viewpoint, please give them the following message:

" 'In case of a resumption of hostilities we are militarily in a position to reconquer, in the east, the province of Posen and to defend our frontier. In the west, we cannot, in view of the numerical superiority of the Entente and its ability to surround us on both flanks, count on repelling successfully a determined attack of our enemies.

" 'A favorable outcome of our operations is therefore very doubtful, but as a soldier I would rather perish in honor than sign a humiliating peace.' "[47]

Groener suggests in his memoirs that had fighting been resumed, the marshal might have assumed command of the troops in the field. Plans to that effect seem to have been drawn up, and General von Seeckt had apparently been selected to serve as his chief of staff.[48]

In Weimar, Groener was faced with indecision and confusion. Two days before his arrival the Allies had addressed a new note to Germany. It contained some modifications of the original terms, but it also made clear that the Allies were not prepared to make any further concessions. It requested the acceptance of the treaty by June 24 and warned that in case of nonacceptance all necessary steps would be taken to enforce the peace terms. The government

[47] Volkmann, *Revolution*, pp. 257, 299–304; Groener, *Lebenserinnerungen*, pp. 492–502. The term "Entente," an allusion to the Anglo-French *entente cordiale* of 1904, was used by the Germans during and after World War I to designate the Allies.
[48] Groener, *Lebenserinnerungen*, p. 504; Friedrich von Rabenau, *Hans von Seeckt: Aus seinem Leben 1918–1936* (Leipzig, 1940), p. 182 n.1.

was uncertain as to the course to pursue: a vote taken on June 19 showed that eight of its members favored rejection while six counseled acceptance. Unable to arrive at a clear decision, the ministers resigned that same day.

If Groener found the political leaders badly divided, he encountered no such indecision among the military chiefs. Discussions with a number of generals disclosed that they were ready to take up arms again regardless of what the government would decide. To his dismay he found them prepared to surrender Western Germany and to content themselves with the defense of the provinces beyond the Elbe River. "The old Prussia," General Reinhardt announced, "must be the core of this Reich." Groener could only shake his head at this fuzzy romanticism that expected to draw its strength from memories of Frederick the Great and was willing to abandon the industrial power of the Rhine and Ruhr. But a meeting with civilian leaders, later that day, put a strong damper on the enthusiasm of the military. Representatives from Silesia and East Prussia who had earlier urged armed resistance had now to admit that given the war weariness of the population, a reopening of hostilities would receive civilian support only if the government were to reject the treaty. When Groener saw Ebert the next morning to hand him Hindenburg's statement, he was convinced that his estimate of the situation was correct. Having fulfilled his mission, he returned to Kolberg.

On June 20 and 21 Ebert tried desperately to form a new government. Since the Democrats refused to sign the peace treaty, either conditionally or unconditionally, the government that was finally appointed consisted only of Centrists and Social Democrats. To avoid complete chaos, the new government presented itself to the national assembly with the proposal that it be authorized to sign the peace treaty, with the understanding, however, that signature did not imply acknowledgment of Germany's war guilt or acceptance of the obligation to surrender the Emperor and others to be tried as war criminals by the Allied and Associated Powers. This mandate it received by a vote of 237 against 138.

The Allies insisted, however, on the unconditional acceptance of the treaty and warned the German government that less than twenty-four hours remained before the deadline of June 24. Once more Weimar was thrown into turmoil. Once more there was talk of resuming the fight, and some of the generals urged Noske to establish a military dictatorship. There were rumors of military revolts; General Maercker, the commander of the troops on duty in Weimar, took it upon himself to warn the Democratic and

Centrist leaders that he could not, in case of acceptance, answer for the continued discipline of his troops. Hindenburg added to the existing confusion by sending a telegram to the president reiterating his earlier message about the hopelessness of military resistance, but warning at the same time that the government could count on the support of the army only as long as it did not sign the peace treaty unconditionally.[49]

In the face of this alarming confusion, Ebert turned once more to the supreme command. Calling Groener, the president declared that he would agree to the acceptance of the treaty only if the supreme command would state unequivocally that armed resistance was out of the question. He would call back after three hours to learn Hindenburg's and Groener's views and would pass on their advice to the government when it took the decisive vote that afternoon.

Again the fate of the republic turned on a decision by Hindenburg and Groener. As always, Hindenburg was reluctant to commit himself; but Groener was ready to shoulder the responsibility. When Ebert called back, the marshal happened to be in the general's office. The latter took the call, and when Hindenburg noticed that Groener was willing to talk to Ebert himself, he quietly left the room. There could be only one answer—resistance was hopeless, and the treaty would have to be accepted on Allied terms. This indeed was the answer that Groener gave Ebert, "not as First Quartermaster General, but as a German who has a clear grasp of the situation." Hindenburg's name was not mentioned, and when Ebert reported back to the ministers and these, in turn, informed the assembly, again there was mention only of Groener's views. Groener of course had spoken as he did because he knew himself in agreement with Hindenburg, and the government and the assembly doubtless understood his reply in that sense. Once more Groener had drawn on the marshal's authority in support of an unpopular decision and yet had made certain that Hindenburg was not too closely identified with it. Hindenburg on his part was satisfied with his background role. When Groener told Hindenburg what he had said to the president, the marshal replied quietly: "Of course you were right; but once more you must be the black sheep." This the general was quite ready to be: "I believed that in the interests of the new army the myth of Hindenburg should be preserved. It was necessary that one great figure should emerge

49 Maercker, *Vom Kaiserheer,* pp. 286–93; Groener, *Lebenserinnerungen,* pp. 506, 504.

from the war free from the blame that attached to the General Staff. That figure had to be Hindenburg."[50]

৵

On the day after the peace treaty had been accepted by the assembly, Hindenburg informed Ebert that he was leaving the supreme command. He had submitted his resignation before, but had agreed to serve until the treaty was signed, and with this understanding Ebert had granted his request. Hindenburg had also informed the ex-Emperor of his wish to resign at the time he first approached Ebert since he had remained at his post at the latter's command.[51] Now that the treaty had been accepted, he felt he had done his duty toward country and Emperor. At the same time his departure was timed so as to dissociate him from the actual signing of the Versailles Treaty on June 28, 1919. His final order to the army was meant to re-enforce this impression: "Soldiers, I recently informed the Government that as a soldier I would rather perish in honor than sign a humiliating peace." But having said this, he at once urged both officers and men to continue to work for the Fatherland's welfare: "What you as individuals may think of the events of these last days is your business. But for your actions there can be but one guiding principle—the welfare of the Fatherland. . . . The preservation of internal peace and the opportunity for constructive work depend essentially on the inner strength of the Army. It is our duty to maintain this strength. As difficult as this may be, we must set aside our personal views. In this way only can we hope, with God's help, to lead our poor German Fatherland out of its deep humiliation toward a better future."[52]

On the eve of Hindenburg's departure, the members of his staff gave him a farewell dinner. Groener made the speech of the evening: he spoke of Hindenburg's life and career; he found words of high praise for the collaboration of Hindenburg and Ludendorff during the war; he noted that the Emperor himself had asked the marshal to remain with the army to help preserve the unity of army and nation. He also thanked him for pointing the way "by which we can and must transplant the good elements of our traditions into the new age, for this was the birth hour of a new age." Groener urged his audience to understand that an effort

---

[50] Groener to Freudenthal, Dec. 31, 1923, in *Gegenwart*, Mar. 23, 1957, p. 174.
[51] Hindenburg-Ebert correspondence, in Schulthess, 1919, I, 200, 266–67; Görlitz, *Hindenburg*, pp. 223–24.
[52] Schulthess, 1919, I, 267.

would have to be made to rebuild the country: "The person of the Field Marshal represents the transition from an old to a new era, he transmits the great and steady forces of the past into our national future. . . . As he served faithfully three royal and imperial masters, he served, in equal loyalty, the Fatherland in its present misfortune. He overcame his misgivings which might have kept him from reaching his decisions freely and in accordance with the dictates of his conscience. . . . We are pledging ourselves to follow his example to the end of our days."

Hindenburg's reply was brief and expressed what was closest to his heart: "When I look back today, I think first, in unending love and loyalty, yet with a heavy heart, of my Most Gracious Royal and Imperial Master whose confidence once called me to my post." He paid tribute to the men who fought under him during the war, to the Free Corps, to the members of the various staffs which he had headed, to his "incomparable Ludendorff" whom he would never forget, and to all his aides. There was also a final word of appreciation for his last adviser, the faithful Groener. "Whether I see the return of better times, God alone knows. But I wish it for you, and I know that you will see once again that old greatness without which we cannot conceive of Germany and Prussia."

The following morning he left. As his last official act, just before he drove to the station, he signed a letter to Marshal Foch in which he urged the Allied commander in chief not to insist on the extradition of the Emperor and offered to submit to a war crime trial in place of his monarch. The entire staff saw him off; Free Corps "Hindenburg" which had been on duty at his headquarters was drawn up for a final review in front of the railway station and there was a special honor guard on the platform. He departed not as a defeated general but as a national hero. "His glory and his person," Groener recalls in his memoirs, "had emerged without blemish from the disaster."[53]

Groener himself retired shortly afterwards after having arranged the incorporation of the supreme command into the regular Reichswehr; he suggested General von Seeckt as his successor. He thought von Seeckt best qualified to build up an effective army within the limitations imposed by the peace treaty and felt confident that the general would not tolerate any political interference on the part of the government or the Reichstag. His advice was disregarded, however, and Reinhardt received the appointment.[54]

[53] Groener, *Lebenserinnerungen*, pp. 510–12; Schüddekopf, *Heer und Republik*, p. 46.
[54] Groener, *Lebenserinnerungen*, pp. 513–15.

CHAPTER 2

INTERIM

HINDENBURG returned to Hanover where he had lived after his retirement from the army until World War I. His reception on his arrival at Hanover was as elaborate and ceremonious as had been his departure from Kolberg. An honor guard saluted him at the station; a committee of municipal and state dignitaries, not a few of them Socialists, participated in the city's official welcome, and Hanover's citizenry lined the flag and flower draped street in an enthusiastic demonstration of their affection for their famous fellow townsman.

A large roomy villa, notably different from his modest prewar apartment, awaited the marshal in one of the city's suburbs. The municipal administration had put the house at his disposal in 1918; the presentation had been made by a conservative city council, but after the revolution Hanover's socialist administration had upheld the gift since it too wished the nation's hero to keep his residence in Hanover.[1]

Though once more retired, Hindenburg was to have neither rest nor privacy. He could not show himself in the streets without attracting a crowd, he was besieged by an unending stream of visitors and delegations, and for many hours each day he kept busy attending to a voluminous correspondence. In addition the wearisome debate about the events of November 9 continued into his first weeks in Hanover.

There was also the new task he had meanwhile assumed of writing his memoirs. Many of his fellow generals, idle now in retirement, were writing theirs. Some were interested merely in recording their experiences for future historians and strategists. Others were anxious to defend themselves against charges of incompetence or to express their resentment because their advice had been ignored at critical moments. Hindenburg belonged to neither of these groups. The plan to write his memoirs had not even been his, but had been suggested to him by Reimar Hobbing, an enterprising publisher in Berlin. What Hobbing had in mind was no conventional record of the marshal's personal and military experiences. Rather, he wished him to write an account of his in-

[1] Görlitz, *Hindenburg*, pp. 228–30; Wheeler-Bennett, *Wooden Titan*, pp. 223–25.

ner development and of those ethical and spiritual values that had guided him, a Prussian and German officer, in an era of unforgettable greatness. The book was to be an inspirational and educational work that would serve as a beacon of hope in the prevailing mood of despair and confusion. Translations would at once be published in other countries since Hobbing felt confident that such an account of the marshal's personal and spiritual growth would prove of immense benefit to Germany's standing in the world. To ensure its speedy completion, he proposed that it be written under Hindenburg's direction by a team of anonymous collaborators.

Hindenburg seems to have been reluctant at first to accept the suggestion, but he had further inquiries made, and the information he received sounded encouraging. He was assured that the work could indeed render a great service to the nation in this hour of turmoil and confusion; it would have an enormous effect on the country since the marshal represented the only remaining support for hundreds of thousands of people. Care would have to be taken of course to avoid all sensationalism, and this could best be accomplished by keeping away from polemics. The book would simply be a "spiritual accounting" to the German people, "ranging high above everyday quarrels and differences of opinion, beyond good and evil." Hindenburg was impressed with these arguments, but he still had his reservations. There was also the problem of choosing the right publisher. Some advisers felt that Hobbing had a penchant for high-pressure publicity and would not content himself with the restrained, dignified promotion that a work by Hindenburg would require. Meanwhile others pleaded with the marshal to write the book. In the end, when the staid old publishing house of S. Hirzel in Leipzig agreed to bring out the work, Hindenburg gave his consent.[2]

Out of My Life, written with the assistance of one of his former aides, Colonel von Mertz, made no attempt to make an original contribution to the debate then raging about the strategy of the War. While military events are covered in some detail, the work deals primarily with the person and views of the marshal, in accordance with its specific objective. Controversial issues are bypassed—Ludendorff's alleged loss of nerve during the Battle of Tannenberg is touched upon only in an oblique aside, without mention of name. There is an allusion to Hindenburg's occasional intervention in political matters, but the crisis centering on the Reich-

---

[2] Mertz to Hindenburg, Mar. 29, 1919 (copy), Groener Papers/8/34–1; Hindenburg to Ludendorff, Aug. 20, 1919, Ludendorff, *Vom Feldherrn,* I, 70.

stag's Peace Resolution and the friction between the government and the supreme command culminating in Bethmann Hollweg's resignation are not even mentioned. The dismissal of Ludendorff and the Emperor's abdication are glossed over; the discussion of the military collapse is equally blurred, but the implication is unmistakable that it was the defection of the home front rather than the exhaustion of the troops that accounted for the collapse of the army: "Like Siegfried, slain by the treacherous spear of the grim Hagen, our exhausted front collapsed."[3] This of course was the essence of the "stab-in-the-back" version of the military collapse, and Hindenburg subscribed to it in his book although he granted in private that the collapse had been caused primarily by military defeat.[4]

The main concern of the book was, of course, to achieve its proposed educational and inspirational purpose. Thus it sought to impress upon its readers the need for a large and strong army, but in stressing the value of the army to the country, it was not so much concerned with its military as with its social and educational function. The army was hailed as an invaluable school of discipline, subordination, and selflessness: it bred character, presence of mind, determination, and responsibility. There could never be a substitute for the kind of national schooling the army had provided. Germans, more perhaps than any other nation, needed the discipline that only military training could give them. Without it the marshal saw no alternative but decay and sterility for the Fatherland.[5]

Next in importance to the army, *Out of My Life* maintained that the country needed the restoration of the national monarchy —the goal to which generations of Germans had aspired and which a half-century before had become the foundation stone of German greatness. Hindenburg's personal concerns lent a special emphasis to this plea; it is obvious that he wished to clear himself with this book of all charges of disloyalty to his monarch and the monarchy. He stresses his allegiance and gratitude to his King and Emperor, and keeps referring to him in terms of deepest devotion, "my Emperor," and "my All-Highest War Lord." He

[3] Mertz, "Zur Entstehung der Lebenserinnerungen des Generalfeldmarschalls von Hindenburg," MS., *BdRPr.*, R 54/269; Ludendorff, *Vom Feldherrn*, I, 71–72; Hindenburg, *Aus meinem Leben*, pp. 87, 200–01, 392–403.

[4] Otto Meissner, *Staatssekretär unter Ebert-Hindenburg-Hitler: Der Schicksalsweg des deutschen Volkes von 1918–1945, wie ich ihn erlebte* (Hamburg, 1951), p. 39. See also Hindenburg to Philipp, March 11, 1924, Bundesarchiv, Kl. Erw./223.

[5] Hindenburg, *Aus meinem Leben*, pp. 9, 17, 64–67; also Schüddekopf, *Heer und Republik*, pp. 18–19.

speaks with similar deference of William I, while Bismarck's name is mentioned but rarely and with notable restraint, as if the acknowledgment of the chancellor's accomplishments might detract from the prestige of his sovereign.[6]

The marshal's aversion to politics is implicit throughout the book—an attitude which Hindenburg, not unnaturally, attributes to his soldierly upbringing. He cautioned his readers specifically against party politics which so easily could become a battlefield of petty intrigues. What he hoped for was the recreation of a strong consolidated state, rooted in the authoritarian concepts of the old Prussia. He was confident that Germany would again attain this objective once the present high tide of disorder and demagoguery had receded: "With this certainty I lay down my pen and put my trust in you—German youth."[7]

The book was warmly received by upper- and middle-class audiences, and though it was sharply attacked in the Socialist press, it also found its way into many a worker's home. Several hundred thousand copies were sold within a short time; it became a favorite Christmas and birthday gift. Its success may seem surprising, allowing even for the veneration its author enjoyed, for it was not a well written book: it lacked vigor and grace, and added little to what was generally known. The merit of *Out of My Life* lay in its very simplicity; it offered an easily understood survey of military developments during the War, much less exacting than Ludendorff's more substantial memoirs. Unpretentious and undemanding, the book became a bestseller as a popular historical account and as such fulfilled well that inspirational and educational purpose for which it was written.[8]

Before the book appeared, Hindenburg was given another opportunity to defend the honor of the old army. In August 1919, the national assembly established a committee to inquire into the responsibility for the outbreak and the length of the war. The

---

6 Hindenburg, *Aus meinem Leben*, pp. 405, 54, 59, 61, 143, 233, 300, 332–33, 13, 43, 215, 77–79. His reservations about Bismarck may also have stemmed from the fact that he had some misgivings about Bismarck's unification of Germany. Like most Prussian conservatives he did not cherish the thought of the union of Prussia with the less tightly structured South German states (*ibid.*, p. 42). Nor did he ever outgrow his specifically Prussian patriotism. To the end of his days he remained rooted mentally in the pre-Imperial world of William I. Cf. Friedrich Meinecke, *Strassburg, Freiburg, Berlin: 1901–1919* (Stuttgart, 1949), p. 248; Dorothea Groener-Geyer, *General Groener: Soldat und Staatsmann* (Frankfurt/M., 1955), p. 279.

7 Hindenburg, *Aus meinem Leben*, pp. 199–200, 218, 393, 215, 405–06.

8 Information from S. Hirzel Verlag, Nov. 11, 1957. Interestingly some of the more serious conservative journals, such as the *Preussische Jahrbücher* and the *Deutsche Rundschau* which paid considerable attention to the literature about the War of 1914–18 ignored the book completely.

investigation was to determine the causes leading to the explosion of 1914, and was also to ascertain whether the war could have been ended earlier on tolerable terms. In addition, this committee was given the task of examining the relationship between military and civil leadership and of investigating the recurrent charges that Germany had violated international law in her military and economic warfare. The hope was that the bitter controversies raging over these questions could thus be settled once and for all. At the same time the investigation was to obviate the extradition of any "war criminals" to the Allied Powers. If the committee found that German nationals had been guilty of breaches of international law, they were to be tried before a specially established state court of justice (*Staatsgerichtshof*).[9]

The committee quickly settled down to its task. Since the Allies would soon present a list of those they wished to have extradited, no time was to be lost. Among the issues that had to be clarified, the German reaction to President Wilson's peace move in 1916–17 ranked as a major one. Could hostilities have been ended on acceptable terms at that time if Germany had not decided to resort to unrestricted submarine warfare? Why had Germany taken that fateful step, and why had the supreme command insisted on it in spite of the chancellor's warnings? To answer these questions, Ludendorff was asked to testify as a witness.

The subcommittee in charge of this phase of the investigation deliberately refrained from calling Hindenburg. The committee was already the target of bitter attacks from the right that condemned the entire procedure as shameful and it did not wish to add to its troubles by requesting the marshal to appear before it as an ordinary witness under oath. The request was bound to touch off new outbursts of vituperation at a time when the political atmosphere was surcharged with tension. Nor could Hindenburg be expected to make any helpful contribution to the inquiry. The committee was aware of the role he had played during the war, and knew that he was unlikely to have any information that Ludendorff could not supply. Yet when Ludendorff was summoned to testify, he refused to appear unless the marshal did. Although this ultimatum was a clear violation of law, the harassed committee gave in and called on Hindenburg to appear before a forthcoming session. The marshal agreed, but as expected the news provoked a new outburst of the rightist press against the committee.

Ludendorff had good reason to insist on the marshal's appear-

9 Heilfron, *Die deutsche Nationalversammlung*, VIII, 150–53.

ance. In his memoirs he claims that an investigation of Hindenburg's conduct of the war would have demonstrated once and for all the absurdity of the entire procedure, but this was doubtless a secondary consideration. His chief motives were clearly less selfless: with his own prestige on the decline, he hoped to benefit from the marshal's unimpaired popularity to gloss over some of the decisions for which he might be taken to task. And if he should not succeed in this, Hindenburg was to be forced to share the responsibility with him.[10]

The two men appeared before the subcommittee on November 18, 1919. Hindenburg's stay in the capital turned into a triumphant ovation for the nation's hero. The government paid its tribute to him by providing a special lounge car for the trip from Hanover. The army, not to be outdone, dispatched a guard of honor to the station; two officers were assigned as his aides, and sentries posted at the gates of the villa of Karl Helfferich, the German National leader, whose house guest Hindenburg was while he stayed in Berlin. Large crowds lined the streets and lustily cheered him wherever he went. If he resented having to account for his wartime decisions, he must have felt amply rewarded for his pains by this heartwarming reception. But when the ovations provoked counter-demonstrations, he was anxious to check them. In an appeal to the people of Berlin he urged them to desist from any actions that might, as he put it, disturb traffic and public order. And when some demonstrators urged him, while he was on his way to the Reichstag, not to appear before the committee, he answered, clearly annoyed: "Don't bother me; I am on duty." If it had not been for a heavy snowstorm that day, a more determined attempt might have been made to keep him from testifying. A few days earlier, when he was thought, erroneously, to be on his way to the Reichstag, a student mob forced him to turn back. On the day he did testify the streets were patroled by troops, and he himself was escorted by mounted guards.[11]

He came to the meeting thoroughly briefed. Helfferich and his party friends had decided to use his appearance before the committee for a well staged attack upon the republican regime and the

10 Ludendorff, *Vom Feldherrn*, I, 70; Moritz Julius Bonn, *So macht man Geschichte* (Munich, 1953), p. 238; *Official German Documents Relating to the World War* (New York, 1923), II, 849.

11 Wheeler-Bennett, *Wooden Titan*, pp. 231–33; Görlitz, *Hindenburg*, pp. 231–32; Gustav Noske, *Erlebtes aus Aufstieg und Niedergang einer Demokratie* (Offenbach/M., 1947), pp. 148–49; Walther Freiherr von Lüttwitz, *Im Kampf gegen die November-Revolution* (Berlin, 1934), p. 108; *New York Times*, Nov. 13, 15, 16, 18, 21, 1919.

democratic left. In consultation with Ludendorff, they had carefully laid their plans. A statement was prepared for the marshal that he was to read to the committee; his statement read, Ludendorff would answer any questions that might be asked. No chance was to be taken on exposing the marshal to the give-and-take of an interrogation in which he might be forced into some damaging admissions. Hindenburg agreed readily to these arrangements that cast him in the kind of background role he always preferred in difficult situations.[12]

The committee received the two men with great deference: as Hindenburg and Ludendorff entered the room, everyone rose; the chairman, the Democratic deputy Gothein, himself showed them to the witness stand that some admirers had decorated with chrysanthemums and black-white-and-red ribbons. Gothein opened the session, and turning toward the marshal apologized for having inconvenienced him, "The Committee would have been glad to spare you the great trouble of appearing before it and, above all, would gladly have spared you the difficulties of your journey in the winter time, but since General Ludendorff placed great importance upon having his testimony taken at the same time as yours was, we could not avoid the necessity of requesting you to appear before us." Hindenburg's answer was courteous, though cool: "I may be permitted to state that I felt it incumbent upon myself to take my place at the side of my faithful companion in arms during great and troubled days, and that I am grateful that the opportunity has been afforded me to do so. I am also grateful for having had my journey made easier for me."

After this exchange Gothein asked the marshal to be sworn as a witness. Now, however, some difficulties arose. Hindenburg insisted on having Ludendorff read a prepared statement in which both denied being under any obligation to testify since anything they might say might expose them to the danger of criminal prosecution; witnesses need not testify, according to the code of criminal procedure, which was here applicable, if their answers tended to incriminate them. They were prepared to testify, but if they waived their right of refusal, they did so merely in order to help establish the historical truth: "It is only by learning the truth that the German people can recover, and it is for this reason, and for this reason alone, that we are ready to give our testimony under oath." The chairman tried to shrug off this statement as merely a

[12] Groener to Rohdewald, Dec. 18, 1919, Groener-Geyer, *General Groener*, p. 392; Ludendorff, *Vom Feldherrn*, I, 74–75; Wheeler-Bennett, *Wooden Titan*, pp. 231–32; Ernst Troeltsch, *Spektator-Briefe* (Tübingen, 1924), p. 92.

"private expression of will" of the witnesses, and the two men were sworn.

Gothein now asked Hindenburg the first of a series of questions which had been submitted in advance to both witnesses. It related to unrestricted submarine warfare. When was it decided that an all-out campaign could not be postponed any longer, and for what reasons? As arranged, Hindenburg ignored the question and instead read the statement that had been prepared for him. It had nothing to do with the points at issue, but was merely a defense of the conduct of the war by the supreme command. In its determination to fight the war through to victory, the statement declared, the supreme command had considered itself but the executor of the will of both nation and army. Yet while the army had fought gallantly until the last moment, the nation had proved itself weak and undisciplined, and in the end its failings had led, inevitably, to the military collapse. He reiterated here not merely what he had said in his book, but went far beyond it. The disintegration of civilian morale, he now claimed, had set in before he and Ludendorff took over the supreme command in August 1916: "When we took command, we submitted to the Government a number of proposals, the purpose of which was to concentrate all our national forces for the purpose of bringing about an early termination of the war, and one that would be favorable to us. . . . However, we all know the fate of our proposals. . . What I sought to obtain was strong and cheerful cooperation, and I was met with weakness and a refusal to act. From this moment on, we were never free from anxiety as to whether or not our people at home would stand fast until the war was won." Plans were being laid, the supreme command noticed, to undermine the morale of both army and navy: "The purposes which the leaders contemplated became now impossible to carry out. . . . So our operations were bound to fail, and the collapse was inevitable; the resolution was but the keystone."

Hindenburg then added these fateful words which were to make history: "An English general has said, with justice: 'The German Army was stabbed in the back.' No blame is to be attached to the sound core of the Army. Its performances call, like that of the officer corps, for our equal admiration. It is perfectly plain on whom the blame rests. If any further proof were necessary to show it, it is to be found in the statement made by the British general and in the utter amazement of our enemies at their victory." In conclusion he noted that he and Ludendorff had always agreed on all important decisions: "We have borne our common share of anxiety and responsibility. And here too, we jointly appear before you as those who stood for the ideas and methods of the Supreme Command ever since August 29, 1916." Ludendorff was satisfied and, as he notes in his memoirs, almost ready to let bygones be bygones.

Gothein had tried repeatedly to interrupt Hindenburg on the grounds that his statement was irrelevant, but the marshal had blandly ignored his protests. Now the chairman once more asked his question concerning the choice of February 1, 1917, as the starting time for unrestricted submarine warfare. Hindenburg answered briefly and referred Gothein to Ludendorff. The session soon became stormy. Ludendorff was discursive and opinionated, and the discussion was frequently punctuated by heated exchanges between him and the chairman and some of the other witnesses. Hindenburg sat by calmly and contented himself with injecting an occasional comment. The session ended inconclusively, but after this frustrating experience the committee decided not to call back either witness. The next day Hindenburg left for Hanover to the accompaniment of new ovations and demonstrations. At the station another honor guard saw him off in proper style.[13]

This, then, was the official birth of the "stab-in-the-back" legend. It had been circulated before though not with this catchy slogan; in fact, the foundation for it was laid even before the final military collapse when Ludendorff, with newly gained confidence in the strength of the army, had warned the government that continued resistance depended on the determination of the home front to carry on the struggle.[14] This legend was inadvertently encouraged by the Allied Powers when they insisted, contrary to customary practice, on conducting armistice negotiations with civilians rather than with the military. The generals thus were spared the onus of accepting the armistice, and they could uphold the myth of the undefeated army which had been betrayed by corrupt politicians. To this version Hindenburg had now given his sanction. In the

[13] *Official German Documents*, II, 849–904, esp. pp. 849–55; Ludendorff, *Vom Feldherrn*, I, 75–85; Bonn, *So macht man Geschichte*, pp. 239–40; Wheeler-Bennett, *Nemesis*, p. 68; Georg Gothein, "Aus meiner politischen Arbeit," MS., Gothein Papers/58/84–85. On the history of the remark attributed to General Sir Frederick Maurice, see the detailed study by Friedrich Freiherr Hiller von Gaertringen, " 'Dolchstoss'–Diskussion und 'Dolchstosslegende' im Wandel von vier Jahrzehnten," *Aus Politik und Zeitgeschichte*, suppl. to *Das Parlament*, Apr. 17, 1963.

[14] Meeting of State Secretaries, Oct. 18, 1918, esp. Solf's comments, *Amtliche Urkunden zur Vorgeschichte des Waffenstillstandes 1918*, Auswärtiges Amt und Reichsministerium des Innern, ed. (Berlin, 1924), No. 54, pp. 119–20; Friedrich Meinecke, *Die deutsche Katastrophe: Betrachtungen und Erinnerungen* (Wiesbaden, 1947), p. 51.

face of such formidable backing, all contrary documentary evidence and expert opinion were to prove utterly ineffective.[15]

❦

Hindenburg's talks in Berlin dealt not only with the preparation for his appearance before the investigation committee. Some of his visitors came on a very different errand. The election of Ebert as Reich president had been a temporary arrangement, on the basis of the provisional constitution which the national assembly had enacted during the first days of its existence. On August 11, 1919, the permanent constitution had been promulgated at Weimar, and in conformity with its provisions plans were now being made for the election of a new president.

Ebert, it was clear, would once more be the candidate of the Social Democrats. Under difficult circumstances he had filled his high office with dignity and apparent effectiveness. He was likely to attract many votes from the bourgeois camp, from Centrists and Democrats, and with their support his election was all but assured. A rightist candidate could hope to defeat Ebert only if he captured the bulk of the bourgeois vote. While Hindenburg's nomination had aroused no enthusiasm in February 1919, some rightist leaders thought the political atmosphere sufficiently changed to turn to him as the man who might defeat Ebert.

The leaders of the German People's Party enthusiastically endorsed the suggestion. There were some objections to the marshal's candidacy in the Rhineland and in Southern Germany, ostensibly on the grounds that Hindenburg ought not to be drawn into a party-political contest, but actually because his Prusso-military background caused some misgivings; yet the bulk of the party supported its leaders. In August 1919, less than two weeks after the new constitution had been enacted, the party's executive committee decided to present Hindenburg's name to the nation. The entire *Bürgertum* would rally around him, Stresemann, the head of the People's Party argued, since no other bourgeois candidate would dare run against him. Nor need his candidacy be considered a monarchist demonstration; his presidency would in fact make it easier for monarchists to accept the new situation.[16]

The German Nationals seized upon the proposal with equal

---

15 If the "stab-in-the-back" legend has today any more adherents in Germany, they can be but few. All leading German historians now reject it; cf. Gerhard Ritter, *Europa und die deutsche Frage* (Munich, 1948), pp. 178, 185–86; Werner Conze, in Peter Rassow, ed., *Deutsche Geschichte im Überblick: Ein Handbuch* (Stuttgart, 1953), p. 653; Hans Herzfeld, *Die moderne Welt: 1789–1945* (Brunswick, 1952), II, 188–89. General Beck who had earlier accepted the legend (see his letter of Nov. 28,

enthusiasm. As the party *par excellence* of monarchy and army, they considered themselves particularly close to the marshal. All objections to him because of his role on the departure of the Emperor on November 9 were swept away in this eager endorsement of his candidacy. Under the cautious leadership of Oskar Hergt, a one-time Prussian minister of finance, the bulk of the party had not yet assumed the obstructionist attitude of later years and was prepared, with some reservations, to cooperate with the Weimar Republic. With the marshal as president, the leaders would find it even easier to pursue their moderate course over the opposition of those party diehards who kept clamoring for a policy of strict noncollaboration with the new regime.[17]

The decisive conference with Hindenburg concerning his presidential nomination took place while he was in Berlin. Hergt and Stresemann called on him and urged him to accept the candidacy. He was not unprepared for their visit; they had earlier approached him by letter, and after consultation with some confidants in Hanover he had carefully worked out his answer. Under certain conditions, he told them, he would be willing to run. He would not accept if he were to be merely a figurehead who might have to work with a Socialist government. His visitors assured him that in view of the manifest trend towards the right he need not worry about such a possibility; the forthcoming Reichstag elections were bound to result in a leftist defeat. They were equally reassuring on the chances of his election since he insisted he would not expose himself to the embarrassment of a defeat. Clearly relieved, Hindenburg stated that he personally had no further objection to his nomination, though it involved heavy sacrifices. As a devout monarchist he did feel, however, that he ought to consult the Emperor before accepting and promised to give them his final decision within the next two weeks.

The ex-monarch approved, and soon preparations were being made to launch Hindenburg's campaign on a nonpartisan basis. When Ludendorff called on the marshal some weeks later, his

---

1918, in Schüddekopf, *Heer und Republik*, pp. 24–26), repudiated it in a lecture he gave in 1941 ("Der 29. September 1918," in Beck, *Studien*, pp. 195–225).

[16] Meeting of Executive Committee of German People's Party, Aug. 24, 1919, Stresemann Papers/207/3088/137870; Stresemann to Brües, Sept. 13, 25, 1919, *ibid.* /207/3088/137915–16, 138950–51; *Kölnische Zeitung*, No. 229, Mar. 8, 1920.

[17] Westarp, *Ende der Monarchie*, p. 159; Lewis Hertzman, "The German National People's Party (DNVP.): 1918–1924," Ph.D. thesis, Harvard, 1954, pp. 113–14, 116–21, 148–49, 308–10; Werner Liebe, *Die deutschnationale Volkspartei: 1918-1924* (Düsseldorf, 1956), pp. 15, 147 n. 218–19.

candidacy was discussed as a definite fact. It was formally announced on March 8, 1920.[18]

The election was never held, and even before the decision was made to forego it, Hindenburg had withdrawn his candidacy. The ill-fated Kapp Putsch in mid-March 1920 upset all political calculations. In the wake of that coup, Hindenburg could no longer have run on anything resembling a nonpartisan basis, nor was there any assurance that he would be elected. Under these circumstances he announced at once his withdrawal. The warning of the Western Powers that they would not tolerate the election of the man who headed the list of the "war criminals" may have confirmed him in the wisdom of his decision, for he was anxious to spare his country —and himself—all avoidable difficulties.[19]

જ

The Kapp Putsch epitomized the immense difficulties in which the young republic was enmeshed from the first days of its existence. In the aftermath of war and defeat, economic conditions kept spiraling downward. The bourgeoisie was deeply concerned about the continuing unrest and longed for the restoration of order and stability. The seemingly unending succession of strikes, demonstrations, and clashes confirmed the suspicions of those who had viewed the advent of the republican regime with some apprehension. Others who had accepted it now concluded that their personal and economic security was predicated on the restoration of the traditional authoritarian government. Their fears grew as the workers, dissatisfied with what the government had done for them so far, drifted in growing numbers into the ranks of the Independent Socialists and Communists. And if the new regime was unable to maintain order domestically, neither was it able, in the eyes of the *Bürgertum,* to vindicate its existence by diplomatic successes—national intransigence seemed to hold out the only chance for a better future. There had been rumors, moreover, of shady deals by prominent government and party leaders; however unfounded most of them were, they added to the existing malaise. Demands for a change were spreading, but most

18 Meeting of Executive Committee of German People's Party, Nov. 24, 1919, Stresemann Papers/208/3088/138060–61; confidential memorandum, No. 3, Dec. 17, 1919, *ibid.*/208/3088/138121; Rauch to Bernstein, Oct. 14, 1920, *ibid.*/218/3091/139776; materials on Kapp Putsch, in Braun Papers.

19 Riesser to Stresemann, Jan. 3, 1920, Stresemann Papers/220/3091/139993; Stresemann to Executive Committee of German People's Party, Sept. 13, 1920, *ibid.*/211/3089/138473–74; Rabenau, *Seeckt*, p. 220; Görlitz, *Hindenburg*, p. 236; Luwig F. Gengler, *Die deutschen Monarchisten 1919–1925* (Erlangen, 1932), pp. 70–74; Ludendorff, *Vom Feldherrn,* I, 108.

of those who favored a change thought of it in terms of new elections by which the Socialist president and the leftist majority in the Reichstag would be removed.

Military circles shared the wish for a change, and even toyed briefly with a plan of establishing a military dictatorship under Noske; but when Noske refused to become a party to any such plot, it failed to develop. The discontent of the officer corps, however, increased, and it looked with growing dismay on the government since some ministers did not conceal their distrust of the military. Most generals, however, were no longer willing to resort to a violent overthrow of the government, for they knew that such an attempt would lack mass support.

Against this background of rancor and dissatisfaction, a military Putsch was staged on March 13, 1920 by those who had always advocated an armed revolt. Given the hesitation of most army leaders, they relied primarily on the Free Corps with their particular stake in an uprising—to ward off disbandment of the Corps which the government, on Allied insistence, was now determined to carry out.[20]

The Kapp Putsch was a direct disavowal of everything for which Hindenburg had stood since the collapse of the monarchy. It repudiated the attempts, so largely associated with his name, of building a bridge from the monarchy to the new state. Those who planned and supported the rising were indeed men who had never shared the deep respect in which Hindenburg was held by the bulk of the nation. Their leader, Wolfgang Kapp, was an ardent admirer of Ludendorff and had long known that Ludendorff rather than the marshal had been the guiding spirit of their victories. He disliked Hindenburg because of his cautious and slow moving ways, and he had not forgiven him for having lent his support to the republic during the first few months of its precarious existence. Of his associates, Ludendorff and his one-time aide, Colonel Bauer, shared Kapp's distrust of the marshal. Nor was Hindenburg a popular figure among the Free Corps that supported the Putsch; in the eyes of these rootless adventurers, the staid and sober marshal in his noncommittal restraint had always seemed a man who looked for an easy way out of every crisis, and many indeed spoke of him with open contempt. They refused to see in Hindenburg a symbol of national unity that could inspire and guide the nation to new greatness. General von Lüttwitz, the military leader of the Kapp Putsch, was more favorably disposed to the marshal,

[20] Noske, *Von Kiel*, pp. 204–06; Groener, *Lebenserinnerungen*, p. 514; Rosenberg, *Geschichte*, pp. 105-12; Troeltsch, *Spektator-Briefe*, pp. 125-33.

but even he did not wish Hindenburg to be associated with that undertaking.[21]

The Putsch was precipitated when the government, forewarned of the plot, attempted to relieve Lüttwitz of his command. Without consulting Kapp, Lüttwitz decided that the time for action had come, and he ordered the Free Corps in his command area to march on the capital. Since the army refused to defend the government, the cabinet had no means of stopping Lüttwitz. It was able, however, to escape from Berlin and establish itself first in Dresden and later in Stuttgart. It thus frustrated one of the basic premises of Kapp's plan—that taken by surprise, the cabinet would immediately be arrested. Kapp's plans also went awry in other respects. Since the understanding had been that the plotters would strike in late March or in April, he had not yet completed the formation of his government and, as it turned out, he was never to do so.

What followed was, inevitably, a tragicomedy of errors and confusion. Even though parts of the Reichswehr sided with him, Kapp realized at once that all was lost. It was a measure of his despair that he was willing to negotiate with the hated Socialists, and in one moment of utter demoralization he even received a delegation of Independent Socialists. A day later, when some deputies of the People's Party urged him to call on Hindenburg to take his place while he, Kapp, would serve under him, he was ready to accept that suggestion too, despite his dislike of the marshal. But given the unwillingness of most generals and officials to support him, nothing could save him and his associates. A general strike proclaimed by the labor unions and approved by the legal government precipitated the inevitable collapse of the Putsch. Kapp fled from Berlin on March 17, four days after he had proclaimed himself chancellor, and Lüttwitz, his "Defense Minister," followed him a few hours later.[22]

Hindenburg remained silent during these days. He had had some general knowledge of Kapp's preparations, and he had hastened to express his strong disapproval of these plans. He ab-

---

21 Ludwig Schemann, *Wolfgang Kapp und das Märzunternehmen vom Jahr 1920* (Munich and Berlin, 1937), pp. 105, 116; Peter von Heydebreck, *Wir Wehr-Wölfe: Erinnerungen eines Freikorps-Führers* (Leipzig, 1931), pp. 68, 81; Lüttwitz, *Kampf gegen November-Revolution*, pp. 107–08.

22 Schemann, *Kapp*, pp. 146–58; Lüttwitz, *Kampf gegen November-Revolution*, pp. 120–22; Waite, *Vanguard*, pp. 156–58; Rabenau, *Seeckt*, p. 219; meeting of German People's Party leaders, Mar. 13, 14, 1920, Stresemann Papers/217/3090/139552; memorandum on discussions of party delegation with Kapp, Mar. 13, 14, 1920, *ibid./* 139529; Volkmann, *Revolution*, pp. 350–51, 364–65; Carl Severing, *Mein Lebensweg* (Cologne, 1950), I, 255–56.

horred the chaos of civil war and may have sensed also the hopelessness of the undertaking. Three days before the coup, the marshal attended the anniversary celebration of the founding of the Free Corps Hindenburg, then stationed near Hanover, but the occasion was purely social and he was as surprised as was the Corps when the Kapp Putsch put a sudden end to the festivities.

During the four days of the Kapp regime he remained closeted in his home. Many saw in him the ideal mediator between the opposing camps. Someone (Groener?) suggested to President Ebert that he ask Hindenburg to exert his influence on the Reichswehr, and informing the marshal of this proposal, urged him to accept the call if he were asked, "since one word from you would be sufficient to lead the Reichswehr back into constitutional paths." The marshal, however, did not move, preferring to let events take care of themselves.[23]

Hindenburg was convinced that the debacle of the Kapp Putsch had ruined his presidential chances and he withdrew as a candidate. He turned a deaf ear on all pleas that his election offered the best safeguard against any further putsches and invariably answered, "no."[24] More even than before, he shunned public appearances and rarely ventured into the streets. He insisted that he had no political ambitions and accepted few invitations to public gatherings. When he did, it was to attend a veterans' congress or the unveiling of a war memorial, and on these occasions, he was anxious to avoid all political demonstrations. He never failed, in the few speeches he made, to pay public tribute to the ex-Emperor, even if members of the government or representatives of the Reichswehr were present. This he considered a matter of personal loyalty (or perhaps of atonement) rather than a political gesture, and he was deeply shocked when one such address in Königsberg, East Prussia, led to a bloody clash between Reichswehr and Communists. He was anxious, he complained, not to add to the difficulties of his troubled country and appears not to have understood why his public appearances became threatening monarchist demonstrations in republican eyes. He embarrassed the government in other ways too. Shortly after the Königsberg incident he predicted to an American visitor that Germany would

23 Görlitz, *Hindenburg*, p. 234; *Das Buch vom deutschen Freikorpskämpfer*, Ernst von Salomon, ed. (Berlin, 1938), p. 375; Joachim von Stülpnagel, *75 Jahre meines Lebens* (Oberaudorf, Obb., 1960), p. 185; copy of unsigned undated telegram to Hindenburg, Schleicher Papers/5/54.
24 Vermittlungsstelle Vaterländischer Verbände, "Richtlinien zu den Wahlen," Apr. 30, 1920, Westarp Papers; Rauch to Bernstein, Oct. 14, 1920, Stresemann Papers/218/3091/139776.

eventually have her revenge on France, "and if it takes a hundred years; . . . what I want more than anything is to take up arms once more against France." Again he was greatly disturbed when the statement touched off a bitter debate in the Reichstag.[25]

After the death of his wife in the spring of 1921, Hindenburg felt even more the need for privacy and seclusion. It is evident from his own words and actions, however, that he thought such aloofness the best way too of retaining his popular standing. He was annoyed when Groener raised some questions in a magazine article about the strategy of the supreme command in 1918. He could accept the fact that the article was going to hurt him, he complained to the general, but he regretted that the German people would no longer have the same faith in him. He was similarly perturbed when Colonel Bauer maintained in his memoirs that Ludendorff had been the actual victor at Tannenberg and the guiding spirit of the supreme command and that the honors and admiration bestowed on Hindenburg should rightly have gone to his chief aide. He asked Ludendorff to issue a public refutation of Bauer's charges, but Ludendorff who agreed fully with Bauer refused to do so and suggested that someone else might be found for this task. However, his greatest concern was the unending debate about his attitude on November 9, the day of the departure of William from Spa; to his dismay this debate would not die down. In 1922, the ex-Crown Prince published his wartime reminiscences, in which he stated that the marshal had been unable to help the Emperor and had stood by silently while the fate of the monarch was being sealed. Hindenburg had been in the midst of preparations for a visit to the East Prussian battlefields when the reminiscences came out and his immediate reaction was to cancel the trip. He was persuaded with great difficulty that he need not fear any adverse repercussions and that his reception in East Prussia would be as cordial as ever.[26]

There were other problems. Sometimes even Hindenburg found it difficult to reconcile his monarchist convictions with the apolitical attitude he wished to maintain. Again he took refuge in carefully worked out compromises in which he tried to adjust his obligations towards his monarch to the obvious fact that monarchism

[25] Hindenburg to Groener, Dec. 9, 1919, Oct. 18, 1921, Groener Papers/7/28; Dehmel to Stresemann, Apr. 7, 1925, Stresemann Papers/23/3166/158703; Hindenburg to Westarp, Aug. 19, 1923, Westarp Papers; Wheeler-Bennett, *Wooden Titan*, pp. 242–43; Schöpflin, Mar. 15, 1923, *Stenographische Berichte der Verhandlungen des deutschen Reichstages* (hereafter cited as "*Verhandlungen*"), Vol. 360, p. 11097.
[26] Groener-Geyer, *General Groener*, p. 211; Ludendorff, *Vom Feldherrn*, I, 168; Freiherr Wilhelm von Gayl, "Mit Schwert und Feder," MS., Gayl Papers/11.

was no longer a national concept but an issue of party politics. He was overjoyed when the ex-Emperor sent him a telegram congratulating him on having escaped unharmed from an attack on him by a burglar; he considered it his duty to attend the funeral of the former Empress in Potsdam in the spring of 1921; and he never neglected to render his sovereign homage in public addresses. All these, however, were personal gestures honoring the past, and they were not intended as calls to political action; he quickly rejected any suggestion that he work actively for a monarchist restoration. When one of his sons-in-law organized an association of monarchists (*Bund der Aufrechten*), he refused to join. He must not belong to any partisan organization, he explained, if he were to continue to work for German unity. He became even more cautious after the Kapp Putsch. Though Kapp does not seem to have aimed at the restoration of the monarchy, the uprising was generally considered a monarchist undertaking and its failure served to discredit further all monarchist aspirations. Hindenburg's caution was so great that when the ex-Emperor suggested that the marshal visit him in his exile at Doorn, he was not certain whether he ought to accept the invitation and consulted Westarp. Only after the latter had assured him that the visit was unobjectionable politically, did he decide to go. (The trip which was planned for March 1925 never materialized. It may have seemed inadvisable after the death of President Ebert on February 28, 1925, in view of the forthcoming presidential elections. Once Hindenburg himself had been elected, the plan had to be abandoned of course.)[27]

There would have been no invitation from Doorn, had not the troublesome old problem of the Emperor's departure for Holland in 1918 at last been settled. It was no easy task, for the marshal proved a wily quarry. In August 1920 he consented to issue another statement in defense of the ex-monarch, but it was no more helpful than his earlier ones: the Kaiser had not deserted his army, but had been deserted by his own people and had departed only in order to spare the country the horrors of a civil war and (what was untrue) the resumption of hostilities by the enemy. Again, nothing was said about Hindenburg's role that day—the crucial question that William wished to have clarified.

The ex-monarch was not the only one to insist on a straight-

---

[27] Hindenburg-Westarp exchange, Feb. 1925, Westarp Papers; Ludendorff, *Vom Feldherrn*, I, 117, 160, 212–13; Görlitz, *Hindenburg*, pp. 235, 240–41; Gengler, *Monarchisten*, pp. 70, 75–89.

forward statement from the marshal. This question of Hindenburg's attitude on November 9, 1918, was still being debated in rightist circles. "What keeps the Marshal from issuing an explanation which would solve the doubts of thousands of us? For we have our doubts . . .," one of the Free Corps leaders wondered. Hindenburg must speak up, Westarp was told by a constituent, he must state clearly what happened and put an end to the vicious allegations about the Kaiser's flight and desertion. These misgivings doubtless came to the marshal's attention; together with the ex-Emperor's recurring demands that he issue a forthright acknowledgment of his role on that ill-starred November day they led him to make finally a somewhat more specific statement on his role in the letter written to the ex-Emperor in July 1922 (quoted in Chapter 1 of this study).

Again the statement did not fully meet the ex-monarch's expectations, and it took two months before he could bring himself to acknowledge receipt of the letter. He made it clear in his reply how much he resented the fact that the marshal's statement had been so long delayed, "I am grateful to you for having finally taken this step which respect for historical truth and for the protection of My family and My personal honor had long required." And in a concluding paragraph he clearly implied that the advice which Hindenburg had finally admitted to have given on November 9 had been poor indeed.[28]

After this outburst the correspondence between the two men settled back into its customary courteous tenor. Hindenburg, the loyal servant of his monarch, would never have thought of showing whatever irritation or disappointment he may have felt toward the Emperor, and William knew that given the marshal's popular standing, he could not hope to return to his throne except with the latter's help. In view of his dependence on Hindenburg, he could not allow their relations to deteriorate.

Inevitably, efforts were also made to enroll Hindenburg's support in behalf of the Bavarian pretender, Crown Prince Rupprecht. To draw him closer to the Bavarian restoration movement, one of the Prince's advisers tried to persuade him to move to Munich. In Munich, with its monarchist atmosphere, he suggested, Hindenburg would feel more at home than in Socialist Hanover, but

28 Hindenburg statement of Aug. 16, 1920, in Westarp, *Ende der Monarchie;* Heydebreck, *Wehr-Wölfe*, pp. 150–52; Letter to Westarp, Sept. 7, 1921, Westarp Papers; William II to Hindenburg, Apr. 5, 1921, Kaiser Wilhelm II., *Ereignisse und Gestalten aus den Jahren 1878-1918* (Leipzig and Berlin, 1922), p. 254; Hindenburg to William II, July 28, 1922, William II to Hindenburg, Sept. 21, 1922, Niemann, *Revolution,* pp. 472–73.

Hindenburg begged off. All he would do was to pay a brief visit to the city in August 1922, on his way to a chamois hunt which had prudently been arranged for him. While in Munich he met with Rupprecht and Ludendorff who now made his home there, and with a number of other monarchist leaders; among those he saw were some members of the Nazi Party, already a force to be reckoned with in Bavaria. Hindenburg, however, carefully kept away from close involvement with any group and the only lasting result of his visit was the friendship he formed with his hunting hosts. He gladly accepted their hospitality and was from then on their house guest during the hunting season each fall.[29]

His personal life became ever quieter—a symbol of past greatness, he was receding into history. Those were years of deep unrest in Germany marked by the occupation of the Ruhr Basin by French and Belgian troops; an inflation that shattered the hopes of millions of ever gaining again any measure of social and economic security; and a political and spiritual malaise that fed radical movements of both the right and the left. Communist risings kept central Germany in turmoil, and in the south Nazi and other antirepublican forces were preparing for a showdown with the Berlin government. These events did very little to disturb the peace of the villa on the outskirts of Hanover; even the effects of the inflation were cushioned by a special fund set up by a group of industrialists that relieved the marshal of all economic anxieties throughout the deepening crisis. In the fall of 1923 he again spent a few weeks hunting with his Bavarian friends. One of Hitler's associates whom he met on this trip asked him whether he might give Hindenburg's greetings to Hitler: "You may, but tell him also I must warn him against any rash action; the Fatherland cannot stand another Kapp Putsch." It was not the kind of advice that the restless Hitler would heed.

When the conflict between Berlin and Munich sharpened, Hindenburg insisted on staying neutral. In October the commander of the Bavarian contingent of the Reichswehr refused to take orders from his superiors in Berlin. Gessler, the Reichswehr minister, pleaded with Hindenburg to use his influence to bring the rebellious general back into the fold, but the marshal refused. Only after the Hitler Putsch in November 1923 did he issue a statement: "I deeply regret that German brothers, all equally inspired by love of their Fatherland, fought each other in Munich and inflicted a painful wound on the nation to the delight of our

[29] Görlitz, *Hindenburg*, pp. 240–41; Ernst Röhm, *Die Geschichte eines Hochverräters* (Munich, 1928), p. 131.

enemies. Take each other's hands across the graves of those who died in this action with faith in the righteousness of their cause, just as we elders did in 1866. More than ever, our poor Fatherland needs unity to cope with its immense difficulties."[30] To him these words were no mere platitudes. He himself had come to accept the republican regime in this spirit of reasonableness, despite his political and emotional reservations, and with good will and self-discipline, he was certain, others could do the same.

With the failure of Hitler's Putsch the wave of unrest that had swept across Germany for five dismal years appeared to have spent itself. After 1923 the Free Corps and other militant organizations that seemed to thrive on strife and confusion receded into the background. Slowly the country lifted itself out of the chaos of inflation and civil war. There was hope that a future could be built within the framework of the new state, and many a foe of the republic now brought himself at least to tolerate it. There seemed good reason to believe that it would soon be firmly established.

Parallel to this change in the political climate, Hindenburg's status too underwent a distinct change. Many who had once looked to the marshal as a leader to a better future now turned to others more likely to satisfy their expectations. The number of visitors and delegations paying their respects to him began to fall off. Occasionally he would still be called upon to serve as a mediator in an officers' dispute of honor. Once or twice Hindenburg was asked to intervene in the interminable quarrels between Ludendorff and his many enemies. In August 1924 he traveled again to East Prussia to attend the celebration of the tenth anniversary of the Battle of Tannenberg and to lay the cornerstone for a memorial. The ceremony was impressive; some 50,000 persons attended, among them all living generals who had participated in the battle and some of the dignitaries of the republic. In contrast to his earlier visit that had provoked demonstrations and counterdemonstrations, his reception on this occasion was calm and restrained. Hindenburg no longer counted as a political force, but was honored as the venerable symbol of a past now gone beyond recall.[31]

[30] On fund, letters of Feb. 4, 1932, May 4, 1925 (copies), Schleicher Papers/20/214–16; Hindenburg's statement to Nazi in Görlitz, *Hindenburg*, p. 241; Gessler, quoted by Anneliese Thimme, in *Welt als Geschichte*, xvii (1957), 21; Hindenburg, quoted in *Türmer*, xxvi (1923–24), 280. In 1866 Bismarck united northern and central Germany in the North German Confederation. Some of the member states of the new Confederation had earlier that year sided with Austria against Prussia in the Austro-Prussian War.

[31] Görlitz, *Hindenburg*, pp. 243–48; Ludendorff, *Vom Feldherrn*, i, 264–65, 399; *New York Times*, Aug. 28, 1924.

CHAPTER 3

THE ELECTION OF 1925

N February 28, 1925, Friedrich Ebert, the republic's first president, died. He had risen far above the limitations of party politics and had filled his high office with dignity and effectiveness. His integrity had gained him the respect of many a rightist opponent—a notable achievement for a one-time harnessmaker and innkeeper who was facing the social prejudices of a caste-bound society. His premature death, at the age of fifty-four, was precipitated by nationalist attacks on his patriotism; it forms part of that series of tragic circumstances that deprived the Weimar Republic of the few men of statesman-like caliber among its leaders.

Although Ebert's term of office would have ended in any event just four months later, the country was unprepared for a presidential election campaign. With conditions more stable again, the nation was turning away from the political arena. Its main concern was now the solution of its material problems, and the first signs of economic improvement encouraged this dissociation from politics.

The left, in particular, had failed to pay attention to the prospect of a new presidential contest. It simply assumed that Ebert would run again and that his reelection was assured. With that easy complacency that characterized the republican forces, it noted the growth of the democratic parties in the last Reichstag election (December 1924) and the striking decline of the radical movements of both right and left. Nor did it appreciate the potential importance of the president's office. Although Ebert had assumed vast authority in more than one crisis, the left looked upon the president as mainly a figurehead, and Ebert's personal modesty and his quiet, unpretentious ways had helped to strengthen this impression.[1] Surely the new president would have few opportunities for initiative and political action now that the republic seemed firmly established. Otto Braun, one of the Socialist leaders, recalls in his memoirs that he was most reluctant to run as his party's candidate because of the obvious unimport-

[1] Friedrich Stampfer, *Die vierzehn Jahre der ersten deutschen Republik* (Hamburg, 1953), p. 440; *Frankfurter Zeitung*, No. 277, Mar. 26, 1925.

ance of the presidency, and he agreed to his nomination only because he was certain that the first campaign would end inconclusively.[2]

The right had given some thought to the forthcoming election. Some weeks before Ebert's death the *Reichsbürgerrat,* an organization representing the conservative bourgeoisie, had set up a committee that was to find a suitable candidate. Its chairman was Friedrich Wilhelm von Loebell, a Prussian minister of the interior under the monarchy. Since the main purpose of the committee was to prevent the election of Ebert (or any other Social Democrat), it was to look for a man of nationwide appeal who would draw a substantial following from the bourgeois left as well. The committee was thus to include spokesmen, not only of the rightist parties and organizations, but also of such middle-of-the-road groups as the Center and the Economic Party, a party representing small business.[3] That the right was more concerned with the presidency was no accident. Many of its leaders were now convinced that it could hope to wield influence only within the republic, not against it, and the German National People's Party had shown therefore an increasing readiness to participate in the government. Part of its Reichstag delegation had supported the Dawes Plan which regulated anew the payment of Germany's war reparations. And in January 1925 members of the German National Party had for the first time joined a republican government. It was obvious that the right's acceptance of the republic would help to strengthen the new state; if it was to control this trend, it had to seize as many positions of power in the state as it could, and the presidency was one of them.

The right was also more aware of the potentialities of that post than its republican opponents. From its antiparliamentary perspective it looked on the presidency as the one post from which a strong leader could effectively check the dominance of the Reichstag. It saw sufficient leverage in the constitution to assure the president a large measure of political influence. "Given the great powers which the Reich President derives from [Articles] 4[8], 50, 53, 25, 73 of the Constitution, the parties of the right must agree on one candidate," one spokesman wrote some weeks

2 Otto Braun, *Von Weimar zu Hitler* (New York, 1940), p. 169; Severing, *Lebensweg,* II, 51.

3 Minutes of preparatory meeting under Loebell's chairmanship, Feb. 12, 1925, Westarp Papers; also memorandum on same meeting, Stresemann Papers/20/3166/ 158154–56; Nationalverband Deutscher Offiziere to Reichstag delegation of German National People's Party, Jan. 24, 1925, Westarp to Nationalverband, Feb. 24, 1925, Secretariat Westarp to Walbaum, Mar. 10, 1925, Westarp Papers.

before Ebert's death, "and under the guise of a supraparty label [present] him to their voters." In consequence the *Reichsbürger-rat* considered it its foremost task, in the words of its executive secretary, "to impress upon the public the importance and great influence of the Reich President on our future political development."[4]

Loebell himself had been among the first to urge upon the German Nationals a more positive attitude towards the republic. Since the fall of 1924 he had been publishing a biweekly journal, the *Deutschen-Spiegel,* that set itself the task of steering them away from the sterile antithesis of monarchy *vs.* republic. He wanted the "national movement" to take control of the state by exercising its constitutional rights and making full use of all administrative possibilities. The strengthening of the executive would have to be the first step; by yielding to political party exigencies the right had lost too much ground to the Reichstag. An editorial in the *Deutschen-Spiegel* warned in October 1924: "Our state requires the strongest possible concentration of power since we live in central Europe. We must once more give ourselves a [genuine] head of state, that is, a president who can act and does not solely depend on the parliament." The *Deutschen-Spiegel* thus sought to prepare the ground for the forthcoming presidential elections—a preparation that the editors considered the more imperative since they felt that the right, by the sterility of its oppositional tactics, had alienated a large number of its one-time supporters.[5]

Despite these long-range plans the right was no better prepared than the left to launch an election campaign after Ebert's sudden death. The Loebell committee had met a few times, but had reached an agreement in principle only on the nomination of a "supraparty" candidate. Loebell now called for the immediate selection of a strong personality not too closely identified with any one party. It was not easy to find an acceptable candidate. The German Nationals proposed Gessler, the Reichswehr minister; Seeckt, the military chief of the Reichswehr; and Tirpitz, the creator of the Imperial Navy. Since they all belonged to the military sphere, the German People's Party rejected them from

4 Letter of Jan. 23, 1925, copy in Stresemann Papers/20/3166/158109; letter of Feb. 2, 1925, *ibid.*/92/3160/172529; Otto Koellreutter, in *Deutsche Juristen-Zeitung,* XX (1925), 555.

5 Loebell, in *Deutschen-Spiegel,* Sept. 5, 1924, esp. p. 15, Sept. 19, 1924, p. 11; Kriegk, in *ibid.,* Oct. 24, 1924, pp. 8–9; editorials, Sept. 5, 1924, p. 5; Oct. 24, 1924, p. 14, Dec. 25, 1925, p. 2457.

fear of foreign political repercussions. Hans Luther, the chancellor, who was close to the People's Party, proved unacceptable to the German Nationals. Hindenburg's name was brought up, but was quickly discarded, primarily because of his age. Religious divergencies also hampered the negotiations; as a result the Center and its Bavarian offshoot, the Bavarian People's Party, gave up the thought of working with the Loebell committee. In the end, Dr. Karl Jarres, lord mayor of Duisburg and a member of the German People's Party, was nominated. An efficient administrator with good industrial connections, he belonged to the right wing of the People's Party and was acceptable to the German Nationals. And as a Protestant who had risen to eminence in the Catholic Rhineland, he was also expected to attract the conservative Catholic vote.[6]

While Jarres could claim the support of more than one party, his fellow candidates were nominees of individual parties. Neither the middle nor the leftist parties could agree on a common candidate. Both Center and Bavarian People's Party chose separate candidates. So did the parties of the left—Democrats, Socialists, and Communists. On the extreme right, Ludendorff ran as the nominee of the Nazis. The election, on March 29, 1925, thus brought no decision. No candidate obtained the majority on which victory depended. A second election had to be held, but a plurality would now be sufficienct to win.

This time the left found it easier to agree on a common candidate. The Center, Social Democrats, and Democrats joined forces in a so called "People's Bloc" and nominated ex-Chancellor Wilhelm Marx, who had been the Center's choice in the first election. The Communists again decided to run their party leader, Ernst Thälmann. The decision was in open defiance of the Comintern, which, on certain conditions, wished to support Otto Braun and possibly even Marx.[7]

Marx's electoral chances looked promising. He was no statesman of caliber, but he was respected as a man of integrity and good

[6] Westarp correspondence, Mar. 1925, Westarp Papers; Stresemann to Gessler, Mar. 11, 1925, Stresemann to ex-Crown Prince William, Mar. 23, 1925, Stresemann, *Vermächtnis*, II, 43–45; Wheeler-Bennett, *Wooden Titan*, pp. 255–56.

[7] Ossip K. Flechtheim, *Die kommunistische Partei Deutschlands in der Weimarer Republik* (Offenbach/M., 1948), pp. 124–25; Miriam Kölling, "Der Kampf der Kommunistischen Partei Deutschlands unter der Führung Ernst Thälmanns für die Einheitsfront in den ersten Jahren der relativen Stabilisierung (1924 bis 1927)." *Zeitschrift für Geschichtswissenschaft*, II (1954), 13–14; Rosenberg, *Geschichte*, p. 209; *Rote Fahne*, Apr. 19 and 22, 1925, quoted in Spartakus, *German Communists* (London, 1944) p. 53.

will. He could look back on a distinguished career as a judge and had attained one of the highest positions in the Prussian judiciary. A skillful negotiator and arbitrator, he had established his political reputation as an umpire rather than as a dynamic and resourceful leader. As a middle-of-the-roader with liberal overtones he was acceptable to the left; but he was also known as an advocate of closer cooperation with the right, and, though himself a supporter of the republic, had fought off recurrent efforts to read all monarchists out of the Center Party. He was clearly a compromise candidate, but was thought to meet well the requirements which the functions of the presidency, somewhat subordinate in the eyes of the left, imposed upon its incumbent. His main handicap was that he was a Catholic—a fact that was bound to alienate some of the Protestant voters.[8]

Given Marx's support by the Center and Socialists, the German Nationals were convinced that Jarres could not defeat him; they had never been very enthusiastic about his candidacy and seized on this chance to insist that he be dropped. Rumors had had it that Hindenburg would run in the second election; many now began to urge openly that the marshal be the candidate of the right. Feelers had been put out already to sound him out about his availability; Hindenburg's answer had been negative, but his "no" had been qualified. On April 1, just three days after the first election, the leaders of the old Conservative Party of Imperial days, now an enclave within the German National Party, decided to support his candidacy in the Loebell committee (recently renamed the Reich Bloc).[9]

Obviously this was a move of desperation on their part; they had expressed no similar interest in Hindenburg at the time of the first campaign. In fact, most old-time Conservatives looked on him with some distrust, for they had never forgiven him for his "betrayal" of the Emperor in November 1918. Yet in their determination to keep the presidency out of republican hands, they suppressed their misgivings and turned to him. Count Westarp, one of the Conservative leaders who voted for Hindenburg's nomination, sounded almost apologetic when he tried to

[8] Otto Gessler, *Reichswehrpolitik in der Weimarer Zeit*, Kurt Sendtner, ed. (Stuttgart, 1958), p. 382; Stresemann to Houghton, June 4, 1925, Stresemann, *Vermächtnis*, II, 242; Stampfer, *Vierzehn Jahre*, pp. 451–52; Walter H. Kaufmann, *Monarchism in the Weimar Republic* (New York, 1953), p. 133.

[9] *Mitteilungsblatt des Reichsblocks zur Durchführung der Reichspräsidentenwahl*, No. 7/8, Mar. 25, 1925, Dingeldey Papers/111; Schwertfeger to Kuhl, Mar. 25, 1925, Schwertfeger Papers; Stresemann to Maltzan, Apr. 7, 1925, Stresemann, *Vermächtnis*, II, 264; personal information.

justify his vote to a constituent: "We assume that your circles too will understand the present settlement of the candidacy."[10]

There had been other objections to Hindenburg's nomination when his name had first been considered. The most serious had been his age, but there had also been some concern about his lack of political experience. Given the importance that the right attributed to the presidency, these considerations had weighed heavily enough with the German National leaders to lead to the speedy dismissal of his name.[11] The German People's Party had given no thought to his candidacy during the first campaign.

All objections were now overruled by those who saw in Hindenburg the one man with sufficient stature to wrest victory from Marx's hands. They were no longer concerned with electing a strong leader, but were only trying to run a sure winner. "[Our] candidate must be a personality," Loebell had said when he had first proposed the establishment of his committee, "who knows exactly what he wants, who is concerned solely with the interests of the Fatherland, who has wide experience in economic and political matters, has dignity, and is able, if need be, to overrule the parties and use his constitutional rights with tact and skill." Through his brother, a high-ranking army officer who had served many a tour of duty with Hindenburg, Loebell had become closely acquainted with him. He knew that the marshal had few of the qualifications he considered essential, but now he chose to ignore these shortcomings as did Westarp and others.[12] Whatever his failings, his election seemed preferable to that of Marx whose presidency would further consolidate the republic and forestall the return of an authoritarian regime.

Not all rightists agreed, however, that the marshal was the right choice as a candidate. Many German Nationals maintained their earlier objections. Almost to the day of his nomination such conservative papers as the *Deutsche Tageszeitung* and the *Kreuz-Zeitung* insisted that Hindenburg was too old to assume the burden of the presidency.[13] Many of the paramilitary organizations objected to him, partly for these same reasons and partly

10 Westarp, *Ende der Monarchie*, pp. 159–60; Secretariat Westarp to Bonin, Apr. 17, 1925, Westarp Papers; also Gayl memorandum, n.d., Gayl Papers/11.

11 Hans Schlange-Schöningen to author, Nov. 9, 1956.

12 Minutes of preparatory Loebell Committee meeting, Feb. 12, 1925, Westarp Papers; Görlitz, *Hindenburg*, p. 32.

13 *Deutsche Tageszeitung*, No. 163, Apr. 6, 1925; *Kreuz-Zeitung*, quoted in *Berliner Tageblatt*, No. 159, Apr. 3, 1925; memoranda on German National objections to Hindenburg from Bavaria, Hamburg, Frankfurt/Oder, and Halle, Dingeldey Papers/111; Hans Schlange-Schöningen, *Am Tage Danach* (Hamburg, 1946), p. 30.

because their members, mostly younger men, did not hold the marshal in the awe their elders did. To these unrelenting enemies of the new state, he was someone who had made his complacent peace with the republic and now was living in ease and comfort. Under the pretext that the venerable old marshal should not be dragged into a sordid election campaign, the *Stahlhelm,* the leading veterans' organization, kept opposing his candidacy until his nomination could no longer be blocked.[14]

The most serious objections were voiced by the German People's Party. Its leader Stresemann, the foreign minister, was at the time engaged in delicate negotiations with Britain and France which eventually led to the conclusion of the Locarno Pact. Under his leadership the party was especially sensitive to the international repercussions of the election. Not unnaturally it feared that Hindenburg's nomination would give offense to the Western Powers; France in particular would not take kindly to the prospect of seeing the field marshal of World War I elected president of her dreaded neighbor. There was some anxiety also that the United States might withhold badly needed credits from German industry in its concern over the election of a reputed monarchist and militarist. On this point industrial groups of the German National Party agreed with their counterparts in the People's Party. Industry wished to see Jarres renominated. But its preference for the latter was due not only to fears of unfavorable foreign reaction. As head of a large industrial city, Jarres could be expected to show more understanding for industrial needs than Hindenburg who called agrarian East Prussia his home. Since industrialists would have to contribute the bulk of the campaign funds, their objections could not be taken lightly.[15]

Despite such widespread opposition the advocates of a Hindenburg candidacy refused to give in. Convinced that only he could prevent Marx's election, they decided to approach the marshal once more and on April 1, a German National delegation called on him at his home in Hanover. The call came as no surprise to him. Ever since it had been obvious that Jarres could not win in the first election, Hindenburg had been urged to run in the second campaign. But he had begged off. Given his age and his political inexperience, he had written to one of his confidants,

14 *Berliner Tageblatt,* No. 155, Apr. 1, 1925; German People's Party, Sebnitz, Saxony, to *Reichsgeschäftsstelle,* Berlin, Apr. 6, 1925 Dingeldey Papers/111.

15 Staff report (*Truppenamtsvortrag*), Apr. 24, 1925, Schleicher Papers/17,ii/9–10; Stresemann diary, Apr. 15, 18, 1925, Stresemann, *Vermächtnis,* II, 48–50; also German People's Party to Freund[t], June 9, 1925, Dingeldey Papers/111; *Frankfurter Zeitung,* No. 257, Apr. 6, 1925, No. 273, Apr. 12, 1925.

he would be most reluctant to become president. Even if there were a widespread feeling that the country's salvation depended on his candidacy and his election were assured, he still believed that there were other and better candidates, and he would therefore prefer to live out his life in the peaceful privacy of his home.[16]

His rejection thus was not unqualified, but Hindenburg did not covet the presidency. Apart from all other objections, no post could hold any attraction for him that would involve him in controversies, and they would be hard to avoid in the presidency. But he also knew that millions of Germans looked to him as one of the few unifying symbols which the strife-torn nation still possessed.

Jarres' defeat led Hindenburg to reconsider his position. If the country were to call on him now, he told some associates, he would consider it his duty to lend his name to the cause of national unity. Accordingly he informed his German National callers, after stating his reservations: "If you feel that my election is necessary for the sake of the Fatherland, I'll run, in God's name." But he wanted to be certain that there was such a need and that the nation, and not just one or two parties, wished him to run, before he committed himself definitely. He received several other German National visitors, but his answer was invariably the same. He would accept only if all parties of the right would support him and if he were convinced that his refusal would indeed endanger the Fatherland.[17]

He learned, of course, of the objections of Stresemann and his associates to his candidacy. On April 5, two representatives of the People's Party called on him to urge him not to accept the nomination. They impressed on him the gravity of the foreign political repercussions which his candidacy could be expected to have. They also warned him that his chances of winning the election were quite uncertain. At this point, however, the marshal's supporters received welcome help from a new quarter. The leaders of the Bavarian People's Party decided to second his nomination. They preferred the Protestant Hindenburg to the Catholic Marx, despite their party's Catholic ties, because support of Marx would have meant cooperation with the Social

---

16 Personal information.

17 Schlange-Schöningen, *Am Tage Danach*, p. 30; Gerhard Schultze-Pfaelzer, *Wie Hindenburg Reichspräsident wurde* (Berlin, 1925), p. 10; Dieter von der Schulenburg, *Welt um Hindenburg: Hundert Gespräche mit Berufenen* (Berlin, 1935), p. 57; Görlitz, *Hindenburg*, pp. 249–50.

Democrats. Any such collaboration was considered abhorrent to their followers; they still remembered the excesses of Bavaria's Soviet regime in 1919 and persisted in associating the Socialists with it. As a monarchist, too, Hindenburg held special attraction for a party which had never abandoned the hope of seeing Crown Prince Rupprecht ascend the throne of Bavaria.[18]

But Hindenburg was too much shaken by the opposition of the German People's Party to be impressed by this increase in his following. On April 7, he decided to withdraw his consent to be considered for the candidacy. A telegram to that effect was drafted and communicated by telephone to the Reich Bloc. It stated that he would not be able, because of his advanced age, to accept the difficult post of Reich president and urged all those "to whom the Fatherland meant more than their party" to vote for Jarres and thus avoid a dangerous split. Not to vote in the election, he warned, would gravely harm the Fatherland in a critical hour.

On receipt of this information the German People's Party decided to cancel the call on Hindenburg of yet another spokesman who was to impress once more on the marshal the dangers of his candidacy. But the German Nationals were not yet ready to give up. Without informing the People's Party, they obtained Hindenburg's consent to a postponement of the telegram's publication (it came, however, too late to prevent all papers from printing it). And again without informing the People's Party, they dispatched that same afternoon a special mission to Hanover to urge him to reconsider his decision.

The two emissaries they sent were well chosen for their delicate task. The chief envoy was Admiral von Tirpitz who belonged to Hindenburg's generation. Only a year younger than the marshal, he knew and understood him better than many a younger man. He was a skillful and experienced negotiator of great persuasiveness and he belonged to that wing of the German National Party that had recognized the futility of blind obstruction and had shown its willingness to cooperate, within limits, with the republic. His conciliatory stand, it was hoped, would appeal to the marshal who too had urged the German Nationals to assume a more cooperative attitude towards the new state. Tirpitz's companion, Walter von Keudell, had qualifications of his own. The grandson of one of Bismarck's aides, he was an East German landowner and belonged to that old agrarian nobility to which

18 *Ibid.*, p. 251; Karl Schwend, *Bayern zwischen Monarchie und Diktatur* (Munich, 1954), pp. 309-13; staff report of Apr. 24, 1925, Schleicher Papers/17,ii/9-10.

Hindenburg felt himself closest socially and emotionally. Forty years old at the time, he could also act as the spokesman of a much younger generation than Tirpitz.

The conference lasted for several hours. Tirpitz impressed on Hindenburg the need for his candidacy and appealed to his sense of honor and duty not to withhold his services from the Fatherland. The result of the meeting was that Hindenburg withdrew his rejection and asked for a new report on the attitude of the various parties represented in the Reich Bloc. He would then give his final decision.[19]

The Reich Bloc met once more on April 8. There were new telegrams from various organizations—the *Jungdeutsche Orden,* the *Viking-Bund,* the Bavarian *Stahlhelm*—urging the retention of Jarres. But there was also a telegram from Jarres himself who proposed to withdraw in order to avoid a split in the vote of the right. Nevertheless the spokesmen of heavy industry and of the German People's Party continued to support him. The Nazi representative likewise maintained his objections to Hindenburg, but felt that since his name had been brought up publicly, his nomination had become imperative. On the other hand, along with the German Nationals, the Economic Party, the agrarian *Landbund,* the Protestant labor unions, and some other organizations came out for Hindenburg. Once more the delegates of the German People's Party explained why they considered the marshal's candidacy inadvisable. But faced with an intransigent majority, they finally gave in, although they still questioned Hindenburg's ability to win. Reached by telephone, Jarres at once withdrew his name. Loebell then called Hindenburg to report on the outcome of the conference. The marshal inquired about the attitude of the German People's Party. Informed of its continued misgivings, he asked for a personal report after which he would decide what to do. But Loebell, fearful of new difficulties, insisted on an immediate answer. Uncertain, the old man asked Loebell what he would advise. The latter of course urged him to agree to his nomination, and thereupon Hindenburg consented.[20]

---

[19] Görlitz, *Hindenburg,* pp. 251–52; memorandum of May 1, 1925, by Stocksieck, minutes of Reich Bloc meeting of Apr. 8, 1925, Dingeldey Papers/111; on need for greater German National cooperation, Hindenburg to Hergt, Oct. 30, 1923, quoted in letter of Hergt to author, May 28, 1958. In a somewhat different account by Otto Schmidt-Hannover, *Umdenken oder Anarchie: Männer-Schicksale-Lehren* (Göttingen, 1957), pp. 192–94, written over thirty years after the event, the developments of Apr. 7 and 8, 1925, are apparently projected into one day.

[20] Görlitz, *Hindenburg,* pp. 252–53; minutes of Reich Bloc meeting of Apr. 8,

Political questions were not taken up with the marshal during the preliminary conferences. Since he was to win on the strength of his personality, there was no need to develop a concrete political program. Nor did it seem necessary, or advisable, to reach specific understandings with him. Loebell and his associates knew that Hindenburg disliked politics; rather than annoy him and possibly jeopardize his candidacy, they decided to postpone such discussions until after his election. Given Hindenburg's need for guidance, they felt certain that he himself would then ask for their counsel. That would be the time to exert their influence on him.[21]

But if Hindenburg's backers had to make concessions to him, he, in turn, bowed on one significant point to the mood of the nation. At some time during the negotiations with the German Nationals and the Reich Bloc he got in touch with the ex-Emperor to obtain the latter's approval of his candidacy. Otto Meissner, his state secretary, reports in his memoirs that "a confidential inquiry sent to the former Kaiser produced the reply that he would face no difficulties from that quarter should he assume the post of the republican Reich President." In a letter addressed to the ex-monarch two years later, Hindenburg himself refers to the fact that he accepted the post only after having obtained His Majesty's approval. The move was entirely in keeping with Hindenburg's personal attitude toward William II. He still felt bound to him in traditional allegiance and sincerely hoped for the day when his monarch would once more ascend the throne.[22]

Nevertheless Hindenburg did not object when his campaign aides dismissed as false all suggestions that he had obtained William's consent. Meissner said a few months later that the denials were issued with Hindenburg's knowledge and the campaign reminiscences of Gerhard Schultze-Pfaelzer who served as one of his press agents bear out this statement. On one occasion, during an interview with an American newspaperman, Hindenburg himself denied that he had consulted the ex-Emperor before

1925, declaration of delegates of German People's Party on committee, Apr. 8, 1925, Dingeldey Papers/111; circular of board of directors, German People's Party, Apr. 9, 1925, Stresemann Papers/83/3161/172627–29.

21 Görlitz, *Hindenburg*, pp. 32, 249; Loebell to Bülow, June 24, 1925, Bülow Papers/101/159–60.

22 Meissner, *Staatssekretär*, p. 147; Hindenburg to William II, Feb. 1927, cited in Görlitz, *Hindenburg*, p. 252.

accepting the candidacy. Later he had Meissner make similar denials on his "special instructions." It is of course possible that he acted from loyalty towards the ex-Emperor whom he wanted to spare all embarrassment; significantly the ex-monarch too had an aide deny flatly that he had bestowed his approval on Hindenburg's candidacy. But his attitude was also entirely in accordance with the cautious reserve he had long maintained in all matters touching on the monarchist issue.[23]

This, then, was the background of Hindenburg's candidacy. He accepted it formally on April 9, 1925, in a brief ceremony at his home in Hanover.

ᔥ

His election campaign was clearly attuned to the manner of his nomination. It was marked by a striking absence of issues except that of his age which was dismissed as irrelevant, with references to Emperor William I, Clemenceau, and others who had served their country well at a more advanced age. The main emphasis was placed on Hindenburg's character—". . . simplicity and honesty, loyalty, sense of duty, integrity." "[Hindenburg] has no specific mandate in terms of a party political program or a party political coalition," a campaign directive of the Reich Bloc proclaimed. "He is the candidate of the entire nation and as the future head of the entire state completely free in his decisions." Marx, on the other hand, was denounced as the captive of the Social Democrats. His candidacy was described as the result of a deal between the Center Party and the Socialists by which the latter hoped to recapture the power to carry out their Socialist program: "The Center is ready to sell out to them. The Weimar Coalition has turned into the bloc of the revolution. The Reich Bloc defends the state against the Social Democrats in this campaign." Special attention was to be paid to the misgivings which many Democratic and Social Democratic voters had about Marx; objections to Hindenburg, on the other hand, because of his alleged monarchism and militarism were to be countered with

---

[23] *Mitteilungsblatt des Reichsblocks*, No. 10, Apr. 14, 1925, Dingeldey Papers/111; Meissner to Bischoff, June 3, 1925, BdRPr., R 54/296. See also Schultze-Pfaelzer, *Wie Hindenburg Reichspräsident wurde*, pp. 22–23; Hindenburg interview with Berlin representative of Hearst papers, Apr. 21, 1925, *Hindenburg: Briefe, Reden, Berichte*, Fritz Endres, ed., (Munich, 1934), p. 148; William's denial in Gengler, *Monarchisten*, pp. 171–72. How much the marshal was concerned with his personal position, he made clear at once to his campaign aides. Their main task was, according to his explicit instructions, not to publicize him, but to defend him against political attacks. Herrwarth (?) to Gayl, Apr. 11, 1925, Gayl Papers/11.

the argument that as president he would devote himself solely to the attainment of "social justice, religious equality, genuine peace at home and abroad."[24]

The campaign proceeded along these lines. Speakers were instructed to stress the apolitical nature of his candidacy which was based solely on the greatness of his person. One proposed speech announced in mystic exultation, "Hindenburg is not a 'candidate' . . . no one could or should bring him 'closer' to the German people. Hindenburg is Germany herself, he stands for national self-confidence, hope and fulfillment at the same time. In these days of indecision, cynical effeminacy, and shallow perorations, the name of Hindenburg echoes almost like a myth across the German chapters of glory [sic] down to us." As a man to whom the Fatherland stood high above everything else, he would be the creator of a new and genuine German unity. "Never," speakers were to reassure any doubters, "did the Marshal violate his loyalty towards the 'new order' so alien to him; for the concept of the Fatherland is no mere slogan to him, but ever the object of his duty and his love." Other appeals stressed his dignity and his integrity. "There is no question of deciding the form of government, directly or indirectly, one way or another or steering a new course in our foreign policy. It is merely a question of placing at the head of the nation the best and most deserving man, the purest character, the most incorruptible guardian of law and morality."[25]

Hindenburg's personal campaign activities ran to similar generalizations. They suited him well in their noncommittal nature. He asked an aide to compile for him a list of pithy patriotic sayings, *vaterländische Kernworte,* and these he used freely in messages to individuals and organizations. Determinedly he clung to what he considered the nonpartisan character of his candidacy, and refused to have dealings with party spokesmen, receiving only representatives of the Reich Bloc. Actually most of the latter were active in the German National People's Party as well, but this does not seem to have worried him. In fact, he did maintain contact also with official party representatives: Martin Schiele,

24 Countess Westarp to Heinrich, Apr. 20, 1925, Westarp Papers; *Mitteilungsblatt des Reichsblocks,* No. 11, Apr. 16, 1925, Dingeldey Papers/111; *Deutsche Tageszeitung,* No. 168, Apr. 9, 1925; "Politische Richtlinien," Apr. 10, 1925, Stresemann Papers/23/3166/158725–28.

25 Leaflets, broadsides, posters, in Duke Collection, Hoover Library; *Mitteilungsblatt des Reichsblocks,* No. 10, Apr. 14, 1925, Dingeldey Papers/111; Appeal of Reich Bloc, "Warum Hindenburg?" in *Deutsche Mittelstands-Zeitung,* Apr. 23, 1925.

the Reich minister of the interior, acted as liaison officer between him and the German Nationals.[26]

On April 11, he issued an Easter Message to the nation. Patriotic Germans, he stated, had offered him the highest office in the Reich, and he had accepted their call after serious consideration. If elected, he pledged himself to serve in accordance with the constitution, without regard to party, person, social background, or economic status—"As a soldier I have always been concerned with the nation as a whole, not with parties." But he assured those who might see a potential dictator in him that he was not going to suppress the parties: "In a parliamentary state they are needed, but the head of the state must stand above them and, independently of them, work for every German." He had never lost faith in the German people or in God's help, but he was too old to believe in a sudden change of conditions. "No war, no internal rising can obtain freedom for a nation which is still in chains and, alas, rent by internal discord. What we must do is to work hard, quietly, peacefully." However, just as the first president had never denied his origins as a Social Democratic worker, no one would expect him to give up his political convictions: "I do not consider decisive the form of a state, but the spirit which inspires that form. I offer my hand to every German who is national-minded, maintains the dignity of the German name at home and abroad, and wants religious and social peace, and ask him to help me work for the rehabilitation of our Fatherland."[27]

The statement was moderate in its tenor and a faithful expression of Hindenburg's beliefs. But the opening sentence must have given pause to perceptive readers. "Patriotic [*vaterländisch gesinnte*] Germans" had called on him, it asserted. There was an unmistakable implication here that patriotism, an attitude that the right long had claimed as its exclusive concern, could be found only in his camp. Even without a specific platform, Hindenburg's campaign did not stay entirely above ideological and partisan issues.

Leaving the speech-making to others, Hindenburg limited his public appearances to two: one, a brief talk before a gathering of German and foreign press representatives and delegates of political, economic, and cultural organizations in Hanover; the

---

26 Schultze-Pfaelzer, *Wie Hindenburg Reichspräsident wurde*, pp. 19, 50; Görlitz, *Hindenburg*, p. 253; Schmidt-Hannover, *Umdenken*, p. 191; Schiffer, *Liberalismus*, p. 55; also Herrwarth(?) to Gayl, Apr. 11, 1925, and protocol on conference with Field Marshal von Hindenburg, Apr. 19(10?), 1925, Gayl Papers/11.
27 Schulthess, Apr. 11, 1925, p. 55.

other, a radio address to the nation. On both occasions he again presented himself as a nonpartisan candidate motivated only by his sense of duty. He would serve his nation, he promised, and work peacefully for its unity and rehabilitation, in strict observance of the constitution. At a press reception after his first speech, he reiterated his position: "I am no militarist, as my opponents claim. . . . Nor am I the old man in a wheelchair, as some people would like to have the country believe. . . . As for the tasks of the future, I have no ready-made answers. I am not going to get involved here in any detailed questions; if I should become President, the Chancellor and my cabinet will have to govern in accordance with the laws and the Constitution."[28]

A theme recurring in his statements was that unlike the republican parties, those gathered in the Reich Bloc were dedicated to great common goals. Unhappily, this was far from true and one of the great problems of the managers of the marshal's campaign was that many of his supporters disliked each other most heartily. There were continual clashes between the German Nationals and the People's Party and continuous charges and countercharges. Hardly a day passed, moreover, without a German National jab at the hapless Stresemann who was considered not "national-minded" in his foreign policy. Stresemann himself went on leave immediately after Hindenburg's nomination to avoid all campaigning on the marshal's behalf since he expected foreign reaction to be so unfavorable that it might put an end to his foreign political plans. Reaction abroad was indeed so violent that Luther thought seriously of suggesting to Hindenburg that he withdraw. The plan was dropped since his resignation could have been made palatable only if Marx too had bowed out in favor of a catch-all candidate, and no such man could be found. The German People's Party remained skeptical of Hindenburg's candidacy up to the day of his election, and so did substantial parts of the Bavarian People's Party. Matters, in fact, reached a point where Hindenburg himself seems to have thought of withdrawing from the campaign.[29]

The full gravity of the rightist predicament was revealed by the liberal *Berliner Tageblatt*. Its editors obtained access to the

28 Endres, *Hindenburg*, pp. 143–47.

29 Schubert memorandum, n.d., *Records of German Foreign Ministry*, Innere Politik/2/2281/136738; Kempner, memorandum, Apr. 15, 1925, *Records of German Reichskanzlei* (hereafter cited as "*Rkz.*"), R 43 I/584; Stresemann Papers/93/3161/ passim; *Mitteilungsblatt der Deutschen Volkspartei Berlin-Mitte*, Apr. 17, 21, 1925, Dingeldey Papers/111; Stresemann diary, Apr. 15, 1925, Stresemann, *Vermächtnis*, II, 47.

minutes of a meeting of German National leaders that abounded in recriminations against the German People's Party, the Economic Party, and the Reich Bloc. But the meeting also voiced its uneasiness about the marshal's chances of victory. This uncertainty it shared with many leaders of Hindenburg's campaign. Stresemann's diary is filled with doubts and complaints about the difficulty of getting financial support. "Utter pessimism prevails regarding the prospects of Hindenburg's candidacy," he noted on April 20. "The Berlin Reich Bloc is apparently without any resources. All is confusion, and there is a complete lack of enthusiasm." Even the well informed Reichswehr ministry was uncertain as late as April 24, two days before the election, whether Hindenburg could be expected to win.[30]

The opposition had its troubles too. They lay partly in the person of Marx, and partly in the special problems that any opposition to a man of Hindenburg's stature presented. Marx, a delightful conversationalist who was at his best in informal talks before small groups, was not a forceful personality or an impressive speaker. His judicial background may have accounted for his sober and colorless style—a flavor of detached legalism always clung to his views. (His lack of popular appeal had concerned many of his party colleagues when his candidacy was first being considered.[31]) Naturally modest and aware of his lack of special status, Marx could not give his appeals the magisterial note that characterized Hindenburg's statements. "The confidence of many sections of the nation has offered me the candidacy for the Presidency of the German Reich," he said in an Easter Greeting (as distinct from the marshal's Easter *Message*). He too considered it his foremost task to preserve German unity which ought to be more than mere linguistic and organizational unity. "National unity is spiritual unity. Spiritual unity implies basic agreement about our social community and the goals of cooperation with other nations. The foundations of our social community, it seems to me, are freedom of the individual and a sense of duty towards the community." This was a time, not just of suffering, but of greatness too. It was truly the time of Easter in which men who had been caught up in the web of material problems were once more looking for the higher values of life. Marx con-

---

[30] Minutes of German National meeting of Apr. 20, 1925, as reported in *Berliner Tageblatt*, in Stresemann Papers/93/3161/172673; Stresemann diary, Apr. 16, 20, 1925, Stresemann, *Vermächtnis*, II, 47–48, 50; staff report of Apr. 24, 1925, Schleicher Papers/17,ii/9–10.

[31] Gessler, *Reichswehrpolitik*, p. 341.

cluded with the wish that "this search and this longing may find its courageous voice, now that the fundamental problems of the nation's life and future are at stake. . . . May freedom and moral duty serve as the guiding principles of the entire nation, beyond special interests and parties. To work for this goal is my greatest wish wherever the will and the confidence of the people may place me."[32]

In his campaign speeches Marx warned against the futility of impotent saber rattling and pledged himself to work for a better understanding in foreign affairs. He promised Germany's cooperation in the expansion of international trade, reminding his audiences of the economy's need for internal stability and foreign credits. His main domestic task he saw in the vigorous defense of the republic's democratic institutions against its enemies on both the right and the left and in the strengthening of these institutions through the promotion of social justice and religious equality.[33] Marx tried very hard to avoid taking direct issue with Hindenburg and preferred to mention the marshal as little as possible. On the few occasions on which he brought up his name, he was almost apologetic about his opposition to him. In one of his speeches he praised him as the victor of Tannenberg. He felt the need to reiterate his profound admiration for the nation's hero and expressed his regret that he had been forced to take up the fight against him. He never touched on Hindenburg's lack of political experience, his age, or his monarchism. Nor did he dwell on the marshal's errors of judgment during the war which might have some bearing on his qualifications as president. Given Hindenburg's stature, he considered such charges little suited to draw new voters into his camp. They might, on the other hand, irritate those who were otherwise willing to vote for him.[34]

Marx's Catholicism proved a handicap too, although it is difficult to estimate the number of votes he lost because of it. Apart from devout Protestants, it also helped to keep away from the polls some of the more radical Social Democrats. These, however, objected primarily to his reluctance to challenge Hindenburg more openly. Severing believes that several hundred thousand

[32] Schulthess, Apr. 12, 1925, p. 56.
[33] Frankfurter Zeitung, No. 283, Apr. 17, 1925, No. 286, Apr. 18, 1925, No. 303, Apr. 24, 1925.
[34] Ibid., No. 277, Apr. 15, 1925, No. 286, Apr. 18, 1925; Nürnberg-Fürther Morgenpresse, No. 113, Apr. 25, 1925; Kölnische Volkszeitung, No. 277, Apr. 15, 1925; Düsseldorfer Tageblatt, No. 114, Apr. 25, 1925; Mss. of Marx's speeches, Marx Papers.

Socialist workers abstained from casting their vote on election day, but this estimate seems too high on the basis of the election returns.[35]

But there were also notable reservoirs of republican strength which made a prediction of the outcome of the election most hazardous. Of these, the most important was the *Reichbanner,* an organization, mainly of veterans, whose members were supporters of the republic. It had been founded a year before, in February 1924, as a defense force of the republic against such antirepublican groups as *Stahlhelm,* Nazi Stormtroops, and the Communist Red Front Fighters League. The *Reichsbanner* grew with surprising speed; the claim of its leaders, on its first anniversary, that it had reached the 3 million mark was most likely exaggerated, but it did quickly attract a substantial following. The desire to defend the new democratic-republican state against extremist assaults was strong, and the soldierly organization of the *Reichsbanner,* its uniforms, marches, and parades had their attractions too. Its effectiveness is evident from the concern with which the right watched its growth and tried to counteract it by strengthening and overhauling its own organization.[36]

The *Reichsbanner* was especially active during the presidential campaign; wherever it made an appearance, it impressed large numbers of people with its strength and its discipline. It provided Marx and his fellow campaigners with escorts at meetings and other functions and arranged parades and torchlight processions, complete with military music and presentation of colors. Its bands attracted huge crowds and supplied that martial-romantic atmosphere that showed the soldierly spirit was not the exclusive monopoly of the Hindenburg camp. Although recruited primarily from the ranks of the Social Democrats, the *Reichsbanner* did draw part of its membership from the Center and Democrats. In this way it served as a further link between these three parties—a fact that was of undoubted benefit to the cohesion of the People's Bloc. Cooperation among the parties supporting Marx was much better than among those working for Hindenburg.[37]

✑

Thus the day of the election approached with the outcome still in the dark. The nation went to the polls on April 26, 1925.

[35] Severing, *Lebensweg,* II, 53–54; *Frankfurter Zeitung,* No. 313, Apr. 28, 1925.
[36] Schulthess, Feb. 21–22, 1925, p. 36; Stampfer, *Vierzehn Jahre,* pp. 396–98; Rosenberg, *Geschichte,* pp. 204–05; Bracher, *Auflösung,* pp. 143–44; Weiss to Westarp, Dec. 6, 1924, in Liebe, *Deutschnationale Volkspartei,* pp. 180–81 n. 479.
[37] Minutes of German National meeting, Apr. 20, 1925, Stresemann Papers/93/

Hindenburg won by the narrow margin of 7 per cent. Against the 13,751,000 votes cast for Marx, he received 14,655,000 votes. Thälmann, the Communist candidate, obtained 1,931,000 votes. The election returns demonstrated that those who had hoped to capitalize on Hindenburg's name had calculated correctly. Almost 3.5 million more voters participated in this second election than had in the earlier one. Of these, close to 3 million cast their vote for the marshal. Marx gained but 500,000 votes over the republican vote of the first election.

Otherwise the returns revealed few noteworthy changes. Like Jarres, Hindenburg was most firmly entrenched in the Protestant rural areas of northern and eastern Germany. Marx, on the other hand, led in the Catholic and most of the major industrial regions, and in traditionally liberal Baden and Württemberg. Even in Bavaria, religious ties proved stronger than expected and a substantial part of the Bavarian People's Party refused to follow its leadership and cast its vote for Marx rather than Hindenburg.[38] While the marshal did much better than Jarres in Bavaria, Marx scored even larger gains for the People's Bloc, compared to the first election. He lost comparatively few votes to Thälmann who gained a mere 60,000 over his first campaign. On the whole Social Democratic discipline was good, and except in Saxony, few Socialists defied their leaders by abstaining or voting for Thälmann.

The most significant changes occurred in the industrial areas. Hindenburg reduced the republican majorities in Rhineland-Westphalia and Upper Silesia, despite the prevalence of the Catholic element in those regions. In Saxony, a Protestant stronghold, where the republican parties had had a narrow plurality in the first election, he even obtained a safe lead over Marx. Not only did he attract most of the new vote, but substantial segments of the Democratic Party also voted for him. The shift was a reaction to the militancy of Saxony's labor movement (Thälmann's few gains were scored mainly in Saxony). But Democrats abandoned their party elsewhere too. Even in Hamburg, traditionally a liberal stronghold, Hindenburg won over Marx, due to a marked shift in the Democratic vote. Once more the moderate bourgeoisie demonstrated its lack of faith in the effectiveness of the Weimar Republic.

3161/172673; Stresemann diary, Apr. 16, 1925, *ibid./272/3113/147782; Frankfurter Zeitung*, No. 277, Apr. 15, 1925, No. 280, Apr. 16, 1925, No. 286, Apr. 18, 1925, No. 290, Apr. 20, 1925.

[38] Haniel to Reich Chancellery, Apr. 1925, *Rkz.*, R 43 1/584.

As for Marx, next to Bavaria, he scored his most notable gains in Berlin. Here he increased the republican lead by over 60 per cent. The capital, politically sensitive, anticipated trouble should the marshal be elected and tried hard to keep him out of the presidency.

Though Hindenburg won, he did not have a majority—the votes cast for Marx and Thälmann outnumbered his. But Marx's victory cannot be attributed solely to the Communists' decision to run their own candidate. Full support by the Catholic Bavarian People's Party would also have assured him of victory. What must have disappointed him most, however, was the defection of several hundred thousand fellow Centrists who cast their ballot for Hindenburg. Taken together with the shift in the Democratic vote to the marshal, these votes for Hindenburg must have amounted to at least 500,000. Thus the defection from Marx's own party and the Democratic Party, supposedly a mainstay of the republic, was in itself large enough to cause Marx's defeat, for Hindenburg won by only 904,000 votes.[39]

৵

An evaluation of the election might best begin by establishing what it did *not* mean: the victory of the Field Marshal of World War I fame was not a manifestation of military aggressiveness. Militarily Hindenburg had remained to the nation the victor of Tannenberg, and Tannenberg was a battle fought *in defense* of German soil. Even if every allowance is made for the exigencies of campaign tactics, the tenor of the Reich Bloc's speeches and writings still provides abundant evidence that it hoped to assure Hindenburg's victory by emphasizing his loyalty to the constitution and his devotion to peace and order—a pledge, that attracted wavering voters weary of the internal strife that beset the Weimar

[39] John K. Zeender, in his paper "The German Catholics and the Presidential Election of 1925," *Journal of Modern History*, xxxv (1963), 366–81, has calculated that some 400,000 Centrists in western and southern Germany and in Silesia voted for Hindenburg rather than Marx. This figure may be somewhat too high, for Zeender assumes that no followers of the Democratic Party preferred Hindenburg to Marx in these areas. Hindenburg's success in Saxony and Hamburg in any event can be explained only by a substantial support from Democratic voters; a very conservative estimate which assumes that Hindenburg got every new vote (most unlikely) and Centrist support was proportionately as large as Zeender has calculated for the predominantly Catholic regions would arrive at 26,000 Democratic votes cast for Hindenburg in the Dresden-Bautzen district, 35,000 in Leipzig, 13,000 in Chemnitz-Zwickau, and 11,000 in Hamburg (figures based on the returns published in *Statistisches Jahrbuch für das Deutsche* Reich, 1924/25 [Berlin, 1925], pp. 392–95). Whatever the respective allocation to the two parties, at least 500,000 Centrists and Democrats voted for Hindenburg rather than Marx in all of Germany.

Republic. As in 1914, Hindenburg's massive presence and the impression of strength and authority that his pictures conveyed, convinced millions of Germans that he would provide the strong leadership they longed for. To a nation that for generations had looked upon the Army as an educational force teaching an essentially undisciplined people the soldierly virtues of order and discipline, he was the embodiment of these very qualities. "The nation did not even want the Marshal," commented one of his biographers, "it simply wanted the soldier."[40]

If Hindenburg's election was no mandate for chauvinist militancy, neither was it a victory of the monarchist movement. The People's Bloc had frequently pictured the campaign as basically a struggle between reactionary monarchism and democratic republicanism, but this was at best a propagandist oversimplification.[41] The campaign tactics of the Reich Bloc provided ample evidence that monarchism was not considered a winning issue and it was consistently played down. Hindenburg's own attitude too attests to this fact, and whatever his political inexperience, he did have a distinct flair for the trend of public opinion. While not a few of his supporters did see in him the forerunner of a monarchist restoration, they were clearly a minority. The bulk of his voters cast their vote for Hindenburg, the nation's hero, rather than for the ex-monarch or any other potential pretender.

In consequence, there was considerable confusion at first as to what Hindenburg's election did mean in specific terms. The rightist press hailed it of course as a vindication of its policies; but underneath its triumphant jubilation the Hindenburg camp wondered uneasily whether the marshal's election would not serve to strengthen the republic since he was swearing allegiance now to its constitution.[42] The left, on the other hand, worried that with Hindenburg's victory the republic had suffered a grievous blow. But this concern, in turn, was tempered by the conviction that Hindenburg was not the man to indulge in wild adventures.[43] Very soon, many observers on both right and left came

[40] Horst von Metzsch, *Hindenburg* (Leipzig, 1932), p. 10; also Schultze-Pfaelzer, *Wie Hindenburg Reichspräsident wurde*, p. 71.
[41] See, f. ex., the appeal of the People's Bloc in *Frankfurter Zeitung*, No. 278, Apr. 15, 1925.
[42] Schulthess, Apr. 26, 1925, p. 59; Westarp, in Reichstag debate, May 19, 1925, *Verhandlungen*, Vol. 385, pp. 1902–03; *Deutsche Tageszeitung*, No. 196, Apr. 27, 1925; Stresemann to Houghton, June 4, 1925, Stresemann, *Vermächtnis*, II, 257–59; Metzsch, *Hindenburg*, p. 73; Meissner, *Staatssekretär*, p. 148.
[43] Schulthess, Apr. 26, 1925, p. 59; Breitscheid, May 19, 1925, *Verhandlungen*, Vol. 385, p. 1888; Stresemann interview, in *Le Matin*, May 14, 1925, Stresemann Papers/25/3143/159044–45.

to the conclusion that Hindenburg's election was not actually of as incisive significance as had at first been assumed; his personality and the narrow margin of his victory appeared to preclude any far-reaching changes. "Anyone who kept a cool head could easily see that the decision was not really too significant," the historian Hans Delbrück wrote in a post-mortem on the election in the *Preussische Jahrbücher,* an organ of the moderate right:

"What actually is the difference between Hindenburg and Marx, if we look at their personalities and their political program. . . . In his views on social policies, the economy, taxes, Marx is certainly much closer to Hindenburg than to his Socialist voters. Hindenburg is to pursue a stronger foreign policy, but will not be able to do so because of Germany's weakness. . . . Hindenburg is to be the pacemaker or herald of a monarchist restoration. This idea will soon be given up. The very opposite will happen, and the election of the Field Marshal will turn out to be a great disappointment to many. He is going to restore the monarchy as little as he is going to give a new direction to our foreign policy. On the contrary, as President he is going to weaken the aversion with which so large a part of the nation has so far looked upon the Republic."

An editorial in the leftist weekly, *Die Weltbühne,* agreed that there was little difference between Hindenburg and Marx. It predicted that Hindenburg would lead Germany into the League of Nations and that he would sign the proposed Security Pact, later known as the Locarno Pact, with Britain and France:

"Monarchist restoration games are precluded for the new President by the weakness of the monarchist victory (if they are not already precluded by the oath which, it may be assumed, was sworn by a man of honor). Just as Ebert had to deal gently with the German Nationals, Hindenburg is going to meet the Social Democrats halfway. That he is not going to free the Republic from monarchist-chauvinist officers, administrators, judges, teachers, professors is obvious. But Marx would not have done that either. Hindenburg and Marx are no sharp opposites."[44]

From the perspective of the day this viewpoint was perhaps not unreasonable. Yet it was obviously predicated on the continued

[44] *Preussische Jahrbücher,* editorial of May 3, 1925, reprinted in Hans Delbrück, *Vor und nach dem Weltkriege* (Berlin, 1926), pp. 447–51; *Weltbühne,* editorial of May 12, 1925, reprinted in Kurt Hiller, *Köpfe und Tröpfe* (Hamburg and Stuttgart, 1950), pp. 22–27.

"normalcy" of conditions in which the powers of the president would be hedged in by government and Reichstag. Even given such "normalcy," it was of some consequence whether Hindenburg, who merely tolerated the republic, served as its president or Marx, who sincerely believed in it. The political-emotional atmosphere of the country was bound to be affected by the marshal's presidency, and such a change could prove important since the election returns had again demonstrated, as they had for some years, that the convinced supporters of the democratic republic were a minority of the electorate and that the quest for a new authoritarian order was far from dead.

If many were inclined to minimize the significance of Hindenburg's victory, others believed that Hindenburg would be in a better position than Marx to bridge the gap between the old Imperial Germany and the new Republican Germany. "The antithesis between the old and the new has far too long cast its shadow over Germany's political development," a Centrist leader, Monsignor Ludwig Kaas, said in the Reichstag some weeks after the marshal's election. "There is now an especially favorable opportunity to create an honest synthesis. It seems to us that our new Reich President ought to be more successful than anyone else to induce those who are ideologically close to him to consider the idea of a reconciliation between 'then' and 'now' . . . and to merge them into a higher unity."[45] This indeed was the task that Hindenburg had specifically set himself; he wished to build a bridge between the past and the present and to counteract the stubborn obstructionism of the right. At the same time he hoped to curb the influence of the leftist parties, considering them even more nefarious and shortsighted.

Given the deep cleavages dividing the nation, these were exacting tasks. They required acumen, initiative, and determination—qualities Hindenburg had rarely displayed during his long life. Nor had he so far given any indication that he had a clear concept of how to approach this difficult mission.

⌒

On May 11, Hindenburg left Hanover to assume his new office in the capital. At the station, Noske, the former Reichswehr minister and now *Oberpräsident* of the province of Hanover, bade him farewell on behalf of the local authorities. As a Social Democrat he had voted for Marx, but he purposely refrained

45 Kaas, May 19, 1925, *Verhandlungen*, Vol. 385, p. 1911.

from partisan remarks and merely stated, with evident reserve, that "millions of people hoped in trusting confidence that the new President would succeed in improving social conditions and bring about an alleviation of outside pressures on our Fatherland." Hindenburg answered in a similar vein, stressing his determination to serve as a mediator between all conflicting interests. But there were at once discordant notes. Social Democratic meetings protested Noske's noncommittal remarks, and Hanover's Socialist paper refused to publish his speech.[46]

Hindenburg's reception in Berlin, while outwardly festive and colorful, was marred by similar tensions. The *Reichsbanner* refused to participate in the ceremonies on the grounds that they were being perverted into monarchist demonstrations. Only rightist organizations lined the streets along which the marshal's motorcade proceeded on its way to the Presidential Palace. The long smouldering dispute over the black-red-and-gold flag (as against the old Imperial colors of black-white-and-red) broke out anew. While government buildings displayed the official black-red-and-gold colors, private homes hoisted black-white-and-red flags. The crowds welcoming Hindenburg from the sidewalks also waved little flags with the old Imperial colors. Republicans, if they were present, preferred to remain unidentified.[47]

On the following morning Hindenburg took the oath of allegiance to the Weimar Constitution in the Reichstag building. Paul Löbe, the Social Democratic president of the Reichstag, spoke briefly; he hoped that the economic improvement that had started under Ebert would continue and that the newly initiated foreign political contacts would be developed further to eliminate the dreadful effects of the war and postwar years. He concluded with the wish that all persons and agencies concerned would work for the integration of the German Reich as a "peaceful member with equal rights" into the European community of nations.

Hindenburg thanked Löbe for his words of welcome "which you have addressed to me in the name of the German parliament after I took the oath as Reich President, in accordance with the republican Constitution of August 11, 1919." Having presented his credentials, with a pointedly awkward bow to the constitution, he outlined his concept of his future role.

[46] Noske, *Erlebtes*, pp. 277–78; Schultze-Pfaelzer, *Wie Hindenburg Reichspräsident wurde*, pp. 54–55.

[47] Schulthess, May 11, 1925, p. 71; Schultze-Pfaelzer, *Wie Hindenburg*, pp. 59–60; Hörsing, Reichsbanner leader, in Berliner Tageblatt, No. 213, May 6, 1925; *Frankfurter Zeitung*, No. 350, May 12, 1925; *New York Times*, May 12, 1925.

"Reichstag and Reich President belong together, for they both are elected directly by the German people. They derive their powers from this common foundation. Together only they are the embodiment of popular sovereignty which today is the basis of our national life. This is the deeper meaning of the Constitution to which I have solemnly pledged my word just now."

Clearly, he viewed his office not merely as that of a figurehead, on the model of the French presidency, but as one which gave him authority equal to that of the Reichstag. As to his specific functions, he felt that:

"while the Reichstag is the arena in which the divergences of of ideologies and political beliefs struggle with each other, the Reich President must work for the cooperation, above all parties, of all those forces of our nation which are ready and willing to make a constructive contribution. . . . This noble task I can fulfill more easily if the parties in this High House will not indulge in petty quarrels about advantages for a party or an economic group, but will compete with each other in serving our hard-pressed people faithfully and effectively. . ."

In an appeal to the nation, he once more urged the country to unite. "The head of the Reich embodies the united will of the nation. Therefore I am offering my hand in this hour to every German."[48]

But the day was also disturbed by charges and countercharges. The Communists staged a brief demonstration in the Reichstag and then walked out. Once more the streets were lined with delegations of rightist organizations, with the *Reichsbanner* conspicuously absent. Its absence, its leader explained, was not directed against Hindenburg who was now the republic's president; it simply did not wish to stand shoulder to shoulder with those who had smeared and derided the national colors of the Reich and who were even on this day displaying black-white-and-red flags, "an open affront against the President of the Republic." It would make a bad impression on the foreign political front if both monarchists and republicans expressed their enthusiasm for Field Marshal von Hindenburg. "If Hindenburg shows that he respects the Constitution we shall show him all due respect. Our absence . . . is not directed against Herr Hindenburg; on the con-

[48] Schulthess, May 12, 1925, pp. 72–73.

trary we decided on it for domestic and foreign political reasons in the interest of the Fatherland."[49]

Nor could the precarious unity among Hindenburg's supporters be long maintained. When Loebell proposed the continuation of the Reich Bloc as a coordinating agency for the achievement of other political tasks, the German People's Party objected at once and insisted on regaining full freedom of action. The German Nationals were equally unwilling to retain that organization for continued cooperation with their fellow campaigners.[50]

Hindenburg's election thus failed to induce the nation to close ranks behind him: more was needed than fatherly exhortations to exorcize the country's divisions. The question now was what else the marshal would do to attain this foremost objective.

[49] *Frankfurter Zeitung,* No. 352, May 13, 1925; *New York Times,* May 13, 1925; Hörsing, in *Berliner Tageblatt,* No. 213, May 6, 1925.

[50] Loebell to German People's Party, May 29, 1925; Kempkes to Loebell, June 14, 1925, German People's Party to Frankfurt/Oder branch, May 9, 1925, Dingeldey Papers/111; *Frankfurter Zeitung,* No. 294, Apr. 21, 1925.

CHAPTER 4

THE CONSTITUTIONAL PRESIDENT

HATEVER the plans of the Reich Bloc leaders when they sponsored Hindenburg's candidacy, he was determined to follow his own course. "No one ought to get the idea that I am going to let any party tell me what to do," he announced to his entourage, "not even those who gave me their special support during the election campaign." Acting strictly within the framework of the constitution, he would let himself be guided by the counsel of his official advisers.[1]

He demonstrated at once that he was ready to take their advice. At his first meeting with Chancellor Luther he proposed to replace the incumbent head of the presidential *Büro* with a man of his own choice. This was a crucial question; as a political novice he would be very dependent on the counsel of his *Staatssekretär*. His campaign managers, knowing how much he had always relied on his staff even in military matters, had urged him therefore to dismiss Dr. Otto Meissner, Ebert's aide, and suspect as such of democratic and even Socialist leanings. In his place they wished him to appoint a man of rightist background who would steer him into the proper conservative-authoritarian channels. Colonel von Feldmann, the Reich Bloc's representative in Hanover, was mentioned as a suitable successor to Meissner. He had been a sort of political aide to the marshal during the election campaign; as a German National Reichstag deputy and onetime general staff officer he seemed properly qualified as Hindenburg's political mentor. Hindenburg, however, had his doubts and preferred a one-time Prussian official who had served in the Emperor's secretariat. Possibly he believed that Feldmann lacked sufficient political and administrative experience, but he may also have feared that this pugnacious ex-officer might be too rigidly antirepublican. Luther, on his part, felt that Hindenburg's candidate had neither political nor diplomatic experience. Since Meissner could not be dismissed without the cabinet's consent, Hindenburg agreed to retain him "for the time being." But he would not admit that he had changed his mind under pressure: "I still remember that much from my days as a captain,

[1] Schultze-Pfaelzer, *Wie Hindenburg Reichspräsident wurde,* p. 45.

you don't change your sergeant when you take over a new company." Luther had cleverly used this simile to dissuade him from parting with Meissner, and the marshal blandly appropriated it as a handy, conclusive argument.[2]

Dr. Otto Meissner, then in his forty-fifth year, had risen quickly through the ranks of the civil service. An official in the state railroad system before World War I, he had served as a transportation expert during the war. His immediate superior, Rudolf Nadolny, had taken him with him as an aide when he became state secretary to the newly elected Ebert in 1919. When Nadolny left to enter the diplomatic service, Meissner succeeded to his post. He was never a Social Democrat, as was widely claimed, but had joined the Democratic Party in 1919. A conscientious worker, suave and affable in his personal relations, he had been primarily a technical and legal adviser to Ebert; but since he had had to maintain liaison with the government, Reichstag, and other official agencies, he had not been entirely without political influence. Now, under Hindenburg, his influence grew quickly, due to the marshal's need for advice and guidance. Since Meissner had no strong political convictions, his Democratic past did not stand in the way of their harmonious collaboration. As he described his role to Chancellor Marx, he considered himself the executive officer of the president charged with carrying out his orders. In his pragmatic attitude he proved a useful aide to his new chief whose own approach to political problems was not unlike Meissner's.[3]

Pragmatism was indeed the guiding principle of Hindenburg's policies. He had stated during the campaign that the form of a state did not matter; what did matter was the spirit behind that form. The statement was not his; it had been in vogue for some time in those monarchist circles which were trying to justify their collaboration with the republic. He had no difficulty in accepting it for he had always conceived of the state as an apolitical entity, untouched in its core by political or ideological disputes. This state he considered it his duty to serve. There were elements in his attitude of that Lutheran ethic which demands that the faith-

[2] Dommes to Westarp, May 11, 12, 1925, Countess Westarp to Baroness Hiller von Gaertringen, n.d., Westarp Papers; memorandum (by Luther?), n.d., *Rkz.*, R 43 1/579; Schiffer, *Liberalismus*, p. 49; Hans Luther, *Politiker ohne Partei* (Stuttgart, 1960), p. 337; Schmidt-Hannover, *Umdenken*, pp. 189, 200–01.

[3] Testimony of Meissner before Internationl Military Tribunal (hereafter cited as "I.M.T.") No. IV, Case No. XI, transcript, pp. 4590, 4468; information from Dr. Zechlin; Wilhelm Marx, "Das Jahr 1927," MS., Marx Papers/24; Holtzendorff to Count Borcke-Stargordt, Feb. 13, 1949, Institut für Zeitgeschichte, *Zeugenschrifttum* hereafter cited as "ZS")/248.

ful Christian serve wherever God's will places him; but basically his was the attitude of the soldier. As a soldier he had learned to do his duty without asking questions; to work and obey had always been a Prussian article of faith. He had accepted the establishment of the Empire without much enthusiasm, and he was ready now to accept the republic.[4] And if he could serve the state despite his misgivings, everyone else could and should too, whatever his personal preferences. Nothing was to disappoint him more than to find the German Nationals as reluctant as ever to assume public office, except on their own partisan terms.

Hindenburg thus was determined to "do his duty" as he had done it throughout his life. As prescribed by the constitution, it meant working with Reichstag and government. He fulfilled it by retaining in office, not only Meissner, but also the cabinet of Chancellor Luther with Stresemann as foreign minister. Would-be advisers of the right, on the other hand, found it difficult to see him. Loebell complained in June that he had not seen Hindenburg since the election and that the Reich Bloc was evidently considered a political liability, despite its effective support at the polls. While Westarp was able to call on the president, Hindenburg made it clear that he did not wish to receive any unsolicited advice.[5]

But doubts, carefully nurtured by old intimates, kept assailing him. One of his first callers was his long-time friend General von Cramon who acted as a liaison man between him and the ex-Emperor. Hindenburg assured Cramon that he considered himself merely a stand-in for the Emperor and that he would like nothing better than to relinquish his post to his monarch.[6] His loyalty to the ex-Emperor no doubt was a matter of deepest conviction to him, but it collided, inevitably, with his determination to be guided by the advice of the government. He knew that an immediate restoration of the monarchy was out of the question, and he neither made nor abetted such an attempt during his presidency. But he could not, and would not, disregard warnings that the policies of the government and Reichstag were destroying the last remaining substance of that monarchic state on which Germany's greatness had once been founded and which alone could recapture it. As a servant of his monarch, as the symbol of that nonparty state whose professed task it was to provide a

---

[4] On his attitude toward the Empire, see Chapter 2, footnote 6 of this study.

[5] Luther, in cabinet meeting, Apr. 28, 1925, *RKz.*/1833/764414, 764416; Loebell to Bülow, June 24, 1925, Bülow Papers/101/159–60; Countess Westarp to Baroness Hiller, May 15, 1925, Westarp Papers.

[6] Personal information.

counterweight against the divisive interests of the parties, he was committed to protect and uphold what remained of that state. From the outset he thus wavered between these two poles of his loyalties, and at times his vacillations rendered cooperation between him and the government exceedingly difficult.

In this inner ambivalence Hindenburg fought out more than a personal struggle. The conflict with which he was faced personally was indeed the basic weakness of the republic: the Weimar state lacked that essential unity which he was to represent in his person—a unity founded on commonly accepted values and goals. Whatever the hopes of the drafters of the Weimar Constitution, that document came to be looked upon by growing numbers of Germans as a compilation of procedural rules without any substantive content. Carl Schmitt, that era's most influential political analyst, expressed a widely held attitude when he described the Weimar Republic as a political neuter without purposes of its own, unable to integrate the various classes and groups into a genuine community, and contenting itself, not very effectively, with keeping the door open to all parties and ideologies.[7] The view that the form of the state did not matter but rather the spirit that filled it, was but a variation on this same theme.

Hindenburg's uncertainties led him to reconsider his earlier rejection of unasked private advice; he was ready to listen to suggestions, he told Count Westarp after some weeks, but he insisted that they be made in strict secrecy. Westarp, on his part, tried to ease Hindenburg's mind by maintaining the pretense of nonpartisan consultations, offering advice in the name of his "friends" rather than that of his party. The marshal also began to listen to some of his old comrades-in-arms; as soldiers they stood implicitly above party politics.[8]

The effects of these back-stage consultations soon made themselves felt. At his first interview, shortly after Hindenburg's inauguration, Stresemann found him objective in his approach and determined to work loyally with the government. Three weeks later, after a second conference, the foreign minister noted in his diary that it was exceedingly difficult to talk with him about

[7] See his essays "Hugo Preuss in der deutschen Staatslehre," *Die neue Rundschau* XL (1930), i, 289–303, esp. pp. 298–300, and "Das Zeitalter der Neutralisierungen und Entpolitisierungen," and "Staatsethik und pluralistischer Staat," in *Positionen und Begriffe im Kampf mit Weimar-Genf-Versailles: 1923–1939* (Hamburg, 1940), pp. 120–45; see also Wilhelm Hennis, "Zum Problem der deutschen Staatsanschauung," *Vierteljahrshefte für Zeitgeschichte*, VII (1959), 22–23.

[8] Countess Westarp to Baroness Hiller, May 15, 1925, Westarp Papers.

the complexities of foreign policy "since he is so set in his views which are quite fixed and naturally rather one-sided. It seems as if some busybodies are trying to direct the attention of the President towards foreign political matters. All newspaper reports which are critical of the Foreign Office are being played into his hands."[9]

Hindenburg thus found himself the target of a bitter tug-of-war. He showed a good measure of common sense in his personal approach to the problems with which the country was faced. But if he was prepared to accept these realities in private talks with Luther and Stresemann, he was unwilling to defend their policies against the importunities of his friends. He thought it his duty to stay above partisan quarrels, and he maintained strict silence therefore on any such disputes. Yet his careful neutrality merely added to the existing tensions: the republican forces mistook his silence for an approval of the government's policies, while the antirepublicans felt encouraged to fight these policies every inch of the way.[10]

Hindenburg's passivity rendered more difficult Stresemann's efforts to conclude a security pact with both Britain and France. In February 1925, before the marshal's election, Stresemann had proposed such a pact to London and Paris. The three Powers (with Belgium and Italy added later) would promise to uphold the Western European boundaries as drawn by the Treaty of Versailles and to consider as their common concern any violation of this commitment. Stresemann's domestic opponents charged him at once with the permanent surrender of Alsace-Lorraine, the two provinces which Germany had lost after World War I. In reality, the pact did not bar any efforts at a peaceful recovery but merely proscribed a forcible change—precluded in any event by Germany's military weakness. There were additional accusations that Stresemann was rendering Germany permanently helpless by accepting her unconditional entry into the League of Nations. His failure to insist on the immediate and complete evacuation of all occupied territory by Allied troops showed, his opponents claimed, that he was unable to defend German interests adequately. These charges, too, were without foundation; far

[9] Stresemann diary, May 19, June 9, 1925, Stresemann to Houghton, June 4, 1925, Stresemann, *Vermächtnis*, II, 59–61, 259.

[10] Stresemann diary, Aug. 11, 1925, *ibid.*, II, 166; same to Count Stolberg-Wernigerode, Sept. 18, 1925, Stresemann Papers/29/3168/159926; Meissner, *Staatssekretär*, p. 184; Werner Freiherr von Rheinbaben, *Viermal Deutschland: Aus dem Erleben eines Seemanns, Diplomaten, Politikers 1895–1954* (Berlin, 1954), p. 170; Severing, *Lebensweg*, II, 58.

from agreeing unconditionally to Germany's League membership, Stresemann obtained some notable concessions to safeguard Germany's relations with Soviet Russia and he also expressly reserved the right to demand a revision of Germany's eastern border with Poland. The German Nationals, however, persisted in their attacks and in the end forced their party colleagues in the cabinet to resign in protest against the Locarno agreements. Their opposition proved ineffective, however, and the Locarno Pact was approved in late November 1925 by a large majority in the Reichstag.[11]

Hindenburg's attitude toward these negotiations fluctuated. Sentimentally he sided with the opposition: "Like most military men he is skeptical about the efficacy of any alternative to war," Stresemann told the British ambassador. The opposition took every opportunity to impress upon him what it considered the dangers of the proposed pact; Luther and Stresemann, however, supported by the rest of the cabinet, were able to convince him that the proposed pact constituted a step in the right direction. Accepting their view, Hindenburg stated to a cabinet meeting after their return from Locarno: "Some misgivings which were felt here and which I shared too are now gone. I am happy to see that [the cabinet] approves the attitude of the delegation [to the conference] and that it [has] also given its consent, in principle, to the initialing of the agreement. I hope we will continue to secure good results."[12]

Hindenburg's support was cautious and noncommittal, and soon he became even more reserved. The German Nationals urged him to withhold his approval, and Tirpitz and Field Marshal von Mackensen were sent to him in the hope that their military background would lend special weight to their warnings. Ludendorff thundered that loyalty to the soldiers of the World War demanded the rejection of the treaty: Hindenburg would sacrifice his soldierly glory and his personal honor were he to sign it; if he did, his presidency would indeed be considered a threat to all national aspirations. These warnings were not without effect, and Hindenburg's dismay increased when the German Nationals insisted on withdrawing their party members from the cabinet. Unversed in the intricacies of foreign policy,

[11] Stresemann, *Vermächtnis*, II, 205–07, 246–48.

[12] Viscount Edgar Vincent d'Abernon, *An Ambassador of Peace: Pages from the Diary of Viscount d'Abernon* (London, 1929–30), III, 169; Stresemann diary, June 9, Aug. 11, 1925, Stresemann, *Vermächtnis*, II, 60–61, 166; cab. mtgs., Sept. 24, 1925, RKz./1835/765957–59, Oct. 19, 1925, RKz./1836/766340.

he could not appreciate the difficulties which Stresemann faced. He had personal misgivings too about the foreign minister; cautious and pessimistic by nature, he viewed Stresemann's optimism with some distrust. "The Locarno soup was dished up to us by Herr Stresemann and must be eaten up now," he confided to his old friend Elard von Oldenburg–Januschau, an East Prussian landowner and one-time Conservative deputy famed for his outspoken antiparliamentarianism. "The Chancellor went with him since it did not seem advisable to let Herr Stresemann loose by himself. The result of the conference is unsatisfactory. . . . As far as I am concerned, I am not happy about Locarno and am trying to check this mess within my constitutional limits."[13]

Against his custom he presided at a number of cabinet meetings which dealt with the Locarno agreements and Germany's entry into the League. Close observers suspected that he did so primarily to put on record his strong opposition to both steps as well as the force of circumstances to which he had to submit. At the first of these meetings he disagreed with the cabinet's view that the Locarno agreements were advantageous for Germany and that they were the best that could be obtained: "I think the basis of the agreement is a very unequal one," he objected, "unequal in the sense that we have disarmed while the others have not; moreover, we are obliged to maintain a neutral demilitarized zone, yet there is no corresponding neutralization of Alsace-Lorraine." He also felt that Germany should press for a more rapid evacuation of the Rhineland and for additional guarantees that her League membership would not impair her treaty with Russia ("which, to be sure, is no very respectable [*standesgemäss*] alliance)." He mentioned some other objections and in conclusion asked the cabinet not to announce as yet its readiness to accept the agreements.

Luther tried to assure the president that his fears were unfounded and that given Germany's lack of power, no better results could possibly have been obtained. He seems to have been successful; when the cabinet met again with the marshal on the following day, Hindenburg made Luther's arguments his own and agreed that in view of Germany's impotence she was dependent on settling for whatever improvements she could get by way of negotiations. He still felt uneasy, however, about the

[13] Gessler, *Reichswehrpolitik*, pp. 349–50; Meissner, *Staatssekretär*, pp. 154–55; Luther, *Politiker*, pp. 388–89; Hindenburg to Oldenburg-Januschau, n.d., Oldenburg-Januschau, *Erinnerungen*, p. 219.

effect of the agreement on Russo-German relations, but Luther and Stresemann assured him that his fears were unfounded.

Hindenburg then turned to another matter, also close to his heart. He was distressed by the bitter attacks on the Locarno agreements, he told the cabinet, and urged it to explain to the country the difficulties of its task. Such public enlightenment would help to restore domestic peace. Without saying so, obviously he was also concerned about the effect of these attacks on his own popular standing and anxious therefore to put an end to these "bad recriminations."

Luther promised to do what he could, but he warned that he could do little: a large part of the press simply ignored official announcements, and the German National Party was clearly committed to carry on a "relentless war against Locarno." If Hindenburg made a reply to these comments, it is not recorded in the minutes. Resigned now to the acceptance of the pact, he seems to have contented himself with expressing the hope, in a concluding statement, that the treaty would secure for Germany the place in the concert of nations to which she was entitled: "Our rise is bound to be slow; it can't be achieved all at once. . . . I too would have liked to see many things arranged differently, but on the whole we probably can't change them any more."[14] His unofficial advisers were not yet ready, however, to give up the fight against the pact. Prompted by them, Hindenburg asked the chancellor just before the treaty came up for a vote in the Reichstag whether the question of Germany's entry into the League could not be separated from the Locarno Pact. The cabinet rejected this suggestion unanimously lest it lead to the abrogation of the entire pact, and Hindenburg did not press the matter.

Two days later the Reichstag passed the law ratifying the pact. The president signed it since this was his constitutional duty once government and Reichstag had approved it. He was shocked when the German Nationals persisted in their opposition. Would not something be gained by Germany's membership in the League, he complained to Westarp—the recognition of Germany's equality and a better chance of obtaining foreign credits? Should one not at least give matters a chance to develop? But above all he considered the continued opposition an unsoldierly lack of discipline. His admonitions fell on deaf ears. Westarp coolly replied that Germany could never expect to enjoy true equality under the existing circumstances.

[14] Cab. mtgs., Nov. 16, 17, 1925, *RKz./*1836/766583–86, 766599–602.

Stresemann noted later in his diary: "We were close to a state crisis . . . in addition to the party and government crisis . . . but the Old Gentleman stuck it out." He knew however, that this was merely a temporary victory and that he could not count on the continued support of the president.[15] Stresemann's fears were quickly confirmed. Hard pressed by Mackensen and others, Hindenburg demanded once more that the government, before entering the League, obtain a reduction of the occupation forces and an early evacuation of the remaining occupation zones. He also reiterated his earlier fears concerning the future prospects of German-Russian relations. He assured the government that he would stand by its policies and that he merely differed on their tactical implementation, but the cabinet was seriously perturbed by this renewed intervention. The cabinet had other reasons to worry about his support: to its dismay Hindenburg claimed that he need not sign Germany's application for League membership since ratification of the Locarno agreements by the Reichstag gave the cabinet the authority to file this request itself and his signature was therefore not required. The ministers were convinced that his signature *was* required by international law; clearly he wished to dissociate himself from the League application. They saw their suspicions confirmed when Meissner rejected the suggestion that the president drop his objections and set his name under the application as evidence of his confidence in the government. Meissner would only promise that Hindenburg would sign any document on which the League would require his signature *after* the cabinet had submitted its application. He added that while the president would not withdraw his objections, he would be willing, *after* Germany's entry into the League, to express his agreement with the policies of the government. With this tenuous arrangement the cabinet had to be satisfied.[16]

The government did not survive the acceptance of the Locarno agreements: with the withdrawal of the German Nationals, it lost its majority in the Reichstag. It stayed in office only until it had steered the pact through the Reichstag. After the formal signing of the treaties in London in early December it submitted its resignation to the president.

For the first time Hindenburg faced the task of forming a new government. His preference would have been to let Luther form

15 Cab. mtg., Nov. 27, 1925, *RKz.*/1836/766700–02; Westarp memorandum on talk with Hindenburg, Dec. 7, 1925, Westarp Papers; Stresemann diary, early Dec., 1925, Stresemann Papers/272/3113/148048–49; Luther, *Politiker*, p. 398.
16 Cab. mtg., Feb. 3, 1925, *RKz.*/1837/767547–60.

a new bourgeois cabinet, but since the new government would have to accept the Locarno Pact, there could be no question of German National participation. Without the German Nationals, however, the bourgeois parties had no majority in the Reichstag. On Luther's advice, Hindenburg agreed to try forming a government which would include Social Democrats along with the pro-Locarno bourgeois parties.

He did not wish to expose Luther to the probable failure of these soundings. He asked the Democratic leader Erich Koch-Weser to attempt such a coalition since his party alone had no reservations about it, but Koch was reluctant to accept the mandate. To concede to the parties so dominant a role in the formation of the new government could only encourage their selfishness and he proposed instead that Hindenburg grant someone full power to form a new cabinet and let him determine the terms on which the new government was to proceed. This course of relying on the strength of a personality, he maintained, corresponded more closely to the intent of the constitution.[17] But Hindenburg would not take his advice. His concept of the "Weimar party state" demanded that the parties be consulted before any final decisions were made, and he was the more determined to follow this course as Ebert too had adhered to it.

Despite his misgivings Koch took the assignment. He worked out a program that combined pledges of a vigorous foreign policy with promises of a series of social reforms. As he had feared, however, he could not reduce the conflicting demands of the parties to a common denominator. The German People's Party accepted his plans with some reservations, but the Social Democrats, hard pressed by an exceptionally severe winter, insisted on an increase in unemployment relief payments and a reduction of the tax burden on low income groups. These demands the People's Party found unacceptable and negotiations had to be broken off. Hindenburg, with obvious relief, asked Luther to carry on until after the Christmas holidays. He had anticipated difficulties and had expected, as he confided to Westarp, that the "Great Coalition" would not materialize in view of the conflicting party interests, but he professed to be shocked at finding his efforts so little appreciated.[18]

[17] In his diary on which this account is based Koch-Weser does not elaborate on this argument. He probably had in mind Article 56 of the Weimar Constitution which stated that the chancellor determined the basic policies of the government. That he was to be more than a *primus inter pares* is confirmed also by Articles 53, 55, and 58. Cf. Koch-Weser diary, Dec. 1925, Koch-Weser Papers/32/167 ff.

[18] Cab. mtg., Dec. 5, 1925, *RKz./*1836/766841–44; Eyck, *Weimarer Republik,* II,

In January a new attempt was made to form a coalition extending from the Social Democrats to the People's Party, but no more successfully than the first attempt. The Socialists thought it good politics to keep insisting on their demands which, as their own leaders admitted, could not be met; the People's Party maintained that these demands would render even more difficult the task of overcoming the severe economic crisis. Once more the center of political gravity shifted to Hindenburg. He now gave Luther the mandate that Koch had asked for in vain—to form a government without prior party agreement. It was to be a "neutral government of the center"—a government without party ties and consisting, at least in part, of men without any party affiliation. Luther was unable to find a majority, however, even on this basis. Once more Hindenburg had to intervene. He summoned the leaders of the parties from which the proposed "center" government was to be recruited. Urging them to put an end to the undignified spectacle of a prolonged government crisis, he asked them to subordinate their special interests to those of the country. "What might happen after the complete breakdown of the efforts of these last weeks," he warned darkly, "no one can tell." This direct appeal had its desired effect. A few hours later Luther was able to report to the president that the new cabinet had been formed. There remained, however, the task of obtaining a vote of confidence from the Reichstag. Hindenburg armed Luther with a decree dissolving that body should it refuse to support him. Faced with this threat, the Reichstag passed a motion of confidence, but it mustered no more than a tenuous majority of 10, with the 130 Social Democrats abstaining.[19]

Hindenburg emerged from the crisis with his prestige greatly enhanced since none but a few insiders knew that he was at least partly responsible for the prolonged negotiations. As the country at large saw it, after weeks of desultory talks his intervention had quickly led to a settlement—the old marshal had proven stronger than the endlessly wrangling parties. On the other hand, the Social Democrats had by their intransigence helped to further

---

71–73; Hindenburg-Westarp talk, Dec. 7, 1925, Westarp Papers; Gessler, *Reichswehrpolitik*, pp. 348–49; Koch-Weser diary, Dec. 7, 11, 12, 15, 18, 1925, Koch-Weser Papers/32/167–71, 181–83, 191, 199–201, 209–15; Meissner memorandum, Dec. 17, 1925, *RKz./* R 43 I/1308; *Kölnische Volkszeitung*, No. 909, Dec. 8, 1925; Severing, *Lebensweg*, II, 78–80; Stresemann diary, Dec. 16, 1925, Stresemann, *Vermächtnis*, II, 382; Görlitz, *Hindenburg*, pp. 272–73; Schulthess, Dec. 7–17, 1925, pp. 189–92.

[19] Eyck, *Weimarer Republik*, II, 73–75; Julius Curtius, *Sechs Jahre Minister der deutschen Republik* (Heidelberg, 1948), pp. 13–14; Koch-Weser memorandum, n.d., Koch-Weser Papers/34/3–5; *Frankfurter Zeitung*, No. 33, Jan. 13, 1926.

discredit the parliamentary system. In the end one of the Socialists' own leaders, Otto Braun, was among those who advised Hindenburg to nominate a middle-of-the-road government and force it upon the Reichstag.[20]

&

Hindenburg may have gained the respect of many for his handling of the government crisis, but he himself was distinctly unhappy. He found the protracted negotiations, the endless wrangling and quibbling bewildering and frustrating—visitors during those weeks found him tired and discouraged. He took it as a personal affront that the German Nationals kept up their attacks on Stresemann's foreign policy; to him, their intransigence showed not only a shocking lack of discipline but also of loyalty. While he had assumed the burdens of the presidency for the sake of the Fatherland, those who had urged that office on him were deserting him rather than helping. If he had to bow to necessity and accept compromises, so should they; they ought not to let him fend for himself. He suffered most under the censure of his old wartime associates who kept criticizing him for his strict adherence to the constitution and the rules of the parliamentary system. And somehow the haunting specter of that never-forgotten November 9, 1918 kept injecting itself into his concerns. When a visitor sought to reassure him by saying that only those who had been at Locarno had the right to blame Luther and Stresemann for not having accomplished more, he burst out with unusual vehemence: "You are quite right, you are absolutely right. They blame me too for having let the Emperor leave the country in 1918. Oh God, only someone who was not there at the time can say something like that. Only those have the right to pass judgment who did live through those days!"

Even a more self-assured person might have found it difficult to ignore these never-ending attacks, and Hindenburg had no such firmness of mind. Two days after Luther had been appointed again, he listened to Westarp's plan for a new cabinet in which the German Nationals would participate and from which Stresemann would be excluded. And on the following day he discussed Luther's replacement with Oldenburg-Januschau.[21]

20 Severing, *Lebensweg*, ii, 79–80; Braun, *Von Weimar*, p. 187; *Frankfurter Zeitung*, No. 33, Jan. 13, 1926.

21 Hindenburg's remark in unsigned memorandum on Escherich talk with Hindenburg, Feb. 4, 1926, Stresemann Papers/35/3144/161126–27; Stresemann diary,

Oldenburg, however, was not interested in merely forming another government that would take the place of Luther's. For some time now rightist circles had been toying with plans to transform the parliamentary regime into an authoritarian one which they alone would control. They saw in the protracted government crisis a welcome opportunity to air their thoughts. "The hope that our venerable President would succeed in unifying the multitude of centrifugal elements in our people, as he so ardently wishes, has not been fulfilled, could not be fulfilled, for one cannot force 60 million individuals into one direction. The individualistic German needs strong governmental guidance," the *Berliner Börsen-Zeitung,* noted for its industrial and military connections, wrote during those days. Conditions are ripe, the paper predicted, for the formation of a government of officials and business leaders free from party ties, who would be steered by the firm hand of a strong chancellor. Other rightist leaders were even more outspoken. Far from making any excuses for Hindenburg, they stated bluntly that he had disappointed their expectations and that it was naive to see in him any longer a "national hope." An "Emergency Association" of which Westarp and the Pan-German leader Heinrich Class were members called for "patriotic self-help." On their visits to the president they left him in no doubt about the sentiments of his one-time supporters. Several former generals petitioned him formally to take Class's advice and establish a dictatorship. His son, Major Oskar von Hindenburg, who served as his military aide, was approached with similar proposals. The ex-Crown Prince too warned the marshal that Germany was facing a new revolution: "The attacks on our Hohenzollern family, against the judiciary, landed property, ultimately against all property is but a systematic preparation for the Bolshevization of Germany. There is still time for a determined government ready to apply its power ruthlessly to fight off these destructive tendencies. But time is running out. If nothing is done, I see us being plunged into a bloody civil war whose outcome is quite unpredictable."

The old man was greatly perturbed and expressed regret to his confidants that he had ever accepted the presidency. He refused to become a party to these plots, but he could not bring himself to ignore the warnings of his conspiratorial visitors; their criticisms of the republic seemed well founded to him, even if their remedies were too radical for his conservative tastes. At

---

Jan. 27, 1926, *ibid.*/279/3100/149458–59, Mar. 25, 1926, 149493; Countess Westarp to Baroness Hiller, Jan. 22, 1926, Westarp Papers.

one point he seems to have promised to appoint to the post of finance minister Alfred Hugenberg, the owner of a newspaper chain and leader of the most intransigent wing of the German National Party; on another occasion he assured Westarp again that Stresemann would be excluded from the next government. But Luther and Stresemann to whom he passed on all complaints were able to reassure him that theirs was the right path. And since they were his official advisers, he grudgingly continued to follow them.[22]

The antirepublican plotters were not easily discouraged, however, and they pursued their various schemes indefatigably. It is not clear at what point they decided to expedite the changeover to a dictatorship by the use of force; possibly Hindenburg's refusal to listen to them convinced them that mere persuasion was not enough. A Communist rising, provoked if need be, was to serve as the occasion for an armed coup, with parts of the Reichswehr cooperating with the semimilitary organizations that continued to lead their shadowy existence under the protection of various political and other organizations. Preparations were carried out in the haphazard way that had characterized and doomed the Kapp Putsch. They were serious enough, however, to induce the Prussian police to search the homes of some rightist leaders, industrialists, and ex-officers. Among the incriminating material discovered were plans for the dissolution of all parliamentary bodies, with continued parliamentary activity punishable by death; the replacement of the Reich president with a regent; and the appointment by this regent of regents for the various states. Significantly, Hindenburg was to be left in office only until the new regime was firmly established; once this had been accomplished, his place would be taken by someone more amenable to the plans of the plotters. In consequence, while they kept urging him to set up a dictatorship lest the country fall prey to the Communists, they actually left him in the dark about their ultimate plans. From what he did learn, he seems to have dissociated himself—in his indecisive way that left all doors at least half-open.[23]

22 Oldenburg-Januschau, *Erinnerungen*, pp. 218–19; Berliner *Börsen-Zeitung*, Jan. 23, 1926; Severing, *Lebensweg*, II, 80; Alfred Kruck, *Geschichte des alldeutschen Verbandes; 1890–1939* (Wiesbaden, 1954), pp. 173–74; Countess Westarp to Baroness Hiller, Feb. 5, Mar. 19, 24, 1926, Westarp Papers; Class to Oskar von Hindenburg, Jan. 26, 1926, in *Tagebuch*, July 2, 1927, pp. 1060–61, same to ex-Empress Hermine, Jan. 26, 1926, in Berliner *Tageblatt*, No. 226, May 15, 1926; ex-Crown Prince Wilhelm to Hindenburg, May 14, 1926, Schüddekopf, *Heer und Republik*, pp. 210–11; Luther, *Politiker*, p. 338.
23 *Frankfurter Zeitung*, No. 352, May 13, 1926, No. 364, May 18, 1926; *Berliner*

As if to highlight the instability of the republic, the plot was uncovered in the midst of another cabinet crisis. This latest fracas grew out of the republic's old and troublesome flag problem. To the great disappointment of his supporters Hindenburg made no attempt to replace the new black-red-and-gold colors with the Empire's black-white-and-red. While he did feel a deep attachment to the old flag, he would not make such a change on his own initiative. Unlike him, however, Chancellor Luther was a man bursting with energy. Impetuous and without much political flair, he did not hesitate to tackle the sensitive flag problem. Diplomatic reports had kept pointing out that many an awkward situation resulted abroad from the flag dispute; German legations and consulates in port cities were showing black-red-and-gold while incoming German ships, hoisting the commerce flag, displayed the old colors, with the new ones barely visible in the upper left corner (see Article 3 of the constitution). German overseas settlements, moreover, had never reconciled themselves to the existence of the republic and kept hoisting the Imperial flag—other countries thus were constantly being reminded of the bitter internal discord in Germany. The official display by German missions and consulates of the commerce flag together with the National black–red–and–gold flag was proposed to help bridge the existing gap; this proposal appealed to Luther, and he decided to act on it.[24]

A suitable opportunity seemed to present itself early in May 1926 when Hindenburg was scheduled to pay a state visit to the port city of Hamburg. By associating the step with the prestige of the president, the chancellor hoped to disarm the opposition of the republican parties more easily. Stresemann, on consultation, voiced no objections, and after a prolonged debate the cabinet accepted the plan. Hindenburg, fearing new difficulties, did not, apparently, welcome it, but obviously could not reject it. When it became clear, however, that there would be considerable op-

Tageblatt, No. 222, May 12, 1926, No. 230, May 18, 1926; Braun to Severing, May 27, 1926, Severing Papers/1926; "Vertrauliche Mitteilungen über wirtschaftliche und politische Tagesfragen," May 18, 1926, Stresemann Papers/38/3145/161481; *Deutscher Geschichts-Kalender* (hereafter cited as "*Dt. Gesch.-Kal.*), 1926, A, I, 221–22; Braun, *Von Weimar*, pp. 198–202; report of *Oberreichsanwalt*, July 13, 1927, Grzesinski Papers/1465.

24 Braun, *Von Weimar*, pp. 188–90; Luther to author, Sept. 20, 1956; Stresemann statement, n.d., Stresemann, *Vermächtnis*, II, 389–90; same to Nadolny, Jan. 1924 (draft), Stresemann Papers/265/3111/146673; Nadolny to Stresemann, Sept. 9, 1925, *ibid.*/16/3119/157146–47; Rauscher to Stresemann, May 3, 1926, copy in *ibid.*/281/3100/149635; Koch-Weser diary, May 6, 1926, Koch-Weser Papers/34/134–35; memoranda by Wienstein, Apr. 29, May 4, 1926, *RKz.*, R 43 I/1833.

position to the move, he refused to announce it on his visit to Hamburg. There were also some constitutional questions that needed to be settled; Luther suggested at a subsequent cabinet meeting that the decree limit the official display of both flags to non-European areas and to European ports of call for German ships, since only there the hoisting of the commerce flag could be justified. In this form the decree was signed by Hindenburg on May 5, after his return from Hamburg.

The decree raised a storm of protest in the republican camp. There were bitter attacks on the government in the Reichstag, and protest meetings were held in all parts of the country. Once more the *Reichbanner* was one of the focal points of this republican activity, and in a number of mass demonstrations it proclaimed its determined opposition to the decree. It became obvious that the government was facing a serious crisis. In order to shore up its position, Hindenburg sent Luther a letter in which he assured the republicans that nothing was further from his mind than to tamper with the national colors: the flag dispute was hurting the country and had to be settled by some compromise that would do justice to both present-day Germany and its goals and to the historical development of the Reich. He concluded with the hope that the time would come "when the German people will once more rally in unity around one and the same symbol of its political existence." He also urged the government to seek a final solution to the flag problem by way of a Reichstag-enacted law.[25] The letter failed to achieve its purpose —instead of helping Luther, it strengthened the impression that the decree constituted an unjustifiable interference on the part of Hindenburg. He, rather than Luther, was held responsible for it, and the measure was widely considered as the first act in a presidental plot to restore the old Imperial colors. The storm did not subside when the government decided to postpone for three months the implementation of the decree in the hope that a solution might be found by way of legislation. Faced with a hostile majority in the Reichstag, Luther was forced to resign.[26]

[25] It was doubtful even whether the change could be properly enacted by an ordinary law. Since the constitution provided that the merchant marine display the old colors, it would seem that only a constitutional amendment could extend their display to diplomatic and consular buildings; cf. Eyck, *Weimarer Republik*, II, 82–83. Significantly, the republicans made no attempt to test the constitutionality of the flag decree.

[26] Eyck, *Weimarer Republik*, II, 92–95; Stampfer, *Vierzehn Jahre*, pp. 491–92; *Berliner Tageblatt*, No. 209, May 5, 1926; Koch-Weser diary, May 7, 1926, Koch-Weser Papers/34/155–57; Stresemann to Luther, Apr. 29, 1926, Stresemann, *Vermächtnis*, II, 388–89; memorandum by Bernhard, May 8, 1926, Stresemann Papers/

Except for his letter to Luther, Hindenburg remained passive throughout this entire episode. Faithful to his self-imposed role, he let himself be carried along by events. When Luther proposed to limit the application of the decree to non-European areas and European ports, Meissner doubted that Hindenburg would accept this distinction; but if the president had any misgivings, Luther had no difficulty in overcoming them, for he obtained the president's signature that very same day. Perhaps he would have resigned, as Stresemann feared, had the decree been repealed, but he was unwilling to fight for it actively. His letter to Luther, in its cautious and moderate approach, obviously was a faithful expression of his attitude. The German Nationals accepted it as such, and Westarp, furious over the letter's conciliatory tone, expressed his displeasure to Hindenburg. Nor did the German Nationals support the government when its fate was being debated in the Reichstag. Resentful of the decision to postpone the execution of the decree, they abstained from voting against both a Socialist motion for a vote of nonconfidence and a Democratic motion of censure. In keeping with parliamentary courtesy, they refrained from mentioning Hindenburg's name in the debate, but it was clear that this gesture was aimed not only at the government, but also at him.[27]

All things considered, however, Hindenburg emerged as the victor from the flag crisis. There followed the usual harried negotiations; among those who tried forming a cabinet was the mayor of Cologne, Konrad Adenauer. In the end Hindenburg's erstwhile opponent, ex-Chancellor Marx, was appointed to head the new government—it was almost an exact replica of its predecessor. The flag decree, too, remained unchanged. Marx agreed with the *Deutsche Tageszeitung,* a paper that faithfully supported Hindenburg, that the president's mandate to the new cabinet carried with it the obligation not to tamper with the flag decree. No change was made in the decree, but its retention aroused no new protests. The republican fervor seemed to have spent itself in the removal of Luther; even the Social Democrats raised no objections. Once again the republican forces saw their victory turned into defeat. Hindenburg, on the other hand, had won a victory for which, as so often before, he could claim little credit.[28]

281/3100/149643; Breitscheid, May 11, 1926, David, May 12, 1926, *Verhandlungen,* Vol. 390, pp. 7158, 7211.

27 Cab. mtgs., May 5, 1926, *RKz.*/1839/768743–44, May 10, 1926, 768784–90; Countess Westarp to Baroness Hiller, May 11, 1926, Westarp Papers.

28 *Deutsche Tageszeitung,* No. 220, May 14, 1926; Marx, "Die Auseinandersetzung

The acquiescence of the republicans was the more astonishing as they were being challenged on other fronts too. The rightist plot, uncovered just then, ought to have warned them not to relax their vigilance. The antirepublicans were also on the offensive in another campaign raging over the disposal of the holdings belonging to the former ruling families. These properties were being held by the state governments, pending a final settlement. The Reich government had tried to settle the matter by law, but failed since there was sharp disagreement about the compensation to be granted to the princes. Meanwhile the latter had taken their claims to court and had won a number of favorable decisions.

Since these judgments placed heavy financial burdens on the states concerned, the Social Democrats had thought of submitting the matter to a popular referendum. The move was still in the planning stage when the Communists learned about it. Recognizing its political potentialities, they decided to appropriate it for their own purposes. The Socialists had been considering a moderate indemnification, but the Communists advocated expropriation without compensation. Fearful of losing followers, the Socialists abandoned their own proposal and adopted the Communists'. Support for a petition to hold the referendum was readily obtained; over 12 million voters signed the petition. The number surpassed by more than one million the number of Socialists and Communist votes cast in the last Reichstag election. Evidently not only Marxists favored the outright expropriation of the property of the princes.[29]

Nevertheless there was little chance that the referendum would get the required support of the majority of the electorate. Hindenburg's friends, however, pleaded with him to state publicly his opposition to the proposed measure. The rumor was being spread, Loebell wrote him, that he would sign the Socialist-Communist bill, should it be approved by the voters. Hindenburg of course was opposed to the measure. As early as March he had warned the government that he considered its bill unconstitutional and that he would not sign it, should it be passed by the Reichstag. He expressed himself in similar terms to the many callers who inquired about his attitude toward the referendum. But the *Kaiserpartei* (Meissner's term) wanted a public commit-

mit den fürstlichen Häusern über ihre Vermögen," MS., pp. 5–6, Marx Papers/24; same, "Die Flaggenfrage, MS., p. 3, *ibid.*/17; *Berliner Tageblatt*, No. 234, May 20, 1926; Marx, May 19, 1926, *Verhandlungen*, Vol. 390, p. 7321.

29 Eyck, *Weimarer Republik*, II, 87–92; Stampfer, *Vierzehn Jahre*, pp. 482–89.

ment. Berg, now the administrator of the ex-Emperor's holdings, kept urging him to issue a public appeal against the referendum. Meissner warned that the chancellor would never countersign such an appeal as required by the constitution, but Berg was not impressed. In that case, he replied, the appeal would have to be published without Marx's signature. Hindenburg of course would not lend his hand to this cavalier disregard of the constitution, but he was also unwilling to ignore the pleas of the ex-Kaiser's spokesmen. That they were asking him to break his self-imposed silence on all partisan issues does not seem to have troubled him. He owed it to his conscience, he insisted, to stand up for the Emperor and for justice. But since he could not speak up as president on behalf of the Kaiser, he would have to resign and then issue his appeal. With each passing day he appeared more determined to adopt this course, and there was every prospect of a major political crisis. To clear the impasse, Meissner proposed in the end that Hindenburg make his views known as a private citizen; if he made a statement in the form of a personal letter, it would not require the countersignature of the chancellor. As a suitable vehicle he suggested a reply to Loebell's letter which the latter might be permitted to publish.

Seizing on Meissner's proposal, Hindenburg agreed to write to Loebell and state his opposition to the expropriation bill. The letter was promptly written and dispatched. Hindenburg called the referendum a "dangerous assault on the legal foundation of the state" and on law and morality in general. He warned that it might lead to the abuse of this plebiscitary instrument; by arousing the passions of the hard-pressed masses in times of misery, the nation might one day find itself without the safeguards of its cultural, economic, and national life. Loebell lost no time in printing the letter in a special issue of his *Deutschen-Spiegel*. Distributed by the hundreds of thousands, the statement caused a sensation; it was received jubilantly by the right and with dismay by the left. The republicans had come to respect the president for the way in which he appeared to be handling his duties; but even those who agreed with the gist of his arguments, objected to this open descent into the political arena. Hindenburg was nonetheless glad to have this opportunity to show the right that despite all disagreements he was at heart on their side, and in this sense Westarp and others used the letter to reassure their increasingly restive constituents.[30]

[30] Severing, *Lebensweg*, II, 89–90; Marx, "Auseinandersetzung," pp. 9–10, Marx Papers/24; Hindenburg to Marx, Mar. 15, 1926, *RKz.*, R 43 I/2206; Koch-Weser

The letter proved useful for other purposes also. What worried Loebell as much as the referendum was Hindenburg's apparent anxiety to form a new government that would enjoy majority support unlike Marx's. To that end the marshal was even prepared to appoint a cabinet that included some Social Democrats. This Loebell hoped to prevent by driving a wedge between the president and the Socialists. In an article in the *Deutsche Tageszeitung,* timed to appear just a day before he published Hindenburg's letter in his *Deutschen-Spiegel,* he asserted again that Socialists and Communists were claiming Hindenburg's support in their referendum campaign: "The real aim of the left is to destroy the only safeguard of a stable political development which we have in Germany, the influence of Reich President von Hindenburg. . . . Hindenburg's name is to be used for the destruction of our present state which is founded on the rule of law (*Rechtsstaat*) . . . . If the plan were to succeed, Germany would be subjected anew to the revolutionary or Socialist-Communist whims of the leaders of 1918." To these alleged aspirations Hindenburg's letter was to provide an answer too. By drawing Hindenburg into the dispute, wrote the Centrist *Kölnische Volkszeitung,* every effort was being made to prevent the formation of a "Great Coalition" government extending from the German People's Party to the Social Democrats. As Loebell had hoped, the interparty struggle did indeed increase in intensity after the letter had been published.[31]

On June 20, 1926, the referendum took place. Votes cast in favor of the bill came to 15.5 million, far from enough to carry it, but a number large enough to indicate again that a great many non-Marxists favored the outright expropriation of the holdings of the former ruling families. The "aye" voters thought of the losses they had suffered from the war and inflation, and wished the former dynasties to share in these losses.[32]

But once more the readiness to protest was not matched by the will to propose a constructive alternative. With the expropriation bill disposed of, the government renewed its efforts to settle the problem by way of an ordinary law. Its proposal provided for a fairly generous compensation and was rejected by both the

---

diary, Aug. 14, 1926, Koch-Weser Papers/34/303–07; Hindenburg to Loebell, May 22, 1926, Schulthess, June 10 1926, pp. 114–15; Westarp's office to Werner, June 10, 1926, Westarp Papers.

[31] Pünder to Marx, July 23, 1926, Marx Papers/1078; Loebell, "Um den Reichspräsidenten," *Deutsche Tageszeitung,* No. 257, June 6, 1926; *Kölnische Volkszeitung,* June 9, 1926, cited in Marx, "Auseinandersetzung," Marx Papers/24.

[32] Stampfer, *Vierzehn Jahre,* p. 487; Eyck, *Weimarer Republik,* II, 91.

right and the left. The German Nationals maintained that it imposed unjustifiable and unconstitutional sacrifices on the princes while Socialists and Communists rejected it as not going far enough. Hindenburg seems to have wavered: first he reiterated his opposition to the government bill and threatened to dissolve the Reichstag rather than sign it. Westarp, however, who knew that the German Nationals would suffer serious defeat in an election convinced him that a dissolution was inadvisable. The president then seems to have made up his mind that if a legislative settlement was inevitable, it ought to be reached as quickly as possible after the turmoil of the preceding weeks. Doubtless he also knew that agrarian circles were by that time in open revolt against the German National leaders and demanded the immediate acceptance of the bill. Anxious to have their say on tariff and other policies, they thus wished to prove that they deserved to be taken into the government. Some of their spokesmen, impeccable members of old Prussian families (Hardenberg, Richthofen, Arnim), even toyed with the thought of establishing a party of their own. When the German Nationals persisted in their rejection of the government bill, Hindenburg tried frightening them by threatening again to dissolve the Reichstag. Horrified at the prospect of new elections, many now reconsidered. Yet Westarp was able to persuade them that the threat was not meant seriously, and that to accept the bill would greatly embarrass the president.

Faced with opposition on all sides, Marx gave up the fight for the bill. He thought of resigning, but stayed on at Hindenburg's urgent request. Nor did he press the unwilling president to dissolve the Reichstag, as the Social Democrats, confident of gaining in new elections, demanded. Once again an opportunity to improve the position of the republican forces could not be exploited.

Negotiations now shifted to the states and each tried to make its own settlement with its one-time rulers. Anxious for speedy action, Hindenburg asked Berg to scale down his claims. But when he went to Bavaria for his annual chamois hunt, his hosts and their friends urged him to give more help to the princes. He asked Marx to press the Prussian Government for an early settlement. Should the matter be brought once more before the Reichstag, he foresaw grave difficulties; the new Reichstag bill might tend too much towards the left or provide for complete expropriation. In that case, he somberly warned, he might have to resign from the presidency.

110

Marx took the hint and conferred hurriedly with one of his party colleagues in the Prussian Government. His colleague saw little prospect of a settlement since the Socialist attitude had become much more rigid meanwhile. A few weeks later, however, the Socialists agreed to a negotiated settlement with the Hohenzollerns that was less advantageous to Prussia than that proposed by the Reich. This they did, Marx explained darkly in his memoirs, "to avoid worse consequences." Obviously they had been forewarned that Hindenburg might resign if they did not accept; whatever their misgivings about him, they were not prepared to face a new presidential election. Once more they presented a picture of indecision and diffidence, arousing the contempt of their foes. "It was a bitter blow to the parliamentary system," Chancellor Marx commented later, and one Center deputy warned that no one should be surprised if each new crisis would lead to more insistent demands for a strong man who would curb the rights of the Reichstag.[33]

Had they acted with circumspection, the republicans might well have turned the crisis to their advantage and Hindenburg would hardly have stood in their way. This became clear a few weeks later when new troubles confronted the president: this contretemps centered on General von Seeckt, the chief of the Reichswehr. In the fall of 1926 Seeckt had permitted the eldest son of the ex-Crown Prince to serve as a liaison officer in Reichswehr maneuvers in Southern Germany. When this became known, the republican press pounced on it as evidence of the army's monarchist aspirations. Seeckt's action was criticized also as a thoughtless embarrassment of Stresemann who was trying just then to obtain the withdrawal of the Anglo-French forces from the occupied Rhineland. Gessler, the Reichswehr minister, had not been consulted about the Prince's assignment and refused to defend the general; he informed Hindenburg that he would have to insist on Seeckt's resignation or would otherwise have to resign himself. Hindenburg had no liking for Seeckt, but he recoiled at the thought of dismissing a general at the request of a civilian. Worse, he was asked to punish Seeckt for having permitted a grandson of his Emperor to serve a tour of duty in the army. Westarp hurried to him to urge him to resist the de-

[33] Braun, *Von Weimar*, pp. 215–16; Marx, "Auseinandersetzung," pp. 11–13, Marx Papers/24; cab. mtgs., June 25, 1926, *RKz.*/1839/769333, July 2, 1926, 1840/769454–57; Westarp to Seidlitz-Sambecki, July 5, 1926, same to Barth, July 28, 1926, Countess Westarp to Baroness Hiller, June 16, 22, 25, 1926, Westarp Papers; Schulthess, July 1–2, 1926, pp. 124–25; memoranda by Pünder, Sept. 8, 1926, and by Pukass, Sept. 13, 1926, *RKz.*, R 43 I/2207.

mand and many others pleaded with him to reject Gessler's ultimatum. Marx, however, sided with Gessler and so did the rest of the cabinet. Faced with a new government crisis, the president decided to give in.

His final meeting with Seeckt was a painful ordeal: What would the Emperor say? He did not criticize the general for his unauthorized action, nor did he even mention the Prince. In a personal memorandum he wrote subsequently, he stressed the fact that he asked for Seeckt's resignation, not because of his invitation to the Prince, but because he did not wish to part with the government. To Seeckt he seemed worried and helpless as he complained: "What else can I do? I just cannot have another cabinet crisis." To ease his mind, he asked Seeckt whether he would be willing to accept an ambassadorial appointment—"in Tokyo or London or Madrid"? The general said that he would, but the call never came. Stresemann, distrustful of Seeckt and mindful of the possible repercussions of such an appointment, raised strong objections whenever Hindenburg suggested it, and Hindenburg, on his part, refrained from pressing the matter.[34]

As his successor Seeckt proposed General Wilhelm Heye, the commander of the East Prussian military district. Without political ambitions, he seemed a suitable candidate. In rightist circles the plan roused furious protests, however, on the grounds that Heye had played a questionable role on the fateful November 9, 1918 (see Chapter I of this study). These protests opened up old wounds, and Hindenburg rejected them angrily: Heye had merely done his duty that day and those who were criticizing him now had not done so in 1918. Heye received the appointment.[35]

Hindenburg was not allowed to forget Seeckt's dismissal. Knowing how much it had embarrassed the president, Stresemann's opponents tried to use it against the foreign minister.

[34] Eyck, *Weimarer Republik*, II, 115–22; Gessler, *Reichswehrpolitik*, pp. 301–11; Hans von Seeckt, "Bemerkungen zu meiner Verabschiedung, 14. Oktober 1926," MS., Seeckt Papers/17; Hindenburg's remarks to Seeckt, in Seeckt to his wife, n.d., *ibid.*/28/371a–b; Hindenburg memorandum of Oct. 13, 1926, cited in Görlitz, *Hindenburg*, p. 283; Countess Westarp to Baroness Hiller, Oct. 12, 1926, Westarp Papers. But here again there were limits to his readiness to subordinate his monarchist loyalty to his republican duties. After the Seeckt incident rumors began to circulate that the ex-Emperor was planning to return to Germany. Though unfounded, they caused serious concern in republican circles and led the Social Democrats to prepare a bill prohibiting the ex-monarch's return. Hindenburg informed the cabinet that he would not sign such a bill should it be passed by the Reichstag and would rather resign. Cab. mtg., Oct. 22, 1926, *RKz.*/1841/770308; German minister to Netherlands to Stresemann, Nov. 2, 1926, Stresemann Papers/46/3147/162905–08.

[35] Countess Westarp to Baroness Hiller, Oct. 12, 1926, Westarp Papers.

Rumors began to spread that Seeckt's dismissal was Stresemann's work: the general had walked into a trap set by the foreign minister. By removing Seeckt, the story ran, Stresemann hoped to improve his relations with France. Care was taken that these tales would reach Hindenburg; one of the ex-Kaiser's sons, Prince Oskar of Prussia, took it upon himself to pass them on to the president.[36] Foolish though they were, they caused Stresemann much concern. He had never had the president's confidence, and he was fearful lest these rumors confirm the marshal's suspicions that he was an ineffective foreign minister. Thus he had to spend much time and effort thwarting those talebearers who had the ear of the marshal, for he knew that his diplomatic successes were worth little without the president's backing. As it was, Hindenburg's reluctant support was insufficient to strengthen his domestic position to any noticeable degree. In consequence, though Stresemann's diplomatic achievements were remarkable, the republic, immersed in its never-ending internal feuds, did not gain in strength correspondingly.

ℒ

Few observers were aware at the time of these difficulties. Despite tensions and crises, the republic seemed to be growing stronger. Much of the credit for its consolidation went to Hindenburg; his apparent acceptance of the republic, his oath to support the constitution were hailed as adding strength to the new state, and behind the giant figure of this republican quasi-monarch, the ex-Emperor receded ever farther into the background.

In reality, Hindenburg's contribution to the stabilization of the republic was not as significant. This consolidation had been under way before his election—his nomination was in fact a last desperate attempt to avert the perpetuation of Weimar democracy. The assistance he rendered to the republic consisted in bowing, though often reluctantly, to the will of the government and to say this is not to attempt to minimize the personal conflicts such acceptance involved. Rarely, however, did he lend his support to the government by a positive action or statement. He did not, for example, second the cabinet after the ratification of the Locarno Pact, when the Pact had become official policy and no longer was a partisan issue, and if this can perhaps be explained by the doubts he had concerning its value, he re-

[36] Raumer to Stresemann, Oct. 13, 1926, Stresemann Papers/45/3147/162735; Stresemann to Raumer, Oct. 15, 1926, and to Priesdorff, Oct. 27, 1926, *ibid.*/278a/3100/149362–63, 149370.

mained, however, just as passive in cases in which he was more appreciative of the government's accomplishments. He congratulated Stresemann when the latter, against all expectations, secured the evacuation of Düsseldorf and Duisburg in the summer of 1925; but when some time later he received a delegation of Rhinelanders who expressed their disappointment about Stresemann's failure to accomplish more for their homeland, he merely observed that they ought not to judge him too quickly, but give him time to continue his efforts.[37]

These ambiguities also helped to bring on some of the recurrent anti-republican crises that kept upsetting the country. In the face of his studied detachment, those who knew him well tended to discount his vaunted allegiance to the constitution. Heinrich Class and his fellow plotters may not have had much confidence in Hindenburg's willingness to help them overthrow the republic, but their plans were clearly predicated upon the assumption that, whether from sympathy or passivity, he would not oppose them. Luther's flag decree was based on similar considerations. Measured against these facts, his service to the republic appears less substantial.

Still, the impression prevailed that under Hindenburg's captaincy the republic was now firmly established. Given this fact, a growing number of rightists gave up hope of restoring the monarchy within the foreseeable future and the feeling grew that to take refuge in rigid obstructionism was self-defeating. A segment of the German Nationals' agrarian wing threatened to break away when the party leadership rejected a legislative settlement of the problem of princely properties and the same group was ready to accept Stresemann's conduct of foreign affairs. Continued all-out opposition seemed pointless to them since it deprived them of all influence on governmental policies and barred them from holding office. It was, however, practical considerations—higher tariffs and increased credits—that really accounted for this change of attitude, not the presence of Hindenburg in the presidency, although his presence made such demands more respectable.[38]

[37] Stresemann to Schoch, July 27, 1925, Stresemann, *Vermächtnis*, II, 61; memorandum on meeting with Rhinelanders, Oct. 21, 1925, Stresemann Papers/30/3169/160182.

[38] Knebel-Doeberitz to Stresemann, Jan. 19, 1927, Stresemann Papers/49/3167/163703–04, Campe to Stresemann, Apr. 24, 1927, *ibid.*/97/3162/173519, Rheinbaben to Stresemann, Dec. 16, 1926, *ibid.*/97/3162/173385–86; Kalckreuth, "Hindenburg und die Landwirtschaft," in Friedrich Wilhelm von Loebell, ed., *Hindenburg: Was er uns Deutschen ist* (Berlin, 1927), pp. 199–202.

In industrial circles, too, there was now a tendency to attain a *modus vivendi* with the republic. It was expressed publicly by a prominent Rhenish industrialist, Paul Silverberg, before the annual meeting of the Reich League of German Industry (*Reichsverband der deutschen Industrie*), the leading association of the country's industrialists. Silverberg acknowledged that business had come to accept the new state and its constitution and also was aware of the fact that there could be no stable government without the active participation of labor. Not every industrialist shared Silverberg's viewpoint, but the speech had been approved in advance by the League's board of directors and was more than the expression of a private opinion. Similar thoughts were voiced in various statements by Carl Duisberg, the League's president.[39]

The right's changing attitude was also reflected in the decline of the paramilitary organizations: many were dissolved for lack of funds as their radical activism became increasingly objectionable to their industrial and agrarian backers and these reduced or withheld altogether their contributions. Banks called in loans on the grounds that nationalist demonstrations were endangering the country's economic stability. Organizations such as the *Landbund* decided that they could further their interests more effectively by lawful parliamentary methods. "The year 1926 was not a good one for the *vaterländisch* movement," Count von der Goltz, one of its leaders, reported in his annual survey: there had been a gradual demoralization of the "national" viewpoint by the skillful propaganda of the opposition. Hindenburg was blamed by implication since he had done nothing to stop the trend; except for a perfunctory mention of the president's name, Goltz's report passed him over in silence. Goltz had opposed the marshal's candidacy the year before and can hardly have been surprised by Hindenburg's inactivity. Indeed, he and the groups for which he spoke must have derived some wry satisfaction from the fact that their doubts about Hindenburg's presidential qualifications had been confirmed so abundantly. Franz Seldte, the *Stahlhelm* leader, declared in his keynote address at the *Stahlhelm's* annual congress in May 1927: "We are [still] waiting for the great leader or statesman who is ready to lead us. . . . The *Stahlhelm* is longing for the great leader. Give us this leader, or we shall look for him in our own ranks, and we shall find him."[40]

[39] Bracher, *Auflösung*, p. 206; "Innenpolitische Rundschau," *Zusammenschluss*, 1 (1926), 60–61; *Berliner Tageblatt*, Sept. 11, 1926.

[40] Cremer to Stresemann, Oct. 18, 1926, Stresemann Papers/96/3161/173303–10;

Seldte knew that this was an empty threat. While the *Stahlhelm* had not been affected by the general decline of the militant leagues and had in fact grown because of the influx from defunct organizations, it was nevertheless in no position to impose its will upon the nation. If it were to exert any influence, this would have to be done within the framework of the republic. "Let us enter the state," a *Stahlhelm* leader proposed in a public address that fall; if the "national" organizations gained control of the state, they could shape politics according to the demands of their conscience. The form of government was no longer important to the "national movement"; it accepted the present state, for no one could change it by simply ignoring it. He himself, the speaker stated, was a convinced monarchist, but the monarchy could not be restored unless it had the support of the bulk of the nation—there could be no monarchy "by the grace of God." The *Stahlhelm* must look ahead, not back. In consequence, the *Stahlhelm* decided, in Seldte's words, to pursue its goal, "no longer as a paramilitary organization (*Wehrverband*), but as a political-national liberation movement." It began to take part in elections, trying to obtain candidacies for *Stahlhelmers* and pledging its support to parties willing to grant *Stahlhelm* members "safe" places on their electoral lists.[41]

The German National Party, too, had to lower its sights and adjust its policies. In July 1926, Westarp informed Hindenburg of the party's readiness to help him form a new government if he so wished and was even prepared to retain Stresemann as foreign minister. That year's party congress likewise offered its collaboration to a new nonsocialist government, trying to make a virtue out of necessity. Participation in the government might enable it to transform the republic into an authoritarian state similar to the old monarchy, and this rather than the actual return of the monarchy was what really mattered. German National leaders began asking for the elimination of Article 54 of the Weimar Constitution which established the dependence of the government on the confidence of the Reichstag, and at its annual congress in 1927 the party made this demand a part of its official program.

unsigned memorandum, Nov. 23, 1927, *ibid.*/61/3172/166661; Count von der Goltz, "Jahresbilanz der vaterländischen Bewegung," *Deutsche Zeitung*, No. 356a, Dec. 31, 1926; Seldte's speech, *ibid.*, No. 106a, May 7, 1927; Junius Alter, *Nationalisten: Deutschlands nationales Führertum der Nachkriegszeit* (Leipzig, 1930), p. 169.

41 Stahlhelm leader's speech, reported in *Stahlhelm*, Oct. 31, 1926; Seldte to Stresemann, Apr. 29, 1927, Stresemann Papers/53/3148/164031; memorandum by Stresemann, Aug. 5, 1926, *ibid.*/41/3146/162183–85; "Stahlhelm und Parteien," *Kölnische Zeitung*, No. 773a, Dec. 12, 1927.

"Without prejudice to its monarchist convictions" it now favored constitutional amendments aiming at a limitation of the rights of the Reichstag and the state parliaments and a corresponding increase of the powers of Reich and state presidents: the Reich president was also to become head of the Prussian state while the Reich chancellor would double as Prussian minister-president. By thus restoring some of the administrative features of the old Bismarck Empire, the executive branch was to recover its former authority.[42]

A measure of expediency, the German National change of tactics clearly did not imply an acceptance of the democratic republic. Nor can Hindenburg be credited with this change, except perhaps indirectly. Some observers thought that they saw in it the result of the marshal's willingness to serve the republic: the right had elected him president and now it was forced to support him. As one German National deputy wrote, "The nation simply would not understand it if because of their basic principles, the German Nationals would at every turn desert the man who had done so much for the Fatherland." There is, however, no evidence that this was the reasoning of the German Nationals or of the *Stahlhelm*. On the contrary, if these groups decided on a change, the change was inspired partly at least by what they considered the disappointing performance of Hindenburg. As the marshal had failed to curb the parliamentary system, they concluded that they would now have to undertake this task themselves. But since the republic had become less vulnerable, their attack had to be launched from within. There was also the hope that by adopting this strategy they might prevail on the president who would not initiate any changes himself to lend his name and authority to their efforts.[43]

The republican leaders made no systematic attempt to use the apparent consolidation of the republic to influence him. This was partly due to their failure to grasp the pivotal import of the presidency and partly to their lack of contact with Hindenburg. They felt him to be inaccessible to them, both physically and mentally—a feeling undoubtedly reenforced by a distinct sense of social inferiority on their part. Unlike men like Westarp, Tirpitz, or Oldenburg-Januschau, most republican leaders never quite

42 Stresemann diary, July 3, 1926, Stresemann, *Vermächtnis*, II, 407; Westarp to Weller, June 12, 1926, Westarp Papers; Berndt, Mar. 10, 1926, *Verhandlungen*, Vol. 389, p. 6140.

43 Graef, in *Der nationale Wille: Werden und Wirken der Deutschnationalen Volkspartei 1918–1928*, Max Weiss, ed. (Leipzig, 1928), p. 51; Spahn and Kalckreuth, in Loebell, *Hindenburg*, pp. 113–15, 199–202.

overcame an air of subservience in his presence and thus were at a disadvantage in presenting their views to him.

This difficulty was compounded by inner uncertainties that beset the moderate bourgeois parties and kept them from giving encouragement to Hindenburg in his cautious cooperation with the republic. The decline of the Democratic Party and bitter internal struggles in Stresemann's German People's Party attest to these vacillations. They were also evident in the Center Party, supposedly one of the mainstays of the republic; held together by the common cultural and spiritual concerns of its Catholic membership, the party's following was socially and economically heterogeneous and included both monarchists and republicans. To satisfy such diversified groups made it imperative to avoid irrevocable commitments. The party leaders rejected therefore demands of the Center's left wing that it call itself a republican party and insisted that the Center was a constitutional party (*Verfassungspartei*), ready to collaborate with any legal government and uncommitted to any specific form of government. The fact was that the Center Party could not be counted among the republic's all-out defenders, and it was neither willing nor able to counteract the antirepublican pressures on Hindenburg.[44]

Under these circumstances the Social Democratic Party, the one major party that supported the republic without reservations, might have thought it imperative to safeguard and strengthen democratic-republican institutions by active participation in the government. Yet except for two interludes in 1921–22 and 1923 the party remained outside of all Reich governments between 1920 and 1928. In part this absence was due to the bitter opposition of the German Nationals as well as large parts of the German People's Party that refused to work with the Socialists. But the Socialists themselves could not make up their minds whether they wished to gain some measure of influence by entering a government coalition with the bourgeois parties, at the price of dropping a part of their social demands and risking the loss of some of their following to the Communists, or whether they wished to retain their program and remain in the opposition, hoping that at some later time they might enter the government on more favorable terms. To wait for such an opportunity was also beset with risks, since if the German Nationals entered the government earlier,

[44] Marx, at Center Party Congress, Nov. 16, 1925, Marx Papers/13; same, "Der Charakter des Zentrums als Partei," MS., Marx Papers/32; also Karl Bachem, *Vorgeschichte, Geschichte und Politik der deutschen Zentrumspartei* (Cologne, 1927–1931), VIII, 256–64.

the republic was likely to move even farther away from the Socialists' hopes and objectives. Rudolf Hiferding, the party's chief theorist, summed up this dilemma: "The German Nationals are making every effort to enter the government. The Social Democrats are now faced with the question whether they can prevent the participation of the German Nationals in the government, in order to further republican policies and whether this can be done at a price which would justify the heavy responsibility of entering the government and would be approved by the working masses. The answer will depend on the contribution the middle parties are willing to make to the policies of the social republic."

Obviously Hilferding was not anxious to have the Social Democrats enter the government. His was not an isolated view. Paul Löbe, the Socialist *Reichstagspräsident*, argued too that the party should concentrate now on the realization of its economic and socialist goals since the republic was firmly established. The issue was no longer "republic *vs.* monarchy," but "capitalism *vs.* socialism." It thus would be more in accordance with the party's aims to remain in the opposition than enter a coalition with the bourgeoisie. Most party leaders shared these views. There were elements of the class-struggle mentality in their attitude, but there was also a basic reluctance to assume power and responsibility and to rely rather on a supposedly irresistible evolution that would bring about the attainment of Socialist goals.[45]

Some of the Social Democratic leaders disagreed strongly, however, with this strategy of the party. Among them were Braun and Severing who as long-time members of the Prussian government could better appreciate the value of active participation in government. Severing kept urging his friends to enter a coalition with the bourgeois parties. To insist on a specified social policy as the *sine qua non* of a coalition seemed to him unrealistic and impractical. Moreover, he thought it unlikely that an advance understanding could be reached with the German People's Party, the spokesman of heavy industry, on working hours, industrial safety, workers' insurance, and workers' rights. "Will these problems be settled more favorably for the workers," he pleaded, "if the influence of [heavy industry] remains unchallenged in the cabinet, or would it not be better from the viewpoint of labor if [the] Social Democrats would participate in the shaping of policies [prior to their presentation to the Reichstag]?"

45 Rudolf Hilferding, "Politische Probleme," *Gesellschaft* III (1926), ii, 303; Paul Löbe, in *Vorwärts*, May 5, 1927; also Hermann Müller-Franken, "Vom deutschen Parlamentarismus," *Gesellschaft*, III (1926), ii, 291–98.

Otto Braun's advice was in a similar vein. Speaking from practical experience, he pointed out that advance agreements on detailed government programs were pointless. Strong men would always obtain a consideration of their viewpoint without any advance commitments, while weak men would be overruled in spite of all such arrangements. Braun was all the more anxious to see the Social Democrats in the government since he knew how much Hindenburg's acceptance of any viewpoint depended on direct access to him. If some of the party's members were among his official advisers, he was certain that the president would listen to them.[46]

Sympathetic liberals urged a similar strategy on the Social Democrats. Hugo Preuss warned them repeatedly that if they did not outgrow their class-struggle dogmatism, they would force the bourgeoisie into a class solidarity of its own. There was great danger in that case that the liberal bourgeoisie would join forces with the antidemocratic bourgeoisie of the right. "Once this happens," he predicted, "the fate of German democracy and of the [people's] state would be sealed." There were other warning voices. In an article in the Socialist monthly, *Die Gesellschaft,* Bernhard Guttmann, an editor of the liberal *Frankfurter Zeitung,* pointed out the pitfalls of the Socialists' policy of staying out of the government. The republic, he warned, was not yet firmly established and it would not survive unless large groups of the middle class were willing to accept the new state. This they would do, he warned, only if they were convinced that it would protect law, order, and property. Otherwise reactionary forces would draw the entire bourgeoisie into their camp and by the skillful abuse of parliamentary methods subvert the republic. "We cannot tell what struggles lie ahead during the next years," Guttmann wrote, "but this much we can say, negatively, that the period during which the Republic must be consolidated cannot also be a period of bitter social tensions. The time for the establishment of a true democracy, of a state of social justice will come later. This we must understand. . . ."[47]

These counsels were not without effect. At the party's biennial congress in 1927, the majority of the speakers voiced similar

[46] Carl Severing, "Der Weg aus der Krise, *Sozialistische Monatshefte,* LXIV (1927), 1–5; same, "Kiel," *Gesellschaft,* IV, ii (1927), 1–5; Braun, *Von Weimar,* pp. 174, 200–04; memorandum by Pünder, Dec. 4, 1925, *RKz.,* R 43 I/1307.

[47] Hugo Preuss, *Staat, Recht und Freiheit: Aus 40 Jahren deutscher Politik und Geschichte* (Tübingen, 1926), pp. 432–33; same, *Deutschlands Republikanische Reichsverfassung* (Berlin, 1923), pp. 65–66; Bernhard Guttmann, "Die nächste Phase der Republik," *Gesellschaft,* III, (1926), ii, pp. 306–15, esp. pp. 308, 311–12, 314.

thoughts, and the tenor of the discussions reflected a much greater concern with the safety of the republic than had been the case at the 1925 meeting. In his keynote speech, Hilferding pointed out that there was no longer any danger of a monarchist restoration, but this meant merely that the struggle against the republic had assumed a different form. The German Nationals, he warned, were no longer interested in the monarchy because they believed that they could establish their social and political domination over the nation within the republic. The struggle was now one of fascism against democracy. He urged the party not to put too much faith in legislative solutions, and like Severing and Braun he pleaded that they seek access to executive power. Most other speakers agreed and when the dissenters moved that the party adopt a policy of "opposition rather than coalition," the motion was defeated by a majority of 255 to 83.[48]

&

Whatever the qualms of some of the Socialists, Hindenburg remained ready throughout 1926 to appoint some Socialists to the cabinet if a majority coalition could thus be formed. In the fall of that year Chancellor Marx and the Socialist leadership, both anxious for a rapprochement, discussed the possibility of closer collaboration. Understandings were reached on the initiation of a number of social reform measures and the government agreed to some changes in the army's recruitment practices and in its dealings with the paramilitary organizations. Hindenburg consented to these military reforms which he must have viewed with some misgivings, and he also reiterated his willingness to appoint some Social Democrats as ministers if Marx and the Socialists should reach an agreement on the latter's entry into the government.[49]

At this point trouble developed. To the president's dismay, Ernst Scholz, the spokesman of the right wing of the People's Party and a personal favorite of his, voiced strong objections to collaboration between the government and the Socialists. The Social Democrats reacted sharply, but thanks to Marx's skill, the incident was smoothed over and the talks about the Socialists' entry into the cabinet were resumed. Soon they ran into new

[48] Sozialdemokratischer Parteitag Kiel, 1927, *Protokoll* (Berlin, 1927), pp. 175–76, 182 (Hilferding), pp. 191–92 (Scheidemann), pp. 201–03 (Severing); but see also pp. 197–98 (Löbe), p. 199 (Aufhäuser); vote on p. 224.
[49] Marx, "Das Jahr 1926," MS., Marx Papers/24; Stresemann, "Betrachtungen zur Krisis," Feb. 1927, MS., Stresemann Papers/50/3148/163836–38; protocol of conference of Government with Social Democratic leaders, Dec. 1, 1926, Schüddekopf, *Heer und Republik*, pp. 214–17; Eyck, *Weimarer Republik*, II, 123.

difficulties. In December 1926 the *Manchester Guardian* published details of Germany's secret rearmament and her close military collaboration with the Soviet Union. The Social Democrats now voiced misgivings about joining a government tainted with such flagrant militarist abuses, but the patient and resourceful Marx was able to patch up this new trouble too. The Socialists, it was agreed, would air some of their grievances in the Reichstag and receive governmental assurances of remedial action. Other issues, however, such as that of Russo-German military collaboration and the question of secret frontier guards would be passed over in silence in the interest of national security. The negotiations about the Socialists' entry into the government would be continued, and since all government parties, including the People's Party, were prepared now to accept their participation and the president too remained ready to appoint Socialist ministers, the reorganization of the cabinet seemed a certainty.

Yet the Socialists' radical wing that had always been opposed to a bourgeois-Socialist coalition considered the compromise a repudiation of the antimilitarist principles in which the party believed. At a meeting of the party's Reichstag delegation, the left wing obtained majority support for a new set of conditions on which Socialist participation in the government was to be made dependent. The new terms demanded: formation of an entirely new cabinet instead of a mere reorganization of the old one; the exclusion of Gessler, the Reichswehr minister, from the new administration; and army reforms that were to go far beyond those agreed upon previously. Marx refused to make any of these concessions, and Hindenburg too rejected these demands. The president resented the attack on Gessler as an unwarranted intrusion upon his own jurisdiction and saw the demand for the resignation of the government as a threat to his presidential prerogatives. It was up to him, he insisted, to initiate negotiations for the formation of a new cabinet.

Bowing to the will of the majority, the Socialist leaders decided to force Marx's hand and moved for a vote of no-confidence in the Reichstag. To prepare the ground for that vote, the party charged Scheidemann, the one-time chancellor, with the task of expressing its unalterable objections to the Reichswehr's clandestine activities. In a lengthy speech in the Reichstag, Scheidemann took the army to task for its continued collaboration with many of the paramilitary organizations of the right, its financial transactions with German industrial enterprises, and its secret arms deals with Soviet Russia. He demanded the resignation of Gessler and the discontinuation of all contacts between Reichswehr and rightist organizations, a radical reform of recruitment practices, an end to financial contributions by heavy industry, and fixed limitations of the Reichswehr's future armaments. The speech revealed no military secrets nor did it mention any data not already in the public domain. Nevertheless it threw the Reichstag into an uproar. German Nationals and rightist extremists staged a walkout, and for a moment the government too seems to have contemplated leaving the hall. Many Centrists and Democrats felt uneasy about the speech, and so did a number of Scheidemann's own party colleagues. The Communists, in turn, resented the critical references to the Soviet Union. Nevertheless Marx was defeated on the no-confidence vote. Whatever their reaction to Scheidemann's revelations, the Communists could not pass up the chance of rejecting a bourgeois government. The German Nationals also supported the motion, confident that their time had come and any new cabinet would have to include them. By forcing Marx to resign, they expected to open the door to their own entry into the government.[50]

However justified the Socialist charges had been, the democratic camp was the main victim of the fracas. Those in the German People's Party who favored a coalition with the German Nationals now gained the upper hand. Among Centrists too there was greater readiness to work with the German Nationals and Hindenburg, embittered by the attacks on the army, now rejected as out of the question the appointment of Socialist ministers. Nor would he approve any longer the military reforms on which agreement had already been reached.[51]

Scheidemann's attack also rendered more difficult the position of those Reichswehr circles that were willing to come to terms with the republic and whose views carried weight with the president. Their most important spokesman was Colonel Kurt von Schleicher, a protégé of Groener since prewar days and his aide at

50 Marx, "Das Jahr 1926," Marx Papers/24; Vorwärts, Dec. 12, 1926; Curtius, Sechs Jahre, pp. 45–46; Stresemann, Vermächtnis, III, 90–92; Eyck, Weimarer Republik, II, 123–35; Schulthess, Dec. 16–17, 1926, pp. 175–80; Severing, Lebensweg, II, 103–04; Hans Simons, "Deutschlands Regierungswechsel," Sozialistische Monatshefte, LXIV (1927), 210; Frankfurter Zeitung, No. 939, Dec. 17, 1926; cab. mtgs., Nov. 11, Dec. 13, 15, 16, 1926, RKz./1841/770710–11, 1842/771252–57, 771311–13, 711315–16; Stockhausen diary, Dec. 6, 13, 15, 16, 17, 1926, Max von Stockhausen, Sechs Jahre Reichskanzlei: Von Rapallo bis Locarno, Walter Görlitz, ed. (Bonn, 1954), pp. 236–39.
51 Görlitz, Hindenburg, pp. 285–86; Bredow to Schleicher, Jan. 17, 1927, Schleicher Papers/17,ii/31; Stresemann diary, Jan. 1927, Stresemann, Vermächtnis, III, 92; cab. mtg., Dec. 18, 1926, RKz./ 1842/771318; Deutscher Volkswirt, Dec. 24, 1926, p. 387.

Kassel and Kolberg. The Reichswehr's political expert, he had steered it through many a contretemps with Reichstag and political parties. As a close friend of Oskar von Hindenburg with whom he had served in the Third Guards, the marshal's old regiment, Schleicher was also a frequent visitor to the Presidential Palace. The president liked the sociable, urbane colonel whose easy banter amused him; as a military man Schleicher could talk to him also on serious matters in terms that he found easy to follow. Gradually he took Schleicher into his confidence and listened to his views and suggestions.

On Schleicher's advice steps were taken to improve relations between the Weimar Republic and the Reichswehr—doubtless he had approved the military reforms agreed upon with the Socialists before Hindenburg consented to them. A memorandum of late December 1926, found among Schleicher's papers and most likely by him, insisted that the army must improve its relations with the republic: it dismissed as illusory hopes for a monarchist restoration and urged a more flexible attitude in the flag controversy—the restoration of the old colors was the ultimate goal, but the officers corps was foolish to openly flaunt its aversion to the official Reich colors. If it accepted them, it would also deprive the army's opponents of an effective propaganda weapon: "For example, wreaths with black-red-and-gold and black-white-and-red ribbons can work miracles." (An official flag decree by the Reichswehr minister, a few months later, incorporated this particular suggestion.) The memorandum turned likewise against loose talk about a dictatorship, Article 48, and similar matters. Only the president could invoke the emergency provisions of Article 48, and the army was merely his executive instrument.[52] In that same vein, collaboration with other organizations was to be kept to a minimum and tolerated only if the defense needs of the country demanded it. Anyone violating these rules would be dismissed at once.

[52] Article 48 of the Weimar Constitution gave the Reich president the right to force states, if need be, by armed force, to comply with their legal duties. It also empowered him to take whatever measures were needed to protect public order and safety if they were threatened. Ebert had often resorted to these emergency powers in the crisis years of his presidency, and many rightists now wanted Hindenburg to use them to put an end to the recurring governmental and parliamentary crises. Carl Schmitt was one of the first legal experts to assert that the president could lawfully do so while the bulk of the constitutional jurists still maintained at that time that such a use of the presidential emergency powers went beyond their intended scope. Class' dictatorship plans had been justified with this wider interpretation of Art. 48. See Carl Schmitt und Erwin Jakobi, "Die Diktatur des Reichspräsidenten," in *Veröffentlichungen der Vereinigung deutscher Staatsrechtslehrer,* 1 (1924).

Admittedly, the concessions proposed here were minor ones, but a skillful republican leadership, gathering all forces disturbed by the policies and practices of the army, might in time have obtained more substantial changes. As it was, the isolated foray of the Social Democrats could only strengthen the hands of those who opposed such a rapprochement. When the German Nationals did join the new government, one of their reasons for doing so was to prevent the Reichswehr from being surrendered to the mercy of "party political interests." And inevitably Hindenburg again became more unwilling to approve of any reforms.[53]

With the cabinet's resignation the initiative shifted once more to the president and he had to submit again to the dreary duty of forming a new government. Since the Center was indispensable to any coalition, Marx expected that he would be asked to sound out the parties. Hindenburg, however, had his own idea: to give the chancellorship to a man of the People's Party. Holding a middle position between Center and German Nationals, it seemed the logical source from which to select the next chancellor. But the Center rejected the two men whom he chose, and so he turned once more to Marx.[54]

Marx was no more successful in his search for support, but he learned one important fact: the German Nationals had their heart set on joining the government since their agrarian and industrial supporters were urging them to exert greater influence on tariff and tax policies. Marx was convinced that he could form a cabinet if Hindenburg was willing to back him. He arranged with the president the dispatch of a letter in which Hindenburg "requested" him to form, as quickly as possible, a government drawn from a bourgeois coalition. The letter addressed an emphatic

[53] Rabenau, *Seeckt*, pp. 482–83; "Zur Lage und Stellung der Reichswehr," n.d., but initialed by various readers, Dec. 31, 1926 to Jan. 4, 1927, Schleicher Papers/ 32/81–90, reprinted in Thilo Vogelsang, *Reichswehr*, pp. 409–13; memorandum by Bredow, July 22, 1927, Schleicher Papers/35/29, and by Hasse, Nov. 1926, 1930, reprinted in Vogelsang, *Reichswehr*, pp. 408–09; also Bussche-Ippenburg, ZS./217; Bracher, *Auflösung*, p. 269; flag decree, Schulthess, Aug. 15, 1927, pp. 137–38; German National statement (by Westarp) in Schüddekopf, *Heer und Republik*, p. 213.

[54] Gessler, *Reichswehrpolitik*, pp. 348–49; Curtius, *Sechs Jahre*, pp. 46–49; Stresemann diary, Jan. 1927, Stresemann, *Vermächtnis*, III, 92; Schulthess, Jan. 10, 14, 1927, pp. 3–4, 10–11; Marx, "Das Jahr 1926," and "Das Jahr 1927," Marx Papers/24; "Zur Entwicklung der politischen Lage," Schleicher Papers/17,ii/26–28 (Görlitz, *Hindenburg*, pp. 302–03, erroneously attributes Schleicher's proposals to Hindenburg and to a later government crisis in 1928, but helps to establish the fact that they did reach the president); Bredow to Schleicher, Jan. 17, 1927, Schleicher Papers/17,ii/31; Stresemann, "Betrachtungen zur Krisis," Stresemann Papers/50/ 3148/163845–46, 163858; Stresemann to Marx, Jan. 30, 1927, Stresemann, *Vermächtnis*, III, 103.

appeal to "all parties in the Reichstag which can be of help to set aside personal objections and differences of opinion for the sake of the Fatherland, to join hands for constructive achievements under your [Marx's] Government and to unite behind its goal of working neither for nor against individual parties, but for the welfare of the Fatherland, in loyal adherence to the Constitution." In conclusion Hindenburg urged Marx to safeguard the justified interests of the working masses "in an effort to serve all classes."

Delivery of the letter was timed to reach Marx while he was meeting with the leaders of the Center's Reichstag delegation. It had the desired effect and the Center declared itself ready to enter a coalition with the German Nationals. This decision, the *Frankfurter Zeitung* reported, was essentially due to the Center's feeling that the German Nationals' determination to obtain access to governmental power offered a certain assurance for the permanence of the cabinet. The Social Democrats, the paper noted, did not seem to have this will to power. The German Nationals, on their part, were willing to work with the Center and negotiations were now resumed.

They brought forth a program which the German Nationals would have dismissed out of hand a year before, pledging them to uphold the Locarno policy, to collaborate loyally with the League of Nations, to protect the republic against slanderous attacks, and to defend it against extremist attempts to overthrow it. Marx, in turn, conceded to them that they need only recognize the legal validity of the constitution; he did not insist on an "unreserved recognition" of the republic as he had done at first. Yet by acknowledging the legality of the constitution they admitted in fact that the monarchy belonged to the past. Not all negotiations went smoothly, however. There were recurrent squabbles about the distribution of cabinet posts, and twice Hindenburg had to settle them personally. In one case he warned the German Nationals that he would dissolve the Reichstag if the government were not set up at once. On January 31, 1927, six weeks after the previous cabinet had resigned, the new one was finally formed. With Marx as chancellor, it included four German Nationals, several members of the German People's Party and of the Center, and one representative of the Bavarian People's Party. "The German Republic has once more a Government," the *Frankfurter Zeitung* commented, "but it is no republican Government. On the contrary. At no time since 1918 has the Republic been represented as weakly in any Reich Government as in Marx's latest cabinet."

Again it had been Hindenburg who had put an end to the tortuous negotiations. The country had watched the party quarrels with increasing dismay, and the demand for determined leadership had steadily grown. Hindenburg alone had seemed able to provide it, and it is a measure of his changing status that in his letter to Marx he no longer *invited* the latter to form a government, but rather *requested* him to proceed. Some even more far-reaching proposals had come to his desk. Schleicher sent him a list of suggestions culminating with the advice that if no majority government could be formed, the president warn all parties concerned that he would appoint a government composed of men of his confidence, without regard to party wishes, and that he would give such a government the authority to dissolve the Reichstag if it would not support it. "I am convinced," Schleicher's proposal concluded, "that this procedure could lead to the creation of a secure and stable government or create the right atmosphere for new elections. The nation appreciates a clear policy and a firm will."[55]

৵

The new government got off to an inauspicious start. An angry Reichstag debate followed Marx's presentation of his program and Westarp, speaking for the German Nationals, all but apologized for having accepted it. This done, he proceeded to qualify that acceptance on numerous points. Guérard, the Centrist spokesman, had almost as many reservations. Yet despite this unpromising beginning the government was to stay in office longer than any of its predecessors, and collaboration among its members, according to Marx's testimony, was exceptionally good. When it resigned, in the spring of 1928, it could look back on a legislative record which surpassed that of almost all other cabinets.

It was especially active in the domain of social legislation. The Center and German Nationals drew a substantial following from labor and employees; to retain their support, the cabinet initiated a program of social legislation that even the wary and critical *Sozialistische Monatshefte* called "the most complete and most sensible government program . . . that has so far been announced in the Reichstag." Among its major enactments were the formal establishment of the eight-hour day and the introduction of a comprehensive system of unemployment insurance.[56]

[55] Schulthess, Feb. 3–5, 1927, pp. 23–37.
[56] Eyck, *Weimarer Republik*, III, 177; Simons, "Regierungswechsel," *Sozialistische Monatshefte*, LXIV (1927), 211.

To Hindenburg these must have been reassuring developments. The German Nationals seemed to have made their peace with the republic; the radicals of both right and left were losing ground; social unrest was being allayed—was the nation at long last ready to attain the higher unity that he kept urging upon it?

The answer, alas, still was, no. Beneath the surface calm the old disputes were kept alive. Unquestionably, the number of the republic's irreconcilable foes had decreased, but many of the remaining ones continued to hold influential positions in business and government, in the judiciary, in schools and universities, and in the professions. They had a relentless spokesman in Hugenberg and a powerful mouthpiece in his farflung chain of newspapers and magazines.

Alfred Hugenberg, who was to play an increasingly fateful role from then on and whose relations with Hindenburg constitute an important chapter in the story of the Weimar Republic, defies easy analysis. In his youth this one-time Prussian official and Krupp director had dabbled in poetry, and his letters and articles still reflected the poet's attention to style and rhythm. But now his days of esthetic concern lay far behind him. Endowed with a bulging embonpoint and an old-fashioned handlebar moustache, the small heavy-set man seemed the embodiment of petty bourgeois complacency. Behind this deceptive appearance, however, there hid a keen business mind and a shrewd organizing talent that earned him the nickname of "Silver Fox." To these attributes was added an unshakable faith in his own judgment and an implacable hatred of the republic. Transcending economic considerations, this enmity would not be appeased by material prosperity; it was rooted in social and political convictions, in his refusal to accept the democratic equalitarianism of the constitution. Hugenberg and those for whom he spoke believed that they representetd a social elite, qualified by education and property to control the fate of the nation. They remained determined to reestablish an authoritarian state with or without the monarchy in which they would regain their privileged status, a state without a Weimar Constitution which, in Hugenberg's words, outdistanced every other constitution in the extent to which it implemented the "nonsense of majority [decisions]," and unhampered by the "socialist doctrine of envy which deprives the other fellow of what he has (the pernicious foundation of present-day German politics)."[57]

[57] Alfred Hugenberg, *Streiflichter* (Berlin, 1927), pp. 90, 79. For some interesting analyses of antirepublican attitudes, see Harry Graf Kessler, *Tagebücher 1918–*

The Hugenberg camp was greatly dismayed by the decision of the German Nationals to enter the government. Hugenberg himself had stayed away from the session in which the Reichstag had expressed its confidence in Marx's cabinet. His attitude is summed up well in a letter he wrote to Count Westarp later that year: "Our party is fundamentally an antiparliamentary one, but must nevertheless operate in a parliamentary state. This dilemma is a fact, and we must never forget it. This awkward situation induces some of our people, at least in the parliaments, to accept altogether the present parliamentary system. Anyone who accepts this parliamentary system, belongs, from the historical perspective, to those [nameless] figures who keep passing (or staggering) [across the historical stage]. History will decide whether they are going to be stand-ins for those elements which will destroy Germany completely, or—if everything goes well—will just be carters attending to their menial job without any creative idea. Whoever believes theoretically in the necessity of a complete innovation and reconstruction of our public life, whoever is contemptuous of today's state and yet builds his personal fortune and future on his collaboration with the parliamentary system is a moral cripple. Soon his ambitions will win out over all theories and convictions. . . . Allow the party a life of its own outside the parliamentary delegations, let the nonparliamentary party be the conscience of the delegations which today are active in the various parliaments. Then we will at least have a formal demarcation line from which we may generate and organize the forces for the real tasks of the party."[58]

Untiringly he devoted himself to those "real" tasks, and kept the readers of his various newspapers and magazines in constant turmoil with lurid reports of governmental inadequacy and corruption. His press campaigns also served to intimidate many who were now prepared to accept the republic. Fearful of Hugenberg's wrath, some of Berlin's hotels refused to hoist the black-red-and-gold flag on official occasions, and so did many banks and department stores. Reichswehr Minister Gessler had to pay dearly for his defiance when he ordered the display of black-red-and-gold (along with the black-white-and-red military flag) on military buildings and private residences of members of the armed forces

---

1937 (Frankfurt/M, 1961), entry of Aug. 14, 1927, p. 530; Braun, in Schulthess, Sept. 7, 1927, p. 149; Nölle, "System Severing," *Germania*, Apr. 8, 1925; Ernst Feder, "Abschied von Severing," *Berliner Tageblatt*, No. 472, Oct. 6, 1926.

[58] Hugenberg to Westarp, Sept. 17, 1927, quoted in Dr. Wahrmund, *Gericht über Hugenberg* (Dillingen, 1932), pp. 49–50.

who wished to show flags. There was an uproar in rightist circles which Hugenberg's papers would not allow to die down. Not surprisingly the republican parties were also roundly defeated in their efforts to proclaim August 11 a national holiday—the day of the promulgation of the Weimar Constitution.[59]

Hindenburg too was drawn into these controversies. Ever since his election he had dutifully attended the ceremonies held in the Reichstag each August 11, but Severing has told in his memoirs how uneasy the president felt during such demonstratively republican functions. Rightist opposition to these ceremonies, carefully nurtured by the Hugenberg press, increased his embarrassment. So did the protests against Gessler's flag decree although the decree called merely for procedures which Hindenburg himself had been following as president. Still, in view of the bitterness that the decree aroused, he hastened to dissociate himself from it. He authorized Westarp to state publicly that he, Hindenburg, had not been informed of the order before it was published and gave Westarp to understand that he disapproved of it.[60]

Hindenburg, however, could not always escape controversy so easily. In the spring of 1927 the Law for the Protection of the Republic expired. It had been enacted in 1922 after the assassination by rightist fanatics of Walther Rathenau, the foreign minister, and prescribed heavy penalties for individuals and organizations engaged in unconstitutional activities. One of its provisions barred the return of William II without the permission of the Reich government. A bill extending the law for another two years was passed by the Reichstag. As usual, many friends scurried to Hindenburg and pleaded with him to reject it and Marx could not get him to sign it. In despair Marx asked Otto Braun to call on the marshal and convince him that his constitutional duty required him to promulgate the law. As a fellow East Prussian and fellow hunter, Braun, though a Socialist, was believed to have the president's ear. Whether he did or not, he knew how to handle the marshal. If Hindenburg did not sign, he explained, he would either have to dissolve the Reichstag and call for new elections or consult the nation by way of a referendum. Hindenburg shuddered at both alternatives with their prospects of renewed political turmoil. With the ground

[59] Stresemann to Vögler, Sept. 25, 1927, Stresemann Papers/284/3115/130128; Kessler diary, Aug. 11, 1927, Kessler, *Tagebücher*, pp. 528–29.
[60] Westarp to Traub, Sept. 9, 1927, Westarp Papers; Hindenburg quoted in Schulenburg, *Welt um Hindenburg*, p. 48.

thus prepared, Braun moved to the attack: the prohibition was meaningless since Germany would have to allow the ex-Emperor's return if no state wished to grant him asylum. Besides, Hindenburg was not asked to promulgate a law barring the ex-Kaiser; rather, Braun pointed out in all seriousness, he was to sign a law that had nothing to say on the former monarch, but merely extended the validity of an earlier law, signed by Ebert. Hindenburg let himself be persuaded and signed the law; as he told his friend Cramon, he did it to avoid another political crisis and with the hope that the damage could be undone later.[61]

The past kept injecting itself on other occasions. On September 18, 1927, Hindenburg, resplendent in his field marshal's uniform, attended the dedication of a memorial erected at Tannenberg. The ceremony might have received little notice abroad if he had not used the occasion to raise once again the war-guilt question and deny categorically that Germany was responsible for the outbreak of World War I. Germany had resorted to war in 1914 as the only means left to her to defend herself against a world of enemies. The moment was poorly chosen for such a statement. Stresemann was attending a League meeting at the time and had just been able to obtain a reduction of the Allied occupation forces. Hindenburg's speech was therefore considered a shocking display of ingratitude, and the foreign minister was faced with considerable bitterness at the League meetings. Stresemann had not anticipated this reaction, partly because he had underestimated the probable effects of the speech, and partly because the draft submitted to him had been worded as a personal rather than an official statement. Hindenburg was to state that as an old man, approaching death, he felt the obligation to go on record once more before the German people, but this key sentence had been omitted from the final version. Whether the address would have caused less of a stir had it been included, is of course open to question. As it was worded, the bluntness grated on foreign ears—in protest against it the heads of the former Allied states decided to snub Hindenburg and not send greetings to him on his forthcoming eightieth birthday.[62]

Hindenburg learned of this reaction with amused surprise. He was pleased with the resounding applause with which his speech was greeted in "national" circles and appears to have shown no

[61] Pünder to Marx, July 31, 1926, Marx Papers/1078; Severing, *Lebensweg*, II, 90–91; Braun, *Von Weimar*, pp. 172–74.
[62] Schulthess, Sept. 18, 1927, p. 153; Stresemann to Marx, Sept. 21, 1927, Hoesch to Stresemann, Sept. 22, 1927, Stresemann Papers/59/3172/166260, 166295–96; memorandum by Stresemann on talk with Hindenburg, Oct. 3, 1927, *ibid.*/6013172/166400.

concern over its unfavorable reception abroad. Nor did anyone suggest to him, it would seem, that it had been improper for him to depart from the draft approved by the foreign minister. What did worry him, on the other hand, was the reemergence on that occasion of those old personal problems that never ceased troubling him: his relations with Ludendorff and with the ex-Emperor.

Ludendorff, too, had been invited to attend the ceremonies at Tannenberg. He had accepted the invitation, but had made it clear that he did not wish to meet with Hindenburg. To make doubly sure that there would be no meeting, he had declined to attend the official banquet tendered by Heye on the eve of the ceremony. Hindenburg who abhorred public scenes was fearful that Ludendorff might provoke an open clash. This the general did not, but he refused to join Hindenburg and took his stand ostentatiously a few feet away from the president when detachments of the Reichswehr marched by them in review. The marshal was deeply upset. Weeks later he still fretted about the incident and sought reassurance from many of his visitors.

The ex-Emperor, too, caused him some anxiety during those days. With growing alarm William II had noticed the waning of monarchist sympathies. The extension of the Law Protecting the Republic, with German National votes, and the promulgation of that law by Hindenburg had been a great shock to him. Hindenburg, William felt, had come to like his office and he personally doubted, as he confided to one of his aides, that the marshal had actually made a sacrifice when he accepted the presidency. In his concern the ex-monarch suggested to the German National leaders that they select now, in view of Hindenburg's age, a reliable monarchist candidate to run in the next presidential election; he did so clearly to avoid as precipitate a choice as in his view had been made in 1925.

Beyond these long-range plans there was need for immediate action. The Tannenberg ceremony seemed a welcome occasion to William to remind the country of his continued existence. He sent Hindenburg a telegram that stressed William's contribution to that victory and presented Hindenburg and Ludendorff in the role of mere executors of the Emperor's instructions. As the former Kaiser condescendingly put it, "Dispatched by me to East Prussia with orders to deliver it from the enemy whatever the cost, you and General Ludendorff succeeded in doing so, thanks to your superior leadership and to the dedicated support of your subleaders and aides, most of whom were the disciples of my old chief of staff Count Schlieffen." Tannenberg had shown the world anew what German strength can achieve "under strong determined leadership," implying that the country was not getting it now. William had expected Hindenburg to read the telegram at the public ceremony, but was disappointed. The president had been warned that a public reading of the dispatch might provoke new internal difficulties and he therefore decided to read it instead to his old war comrades at the banquet. Some of the ex-Kaiser's supporters disliked his caution and to Hindenburg's embarrassment published the message a few days later in the *Kreuzzeitung,* the monarchist mouthpiece. As expected, the telegram provoked an acrimonious debate, opening old wounds and quarrels. But what worried Hindenburg most was that once more he felt himself painfully isolated from those whose good opinion he valued most.[63]

For a fleeting moment the celebration of his eightieth birthday, on October 2, appeared to bridge these differences. In unusual accord the bulk of the nation paid its tribute to him. Solemn ceremonies and joyous festivities attested to the veneration that he commanded; republican spokesman paid as eloquent homage to him as did their rightist opponents. Inevitably, there were some discordant notes in this harmony: Ludendorff's followers, now organized in a "Tannenberg-Bund," were forbidden to attend any of the birthday celebrations "in view of the incredible occurrences at the unveiling of the Tannenberg Memorial"; the *Alldeutsche Blätter,* the organ of the irrepressible Pan-Germans, bemoaned Hindenburg's "bourgeois ethics" that allowed him to retain Ebert's aides—a "basic mistake . . . which kept calling forth new mistakes"; and the Communists reiterated their charges of the marshal's militarism and imperialism. Few people outside of these groups paid any attention to these attacks. Other critics who might have received more attention voiced their misgivings so quietly that they were drowned in the panegyrics in which the celebrants revelled.[64]

The tenor of these celebrations reflected the fact that the political consolidation was more apparent than real. Both right and left agreed that a restoration of the monarchy was no longer a matter of practical politics. Even Loebell had to grant that, "as is generally understood, Hindenburg did not assume the Presi-

63 Same memorandum, *ibid.*/166399–400; on William's attitude, Maltzahn to Westarp, June 2, 1927, Westarp Papers; Görlitz, *Hindenburg,* pp. 288–89; Gessler, *Reichswehrpolitik,* p. 344; Stülpnagel, *75 Jahre,* p. 240.

64 *Frankfurter Zeitung,* No. 730, Oct. 1, 1927; *Alldeutsche Blätter,* Oct. 1, 1927, p. 166.

dency to pave the way for a restoration of the monarchy, but in order to preserve the state, further our rehabilitation, and regain for us our rightful position in international councils." Conservative newspapers, too, saw Hindenburg's foremost task in aims other than the hopeless attempt to revive an irretrievable past. "Let us hope," wrote the agrarian *Deutsche Tageszeitung*, "that Hindenburg will succeed in establishing German strength and greatness by fusing old ideals with new concepts."

The left, in turn, congratulated itself on finding the republic so much stronger and healthier than it had been at the time of Hindenburg's election. "Hindenburg's election as the second President of the Republic has . . . contributed a great deal to the consolidation of the republican form of government which is so evident today," wrote a contributor to the *Berliner Tageblatt*, "Hindenburg's Presidency has restored a realistic perspective to political thinking in Germany." In the same vein the *Frankfurter Zeitung* observed "that the result of his Presidency so far is a remarkable consolidation and invigoration of the Republic." Nor need Hindenburg's monarchist inclinations be a cause for alarm any more; he had shown that he meant to keep the oath he had sworn as president of the republic: "No one ought to demand therefore of this old Prussian officer that he give up at this late date his monarchist convictions which are rooted so deeply in his heart." Not every liberal of course was prepared to discount the marshal's political sympathies so completely—the widely read Theodor Wolff, editor-in-chief of the *Berliner Tageblatt*, was much less certain as to how far republicans could rely on Hindenburg as a guardian of the republic. He limited himself to a few words of courteous appreciation in his editorial of the day before passing on to other matters. But such skepticism was exceptional. So many devout republicans hailed the election of Hindenburg as a triumph of the democratic selection process that one Centrist newspaper asked in alarm whether the republicans did not, by such eulogies, acknowledge the greater political wisdom of the anti-republican right. It wondered too whether the republicans realized that the nationwide Hindenburg celebrations were a boon to the parties of the right much more than to the republic. This was also the view of the Socialist press. *Vorwärts* saw in these festivities, not a manifestation of national unity, but an alarming demonstration against parliamentary democracy. The "Hindenburg Republic," it warned, had still to be transformed into a truly democratic state. This, rather than the question of monarchy *vs.* republic, was indeed the decisive issue now. Yet even those who were aware of this problem proposed no specific solution.[65]

Rightist speeches and editorials that day were far more concrete in discussing their aims. Westarp, addressing a gathering in Hanover, asked for far-reaching constitutional amendments to meet the nation's need for strong leadership. The president ought to have the right to appoint and dismiss chancellors and ministers on his own, he ought to control Prussia, he ought not to be put in a position where he would have to promulgate laws of which he disapproved. "It is our duty," he admonished his audience, "to strengthen the constitutional position of the President." Other rightist speakers expressed similar thoughts, and they were even voiced in the church service Hindenburg attended on that October morning. Commenting on the fact that it was not always those that sow who harvest, the officiating minister, a high Lutheran church official, observed that the Fatherland which the nation had inherited from its forebears had been forged into one Reich, not by majority decisions, but by blood and iron.

In the face of these demands, republican apathy seems hard to comprehend. If nothing else, the flag controversy, always a faithful barometer of the political atmosphere, ought to have warned the republicans of the precariousness of their position. Characteristically the Berlin correspondent of the *Frankfurter Zeitung* noted with obvious satisfaction that while many buildings had hoisted the black-white-and-red flag, black-red-gold was also very much in evidence. But the *New York Times* representative gained a rather different impression: "If the matter were left to the Berlin crowds, the old Imperial colors would win in a walk."[66]

Among the gifts and honors showered on Hindenburg, the most notable one was the deed to Neudeck, his ancestral home in East Prussia. Some months before, the owner, a sister-in-law of the president, had been compelled to put the estate up for sale. Oldenburg-Januschau, who learned of her plans, decided to save it for his old friend. Hindenburg's forthcoming birthday

[65] Loebell, "Hindenburg und das deutsche Volk," in Loebell, *Hindenburg*, p. 287; *Deutsche Tageszeitung*, No. 463, Oct. 1, 1927; Karl Eugen Müller, "Hindenburg und die deutsche Republik," *Berliner Tageblatt*, No. 465, Oct. 1, 1927; Theodor Wolff, "Rückblick," *ibid.*, No. 466, Oct. 2, 1927; *Frankfurter Zeitung*, No. 732, Oct. 2, 1927; *Rhein-Mainische Volkszeitung*, No. 228, Oct. 4, 1927; "Das Fest der Anderen," *Vorwärts*, Oct. 2, 1927.

[66] Westarp's speech in *Hannoverscher Kurier*, Oct. 2, 1927, suppl.; sermon of Giesst in *Frankfurter Zeitung*, No. 734, Oct. 3, 1927; on flagging, *ibid.*; *New York Times*, Oct. 3, 1927.

would provide the occasion to present it to him as a gift from a grateful nation. He approached Chancellor Marx and suggested that Neudeck be purchased from funds of the *Hindenburg-Spende,* a public foundation for invalid war veterans. The chancellor liked the proposal of giving Neudeck to Hindenburg, but he declined to spend funds of the *Hindenburg-Spende;* Hindenburg would never approve of their use for this purpose. He suggested that Oldenburg raise the money among East Prussia's landowners. Acting on Marx's advice, Oldenburg turned to this group, but East Prussia contributed no more than a fraction of the required amount. In the end the funds were raised by public subscription, most of them from industrial circles.[67]

The transaction has often been viewed as a cynical scheme on the part of East Prussia's landowners to promote their agrarian concerns by associating Hindenburg with them. One or the other of them may have harbored such hopes, but their unwillingness to contribute more than a paltry 50,000 toward the needed 1,000,000 marks would seem to refute the existence of any paramount interest on their part in making the president a fellow landowner. There was indeed no need to arouse his interest in the concerns of East Prussian agriculture since he had always served willingly in the cause of agrarian demands and pressures. It was known, moreover, in these circles that he considered the large estates indispensable as producers of foodstuffs in wartime. This was one of the few economic convictions he held, and since it touched on the military domain, he was not likely to give it up. But above all he saw these holdings as the homes of those old Prussian families that to him were the country's backbone. Were they to lose their properties, they would be destroyed as a class, and the nation would thus be deprived of that social elite which alone could recapture its greatness. He therefore considered it his duty to shield them from losing their land, and no material association with East Prussian agriculture was needed to impel him to come to its help.[68]

[67] Oldenburg-Januschau, *Erinnerungen,* pp. 222–23; Görlitz, *Hindenburg,* pp. 291–92; Oldenburg-Januschau to Marx, June 27, 1927, Marx to Oldenburg-Januschau, June 28, 1927 (draft), *RKz.,* R 43 1/580.

[68] Wheeler-Bennett, *Wooden Titan,* pp. 309–13; Olden, *Hindenburg,* pp. 211–23; Braun, *Von Weimar,* pp. 295–96; Hindenburg to Marx, May 2, 1927, on aid to East German agriculture, *RKz.,* R 43 1/1798; Hans Otto Meissner and Harry Wilde, *Die Machtergreifung: Ein Bericht über die Technik des nationalsozialistischen Staats-streichs* (Stuttgart, 1958), pp. 156–57. One other aspect of the transaction has also come in for sharp criticism—the deeding of the estate to Hindenburg's son Oskar who was entered as the owner of Neudeck in the official records. When this pro-

The birthday ceremonies were barely over when new clouds darkened the political horizon. An enterprising staff captain in the Reichswehr ministry had used secret funds of the Navy for some business investments on the Navy's behalf. The venture had failed dismally and had cost the taxpayers some 12 million marks. Gessler had been unaware of these transactions, but the resulting scandal forced him to resign in January 1928 and Hindenburg now had to find a successor. The rightist parties, anxious to obtain control of the post, suggested two candidates. The German Nationals proposed Count Schulenburg, Hindenburg's old adversary on the November 9 issue, and now one of their Reichstag deputies. The German People's Party suggested a retired admiral, Brüninghaus, who served as its naval expert in the Reichstag. But Hindenburg wished to appoint someone less rigidly antirepublican who would not cause him any embarrassment. He thought of Franz von Papen, the future chancellor, who as a one-time member of the general staff seemed to have professional qualifications and as a right-wing Centrist was a moderate monarchist. But the Reichswehr considered this choice "too venturesome." In the end the marshal selected his old associate of the last days of the war, General Wilhelm Groener. The decision was not an easy one for him. Groener was still anathema to rightist groups; Count Westarp lost no time objecting to the appointment, but Hindenburg would not listen to him.

It was Schleicher who suggested Groener to the president. The colonel saw in Groener the right man to head the Reichswehr; here was a distinguished soldier who agreed with him on the necessity of improving relations between the army and the re-

---

cedure was called to public attention some years later by none other than Ludendorff, it was widely suspected that it had been adopted to evade payment of the inheritance tax. Baron von Gayl, the director of the East German Settlement Corporation, who was closely connected with the transaction, has given a different explanation. At Hindenburg's age, he writes, Neudeck would soon have passed to his son. Since it was to be bequeathed undivided to the president's male descendants, it seemed advisable, for clarity's sake, to keep it apart from the marshal's estate and turn it over at once to Oskar. The inheritance tax, according to Gayl, would not have been high in the case of a bequest from father to son; the needed account could have been set aside, moreover, from the collected donations. (Whether this could have been done seems doubtful, however; five years later a new collection had to be made on the occasion of Hindenburg's 85th birthday to pay off the debts incurred in connection with the original gift. Gayl too seems to have had his doubts, for he adds that in case of serious difficulties the Prussian minister of finance would have cancelled the tax out of respect for the marshal.) Cf. Eyck, *Weimarer Republik*, II, 333–34; Gayl, "Neudeck!", MS., Gayl Papers, unnumbered folder; *Meissner to Schwäbischer Merkur*, Dec. 7, 1932, *BdRPr.*, R 54/298.

public. This was now becoming a matter of some urgency; the Reichstag's four-year term was to expire that year, and the results of recent state and municipal elections indicated that the Reichstag elections would produce a marked swing to the left. Consequently, if the appointment was to have any permanence, the new minister had to be acceptable to the left. This Groener was; during the last governmental crisis he had been mentioned as a possible successor of Gessler in a left-of-center government. Schleicher was also certain that the officer corps harbored no ill feelings against Groener and would fully support him. On these assurances Hindenburg consented to Groener's appointment.[69]

This question was barely settled when Hindenburg found himself faced with new trouble. While the government had carried out most of its legislative program, it had failed to enact a long overdue School Law. The problem at issue concerned the extent to which religious instruction ought to be offered in public schools. The proposed law left it up to the parents in each community to settle the question locally. Given the distribution of the parties—Socialist majorities in the industrial areas of northern and central Germany, Catholic majorities in western Germany and Bavaria, and German National majorities in the rural areas of east and north—denominational schools could be expected to predominate in the Catholic and German National areas and nonreligious schools in Social Democratic bailiwicks. Nondenominational schools offering instruction in all faiths would survive only in a few isolated regions. This the German People's Party found unacceptable since in cultural matters it still adhered to its old liberal principles. It proposed therefore an amendment according to which states that had adopted a nondenominationl school system were to retain it—a plan which the Center, in turn, rejected.

There is a good deal of evidence that the Center was deliberately aiming at a breakup of the government. It could not possibly expect a more favorable arrangement in a new government in which, as there was every indication, the Social Democrats would play an important role and there would be no

[69] Eyck, *Weimarer Republik*, II, 191–94; Meissner, *Staatssekretär*, pp. 165–66; on Papen, Stülpnagel, *75 Jahre*, p. 248; Groener-Geyer, *General Groener*, pp. 241–43, 328; Westarp, *Ende der Monarchie*, p. 159. Groener claimed later that Hindenburg obtained the consent of the ex-Emperor before appointing him (Groener quoted by Schnee, in *Dt. Rundschau*, LXXVII [1951], 795), but this seems to be refuted by a contemporary letter of Meissner who stated that Groener's appointment caused great excitement among the "old generals of day before yesterday . . . , also in Doorn." Meissner to Nadolny, Jan. 24, 1928, *Welt als Geschichte*, XIX (1959), 90–91.

German Nationals to support its position. Yet the Center effectively sabotaged all efforts of Stresemann to act as a mediator. Evidently the leaders wished to appease the increasingly restive labor element of the party which chafed at the coalition with the German Nationals. Labor also resented a recent salary raise for public officials, while an increase of old-age pensions and invalids' rents had been rejected. In view of the evident trend toward the left, the Centrist leaders may well have felt that they ought to part ways with the right. But the German Nationals, too, were faced with difficulties in their own ranks and on some points of the School Law proved even more recalcitrant than the Center. The breakup of the government thus became inevitable.[70]

Once again Hindenburg had to step in. He asked Marx to stay in office until such urgent legislative measures as the passing of the budget, agricultural relief measures, and compensation for war losses had been settled. Copies of the letter in which the president expressed his wishes were transmitted to all party leaders, and under this presidential prodding, government and parties agreed to complete the most pressing legislative tasks. By the end of March 1928, they were achieved, with Hindenburg putting in an occasional word of admonition when new difficulties threatened to block these efforts. Once more he had rescued the country from an impasse into which partisan quarrels had led it, and he was widely acclaimed for his statesmanship.[71]

On March 31, 1928, the Reichstag was dissolved and new elections were scheduled for May 20.

[70] Eyck, *Weimarer Republik*, II, 158–59; Marx, "Die Reichstagswahl vom 20. Mai 1928 und das Kabinett Müller," MS., Marx Papers/19; memorandum by Stresemann, Dec. 15, 1927, same to Weissmann, Feb. 15, 1928, Stresemann, *Vermächtnis*, III, 272–75; Schulthess, Oct. 11, 1927, pp. 168–69, Jan. 15, 1928, pp. 7–8, Feb. 9, 1928, p. 58.

[71] Cab. mtg., Feb. 15, 1928, *RKz.*/1696/775950–53; Hindenburg to Marx, Schulthess, Feb. 9, 1928, pp. 57–78; Pünder to Stresemann, Feb. 27, 1928, Stresemann Papers/65/3149/165136–37; Koch-Weser diary, Feb. 18, 1928, Koch-Weser Papers/37/105–09.

CHAPTER 5

REPUBLICAN INTERLUDE

N keeping with the mood of the country, the campaign for the May election of 1928 was quiet and restrained, the slogans familiar, and the speeches uninspired.[1] The political issues were of little interest to an electorate preoccupied with material concerns. Most parties tried nonetheless to keep up the pretense of ideological aspirations and dealt only vaguely with the economic problems close to the hearts of their constituents. Only the Economic Party presented itself unashamedly as an economic pressure group; catering to small business, it boasted that it was little concerned with the question of monarchy *vs.* republic or the colors of the national flag, but saw its primary *raison d'être* in promoting the interests of its supporters. It was the one bourgeois party, not surprisingly, that increased its following in the elections, for it clearly appealed to a widespread mood.[2]

The German National Party, on the other hand, refused to adjust itself to the changing temper of the country and paid dearly for it. Agrarian circles, tired of its obstructionism, broke away and formed their own party. (A similar split took place in the German People's Party, in protest against the predominance of industrial interests in its leadership.) Too late (in April) the German Nationals finally cut their ties with the irreconcilable monarchists in the party, still gathered in a Conservative *Hauptverein*. This gesture was pointless since the leaders announced that the restoration of the monarchy remained their ultimate, though by now rather distant, goal.

The main campaign effort of the German Nationals centered on the familiar demand for "more power to the President." There was, however, some concern in their ranks as to the wisdom of this plank. An official of the National Association of German

---

[1] There were, however, some ominous incidents. The most serious occurred in Munich where the Nazis broke up a meeting at which Stresemann spoke, with the Bavarian police unable to restore order. Eyck, *Weimarer Republik*, II, 204.

[2] *Deutsche Mittelstands-Zeitung*, June 3, 1928; also statements of the party's chairman, Drewitz, *ibid.*, and at party congress, Schulthess, Aug. 25, 1927, p. 139. See also *Kölnische Volkszeitung*, No. 375, May 21, 1928; *Kölnische Zeitung*, No. 289, May 27, 1928, both quoted in *Krauss Pressedienst*, May 27, 1928, Marx Papers/19; *Frankfurter Zeitung*, May 14–17, 1928; *Dt. Volkswirt*, May 18, 1928, p. 1107.

Officers (*Nationalverband Deutscher Offiziere*) wrote Westarp that he was very much in favor of a restriction of the rights of the parliament, but he did not think that an increase of the president's powers would produce that result. He was afraid that "in the case of the present occupant of the currently highest office in the Reich" an increase in the president's powers would be abused by his entourage. Matters would get even worse, he warned, when a successor took over; he would most likely be an out-and-out party man, possibly even one infected with pacifist leanings. Westarp admitted these misgivings were understandable and were shared by some members of the party's governing board. Yet the party leadership felt that as a matter of principle, it ought to take up the fight against the power monopoly of the parliamentary majority. There was little chance, he added, that the proposal would be accepted by a two-thirds majority of the parliament which would thereby deprive itself of its powerful position. Nevertheless the German Nationals pursued this demand with as much vigor as they could muster in this sluggish campaign; at one point they even tried to arouse greater interest by distributing pictures of Hindenburg with their plank as the caption. Circulation had to be stopped, however, when Hindenburg protested against the use of his picture for partisan purposes. He also objected to claims of the People's Party that it was the "Party of Hindenburg," since "he did not belong to any party." Little was lost, for these attempts to make use of his name failed to spark any greater enthusiasm among the voters.[3]

The elections on May 20, 1928, produced a marked swing to the left. Social Democrats and Communists increased their votes by 14 and 17 per cent, respectively. The Socialists drew some of their new voters from the Center Party whose working class wing had objected to the Center's coalition with the German Nationals; the Communists, in turn, gained the support of disillusioned Social Democrats who despaired of the Socialists' ability to be their effective spokesmen. Both parties were also the main beneficiaries of the influx of some 4.5 million new voters.[4] Except for the Economic Party, the nonsocialist parties—German Nationals, People's Party, Center, and Democrats—suffered considerable

[3] Georg Decker, "Der Tod einer Partei," *Gesellschaft*, v (1928), i. pp. 397–99; Schulenburg to Schleicher, June 2, 1928, Schleicher Papers/17,ii/32; official to Westarp, May 14, 1928, Westarp to official, May 22, 1928, Westarp Papers; *Frankfurter Zeitung*, May 19, 1928.
[4] Marx, "Die Reichstagswahl," MS., Marx Papers/19; also Houben to Marx, June 14, 1928, *ibid*; see also memorandum by Priesdorff, Feb. 17, 1928, Stresemann Papers/99/3162/173870.

losses. Many of their former supporters cast their votes for parties catering more directly to their economic interests or, indifferent or dispirited, did not bother to go to the polls.[5]

Most radical rightists had similar setbacks; only the National Socialists elected a handful of deputies to the Reichstag. While they suffered losses in some districts, in others they received more votes in 1928 than they had in December 1924. Moreover, their victory over all rival groups made Hitler the unchallenged leader of rightist radicalism.[6]

If the voters seemed unconcerned with the larger political issues, their leaders appeared no more ready to shoulder the burdens of government. The salient impression of the weeks following the elections is that no party was anxious to assume power and the Social Democrats in particular seemed reluctant to reap the fruits of their victory. In an editorial, noteworthy for its restrained satisfaction, *Vorwärts*, their main party organ, urged the leaders not to shy away from the difficult task of forming a new government. Whatever the obstacles, they would have to approach it in good faith and not simply in the hope of seeing the negotiations fail or with the secret intention of wrecking them on their own. To play a waiting game and refrain from assuming power, the editor warned, would merely help the German Nationals to achieve their demand for "more power to the President." It was not until June 6, more than two weeks after the elections, that the party directorate decided, against the votes of the leftist opposition, to demand the chancellorship in the forthcoming negotiations. But it was obvious that the decision had not been reached in a spirit of confident anticipation, and *Vorwärts* revealed something of the party's misgivings when it all but pleaded with the prospective partners in the new government coalition to approach the future collaboration in a spirit of good faith. Mindful of their dearth of strong personalities, the Socialists worried lest the bourgeois parties would block their attempts at social reforms so effectively that their supporters would desert them for the Communists—the dreaded possibility overshadowing all their decisions and policies.[7]

[5] Kempkes to Stresemann, Feb. 24, 1928, *ibid.*/173885–87; Stresemann to Reinhold, June 2, 1928, *ibid.*/100/3163/174106; Hans Zehrer, in *Tat*, xx (1928), pp. 204–05, 285; Gustav Stolper, in *Dt. Volkswirt*, May 25, 1928, p. 1151.

[6] Eduard Stadtler, *Bahn frei für Hugenberg* (Berlin, 1930), p. 14; Albert Krebs, *Tendenzen und Gestalten der NSDAP: Erinnerungen aus der Frühzeit der Partei* (Stuttgart, 1959), pp. 60, 63; Carl Mierendorff, "Gesicht und Charakter der nationalsozialistischen Bewegung," *Gesellschaft*, vii (1930), i, 491–93.

[7] *Vorwärts*, No. 248, May 27, 1928; Braun, *Von Weimar*, p. 245; Schulthess, May 31, 1928, p. 110; Cuno Horkenbach, *Das Deutsche Reich von 1918 bis heute* (Berlin,

While the Socialists were reluctant to assume governmental responsibility, the bourgeois parties were anxious to see them do so. Some liberal papers suggested that the new chancellor be selected from the Center Party since a Socialist might be too inflexible due to his fear of the Communists, but the Center curtly turned down the proposal: it would not lend its hand to any arrangement that would relieve the Social Democrats of their responsibility. Similarly, the German National leadership rejected suggestions that Hindenburg be asked not to appoint a Socialist as chancellor. Speaking for the party, Westarp maintained that there was no better way of discrediting the Social Democrats than by letting them govern for a time. He hoped that the cost to the nation would not be too high; it would mainly have to be borne, he added grimly, by the agricultural sectors and others responsible for the German National setback.[8]

Hindenburg thus was faced with the familiar difficulties accompanying the formation of all new governments. Never pleasant, the task was even more unpleasant this time since he had to entrust the chancellorship to a Social Democrat. That he would have to appoint a Socialist, he never seems to have doubted; to ease his task, he asked Westarp not to attack such a Socialist government too sharply. To his surprise he found the Socialist candidate, Hermann Müller-Franken, a likable person whose dry humor and businesslike ways he quickly learned to appreciate. He later confided to Groener that Müller had been the best chancellor he had had until that time, adding sadly that it was too bad that he was a Social Democrat. But the bargaining and maneuvering of the parties was as frantic as ever, and Müller, a skillful tactician in parliamentary in-fighting, but no forceful leader, lacked the confident strength to fuse their conflicting interests into some measure of unity. The main difficulties arose over differences of opinion with the German People's Party whose votes were needed to secure a majority in the Reichstag. Had Stresemann been in Berlin, these disagreements would probably have been settled, but the foreign minister was convalescing in southern Germany and unable to exert his authority over the recalcitrant elements in his party.[9]

1930), p. 254; memorandum by Pünder, May 26, 1928, Stresemann Papers/67/3174/167803.

[8] Marx, "Die Reichstagswahl," Marx Papers/19; Feldmann to Westarp, June 11, 1928, Westarp to Feldmann, June 18, 1928, Westarp Papers.

[9] Pünder memorandum, May 26, 1928, Stresemann Papers/67/3174/167803; Countess Westarp to Baroness Hiller, May 31, 1928, Westarp to Feldmann, June 18, 1928,

After weeks of futile discussions Müller gave up the attempt to assemble a government based on a formal party coalition. At this point Hindenburg seems to have made an attempt to form a government more after his own heart. Through Meissner he approached Dr. Scholz, the leader of the People's Party's right wing, to inquire whether Scholz would be willing to head a new cabinet. But his hopes were at once disappointed. Scholz did not wish to commit himself—he probably considered the plan unfeasible.[10]

Meanwhile Müller and Stresemann had reached the conclusion that further negotiations between their parties would hardly produce more constructive results. They agreed that Müller ought to form a government, not on the basis of formal compacts with the parties concerned, but through understandings with individual leaders—men who carried sufficient weight in their party councils to ensure the support of the government even without any formal commitments. The move was meant to check the obstructionist tactics of the People's Party and force it to follow Stresemann's lead. There were some bitter protests, but Stresemann was able to quash the rebellion by threatening to leave the party if he as its leader were forced to submit to the dictates of its Reichstag delegation.[11]

More serious difficulties arose in another quarter. The Center Party made its toleration of such a "Cabinet of Personalities" dependent on securing the post of vice-chancellor for one of its members. Müller apparently had no objections, the less so as the candidate for that post was Joseph Wirth, who had been so bitterly opposed to his party's collaboration with the German Nationals that he had come close to being read out of the party. For that very reason, however, Hindenburg objected to Wirth's appointment as vice-chancellor. He saw no need for such an appointment, he wrote Müller, and ever mindful of his presidential prerogatives, he added that he was not going to have a party dictate to him the composition of the Reich cabinet. He had his way, but the Center, offended by this rebuff, refused to be represented in the new government by more than a mere liaison man. For this function it selected von Guérard, an undistinguished member of its Reichstag delegation who fitted poorly into this cabinet of "personalities." Guérard took over the unimportant ministry of

Westarp Papers; Groener to Gleich, Apr. 4, 1930, Groener Papers/7/27; Wilhelm Keil, *Erlebnisse eines Sozialdemokraten* (Stuttgart, 1947–48), II, 371.

10 Morath to Stresemann, June 29, 1928, also Scholz, in meeting of Reichstag delegation leaders of German People's Party, June 26, 1928, Stresemann Papers/101/3163/174198, 174200.

11 Eyck, *Weimarer Republik*, II, 206–08; Stresemann, *Vermächtnis*, III, 297–304.

transportation, and, temporarily, the ministry of occupied territories.[12]

It was not until June 28, some five weeks after the elections, that Müller was able to complete his cabinet. At that, it was merely provisional in character, for the understanding was that the Center Party would be given one or two additional ministries as soon as the Wirth incident had been forgotten. But the main question was whether it would prove to be a cabinet of genuine "personalities" able to carry their parties with them. Here again its beginnings were inauspicious; unsure of the extent of the support it enjoyed in the Reichstag, it did not dare ask for a vote of confidence, but contented itself with a motion approving its program.[13]

Nor did Hindenburg lend it the prestige of his authority. He accepted it as noncommittally as he had accepted its predecessors, and in view of the fact that some of its members were Socialists, perhaps no more was to be expected. Yet in a sense the new government, extending from the socialist left to the moderate right, came closer to Hindenburg's oft-proclaimed hope for national unity than any other cabinet that had been established during his presidency. Nor was this, supposedly, a party government in the usual sense. For that very reason a word of support from the president was essential; it would also have strengthened Stresemann's hand in his efforts to line up the People's Party behind the new cabinet.

Hindenburg, however, preferred to remain quiet, and subsequent developments convinced him of the wisdom of silence. Except for the irrepressible Pan-Germans and the intransigent wing of the German Nationals,[14] the right had accepted the necessity of including the Socialists in the new government. But a reaction soon set in against such passivity, and in the ensuing debate Hindenburg too was openly taken to task for his acquiescence in this deplorable step.

The *Stahlhelm* was the first to open fire. Shocked by the electoral gains of the left, the *Stahlhelm* leaders returned to the attack on the republic. Thus they warned at the *Stahlhelm's* annual Front Soldiers Day a few weeks after the elections: "The parties which claim to fight for German freedom and against international Marxism will either have to prove their ability to carry this fight

---

12 Marx, "Die Reichstagswahl," Marx Papers/19; *Germania*, No. 297, June 29, 1928; Wolfgang Stresemann, telephone message, June 27, 1928, Stresemann Papers/101/3163/174186–87.

13 Eyck, *Weimarer Republik*, II, 210.

14 *Alldeutsche Blätter*, May 26, 1928, p. 85; Kruck, *Alldeutscher Verband*, p. 15.

to a victorious conclusion or will have to let others take over." Soon they became more outspoken and openly vented their hatred of the republic; if earlier the form of the state had no longer mattered, it now aroused their fury again: "We hate the present form of state with all our heart," one of the *Stahlhelm's* provincial organizations declared publicly, "we hate it. . . . we hate it. . . , we hate it. . . . We shall fight the system which governs the present state, we shall fight those who support it by their compromises!"[15]

Old frustrations, hurt pride, and social prejudices were again bursting forth against the parliamentary methods of negotiation and compromise. Despite the many solid achievements of the republic in the field of foreign, social, and economic policy, the aimless maneuvering of the Socialists and the quibbling of the bourgeois parties kept feeding the fires of this reviving rebellion. What was needed, in the eyes of the *Stahlhelm,* was the natural vigor and the unspoiled integrity of a movement unhampered by formal programs and specific commitments; countering the sterile rationalism of the republic, it would inspire the nation with the vitality of faith and feelings. As Eduard Stadtler, one of its spokesmen, exulted: "What to us is so much more 'programmatic' in the politics of the *Stahlhelm* movement than the elaborate programs of the parties is the spirit of the movement which has never been defined expressly and which cannot be defined . . . For this is the essence of the policies pursued by the militant *Bünde* and the *Stahlhelm,* that their driving power is bearing, faith, myth, life for an idea, the exemplary deed, heroic preparedness, fighting leadership, radiantly believing followers, the solidarity of men eager to give battle, the community of youth, marching columns, the ethos of the trenches, waving flags, the rhythm of martial music, windbreaker pride . . . To us program means hardly anything, life, human beings, everything."[16]

What expressed itself here was an emotional activism that valued action for its own sake, unmindful of its effects and unhampered by moral or social conventions. In the words of the above quoted *Stahlhelmer,* it was the credo of one who was driven by an "inner commitment toward that voice of his blood which forces him to remain irrationally vague and to express his youthfully erratic ways with corresponding unpredictability."[17]

[15] Wilhelm Kleinau, *Soldaten der Nation: Die geschichtliche Sendung des Stahlhelms* (Berlin, 1933), pp. 51, 57.

[16] Bothmer to Stresemann, June 26, 1927, Stresemann Papers/98/3162/173587–92; Stadtler, *Bahn frei,* p. 57; also pp. 21–22.

[17] Edgar Jung, "Die Tragik der Kriegsgeneration," *Süddeutsche Monatshefte,* (1929–30), 514; Stadtler, *Bahn frei,* p. 38.

To such primordial exuberance the president's cool sobriety could only seem weak and contemptible. While never enthusiastic about Hindenburg, the *Stahlhelm* had, however, refrained from criticizing him publicly. In fact, it had welcomed him into its ranks as an honorary member, though never as its honorary president, as was widely believed,[18] and it had never failed to express its respects to him in official messages and proclamations. It did not abandon this reserve now, and its publicists slapped, if ever so gently, the hands of the Pan-Germans, when their leader Class attacked the president at the League's annual convention that fall. But the *Stahlhelm's* attitude was changing; its criticism of those who were supporting the existing "system" with undignified compromises was directed against Hindenburg too and was so understood. Its labored efforts to uphold him nevertheless as a symbol of national greatness were perhaps even more revealing. "Hindenburg represents to us timelessness, history, myth, and national faith," Stadtler mused, "so that the task of national leaders can only consist in utilizing as a specific Hindenburg faith the moral strength which he represents in their own work. The quarrel about Hindenburg cannot help us. We can progress only inspired by a sincere, humble, dynamic faith in Hindenburg. And the nation is going to follow whoever, inspired by this faith in Hindenburg, will renew and reshape that Prussia and that Germany which is so shiningly reflected in Hindenburg."[19] The marshal was assuming the "role of a monument from days long past that could not be brought to life," an army officer later recalled, "people passed it in reverence, they took off their hats, but they did not stop—they went on as they always do when they see a monument."[20]

While the *Stahlhelm* maintained the outward forms of reverence and respect toward Hindenburg, other groups on the right no longer did so, and soon, except for the Communists, no one assailed him more bitterly than did these rightist critics. The most venomous attacks were launched by *Justizrat* Class, the indefatigable leader of the Pan-German League. Like all Pan-Germans he had long been critical of the president. Abandoning all restraint now, he poured forth his contempt for the marshal at a board meeting of the League: "No objective observer can deny that things have gone from bad to worse from the day on which

[18] Curtius to Stresemann, Oct. 4, 1928, Stresemann Papers/72/3149/165529.

[19] Stadtler, *Bahn frei*, pp. 102–05; also *Berliner Börsen-Zeitung*, Sept. 28, 1928; Stresemann to Gilsa, Oct. 14, 1928, Stresemann, *Vermächtnis*, III, 320.

[20] Moriz von Faber du Faur, *Macht und Ohnmacht: Erinnerungen eines alten Offiziers* (Stuttgart, 1953), p. 141.

Herr von Hindenburg took office. For this the President is responsible to the present and the future Germany."[21] Other "national" standard-bearers voiced similar feelings, among them, not surprisingly, the ex-Crown Prince.[22]

If these critics could perhaps be dismissed as outsiders, the same could not be said of the German National Party. Shortly after the elections Walter Lambach, one of its younger deputies in the Reichstag and head of a leading white collar union, called on the party to tone down its monarchist aspirations and welcome republicans into its ranks. Hindenburg, he stated, had come to overshadow the Hohenzollerns so completely that they no longer commanded much affection among the German people. The party ought to appeal to all Germans and transform itself into a truly national conservative party if it wished to play any role in the future. But the party's immediate reaction was to expel him, and only on second thought, to avoid a further secession, it reinstated him—with a severe reprimand.[23]

So tenuous a settlement could not heal its internal cleavages. When Lambach's proposals were answered, this was done, not by Westarp, the party's official head, but by Hugenberg, the spokesman of the intransigents. Lambach, he charged, was an opportunist; if he wished to fight the monarchist movement, he would have to do this from outside the party. Yet on Hindenburg he remained silent although Lambach had paid him such eloquent tribute. This omission was not accidental; as a leading Pan-German, Hugenberg had always objected to the marshal's acceptance of the republic. Nor had he left any doubt that he approved Class' public criticism of Hindenburg's policies. One of his closest associates had shared the speaker's rostrum with Class when the latter had launched his attack on the president.[24]

As the spokesman of the intransigents Hugenberg became head of the party in October 1928, after Count Westarp had resigned in

---

21 Class, in *Alldeutsche Blätter*, Sept. 15, 1928, p. 150; also Kruck, *Alldeutscher Verband*, pp. 173, 175. The civilian address "Herr" was meant as an expression of contempt. Cf. the letter of a former officer to Hindenburg, Feb. 2, 1930, copy in Schleicher Papers/3/23–24: "For some time now national circles no longer accord Your Excellency the honor of calling you 'Hindenburg,' but add a 'Herr von' by which they wish to suggest their dissociation from you."

22 Karl Litzmann, *Lebenserinnerungen* (Berlin, 1927–28), II, 308–09; Müldner von Mülnheim to Schleicher, Nov. 23, 1928, Schleicher Papers/21/11–12.

23 Lambach, in Kaufmann, *Monarchism*, pp. 182–85; Stampfer, *Vierzehn Jahre*, pp. 529–30; Bracher, *Auflösung*, pp. 313–15; Schulthess, July 24, Aug. 29, 1928, pp. 141–42.

24 Kaufmann, *Monarchism*, pp. 185–86; Alter, *Nationalisten*, p. 274; Bracher, *Auflösung*, pp. 313–14; Westarp to Philipp, Apr. 4, 1928, in *Frankfurter Zeitung*,

disgust over the party's internal feuds. His election, carefully engineered, was close; many of his colleagues had serious misgivings about entrusting him with the leadership, and all indications pointed indeed to the party's need for more flexibility. Thanks to his financial and press resources and his great organizational skill, Hugenberg succeeded quickly, however, in making himself its unchallenged master. Hindenburg, watching this change with mixed feelings, saw his pleadings for unity farther than ever from realization. With Hugenberg in command, there was little chance that the party would continue its cautious cooperation with the republic. He also worried lest Hugenberg's ties to industrial interests might lessen the party's support of agrarian concerns. When Hugenberg came to pay his respects as the new head of the German National Party, the president cautioned him not to promote the interests of industry at the expense of agricultural needs.[25]

If the growing recalcitrance of the right deterred him from coming to the aid of the Müller government, the attitude of the Socialists was even less suited to kindle his enthusiasm for the new cabinet. One of the major issues of the election campaign had centered on a new pocket battleship, or *Panzerkreuzer,* which the Navy wanted to build; the first installment on construction had already been granted by the previous Reichstag, and the Reichsrat too had approved it, provided the required amount could be drawn from available funds. During the election campaign the Social Democrats had opposed construction of this ship and had tried to win votes with the slogan, "Free meals for children instead of battleships!" Soon after the formation of the new government, Groener insisted however that funds be allocated at once for the projected pocket battleship. Hilferding, the Socialist finance minister, found that the required amounts were available, and the cabinet agreed to start construction. The decision was unanimous; to avoid a government crisis at this early stage, the Socialist ministers too voted for it. Even more was at stake than Groener's departure; should he resign, Hilferding intimated to a Centrist deputy, Hindenburg too might leave office. Republican diffidence thus was as great as ever; even after a striking victory at the polls, the Socialist leaders were anxious to avoid a new

May 19, 1928; Anger to German National People's Party, Sept. 10, 1928, copy in Westarp Papers.

[25] Alter, *Nationalisten,* pp. 151, 154–55; Stampfer, *Vierzehn Jahre,* p. 530; *Dt. Gesch.-Kal.,* 1928, A, 401; Westarp memorandum on talk with Hindenburg, Jan. 15, 1930, Westarp Papers.

presidential election and would rather have Hindenburg, the reluctant supporter of the republic, continue in office.[26]

The need and the wisdom of the Navy's proposals could well be questioned. As the initial part of a larger program, the building of the pocket battleship constituted a heavy financial commitment. Yet at that very moment, Stresemann was trying to obtain a reduction of Germany's reparation payments on the grounds that they put an intolerable burden on the country's economy. During that same month too the government signed the Briand-Kellogg Pact by which war was renounced as an instrument of national policy. There was also the nagging question whether the building of the *Panzerkreuzer* was justified militarily, and the additional problem of reviewing the issue in the light of the political shift the recent elections had disclosed. Groener's urgency struck the left as evidence that the pervading power-hungry militarist spirit chose to ignore the nation's more pressing social and economic needs.

On these and other grounds the Social Democrats and Communists attacked the decision of the cabinet. The Social Democrats insisted that their ministers who had agreed to the allocation of funds disavow themselves and vote with them (instead of abstaining); the ministers did so since they were anxious to maintain party unity. The incident showed how sadly Müller had failed to set up a "Government of Personalities." It was not the ministers who carried their Reichstag delegations with them, but the delegations that, as usual, imposed their will on the ministers.[27]

If the fracas furnished new proof of republican ineptness, it also revealed the weak position of Groener and Hindenburg. Neither man was convinced that the naval program was justified. Groener admitted frankly that he was anxious to build the ship to avoid being put under pressure by some of the rightist papers, and he wrote later that the president had been ready to shelve the program and that it was only due to his efforts that the marshal insisted on its implementation. When Hindenburg explained his position to Müller, he justified it primarily on political, not on military, grounds. And he too had his eye on the right when he let it be known that he might have to resign if the program were dropped by the Reichstag.[28]

---

[26] Severing, *Lebensweg*, II, 157–58; Stegerwald memorandum on talk with Hilferding, Sept. 12, 1928, Marx Papers/19.

[27] Wheeler-Bennett, *Nemesis*, pp. 191–92; Eyck, *Weimarer Republik*, II, 210–13; Schüddekopf, *Heer und Republik*, pp. 212–13; Nuschke, in *Berliner Volks-Zeitung*, No. 391, Aug. 19, 1928.

[28] Groener, in cab. mtg., Nov. 15, 1928, *RKz.*/1699/778479–80; also Schleicher to Groener, Aug. 18, 1928, in *Welt als Geschichte*, XI (1951), 124. The letter suggests

He could not but feel drawn to the right, whatever its failings. The German Nationals were the ones who had seen in the *Panzerkreuzer* the symbol of a strong and self-reliant Germany, the signpost to a better future. The Socialists, on the other hand, had shown themselves vacillating and unreliable, and their behavior confirmed him in his conviction that party politics and the parliamentary system were Germany's ruin.

Groener as well as Schleicher, whose advice carried increasing weight with the president, began to feel that their policy of cooperation with the republican forces was placing them in an ever more difficult position. The Socialists seemed little concerned with the problems the generals faced while the latter's endeavors to reach a *modus vivendi* with Socialists and Democrats earned them the distrust of "national" circles. It was expressed with increasing frequency in attacks on the "tired resignation" and the "misplaced tolerance" of the Reichswehr ministry. Soon Nazis and German Nationals vied with each other in expressing their lack of confidence in the "system of desk generals" who ran the ministry and knew nothing of the true frontline spirit.[29] Sustained long enough, such charges might lose Groener not only the respect of his officer corps, but might also alarm Hindenburg, whose backing was indispensable.

These considerations strengthened Groener's determination to seek a showdown on the *Panzerkreuzer* issue; he knew that to yield on this matter would discredit him forever in the eyes of the right, and this he could not afford. Yet in the long run the course he had set for himself and the Reichswehr could not be pursued without firm and consistent support in the Reichstag, and the question that increasingly came to preoccupy him and Schleicher was where that support could be found.

ᔍ

Hindenburg kept watching developments with growing concern. The uneasy coalition supporting the government threatened to break up at any moment. The hope had been that the Center Party would dispatch into the cabinet one or two additional mem-

---

that neither Groener nor Schleicher thought much of the military value of the proposed ship. On Hindenburg's attitude, see Groener, in *Deutsche Allgemeine Zeitung*, Oct. 8, 1932, quoted in Groener-Geyer, *General Groener*, p. 258; also Müller, in cab. mtg., Nov. 14, 1928, *RKz.*/1699/778461.

[29] Letters to Schleicher, Nov. 18, 1928, Schleicher Papers/3/6–7, Mar. 23, 1929, *ibid.*/67/63, Jan. 17, 1930, *ibid.*/ 34,ii/94–95; Strasser, Mar. 15, 1928, *Verhandlungen*, Vol. 395, p. 13426; Epp, June 15, 1929, ibid., Vol. 425, p. 2520; Schmidt-Hannover, June 17, 1929, *ibid.*, Vol. 425, p. 2549.

bers that fall and enhance the prestige of the government, but the negotiations between Chancellor Müller and Centrist representatives dragged on inconclusively. For several weeks the country was treated to the melancholy spectacle of bitter wrangling over cabinet seats until, in early February 1929, the Center "withdrew" its lone representative, von Guérard, from the Reich government. Once more the "Cabinet of Personalities" submitted meekly to the demands of a party.[30]

The president, following the crisis uneasily, refrained from intervening. Had he done so, he might well have prevailed on the parties to come to terms with each other. For his authority was still such that, as Stresemann stated, "many a crisis would end as soon as the President would say a decisive word and the formation of the cabinet would be taken out of the hands of the parliamentarians." Yet Hindenburg would not seize the initiative if there was an alternative. When Müller conveyed to him the cabinet's willingness to carry on after Guérard's withdrawal, he readily gave his consent.[31] He sensed, however, that he might not be able to remain inactive much longer. Many of his intimates besieged him with their "I told you so's," and urged him to intervene. "What are you going to do now?" the irrepressible Oldenburg asked him at the height of the crisis, "the whole mess is blowing up right into your face." He did not know yet, Hindenburg answered wearily, but some time later he had a long talk with Westarp. Should he step in soon, he wanted to know, or should he wait and see how things would turn out? He did not want to be charged with passivity by the right. Westarp suggested that he wait until the ineptness of the Müller government had been demonstrated even more fully. He accepted this counsel the more willingly as Westarp assured him that he would not be accused of inactivity by the German Nationals.

Yet he feared that he had merely gained a little time before he would have to take action. Westarp confirmed his belief that the government could survive for only a few more months. When it fell, the marshal announced, he would not allow the parties to engage in any protracted bargaining before a new cabinet would be formed, and Westarp had to explain to him what rights he had in that case. He also discussed with his visitor some possible candidates for the chancellorship. He was thinking of a man who was acceptable to the right without being an inflexible doctrinaire.

[30] Schulthess, Feb. 6, 1929, p. 27–29; Stresemann, speech of Feb. 26, 1929, Stresemann, *Vermächtnis*, III, 428–29.
[31] Stresemann, *ibid.*; Schulthess, Feb. 6, 1929, p. 29.

Hugenberg, he rejected, and he found Groener unsuitable because of his many rightist opponents. He asked Westarp about Schleicher as a possibility and also inquired about Noske. Seeckt's name was mentioned, but on second thought Hindenburg wondered whether it would be wise to appoint a general; this might be mistaken in some quarters as an indication of dictatorial aspirations. Westarp seized on this opening to test the president's ultimate plans. It would depend on what he wished to accomplish, he pointed out. Did Hindenburg intend to govern without and against the Social Democrats? This would be necessary, the president replied. In that case, Westarp answered gravely, he ought not to shy away from a personality who suggested the use of force. "The chancellor problem is tough," sighed Hindenburg, and having been reassured once more that the right would not accuse him of a lack of initiative, he was clearly relieved that he did not have to make up his mind at once. How he was looking forward to the day when he could retire to Neudeck, he confided to Westarp. And to show him that his heart was in the right place, he blandly added that he too would then join the "Opposition."[32]

As it turned out, a year passed before he did have to act. Shortly after Westarp's visit, Müller settled his differences with the Center Party and three of its members, among them two prominent leaders, Wirth and Stegerwald, entered the government giving it a new lease on life. The formation of a viable government had become a matter of urgency since negotiations were soon to open to review the problem of reparations. In the face of this necessity party rivalries were finally cast aside.

Though the fate of the government was no longer of immediate concern to the president, the "Opposition" saw to it that he was to have little peace that year. Earlier, in January, it had already confronted him with that ever sensitive problem of clarifying and reconciling his loyalty to both the ex-Emperor and the Weimar Republic. On the occasion of the seventieth birthday of William II, the *Stahlhelm* had proudly proclaimed that its members still felt themselves bound to the monarchy by their oath of allegiance. The statement gave rise to the question whether a government official could remain a *Stahlhelmer* and as an honorary member Hindenburg was drawn into this controversy. He had so far ignored the *Stahlhelm's* antirepublican utterances on the ground that he considered his membership suspended during his presi-

---

[32] Oldenburg quoted in Westarp to Hiller, Jan. 28, 1929, Westarp Papers; Westarp memorandum on talk with Hindenburg, Mar. 18, 1929, *ibid.;* Bracher, *Auflösung,* p. 306 n. 75.

dency,[33] but he could not keep silent in the face of this brazen defiance of the republic. Intervention, however, was the more distasteful to him since the *Stahlhelm* had expressed sentiments that he fully shared. To his relief the matter was settled quickly. Asked for an explanation, the *Stahlhelm* leaders provided an "authentic" interpretation of their proclamation: the *Stahlhelm* wished to attain its goals solely by legal means and the oath of office of present officials was in no way affected by this purely personal declaration of loyalty of old soldiers to their one-time commander-in-chief. Although this explanation could hardly be reassuring to supporters of the republic, Hindenburg accepted it as satisfactory and considered the matter closed.[34]

Nevertheless his difficulties with the *Stahlhelm* and other groups of the "Opposition" were only beginning. In September 1928, the *Stahlhelm* announced that it would submit to a popular referendum the demand for a strengthening of the president's powers. The proposal demonstrated a singular lack of political flair; considering the recent setbacks of those parties that would normally support this demand, a worse time could not have been chosen. The German National Party, however, was in no mood to engage in another lost cause, and it persuaded the *Stahlhelm* to postpone any action until a more promising issue had been found.[35]

It took them some time to find such an issue. Casting about for a suitable cause, they decided to submit the repudiation of the "war-guilt lie" to a popular referendum. This issue seemed especially opportune since the vote could be timed to coincide with the decision on the new reparations plan that had been worked out meanwhile by a committee of financial experts at Paris.[36] This plan, known as the Young Plan after the committee's American chairman Owen D. Young, was to replace the earlier Dawes Plan and establish a permanent basis for Germany's reparation payments. The product of long and frequently embittered negotiations, the plan fixed the annual installments to be paid by the Reich, provided for certain safeguards to protect the German economy, and eliminated the creditors' control over the German railways, the Reichsbank, and other collateral that had been

[33] While this was his attitude as officially reported in 1928 (Curtius to Stresemann, Oct. 4, 1928, Stresemann Papers/72/3149/165529), in 1932 Hindenburg stated: "I refused to give up my honorary membership in the Stahlhelm when this was suggested to me by the Government." Hindenburg to Berg, Feb. 5, 1932, *Vierteljahrshefte für Zeitgeschichte*, VIII (1960), 82.

[34] Horkenbach, *Dt. Reich*, Feb. 23, 1929, p. 269.

[35] Westarp to Hiller von Gaertringen, Jan. 28, Feb. 6, 1929, Westarp Papers.

[36] Westarp to Oldenburg-Januschau, June 13, 1929, Westarp to Maltzahn June 19, 1929, Westarp Papers.

granted to them by the Dawes Plan. From the German viewpoint the advantages of the new plan were limited, and they could well be questioned, but the plan did establish a ceiling, however unrealistic, to Germany's obligations, reduce somewhat the immediate installments, and mark an important step toward the restoration of Germany's full sovereignty. Acceptance of the plan, it was hoped, would also restore confidence in Germany's solvency and help her to get foreign credits. During the final negotiations at the Hague, moreover, Stresemann was able to secure from Briand the promise that the last Allied soldier would leave the Rhineland by June 30, 1930.

The German Nationals were nevertheless determined to prevent the acceptance of the plan. A case could of course be made against it simply on the grounds that it established financial commitments for sixty years and that the grandchildren of the generation that had fought the war of 1914–18 would still be paying reparations for a conflict that would be no more than a historical date to them and the recipients. But as Stresemann suggested, the payments would most likely come to an end before the next generation had grown to manhood; besides, his task was to help the present one, and no one had yet suggested how he could have done better for it.[37]

Originally the German Nationals had been confident that the Young Plan would call forth a serious internal crisis. They found, however, that they were mistaken in this assumption and it became clear that the Reichstag would ratify the new plan. They now tried to enlist Hindenburg in their fight against acceptance. Whatever their attitude towards the president, his help was indispensable if their campaign were to have any chance of success. If Hindenburg could be persuaded to suspend for two months the promulgation of the law by which the Reichstag would enact the Young Plan, they could submit the law to a plebiscite—a procedure provided for in the constitution. The hope was that the president's decision could also be interpreted as an expression of his opposition to the plan and would thus give additional impetus to their campaign.[38]

It was unlikely that Hindenburg would accede to this scheme. When Westarp talked to him about the German Nationals' opposition to the Young Plan, his immediate reply was that the plan constituted a definite improvement over the Dawes Plan, and "all

[37] Werner Conze, in Rassow, *Dt. Geschichte,* p. 652; Stresemann, *Vermächtnis,* III, 563.
[38] Westarp to Oldenburg-Januschau, June 13, 1929, Westarp Papers.

counterarguments," in Westarp's melancholy phrase, "bounced off him without effect." Oldenburg apparently was no more successful when Hindenburg, vacationing in Neudeck, visited him at Januschau. The German Nationals, doubtful of changing the president's mind, agreed therefore with the *Stahlhelm* to attack the plan indirectly by launching the referendum against the "war-guilt lie."[39]

But other forces were at work in the nationalist camp that were not willing to content themselves with this compromise. On July 9 a Reich Committee for the German Referendum was formed in Berlin. Going beyond the earlier plan, it announced the preparation of a referendum against both the Young Plan and the war-guilt lie. Among the signers of the announcement were Hugenberg, Class, Seldte, and Hitler.

The initiative for this alliance which brought together the chief exponent of big-business interests and the Nazi leader who had never made a secret of his contempt for the bourgeoisie, seems to have come from Class. Busily hatching new plots to destroy the republic, Class had decided that the German National Party could not achieve this goal without the support of a vigorous, militant organization. He did not see such a force in the *Stahlhelm* and insisted that the help of the Nazis was needed. Class was no blind admirer of Hitler and urged caution in his dealings with him, but he detected a ruthless vitality in his movement that seemed to be lacking in the *Stahlhelm*.[40] Hugenberg, who prided himself on his skill at the conference table, was confident that he could handle Hitler and agreed to Class's plan. An emissary was dispatched to Munich. Hitler, however, was not easily persuaded to ally himself with such "reactionaries" as Hugenberg and Class, and when he did, he did so entirely on his own terms. The price he demanded was the right to full independence in his campaign and a sizable part of the available funds to finance it. And in case his new allies had not understood how determined he was to go his own way, he picked as his liaison man Gregor Strasser, the most prominent "socialist" in his party.[41]

Soon Hugenberg had to pay an even higher price for the collaboration of his new ally. The opposition to the Young Plan was to be mobilized by submitting to a popular referendum a "Law Against the Enslavement of the German People," the so-called "Freedom Law." This law requested the government, not only to

---

[39] *Ibid.;* Schulthess, June 15, 1929, p. 110.
[40] Kruck, *Alldeutscher Verband*, pp. 200–01.
[41] Alan Bullock, *Hitler: A Study in Tyranny* (New York, 1953), p. 132.

repudiate the "war-guilt clause," but to obtain also its formal repeal by the former enemy powers and to secure, at once and unconditionally, the evacuation of the occupied territories, regardless of the acceptance or rejection of the decisions of the Hague Conference. Finally, the government was not to assume any obligations based on the war-guilt admission such as those provided for in the Young Plan. "Chancellor, Reich ministers, and other Reich plenipotentiaries" who would sign treaties with foreign powers in violation of this prohibition were to be prosecuted for treason (Article 4).[42]

Clearly the product of demagogic vindictiveness, the law made no sense. Exactly how the government was to induce other powers to cancel the war-guilt clause or to evacuate the Rhineland immediately and unconditionally was not explained. Nor was there any indication of what would have to be done should the Hague agreements be rejected. The "Freedom Law" was simply an appeal to the lowest instincts of the nation, and this was made even clearer by the punitive provisions of Article 4.

Article 4 did, in fact, lead to heated debates within the "national" camp. To their dismay German Nationals and *Stahlhelm* discovered, too late, that it might have to be applied to Hindenburg too. They hurriedly asked for an amendment exempting the president, but the Nazis balked. Considering him a mainstay of the republic, they had begun to attack him in speeches and editorials and did not see why he should be privileged.[43] But Hugenberg, however critical he was of the president, feared that any threat against Hindenburg would alienate large numbers of potential supporters of the referendum. Besides, he had not yet given up hope of enlisting the president's help in his campaign against the Young Plan. In the end the Nazis relented and Article 4 was reworded so as to read: "Chancellor, Reich ministers, and their plenipotentiaries . . ." But if the president was thus relieved of all legal responsibility, he would still remain morally responsible.[44]

The Nazis refused, however, to strike out the entire article, as the German Nationals of Westarp's persuasion suggested on second thought. While Hugenberg did not share their misgivings, he was willing to go along with them. But the Nazis would not, and faced with their secession or a possible revolt in his own ranks,

---

[42] Stampfer, *Vierzehn Jahre*, p. 547.

[43] *Ibid.;* Eyck, *Weimarer Republik*, II, 281–82; compilation of anti-Hindenburg Nazi speeches and editorials, in *Sozialdemokratische Partei-Korrespondenz*, No. 11, 1929; Görlitz, *Hindenburg*, p. 307.

[44] Schulthess, Sept. 21, 1929, p. 174; memorandum about opposition of *Reichslandbund* against Art. 4 of referendum, Sept. 17, 1929, Westarp Papers.

Hugenberg opted for Hitler. This he could do the more easily as he had serious doubts that the Freedom Bill would become law. The referendum was to be above all therefore a roll call of the rightist opposition. In the words of one Stahlhelm leader, it was to lay a "firm foundation for the future so that we can reach all those elements . . . who are dissatisfied with present conditions."[45] There was also the hope that the time gained by delaying the promulgation of the Young Plan could be used to induce the president to change his mind. Knowing Hindenburg, the initiators of the referendum believed that he would find it easier to oppose the Plan if a referendum were held than if he had to decide by himself whether or not to veto its promulgation.[46] The one would not require as much initiative on his part as the other.

To have Hidenburg take a stand against the Plan was Hugenberg's most immediate concern. Even if the president's opposition should prove ineffective, it would drive a wedge between him and the government, and this in itself would constitute a major victory in the campaign against the republic. For to destroy the Weimar Republic was the real objective of the "National Opposition." One ex-general wrote in the *Münchener Neueste Nachrichten,* "Let's state it frankly, the movement is directed against Germany's present regime." Or, as the *Völkischer Beobachter* put it: "This is a struggle for control of the state."[47]

As part of the campaign, pressure was brought to bear on the president from many sides. He was urged to express his opposition to the Young Plan by old friends and confidants such as Berg who pleaded with him to reject the Plan and to dissociate himself from the government. At the request of the Referendum Committee a group of twenty-two former generals and admirals, among them Mackensen, Tirpitz, and the trusted Cramon, sent a petition in which they begged him to put himself at the head of the "revolt against [Germany's] suppression" and to disavow the Hague agree-

---

45 Gilsa to Mahnken, n.d., in Severing, *Lebensweg,* II, 220–21; also unsigned MS. in Severing Papers/1929.

46 Schulthess, Sept. 21, 1929, p. 174; Westarp to Hugenberg, Aug. 22, Sept. 17, 1929, *Reichslandbund* memorandum, Sept. 17, 1929, Hugenberg to Westarp, Aug. 24, 1929, memorandum on meeting of German National Reichstag delegation, Sept. 20, 1929, Hugenberg to Schiele, Sept. 30, 1929, Westarp Papers.

47 Otto Schmidt-Hannover, "Vertrauliches Rundschreiben an Vorsitzende der Landesverbände der DNVP," June 1932, Schmidt-Hannover Papers; Hugenberg to Westarp, Aug. 24, 1929, Westarp Papers; Meissner, *Staatssekretär,* p. 178; Curtius, *Sechs Jahre,* pp. 109–10; *Münchener Neueste Nachrichten* and *Völkischer Beobachter* quoted in Severing, *Lebensweg,* II, 218; also Stresemann, "Betrachtungen zum Verfassungstage," 1929, MS., Stresemann Papers/84/3178/170681–82.

ments. The Committee even mobilized some of the president's relatives to urge him to support its endeavors. Possibly it was also the source of some rumors, promptly reported to Hindenburg, that the *Reichsbanner* was planning to stage a Putsch on Constitution Day, August 11, and he was warned not to attend the official ceremony that day. It would have been fully in keeping with the Committee's strategy to embarrass the government by engineering the president's absence from that commemoration; but the plan misfired—on Meissner's advice Hindenburg decided to ignore these warnings.[48]

To all those who pleaded with him to oppose the Young Plan, Hindenburg gave the same answer: he personally believed that the Plan, while far from satisfactory, did constitute an improvement over the Dawes Plan; besides it might be revised at a later date. But he added that he would not make his final decision nor take a public stand until his turn came in accordance with constitutional procedures. By keeping silent, he hoped to remain aloof from the struggle.[49]

He was furious therefore when the Referendum Committee tried nevertheless to draw him into the public debate. It was characteristic of the tenuous alliance Hugenberg and Hitler had formed that their attempts to force him to take a stand conflicted with each other. While Hugenberg's newspapers pictured the president as demanding the rejection of the Young Plan and his film concern produced a movie against it centering on the marshal, Nazi speakers and writers charged Hindenburg with supporting it and indulged in bitter personal attacks against him. In mid-October Hindenburg felt impelled to defend himself publicly against his involvement in the controversy. In a letter to Müller he protested against the attempts of both supporters and opponents of the referendum to quote his alleged views on the "so-called" Young Plan. "One side claims that I favor the referendum and the other emphasizes that I am committed to accept the Young Plan. I wish to state that I have not authorized anyone, directly or indirectly, to make known my personal views on this question. I have, on the contrary, always made clear that I shall reserve my final decision until the time when this most important question is ready to be settled. I shall then determine, in accordance with Articles 70, 72, and 73 of the Constitution, whether to promulgate it or suspend its promulgation. By this procedure I

[48] Görlitz, *Hindenburg*, pp. 307–11; Severing, *Lebensweg*, II, 207.
[49] Görlitz, *Hindenburg*, pp. 310–12; Hindenburg to Brünneck, Jan. 1, 1930, Schulenburg, *Welt um Hindenburg*, p. 159.

stand as always." Two days later he went a little farther and told Müller that he considered Article 4 of the Freedom Bill a nonpertinent and personal attack; the chancellor was authorized to quote him as opposing that provision, and an official communiqué was published. Yet when the government wished to distribute a poster quoting the words he had used, a German National caller persuaded him that his good name was being exploited by the republicans, and he insisted that the poster be withdrawn since it drew him too deeply into the debate.[50]

These were trying days for the president. Once more he found himself at odds with many of his oldest associates, and the necessity to reject their advice left him unhappy and lonely.[51] Even if he did not grasp the immensely complex issues involved in the new plan, he did understand that it offered Germany some advantages and that above all the evacuation of the Rhineland five years ahead of schedule was an important gain. Unlike Berg, Oldenburg, and others, he understood also that Germany's power-political weakness imposed clear limits on her bargaining ability, and that there was no practical alternative to what had been accomplished. His attitude was the more remarkable since, except for his official advisers, no one else who favored acceptance of the Young Plan seems to have counseled him on this issue. His biographer Walter Görlitz who had access to his personal papers discusses at length the many appeals of Young Plan opponents that reached him, but does not mention a single letter or plea urging acceptance of the plan. The assumption that no such approaches were made at that time seems to be borne out also by Görlitz's report that *after* he had signed the Young Plan Law, a good many people did write to him to express their appreciation.[52]

The Reich Government did not remain inactive in the face of the agitation promoted by the Referendum Committee; by broadcasts, pamphlets, and public meetings it sought to refute the attacks on the Young Plan. It also invoked disciplinary measures against officials who worked actively on behalf of the referendum.

---

[50] Görlitz, *Hindenburg*, pp. 310–11; Schulthess, Oct. 16–18, 1929, pp. 190–91; cab. mtg., Oct. 18, 1929, *RKz./1703/781718*; Pünder to Meissner, Oct. 21, 1929 (copy), RKz., R 43 I/1889; Schmidt-Hannover, *Umdenken*, pp. 245–46, whose account is, however, in part inaccurate; personal information.

[51] As if to righten the balance, he intervened (unsuccessfully) with the chancellor on behalf of the *Stahlhelm* whose Rhenish-Westphalian units had been disbanded by the Prussian Government because of illegal military activities. Görlitz, *Hindenburg*, p. 311; Hermann Pünder, *Politik in der Reichskanzlei: Aufzeichnungen aus den Jahren 1929–1932*, Thilo Vogelsang, ed. (Stuttgart, 1961), entry of Oct. 23, 1929, p. 18.

[52] Görlitz, *Hindenburg*, p. 319.

Going farther, the Prussian Government forbade its officials to sign the initiating petition or to vote for the referendum on the grounds that Article 4, slandering the highest officeholders of the Reich, exceeded the constitutional right of public officials to voice their political views. The Reich postal minister discovered, however, that in some parts of the country the opposition of his officials to the Young Plan was so strong that disciplinary courts which were composed of postal officials tended to acquit anyone who did participate in the referendum campaign, and the Prussian decree was declared unconstitutional by the *Staatsgerichtshof*.[53]

The initiating petition was signed on November 2. It secured the signatures of the required 10 per cent of all voters, and its sponsors could now demand the consideration of the "Freedom Bill" by the Reichstag. But the actual percentage of 10.02 per cent was so small that it rendered illusory all hope of preventing the acceptance of the Young Plan. Since this was not their real objective, however, the sponsors of the referendum saw no reason to drop the matter. At their request the Freedom Bill was now submitted to the Reichstag. While its fate was a foregone conclusion, the ensuing debate provided another opportunity to assail the hated republic. Again the supporters of the bill were frank about their true motives; as one German National speaker gleefully boasted, "the fight for the Freedom Bill is a fight against the present system." And since Hindenburg in their eyes was an integral part of that "system," the Nazis considered him now a legitimate target for an open attack. For the first time in anyone's memory the Reichstag was treated to an uninhibited onslaught on the president by a non-Communist deputy. Assailing his attitude toward the Young Plan, the Nazi spokesman derided him as completely devoid of political understanding and simply echoing the views of his advisers. A few months earlier Goebbels, in criticizing the president, had still avoided mentioning his name and had referred to him merely as a "higher Reich agency" (*"eine höhere Reichsstelle"*); but such restraint was now no longer thought necessary.[54]

The bill was overwhelmingly defeated in the Reichstag, yet the Referendum Committee insisted on submitting the Freedom Bill to a national plebiscite. When it was held on December 22, it produced 5.8 million supporting votes, just a little more than one fourth of the votes needed for the enactment of the bill.

[53] Cab. mtg., Oct. 3, 1929, *RKz.*/1703/781469–74; Schulthess, Dec. 19, 1929, p. 229.
[54] Reventlow, Nov. 30, 1929, *Verhandlungen*, Vol. 426, pp. 3344–45; *Goebbels Spricht: Reden aus Kampf und Sieg* (Oldenburg, 1933), p. 11.

After a second conference at the Hague in which some remaining questions were settled, the Young Plan was submitted to the Reichstag for ratification. Once more Hindenburg was subjected to a barrage of letters and petitions urging him to oppose its acceptance. Many of his East Prussian friends besieged him, moreover, to reject a German-Polish agreement on monetary and property claims that had been negotiated along with the Young Plan.

As these pleas kept pouring into the Presidential Palace, Hindenburg grew increasingly restless. At the prompting of some of his confidants, he insisted on new assurances that the Young Plan could be revised; he wanted it rewritten to prepare the way for the evacuation of the Saar Territory which the French were entitled to hold until 1935. He also requested specific proposals as to how the reparations were to be financed in the face of the country's worsening economy. Müller was able to reassure him about the Plan's advantages and possibilities of revision, and coming again to his aid, Hindenburg tried hard to explain to his critics why it should be accepted. He encountered little understanding for his efforts, and a meeting with Hugenberg ended on a note of resentful tension. The mental anguish he suffered during those days was written deep in his face. "You know I am a calm man," he confided to Westarp, "but now I have not slept for several nights, this is a terrible time." Other visitors too found him worried about his alienation from old associates and comrades-in-arms. And he was left under no illusion about the bitter hostility that existed in circles that used to claim him as one of their own. "Is it of no concern to Your Excellency," a former officer wrote to him, "that a well known Dresden personality said recently with the approval of strictly national circles: 'Herr von Hindenburg is impartial towards Reds and Pinks to the point of self-emasculation.'? A well known Silesian personality put it this way: 'When will Herr von Hindenburg announce his availability as President of the future Soviet Republic of Germany?' Is it of no concern to Your Excellency that for some time now not only the Imperial princes, but also many other respected persons in all fields and activities leave the hall when Your Excellency makes his entry?" In a similar spirit of angry defiance the annual party convention of the German Nationals refrained from sending him a word of greeting as had been its custom on these occasions.[55]

[55] Görlitz, *Hindenburg*, pp. 315–18; Countess Westarp to Baroness Hiller, Feb. 20, 1930, Westarp Papers; former officer to Hindenburg, Feb. 20, 1930, copy in Schleicher Papers/3/23–24; German Nationals, in *Dt. Gesch.-Kal.*, 1929, A, 323; also

But his mind was made up, and when the right made a last-ditch attempt, after the Reichstag's acceptance of the Young Plan and Polish settlement in March 1930, to persuade him to suspend their promulgation and arrange for another plebiscite, he ignored the request. On the day after the Reichstag had passed both bills, he signed the Young Plan Laws. He was more reluctant to accept the Polish settlement since it had been enacted by a slim margin and some of his agrarian friends had also questioned its legal validity. Yet after some days, having been assured that it was constitutional, he signed it too. The next day the Pan-German *Deutsche Zeitung* featured on its front page a black-bordered editorial, "Farewell from Hindenburg," in which Class bemoaned the disastrous incompetence of the president. Some *Stahlhelm* units demanded that he be deprived of his honorary membership— after a heated debate in a leadership meeting the motion was defeated by a narrow margin. But the *Stahlhelm* leaders did express publicly their deep disappointment in him through an official resolution: "The frontline generation cannot, from its sense of responsibility, follow the President who believes that he ought to assume the responsibility for the German people's enslavement for several generations."[56]

In a message to the nation Hindenburg explained why he had signed the laws. He urged the country to consider the issue settled and to work now in unity for a better future. He pointed to the grave economic problems which confronted the nation, the large unemployment and the desperate plight of German agriculture, and asked that they be attacked right away. "In a letter to the Chancellor," he concluded, "I have today set the Government the task of accomplishing this job, and I hereby call on all Germans to join hands across the dividing lines of the parties."[57] The statement was worded in marked contrast to earlier declarations: before there had been appeals to the nation and at most requests to the government, now there were instructions and summons. In fact, the message was ushering in a new phase in the tortuous history of the Weimar Republic.

៙

The passage of the Young Laws was the last major accomplishment of Weimar democracy. Two weeks to the day after the

---

Hahnke to Mackensen, Feb. 15, 1930, in Groener-Geyer, *General Groener,* pp. 400–02; Curtius, *Sechs Jahre,* p. 144.

[56] Eulenburg, Mar. 10, 1930, *Verhandlungen,* Vol. 427, pp. 4309–12; Zweigert, *ibid.,* pp. 4316–17; Kruck, *Alldeutscher Verband,* p. 173; *Hannoverscher Kurier,*

president had signed the laws, Müller's cabinet was forced to hand in its resignation. A new kind of government deriving its authority from the confidence of the president rather than that of the Reichstag succeeded it.

The change did not come unexpectedly. Since the elections of 1928, the country had become more dissatisfied with its political system. The election returns revealed political indifference and preoccupation with material concerns alarming to many thoughtful observers. The difficulties Müller had faced in forming and retaining his cabinet added to these problems. The feeling was widespread that party activities could not be allowed to continue in their erratic and unpredictable way. Suggestions were made to reform the electoral system, to abolish the splinter parties, or to give the government greater powers.

Most critics, however, were not concerned with procedural changes; they judged the politics of the country in terms of the men who shaped policy, and what they missed most was confident, able leaders. Many had cast their vote for Hindenburg in the hope that he would be a strong helmsman, steering the state with a firm hand along a fixed course, maintaining order and authority, and relieving them of political responsibilities for which they had never cared and which they did not like to see entrusted to the entire nation. But the marshal had disappointed their expectations; he had been unable to integrate the divergent classes and interests into a cohesive, purposeful whole, nor had he provided the political leadership for which they longed. The need for order and for a sense of direction gradually grew into the country's overriding concern. As one rightist youth leader summed up a widespread attitude: "We are not concerned with the form of the state, but with its essence—its ability to safeguard order." By failing to assert themselves, by failing to imbue the state with the strength to fulfill its most basic function—to maintain order—the republican forces had forfeited their right to govern. "These times long for authority," noted the *Tat*, a neo-conservative monthly that was just beginning to receive considerable attention among the younger intelligentsia, "they are tired of liberal ideals."[58]

No. 142–43, Mar. 26, 1930; *Tagebuch,* July 19, 1930, p. 1133; Stahlhelm resolution, in Deutsche Zentrumspartei, *Die deutschnationale Volkspartei* (Berlin, 1932), p. 10. (Hoover Institute)

[57] Schulthess, Mar. 13, 1930, pp. 74–75.

[58] Curt Hötzel, *Tat,* xx (1928), 231; Zehrer, in *ibid.,* xxi (1929), 195. An indication of how unsettled the country considered conditions is revealed in the idiomatic use

The demand for strong leadership was not confined to the right. A Centrist deputy noted in 1926 that as confidence in the parties was declining, the call for a *people's* leader was gaining ground: "It reflects a deep spiritual need of the voters and is going to hurt most those parties which do not have such people's leaders or for some reason shy away from strong and courageous leadership." Monsignor Kaas, who was elected chairman of the Center Party in 1928, voiced similar thoughts: "Never has the German soul asked more vehemently and impatiently for leadership in the grand style than in these days when we are worried about our national and cultural problems." "A deep longing for the strong will of a leader and saving ideas is sweeping across Germany," the liberal *Deutscher Volkswirt* observed at this time, "the hour to prove itself has come for German democracy."[59]

The Social Democrats, on the other hand, seemed unaware of the depth of this feeling. Their leading theoretical journals all but ignored the proposals for the overhauling of the political and parliamentary system, and the growing demands for strong leadership. In Otto Braun they did have a man of strength and ability who also enjoyed the respect of the opposition.[60] "The esteem in which the Prussian Minister-President Braun is held in rightist circles," wrote the *Deutsche Führer-Briefe,* a newsletter close to the industrial wing of the German People's Party, whose very name was a significant tribute to the signs of the time,[61] "is not being paid to his political beliefs and even less to his actions, but to the *way* in which he acts, purposefully, without much

---

of the term "peace." By common understanding the phrase "in peacetime" referred even then, more than ten years after World War I, to the pre-1914 era. At a cabinet meeting in April 1931, the minister of agriculture (Schiele) complained that while the butter price had reached peacetime levels *("Friedenshöhe"),* prices for pigs and cows amounted to only 76 and 66 per cent, respectively, of the "peacetime" prices *("Friedenspreise").* Cab. mtg., Apr. 25, 1931, *RKz.*/1683/786399.

[59] Joos to Stocky, Jan. 1926, copy in Marx Papers/13 (italics in copy); Kaas quoted in *Das Ende der Parteien 1933* Erich Matthias und Rudolf Morsey, eds. (Düsseldorf, 1960), p. 291; *Dt. Volkswirt,* 1928, quoted in *Z. f. GeschWiss.,* 1 (1953), 885. The annual report on high school programs in Prussia for the academic year 1927–28 showed that a large part of the themes assigned during that year centered on great men and leaders. "The longing for the hero shines through a thousand times—Frederick the Great, Bismarck, Stein," commented *Das Tagebuch. Tagebuch,* Oct. 18, 1930, pp. 1676–77.

[60] This estimate of Braun applies to the years under discussion here, 1928–1930, and cannot be affected by the fact that beginning in 1932 Braun, worn out by family and health problems, lost his fighting spirit.

[61] In the same vein the Committee on Organization of the German People's Party proposed shortly before Stresemann's death that the title of *Parteivorsitzender* (party chairman) be changed to *Parteiführer* (party leader). Stresemann Papers/106/3165/175231.

wavering, after calm and sober reflection."[62] But the Socialist Party did not select him as chancellor, nor did his views carry much weight in the party's councils. More from lethargy perhaps than from conviction the Social Democrats remained unshaken in their faith in Weimar democracy as it existed, and this faith seemed incompatible with reliance on a strong leader.

Thus the breach between the Socialists and the bourgeois parties was steadily widening when the decline of the economy further aggravated the tensions between them. The political impact of the depression did not manifest itself fully, however, until after the Young Plan had been ratified by the Reichstag. A substantial number of Reichstag deputies opposed the Müller government, but saw the need to accept the Young Plan. Since acceptance required the support of the Social Democrats, they allowed the government to continue in office until the Plan had been ratified.

Once the Young Plan had been accepted, however, the conflicting interests of the coalition partners forced the smouldering crisis into the open. Not surprisingly it centered on a reorganization of the unemployment insurance system and on the focal question of how to distribute the increasing financial burdens that resulted from the deteriorating employment situation. This was more than merely a financial problem, for it struck at that basic and never-solved problem of the relationship between business and labor.

Business maintained that it could not assume any further financial burdens and thought it essential, in a declining economy, to reduce the costs of production; rather than increase their contributions to the insurance fund, the employers demanded that payments to the beneficiaries be cut substantially. Labor, on its part, insisted that the unemployed were getting barely enough to meet their minimum needs; a further reduction of relief payments was therefore out of the question. But beyond these economic issues something more fundamental was at stake. To labor, the unemployment insurance system provided not only a guarantee that its living standard would be kept at a tolerable level; it saw in it also a safeguard against attempts by business to play off the unemployed against those who still had work. To employers, on the other hand, the insurance system seemed wasteful and open to abuses (not denied by labor, though their extent was disputed) and financially intolerable. But they saw it above all as a symbol of labor's self-assertion, and as such they wanted to curb its growth along with collective bargaining and arbitration.[63]

[62] *Deutsche Führer-Briefe,* Aug. 1931, quoted in Braun, *Von Weimar,* p. 365.
[63] Helga Timm, *Die deutsche Sozialdemokratie und der Bruch der Grossen*

Politically this conflict of interests was reflected in new disruptive tendencies that threatened the continued existence of the Müller government. The People's Party became more outspoken in its opposition to "Marxist" policies; after Stresemann's death in October 1929 it showed a growing desire to dissociate itself from coalition with the Socialists, while a growing minority in the Social Democratic Party wished to withdraw from the government on the grounds that only by vigorous opposition to the bourgeoisie, not in collaboration with it, could labor be aided effectively.[64]

Still, after long and complex negotiations, the government succeeded in preparing a finance program early in March 1930 which all of its members, from the Social Democrats to the German People's Party, found acceptable. The Reichstag delegation of the People's Party, however, rejected the proposed solution as inequitable although it had been worked out by a member of its own party, Professor Paul Moldenhauer, who had become finance minister in December 1929 as the successor of Hilferding. For two weeks the government program faced an impasse, until Heinrich Brüning, the Center Party's financial expert and now the head of its Reichstag delegation, suggested a complicated compromise plan by which the final settlement of the unemployment insurance problem was to be postponed temporarily. His hope was that at a later date calmer minds might find it easier to work out a mutually satisfactory settlement.[65]

Brüning's plan was accepted by Center and Democrats and, after prolonged deliberations, by the German People's Party as well. The death blow was dealt to the plan by the Socialists. Under pressure from the labor unions and the radical wing of the party, they decided to reject Brüning's formula. They did so in full awareness of the fact that their refusal would probably lead to the cabinet's resignation and to the formation of a new one in which they would not be represented. But the old argument of its moderate elements that the party could work more effectively for its aims in the government than outside of it was once more dismissed. The Social Democrats may have hoped that the government would now present this plan to the Reichstag, and there it would either be accepted under public pressure or be rejected

---

Koalition im Marz 1930 (Düsseldorf, 1930), pp. 128–30; Stampfer, *Vierzehn Jahre,* pp. 549–50.

[64] Werner Conze, "Die Krise des Parteienstaates in Deutschland 1929/30," *Historische Zeitschrift,* CLXXVIII (1954), 58–63.

[65] Timm, *Dt. Sozialdemokratie,* pp. 172–73, 180–81; Conze, "Krise," p. 65.

due to the opposition of the People's Party. Even this outcome they would have considered a gain, for the defeat of the bill would have pointed up the antisocial attitude of the German People's Party and the groups supporting it, while the Social Democrats would have emerged as the true champions of the people.[66]

But it was too late for this. Moldenhauer, who had earlier been prepared to back the plan even against his own party, was no longer willing to support it before the Reichstag. Müller, worn out and ill, decided to give up the fight. Without the full backing of his own cabinet he knew that the battle was lost. He also knew that while two weeks before Hindenburg might have consented to introduce the plan by presidential emergency decree, he was now no longer willing to do so in view of the government's inability to reach an agreement. The cabinet decided therefore to submit its resignation to Hindenburg and the last truly parliamentary government of the Weimar Republic left the political stage.[67]

෴

There was, it might be said, a melancholy logic in this. With few exceptions, the members of the cabinet had proved incapable of transcending party ties to adhere to policies they thought correct. At one point Curtius and Moldenhauer had been prepared to defy their own party; at Hindenburg's request, they would have stayed in the government over their party's opposition had Müller been empowered by Hindenburg to impose his program with the help of Article 48. But when Hindenburg withdrew his request, Moldenhauer bowed at once to his party, and Curtius evaded the issue by going on a skiing vacation to Switzerland. The Centrists too were unwilling to challenge their Reichstag delegation; they refused to revive the original program once their party accepted the Brüning plan. Nor did the Social Democrats display any greater independence. They made only a half-hearted gesture to carry their party with them during the decisive meeting that rejected Brüning's proposal. The ministers, Stampfer recalled later, remained in the room only briefly and made no serious effort to fight for the plan they thought imperative. Abandoning their leadership role to their Reichstag delegations, these men virtually renounced their government functions. Weimar democ-

66 *Ibid.*, pp. 69–70; Timm, *Dt. Sozialdemokratie*, pp. 172–77; Stampfer, *Vierzehn Jahre*, pp. 561–63; Hilferding, "Der Austritt aus der Regierung," *Gesellschaft*, VII (1930), i, 388–89.
67 Cab. mtg., Mar. 27, 1930, *RKz.*/1705/783196, 783203–06.

racy collapsed from its own internal weakness rather than from assaults battering it from without.[68]

Those who wished to establish a government backed by the presidential emergency powers of Article 48 had followed these developments with close attention. Anticipating the outcome, they sensed that their time was approaching and felt more confident since their number was rapidly growing. The idea of a presidential government now appealed to many because its authoritarian character suggested a return to the stability of the Empire; it seemed to promise speedy and efficient action and would deal the parliamentary system a possibly fatal blow. Business groups clamored for it, hopeful that the new authoritarianism would help them curtail the rights of labor and restore the old hierarchy of command and allegiance. Agrarian circles shared these hopes, and so did all those who longed for the security of a fixed status. Even among republicans, the demand for strong leadership independent of the whims of the Reichstag was rapidly gaining ground.[69]

At the same time political scientists were gathering evidence in support of the legality of a government based on the authority of the president rather than the confidence of the Reichstag. Carl Schmitt had argued as early as 1924 that the emergency powers of the president were almost unlimited as long as they were not concretely delineated by a specific law, and such a law had never been enacted. A colleague seconding Schmitt at the time even quoted Hugo Preuss, the drafter of the constitution. Preuss had written in 1924 that the time to pass such a law had not yet come and that it was essential "to preserve as much scope as possible for the constitutional dictatorship. The chances are that it will be needed even more than before." At that time most of Schmitt's colleagues had disagreed with him, but by 1930 his views had been widely accepted. The influential *Bund zur Erneuerung des Reiches* (League for the Reorganization of the Reich), headed by ex-Chancellor Luther, publicized them widely, and so did a growing number of newspapers and periodicals. "For us," wrote the *Bund,* "the decisive point is that the popular conviction of the exalted position of the President is gaining ground. We want to do our part to strengthen the rights of the President." Not only conservatives supported these arguments. "The Constitution,"

[68] Curtius, *Sechs Jahre,* p. 162; Noeldechen memorandum, n.d., Schleicher Papers/ 23/1–3, reprinted in Vogelsang, *Reichswehr,* pp. 414–15; Stampfer, *Vierzehn Jahre,* pp. 562.

[69] *Veröffentlichungen des Reichsverbandes der deutschen Industrie,* No. 50, Jan. 1930, quoted in Z. f. *GeschWiss.* 1 (1953), 887; Morsey, in Matthias and Morsey, *Ende der Parteien,* p. 292; Vogelsang, *Reichswehr,* p. 66.

wrote a prominent liberal jurist, "grants the President all the rights which he needs for the execution of his task. They have merely been pushed into the background. The more the parliament eliminates itself, the stronger the position of the President, the more real his rights which so far have been mere paper rights."[70]

The formation of a government independent of the parties and equipped with the emergency powers of Article 48 had been discussed for some time by Hindenburg and his advisers. Friends and other self-appointed counselors had urged the same step, and while the marshal still hesitated to take it, his reluctance was a matter of timing rather than principle. From the early years of his presidency, he had opposed the enactment of any law defining the specific powers of Article 48, lest such a law limit his powers beyond what he considered safe.[71]

Among his advisers General von Schleicher was the most active promoter of an "independent" presidential government. He had had a first taste of it in the crisis days of 1923 when the Reichswehr had been entrusted with full emergency powers. Since that time he had always hoped that some day another constitutional dictatorship could be established, though preferably not a military one. Two of his aides were good friends of Carl Schmitt, and Schmitt provided the legal underpinning for the plans by which Schleicher hoped to reduce the influence of the Reichstag and restore domestic stability. This hope assumed a new urgency as the general watched the growth of Nazism. Ever sensitive to possible dangers, Schleicher was worried lest Nazis and Communists might rise simultaneously and draw the Reichswehr into a civil war. Recurrent reports indicated, moreover, that a growing number of the younger Reichswehr officers sympathized with the Nazis and might thus prove unreliable in the case of a showdown. His worst fears appeared confirmed with the discovery in the spring of 1930 of a plot aimed at the army's neutralization in the event of a Nazi rising. In such an emergency the impotent Müller government would be helpless. Schleicher wished to replace it therefore by one

[70] Carl Schmitt, "Die Dikatur des Reichspräsidenten," *Veröffentlichungen des Vereins deutscher Staatsrechtslehrer,* I (1924), 70–90, 103–04; Preuss, quoted by Jacoby, ibid., pp. 135–36; Bund zur Erneuerung des Reiches, *Die Rechte des Deutschen Reichspräsidenten nach der Reichsverfassung* (Berlin, 1930), pp. 40, 53–54, 58–62; Hachenburg, in *Dt. Juristen-Zeitung,* Apr. 15, 1930, p. 540.

[71] Unsigned memorandum, Dec. 10, 1927, cited in Görlitz, *Hindenburg,* pp. 297–98; memorandum by Westarp, Mar. 18, 1929, Westarp Papers; Oldenburg-Januschau, *Erinnerungen,* p. 218; Hindenburg's opposition to law implementing Art. 48 in Hindenburg to Marx, Nov. 22, 1926, *RKz.,* R 43 I/1870.

that would be more independent of parties and parliament, display greater strength, and deal more effectively with the extremists of both right and left. At the same time, it would have to be sympathetic to the aims of the Reichswehr and ready to support its rearmament plans. And given Hindenburg's age, it ought also to have sufficient authority to steer the country through any crisis that might follow the president's death.[72]

Schleicher thus set out to prepare the ground for a government that would meet all these requirements. He was especially anxious to draw at least parts of the German National Party into these plans. Since collaboration with the intransigent Hugenberg seemed out of the question, he encouraged the dissident elements of the party to challenge Hugenberg's leadership. In addition to this group headed by the Reichstag deputy Gottfried Treviranus, Schleicher hoped to base his new government on the People's Party, Center, and Democrats and thought of Brüning as the right man to head it. The Centrist leader had impressed him as a capable financial expert of conservative leanings and as a man of impeccable integrity. As a veteran with a fine war record and as a participant in the fight against the Spartacists in 1918–19, Brüning commanded the respect of "national" circles and was likely to be acceptable to Hindenburg too. His war service had been, moreover, an incisive experience in his quiet and unexciting life and had left him with an abiding interest in military affairs. More than once he had come to the aid of the Reichswehr when the Reichstag threatened to cut its appropriations, and he could be expected as chancellor to look with benevolence on the army's special concerns. To the Social Democrats he might also prove tolerable since he had long been associated with the Catholic labor movement.[73]

Yet when Schleicher approached Brüning, the latter rejected all thought of replacing Müller. He felt that the call ought to go to Hugenberg as the leader of the "Opposition," but the change-over to a German National government should be postponed until the Rhineland had been evacuated. When told that Hugenberg

[72] Carl Schmitt, *Verfassungsrechtliche Aufsätze aus den Jahren 1921–1954* (Berlin, 1958), p. 350; Heinrich Brüning, "Ein Brief," *Deutsche Rundschau* LXX (1947), 2–3; naval officer to Schleicher, Jan. 17, 1930, Schleicher Papers/34.ii/94–95; Sauer in Karl Dietrich Bracher, Wolfgang Sauer, and Gerhard Schulz, *Die nationalsozialistische Machtergreifung: Studien zur Errichtung des totalitären Herrschaftssystems in Deutschland 1933/34* (Cologne and Opladen, 1960), p. 703.

[73] Groener to Gleich, Jan. 4, 1930, Groener-Geyer, *General Groener*, p. 262; Meissner, *Staatssekretür*, pp. 187–88; Eschenburg, "Rolle der Persönlichkeit," p. 12; information from Dr. Zechlin.

would not cooperate, Brüning suggested that Müller be kept in office.[74]

Hindenburg himself had assumed that a chancellor deriving his authority from his special confidence should be someone whom he knew well personally. He had in mind such men as his old comrade-in-arms General von Gallwitz, or Count von Arnim-Boitzenburg, a Brandenburg landowner, or possibly even Schleicher himself. If it had to be a leader of a political party, he wanted a moderate German National or a right-wing man of the People's Party. On another occasion he talked of a cabinet of officials backed by all non-Socialist parties. His greatest concern was to obtain the support of the German Nationals since without them this government would have no majority in the Reichstag. Hugenberg, when approached, was evasive, and to his great disappointment Westarp too had his doubts whether the German Nationals would back such a government. Should this prove true, Hindenburg wanted to go on working with the Social Democrats. Nor was he ready as yet, it would seem, to invoke the emergency powers of Article 48 or to dissolve the Reichstag.[75]

During the following weeks, at the height of the anti-Young Plan campaign, he was subjected to mounting pressures to dissociate himself from the Müller government. Although he was deeply unhappy, he refused to give in. When Arnim-Boitzenburg urged him to reject the Young Plan and Polish Treaty and to replace the Müller government with one consisting of rightists, he noted sadly in the margin of the letter: "The right is again deserting me (H[u]g[en]b[erg]), as it did twice before." And when Oldenburg-Januschau suggested that he resign rather than sign the laws, his melancholy comment was: "What happens when I leave? If I remain, let me do what I think right."[76]

Unable to secure German National support for a government of his choice, he kept working with Müller. Once he had reached this decision, he became remarkably active in his efforts to help the government to complete its financial program. When the People's Party balked at a proposed emergency tax, he intervened and in a personal talk with Scholz urged him to accept the measure. In a critical situation such as this, he warned, those who were safe from unemployment would have to come to the aid of the unemployed. But the People's Party refused to yield, and the president

[74] Gottfried Treviranus, in *Parlament,* Jan. 28, 1953; Wheeler-Bennett, *Wooden Titan,* pp. 339–40.

[75] Görlitz, *Hindenburg,* pp. 303–04; memorandum by Westarp, Jan. 15, 1930, Westarp Papers.

[76] Görlitz, *Hindenburg,* p. 317.

was attacked by some rightist papers for helping the labor unions to establish a dictatorship under parliamentary cover.[77]

Another budgetary crisis, involving naval appropriations, struck closer to home. Groener had asked for funds for a second pocket battleship and had also requested increased allocations for training purposes and the purchase of ammunition. The Social Democrats objected to both items in view of the Reich's strained finances, and the Center opposed the ship-building program. Hindenburg got Groener to postpone work on the ship, but Groener was adamant on his other requests. When he threatened to resign, the president insisted that his demands must be met. There was the usual veiled warning that he too would have to resign otherwise, and his arguments were again personal and political rather than military. He did not wish to part with the Reichswehr minister, he told Müller, nor could he be expected to accept the distasteful Young Plan and at the same time have Groener resign on the grounds that the Reich was not exhausting all rearmament possibilities left open to it by the Versailles Treaty. Two days after Müller had received this presidential ultimatum, the harassed cabinet gave in to Groener's requests.[78]

Late in January the Center Party announced that it would not accept the Young Plan unless the budget were approved simultaneously. With the Young Plan in serious danger, Hindenburg had to step in again. He received Brüning on the day before the Plan came up for a vote: while it might be accepted without Centrist support, he warned that acceptance by a close vote might force him to submit the Plan to a plebiscite. Brüning insisted that the Center Party had to be certain, in the national interest, that the Plan would be supplemented by adequate financial safeguards internally. Hindenburg promised that he would use his full powers to secure an orderly financial program. Thus reassured, the Center relented and cast its vote in support of the Young Plan.[79]

Hindenburg's pledge included the promise that he would, if necessary, authorize Müller to dissolve the Reichstag and impose the budget by emergency decree. (That he would do so is evident from a memorandum that one of Schleicher's aides drew up for Groener.) Hindenburg also took care to prevent a premature breakup of the government; should the People's Party try to withdraw Curtius and Moldenhauer, the two men agreed to remain

[77] Timm, *Dt. Sozialdemokratie*, pp. 168–71; *Dt. Allgemeine Zeitung*, No. 101–02, Mar. 2, 1930.
[78] Memoranda by Pünder, Nov. 23, 1929, Feb. 15, 1930, unsigned memorandum, Feb. 17, 1930, *RKz.*, R 43 I/606 and 2654.
[79] Timm, *Dt. Sozialdemokratie*, pp. 172–75; Schulthess, Mar. 10–11, 1930, p. 67.

in the cabinet, even at the price of being expelled from the party.[80]

But if Hindenburg was willing to grant Müller emergency powers, Schleicher was not. The general worried, the aide-memoire shows, lest such authority would strengthen the anti-militarist Social Democrats. At the same time he foresaw furious new attacks by the right. The losers would be those moderate conservatives on whose support he was basing his plans to restore stable conditions. All trouble could be avoided, however, if a new cabinet above the parties (*überparteilich*) would be formed—one headed by Brüning or Scholz, should the former be unavailable. (A subsequent footnote states that Brüning had agreed to become chancellor and would stay at his post whatever the problems that might arise.) Schleicher had earlier called Hindenburg's attention to Brüning, and he now redoubled his efforts.[81]

The president first met Brüning early in February when the latter called on him to pay his respects as the newly elected leader of the Center's Reichstag delegation. He was impressed with Brüning's sober and unpretentious factualness, and an exchange of war experiences suggested some common ground on values and interests. But to appoint him chancellor was a different matter. As an orthodox Lutheran, the marshal had never outgrown his distrust of Catholics, and his Protestant heart must at first have rebelled at picking a Catholic Centrist as the man of his confidence. Yet Schleicher knew how to overcome his misgivings.[82] He painted the effectiveness of a Brüning-led government in bright colors: it would restore order and discipline; it would be strong enough to relieve the plight of East Germany's agriculture (which, in fact, he believed was being exaggerated by Hindenburg's friends[83]); and it would expedite the Reichswehr's rearmament plans. But he also exerted more direct pressures on the president.

[80] Memorandum by Noeldechen, n.d., but internal evidence shows that it must have been written after the government agreed on the budget on March 5, in Vogelsang, *Reichswehr*, pp. 414–15; *Germania* editorial, reprinted in Schulthess, Mar. 10–11, 1930, pp. 67–68; also Pünder, *Reichskanzlei*, entries of Mar. 9, 14, 23, 1930, pp. 42, 44, 45.

[81] Noeldechen memorandum, Vogelsang, *Reichswehr*, pp. 414–15. Footnote, however, is not reprinted there. See Schleicher Papers/23/2.

[82] According to one account, in this form undoubtedly apocryphal, Schleicher told Hindenburg when he suggested Brüning as a suitable chancellor: "Your Excellency ought to take this man, he wears his Iron Cross, first class, even on his dark suit. He was a reserve officer." To which Hindenburg is said to have answered: "Well, that's excellent. Then he must be a decent fellow. Have him come and see me." Schüddekopf, *Heer und Republik*, p. 248 n. 658; see also Magnus Freiherr von Braun, *Von Ostpreussen bis Texas* (Stollhamm [Oldb.], 1955), p. 211; Meissner, *Staatssekretär*, pp. 187–88.

[83] Schleicher to Groener, Aug. 10, 1929, in *Welt als Geschichte*, XI (1951), 127; Schleicher to Meissner, Mar. 18, 1930, Schleicher Papers/44,i/19.

The Reichswehr, he insisted, ought not to be asked to help enforce the emergency decrees of a Socialist chancellor, and Groener, probably on Schleicher's prompting, resorted to that ever-effective threat of resigning should Müller be granted the right to draw on the special presidential powers of Article 48.[84]

Hindenburg did not find anything improper in Schleicher's activities that now went far beyond those of an informal adviser. That the general, as the spokesman of the Reichswehr, would want to defend the interests of the army and protect it from the incompetent civil authorities seemed only natural and probably even desirable and necessary to the marshal. He and Ludendorff had done the same in the days of the Empire, and Schleicher and Groener were merely following a customary procedure. Schleicher, moreover, found a useful ally in Meissner who agreed that a right-of-center cabinet backed by the president's confidence and equipped with all necessary emergency powers would be the best way to put an end to the existing impasse.[85]

Unwittingly the Müller government played into Schleicher's hands. On March 18, Hindenburg sent Müller a letter in which he requested new aid for the agricultural east. The importunities of his agrarian friends were becoming more pressing—to satisfy their complaints the marshal asked as the price for his signing of the Young Plan and Polish Treaty that Müller complete with the greatest possible speed the agricultural aid program now being drafted, and that he initiate in addition a generous special aid program for the east since it was hit even harder than other parts of the country. The letter was written in the same peremptory tone he had used in his earlier message, and to put the government under greater pressure, it was published immediately in the press. Meissner, calling it to Schleicher's attention, hailed it as the inauguration of the "best we can have, the *Führertum* 'Hindenburg' and the first phase and the bridge to your solution!"[86]

To Hindenburg's dismay the government was reluctant to act as speedily as he wished. He had generally had his way whenever he had made such requests on earlier occasions, and for several years now he had forced all the cabinets to set aside substantial amounts for agricultural aid. He also had seen to it that these demands were taken care of ahead of much other but no less urgent business. His insistence had been such that in the words of

[84] Rabenau, *Seeckt*, pp. 650–51; Kurt Caro and Walter Oehme, *Schleichers Aufstieg* (Berlin, 1933), p. 196.

[85] Meissner to Schleicher, Mar. 18, 1930, Schleicher Papers/44,i/19.

[86] Hindenburg to Müller, Mar. 18, 1930, Schulthess, Mar. 18, 1930, pp. 78–79; Meissner to Schleicher, Mar. 18, 1930, *loc. cit.*

State Secretary Pünder even the Müller government had been forced to accept agrarian policies "which a short while before would have been inconceivable for Social Democrats." But now, when his agrarian friends were particularly critical of him, he was suddenly faced with difficulties in coming to their rescue. Nor were his friends satisfied when the cabinet did comply with Hindenburg's wishes, dismissing its proposals as inadequate. The *Ring*, the house organ of the country's social elite, added insult to injury in a sneering editorial comment:

"The old Field Marshal has seen fit, like Zeus, to appear himself on the stage to say something too. But what came was mere words, and these words were not inspired by the convincing power of a firm will of his own. To Jupiter's thunder belongs lightning. The words of a man like Hindenburg must be accompanied by action, or at least by the will to action. But the parties are going to wreck any action. The President still does not see that any action in which the parties are allowed to participate directly or indirectly is doomed to be futile." [87]

Hindenburg seems to have dropped whatever misgivings he may still have had about Schleicher's plans at this point. If he had not yet done so, he now agreed to the appointment of Brüning as head of the government that would succeed Müller's once the latter broke up. Moldenhauer was apparently told that the president was no longer interested in his remaining at his post since he changed his stand on the budget and gave in to his party. When Müller asked Meissner on March 27, after the Socialists had rejected Brüning's compromise formula, whether the president was willing to grant him emergency powers, Meissner's answer was evasive: "The President would not commit himself at the present time and would make up his mind only after the cabinet had reached an agreement." Since an agreement was no longer possible, the answer was no, and the cabinet submitted its resignation. [88]

On the following day Brüning was asked to form a new cabinet. The Centrist leader had tried to the last to find a parliamentary solution to the financial impasse since he felt the time was not yet ripe for Schleicher's solution. The general's plan could be

[87] Cab. mtgs., Mar. 20, 1930, *RKz.*/1705/783155–63; Dec. 1, 1928, 1699/778685–86; Feb. 25, 1929, 1700/779633; Mar. 20, 1929, 1701/780080–82; Hindenburg to Müller, Feb. 20, 1929, *RKz.*, R 43 I/2541; also materials in R 43 I/1853; Pünder to Heukamp, Dec. 2, 1930, quoted in Bruno Buchta, *Die Junker und die Weimarer Republik: Charakter und Bedeutung der Osthilfe in den Jahren 1928–1933* ([East] Berlin, 1959), p. 61; Schulthess, Mar. 24–25, 1930, pp. 87–88; "Um den Reichspräsidenten," *Ring*, Mar. 23, 1930, p. 222.

[88] Severing quoted in *Volks-Zeitung für das Vogtland*, No. 92, Apr. 19, 1930, Severing Papers/1930; cab. mtg., Mar. 27, 1930, *RKz.*/1705/783204, 783206.

made to work only if a sufficient number of German Nationals would turn against Hugenberg, and of this, there was no assurance. Schleicher himself had been warned of Hugenberg's hold on the party; even Westarp was still willing to follow him and to take up the fight against Brüning. Apparently Schleicher did not expect Hugenberg's followers to leave him, but hoped, quite mistakenly, that the very existence of the Treviranus group and the threat of its growth would force Hugenberg to be more cooperative. But possibly he never thought through very thoroughly the realities of the political situation. Impatient, overconfident, anxious to see Müller depart from the chancellery, Schleicher simply would not wait any longer.

Hindenburg overcame Brüning's misgivings by threatening to resign should Brüning refuse to be chancellor. At the same time he appealed to Brüning, the one-time lieutenant with a sense of duty and discipline, not to desert the Fatherland in its hour of need. If this was inconsistent, it nevertheless had the desired effect. "In the end I could not reject the President's appeal to my soldierly sense of duty," Brüning later wrote to a friend.[89]

Brüning set out at once to assemble his cabinet. The special character of the new government limited the choice of ministerial candidates; feelers had been put out, moreover, to several potential candidates, and Schiele, the *Landbund* president, had been enlisted by Hindenburg as minister of nutrition and agriculture before Brüning had even been designated as chancellor. Yet Brüning had to surmount a number of difficulties before he completed his task. Hindenburg had assured Schiele that he would have his full support and had promised to dissolve the Reichstag and issue emergency decrees should Schiele's agrarian aid program be rejected. Fortified by such strong presidential backing, Schiele insisted on farther reaching demands than Brüning was ready to grant; in the end Hindenburg intervened, and the differences were settled on Schiele's terms. On March 30, only two days after his appointment, Brüning could present his cabinet list to the president.

In its personal composition the new government differed less from its predecessor than might have been expected. The four Socialist members had been replaced by four newcomers: Brü-

89 Brüning to Reich Committee of Center Party, Schulthess, Apr. 6, 1930, p. 182; also Zehrer in *Tat*, XXII (1930), 165; Decker, in *Gesellschaft*, VII (1930), i, 482; Osten-Warnitz to Schleicher, Jan. 21, 1930, Schleicher Papers/23/12–13; memorandum by Westarp, Mar. 1930, Westarp Papers; Bussche-Ippenburg, ZS./217; Wheeler-Bennett, *Wooden Titan*, p. 345; Brüning, quoted in Rüdiger Robert Beer, *Brüning* (Berlin, 1931), p. 54.

ning, the new chancellor; Schiele, who was to serve also as a sort of liaison officer to the German National Party of which he remained a member; Treviranus who represented the dissident German Nationals; and Professor Johann Victor Bredt, a specialist in constitutional law at the University of Marburg and one of the leaders of the Economic Party whose support could thus be secured. All other members of the new cabinet had belonged to the Müller government, although in different capacities in some cases. The changes gave the new cabinet a right-of-center complexion that was to make it attractive to the German Nationals. It claimed, however, to be no ordinary party government, and no interparty agreement preceded its formation. It was widely hailed as a new type of government, a "Hindenburg Cabinet," which derived its strength not so much from party support as from the confidence of the president. As such it was to revitalize the authority of the state and raise it once more to a respected national institution. The fact that six members of the new government had seen frontline service in World War I and had been decorated with the Iron Cross, first class, was welcomed as a happy omen of this new spirit: it suggested youth, comradeship, and idealism; it implied action and initiative; and promised an end to the passivity and selfishness that had plagued for so long the politics of the republic.[90]

The Weimar Republic, it seemed, had entered upon a new and happier phase of its melancholy history.

[90] Westarp quoted in Conze, "Krise," p. 81 n. 3; Keil, *Erlebnisse,* II, 371; Schulthess, Mar. 30, Apr. 1, 1930, pp. 93–94; also Brüning quoted in *ibid.,* Apr. 6, 1930, p. 102; Curtius, *Sechs Jahre,* p. 162.

CHAPTER 6

THE BRÜNING ERA:

PARLIAMENTARY PRELUDE

RÜNING'S appointment actually ushered in a phase that was new only in a limited sense: his program contained little that distinguished it from that of his predecessor; he retained the financial and agricultural plans of the Müller government, and while Müller had not yet worked out a specific eastern aid program, he had been committed to its introduction. Above all Brüning's program resembled that of earlier cabinets in its lack of any great goal that might inspire the nation. There was no promise of constitutional reform to remedy the obvious structural deficiencies of the republic; no plan to improve the electoral system; no reform of relationships between the Reich and the constituent states; nor did Brüning have any over-all plan to deal with the growing economic crisis.

These omissions were not simply a consequence of the speed with which the cabinet had been formed; while its specific composition was arranged in a matter of days, the concept of this cabinet had evolved over many months. If its program differed little from earlier ones, this was due to lack of vision on the part of its planners. Hindenburg had some vague sentiments as to the direction in which he wished the country to move; unwilling and unable to express them concretely, however, he had preferred, in Friedrich Meinecke's words, to "allow himself to be shoved with dignity" (*sich mit Würde schieben lassen*). Nor were his advisers and confidants men with political imagination and foresight. To Schleicher the new government was simply a tactical device to create "order" and further the concerns of the Reichswehr. As one of Schleicher's intimates suggested, the Brüning government was an "experiment" to which "one" was in no way completely committed.[1] Meissner, anxious to shield his master against the recurrent political crises, did not have a more substantive concept of the new cabinet. Neither did any

[1] Friedrich Meinecke, *Die deutsche Katastrophe: Betrachtungen und Erinnerungen* (Wiesbaden, 1947), p. 104; Friedrich J. Lucas, *Hindenburg als Reichspräsident.* Bonner Historische Forschungen, Vol. XIV (Bonn, 1959), p. 76; also Dorothea Groener-Geyer to author, Oct. 2, 1956.

of the agrarians, industrialists, or political leaders whom Hindenburg had consulted. They all saw Brüning's main task to be the stabilizing of conditions—to some this meant simply political quietude and to others a political and economic climate in which they could pursue, undisturbed, their individual interests. Brüning himself, an ascetic, self-centered man, was so preoccupied with the task of balancing the budget that all other issues seemed secondary to his precise and orderly mind. None of these men understood that what the country needed most was an inspiring objective that would give it the moral strength to transcend the concerns of the moment.

Even in the tactical sphere, Brüning did not inaugurate any changes. He had been given the mandate of restoring to the government the leadership functions that Müller had largely abandoned to the Reichstag and the parties. To this end he had been equipped with the right to invoke the emergency powers of Article 48 and to dissolve, if need be, the Reichstag. Yet his government was not *a priori* an antiparliamentary one, and he was to resort to exceptional measures only if parliamentary support should prove unattainable.

Presenting himself before the Reichstag, Brüning announced that he felt himself bound to no party; there was a veiled warning that he might resort to the emergency powers of Article 48 to meet his responsibilities, and a clear threat that if the Reichstag would not support him, it would be dissolved. (The dissolution decree, signed and sealed, was ostentatiously held in readiness in its well known red briefcase by one of his aides.) At the same time, however, the chancellor did state that he would not ignore the parliamentary power constellation, and presently he found himself involved in the usual effort to secure a majority for his program.[2]

In this endeavor he faced special difficulties. Unlike other minority governments he could not choose between right and left in his search for party support. His cabinet had been formed with a specific anti-Social Democratic mandate, and he could turn only to the right to secure his needed majority. Indeed, his program was expressly designed to appeal to the rightist parties, promising rigorous economy in public expenditures and a shift in the tax burden to provide some relief to property owners; above

[2] Stolper, in *Dt. Volkswirt*, Apr. 4, 1930, pp. 492–93; Brüning, Apr. 1, 1930, *Verhandlungen*, Vol. 427, pp. 4728–30; Meissner to Hitler, Nov. 22, 1932, in *Jahrbuch des öffentlichen Rechts*, XXI (1933–34), 169; Waldemar Besson, *Württemberg und die deutsche Staatskrise, 1928–1933: Eine Studie zur Auflösung der Weimarer Republik* (Stuttgart, 1959), pp. 139–40; Pünder, *Reichskanzlei*, entry of Apr. 4, 1930, p. 50.

all, however, it pledged generous help to debt-ridden agriculture and special emergency measures for the agricultural east.

Despite these inducements many German Nationals were as hostile as ever. Unimpressed by the government's "Hindenburg mandate," they found it tainted with too many liberal elements, and the continued cooperation in Prussia of the Center and Social Democrats appeared to confirm their suspicions of Brüning's leftist proclivities. Under heavy agrarian pressure, the German Nationals did cast their vote in the end against the no-confidence motion of Social Democrats and Communists, but Hugenberg made it clear in one of his rare speeches to the Reichstag that his was merely a tactical move that did not imply support of the government's program: "We are very distrustful of the intentions and the composition of the new cabinet. . . . At the right moment we shall draw the consequences of this lack of confidence."[3]

The "Hindenburg cabinet" thus failed to produce the hoped for turn of events. This continued impasse was due, however, not merely to party obstruction, but also to Hindenburg's renewed withdrawal from the political stage once Brüning's government had been launched on its course. It had been welcomed as a cabinet bearing the president's personal imprint, and having the presidential emergency powers at its disposal, it was to demonstrate Hindenburg's determination to counteract the disunity of parties and parliament. Though the president was ready to back the Brüning government with the full *legal* weight of his office, he did not support it by any *political* gestures. While Brüning was engaged in his bitter struggle with Hugenberg, Hindenburg remained silent; there is no indication that he had any sense of personal involvement in the success of this government. But it is also true that Brüning did not ask for any overt help. He was careful, in fact, to keep the president out of his difficulties with the Reichstag and preferred to fight his battles without identifying the president with them. Without Hindenburg's open support, however, the government was in a sense cut off from its greatest source of strength, and the nation came quickly to look upon it as merely another cabinet helplessly struggling against the vagaries of the Reichstag. The opposition parties, in turn, tried to discredit the cabinet by denouncing it as an ordinary party government that was shamelessly abusing the presidential name and prestige.

3 Decker, in *Gesellschaft*, VII (1930), i, 481; Brüning, in cab. mtg., Apr. 2, 1930, *RKz./*1705/783225; Hugenberg, Apr. 3, 1930, *Verhandlungen*, Vol. 427, pp. 4770–72; Schmidt-Hannover, *Umdenken*, pp. 260–61.

The ambiguity of Hindenburg's attitude was to plague Brüning throughout his chancellorship. Not only did it prevent him
from drawing on the prestige of the marshal-president which still
was great, but it also affected the collaboration between chancellor
and president, leaving the latter largely uncommitted while the
former retained little freedom of action. The fault was perhaps
as much Brüning's as it was Hindenburg's. Unlike Stresemann,
Brüning rarely seems to have wished for that presidential intervention which might have resolved a critical issue. Both he and
Hindenburg were convinced that Hindenburg's stand "above
the parties" was preferable to any direct involvement that might
impair his carefully nurtured nonpartisan authority. Given his
natural passivity, Hindenburg did not object to this background
role, for it relieved him, in his as well as the nation's eyes, of
any direct responsibility for the chancellor's policies. But his
aloofness made a mockery of his alleged presidential leadership.

While Hindenburg kept out of the public limelight, he was
less restrained behind the scenes and his views and wishes had a
marked impact on the cabinet. In keeping with Brüning's promise, the government drafted at once an agrarian emergency
program providing for higher tariffs and other import controls.
There was some half-hearted opposition on the part of those
ministers whose parties were associated with industrial and small
business interests, but as Hindenburg's spokesman, Schiele was
in an unassailable position. All understood, moreover, that the
German Nationals could be split only if the government succeeded in attracting their agrarian wing, and no one wished to
interfere with this process. Yet the president was not satisfied.
He persisted in his demands for the speedy completion of the
special eastern aid program and kept complaining about its slow
progress. The cabinet had serious doubts whether the granting
of subsidies would by itself end the difficulties of the east. Some
ministers felt that there was need for greater initiative on the
part of the farmers and that more attention ought to be paid in
the plans to such personal factors as indolence and incompetence.
But at the president's insistence the programs were rushed
through unamended to satisfy his impatience.[4]

Encouraged perhaps by the president's special pleadings, some
of the government parties with special interests and plans of
their own, pursued them as if Brüning's were an ordinary

---

[4] Letters by Fessler, Apr. 1930 (drafts), *RKz*. R 43 I/2543; memorandum by same,
May 14, 1930, *ibid./*1801.

parliamentary government. The Bavarian People's Party rejected a proposed increase in the beer tax (always a sensitive issue in beer-loving Bavaria), while the Economic Party objected to a raise in the turnover tax. For once Hindenburg did intervene and make a personal appeal and compromises were arranged. Critics, however, were quick to see proof in these maneuvers that the "Hindenburg Government" differed little from its ill-fated predecessors. As Hans Zehrer wrote in the *Tat:* "Brüning's appeal to a new state concept might have been successful had it been used at once against economic interests, but it is being used in fact to support these interests. In consequence the fate of the Brüning era is sealed. It does not inaugurate a new positive era; it merely accelerates the disintegration, it speeds up the crisis. In this sense it still has its use and significance, but not in that in which it wished to make its mark."[5]

The ineffectiveness of the "Hindenburg mandate" continued to make itself felt during the following weeks. Hardly had the new budget been introduced in the Reichstag when the worsening unemployment crisis required additional appropriations. Casting about for a new source of income, the cabinet decided on an emergency levy (*Notopfer*) to be imposed on persons with fixed salaries and some other selected groups. The opposition to this proposal extended again into the ranks of the government parties and the German People's Party decided, as a gesture of protest, to withdraw Moldenhauer, the finance minister; anticipating this move Moldenhauer submitted his resignation. Fearful for the future of his cabinet, Brüning tried to dissuade him from leaving but Moldenhauer would not remain. An attempt was made to invoke the authority of the president, but when Meissner asked if an appeal from the president might induce him to change his mind, Moldenhauer said at first it would not. Later he reconsidered and thought that it might; since he would have to leave his party if he stayed in the cabinet, he implored his colleagues to spare him this step. Again the inability of the government to transcend party politics was made painfully evident.[6] Party parochialism was demonstrated once more when Hermann Dietrich, the economics minister, took Moldenhauer's place. The Democratic Party to which he belonged insisted that Dietrich did so on his own responsibility and that

[5] Cab. mtg., Apr. 9, 1930, *RKz.*/1705/783289–90; Horkenbach, *Dt. Reich,* Apr. 12, 1930, p. 306; press comments, quoted by Keil, May 2, 1930, *Verhandlungen,* Vol. 427, pp. 5025; Zehrer, in *Tat,* XXII (1930), 166–67.

[6] Cab. mtg., June 8, 1930, *RKz.*/1706/784061–68.

his assumption of the post did not commit the party to accept the budget in its entirety.[7]

Nor did the president always stay in the wings. On some issues close to his heart he did claim the limelight, and since these moves were always designed to ward off some rightist complaints, he worried little about the effect of his actions. One such intervention occurred at the height of the parliamentary crisis. On June 30, 1930, the last Allied occupation forces were to withdraw from the Rhineland. A series of celebrations were being planned in the area, and some were to be attended by the president. Such participation required association with the Socialist-led Prussian government that was under constant attack from Hindenburg's German National friends. In an effort to keep aloof from the Braun ministry, Hindenburg objected to signing a joint proclamation, asserting that he wished to avoid all signs of disunity that might arise in the formulation of a mutually acceptable text. Braun assured him that he would sign any proclamation approved by him, and Hindenburg then gave in. New trouble arose when Braun discovered that the text proposed by the president made no mention of Stresemann though the evacuation had been largely his work. Since the president refused to make any changes, Braun in the end issued a proclamation of his own.[8] Later on Hindenburg in an attempt to please everyone made a half-hearted conciliatory gesture: while he would not pay honor to Stresemann publicly, he asked Brüning to place a wreath on his grave on the day of the evacuation.[9]

The shadow this incident cast over what should have been a time of rejoicing was not allowed to pass. In the fall of 1929, the *Stahlhelm's* regional organizations in the Rhineland and Westphalia had been dissolved by the Prussian government because they had held illegal military drills. These activities had violated the demilitarization provisions of the Versailles Treaty and had also endangered the difficult negotiations for an early Allied withdrawal in which Stresemann was then engaged. Nevertheless Hindenburg had intervened with the chancellor at the *Stahlhelm's* request and asked for a repeal of the dissolution. He had

---

[7] Eyck, *Weimarer Republik*, II, 336.

[8] Braun, *Von Weimar*, pp. 298–99. Many a member of the Reich Government agreed with Hindenburg's stand. It is indicative of the decline of Stresemann's standing during the few months since his death that when the cabinet was invited to join a committee set up to erect a Stresemann Memorial, it was decided to leave it up to each individual minister whether he wished to join. Cab. mtg., Apr. 16, 1930, *RKz./*1705/783341–42.

[9] Meissner, in cab. mtg., June 17, 1930, *RKz./*1708/784046–47.

not pressed the matter as long as the Young Plan had not been accepted, but once he had signed the Plan Laws he became more insistent. He was anxious to show his true sympathies, and the fact that the *Stahlhelm* almost expelled him for signing the Young Laws seemed to act as a spur on his efforts. With the evacuation of the occupied area assured, there were renewed pleas, moreover, for the readmission of the proscribed groups. The Presidential Palace was flooded with *Stahlhelmers'* telegrams expressing their urgent desire to pass in review before the marshal when he visited the Rhineland.

Müller promised to intercede with the Prussian government, but he left office before he could take any action. Hindenburg approached Brüning two days after he became chancellor and asked for his help. While Brüning was ready to comply with his wishes, Wirth, the minister of the interior, and Curtius, the foreign minister, were not. Wirth considered the prohibition legal and justified and saw no reason to intervene; Curtius believed an immediate readmission inopportune for foreign political reasons and suggested postponement for six months after the evacuation. But the *Stahlhelm* kept up its pressure. Colonel Duesterberg, its second-in-command, announced in a public speech that the *Stahlhelm* had no confidence in Curtius and Wirth. Rather than back "his" ministers against such presumptuous attacks, Hindenburg redoubled his efforts on behalf of the *Stahlhelm*. He saw no reason, he informed Brüning, Curtius, and Wirth, to postpone the negotiations with the *Stahlhelm* simply because "a [!] speaker had said about two ministers 'that the *Stahlhelm* had no confidence in them.' " To avoid incidents with the occupation forces, he was willing to wait with the readmission until the evacuation had been completed, but he did not want it postponed for another six months.

Brüning tried hard to prevail on the Prussian government to rescind its decree. Braun was willing to talk with the *Stahlhelm* leaders, but he insisted that they approach him directly since Hindenburg's jurisdiction did not extend to internal Prussian concerns. Negotiations between *Stahlhelm* and Prussian authorities were now initiated, but they proceeded slowly. As their price for the revocation of the dissolution decree, Braun and Severing requested that the *Stahlhelm* confirm the legality of the original prohibition and pledge itself not to engage in any further unlawful activities. Furious over what he considered humiliating and dilatory demands, Hindenburg intervened once more. In a pointedly discourteous letter to Braun he denounced the dissolution of the *Stahlhelm* units as unjustifiable and illegal and gave notice that he would not attend the Rhineland celebrations unless they were readmitted. Contrary to the customary courtesies, he turned over this letter to the press at the same moment it was sent to the minister-president. Braun, however, refused to give in to such pressures, and the *Stahlhelm* was readmitted only after its leaders had solemnly pledged to bar all further illegal military training— a formulation expressly acknowledging the legal validity of the original prohibition.[10] This was little more than an academic point, however. Few noted the legal implications of the *Stahlhelm's* commitment, but everyone felt that the Prussian government had been compelled to back down. By his brusque intervention Hindenburg had helped to discredit the Prussian authorities, and so had Brüning since Hindenburg's letter was written and sent with his knowledge. The chancellor approved of the step not only because he sympathized with the *Stahlhelm,* but also because he needed the president's backing during the critical days ahead. Events were now moving toward a showdown.[11]

The prospects of acceptance of the government's budget were far from good. The Hugenberg wing of the German Nationals was as hostile as ever, and several of the government parties were becoming increasingly restless. Collaboration with the Social Democrats, on the other hand, was still out of the question for Brüning. The Socialist leaders had meanwhile come to regret the removal of Müller and were sounding out Brüning about a rapprochement. The chancellor ignored their approaches. The president had asked him to steer a non-Socialist course, and he felt honor bound to pursue it. An accomodation with the left would have lost him, moreover, substantial support on the right. And given the internal divisions of the Socialists, he had no assurance that they would not repudiate any agreement reached between him and their leaders, just as they had disavowed their own Chancellor Müller a few months before. Besides, it was unlikely that Hindenburg would grant him the emergency powers of Article 48, should he turn to the Socialists and fail to obtain a majority.[12]

His course thus seemed clear to him. If a majority could be assembled at all, it would have to be found on the right. His hope was that the Eastern Aid Bill, recently completed and submitted

[10] Braun, *Von Weimar,* pp. 299–303; Severing, *Lebensweg,* II, 250–51; *Tagebuch,* July 19, 1930, p. 1134; *Stahlhelmers'* telegrams in *RKz.,* R 43 I/2735.

[11] Memorandum by Pünder, July 15, 1930, *ibid.;* Leopold, in meeting of German National Reichstag delegation, July 17, 1930, evening, Schmidt-Hannover Papers.

[12] *Dt. Tageszeitung,* No. 234, July 12, 1930; Brüning to author, May 12, 1957; Breitscheid, in *Gesellschaft,* VII (1930), ii, 100–02; Curtius, *Sechs Jahre,* p. 165.

to the Reichstag, would convince the German Nationals that they ought to vote for his budget. If they did not, he was determined to enact the budget by way of Article 48. A call on Hindenburg vacationing at Neudeck assured him of the president's full support for his proposed course of action.[13]

Brüning quickly dismissed any thought of resigning, should he fail in his quest for parliamentary approval. He had accepted his appointment as a soldierly commitment to the marshal-president which made resignation appear like desertion. He had promised Hindenburg to restore the country's fiscal stability, and he was determined to fulfill his pledge. Theirs was no ordinary government, he admonished his colleagues; it had not been formed simply to accomplish its task in the customary way. Rather it was committed to attaining its ends by all constitutional means that might be required. Given the special nature of the cabinet, every single member would have to stand by it and support it in the pursuit of its goals. A withdrawal of even one member would doom the government to failure. Whatever the political obstacles, its task was to push through the new budget.[14]

Impelled by his sense of mission, Brüning had fewer compunctions about using the emergency provisions of Article 48 than most of his colleagues. Less tenacious than he, they urged him to adhere as long as he could to normal parliamentary procedures. Their wishes prevailed, and on July 15, at the second reading of the budget, the chancellor pleaded once more with the Reichstag to accept the government's program. Even at this critical moment, except for a passing reference to the president, he made no attempt to stress his "Hindenburg mandate" and to brand a negative vote as a repudiation of the marshal. As always, he carefully kept Hindenburg's name out of the debate and contented himself with warning the Reichstag that if it did not live up to its responsibilities, the government would make use of all constitutional means to eliminate the deficit in the budget.[15]

The reply of the German National spokesman was not encouraging. The Socialist speaker, on the other hand, suggested talks between the government and his party. But, at Brüning's urging, the cabinet decided against such negotiations since they would lead to the loss of all rightist support.[16] When it became

13 Cab. mtgs., June 25, 27, 1930, *RKz.*/1706/784105–06, 784115–16.

14 Cab. mtg., July 9, 1930, 9:30 P.M., *RKz.*/1706/784349.

15 *Ibid.*/784348; *Verhandlungen,* July 15, 1930, Vol. 428, pp. 6373, 6375.

16 Cab. mtg., July 15, 1930, *RKz.*/784395, also July 14, 1930, 1706/784380; *Verhandlungen,* July 16, 1930, Vol. 428, pp. 6400–03; Dietrich, July 18, 1930, *ibid.,* p. 6515; Keil, *Erlebnisse,* II, 393; Stampfer, *Vierzehn Jahre,* pp. 574–75; *Tagebuch,*

clear on the following day that the government would not obtain a majority, Brüning withdrew his budget bill and later that day the budget was promulgated by presidential decree.

Clearly there could be serious doubts whether Brüning's procedure was compatible with the constitution, and it did give rise to a heated debate among constitutional experts. Yet in the debate in the Reichstag only a minority was concerned with the constitutional aspects of the government's moves. German Nationals, Nazis, and Communists attacked the decree for substantive reasons or merely from opposition to the government. Among those who supported it without asking questions were such mainstays of the parliamentary system as the Center Party and the Democratic Party. The one party opposing the decree on constitutional as well as substantive grounds was the Social Democratic Party. Yet its legal argumentation failed to carry conviction since its own leader, Hermann Müller, had thought, as chancellor, of using Article 48 to push through his budget, and there were others among the Socialists who had even earlier recommended this course. In the face of unemployment and depression, the supporters of the republic too were much more concerned with finding solutions to these difficulties than with the legal problems such solutions entailed. "At the present moment," Finance Minister Dietrich told the Reichstag in defense of the budget decree, "it does not matter so much how this thing is done as that it is done." Doubtless the bulk of the nation agreed with him. "The brutal truth is," one Socialist writer concluded, "that when the constitutional conflict developed, there was no longer a majority in the Reichstag willing to defend the Constitution." Even the Social Democrats reconciled themselves quickly to legislation by decree; two years were to pass before the constitutional validity of any decree was challenged before the *Staatsgerichtshof*.[17]

By promulgating the budget while the Reichstag was still in session, Brüning hoped also to force the hand of the German Na-

---

July 19, 1930, p. 1135. It was later claimed that even minor concessions by Brüning such as those incorporated in the subsequent Presidential Decree of July 26 would have led to an understanding between government and Socialists. This seems unlikely, however, in view of the negative attitude which the official *Sozialdemokratische Pressedienst* and the *Sozialistische Monatshefte*, the mouthpiece of the moderate wing of the party, took toward these modifications. Keil, *Erlebnisse*, II, 393; *Sozialdemokratischer Pressedienst*, July 27, 1930, quoted in, and editorial comment by, *Sozialistische Monatshefte*, LXXI (1930), pp. 742–43.

[17] Severing, *Lebensweg*, II, 247; Dietrich, July 18, 1930, *Verhandlungen*, Vol. 429, p. 6516; Decker, in *Gesellschaft*, VII (1930), ii, 196; Julius Leber, *Ein Mann geht seinen Weg: Schriften, Reden und Briefe*, ed. by his friends (Berlin, 1952), pp. 232–33.

tionals. He expected that most German Nationals would uphold the budget decree so as not to delay the early enactment of the Eastern Aid Bill. Coming to Brüning's aid, Hindenburg too urged them to support the government and warned that their rejection of the budget would force him to either resign from his office or dissolve the Reichstag. Since new Reichstag elections were not opportune at this time, he would have to consider seriously whether he should resign. The warning was conveyed to a number of German National deputies by Schiele, and Meissner too spread it wherever he went. Its logic was perhaps less than convincing since a new presidential election would have been equally inopportune; but it did confirm the opponents of Hugenberg in their decision to vote for Brüning. Hugenberg himself refused to be impressed by Hindenburg's threat, yet he was concerned about its effect on his party and the reluctance of many party colleagues to disavow publicly the president who was now tending toward the right. He proposed a postponement of the vote on certain conditions—among them the inclusion of the German Nationals in both the Reich and Prussian governments by that fall. When Brüning rejected these terms, Hugenberg suggested an unconditional three-months postponement of the decision. But Brüning, anxious to proceed with his program, insisted on an immediate vote.[18]

As anxious as Hugenberg was to avoid a showdown, he would not vote for the budget. The fact was that he was no longer the master of his own decisions. As he later explained to the German National leadership, he had received many warnings that he would lose large parts of his following to the Nazis if he supported the government. "We were facing a split one way or the other, we could not avoid taking a stand. Given this situation, you will understand why in view of the mood of the country . . . I made the known decision."[19]

That decision sealed the fate of the presidential budget decree. When its repeal was voted upon, 25 German National deputies supported the government and voted against repeal; 32, however, sided with Hugenberg—a number sufficient to provide a majority

18 Cab. mtg., July 14, 1930, RKz./1706/784383; on Hindenburg's threat to resign, Schiele, quoted in Jahrb. d. öff. Rechts, xxi (1933–34), 150; Meissner to Schiele, Mar. 9, 1931, BdRPr., R 54/298; Meissner, quoted in Saemisch diary, July 1930, Saemisch Papers/27.

19 Minutes of meetings of German National Reichstag delegation, July 17, 1930, minutes of party leadership meeting, July 24, 1930, Schmidt-Hannover Papers; Hugenberg, in Unsere Partei, Sept. 2, 1930; memorandum by Pünder on Hugenberg-Brüning negotiations, July 19, 1930, RKz., R 43 I/1870; als memorandum by Dietrich, July 17, 1930, Dietrich Papers/254/1.

of 14 (236:222) in favor of the repeal. Brüning had been empowered by Hindenburg to dissolve the Reichstag, and he did so at once. Again, there was no thought of resignation. Since the cabinet's commitment was to the president and not to the Reichstag, it ignored the parliament's verdict. In any event no other government could have been formed since the Social Democrats were hopelessly isolated. An appeal to the country was indeed the only solution—the nation would have to decide on the course it wished to pursue.

෴

The Reichstag had been dissolved because the contest between the presidential cabinet and parliament had reached a stalemate from which the election of a new Reichstag appeared as the only way out. There was no assurance, however, that a new Reichstag would prove more cooperative. Recent state and local elections suggested that the Nazis were likely to score major gains, drawing support away from the middle parties from which Brüning had obtained his basic support. The German National dissidents, on the other hand, would have little time to present themselves to the voters. Organized in the Conservative People's Party, they lacked both money and organization to launch an effective campaign.

Given this outlook, a recourse to the full weight of presidential authority seemed to offer the best chance of assuring the government of an electoral victory. The campaign thus had to be fought over the basic issue of presidential vs. parliamentary power, to decide whether the presidential regime, as conceived in the Brüning government, was to be retained or abandoned. This meant that the political role of the president ought to be the major campaign issue.

The group that understood this most clearly was the Conservative People's Party. It would be wrong, wrote the *Deutsche Tageszeitung*, which supported the new party, to try to keep Hindenburg out of the debate. To deny that he was largely responsible for the developments that led to the dissolution of the Reichstag would be a serious mistake. "All those who wish to strengthen the constitutional position of the German Reich President must see to it that Hindenburg's struggle against an excessive parliamentarism shall not be obscured." Hindenburg's emergency decrees could not be compared to those of Ebert; while Ebert had always had the approval of a Reichstag majority for his decrees, Hindenburg's had no such support, "they are consciously directed against an irresponsible parliamentarism." Westarp, Treviranus, and their associates voiced similar views. The campaign, a former general wrote to Schleicher, "must be fought over the question, 'For or against Hindenburg.' Hindenburg will have to draw a sharp line between himself and Hugenberg. Too much is at stake to be squeamish. . . ."[20]

Yet there were few outside the Conservative People's Party who shared these views. Some segments of the German People's Party voiced similar thoughts. "Does it not seem," mused the *Magdeburgische Zeitung*, "as if there were standing above this campaign, setting its tone and fixing its goal, one man who is stronger than all party officials put together? Is it not quite clear that this campaign, reduced to its simplest formula, means 'For or against Hindenburg'?" It was he who had dissolved the Reichstag and appealed to the nation and called on it to render its verdict "for or against him." "What matters," the editorial concluded, "is to broaden the narrow foundation which the cabinet had in the old Reichstag—the cabinet which rests on his trust." But the party leadership was divided on the question of Hindenburg's role in the campaign, and the issue gave rise to a heated debate in a meeting of its central directorate.

That meeting had been called to examine the draft of a campaign platform prepared by the party's executive committee. Mindful of the president's special role, the document mentioned the name of Hindenburg several times. At once objections were voiced against drawing the president into the campaign. "The President," one deputy warned, "enjoys the confidence of many who do not belong to the parties which voted for the emergency decrees. The national interest demands that this confidence be preserved. The national interest would be poorly served, were we to create a Presidential crisis in addition to a governmental and parliamentary one if the elections should not produce the results for which we hope." Curtius and others felt equally defeatist. Scholz, the party leader, expressed the predicament that confronted the government's backers: "I, too, don't like the idea of constantly using the name of Hindenburg. But I must point out that we cannot help mentioning him when we are to defend the decrees he has signed. Perhaps his name might be mentioned only once, not three times. . . . But it will be the main task of the new Reichstag to defend the decrees of the President. After all, this

20 P[aul] B[aecker], "Hindenburg als Führer," *Dt. Tageszeitung*, No. 339, July 22, 1930; Westarp quoted in *ibid.*, No. 402, Aug. 27, 1930; Treviranus, quoted in *Berliner Tageblatt*, No. 425, Sept. 9, 1930; Letter to Schleicher, July 22, 1930, Schleicher Papers/17,iii/6; als editorials in *Dt. Tageszeitung*, No. 352, July 29, 1930, No. 413, Sept. 3, 1930, No. 431, Sept. 13, 1930.

is why we are voting. We cannot very well ignore these matters." The party platform was amended accordingly, and the name of Hindenburg was used only sparingly in the party's campaign activities.[21]

The problem of centering the campaign on the president created still other complications. Not all of the middle parties were fully committed to him. The Democrats feared that the continued stress on his role might preclude any future coalition with the Socialists for which they continued to hope. Similarly the Center could not ignore altogether its participation in the Prussian Braun-Severing government. Nor did the Democrats change their mind when their leaders merged the party late in July with the *Jungdeutscher Orden*, one of the more moderate paramilitary organizations with whose help they hoped to revitalize their declining fortunes. Somehow, however, they now found it proper to display at their meetings both black-red-and-gold and black-white-and-red flags. This, as they staunchly proclaimed, was to show that their loyalty belonged to the state rather than to any special interest or pressure groups. While they would not use Hindenburg's name, they wished to embody his spirit. They also renamed their party the "State Party" to give further emphasis to their foremost concern.[22]

Like the State Party all other bourgeois parties professed to express that spirit of selfless dedication, of duty and righteousness, that the nation had come to associate with the marshal-president. Anxious to dissociate themselves from the discredited "interest groups," they hastened to assure their voters that they had always been opposed to "interest peddlers" and wished to serve no one but state and nation. It was a hopeless attempt, for it denied the very nature of these parties, and it was quickly defeated by the existing realities. When efforts were made to have these parties join a "Hindenburg bloc" or collaborate in a "Hindenburg program" (with or without mention of the president's name), vested interests, ideological differences, and personal rivalries frustrated all such endeavors. They produced nothing more than a few joint election appeals, and in one or two cases some limited technical collaboration.[23]

[21] *Magdeburgische Zeitung*, No. 432, Aug. 10, 1930; meeting of *Zentralvorstand* of German People's Party, Aug. 24, 1930, *Deutsche Volkspartei* Papers, R 45 II/142, pp. 32, 56, 62, 80.

[22] Hermann Höpker-Aschoff, in Gotthold Egelhaaf, *Politische Jahresübersichten* (hereafter cited as "Egelhaaf"), 1930, pp. 185–86; *Hannoverscher Kurier*, No. 408, Sept. 1, 1930; *General-Anzeiger für Dortmund*, No. 251, Sept. 12, 1930.

[23] Dietrich July 18, 1930, *Verhandlungen*, Vol. 428, pp. 6516–17; election campaign

Ultimately, the failure of these endeavors must be ascribed to Hindenburg himself. Since they centered around his person and policies, he alone could provide the integrating momentum to which party parochialism might have yielded. Beyond that a forthright stand on his part would have focused attention on the overriding issue of the campaign. If the country was to pass judgment on his exercise of his powers, it had to be told of the uses to which he had put them. Granted that age and office set limits to what he could do, they would still have allowed for some speeches and statements on his part. But the country neither saw nor heard him. Hindenburg refrained from any public involvement in the campaign. He seems to have shown some interest in the activities of the Conservative People's Party and had a few encouraging words for a visiting candidate of the moderate wing of the German Nationals; but as his office announced at his express request, "as a matter of principle the Reich President does not intervene in the election campaign."[24]

His passivity helped to blur further the issues of the election, for the explanation he gave for his silence rested on a confusion of his nonpartisan status with a nonpolitical one. While he was not beholden to any party or parties, his was not and had never been a nonpolitical office. Moreover, in recent months it had gained greatly in political import; if ever he had been merely an arbiter of the nation's problems, he was now its official leader: the Brüning government was "his" government, the budget decree a presidential decree, and the election revolved around his leadership. By dismissing it as another contest among the parties, he helped to obscure its real significance, and the task of Brüning and his supporters was rendered even more difficult.

It is unlikely that Hindenburg understood this. As always, he was anxious to steer clear of controversy, and he was also concerned that the people to whom he felt closest by background and upbringing would turn against him. Even now there were indications that many of his friends and associates disapproved of the course of developments. The Conservative League (*Hauptverein*

---

materials, in Hoover Institute, Munich Collection/26; Groener to Gleich, July 21, 1930, quoted in Bracher, *Auflösung*, p. 352 n. 71; Schleicher to Schulenburg, July 25, 1930, Schleicher Papers/17,iii/21; "Bericht über die Verhandlungen mit der DVP wegen Zusammenwirkens für das Hindenburg-Programm," n.d., Westarp Papers; Egelhaaf, 1930, pp. 195–96; "Meine Verhandlungen zwischen dem 18. Juli und 18. Oktober 1930," n.d., Westarp Papers.

24 Hindenburg, marginal comments on newspaper clippings, *BdRPr.*, R 54/297; Treviranus, statement of Feb. 5, 1953, ZS./630; Alvensleben to Schleicher, Aug. 7, 1930, Schleicher Papers/65/25; *Berliner Tageblatt*, No. 387, Aug. 18, 1930.

der Konservativen), the residual organization of the Conservative Party of Imperial days, urged its followers to support the German Nationals as the only monarchist party. The *Stahlhelm* to whose rescue he had gone only recently, left it up to its members whether to support Hindenburg by voting for the People's Conservatives or whether to cast their ballot for the Nazis or German Nationals. And the German Nationals busied themselves with publishing pro-Hugenberg statements by such wartime associates of the marshal as Field Marshal von Mackensen and Generals von Einem, Gallwitz, and Below. His old friend, Admiral von Schröder, in his capacity as chairman of the National League of German Officers, came out for Hugenberg. At the same time the German Nationals warned solemnly against the unwarranted use of Hindenburg's name, although they themselves had no hesitation in using it whenever it suited their purposes. Thus one German National leaflet protested against calling the Brüning government a "Hindenburg cabinet," on the grounds that every cabinet, even that of the Socialists Müller and Hilferding, had been appointed by the Reich president. In a brazen perversion of the facts it even claimed that the Brüning government was undermining Hindenburg's position by trying to destroy the German National Party, the "party of the Hindenburg voters." The president's silence encouraged these distortions; a word from him could have put a quick end at least to the worst ones.[25]

In spite of the fact that Hindenburg's inaction rendered the task of government much more difficult, Brüning discouraged even the issuing of a general appeal by the president to the voters. Such an appeal would at least have recalled to the public the fact that the marshal was the central figure on the political stage. Late in July, Loebell suggested that he publicly request Hindenburg to address such an appeal to the nation. The message was to "dispel the fog of mutual distrust, give new courage to those who had lost hope, and show them that no one group or class could free itself by itself from the present misery and that only loyal cooperation can save us." Meissner feared that a move of this kind would draw Hindenburg into the campaign and advised against it, but Hindenburg did not at once reject the proposal. He asked Brüning for his opinion and also inquired whether independently of any request by Loebell, president and government should issue a

25 Meissner, *Staatssekretär*, p. 384; Conservative League, resolution of Aug. 4, 1930, *Dt. Gesch.-Kal.*, 1930, A, 430–31; "Deutsche Heerführer über Hugenberg," election campaign materials, Munich Coll./26; article by Hans Hilpert, German National leaflet, *ibid.* German National election appeal, July 19, 1930, *Dt. Gesch.-Kal.*, 1930, A, 427.

joint proclamation. Brüning seems to have pondered the matter for a considerable time since his formal reply was not sent for six weeks, but in the end he declined both suggestions. He shared Meissner's misgivings about Loebell's plan, but wondered also about public reaction to an independent appeal. No matter how general its contents, a malevolent opposition might seize on it and denounce it as one-sided support, not only of the government, but also of the parties backing the government. The chancellor felt he could not afford to expose the president to such attacks. There was every prospect that the president would have to intervene later on to help settle the crisis; "in fact, the solution of the difficulties into which we are moving will most likely depend on his influence." Under these circumstances he thought it unwise to have recourse now to this ultimate and decisive influence and possibly weaken it prematurely.

Brüning knew that this was no ordinary election campaign, and as he granted himself, it would have been very desirable, for both domestic and foreign political reasons, to stress the president's leadership. It was, in fact, one of the great fears of the German Nationals that he might do so and thus force them to fight the campaign in open opposition to Hindenburg. He also knew that the campaign was not going well and that his efforts to beat back the relentless assaults of the Nazis and German Nationals did not have the desired effect. Even so he would not ask Hindenburg for that full and active support needed to point up the true issues of the campaign, and it is of course most unlikely that the president would have given him such unreserved backing.[26]

Hindenburg's inactivity was not the only obstacle to an effective government campaign. Had Brüning himself been a strong personality, his own forcefulness might have overcome the drawbacks of Hindenburg's silence. But this shy, withdrawn man was unable to arouse the nation whose support he so desperately needed. His aloofness, his sober realism, his dispassionate speeches did not appeal to the millions without jobs and hopes who wanted excitement and promises. In the words of the worried *Tagebuch*, "What Brüning lacks and what prevents him from strengthening his position to any decisive degree is contact with the country at large, with the people itself whose faith and confidence he should attempt to gain by all means. For if he wants to cope with the parties . . . he must mobilize those who stand above the parties—

[26] Meissner to Brüning, Aug. 1, 1930, Pünder to Meissner, Sept. 10, 1930, *RKz.*, R 43 I/576; Pünder to Warburg, Sept. 11, 1930, *ibid.*/580; German National Reichstag delegation, meetings of July 17, 1930, Schmidt-Hannover Papers.

the voters. He must enlist one hundred talented speakers able to defend his policies clearly and aggressively in the country, he must win the faith of the masses in thousands of articles in thousands of newspapers. . . . He must develop a comprehensive long-range program. . . ."

But to the end Brüning's speeches continued to suffer from a "chilling lack of blood," in the *Tagebuch*'s phrase, and he remained unable to convince the country that he had the "needed prescriptions, energies, passions." Nor was he able to find articulate spokesmen who could have communicated his aims to the country as effectively as thousands of Nazi speakers transmitted Hitler's. There were few stirring speakers among the advocates of the government's case.[27]

Without unity and coordination, moreover, the government camp presented a picture of confusion and inconsistency. The main battles of the campaign were fought over the issue of the democratic republic, and the fight between those who wished to see it preserved and those who hoped to destroy it extended right into the ranks of the cabinet. While Schiele expressed the hope that "this whole system would go to hell as soon as possible," Brüning and Kaas assured the electorate that the chancellor wished to safeguard democracy and was merely trying to discipline it. Similarly, Westarp and Treviranus maintained that Germany's salvation depended on the permanent exclusion of the Social Democrats from all political influence, but Brüning offered to work with anyone willing to serve the Fatherland. As Stresemann's heir and disciple Curtius tried to pursue a cautious and moderate foreign policy, yet Treviranus felt impelled to suggest that the time had come for a revision of Germany's border with Poland. Treviranus, in turn, was repudiated by Brüning who declared that Curtius and he were in charge of Germany's foreign policy and that "any such adventures were therefore out of the question." At the same time Center Party campaigners were instructed to assure their audiences that if the Center's foreign political tactics differed from those of Hugenberg, its goals were essentially the same.[28]

Inevitably these ambiguities conveyed an impression of inde-

[27] *Tagebuch*, June 28, 1930, pp. 1007–08, Sept. 27, 1930, pp. 1531–32.
[28] Schiele, quoted in *Berliner Tageblatt*, No. 420, Sept. 6, 1930; Kaas and Brüning, in Schulthess, July 29, 1930, pp. 184–85; Westarp, in *Ring*, July 30, 1930, p. 123; Treviranus, quoted in *Berliner Tageblatt*, No. 427, Sept. 10, 1930; Brüning in *ibid.*; Curtius, *Sechs Jahre*, pp. 165–66; Treviranus and Brüning in Horkenbach, *Dt. Reich*, Aug. 11, 1930, p. 317; Center Party, "Redeskizze," Aug. 1, 1930, p. 16, Munich Coll./26.

cision, and they sharpened the widespread fear that a government victory would produce still graver uncertainties. Coupled with Brüning's concern for a majority in the new Reichstag, such vacillations seemed to suggest the revival of the old parliamentary system with its sterile wrangling and arguing. Those who saw the country's salvation in an authoritarian regime were more certain than ever they ought not to support a government party; the inability of the People's Conservatives to elect a single deputy on their own strength was perhaps as much due to this fact as to the organizational and financial difficulties which the party experienced.[29]

Since Brüning could not be certain, moreover, of finding sufficient support on the right, he did not completely exclude the possibility of a future collaboration with the Socialists. Given his anti-Socialist mandate, he hesitated to turn to them openly, and the hints he threw out towards them were so vague that the Social Democrats could derive little comfort from them. Even so they provided Nazis and German Nationals with fresh ammunition in their anti-Marxist crusade.[30]

The election returns of September 14 revealed the strength of the nation's longing for determined leadership and authoritarian discipline. Despairing of Brüning's ability to provide them, many abandoned the parties that had supported him. Except for the Center and the Bavarian People's Party, which derived their cohesion from the spiritual discipline of the Catholic Church, and the agrarian *Landvolk* and the Economic Party which had not lost their material appeal, the moderate parties suffered a catastrophic defeat, and even the Center lost many young Catholics to the radical parties. The Nazi Party was the main beneficiary of this rout, and since it was most successful in mobilizing the new and non-voters, it emerged as the second strongest party with 107 deputies, compared to 12 deputies elected just two years before. Next to the Nazi Party, the Communists were the chief gainers in the election with 77, rather than 54 seats. They increased their vote partly at the expense of the Social Democrats and partly because of their effective appeal to new voters. The striking successes of both these parties were won on promises of strong pur-

[29] See the joint appeal of Conservative People's Party, Economic Party, and German People's Party, Aug. 21, 1930, Schulthess, Aug. 18, 1930, pp. 191–92; *Magdeburgische Zeitung*, No. 432, Aug. 10, 1930; Plehwe-Dworischken to Schleicher, Sept. 22, 1930, Schleicher Papers/69/31–32; also "Was sollen wir wählen?" *Ring*, Aug. 10, 1930, p. 558.
[30] See the Braun-Brüning debate, in *Berliner Tageblatt*, No. 415, Sept. 3, 1930; No. 419, Sept. 5, 1930; No. 423, Sept. 8, 1930; No. 427, Sept. 10, 1930.

poseful leadership and radical changes, and demonstrated how inadequately the new presidential regime had presented its case to the nation.[31]

ᗡ

There were few, however, who interpreted the election results in this sense. According to the general consensus, the returns reflected the breakdown of the democratic-parliamentary system and the disavowel of the Brüning government as the embodiment of that system.[32]

Of those opposing the parliamentary system, large numbers had never had, or had quickly lost, faith in Brüning (and, ultimately in Hindenburg too), and they were looking for another leader to guide them out of the existing impasse. Among them there were those who detested the freedom of Weimar democracy and were casting about for a "strong man" who would assign them their fixed place in state and society. There were others whom the deepening crisis had plunged into helpless despair and who were longing for the savior who would restore their jobs and their self-respect. Still others set their hopes on an authoritarian regime to keep the masses and their aspirations in check, and some simply fought the republic from wanton destructiveness. But beyond all personal motivations, there were many who hoped that a strong charismatic leader would show them the way once more to national power and greatness.

From all these elements Hitler had drawn his following in the elections. For this man of the masses who had emerged from the obscurity of the Viennese slums and the trenches of World War I, a social misfit himself who throve on crisis and chaos, had a superb flair for expressing the hopes and anxieties of a despairing people. He had long been aware of the German longing and need for strong leadership, and he was confident that he was the leader to rescue the country from the morass into which ineptness and treason had pushed it. This self-assurance lent his campaign its immense forcefulness, and his confidence that victory would be inevitably his increased the fury of his attacks.[33]

Hitler was as certain that Hindenburg had no leadership gifts

[31] Morsey, in Matthias and Morsey, *Ende der Parteien*, p. 297; Milatz, in *ibid.*, pp. 753–54.

[32] See press comment, in *Dt. Gesch.-Kal.*, 1930, A, 389–94; ∴, "Die kalte Revolution," *Tat*, XXII (1930), pp. 484–511.

[33] Hitler, speech before *Völkischer Führerring*, in Thuringia, early 1927, *Records of the German National Socialist Labor Party* (hereafter cited as *"Nazi Party Records"*)/116/136456.

as he was sure of his own predestination. He felt deep contempt for the old marshal who represented to him the saturated contentment and the cautious timidity of the bourgeoisie. In his personal relations with Hindenburg feelings of contempt blended, however, with a strong sense of awe of this elderly man. Hitler never overcame a distinct uneasiness in the presence of Hindenburg, for the president seemed so impressive a representative of that self-assured social elite from which he himself felt excluded. The old marshal, moreover, bore a striking physical resemblance to Hitler's father; Alois Hitler's powerful personality had overshadowed Adolf's youth, and the marked restraint and courtesy he was to show in his personal contacts with Hindenburg were quite possibly reflections of that old filial submission to a feared parent.[34]

But Hitler would not allow such personal feelings to affect his political judgment. He despised Hindenburg for using so sparingly the powers the Weimar Constitution had put at his disposal. When in 1928 the *Stahlhelm* proposed its referendum on the increase of the president's rights, Hitler rejected the plan. Such an amendment might reconcile many people to the Weimar state, he warned, but his main argument was that the step would be pointless: nothing would be gained by giving the president additional powers since he was the product of "democratic" elections and thus infected with the same flaccid spirit that poisoned the parliament. The Marxists, Hitler warned, would try to elect determined and brutal men; the bourgeois parties, true to their natural flabbiness, would pick "mollusk-like weaklings, ignorant, unimaginative old men, or cowardly worshipers of the existing situation . . . Any attempt to transform a weakling into a pillar of strength by legal manipulations is self-deception . . . The history of the leading minds of the German bourgeoisie from Bethmann Hollweg . . . to Hindenburg should disabuse anyone"; men born to rule would not need the guidance and the support of parliamentary institutions, nor would they permit constitutional checks to limit their freedom of action in times of crisis; someone selected by others to become the "dictator," who would accept his task on condition that his constitutional powers be expanded, would never accomplish anything. Obviously so weak a man lacked that higher compelling call for such a mission. Hindenburg, then, was much too passive, too indecisive, too ready for compromise, to be the nation's leader and savior. Or

[34] Andreas Dorpalen, "Hitler—Twelve Years After," *Review of Politics*, xix (1957), 493-94, 498.

as Hitler put it on another occasion: "Only a hero can be a leader."[35]

However deeply he despised the marshal, during the early years of Hindenburg's presidency Hitler confined such critiques to the privacy of personal letters or closed meetings. His contempt for the president did not blind him to the fact that Hindenburg's stature was such that open attacks on him would alienate many potential supporters. By 1929, however, the Nazis felt that his prestige had declined sufficiently to permit public criticisms of him. One of their deputies, Count Reventlow, assailed him by name in a Reichstag debate; he spoke bluntly of Hindenburg's lack of political understanding and judgment, and claimed that every one of his decisions had been suggested to him by his entourage. His charges were circulated as suitable campaign material by the party's official speakers bureau, and they were followed up by sharp editorials in the party press. "Is Hindenburg Still Alive?" ran a headline condemning his acceptance of the Young Plan. "The helpless stammer of the President leaves us cold," sneered another paper in dismissing his defense of the step. Losing all self-control, a third grimly predicted that "we can see the day when the curse of an entire nation will echo across the grave of an old man." The Nazis revealed the full measure of their hatred when they wished to see Hindenburg among those whom the proposed Freedom Law threatened with imprisonment should they accept the Young Plan.[36]

Their contempt was directed not only against the person of the cautious president, but as much against those bourgeois concerns—law, order, property—of which Hindenburg, that epitome of stability, was the most venerable symbol. For millions, faced with unemployment and penury, these values were losing their meaning. Bewildered and helpless, they were ready to embrace the ideology of those homeless and rootless war veterans who had never found a place in civilian society and had turned their back on civil pursuits and aspirations. Having lost their livelihood, they took comfort in scoffing at those material ambitions they could no longer satisfy. The goals Hitler held out to them,

[35] Hitler to *Stahlhelm* leaders, spring of 1929 (copy), *Nazi Party Records*/116/ 136556-77, esp. 136560, 136565, 136566; same, quoted in *Tagebuch*, June 14, 1930, p. 932.

[36] Reventlow, Nov. 30, 1929, *Verhandlungen*, Vol. 426, pp. 3344-45, also Apr. 3, 1930, *ibid.*, Vol. 427, p. 4765; speakers' campaign material, in *Nazi Party Records*/ 63/72248; editorials quoted in Wheeler-Bennett, *Wooden Titan*, p. 332, and by Wirth, June 17, 1930, *Verhandlungen*, Vol. 428, pp. 5521; also Wilhelm Weiss, in *Nationalsozialistische Monatshefte*, I (1930), 133-34.

transcending the drabness of everyday life, made their own problems seem unimportant. "Individuals are like leaves," he told
them, "they are green today, they wilt and rot, and new leaves are
growing. We live, we must remain, our German people must
remain—this is the eternal, the permanent value that must be preserved." Most people considered themselves much too important,
he complained, and he assured them that position and money did
not matter: "We all must learn once more to think generously,
we must once more become selfless, and the German people must
learn again to live without envy." If they did, glorious vistas of
national and human greatness were awaiting them: "A new spirit
will come alive in the German people and will take up the struggle against the decay of the world." There was here a new dynamism, a self-certainty and breadth of view that contrasted
sharply with the cautious restraint, the dry and sober realism
with which bourgeois speakers addressed themselves to their audiences. They imparted to Hitler's rapt listeners a new sense of
mission and seemed to release them from the dreariness of their
present existence.[37]

Yet whatever hope his speeches inspired, they did not promise
an easier, more prosperous future. What he saw ahead was hard-
ship and danger: "The road a people must travel if it wishes to
scale greater heights, is not the road of comfort and ease, but the
road of relentless struggle. . . . Everything on this earth is strife
and struggle. Work and struggle are two concepts which are in
reality one and the same. The nation which makes the greatest
sacrifices will achieve the most." Not order and security, then,
were the touchstones of the good life, nor the welfare of its
citizens the prime objective for the good state, but the readiness
of the citizen to die for his country.[38] Similar views were expressed
by a multitude of other writers and speakers. As one exultantly
put it, "The bourgeois who rules today by way of his business
is going to be replaced by the warrior. His world—this is the
unshakable faith of a young frontline generation—will be rebuilt
in the spirit of the soldier,—that spirit which draws its inspiration
from authority and ability, command and obedience, responsibility and subordination." It would be a world in which status

[37] Konrad Heiden, *Der Fuehrer* (Boston, 1944), pp. 272–73; E. Günther Gründel,
*Die Sendung der jungen Generation: Versuch einer umfassenden revolutionären
Sinndeutung der Krise* (Munich, 1932), p. 452; Hitler, at Eutin, May 6, 1931, *Nazi
Party Records/176/317915–16.*

[38] Speeches of Feb. 5, 1928, Apr. 12, 1931, in Gordon W. Prange, ed., *Hitler's
Words* (Washington, 1944), pp. 8, 13; Adolf Hitler, *Mein Kampf* (New York, 1941),
pp. 407–08.

would be based on honor rather than money and in which there would be neither caste nor class. It would also be a world which in its militant restlessness and repudiation of all established values would tear down the very foundations of bourgeois society, but this prospect his followers denied or shrugged off. Many saw anyhow little in bourgeois society that seemed worth preserving.[39]

Hitler's overwhelming success thus was not due to the worsening economic crisis alone. In his very ruthlessness he expressed and appealed to the revolt against contemporary society, the sense of moral despair that was shaping the thinking of substantial parts of the nation and propelled them into nihilist daydreams and a repudiation of that soldierly order and discipline which Hindenburg had always embodied. The marshal's apolitical conservative world rested on a social hierarchy that the bulk of the nation had come to reject. Responding to this popular mood, Hitler created within the framework of the Nazi Party and stormtroops a new type of "political soldier" that satisfied both the need for political activism and for soldierly discipline.[40]

The full measure of disillusionment in these groups can be gleaned from their willingness to surrender their most cherished beliefs. They had always prided themselves in their staunch defense of the state, the symbol of national power and greatness, which existed beyond party politics and economic concern. They had fought the republic because to their mind it permitted a selfish society to subvert the integrity of the state. Nevertheless they did not object when the Nazis proposed to reduce the state to a mere instrument of the people. Nor did the Nazis leave any doubt as to their real intentions. The *Nationalsozialistische Monatshefte*, the doctrinal organ of the party, took issue with the view of the state as an end in itself and declared that that concept merely called forth a civil and military bureaucracy. Hitler too dismissed the state as a technical apparatus that could be discarded at will if it no longer met the needs of the nation. He also rejected the ideal of a nonpolitical army whose loyalty belonged to the state as such, and openly urged the Reichswehr to place its loyalty to the nation, as personified in his movement, above any obligation it might have to a "rotten and decaying state."[41]

---

[39] Gründel, *Sendung*, pp. 321–22, 330–31; cf. also Heiden, *Fuehrer*, pp. 309–10, 351–52; Peter F. Drucker, *The End of Economic Man* (New York, 1939), pp. 191–92.
[40] Hitler, before *Völkischer Führerring, Nazi Party Records*/116/136458–59; campaign materials, Jan. 15, 1930, *ibid.*/63/72181; Friedrich Wilhelm Heinz, *Die Nation greift an: Geschichte und Kritik des soldatischen Nationalismus* (Berlin, 1932), p. 11.
[41] *Nationalsozialistische Monatshefte*, II (1931), p. 522; Hitler, *Mein Kampf*, pp. 592–96; same, before *Völkischer Führerring, Nazi Party Records*/116/136461; Reichs-

The effectiveness of this appeal was demonstrated in the fall of 1930, at the trial of three Reichswehr officers who had sought to persuade their fellow officers not to fire on Nazis in the event of an armed rising. This trial revealed that Nazis sympathies were fairly widespread among the Reichswehr's junior officers and that discontent thus was spreading into the very structure of the state. The army trial also disclosed that the attraction of Nazism for many young officers lay in its activism much more than in hopes for promotion and glory. "Junior officers are drawn to the Nazis," a naval officer reported to Schleicher, ". . . not because of better material prospects under a Nazi government; they may not even think of the need for a livelihood. They feel attracted to the Nazis, not because of the latter's program, but rather because they believe that they can see here an effective force determined to prevent the collapse of the Reich—because for lack of proper instruction they see only aimlessness on our side."[42]

Action as such, not its purpose, seemed to become all-important. Among the unemployed millions, among those faced with the imminent loss of their jobs, among businessmen confronted with bankruptcy, and among farmers fearful of foreclosure of their farms—everywhere the feeling was spreading that one could not wait any longer and that "something had to be done." Any action seemed better than continued inaction and non-Nazis, liberals as well as conservatives, agreed. Finance Minister Dietrich, of the Democratic Party, stated openly in the Reichstag that it did not matter so much how something was being done, as that something was being done, and even the cautious Hindenburg was soon to boast that he had let himself be guided in his decisions by the principle of the old Prussian *Felddienstordnung* that any action was better than no action at all.[43]

Under these circumstances it did not matter that the Nazi program was vague and its promises contradictory. "Our task cannot be," Alfred Rosenberg, the party philosopher, announced in the

---

wehr speech of Mar. 15, 1929, reprinted in Schüddekopf, *Heer und Republik,* p. 281.

[42] Verdict in trial of Reichswehr officers, *Justiz,* VI (1930), 194–95. Significantly the defendants gave no thought to the fact that they were defying the authority of their commander in chief, Hindenburg. Nor did the person of the marshal-president play any role in the trial or in the ensuing parliamentary and press debates. Cf. Bracher, *Auflösung,* p. 282 n. 189. See also naval officer to Schleicher, Jan. 17, 1930, Schleicher Papers/34,ii/94–95; Maj. Gen. Friedrichs, statement of Aug. 1951, ZS./171; Richard Scheringer, *Das grosse Los unter Soldaten, Bauern und Rebellen* (Hamburg, 1959), pp. 174–99.

[43] Dietrich, July 18, 1930, *Verhandlungen,* Vol. 428, p. 6515; Hindenburg to Berg, Feb. 25, 1932, *Vierteljahrshefte für Zeitgeschichte,* VIII (1960), 81; also Brüning, in Schulthess, Aug. 4, 1931, p. 173.

Völkischer Beobachter, "to jabber in detail about the things which grow out of our *Weltanschauung* and to expound our theories. All this must burst out of the National Socialist oak." Presented with enthusiastic self-assurance, the program carried conviction despite its vagueness and inconsistencies. "We don't want lower bread prices," one party speaker told a rapt small-town rally, "we don't want higher bread prices, we don't want unchanged bread prices—we want National Socialist prices!" His solution was greeted with enthusiastic applause although he would have been hard put to say what it actually meant. But it did seem to promise some change, and the Fuehrer, strong, wise, inspired, would know how to carry it out. "The psychosis to which the September elections have testified," noted the *Tagebuch,* "revolved around the [three] words: Things must change! In such manic drive people can succumb to terrifying illusions as to what kind of change there ought to be, which one is possible, and which one useful."[44]

If the vagueness of its program did not hamper the party's growth, neither did the tarnished reputations of many of its members. It was widely known that among the party leaders there were many unsavory elements—ex-convicts, sex perverts, blackmailers; the newspapers were full of the intrigues and scandals that rocked the party in unending succession. People either refused to believe these reports or were ready to shrug off such matters as the price to be paid for the movement's redemptive energies. In the words of the writer Ernst Jünger, perhaps the best known of the ideologists of the radical right, the bourgeois need for security was no longer strong enough to hold back those elemental demonic forces that are not ruled and controlled by reason. "Danger . . . dominates our time," he exulted, ". . . There is a need for a new order which encompasses the extraordinary—an order which does not aim at the elimination of danger, but owes its emergence to a new fusion of life and danger." It would be an order in which, as Hitler stoutly predicted, war and peace would be one.[45]

How fully he meant this, his followers did not perceive. For they did not understand that the man to whom they were looking for their salvation saw in them nothing more than the "raw ma-

44 Drucker, *End of Economic Man,* pp. 17–18, 13–14; Rosenberg, quoted by Tarnow, Feb. 12, 1931, *Verhandlungen,* Vol. 444, p. 961; Leopold Schwarzschild, in *Tagebuch,* Mar. 14, 1931, p. 402.

45 Ernst Jünger, *Der Arbeiter: Herrschaft und Gestalt* (Hamburg, 1932), pp. 46–50, 55–56; General Jodl, in Office of U.S. Chief Counsel for Prosecution of Axis Criminality, *Nazi Conspiracy and Aggression* (Hereafter cited as *"Nazi Conspiracy"*) (Washington, 1948), VII, 668–69; Hitler, in Schüddekopf, *Heer und Republik,* pp. 281–82.

terial" from which he could forge the weapon with which to rebuild his world. Individually, they were to him mere bricks for the structure, and as such they could, as he had boasted with cynical frankness in *Mein Kampf*, be used and molded at will. Although there were implications in his words that as individuals he thought them expendable, he skillfully obscured his contempt for them by his impassioned appeals to their national mission. He was careful, moreover, to conceal the full scope of his plans. His real intentions he confided to only a handful of individuals and these were carefully chosen and either lacked the intelligence to grasp what he meant or were willing to go along with their Fuehrer wherever he decided to take them. And had any one of them spoken up and revealed Hitler's true designs, they most likely would have been taken no more seriously than were his own ominous hints and allusions.[46]

[46] Hitler, *Mein Kampf*, pp. 477, 576–77, 583, 678–79, 847–49; Dorpalen, "Hitler," pp. 499–501.

CHAPTER 7

THE BRÜNING ERA:

PARLIAMENTARY DICTATORSHIP

ANY may have been wondering what course the country ought to pursue after the September elections, but Hindenburg did not share their uncertainty. He was determined to keep Brüning as chancellor, and so was the trusted Schleicher. Two days after the elections, Brüning could report to the cabinet that the president had decided to retain the government in its present form. Hindenburg wondered, however, whether some German Nationals should not enter the cabinet, and Brüning promised to explore the feasibility of such an arrangement.[1]

It is doubtful that the chancellor considered an accommodation with Hugenberg likely, but since he was more than ever dependent on the marshal's support, he had to make the attempt. The effort was wasted. Hugenberg renewed his demand for the elimination of the Socialist-led government in Prussia—a price that Brüning was neither willing nor able to pay. Even if he had done so, he still would have been without a majority, for the German Nationals were no longer strong enough to provide it by their support. Unable to reach an agreement with Hugenberg, the chancellor offered to resign, but Hindenburg would not hear of it.

While the president regretted Brüning's inability to come to terms with the German Nationals, he had no such qualms about the chancellor's failure to reach an understanding with Hitler. He thoroughly disliked the loud-mouthed, unrestrained Nazi leader, and the noisy emotional meetings and demonstrations of Hitler's followers were abhorrent to his orderly mind. Hitler, moreover, asked for the posts of Reichswehr minister and minister of the interior for two of his followers, and this the marshal found unacceptable.[2]

[1] Cab. mtg., Sept. 16, 1930, *RKz.*/1707/784833; Noeldechen in *Vierteljahrshefte,* I (1953), 273; Schleicher to Reichswehr commanders, Oct. 25, 1930, *ibid.,* II (1954), 407; Hindenburg and Meissner, "Niederschrift über die Entwicklung der Krise und Demission des Kabinetts Brüning," June 10, 1932, in Vogelsang, *Reichswehr,* p. 459.
[2] Cab. mtgs., Sept. 29, Oct. 4, 1930, *RKz.*/1707/784989, 785031; Westarp, "Meine Verhandlungen," Westarp Papers; memorandum by Pünder, Dec. 3, 1930, Schleicher

As matters stood, Brüning could secure a majority only with the votes of the Social Democrats. In his entourage there was some sentiment in favor of taking them into the government, and for a moment the chancellor himself may have toyed with this thought. He received encouragement for this plan from some unexpected quarters; the League of German Industrialists, shocked by the success of the Nazis, informed him that it felt he should look for support from the left; a memorandum of State Secretary Pünder on a talk with one of the League's board members suggests that that body would not have objected to the entry of Socialists into the cabinet. Similar suggestions reached the chancellor from other industrial circles, and Papen, the future chancellor, who saw him a few days later, learned that banking circles too had been urging Brüning to take some Social Democrats into his government. But Hindenburg, determined to stay on his course to the right, did not want to have any Socialists in the government, and his stand proved decisive.[3] Brüning set out to obtain the support of the Socialists without inviting them into his cabinet—a solution he preferred in any event since he wished to conduct his government without interference from a multitude of divergent party interests in the cabinet. What he looked for was party support rather than collaboration.[4]

To Brüning's relief the Socialists were quite prepared to support his government without participating in it. There had been demands for such a participation—Otto Braun had called for a "front of all reasonable people"—but his party friends preferred not to press the point. They had learned of the chancellor's plans to reduce unemployment relief and other social benefits, and they did not wish to be associated with these measures. They were also aware of the great difficulties that Brüning was facing, and they knew with what hatred the right, including now the more moderate German People's Party, was looking upon them. Thus they threw their 143 votes in the Reichstag into the scales without attempting to obtain some pledge or concession from the chancellor. Their overriding concern was that any demands on their part might lead to Brüning's removal and that his departure from the chancellery would mean the end of German democracy. Hugenberg would

Papers/17,iii/35–36; Brüning in *Märkische Volkszeitung*, 3d Special Election Issue, July 1932, Hoover Institute.

[3] Pünder, *Reichskanzlei*, entries of Sept. 14, 16, 1930, pp. 59–60; memorandum by same, Sept. 15, 1930, *RKz.*, R 43 I/1308; Papen to Schleicher, Sept. 24, 1930, Schleicher Papers/69/6.

[4] Matthias, in Matthias and Morsey, *Ende der Parteien*, pp. 107–08; memorandum by Pünder, May 9, 1931, *RKz.*, R 43 I/678.

be his most likely successor, a memorandum of the Social Democratic Reichstag delegation warned, and Hugenberg would include the Nazis in his cabinet: "Such a Hugenberg-Hitler Government would not call the Nazis' bluff. A Hitler Government would follow the Italian example. This would mean the destruction of all labor organizations, a permanent state of military emergency, suspension of freedom of press and assembly and other political rights, constant danger of civil war at home and of a war of revenge abroad." [5]

While Brüning's political survival was thus assured, his position continued to be precarious. Hindenburg accepted his collaboration with the Socialists, and while Brüning doubtless explained to him that he had made no concessions to them, the very fact, that the chancellor was collaborating with them did bother him. Besides, he was left in no doubt by friends and associates about their reaction to Brüning's reliance on "Marxist" support. To the chancellor's dismay, moreover, even in his own camp there was opposition to his acceptance of help from the Socialists. On the opening day of the Reichstag, the Economic Party announced that it was asking Justice Minister Bredt to resign from the cabinet to "facilitate" the government's reorganization. But Hindenburg came to Brüning's aid and let it be known that he was not willing to make any changes at the request of a Reichstag delegation, and Bredt remained in the cabinet.

More ominous was the attitude of the opposition parties. The Nazis staged a series of anti-Semitic demonstrations in various parts of Berlin, beating up Jews and smashing the windows and showcases of Jewish firms. Abusing their parliamentary immunity, Nazi deputies appeared in the Reichstag clad in their brown uniforms, in open defiance of a law against the wearing of party uniforms in public. At once they set out to sabotage all orderly discussion: the Reichstag had long been notorious for its lack of self-discipline and discourtesies, but the insults and epithets which rang through its halls during those opening days were unprecedented even in the tortured history of German parliamentarism. The obvious purpose was to render the Reichstag unable to fulfill its proper function and undermine what little prestige it still enjoyed in the country. At the same time the extremists hoped to destroy the authority of the Brüning government since it could not be removed by a no-confidence vote. [6]

[5] Hilferding, in *Gesellschaft*, VII (1930), ii, 296; Mierendorff, in *Sozialistische Monatshefte*, LXXII (1931), 315; memorandum in Stampfer, *Vierzehn Jahre*, pp. 580–81.

[6] Schulthess, Oct. 13, 1930, pp. 202–03; Pünder, *Reichskanzlei*, entry of Oct. 15, 1930, pp. 66–67.

While the Nazis relied on verbal and physical disturbances to bring down Brüning, *Stahlhelm* and German Nationals tried to arouse the president against him. Their first effort was launched at the *Stahlhelm's* annual congress that fall. Over 100,000 of its members gathered at Koblenz in the recently liberated Rhineland in the presence of the ex-Crown Prince, General von Seeckt, and other "national" dignitaries. In a resolution accepted by acclamation, the meeting demanded the elimination, by means of a referendum, of the "sterile Marxist dictatorship" in Prussia and the assumption by Hindenburg of the post, newly to be created, of state president of Prussia. Hindenburg was to be impressed with the widespread demand for removal of the Socialist-Center government in Prussia in the hope that he would bow to this display of popular disapproval, put an end to Brüning's continued collaboration with the Social Democrats, and insist on the inclusion of the right in the Reich government. Once the Braun government had been removed in Prussia, the Social Democrats would no longer control the Prussian police. With Hindenburg at the head of the Prussian state, the police force would be entrusted to the right, and Brüning, should he still be the chancellor, would find himself outflanked since the new police commanders would not be available to help him enforce his emergency decrees.[7]

The German Nationals in the Reichstag followed a similar line. A "Hindenburg cabinet," they complained, should have nothing to do with the Socialist government in Prussia, and the leader of their delegation, Dr. Oberfohren, described the Brüning cabinet as the "most repudiated" of all Weimar governments. The most trenchant criticism, however, was voiced by Hindenburg's old friend, Oldenburg-Januschau. The old Junker acted as a sort of liaison officer between the German Nationals and the president, on the assumption, not fully justified, that he had the president's ear. Taking his turn in the Reichstag debate, Oldenburg announced, for Hindenburg's benefit, that "the Prussian Government does not have the confidence of agriculture." He was also entrusted with the rather more sensitive task of driving a wedge between the president and Reichswehr Minister Groener. Discussing the trial against the three Reichswehr officers, he charged that Groener had humiliated the army by permitting the arrest of the three offenders in front of their regiment. By tolerating such a procedure, Oldenburg added, Groener had also abused the authority and prestige of Field Marshal von Hindenburg.

[7] Schulthess, Oct. 5, 1930, p. 200; Ludwig Preller, *Sozialpolitik in der Weimarer Republik* (Stuttgart, 1949), p. 393.

Oldenburg knew that the president felt uneasy about that disturbing incident and had tried to wash his hands of the matter. Hindenburg had allowed the word to be passed that he too considered improper the manner in which the officers had been arrested, and had made a characteristic conciliatory gesture. While he could not grant the defendants a pardon lest the army's discipline suffer, he insisted that the public announcement make clear that he had rejected the officer's plea merely "for the time being." Nevertheless he strongly resented Oldenburg's complaints. Whatever his qualms, he would not tolerate attempts to endanger the army's authority. He had Brüning assure the Reichstag of his full confidence in Groener, and he requested Oldenburg to go at least through the motions of an apology to both Brüning and Groener.[8]

Undismayed by this setback, the German Nationals persisted in their attacks on the government. They kept assailing it for its "creeping socialism," its inadequate assistance to agriculture, and its failure to give the "national" elements a voice in the cabinet. They impugned its integrity for retaining men lacking in the proper "national" spirit, such as Foreign Minister Curtius, Interior Minister Wirth, and the much maligned Groener. As they had hoped, these charges had their effect on Hindenburg. In December Groener wrote to a friend that the president was considering the dismissal of Wirth. He also wanted Baron von Neurath, the ambassador to Britain, to take Curtius' place since Curtius had long been anathema to the "national" parties. But Brüning was able to convince him that any cabinet changes would be inopportune, and he relented once more.

If Hindenburg was willing to consider rightist complaints in matters of foreign policy and domestic administration, he was less receptive to criticisms pertaining to agriculture. Despite the substantial relief measures which the government had granted to the agrarians, complaints and petitions continued to pour into the Presidential Palace, and a never-ending stream of individual callers and delegations tried to arouse Hindenburg's distrust of the chancellor's competence and good faith. As always, Hindenburg would patiently listen to these complaints, but while on earlier

---

[8] Schmidt-Hannover, Oct. 18, 1930, Oberfohren, Oct. 17, 1930, *Verhandlungen*, Vol. 444, pp. 79, 144; Oldenburg, Oct. 18, 1930, *ibid.*, pp. 166–67; Brüning, *ibid.*, p. 174; Oldenburg to Groener, n.d., *Vossische Zeitung*, No. 498, Oct. 23, 1930; Meissner to Schleicher, Oct. 7, 1930, Schleicher Papers/35/131–32; "Vortragsnotiz," Oct. 1930, *ibid.*/1/55; Brüning, "Ein Brief," p. 5. Actually care had been taken that the officers were not arrested in front of their regiment (see the statement by *Landgerichtsdirektor* Braune, in Vogelsang, *Reichswehr*, p. 417), but the contrary rumor was widely believed.

occasions he had simply promised to take up all grievances with the chancellor, he now came to Brüning's defense. This, after all, was "his" government, and he insisted that chancellor and cabinet were doing their best and had already achieved a good deal for agriculture. He also rejected suggestions that the cabinet was prejudiced against large estate owners in its relief measures and that it applied political tests to the officials in charge of the aid program. And for once he refused to put pressure on the government to expand and speed up its agrarian assistance. He was certain that Schiele, his personal choice, was providing whatever help he could get. (His confidence was not misplaced; Schiele did force his colleagues to make many concessions against their better judgment, threatening more than once to resign should he not have his way. Hindenburg had another effective supporter in Groener who always obtained specific instructions from him on the stand he should take in the cabinet on agricultural matters.) For once Hindenburg also aknowledged the fact that agriculture was only part of the German economy and that it could be rehabilitated only within the framework of the entire economy. "Herr von Hindenburg is very quiet and does not press us," Pünder noted in his diary in November while a new agrarian relief program was under discussion. "He realizes that Brüning has to distribute his several 'candies' *at the same time* so that the whole can be saved." [9]

Other indictments that came from the right he continued to accept at face value. That winter a Berlin movie house showed the picture "All Quiet on the Western Front," a realistic and moving presentation of wartime conditions at the front and at home. Nazi demonstrations were organized to obtain its withdrawal on the grounds that it slandered the German army, and Hindenburg too was urged to intervene. He took up the question with Otto Braun since this was a Prussian police matter. Braun who saw nothing objectionable in the picture suggested that Hindenburg have it shown to him. There was no need for that, Hindenburg replied, since his information had been supplied to him by a competent authority. Besides, there was ample evidence of its objectionable character in the bitter indignation it had aroused

[9] Groener to Gleich, Dec. 28, 1930, *Dt. Rundschau*, LXXVI (1950), 1015; materials in *RKz.*, R 43 I/1805, 2545, esp. Hindenburg to Eulenburg-Prassen, Nov. 20, 1930 (copy), and memorandum by Meissner on Hindenburg's conference with Landbund delegation, Dec. 9, 1930; Pünder, *Reichskanzlei*, entries of Nov. 13, Dec. 2, 1930, pp. 73, 78 (italics in original); Schiele, in cab. mtg., Mar. 31, 1931, *RKz.*/1683/786363; on Groener's attitude towards agricultural issues, see Eschenburg, "Rolle der Persönlichkeit," p. 11.

in the national youth.[10] (The picture was withdrawn after further disturbances and demonstrations; the Nazis broke up one showing by letting loose hundreds of white mice in the theatre.)

Hindenburg's greatest fear was that the embittered nation would turn against him. He spent countless hours drafting memoranda and letters that he never mailed in which he defended his policies or tried to assign responsibility for policies where he believed it belonged. "How is history going to judge me?" he mused in an unguarded moment. "I lost the greatest war. I was unable to help my people which called me to the most responsible post in its gift. . . ." And as always he answered resignedly: "I believe the most important thing is to try to do your duty as best you can." [11]

Yet what was his duty? In the days of the Empire, there had always been somebody to tell him—his teachers, his commanding officer, his Emperor, and during the war the self-assured Ludendorff. During the early years of his presidency the Weimar Constitution had provided some guidance; his functions, moreover, had been primarily ceremonial ones. But now the constitution had become largely inoperative, the Reichstag had abdicated its legislative functions, and the ultimate decisions rested with him. Unable to make these decisions on his own, he had to rely on his three main advisers. Fortunately this trio—Schleicher, Meissner, and Brüning—were in basic agreement on the policies to be pursued. As a newcomer Brüning did not enjoy the president's confidence in the same degree as did the two others whom the marshal had known for years, but they both backed him effectively and helped him convince the president of the propriety and necessity of the measures he proposed. Schleicher, by background and training closest to Hindenburg, could discuss with him the chancellor's plans in terms the marshal could understand, while Brüning's penchant for highly technical explanations often left him bewildered and irritated. The general, moreover, provided a link to the right, and his advice was valued therefore as a reinsurance against importunities from that quarter. Meissner, on the other hand, as the legal expert, provided the guarantees that the contemplated measures were constitutionally unobjectionable.

In spite of their agreement on the immediate measures to be adopted, the three men differed in motives and objectives. Meissner, as the servant of his master, was primarily concerned

---

10 Braun, *Von Weimar*, pp. 314–15.

11 Information from Dr. Zechlin; Gert von Hindenburg, *Paul von Hindenburg: Vom Kadetten zum Reichspräsidenten* (Leipzig, 1932), p. 232.

with protecting the latter's rights and easing his duties. Schleicher, the army's spokesman, was anxious to strengthen the Reichwehr and guard it against the risks of a civil war. Brüning's objective was to balance the budget and practice rigid economies as the best way of restoring the country's economic health and stability. Both Schleicher and Meissner supported him because his policies promised to further their own plans as well. Yet the divergence of their primary interests was the source of some difficulties even then and eventually did lead to the breakup of their collaboration.

One of Schleicher's foremost concerns was to achieve a *modus vivendi* with the Nazis. Outwardly a glib cynic, Schleicher was a high-strung individual whose moods varied from cheerful self-confidence to spells of deepest anxiety. The continued growth of the Nazis presented special problems with which Schleicher in his emotional instability could not easily cope. He was pleased with the military ardor of the stormtroopers and welcomed them as a manpower reservoir for the Reichswehr, but he worried about the increasing hostility developing between the government and the stormtroopers. His greatest fear was that the struggle between the government and the Nazi Party might eventually explode into a civil war in which the army would have to fire on fellow Germans—a duty it would find the more distasteful since pro-Nazi sympathies kept spreading among junior officers and enlisted men. But an even more terrifying thought kept haunting him: the Nazis and Communists would rise simultaneously and with the Reichswehr engaged in putting down these internal revolts, Poland might send troops across the border to seize German territory. Schleicher urged Brüning therefore to use caution in his dealings with the Nazis, and the chancellor was forced to assume a more passive attitude toward them than he might have done otherwise. Meissner too favored closer contacts with Hitler, and while for the time being neither he nor Schleicher saw any possibility of taking the Nazis into the government, their attitude was not without effect on Hindenburg. Ever reluctant to take strong measures, the president became even more opposed now to any forcible repression of Nazi activities whenever this question was raised.[12]

The chancellor thus had to proceed with great patience and subtlety to achieve his objectives. His task was rendered more difficult still by the fact that these objectives were rather elusive.

[12] Brüning, "Ein Brief," pp. 3–6; information from Dr. Zechlin; Eschenburg, "Rolle der Persönlichkeit," p. 13; Noeldechen, in *Vierteljahrshefte*, 1 (1953), 268–69, 273; cab. mtgs., Oct. 30, 1930, *RKz.*/1707/785226–30, Dec. 19, 1930, 785532–37.

Basically there were two, and they were mutually related. Domestically he strove to cope with the economic crisis, while in foreign affairs he was aiming primarily at a reduction, if not cancellation, of the reparation payments. A revision of the Young Plan would in turn alleviate the country's economic difficulties; yet in order to achieve this he thought it imperative to balance the budget and keep the currency stable. This obligation Germany had assumed when she accepted the Young Plan, and unless she lived up to it, he feared he might be unable to convince the creditor nations of the need for any reparations revisions. In addition the chancellor considered strict retrenchment imperative to assure Germany's competitiveness in the world market. More than ever she depended on exports to finance her imports and fulfill her reparations obligations. Reduced public expenditures, salary cuts, and tax increases finally were required because any other policy would have inflationary effects, and Brüning was determined to avoid any semblance of an inflation. After the tragic experiences of the early nineteen-twenties, any hint of a new inflation might create an uncontrollable panic that would plunge the country into social and political anarchy.[13]

Whether this fear was justified, no one can say. The deflationary effects of Brüning's financial and economic policies, on the other hand, were little short of disastrous. By slashing public expenditures, by lowering wages and salaries, and by further decreasing unemployment benefits, he reduced what purchasing power there remained; the demand for goods kept dwindling away, and unemployment increased. Price cuts proved an ineffectual remedy since they never kept pace with the decreases in wages. In part this was due to the fact that in many cases wages and salaries constituted only a comparatively small part of the cost of production, but the main reason was political. With Hindenburg shielding agriculture, agricultural prices were exempt from any reductions. Industry often fought off price cuts since the manufacturers were politically in a stronger bargaining position than workers or employees, let alone consumers.[14]

In addition to his many other concerns, Brüning also had to worry about preserving his frail majority in the Reichstag. Although that majority was no longer willing or able to enact any

13 Brüning, Oct. 16, 1930, Feb. 5, 1931, *Verhandlungen*, Vol. 444, pp. 17–22, 680; same in cab. mtg., Oct. 2, 1931, *RKz.*/1685/788363, and in Schulthess, Nov. 5, 1931, pp. 247–48; Wolfgang J. Helbich, "Between Stresemann and Hitler: The Foreign Policy of the Brüning Government," *World Politics*, XII (1959), 32–35, 38–39; Bracher, *Auflösung*, p. 381.

14 Ferdinand Fried, in *Tat*, XXII (1930), pp. 657–59; Bracher, *Auflösung*, p. 405.

legislation for him, he still depended on it to ward off efforts to repeal his decrees or to pass a no-confidence vote. Of the parties supporting him, the Social Democrats, though numerically the most important group, caused him the least concern. While they objected to his financial and economic policies, they were compelled to support him. A break with Brüning would have been followed immediately by the breakup of the Center-Socialist coalition in Prussia and would have deprived them of their last political stronghold. Brüning, moreover, would have had to resign and the door would be opened to a new antidemocratic and antiparliamentarian era. The Socialists understood also that the chancellor was not a free agent and that his dependence on the president forced him to adopt policies they found difficult to accept.[15]

Brüning found it much harder to keep his rightist support aligned behind him. In the aggregate his rightist allies controlled some 85 votes, but in view of the slimness of his majority such small groups as the German People's Party (30 seats), the Economic Party (23), and the *Landvolk* (19) could embarrass him seriously by their defection. In spite of their limited size, these parties were in a much stronger position than the Social Democrats. They faced the formation of a Hitler-Hugenberg government with relative equanimity, and they did not consider the collapse of the Brüning cabinet an unmitigated disaster. In fact, there were factions in all these parties that would have welcomed a rightist dictatorship. Taking advantage of Brüning's need for their votes, these groups pushed their demands for subsidies, tax relief, and other considerations, but blocked all concessions to the Socialists. In late November, the Economic Party did withdraw Bredt from the cabinet in protest against the allegedly pro-Socialist attitude of Brüning.[16]

These political realities were clearly reflected in the emergency decree of December 1, 1930, which dealt with the country's economic and financial problems. It contained a few minor concessions to workers and low-salaried employees, but the bulk of its relief measures went to agrarians and businessmen. For the rest, the decree exacted substantial pay reductions from public officials and employees and imposed further limitations on public ex-

[15] Brüning and Prussian State Secretary Weissmann, cab. mtg., Nov. 30, 1930, *RKz./1708/785385*; "Verwaltungsmacht gegen Reaktion," MS., Severing Papers/1931 II; Hilferding, in *Gesellschaft*, VIII (1931), ii, 7; Braun, *Von Weimar*, p. 309.

[16] Dingeldey, in Schulthess, Nov. 30, 1930, pp. 230–31; Westarp, "Meine Verhandlungen," Westarp Papers; Economic Party, in Schulthess, Nov. 25, 1930, p. 230; Freybe, Dec. 6, 1930, *Verhandlungen*, Vol. 444, p. 421; district group resolutions of German People's Party, Feb. 1931, Dingeldey Papers/16.

penditures, in compliance with demands of the German People's Party.[17] Inevitably, economic activities would suffer another cutback, and the country would be faced with new hardships and deprivations.

Hindenburg, as usual, kept silent when the decree was issued, and once more the full burden of the new sacrifices rested on Brüning. But Brüning was not an effective advocate of his case; he lacked the human warmth, the imagination, and the eloquence to convince the nation of the need for imposing these new hardships. Frugal to the point of asceticism in his personal life, he could not, perhaps, fully appreciate how heavily the privations of the crisis weighed on the country. Nor was he willing, in his integrity, to minimize the immensity of the existing difficulties: his speeches were capable expositions of the country's predicament —precise, logical, and packed with factual information—but they lacked the burning conviction and sweeping appeal that might have rallied the nation behind him. Occasionally he would try to make such appeals, but he failed sadly in these attempts. Thus he told the nation in a New Year's message in 1931: "We are on the threshold between the old and the new year, like men returning from hard and far from esthetic work and showing it, men who know that tomorrow they will have to start in again because the job is not yet finished—who know in fact that it will never be finished because politics is a part of life and will last as long as there is life. But like true workmen who have started a job and would not willingly leave it half-finished, we shall not give up our task to work at the improvement of our conditions as long as we have life and strength. . . . And let us be moderate, not only in our political actions, but also in our political demands. Politics can do much for us, but it cannot make people happy. Just today I am anxious to stress the limitations of any policy so that you will not indulge in any illusions. This would only cause disappointment, and disappointment may keep us from accomplishing what might otherwise be possible."

Some of his supporters urged him to develop a long-range program that would hold out hopes for a better and happier future and would make the existing hardships more tolerable and meaningful. As one deputy in the Reichstag pleaded: "The Government ought to show the people that it has a plan and what it wants to accomplish so that people can see the road ahead of them. In the long run it is impossible that a Government which wants to lead keeps living from hand to mouth. . . . The

[17] Brüning, Feb. 5, 1931, *Verhandlungen,* Vol. 444, p. 681.

216

Russians have drafted a Five-Year Plan. It is doubtful whether it can be carried out. But I will say this for it—those people are working with fanatical enthusiasm at this plan. They are leading a dog's life, but they keep hoping that some day things will be better. I wish the German people too could be inspired with the suggestive powers of such faith to carry it beyond this crisis and lead it out of its present stagnation to new hopes and aspirations." "This people," warned the liberal *Deutscher Volkswirt*, "is longing for a strong personality, for the color and blood of a determined mind, for purposeful leadership; it is incredibly weary of a policy of bloodless formulas. . . . The last years have released immense energies in this people. The task must be to point out a positive goal to these energies which threaten to destroy the state." Yet absorbed in his work, tending to deal with details that should have been handled by his subordinates, the chancellor missed many opportunities to carry his case to the people. Schleicher, mindful of the country's need for games as well as for bread, once told him in jest that he should take a daily ride up and down Berlin's *Unter den Linden* in a carriage drawn by four white chargers with an escort on horseback, but Brüning was not amused. "He lacked the demonical passion of Bismarck and Stresemann," Gessler wrote later, "and perhaps also the ultimate faith in himself." In his self-effacing, disciplined modesty, the chancellor embodied in himself the finest attributes of the traditional Prussian official, in sharp contrast to the charges of his loud-mouthed opponents who claimed to be the sole guardians of the Prussian inheritance. The nation, however, in its highly emotional state could no longer appreciate this fact; in its desperation it mistook the chancellor's sober factualness for cynical coldness—to millions he became the unfeeling "Hunger Chancellor." [18]

Had Brüning been able to reach the nation by direct appeals, he would also have found it easier to deal with the president. Hindenburg had always been inclined to side with the stronger battalions, and these were clearly moving into the camp of the opposition. He was not willing to take strong measures against that opposition and made it clear that he would not sign any emergency decrees that the Reichstag might find unacceptable. [19]

---

[18] Same, in Schulthess, Jan. 1, 1931, p. 4; Schlange-Schöningen, Mar. 6, 1931, *Verhandlungen*, Vol. 445, p. 1429; Papen to Schleicher, Sept. 24, 1930, Schleicher Papers/69/6; Stolper, in *Dt. Volkswirt*, Oct. 24, 1930, p. 107; Schleicher's advice to Brüning, in Lutz Graf Schwerin von Krosigk, *Es geschah in Deutschland: Menschenbilder unseres Jahrhunderts* (Tübingen and Stuttgart, 1951), p. 119; Gessler to Pechel, Aug. 13, 1947, Gessler, *Reichswehrpolitik*, p. 510.

[19] Meissner, in cab. mtg., Nov. 30, 1930, *RKz./1708/785390*.

Nothing perturbed him more than the spreading unemployment and misery with their prospect of continued internal disturbances, and he would have felt greatly relieved, had he seen any signs of a growing public confidence in Brüning's government. As it was, the chancellor's lack of rapport with the country rendered him even more dependent on the president while putting a growing strain on their relationship.

∽

In parliament, it is true, things were not going too badly that winter. Brüning got the necessary support for his emergency decrees in the Reichstag. By incorporating all essential legislation into these decrees, he succeeded in limiting the Reichstag sessions to fairly short periods.[20] During the second of these sessions, in February-March 1931, he also won a procedural victory of some usefulness. The parliament agreed to a change in its rules to render more difficult purely demagogic motions. One of these amendments stipulated that parliamentary requests for an increase in appropriations or a reduction of revenues would be considered only if supplemented by bills proposing a corresponding increase of revenues or decrease of expenditures, respectively. Acceptance of this change, as well as of a few others intended to expedite parliamentary business and the enforcement of order, led to the exodus, in protest, of Nazis and German Nationals from the Reichstag. After their departure the Reichstag could settle down to a more orderly transaction of business. The budget for the fiscal year 1931 was passed on time, and a number of laws on Eastern aid, tax reform, and further financial measures were likewise enacted without much difficulty. Finally, at the urging of the government, the Reichstag adjourned until October. Brüning had six months to work at his tasks without parliamentary interference.[21]

If on the surface the government seemed to be in a stronger position, in reality the problems it faced were greater than ever. Unemployment reached 5 million during the winter. Brüning saw much of the misery and despair on a trip through the eastern provinces in January. The surveys and statistical reports that came to his desk told the grim story of business closures and bankruptcies. While millions lived resignedly in quiet desperation, others refused to accept their lot; every state and local election showed that

[20] Brüning, Nov. 24, 30, Dec. 9, 1930, *RKz.*/1708/785350, 785378–83, 785486–87.
[21] Schulthess, Mar. 18–21, 1931, pp. 83–84.

the Nazi Party continued to grow at an unprecedented rate, and the Communists too kept growing. Pent-up discontent and energies, stirred up by untiring demagogues, were discharged in the never-ending street skirmishes and beerhall battles, political meetings, and demonstrations. Nihilist brutality, fighting merely for the sake of fighting, created an atmosphere of latent civil war, of spreading terror, and governmental weakness. Rarely was there a night in which no life was lost in this domestic guerrilla war, and the number of casualties often ran into the dozens.

Besides there was always the president to worry about. As Brüning well knew, attempts to influence Hindenburg against him were kept up persistently. Hindenburg was so far willing to support the chancellor despite Nazi and German National charges, but given his susceptibility to rightist suggestions, there was no assurance that he would continue to do so.[22]

Efforts to drive a wedge between the chancellor and the president grew in intensity after the turn of the year. In December the insatiable *Landbund* had called on Hindenburg and had pleaded with him for new emergency aid, but this time the cabinet was very reluctant to grant additional credits or tariff increases. Stegerwald, the minister of labor, was outspoken in his opposition to tariff raises at a time when wages were being cut and working hours reduced. The high agricultural tariffs already ran counter to the government's price-slashing program and burdened the economy with a mortgage which Lujo Brentano, the noted economist, estimated at more than twice the amount of Germany's reparation debt. Stegerwald felt also a moral commitment to the Social Democrats to proceed with the greatest caution in tariff matters and at one point during the cabinet debates threatened to resign should he be overruled. Curtius, in turn, voiced objections on behalf of the export industries that would be seriously hurt by any new tariff increases. Schiele, however, clung just as determinedly to his request for the increases and threatened on his part to resign if his request were not granted. Given his dependence on Hindenburg, Brüning had no freedom of action. After some hesitation he sided with Schiele, but when confronted with Stegerwald's ultimatum, he found it expedient to postpone the formal decision.[23]

[22] Groener to Gleich, Dec. 28, 1930, Groener-Geyer, *General Groener*, p. 278; Meissner, in cab. mtg., Nov. 30, 1930, *RKz.*/1708/785390; Hindenburg to Oldenburg-Januschau, Nov. 29, 1930, cited in Görlitz, *Hindenburg*, p. 331.

[23] Cab. mtgs., Dec. 9, 1930, *RKz.*/1708/785480–82, Feb. 17, 1931, 785858–60, Feb. 23, 1931, 1683/786047–63, Mar. 31, 1931, 786356–67; Brentano to Severing, May 31, 1931, Severing Papers/1931 II.

The *Landbund*, vindictive and furious, stepped up its efforts to arouse the president against the government. In an official statement it charged that the government had failed to live up to its "Hindenburg mandate." Rather than save German agriculture, it was catering, with the help of the "Marxists," to exporting and commercial interests. Similarly the Pan-German *Deutsche Zeitung* refused to accept Brüning's agricultural program as a fulfillment of Hindenburg's pledge. A few weeks later Hugenberg accused Brüning of misinforming Hindenburg. Since the chancellor was at the mercy of the "black and red" coalition in Prussia, he had been unable to adopt the realistic policy designed to save agriculture that Hindenburg wished to pursue. Brüning, the German National leader warned, was hiding behind Hindenburg, slyly abusing the president's authority. And to make doubly sure that the president would hear of the chancellor's failings, he asked Oldenburg-Januschau to call on the marshal and report the true facts to him "since you are one of the few [national-minded men] who still has access to the President." Hugenberg also suggested that Oldenburg point out to the president that if he wished to be reelected for a second term, this would be assured only if he had the support of the "national forces." Seconding his party chief in the Reichstag, a German National deputy reiterated Hugenberg's charges and accused Brüning of sabotaging the directives of the president. This indirect reference to Hindenburg was the only occasion on which the "national" parties mentioned his name during the eight-week session in February-March 1931. One of the few positive references to Hindenburg, on the other hand, came from a Socialist deputy. Praising Hindenburg's "oft-proven" sense of duty, he saw in it a firm bulwark against such "wild experiments" as the dissolution of the Reichstag that could lead only to an aggravation of the existing difficulties. The debate foreshadowed the realignment of forces that took place in the presidential campaign a year later.[24]

The agrarian offensive achieved its objective. Hindenburg had watched it with deepening concern and after some weeks had abandoned his earlier reserve. He asked Brüning to complete the eastern aid program with the greatest possible speed. All complaints he received were passed on to the chancellor at the presi-

[24] Landbund statement, Feb. 1, 1931, *Dt. Gesch.-Kal.,* 1931, A, 138–39; *Dt. Zeitung,* No. 41, Feb. 18, 1931; Hugenberg, in *Braunschweigische Neueste Nachrichten,* No. 49, Feb. 27, 1931; Hugenberg to Oldenburg-Januschau, Feb. 16, 1931, Schmidt-Hannover Papers; Kleiner, Feb. 5, 1931, *Verhandlungen,* Vol. 444, pp. 702–05; Sollmann, Feb. 5, 1931, *ibid.,* p. 696.

dent's "special request" and "for immediate consideration."[25] Under Hindenburg's insistent prodding the government had no choice but to give in to the agrarian demands. To try to convince him of the economic pitfalls or the social injustice of such concessions would have been futile; given his anxious concern, he would not have listened. Most of the "Green Front's" requests for tariff increases were therefore granted—but only after the Reichstag had passed the budget and had adjourned.[26]

At the time, the government was in particular need of the president's confidence. To its many domestic difficulties was added just then the embarrassment of a grave diplomatic defeat; and to compound the cabinet's troubles, the immediate effect of this setback was a further drain on its meager financial resources. In an attempt to score a badly needed foreign political success which might strengthen the government's domestic position (and reassure the president as well) Curtius had negotiated that winter, with Brüning's approval, a German-Austrian customs union. News of the discussions had leaked out prematurely, and France, fearful of an eventual political merger of Austria into Germany, had put Vienna under heavy financial pressure to block the project. As a large-scale investor in Austria, Germany too had been affected by these maneuvers, and by early June the Reichsbank had lost over one billion Reichsmark in gold and foreign currency due to hurried withdrawals.

Hindenburg did sign another presidential decree that tried to cope with these new difficulties, but except for a cutback in prices, the government could do little to relieve the country's desperate shortage of gold and foreign exchange. Early in June 1931, Brüning and Curtius paid a visit to England to impress upon the British government the gravity of the German crisis. No decisions were reached during these talks, but Brüning returned confident that he would soon be granted a suspension of reparations pay-

25 Cab. mtg., Apr. 28, 1931, *RKz.*/1683/786424; Schulthess, Apr. 29, 1931, p. 109; materials on Hindenburg's actions in *RKz.*, R 43 I/1858; Lucas, *Hindenburg*, p. 65.

26 The issue was complicated by the fact that it was not a purely economic one and that the agricultural aid programs were defended also on political and military grounds. Much emphasis was put on the fact that a prosperous agrarian population was needed in East Germany and especially in East Prussia as a "human wall" to fend off any Polish designs. This argument which the Social Democrats accepted as readily as did Nazis and German Nationals carried much weight with Hindenburg too. Hindenburg, in cab. mtg., Mar. 20, 1929, *RKz.*/1700/779633; same to Eulenburg-Prassen, Nov. 20, 1930 (copy), *ibid.*, R 43 I/1805; Görlitz, *Hindenburg*, p. 335; *Sozialdemokratische Partei-Korrespondenz*, No. 9, Sept. 1931, p. 614. Yet from that viewpoint the settlement of a large number of small farmers in that area would have been a more constructive solution than the salvaging of large bankrupt estates that relied on cheap Polish labor for their operations.

ments. The country, however, was deeply disappointed in the inconclusive outcome of the discussions, and there was a widespread demand that the Reichstag be reconvened to examine the government's recent decrees and its foreign policy. The chancellor, however, was sharply opposed to such a session. Irresponsible statements, he feared, would merely heighten domestic tensions and undermine what little confidence other countries still had in Germany's stability and economic resilience. Nor was he willing to yield to the renewed clamor for a reorganization of his cabinet; he was certain that any change acceptable to the right would be viewed with distrust by the Western Powers and could thus only add to his difficulties.[27]

He was prepared to stake everything on his right to use his own judgment. He would resign should the Reichstag or its budget committee reconvene, he announced to the cabinet, and he so informed the parties. To assure himself of Hindenburg's support he went to call on the president who was spending the summer at Neudeck. Hindenburg agreed that the Reichstag should not be permitted to meet, but he was less certain that a change in the composition of the cabinet was inadvisable. He had been in favor of a rightward realignment since the September elections, and he was anxious to replace Curtius, Wirth, and Guérard with men of the right. After the debacle of the customs union project he now pressed hard for Curtius' removal. Brüning convinced him that any immediate change in the cabinet's composition, and especially the substitution of a more "national-minded" foreign minister for Curtius, would diminish the chances for an early reparations moratorium; but he promised Hindenburg that he would arrange for a change at an opportune moment.

Whatever Hindenburg's misgivings about Brüning's colleagues, his confidence in his chancellor was still unimpaired. While he agreed that Brüning ought to resign if the Reichstag defied him, he was not willing to part with him permanently. Should the chancellor leave his post, Hindenburg proposed to go through the motions of asking both Hugenberg and the Socialist Breitscheid to form a majority government. He expected neither to do so— Hugenberg would refuse to head a government not entirely independent of the Reichstag, while Breitscheid would be unable to find a majority. In that case Hindenburg would turn to Brüning again, and since Brüning presumably would not be able either to secure a majority he would not insist that his new cabinet

27 Brüning, in cab. mtg., June 11, 1931, *RKz.*/1684/786812–13, 786815; Pünder, memorandum of May 1931, *ibid.*/1683/786473.

rest on the assured support of a parliamentary majority, but would allow him to find his majority as he went along. Brüning was reluctant to accept another appointment should he be forced to resign, yet in the end he bowed to the president's wishes. He knew, however, that any such reappointment, after the Reichstag had had its way, would leave him in a greatly weakened position both at home and abroad. He redoubled his efforts to prevent the Reichstag from meeting, and in the end the Reichstag's council of elders voted against a recall of the parliament.[28]

Brüning's diplomatic endeavors were rewarded earlier than he dared hope. Four days after the demand for the Reichstag's recall had been rejected, on June 20, the American ambassador, Frederic M. Sackett, brought news that President Hoover was ready to intervene in the crisis. Deeply concerned about Germany's plight, Hoover proposed a one-year moratorium, beginning on July 1, for the payment of all war and reparation debts. To lend his proposal greater urgency, Hoover suggested that Hindenburg cable him an appeal for help. In answer to such a plea Hoover would then communicate his proposal to the other creditor nations. There was no time to consult the cabinet; Brüning therefore called Neudeck at once and urged the president to accept Hoover's suggestion. Hindenburg was reluctant to send an appeal, but in the end consented. He was, moreover, assured that the text of his letter would not be published. A draft was prepared and corrected by him, and the approved version was cabled that same night to Washington; it arrived, however, after Hoover had sent off his own proposal. Hindenburg's plea was succinct: "The misery of the German people . . . compels me to take the unusual step, Mr. President, to address myself to you personally. The German people has suffered for years the greatest difficulties, they reached the limit [of the bearable] during the last winter. The economic recovery which had been expected this spring has not taken place. I have therefore taken steps, on the basis of the emergency powers which the German Constitution has given me, to assure the execution of the most urgent tasks with which the Government is faced and to provide the necessary means of subsistence for the unemployed. The measures which I have taken affect radically all economic and social conditions and demand the heaviest sacrifices from all parts of the population." There was, Hindenburg warned, no further way of improving con-

---

[28] Brüning, cab. mtg., June 11, 1931, *RKz.*/1684/786812–13; also same and Meissner, June 15, 1931, 786817–19, 786823–26; Schulthess, June 12, 16, 1931, pp. 136–37, 141–42.

ditions without some help from abroad. He concluded by urging Hoover to take those steps "by which an immediate change in the situation so threatening to both Germany and the rest of the world could be brought about." [29]

Given his reluctance to be identified with the emergency decrees, Hindenburg's cavalier claim to exclusive authorship, as it were, comes as a surprise. So of course does his failure to acknowledge the contribution of Brüning. Evidently he still felt, as he did as commander in chief, that by assuming the final responsibility for an action, he could also claim credit for its success whether or not he had planned it. Thus he claimed authorship now of the emergency decrees in a situation where they would be considered commendable efforts at self-help. The confidential nature of the letter assured him, moreover, that its specific contents would not become known at home where the decrees were viewed with less favor. (The letter was made public, however, during a debate in the United States Congress six months later.)[30]

Over two weeks passed before Hoover's proposal was accepted by all countries concerned. While most of them welcomed the move, France balked, and extended negotiations became necessary to assure her of the temporary nature of the moratorium. She was moreover afraid lest Germany spend the amounts thus saved for military rather than economic purposes. To reassure her on this score, London and Washington suggested that Germany postpone the construction of her new *Panzerkreuzer*. As reasonable as the demand was, Brüning's hands were tied. Any such concession, he knew, would be rejected by Groener and Hindenburg, and was bound to provoke renewed attacks from the rightist parties and possibly even from some of his own supporters. The chancellor warned that any reduction of the naval budget would lead to Hindenburg's resignation. A proposal by the Western Powers that the customs union project be formally renounced met with a similar rebuff although the plan was obviously already dead. Caught between the president and the "National Opposition," Brüning had little scope left for diplomatic maneuver.[31]

On July 6 France agreed to the moratorium after some face-saving arrangements had been made which Brüning could be

---

[29] Brüning, cab. mtg., June 23, 1931, *RKz.*/1684/786781; Pünder, *Reichskanzlei*, entry of June 24, 1931, p. 101; memorandum by same, June 21, 1931, Saemisch Papers/162a; Hindenburg to Hoover, June 20, 1931, Schulthess, June 20, 1931, pp. 491–92.

[30] *Ibid.*, pp. 145, 491.

[31] Edward W. Bennett, *Germany and the Diplomacy of the Financial Crisis, 1931* (Cambridge, 1962), pp. 184–86, 191–93, 199–202.

sure would be unobjectionable to both Hindenburg and Groener as well as to the nation. But valuable time had been lost, and Germany's financial plight which had improved slightly after Hoover's original announcement had suffered a further setback by then. Less than a week later, on July 11, one of the country's largest banks, the Darmstädter und Nationalbank, closed its doors, and on July 13 the government was forced to proclaim a bank holiday. Brüning and Curtius hurried to Paris and London in search of help. Neither Britain nor the United States could offer immediate assistance, and the French who might have been able to help insisted on a political quid pro quo—no revision of the Versailles Peace Treaty for at least ten years. This condition the chancellor was unable as well as unwilling to accept.[32]

Brüning did not return entirely empty-handed, however. Since Germany's financial collapse would have spelled disaster for their own economies, the creditor nations promised to urge their private investors not to recall their short-term credits. In this way the ruinous pressure on Germany's foreign exchange situation would be somewhat eased. The private creditors agreed to this plan, and so-called "standstill agreements" were concluded between them and Germany to establish new payment procedures.

❧

Hindenburg had gone to Neudeck early that summer to find peace and relief there from the exacting demands of the preceding winter. Shortly before he left, the Nazis and German Nationals had subjected him to a new barrage of indignities. The Nazis protested in a series of public statements against the "incredible" and "indescribable" violations of the constitution that both the courts and police had committed in their dealings with the Nazi Party. They warned Hindenburg that they would hold him responsible for the "inevitable consequences" of these crimes and "admonished" him "in the name of millions of persecuted and terrorized Germans to do his duty and defend their constitutional rights against the abuses of the parliamentary majority coalition; or to resign if he can not or does not want to do this and leave the protection of his one-time voters to a newly elected national-minded President." In a similar vein, the German Nationals reiterated their familiar charges that he allowed his person and authority to be misused against the very people who had elected him. Just before his departure for Neudeck, Berlin's Nazi organ,

[32] Brüning, in cab. mtg., July 25, 27, 1931, *RKz.*/1684/787118, 787138–39; Bennett, *Germany and Financial Crisis*, pp. 263–74.

Der Angriff, published an editorial, "The Marshal-President," whose opening paragraph expressed the caustic contempt in which the president was held by the Nazi leaders:

"The Presidency of the man with whom we wish to deal here was a deadly tragicomedy; it was shaped by his basic lack of character and by his inability, carefully concealed behind an air of statesman-like dignity, to see things as they really were.

"It is indeed embarrassing to take note of a man simply because he happened to be President of the Republic, a man whose grotesque insignificance makes us wonder: How could this bumbler ever become an army leader in the Empire and later on President of the Republic?"

After running on in this vein for the better part of two columns, the article mentioned off-handedly at the end that the man it had been discussing was Marshal Maurice de MacMahon, one of Napoleon III's army leaders during the Franco-Prussian war of 1870-71 and later president of the Third Republic. The article was timed to appear on May 31, the anniversary of the Battle of Jutland, when it could count on a particularly large number of readers. As always the day was the occasion of special "national" demonstrations and gatherings; that year the *Stahlhelm* held on that day its annual Front Soldiers Day, attended by some 150,000 members and such guests of honor as the ex-Crown Prince and Field Marshal von Mackensen.[33]

Even Neudeck was no longer the sheltered refuge for which he was longing. While there was not an atmosphere of permanent crisis in the fields and forests of East Prussia, the political tensions did reach into the seclusion of his rural retreat. There were, as always, his old friends and neighbors pouncing upon him with dire reports about the agrarian crisis and the growing despair of the population. They warned against the "Jesuit" tactics of Brüning whom they detested as much as a Catholic as they did as a policy-maker, they complained about Brüning's "flirting" with the Socialist left and clamored for a reshuffling of the cabinet to obtain the support of the right. And there was also that never-ending stream of letters grimly predicting that he would lose what authority he still enjoyed in "national" circles if he persisted in his present course.

As if to bear out these ominous warnings, he had some perturbing personal experiences. On drives through the countryside,

[33] Schulthess, Apr. 27, May 30-31, 1931, pp. 109, 117; *Dt. Gesch.-Kal.,* June 4, 1931, A, 270; Bracher, *Auflösung,* pp. 396-97; *Angriff,* May 31, 1931, quoted in Braun, *Von Weimar,* pp. 366-67; also Heinz, *Nation,* p. 123.

organized groups of Nazis greeted him with derisive shouts and hostile demonstrations; even on a visit to the Tannenberg battle-field he was subjected to a similar humiliation. To one who had always cultivated his national stature this came as a painful shock, and he kept fretting over the fact that this could happen to him, "the Field Marshal General and Liberator of East Prussia." At the same time the rightist newspapers, the only papers he read, kept up a barrage against Brüning's policies and gloated over the deepening economic crisis.[34]

On his visit to Neudeck, Brüning promised to reorganize the cabinet at the first suitable moment, but advised against any change while he was engaged in delicate negotiations with Germany's creditors, and Hindenburg accepted the chancellor's counsel. But then came the bank crisis, and in its wake a new wave of emergency decrees. Hindenburg could not grasp their significance and had to rely on Brüning's and Meissner's counsel. Both agreed that the proposed measures were needed, as did Schleicher who took part in their preparation, and so he put his signature to these decrees. Yet he kept worrying about assuming the "responsibility" for something beyond his comprehension, and many of his visitors and correspondents were quick to encourage his doubts.[35]

Late in July, Hindenburg left Neudeck for some weeks of hunt-ing at Dietramszell in Bavaria. There was the usual crowd to see him off at the nearby railroad station at Rosenberg, but this time the reverent silence with which he was customarily received was broken by shouts of "Germany Awake!," the battlecry of the Nazis. For once he lost his composure and shouted back, furiously, if somewhat obliquely: "Today men are governing [Germany] and not rowdies!" In this grim mood he set out for Berlin en route to Bavaria.[36]

He stopped off in the capital for a series of urgent talks. Among his first callers were Schiele and Brandes, one of East Prussia's agrarian leaders, who called his attention anew to the plight of East Germany's agriculture. That same day the *Reichslandbund* en-joined its members, as a measure of self-help, to refuse to sell more than specified minimum amounts of bread cereals in order to

[34] Memorandum by Meissner, Aug. 1, 1931, reprinted in Matthias and Morsey, *Ende der Parteien*, p. 624.

[35] Hindenburg and Meissner, "Niederschrift," in Vogelsang, *Reichswehr*, pp. 459–60; Brüning, cab. mtg., June 15, 1931, *RKz./*1684/786818; Meissner, Aug. 7, 1931, 787499; Hindenburg to ex-Crown Prince William, July 11, 1931, copy in Schleicher Papers/17,iii/43; information from Dr. Pünder.

[36] *Siegener Zeitung* to Büro des Reichspräsidenten, July 28, 1931, Meissner to *Siegener Zeitung*, July 31, 1931, *BdRPr.*, R 54/298.

force prices up. He promised, as always, whatever help he could give, but he must have wondered how much his help was deserved, and doubtless let Brandes know what he thought of East Prussia's Nazis.[37]

This point he also took up when Hugenberg called on him three days later. Hugenberg did not improve matters when he blandly replied that he too had been heckled by Nazis and had not been able to prevent such demonstrations. Ignoring Hindenburg's sensitivity to any such slight, he tried to allay the marshal's concern by suggesting that he ought not to take such incidents too seriously. Nor would he promise to direct his newspapers to protest against any such occurrences which, as Hindenburg took pains to point out, were especially embarrassing in view of his person and age. Evidently Hugenberg thought it unwise to take the Nazis to task. At the same time, he seemed convinced that he was exerting a salutary influence on them—he had forced them, he proudly maintained, to assume a more "national" attitude and had kept them from sliding into socialist or communist aberrations. But Hindenburg was not satisfied. By collaborating with the Nazis and walking out of the Reichstag with them, he complained, Hugenberg had forced Brüning to move closer to the left since the chancellor had to have a majority. He pleaded with Hugenberg to lend his support to Brüning "since Brüning was inspired by the noblest motives, was working wisely and energetically, and was altogether one of the finest men whom he had ever met in his long life."

On the whole the conference was a failure. Hindenburg had not received Hugenberg for a year and a half since the German National leader had refused to support him, and their last previous meeting had ended on a tense and unfriendly note. He had agreed to receive him now in the hope that he might persuade him, in the face of the pressing crisis, to break with the Nazis and seek an understanding with Brüning. With Hugenberg's help the chancellor would be able to reorganize his cabinet and give it that rightist slant for which the marshal had been hoping so long and his friends and war comrades had been clamoring. Yet Hugenberg proved as inflexible as ever; if he were to work with Brüning, he insisted, the latter would have to end all collaboration with the Social Democrats, and the Prussian situation would have to be clarified too. Beyond these statements he would not commit himself, except to express his readiness to confer with the chancellor.

[37] Schulthess, July 29, 1931, pp. 166, 168.

A meeting between the two men finally took place late in August, due to Hugenberg's dilatory tactics. It produced no rapprochement, nor could it have done so since by that time Hugenberg had decided on a closer and more systematic collaboration with Hitler.[38]

If the talk with Hugenberg was unpleasant, Hindenburg had soon afterwards a much more disheartening experience. Among the recent decrees he had signed was one authorizing Reich and state governments to compel the press to publish official appeals and statements. The measure was to enable these governments to present their case to those who read only opposition papers in which governmental policies were either ignored or distorted.

On the strength of this newly acquired authority the Prussian government requested all papers under its jurisdiction to publish on August 6, an "Appeal to the Prussian Voters." The "Appeal" was directed against a *Stahlhelm*-initiated referendum, subsequently defeated, that called for the dissolution of the Prussian *Landtag* in which the democratic parties still held a majority. It branded the referendum as a pointless and dangerous maneuver of rightist and leftist extremists designed to destroy one of the last citadels of democracy and to create confusion and chaos. "Let those who want a Soviet Prussia or a fascist Prussia vote 'Aye'," the appeal concluded. "Those, however, who are in favor of the social and democratic development of the German Republic and the Prussian State, those who wish to help the Prussian Government in its untiring efforts to lead us away from the frightful misery of economic crisis and unemployment toward recovery and stability, those who want to show common sense, sober judgment, and deep passionate love for people and Fatherland in these grave times— may they be guided by the slogan: Stay away from the polls! Do not take part in the referendum!"

The appeal caused an uproar in rightist circles and at once there were counterappeals and protests. A new barrage of letters and telegrams descended on Hindenburg in his Bavarian retreat. Once again there were the customary solemn warnings that if he did not prevent the abuse of government powers for purely partisan purposes, he would lose the last residue of respect that "national" Germany was still willing to pay him. In the face of these threats, Meissner reported to the Reich cabinet, the president's first impulse had been to repeal the press decree at once. Yet Brüning

[38] *Ibid.*, July 29, Aug. 6, 10, 1931, pp. 165, 167, 175–77, 179; Meissner memorandum, Aug. 1, 1931, in Matthias and Morsey, pp. 623–25; Meissner, cab. mtg., Aug. 7, 10, 1931, *RKz.*/1684/787499–501, 787507; memorandum by Pünder, Aug. 8, 1931, *RKz.*, R 43 I/2701 A.

wished to avoid so sharp a disavowal of the Prussian government, and Hindenburg gave in to him; he demanded, however, an immediate amendment that would preclude any further misuse of the decree. He also insisted on the publication of a statement indicating his strong disapproval of the Prussian government's action and noting that he had "requested" the Reich government to propose appropriate changes in the press decree. "The Reich Government," the statement concluded, "will at once submit such proposals to the President."

The amendments to the press decree were published three days later. Among other changes, they made the compulsory publication of statements other than those of the Reich government contingent on the approval of the Reich minister of the interior. Although the new decree affected the state governments directly, they were not even accorded the courtesy of a pro-forma consultation—at the insistence of Hindenburg who pressed for the immediate promulgation of the amendments.[39]

Brüning reacted almost as sharply to the action of the Prussian government as did Hindenburg. To the chancellor the appeal proved a serious embarrassment both diplomatically and domestically. Its open deprecation of Fascism ("fascist Prussia") came at the very moment the chancellor was in Rome trying to obtain Mussolini's support for a reparations settlement. Above all, however, the Prussian move endangered his unending energy-consuming efforts to retain the president's support. He knew he would be successful with the president only if he could offer him a modicum of personal peace. He knew equally well how much Hindenburg hated to be involved in controversies, and he was also aware of the relentless pressures to which the president was being subjected by friends and acquaintances. He had thought it his task and his duty therefore to keep Hindenburg out of the political firing range, just as Groener had done in 1919. At the chancellor's insistence decrees that were issued over Hindenburg's name had to be rewritten many times so as not to identify him too clearly with the most unpopular measures, and some were shelved altogether to save him embarrassment.

But now, despite all his efforts to shield him, Hindenburg had been drawn into the political arena and over a secondary issue at that. As Brüning knew well, it was one on which the president felt strongly; just recently, when he had stopped off in Berlin, he had made it clear to the chancellor that he disapproved of the se-

[39] Brüning, cab. mtg., Aug. 10, 1931, *RKz.*/1684/787505–06; Dietrich and Meissner, July 20, 1931, 787078–80; also Meissner, Sept. 30, 1931, 1685/788297–98.

verity with which the Prussian authorities were dealing with the press and political demonstrations of the right while showing great leniency, as he claimed, to the left. He would see to it, the chancellor assured the cabinet after the publication of Prussia's anti-referendum appeal, that the wishes of the president would be carried out at once, and he added for the benefit of Meissner who could be expected to report this to Hindenburg that he would not tolerate a recurrence of this kind of action.[40]

Brüning did not content himself with these pledges, for new dangers appeared to be threatening his relationship with the president. Hindenburg, he learned, had been advised at Dietramszell that the chancellor's negative attitude towards the Nazis was unwise. The president seemed impressed by what he was told, and when Brüning maintained that there existed no basis for a collaboration with Hitler or Hugenberg, the chancellor thought he could sense a certain reluctance on Hindenburg's part to go along with his views. To assure himself of the president's continued benevolence, he felt that he would have to take additional steps.

He did not take the most obvious one: a personal call on the president to remove any misunderstandings. Anxious not to disturb Hindenburg at Dietramszell, he decided to enlist Schleicher's help. To his relief the general had sent him a few cordial lines at the height of the Prussian crisis; with his backing Brüning was confident of regaining the president's trust if he had lost it. Schleicher was not in Berlin at the time; in his forty-ninth year he had belatedly married and was spending his honeymoon at a South German spa. Brüning met with the general in late August when he was scheduled to address a Center Party meeting at Stuttgart. Schleicher assured the chancellor that he fully agreed with his plans and policies, and was just as opposed as Brüning himself to the inclusion of Nazis and German Nationals in the government. The general promised to use his influence with the president on Brüning's behalf. Word went to Oskar von Hindenburg that Schleicher was in full accord with the chancellor, and General von dem Bussche-Ippenburg, the head of the army personnel office, who was to see Hindenburg on official business at Dietramszell a few days later, was also instructed to report this to the president. Bussche did and came away from the conference with the impression, as he told Brüning, that Hindenburg had accepted Schleicher's message with evident satisfaction. His impression was

---

[40] Brüning, cab. mtg., Aug. 10, 1931, *RKz.*/1684/787505.

231

not mistaken; to a German National deputy, Hindenburg said at that time in the quaint way he sometimes affected: "[Brüning] is pure and has noble aspirations." [41]

But Brüning did not remain reassured for long. Attempts to turn Hindenburg against him continued without let-up, and they grew in intensity after the president's return to Berlin in September. Those were exhausting weeks for the marshal. He was now in his eighty-fourth year—an age when mere physical existence constituted an effort and the problems connected with his age claimed much of his interest and energy. Never very much at home in the uncertain present, he longed more than ever for the stability of the long gone days of his youth. Official callers found him anxious to settle whatever business they brough him; once this was done, the conversation would wander off to those happier days of the Prusso-Austrian War of 1866 and the Battle of König-grätz in which he had undergone his baptism of fire. He would reel off the names of the noncoms and men who had served under him, and of the villages in which he had stayed. But while he still remembered small details about the war of 1866 or the campaign against France in 1870–71, visitors noted that his memories of Tannenberg were getting hazy. Tannenberg, it seemed, did not belong to that friendlier world to which he retreated from the trials of the day; perhaps it brought back other, unhappier memories— the lost war, Ludendorff, and the abdication of the Emperor.

John Wheeler-Bennett, the English historian, had occasion to watch him at a military ceremony that fall and has given a perceptive description of the old marshal as he was shifting between the world of reality and the world of his dreams:

"A large closed car drew up, an orderly opened the door, and out jumped two smart young staff officers. Then a pause, and slowly, very slowly, there emerged, backwards and bare-headed, an enormous figure. Again a pause, though shorter this time, while one of the young officers extracted from the interior of the car a *Pickel-haube*, which was ceremoniously placed upon the great square head with its hair *en brosse*. Then the figure turned about and one had the momentary impression of a gigantic clockwork doll waiting for the spring to be released which galvanized it into movement. His eye caught the motionless line of soldiery. At once the absent glance changed—the spring had been released—and, one hand

41 Planck to Schleicher, Aug. 11, 1931, in Vogelsang, *Reichswehr*, pp. 427–28; Schleicher to Groener, Aug. 28, 1931, in *Welt als Geschichte*, XI (1951), 129; Brüning, "Ein Brief," pp. 5–6; Bussche-Ippenburg to Mau, Jan. 25, 1952, *Vierteljahrshefte*, I (1953), 267; Schmidt-Hannover, *Umdenken*, p. 277.

grasping his baton and the other resting on his sword hilt, Hindenburg moved stiffly and erect towards the guard of honor."[42]

Nor did Hindenburg ever, as head of state, fail to pay meticulous attention to the rules and conventions of the monarchy. At the annual dinner of the *Herrenklub* that year, one of the guests present was one of the former Grand-Dukes of Mecklenburg. As a sign of respect to the duke, Hindenburg wore his Mecklenburg Great Cross on his dress coat, and when he entered the dininghall, he was careful to walk a little to the left and behind the prince.[43]

But he was never allowed to seek refuge for long in this ordered world of established hierarchies and military achievements. The pressures on him to dismiss Brüning increased, as did the demands of the right for adequate representation in the government. There were also the never-ending warnings that many of Brüning's decrees were unconstitutional. "We who represent the majority of the German people," Hugenberg fulminated at the German Nationals' party convention, "we shall point to Constitution and parliament and shall hold the President to the oath which he has sworn!" Although these warners had never before shown much regard for the Weimar Constitution, their admonitions worried the president, as they well knew they would. And there were the unceasing alarming reports about the deepening agrarian crisis; the cries for help from bankers and industrialists; the renewed rise of the unemployment figures after the brief seasonal improvement of the summer months. The old man grew weary; visitors found him tired and run down. An attack of flu kept bothering him for some time, and in his dispirited condition he found it difficult to shake it off. Yet throughout he tried to attend to his official duties.[44]

At this moment, when he had barely recovered from his illness, Brüning asked him to make an important decision. Never an easy task, it was doubly unwelcome in his state of physical and mental discomfort. But Brüning sensed Hindenburg's vacillations, and he insisted that the president take a clear stand on his attitude toward him. Nazis and German Nationals were just then girding themselves for a mass demonstration aimed directly at him. In mid-October they intended to meet at Bad Harzburg, a resort town in the

[42] Information from Dr. Zechlin; Bussche-Ippenburg, *ZS./217*; Schlange-Schöningen, *Am Tage Danach*, p. 56; Wheeler-Bennett, *Wooden Titan*, p. 351.

[43] Erwin von Aretin, *Krone und Ketten: Erinnerungen eines bayerischen Edelmannes*, ed. by Karl Buchheim and Karl Otmar von Aretin (Munich, 1955), p. 41.

[44] Brüning, "Ein Brief," pp. 6–7; *Frankfurter Zeitung*, Reich ed., Oct. 8, 1931; Görlitz, *Hindenburg*, p. 345; Hugenberg, in Schulthess, Sept. 19/20, 1931, p. 204; Meissner, cab. mtg., Sept. 24, 1931, *RKz./1685/788132*.

Harz Mountains, for a display of their strength. Some of the smaller parties that had thus far supported the chancellor were beginning to waver; the hope was that they would be so impressed by the might of the "National Opposition" that they could be enlisted in the campaign to bring down Brüning. The chancellor felt that he could weather this new assault only if Hindenburg openly demonstrated his continued confidence in him.

Writing some sixteen years later, Brüning recalls that he went to the president to discuss with him the possibility of a change of policy. As he saw it, the president had two choices; he could either forcibly suppress the Nazi Party as a threat to the constitutional order, a task Brüning was apparently willing to undertake with the president's backing; or he could form a new government including the Nazis. If he chose the second alternative, the chancellor warned, in order to keep the Nazis in check, Hindenburg must not permit new elections before the term of the present Reichstag expired in 1934. Brüning doubted that such a government would achieve any success in the forthcoming reparations and disarmament negotiations, and feared that its failure in coping with the internal and external problems of the country might drive many disillusioned Nazis into the arms of the Communists. He made it clear also that he himself would not serve in a government in which the Nazis took part.

Hindenburg found both alternatives unacceptable. He was repelled by the radicalism and the uncouthness of the Nazis and found abhorrent the thought of including them in the government. But cautioned by his Dietramszell friends, he was equally opposed to the forcible suppression of this "national" movement. Shying away from any incisive action, he could not make up his mind. Brüning found him tired and unable to concentrate, and thought he showed signs of mental decline. Possibly Hindenburg simply found it too hard in his weakened condition to follow Brüning's involved explanations. "For Hindenburg," one observer has written, "Brüning's visits always meant a great strain because the latter expected too much [from the president] when he reported to him," and this must have been especially true when Hindenburg was not well. The discussion ended inconclusively, and both Groener and Schleicher had to intervene on the chancellor's behalf before the president assured him once more of his confidence.[45]

---

[45] Brüning, "Ein Brief," pp. 7–8; Meissner, *Staatekretär*, pp. 213–14; Görlitz, *Hindenburg*, pp. 347–48. Some misunderstanding concerning Hindenburg's condition arose from the fact that Brüning's reference to a temporary "mental blackout" was

Brüning, however, had to pay a price for Hindenburg's support: the president would not permit the reorganization of the cabinet to be postponed any longer. At his insistence three of its members had to be dropped—Curtius who was considered too "soft" as foreign minister; Wirth whom Hindenburg disliked personally and who as a representative of the Center's left wing was objectionable to the right; and Guérard whose only offense was that he too was a member of the Center Party. Although he was one of its more conservative leaders, his presence in the cabinet gave the Center, in Hindenburg's eyes, an unduly strong representation.[46]

In the new cabinet Brüning took over the foreign ministry himself. Hindenburg would have preferred the appointment of Baron von Neurath, the German ambassador in London, a jovial Swabian whose conservative-nationalist views might have made him more acceptable to the right. But Brüning whose entire policy was based on the hope of scoring an early diplomatic success wished to conduct himself the forthcoming reparations and disarmament negotiation. Guérard's place was taken by Treviranus who had proven an ineffective administrator of the agricultural aid program. That post was entrusted a few weeks later to an East German landowner and recognized farm expert, Hans Schlange-Schöningen, a one-time leader of the German Nationals who had broken with Hugenberg in the summer of 1930.

There was some question as to who was to assume the strategic ministry of the interior as successor of Wirth. The name of Otto Gessler, the former Reichswehr minister, was brought up. His administration of the Reichswehr ministry had had the approval of the right—largely because he had proved a very lenient taskmaster to the generals; he had no party ties, and Hindenburg was known to like him. (Hindenburg's feelings carried much weight since his personal attitude toward candidates became an increasingly important consideration.) Gessler, moreover, had taken an active part in efforts to reform the country's federal structure and thus seemed well qualified to become minister of the interior.

Gessler was approached and was willing to take the post. He had a ready-made plan to cope with the crisis: the government would have to assume full dictatorial powers. Equipped with these pow-

---

erroneously translated as a *"geistiger Zusammenbruch"* (mental collapse) in the German version published in the *Deutsche Rundschau*. Brüning to author, Feb. 28, 1957. On Brüning-Hindenburg relationship, Eschenburg, "Rolle der Persönlichkeit," p. 13.

[46] Brüning, "Ein Brief," p. 8; Groener to Gleich, Sept. 20, 1931, Groener-Geyer, *General Groener*, p. 280; Meissner, *Staatssekretär*, pp. 206–07.

ers, it could effect a comprehensive reorganization of the state and take sweeping measures against the disastrous unemployment situation. For his plans Gessler found strong support in Brüning's own party; Monsignor Kaas had long favored the establishment of an outright dictatorship under Brüning's leadership. Gessler also gained the impression that at least some of the Socialist leaders approved of his plan. The chancellor, however, was much less encouraging; Gessler's plans resembled closely one of the alternative policies he had discussed with Hindenburg only a few weeks before. Brüning knew that the president would never agree to the suspension of the constitution which Gessler proposed.

Gessler, however, insisted on submitting his plans to the president. He reminded the marshal of that critical hour in Prussia's history, some seventy years earlier, when King and parliament were locked in a bitter struggle over the question of the expansion of the Prussian army. At that time William I had taken Bismarck's advice to proceed with the army reform over the head of the Prussian House of Delegates. Gessler skillfully marshaled other arguments to overcome Hindenburg's scruples: the pseudodemocratic character of Brüning's government, and Ebert's statement that if he had to choose between Germany and the constitution, he would choose Germany. One would not allow an insane monarch to keep ruling simply because there was no constitutional provision for a regency; by the same token one could not allow an impotent Reichstag to keep legislating merely because there was no formal constitutional answer to such an emergency. Hindenburg was impressed: "What you say sounds reasonable enough. I shall think about it." But if he was ready to consider Gessler's solution, Schleicher quickly convinced him that it entailed the grave risk of plunging the country (and the Reichswehr) into civil war. Gessler's candidacy had to be dropped.[47]

Brüning now offered the post to Ernst Scholz. Hindenburg liked him, and Scholz's views would have carried some weight with the president. Through Scholz, moreover, Brüning hoped to salvage the support of the German People's Party. Stresemann's party had kept moving close to the "National Opposition," and some of its leading members, among them Seeckt, now a deputy in the Reichstag, were scheduled to attend the forthcoming meeting at Bad Harzburg. Through Scholz and the People's Party, Brüning would also be able to establish closer contact once more with business and industry, a development Hindenburg too would have welcomed

47 Gessler, *Reichswehrpolitik*, pp. 84–85; Brüning to Gessler, Jan. 31, 1955, Gessler to Pechel, Mar. 18, 1947, *ibid.*, pp. 508–09.

since it would have balanced off in his eyes the Social Democratic support on which Brüning depended. The chancellor's ties with industrial groups had grown very tenuous; he had so far persuaded only one industrialist, Hermann Warmbold, a director of I.G. Farben, to enter the cabinet as minister of economics. Other industrialists to whom he had offered portfolios, Albert Vögler, board chairman of the Vereinigte Stahlwerke, Paul Silverberg, president of a major Rhenish lignite concern, and Hermann Schmitz, another Farben director, had all rejected his invitation, since they did not wish to be associated with Brüning's middle-of-the-road cabinet. Scholz too declined the chancellor's offer on the grounds that the time had come "to draw for responsible collaboration on the strong forces which are gathered in the parties of the right."[48]

In the end Groener took over the administration of the ministry of the interior temporarily. This plan had been hatched some months earlier in Schleicher's fertile mind and according to Groener, had for some time been a "pet project" of Hindenburg, who accepted it readily. Schleicher hoped to obtain some measure of control over the paramilitary organizations with the help of that strategic office. Perturbed by the violence of the Nazi stormtroopers, he was thinking of placing these groups under some government supervision; an agency set up under the aegis of the Reich ministry of the interior was to direct their energies into channels less dangerous to the stability of the state. Whether Schleicher had farther reaching plans, as has been suggested, of using the ministry of the interior as a haven for Groener should he himself wish to take over the Reichswehr ministry is not clear from the available evidence.[49]

Brüning's new cabinet thus differed little from its predecessor. The two "liberals," Wirth and Curtius, had been eliminated, and the representation of the Center Party had been reduced, for the newcomers, Warmbold, the new economics minister, and Joel, the new minister of justice, a career official, were men of conservative leanings, though without party affiliations. But the over-all complexion of the cabinet had barely changed; Brüning had been

48 Schulthess, Oct. 7–8, 1931, p. 23; Brüning, cab. mtg., Oct. 7, 1931, *RKz./*1686/788466–67; Eburwin, in *Tat*, XXIII (1931), 656; *Frankfurter Zeitung*, Reich ed., Oct. 10, 1931; Scholz to Brüning, Oct. 9, 1931, *RKz.*, R 43 I/1308; on Hindenburg and industry, Vogelsang, *Reichswehr*, p. 129.

49 Noeldechen, in *Vierteljahrshefte*, I (1953), 273; Brüning to Gessler, Jan. 31, 1955, in Gessler, *Reichswehrpolitik*, p. 508; Groener, in Oehme questionnaire, Groener Papers/25/224; "Hindenburg's pet project," in Vogelsang, p. 133 n. 517. That the plan of a personal union between the two ministries had been considered for some time is evident from Pünder, *Reichskanzlei*, entry of Dec. 8, 1930, p. 80.

unable to extend the basis of the government significantly towards the right, and the dominant minds in the new cabinet were the same as in the old one: the chancellor himself, Dietrich, the finance minister, and Stegerwald, the minister of labor.

The reorganization thus failed to achieve Hindenburg's two major objectives: it did not satisfy his rightist critics, nor did it avert the defection of the People's Party and the industrial groups of which it was the political mouthpiece. The over-all result was that the new cabinet was even more dependent on Hindenburg's confidence than its predecessor, while Hindenburg from the outset was not too pleased with its composition. This became evident immediately. Hindenburg was greatly concerned about Brüning's failure to establish closer ties with business and agriculture, the two groups that kept worrying him with their relentless complaints. He therefore requested the establishment of an economic council to assist the new government in the solution of the country's economic problems. This council was to serve as a "sort of appendix toward the right," as Pünder phrased it, to develop the closer contact with agrarian and industrial groups that the cabinet change had failed to establish.

The plan had been suggested to Hindenburg by ex-Chancellor Cuno, a director of the Hamburg-America Line. Cuno had urged Hindenburg to reorganize the government by bringing into the cabinet a number of leading industrialists and right-wing career officials. This new government, of which Brüning was to remain the chancellor, was to permit the unilateral revision of labor union contracts so as to eliminate their "Bolshevik equalitarianism"; to reduce the scope of social insurance programs; to lower interest rates and reorganize the Eastern Aid Program; and to promote the reduction of wages, taxes, and social contributions allowing Germany to regain her competitive position in the international market. As for the council, it was to be, in the words of one industrial spokesman, "a sort of Crown Council under the auspices of the President, not the Government; it must never be under the Government, but rather above the Government . . . as a permanent institution."

Brüning acceded to the president's request that he seek a rapprochement with business and agriculture by means of such a council, but he was able to dissuade the president from appointing a body that in personal composition and program would pursue the employers' interests as one-sidedly as Cuno proposed. In its final composition the council included representatives of small tradesmen and labor unions as well. Hindenburg himself was as usual

interested primarily in the appointment of the agrarian representatives, and proposed two spokesmen for the large landowners.
But in the end Brüning obtained as well some representation for
the small farmers.

To the president's great disappointment the council failed to
improve relations between the government and business and agriculture. It met for three weeks in November, made a number of
recommendations, and then disbanded. The agrarian members
withdrew even earlier.[50]

Brüning's position was threatened also from another quarter.
Since the early days of his chancellorship, he had been dependent
on the support and good will of Schleicher. As Hindenburg's
special adviser, Schleicher occupied a unique position which Brüning could not ignore. Cooperation between the two men seems to
have presented no problems at first though the chancellor was
never allowed to forget the general's presence. One of Schleicher's
associates, ex-Captain Erwin Planck, a son of the famous physicist,
held a key post in the chancellery and kept Schleicher informed
on Brüning's plans. Through Planck, Schleicher tried subtly to
guide Brüning's plans. Obviously these efforts are hard to trace,
but what few records exist indicate that until the spring of 1931
Schleicher and Brüning agreed on all basic questions. On the
touchy agrarian question Schleicher expressed himself in full accord with the chancellor; similarly, Schleicher understood and
accepted Brüning's cooperation with the Social Democrats and
with the Prussian government of Braun and Severing. He, as well
as his spokesmen, kept assuring the officer corps that the chancellor
was an "excellent man" who, "in addition to all his other qualifications was also very much concerned with all matters military."[51]

Nonetheless as the economic crisis deepened and opposition to
Brüning increased, Schleicher's attitude began to change. Like
Hindenburg he was subjected to incessant complaints from rightist politicians and disgruntled landowners who knew how much
weight his counsel carried with the president. The politicians objected to Brüning's collaboration with the Socialists in Prussia and

50 *Frankfurter Zeitung*, Reich ed., Oct. 7, 1931; materials on Economic Council in
Z. f. GeschWiss., I (1953), 897–901; quotation from Brandi to Bernhard, Oct. 19,
1931, *ibid.*, pp. 900–01; Bracher, *Auflösung*, pp. 438–39; Brüning, cab. mtg., Oct.
10, 1931, *RKz.*/1686/788471–72; Pünder, *Reichskanzlei*, entry of Nov. 23, 1931,
p. 108.

51 Planck to Schleicher, Aug. 11, 18, 1931, in Vogelsang, *Reichswehr*, pp. 427–29;
Schleicher on agriculture in Schleicher to Brüning, Feb. 24, 1931, Schleicher
Papers/44,i/69; on cooperation with Social Democrats see unsigned memorandum of
Jan. 10, 1931, *ibid.*/44,i/56; on attitude towards Brüning see also Hammerstein-
Equord, Apr. 24, 1931, in *Vierteljahrshefte*, II (1954), 410–11.

demanded his replacement with a "national" leader, and the agrarians painted a somber picture of the agricultural situation. Nor was the mood of the officer corps reassuring. Reports of growing pro-Nazi sympathies kept reaching the general, as did warnings from officers who did not feel themselves drawn to the Nazis, but nevertheless questioned the wisdom of Brüning's collaboration with the "pacifist" Socialists.[52]

Obviously Brüning was not serving the purpose for which he had been appointed. Schleicher had hoped that the chancellor would rally the moderate elements of the right and thus take the wind out of the sails of the rabid extremists. The attempt had failed, and the radicals kept gaining ground. Civil war, that haunting specter, became a concrete possibility; to spare the army this trial, Schleicher began wondering whether an accommodation with Hitler might not be advisable. Up to a point Brüning was ready to go along with him. With the chancellor's approval, Schleicher had earlier that year repealed an old order requiring the dismissal of civilian workers employed by the armed forces who were found to have Nazi affiliations. Yet they did not agree on the extent to which such conciliatory measures should be adopted. Brüning was concerned with the domestic aspects of the problem and worried over the growing violence of the stormtroopers and the lawlessness of the Nazi Party; Schleicher on his part fretted over its military implications. That year a new Polish mobilization plan had fallen into German hands and had aroused great concern in the Reichswehr; the army's chief of staff was "terrified" at the prospect of an early Polish invasion of East Prussia and Silesia. In his anguish Schleicher decided that a more positive *modus vivendi* with Hitler was now imperative.[53]

To pave the way for such a rapprochement, Schleicher began to shift his position. Directly and through Planck, he exerted pressure on Brüning to curtail his collaboration with the Socialists. When Brüning decided to come out publicly against the *Stahlhelm* referendum in Prussia, Planck urged him to tone down his plea and took a hand at rewording his original draft. He also advised against a project coordinating the Reich and Prussian governments by presidential decree which would have given the Reich control of the Prussian courts and police, and in return would

[52] Letters in Schleicher Papers/44,i–ii/48; Heinrici to Groener-Geyer, Mar. 29, 1953, Groener-Geyer, *General Groener*, pp. 273–74; Noeldechen, in *Vierteljahrshefte*, I (1953), 274.

[53] Brüning, "Ein Brief," p. 2; Hans Roos, *Polen und Europa: Studien zur deutschen Aussenpolitik: 1931–1939* (Tübingen, 1957), p. 37 n. 43.

have brought Braun and Severing into the Reich government, and he immediately notified Schleicher. Forewarned by Planck, Schleicher compelled the chancellor to abandon this plan that threatened to block his own program.[54] Shortly afterwards he sent General von Hammerstein-Equord, the chief of the army command, to sound out Hitler on a rapprochement between the Nazi Party and Reichswehr. Early in October Schleicher himself met with Hitler. These contacts produced no tangible results, but Schleicher seems to have gained the impression that given time, he might reach an understanding with the Nazi leader.[55]

While Schleicher felt confident that diplomatic finesse could somehow induce Hitler to become more cooperative, the chancellor was just as certain that these were futile hopes. He felt too weak, however, to insist that Schleicher give up these approaches, nor did he dare protest to Hindenburg against Schleicher's activities. Not only did he fear to irritate Hindenburg by criticizing the general—Brüning never outgrew the lieutenant's awe of the marshal which made any direct opposition on his part seem somehow improper. He decided therefore to counteract Schleicher by convincing the marshal of Hitler's intractability. Once the president had seen for himself that there could be no collaboration with Hitler, Brüning's position would be much stronger. As the gathering of the "National Opposition" drew nearer, the chancellor decided to act, and a meeting was arranged between Hitler and Hindenburg. Brüning's hope was that Hindenburg would find Hitler so offensive as to reject out of hand any demands for a Hugenberg-Hitler government that might be made at the Harzburg meeting.

Hitler saw Hindenburg on October 10, one day before the "National Opposition" gathering in Bad Harzburg. As Brüning expected, the meeting was not a success. Hitler felt ill at ease in the presence of the old marshal; Hindenburg, in turn, was repelled by the torrential loyalty protestations and angry complaints of the Nazi leader. When Hindenburg urged him to assume a more tolerant attitude toward the government, Hitler parried his pleas with evasive replies. The president resented such lack of cooperation and the next day he warned Brüning never again to have him meet with "that Czechoslovak corporal."[56]

[54] Cab. mtg., Dec. 19, 1930, *RKz.*/1708/785532–37; Planck to Schleicher, Aug. 11, 18, 1931, in Vogelsang, *Reichswehr*, pp. 427–29; same to same, Aug. 26, 1931, Schleicher Papers/17, ii/61; Severing, *Lebensweg*, II, 303–04.

[55] Bracher, *Auflösung*, pp. 424, 429.

[56] Meissner, *Staatssekretär*, p. 207; Görlitz, *Hindenburg*, p. 350; personal information. On Hindenburg-Brüning relationship, see also Braun, *Von Weimar*, p. 303.

Even though the meeting ended in failure, the very fact that Hitler had been received by Hindenburg greatly enhanced his prestige. Hugenberg later charged that his reception was timed to torpedo the gathering at Harzburg since it was bound to increase Hitler's sense of his own importance. Whether or not this was one of its incidental purposes, the fact is that Harzburg failed to produce that display of unity that the German National chief had hoped for. The Nazis left no doubt that they were participating with great reservations and that their presence was merely a matter of expediency. The beginning of the proceedings had to be delayed until Hitler saw fit to appear and when the gathering adopted resolutions to be submitted to the Reichstag at its forthcoming session, the Nazis insisted that each party present separate motions. Hitler and his subleaders refused to attend the official dinner, and the Fuehrer left a military parade in the afternoon as soon as his stormtroopers had passed in review. For the non-Nazis the day was a bitter disappointment.[57]

Nothing could have demonstrated more clearly than this meeting that those who were trying so hard to "tame" Hitler were unable to understand either him or his movement. To the Nazi leader the forces gathered at Harzburg—the German Nationals, the People's Party, the leaders of business and agriculture, the princes and noblemen—were all spokesmen of a past era and defenders of a moribund way of life. "Money has come to the end of its success," Spengler had written a decade before in the concluding section of his *Decline of the West*, "and that last struggle is getting under way in which civilization will assume its final form—the struggle between money and blood." Hitler acted accordingly. Rightly, the *Tat* observed at the time that Hugenberg's German Nationals had more in common with the Social Democrats whom they despised than with the Nazis they were wooing. However divergent their social and political aims, German Nationals and Socialists shared certain civil and moral standards, while there was no such tie that held German Nationals and Nazis together.[58]

Brüning could derive little comfort from the failure of the Harzburg meeting since the disunity of its participants did not weaken their opposition to him. The chancellor was a very lonesome man

---

[57] Hugenberg to Borchmeyer, Dec. 6, 1948, in Dr. Borchmeyer, *Hugenbergs Ringen in deutschen Schicksalsstunden* (Detmold, 1951), I, 15; Schmidt-Hannover, *Umdenken*, pp. 280–85; Meissner, *Staatssekretär*, p. 207; Schulthess, Oct. 11, 1931, pp. 224–28; Bracher, *Auflösung*, pp. 408–14.

[58] Spengler quotation, *Tat*, XXIII (1931), 669; see also *ibid.*, p. 518.

during those days; never one to give his confidence easily, he was now more tight-lipped than ever. Fearful of indiscretions, he did not share his concerns with his ministerial colleagues; he worried moreover that if he confided to them the full measure of his anxieties, his frankness would hurt their morale. He tended increasingly to make decisions by himself and informed his colleagues only of what was essential; cabinet meetings were limited to the discussion of technical questions, while problems of policy were settled in informal talks with the individuals directly concerned.[59]

This was harmful in more than one way. Overburdened with work, the chancellor had little time to gain a perspective on his policies. There was barely a free moment to weigh their effect and validity. Nor could he, from his study, test their true impact on the country. To most Germans, the Spartan self-denial he imposed upon them was merely a make-shift attempt to patch up the crumbling structure of the German economy. In their anguish they mistook his caution for irresolution, and his factualness for lack of concern. Brüning seemed to do little to alleviate the country's economic distress and did nothing to relieve its deep spiritual crisis. Neither, of course, did Hindenburg whose prime function this ought to have been. "The nation is weary, demoralized, and tired," Hans Zehrer complained in one of his editorials in the *Tat*, "It is disgusted with the parliament. It is waiting for the great call. The Chancellor is standing on the highest platform, visible to all, audible to all. When he speaks, sixty-five million hear his words. If he would speak the language of this people, if he would free this people from its tensions, there would be the great contact between leader and following. Parliament, bureaucracy, business leaders, and party officials would be swept away with one wave of the hand, the masses would start moving and marching, we would be rid of the worry about the uncertainty of the road. But to do this the Chancellor would have to be robust. The Chancellor is not robust." [60]

These words were written by one who was not an admirer of Brüning. Yet Zehrer sensed the dilemma and the personal tragedy of Brüning. He needed the support of the country to convince

---

[59] Brüning, "Ein Brief," p. 8; same, cab. mtg., July 17, 25, 1931, *RKz.*/1684/ 787044-45, 787115; also Nov.-Dec., 1931, 1686/passim; Groener to Gleich, Sept. 20, 1931, Groener-Geyer, *General Groener*, p. 280; Schlange-Schöningen, *Am Tage Danach*, p. 52; testimony of Schwerin-Krosigk, I.M.T., War Crimes Case No. 11, transcript, pp. 22904-05; Schaeffer, affidavit of May 28, 1948, Doc. No. 302, *Dokumenten-Ergänzungsband* II for Schwerin-Krosigk, *ibid*.

[60] Zehrer, in *Tat*, XXIII (1931), pp. 667-68; also *Frankfurter Zeitung*, Reich ed., Oct. 4, 1931.

the fearful, diffident Hindenburg; to neutralize the maneuvers of the vacillating, volatile Schleicher; and to override the pressures of the economic interest groups and the parochial demands of the parties. But to make himself heard, he had to have the strident voice and the drive of a Hitler, and these he had not. When he spoke of the grievances of the nation and of the sacrifices he had to exact from it, he sounded aloof and uninvolved.

Brüning's position that fall resembled that of his ill-fated predecessor, Bethmann Hollweg, fifteen years earlier: Hindenburg played the part of the wavering William II, Schleicher that of Ludendorff, his one-time chief. (What Schleicher lacked in Ludendorff's domineering aggressiveness, he made up in greater suavity.) In turn, Groener's part came to resemble somewhat the wartime role of Hindenburg. A year before Groener had married again after some years of widowhood and had at the age of sixty-four become the proud father of a son. In the enjoyment of his family bliss the Reichswehr minister had given Schleicher a rather free hand in running the Reichswehr's affairs. "The new family idyll has so increased my laziness and my indifference towards all political developments," he confessed to a friend, "that I pass on to Schleicher whatever comes to my desk." Even more serious from Brüning's viewpoint, was the fact that Hindenburg had disapproved of Groener's remarriage. The resulting estrangement between the two men impaired Groener's usefulness as an ally of Brüning, and the chancellor could not be certain that Groener's support was any longer as useful to him as it had been before in his dealings with Hindenburg.[61]

Thus the outlook for Brüning was grim that fall. It was against this dark backdrop that, in mid-October, he had to present himself to the Reichstag.

∽

Brüning could be reasonably certain that once again the perennial no-confidence motion of Nazis, German Nationals, and Communists would be defeated. What he did not know was how large, or how slim, his majority would be. He had assured himself of the continued support of the wavering Economic Party by a promise of special attention to the needs of small business,[62] but he had not been able to obtain the backing of the German People's Party.

[61] Groener to Gleich, Apr. 26, 1931, Groener-Geyer, *General Groener*, p. 279; Eschenburg, "Die Rolle der Persönlichkeit," p. 14.
[62] Mollath, Oct. 16, 1931, *Verhandlungen*, Vol. 446, p. 2191.

Under the leadership of Eduard Dingeldey, a protégé of Stresemann more distinguished for social charm than political gifts, that party had reached a melancholy impasse. Dingeldey might personally have preferred to back Brüning, but the bulk of the party insisted on siding with the "National Opposition." Seeckt had been joined at Harzburg by several colleagues who represented the party's industrial element, the heart of the anti-Brüning fronde. Dingeldey, on the other hand, participated in the unveiling of a Stresemann memorial on the day of the Harzburg meeting. At the same time, there remained a minority in the party determined to support the chancellor, regardless of what the majority did. Thus the German People's Party came to the October session of the Reichstag still undecided as to what course it should take.[63]

To Brüning the support of the People's Party meant more than a numerical increase of his majority. With its industrial affiliations, the party was the mouthpiece of groups whose support Hindenburg had been especially anxious to secure in recent weeks. Their backing was vital to the chancellor politically as well as economically. Perhaps for this reason he did not content himself with reading a prepared statement to the Reichstag; having made his official announcement, he dropped his usual dispassionate manner and launched into a spirited defense of his policies. He failed, however, to win back the People's Party; Dingeldey, when his turn came, announced that his friends were no longer in a position to support the chancellor. Actually, of the 29 members present, only 21 cast their vote against the government, while 5 sided with Brüning and 3 preferred to abstain.[64]

The no-confidence motion was rejected by 295 to 270 votes. Brüning's margin was narrow, and his victory was the more tenuous since his 25-vote majority consisted almost entirely of the "ayes" of the Economic Party. That party, however, supported him only with great reservations and might not have done so at all had Nazis and German Nationals agreed on a joint course of action. It wished it to be known, the spokesman of the Economic Party announced in an involved explanation, that its vote was meant to express confidence in Hindenburg rather than Brüning: "Along with many other parties, we have . . . the most serious misgivings about the new Brüning cabinet. We assume that President von Hindenburg knows these basic difficulties and misgivings and

63 Dingeldey to Bredt, Sept. 15, 1931, Dingeldey Papers/38; Schulthess, Oct. 7, 1931, p. 223; *Frankfurter Zeitung*, Reich ed., Oct. 12, 1931.

64 *Ibid.*, Reich ed., Oct. 14, 1931; Dingeldey, Oct. 15, 1931, *Verhandlungen*, Vol. 446, p. 2135, also p. 2239.

will at the right time insist on the indispensable change of the system—even against the will of those who are opposed to any change—, if no such change has meanwhile taken place, as promised. We shall follow President von Hindenburg in unshakable loyalty, and despite our misgivings we shall therefore tolerate the cabinet which he has appointed." [65]

Brüning thus weathered the Reichstag session. He also obtained another prolonged adjournment of the parliament until late in February. Yet the tenor of the debate made clear how reluctant even the moderate bourgeois parties were to follow him any longer —a fact that would not be lost on the president.

The first one to trim his sails accordingly was Schleicher and he resumed his talks with Hitler. They were held in deepest secrecy, but the inevitable leak occurred, and a Berlin newspaper disclosed that the discussions had eliminated the sharp differences of opinion that had so far existed between the Nazis and Schleicher. The general was reported to be aware of the necessity of giving the Nazi Party some influence in governmental affairs. Schleicher denied that the talks had covered so broad an area; according to him, they had dealt only with the attitude of the Nazis towards the Reichswehr. Yet the *Berliner Börsen-Zeitung*, the unofficial mouthpiece of the Reichswehr ministry, commented a few days later that "after the open-minded talk between Adolf Hitler and the Reichswehr Ministry we may hope that the relationship between other governmental agencies and the strongest German party on the right will also be re-examined." [66]

Schleicher's negotiations with the Nazis were carried on with Brüning's knowledge, and possibly with his approval, but Schleicher's and Brüning's objectives were not the same. Brüning's attitude toward the Nazis during those months still remains to be clarified; since Hindenburg would not permit him to take strong measures against them, most likely he hoped to keep them, and Schleicher as well, in check by means of some minor concessions. He thought them unfit, however, to share governmental responsibilities, if only because Britain and France would never concede an alleviation of the reparations burden to a Nazi-influenced government. Schleicher, however, was willing to give them some portfolios to obtain their support, and he could do this all the more readily as Hitler and Röhm, the chief of staff of the stormtroops, had been able to convince him and Groener that they would always

[65] Hugenberg to Hitler, Mar. 20, 1932, in Matthias and Morsey, *Ende der Parteien,* p. 629; Mollath, Oct. 16, 1931, *Verhandlungen,* Vol. 446, p. 2191.
[66] Caro and Oehme, *Schleichers Aufstieg,* pp. 218–19.

act legally.[67] Schleicher's faith in the legality of the Nazi movement was the more important since his advice carried greater weight with the president than ever before. "In times of political tension," one of his aides has stated with reference to that winter of 1931–32, "hardly a day went by that Oskar von Hindenburg did not come to us or that [Schleicher] was not consulted by phone." [68] Brüning, on the other hand, found it increasingly difficult to convince the marshal of the validity of his policies.

In this context the struggle between the chancellor and the general for the ear of the president continued. Reporting to him on his talks with Hitler, Schleicher asserted, according to Meissner, that he had reached a basic understanding with Hitler. He gave Hindenburg to understand that Brüning's opposition to the Nazis was the main obstacle in the path of their collaboration with the government. Evidently he was beginning to wonder whether the Nazis could ever be drawn out of their opposition as long as Brüning headed the government. If he were to come to terms with the Nazis, he seems to have felt, Brüning might have to be dropped, a conclusion that Hitler doubtless confirmed. Subtle hints of the chancellor's limitations would prepare the way with the president and at the opportune moment Hindenburg could then be persuaded to replace him with someone more willing to follow the general's lead.[69]

Schleicher knew how dissatisfied Hindenburg was with the recent cabinet changes and how much he hoped for a rapprochement with the right in order to purge himself of the unending charges that he was abandoning the "national" elements. Schleicher knew also how much the marshal had come to dislike signing unpopular emergency decrees. He kept complaining that he had not been elected for that purpose and that it was the task of the chancellor, according to the constitution, to determine policies. By a proper approach, the general began to suggest, an arrangement with the right would be possible, and such an arrangement might produce a workable majority in the Reichstag; with its legislative functions restored there would be no need any longer to sign burdensome emergency decrees.

Happy to learn about these possibilities, Hindenburg urged Brüning to try anew to expand his cabinet toward the right. He

67 Vogelsang, *Reichswehr*, pp. 137–42; also Schleicher to Röhm, Nov. 4, 1931, in Severing, *Lebensweg*, II, 322.

68 Noeldechen, in *Vierteljahrshefte*, I (1953), 273.

69 Meissner, *Staatssekretär*, pp. 212–13; same, testimony, in I.M.T., Case No. 11, transcript, pp. 4513–14; Holtzendorff and Noeldechen, in *Vierteljahrshefte*, I (1953), 269–70, 273–74.

wished contact to be established primarily with the *Stahlhelm* and the German Nationals, but his hope was that a successful collaboration with them would produce a change of attitude on the part of the Nazis too. To his dismay Brüning's reply was still the same: his own contacts with the right had shown that there was no basis for a fruitful collaboration; a change of government including the nationalist forces of the right might also have unfavorable repercussions on the reparation discussions on which he had just then embarked. One might as well wait a little while longer; changes would have to be made in any event after the Prussian elections the following spring. They would undoubtedly lead to the breakup of the Socialist-Center coalition in Prussia and give the Center greater freedom of action in the Reich too. But Hindenburg was not satisfied with these explanations; impressed by what Schleicher had told him, he failed to see that neither Hitler nor Hugenberg wished to reach an agreement with Brüning. Averse to any incisive changes, he was not willing to part with Brüning whom he continued to hold in high regard, but he felt that the chancellor ought to pay greater heed to his wishes. In December, he pleaded once more with him to come to terms with the right, but Brüning's answer still was that this was out of the question. Yet again Brüning on his part thought it impossible to suggest that Schleicher was trespassing into an area which was properly his, the chancellor's.[70]

Hindenburg's restlessness manifested itself in other ways. There was hardly a cabinet meeting during those months at which either Brüning or Meissner did not have to report some special request or complaint of the president. As usual, he was mainly concerned with measures affecting the army or agriculture, and these he pursued with his customary persistence. He felt that the reduction of the retirement pay of former officers was too severe, and kept insisting on new agricultural aid measures, especially for the eastern provinces. In his anxiety to conciliate his East German friends, he would not even wait for the government to complete its assistance plans for all of Germany's agriculture. At his special request Brüning was forced to obtain the cabinet's approval for another rush program for the agricultural east in spite of Brüning's serious misgivings. He had to pay a high price for his pains: the immediate consequence was that the agrarian members of the economic council withdrew from that body. They could not cooperate with a government, they complained, that ignored so manifestly the

[70] Meissner, *Staatssekretär*, p. 212; Brüning, "Ein Brief," pp. 4, 6; Hindenburg and Meissner, "Niederschrift," in Vogelsang, *Reichswehr*, p. 460.

interests of the farmers in Western and Southern Germany. The government could merely reply that it had been guided by the best available advice. To put the blame for the measure on the president was clearly out of the question, and he was not one to assume that responsibility on his own.[71]

Hindenburg, however, earned few thanks for his efforts. On December 15, the East Prussian chamber of agriculture passed another of those shrill resolutions with which it kept pressuring the president into further aid measures. This time it bluntly requested him to clear the road, both personally and in the cabinet, for men tested in their fight for and in their faith in their country—men capable of saving not only its agriculture but the entire nation. The president of the chamber hastened to explain that East Prussia appreciated what Hindenburg had done for the province; it merely wished to see a change of the political system so that the president would have sufficient power to carry out his intentions to help East Prussia. But this after-thought could hardly soften the bitter shock Hindenburg must have felt when he saw himself disavowed so bluntly by his fellow East Prussians.[72]

To the hapless Brüning the demarche could not have come at a worse moment. The expiration of the president's term of office was drawing nearer; to spare the hard-pressed country the disruptions of an election campaign, he was hard at work to arrange a parliamentary extension of Hindenburg's term. One of the major obstacles in the path of this plan was the latter's unwillingness to serve beyond his appointed time. The weary old man was longing to be relieved of his "responsibility" and to withdraw into peaceful retirement at Neudeck. Yet Brüning knew that unless the marshal ran, Hitler was certain to be elected the next president. The East Prussian protest was issued at the very moment at which Hindenburg showed the first signs of wavering in his determination and could but render more difficult Brüning's delicate task of persuasion. The chancellor also needed the president's signature for another emergency decree. Again it was one that the president could be expected to accept with the greatest reluctance. There were to be new wage and salary cuts, a further reduction of pensions, some shifts in the tax structure, but also an over-all reduction of prices, rents, and interest rates so as to enable German exports to compete with Britain's after that country had devalued its currency. The effectiveness of these measures was again weak-

---

[71] Meissner, cab. mtg., Oct. 3, 1931, *RKz.*/1685/788412, Jan. 15, Feb. 18, 1932, 1709/789063, 789273–74; Brüning, Nov. 16, 1931, *RKz.*/1686/788670.

[72] Schulthess, Nov. 19, Dec. 15, 1931, pp. 254–56, 271.

ened, however, by the artificially high food prices that continued tariff increases kept far above the world market price.[73] In its last section the decree introduced some new measures to maintain public peace and order: stiffer penalties against the unauthorized use of weapons, more effective protection of the government against libelous and slanderous attacks, and above all a provision prohibiting members of political organizations from wearing uniforms. This latter step had been considered for over a year since the lack of identifying uniforms or insignia might reduce clashes and street battles, but Hindenburg had consistently refused to approve such a measure. His fear was that it would do great harm to the *Stahlhelm* over which he still watched with a fatherly eye, despite that group's obstructionist tactics. While Nazi stormtroopers and Socialist *Reichsbanner* men had their parties to provide them with programs, the *Stahlhelm* lacked such a reservoir of ideological inspiration. Once it was deprived of the identification tag of a common uniform, it was in danger of losing its followers.

Yet an intervention against the militant organizations had become indispensable. Hardly a day passed without at least half a dozen street battles, almost always with fatal results and a growing number of casualties. In November, documents had been turned over to the Hessian police which showed that the local Nazi organization was drawing up blueprints for the administration of that state after the overthrow of the government. Many state governments had long demanded the intervention of the Reich government against this open defiance of governmental authority; now they became more insistent and could not be put off any longer. Foreign political considerations, too, demanded a crushing of the growing Nazi threat although the government considered it politic to deny this. Yet due to Hindenburg's opposition, the promulgation of the decree had to be postponed several times. After the president had finally given his approval, Meissner warned the cabinet that the president had signed it with great misgivings. The implication was that he would not be likely to sign another decree of this nature. (On the very day Meissner served this notice on the cabinet, Grzesinski, the police commissioner of Berlin, was forced, at Hindenburg's express request, to cancel an order for Hitler's deportation from Prussia "as an undesirable alien whose conduct jeopardizes the interests of the state.")

[73] Brüning, cab. mtg., Oct. 2, 1931, *RKz./*1685/788364–65, Nov. 9, 1931, *RKz./*1686/788630; Franz Oppenheimer, in *Tagebuch*, Jan. 17, 1931, p. 98; *Dt. Volkswirt*, Oct. 2, 1931, p. 5.

Once the decree had been issued, there was the usual flood of protests and complaints to the Presidential Palace. To Hindenburg's relief, Groener, in his capacity as minister of the interior, suggested an amendment to permit the wearing of group insignia and pins since an enforcement of this prohibition proved impossible. The president readily gave his approval.[74]

Another contretemps arose over a Socialist proposal to reduce the annuities paid to the former ruling families by the various state governments. Since every German had suffered large cuts in his income, the demand was morally and legally justified and would have eased the financial burdens the states had to carry. Hindenburg made it known that he opposed any reduction of these payments, and justified his refusal on the grounds that the demand was unconstitutional. Nor did he change his mind when the ministry of justice advised him that the proposal was compatible with the constitution. He persisted in his opposition even when there were indications that a majority would support a bill enacting the plan in the Reichstag. With Hindenburg's backing needed for other measures, the chancellor could not afford a showdown. He had to prevent consideration of the request by the Reichstag that was about to reconvene. Since his own party favored the proposal, his task was especially difficult, and great skill and diplomacy were required to keep it off the Reichstag's agenda.[75]

Despite the growing strain on his relations with Hindenburg, Brüning was hopeful that he would ultimately master his troubles. The moment was approaching at last when he would reap the fruits of his efforts—the foreign political successes he needed so badly appeared to be near. In November 1931, he invoked a clause in the Young Plan that permitted a reexamination of some of the German commitments in the event of a serious economic decline. Specifically it made provision for the suspension of part of the German annuities. Going beyond these limited rights, Brüning asked for a complete reexamination of Germany's reparation debts. The economic crisis, he argued, had reached dimensions never anticipated by the drafters of the Young Plan. A special committee of financial experts was at once appointed by the creditor nations to meet at Basel. Within less than a month

74 Cab. mtg., Sept. 30, 1931, *RKz.*/1685/788284–86; Brüning, Dec. 6, 1931, Meissner, Dec. 11, 1931, 1686/788930, 788974; Groener and Meissner, Jan. 15, 1932, 1709/789065; Groener to Gleich, Nov. 1, 1931, Groener-Geyer, *General Groener*, p. 283; Schleicher to Reichswehr commanders, Jan. 11–12, 1932, *Vierteljahrshefte*, II (1954), 415–16.

75 Cab. mtgs., Feb. 15, 17, 1932, *RKz.*/1709/789255, 789262–63.

it submitted a report confirming Brüning's claims, and plans were now laid for another reparations conference to be held in Lausanne in late January. Yet while the Basel report had implied that Germany might resume payments at some later date, the German press announced at once that the only possible solution was the complete and permanent cancellation of all reparation debts. Brüning also made this demand in a talk with the British ambassador, insisting that he would not be satisfied with a temporary suspension of payments; rather than accept a partial settlement, he would request an adjournment of the conference in the expectation that the deepening crisis would vindicate the German position. The statement, made to placate his domestic opponents, provoked a sharp French reaction; greatly incensed, Paris insisted on a postponement of the conference until June, on the grounds that French elections were to be held in May and no fruitful agreement could be expected until after that event.

Meanwhile all Brüning could obtain was a rather noncommittal statement on the part of the creditors: the conference would seek "to agree on a lasting settlement of the reparation question raised in the Report of the Basel Experts and on methods necessary to solve other economic and financial difficulties which are responsible for the present world crisis." But June was a long way off, and once more Brüning had to ask the country and the president to be patient, while his enemies seized on the delay as new evidence of his weakness.[76]

Time was also needed in another endeavor. In February 1932, after preparations of more than a year, a Disarmament Conference convened at Geneva. Here Brüning hoped to secure an acknowledgement of Germany's equality in military matters, a matter which of course was also especially close to the marshal's heart. This acknowledgement was to be implemented by a reduction of armaments on the part of the other Powers, while Germany would be allowed to equip her armed forces with any weapons retained by the others. She was to have the right to set up a militia that would train 100,000 men yearly for a period of eight to twelve months. At the same time the term of enlistment for members of the regular Reichswehr was to be reduced from twelve to five years allowing for the training of additional men.

These objectives, moreover, could not be achieved overnight.

---

[76] *Documents on British Foreign Policy* (hereafter cited as *"DBFP."*), E. L. Woodward and Rohan Butler, eds., 2d ser., vol. III, *passim;* esp. Brüning, as quoted in Rumbold to Simon, Jan. 8, 1932, p. 12; Pünder, *Reichskanzlei,* entries of Jan. 7, 11, 1932, pp. 111–12.

In fact, the reparations and rearmament problems were mutually exclusive. The demand for a reparations settlement was based on Germany's desperate financial plight and the fact that she had reached the limit of her endurance. Rearmament, on the other hand, required substantial expenditures. Brüning decided therefore to secure an acknowledgement in principle of Germany's military equality before advancing his specific demands. Once Germany's reparation commitments had been removed and with them the restrictive financial regulations of the Young Plan, an increase of the country's armed forces could be financed by a credit expansion.[77]

Ultimately, however, the success of all these plans depended not only on Brüning's diplomatic skill, but was predicated as much on his ability to ward off his domestic opponents long enough for his diplomatic endeavors to bear fruit. This, in turn, he could accomplish only with Hindenburg's backing. What mattered above all, therefore, was to assure the reelection of Hindenburg whose term of office was about to expire.

[77] Wilhelm Deist, "Brüning, Herriot und die Abrustüngsgespräche von Bessinge 1932," *Vierteljahrshefte für Zeitgeschichte*, v (1957), 266, 268; "Richtlinien für die deutsche Delegation zur Abrüstungskonferenz," append. to cab. mtg., Jan. 15, 1932, *RKz*./1709/789066; Wheeler-Bennett, *Wooden Titan*, pp. 381–82.

CHAPTER 8

REELECTION

T HE presidential election of 1925, while a matter of serious concern to many people, had caused deep anxiety to few, if any. The republican parties had hardly appreciated the political potentialities of the presidency and had considered that office primarily a ceremonial post. The rightist leaders, on the other hand, had been aware that control of the office might help them overhaul the country's political structure. They had understood, too, that the victory of the republican candidate would put an end to their hopes of establishing an authoritarian state on the prewar pattern in the foreseeable future. They knew, however, that the defeat of their own candidate would not turn them into outcasts without rights and legal protection. Their misgivings were, moreover, tempered by the knowledge that even a victory of a rightist candidate might not prove an unmitigated blessing. Field Marshal von Hindenburg would have to swear allegiance to the republican constitution, and his acknowledgment of the new order might root it more deeply in the mind of the nation.

Since that time, however, the importance of the presidency had grown beyond all expectations; the Reichstag had all but ceased to function and new forces had emerged, determined to supplant the remnants of the democratic-republican system with a brutal totalitarian dictatorship. There was every reason then to assume that the outcome of the approaching elections in the spring of 1932 would have a crucial impact on the course of German developments.

Despite this fact the question of candidates received little attention until a few months before the election was held. In fact, there had been more interest in that problem immediately after the first election of Hindenburg when few expected him to live out his term.[1] But Hindenburg's unexpected longevity and the deepening political and economic crisis diverted attention to the more pressing problems of the day. Hindenburg himself had at one time thought of Admiral Scheer, the chief of the German

[1] Westarp Papers, *passim;* Stresemann Papers, *passim;* Wegener to Levetzow, July 17, 1929, Wegener Papers/30; *Deutsche Führerbriefe,* Nov. 29, 1929, Braun Papers.

naval forces in World War I, as a suitable successor. Later he may have considered Groener, yet no effort was ever made to groom the Reichswehr minister for that post. His growing unpopularity with the right and his estrangement from Hindenburg deprived him of whatever presidential prospects he may have had.[2]

Interest in the presidential successor revived as the end of Hindenburg's term was approaching. In the first half of 1931 there were some suggestions of extending Hindenburg's term beyond its appointed time. Westarp, convinced of the marshal's indispensability, proposed that he be given lifetime tenure by parliamentary vote. The plan was well received in conservative Reichstag circles. The German People's Party showed some interest in it, but did not pursue the matter, possibly because some of its leaders favored the candidacy of Seeckt. Seeckt's candidacy, however, was bitterly opposed in nationalist circles. "We would get some sort of Hindenburg again," a former Reichswehr general complained, "who may not be touched for national reasons, and who would make some fine gestures and utter some noble phrases, but would actually act quite differently." In May, a leadership meeting of the *Volksnationale Reichsvereinigung,* the party organization of the Young German Order, expressed the wish that Hindenburg remain president beyond his present term of office. Some months later, Papen and a leading Rhenish industrialist called on Brüning to propose a parliamentary extension of Hindenburg's term in order to avoid the disruptive effects of an election campaign. At that time Westarp, too, resumed his efforts to promote Hindenburg's continuing in office. To his happy surprise Westarp was told that the *Stahlhelm* was ready to support a renewed candidacy of its honorary member. He welcomed this news, not merely as an encouraging improvement of Hindenburg's chances, but as a first sign in the breakup of the "National Opposition." Reports of what transpired at the Harzburg meeting that fall seemed to confirm his hopes.[3]

At the same time other forces were hard at work to prevent the reelection of Hindenburg. As usual, Hugenberg was the guiding spirit of these efforts. His plan to take over the government with

2 Wilhelm Widenmann, *Marine-Attaché an der kaiserlich-deutschen Botschaft in London 1907–1912* (Göttingen, 1952), p. 301; memorandum by Dorothea Groener-Geyer, Schleicher Papers/70/8–14.

3 Westarp correspondence, quoted in Bracher, *Auflösung,* pp. 444–45; letter to Epp, Feb. 14, 1931, and Epp's reply, Feb. 21, 1931, *Miscellaneous German Records Collection,* Pt. I/9/9293–96, 9299; resolution of leaders of Volksnationale Reichsvereinigung, May 14, 1931, *Dt. Gesch.-Kal.,* 1931, A, 265; Papen, *Wahrheit,* p. 168; Rademacher to Westarp, Sept. 24, Oct. 5, 1931, Westarp to Rademacher, Oct. 12, 1931, Westarp Papers.

the help of the Nazis had been wrecked by the Reichstag election returns in September 1930. The Nazi Party had grown to four or five times the size of Hugenberg's following, and Hitler was now more outspoken than ever in his contempt for Hugenberg and his industrial and agrarian backers. Hugenberg's hatred of the Weimar "system" precluded any accommodation with Brüning, and he submitted resignedly to the calculated insults with which Hitler chose to offend him. Even if he had wanted to, Hugenberg could no longer have come to terms with the chancellor; few of his followers would have accepted such a complete turnabout. All that he could hope to do was to keep Hitler from getting complete control of the government so that his own German National Party might exert some restraint on the Nazis and safeguard the economic interests of his industrial and agrarian following against any "socialist" excesses.

This opportunity appeared to present itself in the approaching presidential election. Hugenberg was opposed, not only to the candidacy of Hindenburg, but also to that of Hitler. Once elected, he was afraid, Hitler might use the presidency to establish a Nazi dictatorship. To his relief Hitler assured him when he met with him at a Bavarian spa late in August that he was not going to run for the presidency since he could not afford a defeat.[4] Hugenberg suggested that they join forces in support of a candidate who was not formally tied to any party and would be acceptable to both German Nationals and Nazis as well as to the middle parties. By such a joint effort the reelection of Hindenburg might be prevented. As suitable candidates he proposed several men: Karl Jarres, the ill-fated candidate in the first presidential election in 1925; Count von der Goltz, head of the League of Patriotic Societies; and General Otto von Below, a World War I commander who was the favorite choice of the German Nationals and seems to have enjoyed some popularity also in Nazi circles. Hitler agreed in principle, or so Hugenberg thought, but asked postponement of the choice of a candidate, and no selection was made. But Hugenberg was confident that his

---

[4] Actually Hitler did not qualify for the presidency since he was not a German citizen; but if this question was discussed at the meeting, none of the available sources mention it. It is possible that both men had reached an understanding already that at an opportune moment Hitler would be naturalized, as he was some months later, by way of a civil service appointment in the little state of Brunswick. Two weeks after Hitler and Hugenberg met, Brunswick's German National government was transformed into a German National-Nazi coalition. See Rudolf Morsey, "Hitler als braunschweigischer Regierungsrat," *Vierteljahrshefte für Zeitgeschichte*, VIII (1960), 434 n. 69; Schulthess, Sept. 15, 1931, p. 202.

plan would succeed, and he looked forward to the Harzburg meeting as an opportunity to demonstrate the unity of the "National Opposition." After such a public commitment the Nazis would have to accept a common candidate.

Harzburg did not fulfill his hopes; instead of unity it demonstrated the glaring disunity of the "national" camp, and Hitler took pains to impress on his bourgeois partners how contemptuous he felt of them. Yet Hugenberg would not give up; twice he tried to meet with Hitler during the following days, twice meetings were arranged, and only after Hitler had cancelled both, Hugenberg dropped his plan. Hitler had probably never been interested in it, but had merely wished to keep all doors open. A Nazi editor who sounded him out in November got the impression that he had not yet given much thought to the presidential election. His hope apparently was that the problem might be solved by the early death of that "old fool." In that case of course he would run himself.[5]

As in 1925, the leftist parties were even slower than their rightist opponents to consider the candidacy problem, but this time the delay was not due to an underestimation of the importance of the presidency. Rather, it stemmed from the fact that the republican-democratic forces either felt that they had no presentable candidate or that, if they had such a man, Otto Braun, for example, he had no chance of being elected. Preoccupied with the ever increasing day-to-day problems, they had made no attempt to groom a candidate who by means of a constructive and hopeful program could appeal to the nation and provide an antidote to the demagoguery of the Nazis.

In September 1931, the *Reichbanner* decided to support a second candidacy of Hindenburg as the "only way . . . of preventing the Presidency of a National Socialist without civil war," and some Socialist leaders also began to work for Hindenburg's reelection. In November, the Social Democrats sounded out the Communists about the creation of a common front against Nazism; but if there were individual leaders who welcomed the move, the dominant Communist faction, guided by Moscow's instructions, was not averse to the prospect of a Nazi dictatorship. The hope of these leaders was that the ensuing chaos would enable them to seize power more speedily, and they preferred to fight the Socialists rather than Nazis and German Nationals. The terms they

---

[5] Hugenberg to Hitler, Mar. 20, 1932, in Matthias and Morsey, *Ende der Parteien*, pp. 627–29; Borchmeyer, *Hugenbergs Ringen*, I, 18–19; Schmidt-Hannover, *Umdenken*, pp. 271–75; Hitler, quoted, in Krebs, *Gestalten*, p. 34.

proposed for any collaboration were clearly intended to wreck the Socialist Party; they insisted that the Socialists would not only have to withdraw their support from the Brüning Government, but would also have to expel all leaders who had been responsible for this support. If accepted, this demand would have meant the unconditional surrender of the Socialist rank-and-file to the Communists. This, indeed, was the Communists' plan, and it was clearly revealed in their insistence that they wished to establish a united front "from below."[6]

Individual last-minute attempts to find an anti-Nazi to take Hindenburg's place also ended in failure since all those who were approached refused to face Hitler: Carl Petersen, the lord mayor of Hamburg and one of the leaders of the moribund State Party; Dr. Wilhelm Solf, who had held high governmental offices in the Empire and during the first days of the Weimar Republic and had more recently been the German ambassador to Japan; and Dr. Heinrich Sahm, for many years president of the Free State of Danzig and now the lord mayor of Berlin. At this late hour these little-known men had indeed no hope of defeating him. One final effort was made late in 1931. Severing thought he had found a promising candidate in Dr. Hugo Eckener, of Zeppelin fame. Unlike the other men who were approached, the airship commander had at least the advantage of being a well known and popular figure. Politically he stood on the right—his political views had long been close to the *Stahlhelm's*. "One must assume a criminal intent on the part of those states which imposed the Young Plan on Germany," he had declared in a public address in 1930, and "only a warrior people will get ahead in the world." But his nationalism was tempered by his disgust for Nazi excesses and their contempt for the most elementary human rights. If nothing else, he could at least be expected to curb them more vigorously than Hindenburg had been willing to do. Though reluctant to enter the political arena, Eckener did not reject the proposal. Yet before his candidacy could be explored any further, Brüning had placed before the country his plan of extending Hindenburg's term of office by a constitutional amendment.[7]

[6] Reichsbanner resolution, in Schulthess, Jan. 8, 1932, p. 5; Braun to Kautsky, Feb. 9, 1932, *Vierteljahrshefte*, VIII (1960), 83; Stampfer, *Vierzehn Jahre*, pp. 608–09; Flechtheim, *Kommunistische Partei*, pp. 168–70; Remmele, Oct. 14, 1931, *Verhandlungen*, Vol. 446, p. 2096; Bahne, in Matthias and Morsey, *Ende der Parteien*, p. 669.
[7] Walter Zechlin, *Pressechef bei Ebert, Hindenburg und Kopf* (Hanover, 1956), p. 118; Severing, *Lebensweg*, II, 314–15; Arnold Brecht, "Die Auflösung der Weimarer Republik und die politische Wissenschaft," *Zeitschrift für Politik*, n. s.,

The chancellor of course had also been pondering the problem of candidates. That Hitler or any other Nazi would have to be barred from the presidency was self-evident to him. Some of his Centrist friends suggested that he run himself for the presidency, and so did the leaders of the Bavarian People's Party. The Bavarian Party had been among the first to endorse Hindenburg in 1925 but now had its doubts whether he was still strong enough to defend the constitution against the assaults of the Nazis. But Brüning dismissed these plans. He knew that he lacked the mass appeal and the eloquence to rally the nation behind him; his record as chancellor, moreover, had earned him a measure of unpopularity that he could not possibly overcome. Canvassing the field, he found no one who could challenge a Nazi candidate with any hope of success except Hindenburg.[8]

Brüning did not reach this conclusion lightly. He knew that the president was longing for the day when he could relinquish his office and retire to Neudeck to live out his life there free from political responsibilities and at one once more with his old friends and comrades-in-arms.[9] The president's age, his mental and physical decline, his doubts about Brüning would moreover make any future collaboration increasingly difficult. Yet whatever problems he might face later with Hindenburg, the chancellor knew that he would have to work for the president's reelection if his policies were to have any chance of finally bearing fruit.

To make a renomination more palatable to Hindenburg, Brüning took up the plan of having his term extended by a vote of Reichstag and Reichsrat. This procedure would also spare the country the strains and stresses of an election campaign, and it would provide a demonstration of German unity that would strengthen his own bargaining position at the forthcoming reparations and disarmament conferences.

Given Hindenburg's age, however, this arrangement could provide no more than a temporary solution to the problem of keeping the Nazis out of the presidency. If Hindenburg should die within the next two or three years, Hitler might still become president. The chancellor decided therefore to couple the re-

---

II (1955), 306–07; Eckener statements in *Tagebuch*, Mar. 22, 1931, p. 443; but see also on Eckener, *Sozialistische Monatshefte*, LXXV (1932), p. 113.

8 Wheeler-Bennett, *Wooden Titan*, p. 352; Schwend, *Bayern*, pp. 418–19; Schäffer, quoted in Matthias and Mosey, *Ende der Parteien*, p. 459.

9 Preparations for that day had been under way for some time. Beginning in June 1931 a special file was kept in the presidential *Büro* concerning the honors to be shown to him when he left office. *BdRPr.*, R 54/323.

election of Hindenburg with an attempt to restore the monarchy. Since a return to prewar conditions was out of the question and since both the ex-Emperor and the ex-Crown Prince were too discredited to be restored to the throne, he envisaged an English-style limited monarchy, with Hindenburg acting as Regent during the remainder of his life and one of the Crown Prince's sons assuming the crown upon the death of the marshal. He discussed the matter with several Reichstag deputies, and since they approved of the plan, he felt encouraged enough to pursue it further. He understood, however, that the proposal would meet with strong opposition, although he seems to have underestimated the intensity of antimonarchist feelings. The implementation of the plan, by plebiscite, therefore would have to wait until he had strengthened his own position by a major foreign political success. Once he had secured the cancellation of all reparation payments and had scored some success in the disarmament talks, the nation, impressed with these achievements, would be more inclined to accept his proposal. The plan, he felt confident, would also enable him to drive a wedge between the German Nationals and the Nazis; while the latter might well oppose it, the former could not possibly do so. But above all, Brüning expected it to ease his task of persuading Hindenburg to run once more for the presidency. The marshal, he thought, would gladly seek reelection if by so doing he could help to restore the monarchy and thus purge himself of whatever guilt attached to his actions on that fateful November 9, 1918. As the chancellor reasoned, Hindenburg would look upon the return of the monarchy as the crowning achievement of his long life.

To his surprise and disappointment, Hindenburg rejected the plan out of hand. He would never, he told Brüning, lend his hand to the restoration of anyone but "the Emperor himself." To let someone else occupy the throne was a violation of the oath of fealty he had sworn to his monarch. Nor would he give his consent to a monarchy on the British model which to his mind was no genuine monarchy. Even Bismarck's Empire had been unsatisfactory, he maintained, and his thoughts returned to the long-past days of the old Prussian monarchy which had always remained his true home. "Though I spoke with the tongues of men and of angels," Brüning recalled later, "I could have made no impression on him."

It was unlikely, then, that Hindenburg would change his mind, but if anyone could convince him of the soundness of Brüning's proposal that man was obviously Schleicher. Schleicher, however, appears to have shown no enthusiasm for the chancellor's plan. "The idea," Brüning has written, "was rejected not only by Hindenburg but also by the leaders of the Army [and obviously this meant, above all, Schleicher whom the chancellor must have consulted before anyone else]. They were highly skeptical of the possibility of realizing the plan by constitutional means, that is, by a plebiscite. Any unconstitutional means would have been rejected by the leaders of the Army as sharply as by me." The plan thus had to be dropped.[10]

Though the Nazis might no longer be barred permanently from the presidency, it still remained as important as ever to keep them out of that office as long as possible. Brüning now had to persuade the president to agree to an extension of his term without any change in the governmental system. But once more Hindenburg balked. He brought up the familiar arguments which militated against his renewed candidacy—his age, his aversion to politics, his right to quiet and privacy after seven long years at his post. He also pointed to his alienation from his one-time supporters. They would be unlikely to cast their vote for him; in opposing him they might bring up again his role on that unforgotten November day. And he certainly would not want to be the candidate of the left.[11]

Yet Brüning would not give in. Anyone whose counsel carried weight with the president—Schleicher, Neurath, Otto Braun—was enlisted to help change his mind. But for everyone who urged him to seek reelection, there were others who warned him against becoming the candidate of the Socialists and thus betraying everything for which he had stood during his long life. How effective these counsels were, Otto Braun learned when he came to call on Hindenburg. The president willingly listened to Braun's arguments and promised to think them over, but when Braun left, he asked him to keep his call confidential. If the news leaked out that a Socialist had visited him, it would have provoked new angry complaints from old friends and associates, and the weary old man wanted so much to be left in peace.[12]

In the end he let himself be convinced that unless he remained

---

[10] Wheeler-Bennett, *Wooden Titan*, pp. 352–55; Brüning to Kaufmann, n.d., Kaufmann, *Monarchism*, p. 286 n. 55. The only source for this episode is Brüning himself on whose information all other accounts are based; cf. also Kessler, *Tagebücher*, July 20, 1935, p. 738.

[11] Wheeler-Bennett, *Wooden Titan*, pp. 355–56; Braun, *Von Weimar*, pp. 368–69; information from Dr. Zechlin.

[12] Simon to Rumbold, Jan. 12, 1932, *DBFP.*, ii, iii, 18–19; Braun, *Von Weimar*, pp. 368–69; Mackensen to Westarp, Feb. 18, 1932, Westarp Papers.

in office, an extremist of either the right or the left might become president and the country be plunged into civil war. He seems to have had some objection, though, to a parliamentary extension of his term. Otto Braun, for one, had urged him to seek reelection through direct election, and he had agreed with him. Yet Brüning assured him that his proposed strategy was constitutional,[13] and the prospect of being spared the harassments of an election campaign was not unwelcome either. He agreed to a parliamentary extension of his term, provided it would be supported unconditionally by all parties except the Communists. He also reserved the right to resign whenever he considered conditions sufficiently stabilized to permit the holding of new presidential elections.

The chancellor now turned to the task of getting the necessary parliamentary support for his plan. The middle parties readily saw its advantages. The Social Democrats were somewhat more reluctant to accept it, but since they too wished Hindenburg to remain in office, they approved on condition that the rightist parties would back it without being granted special concessions. Obviously the Socialists would gain nothing from an extension of Hindenburg's presidency if Nazi and German National support were bought with the replacement of the Brüning government by one made up of rightists or with new Reichstag elections.[14]

Brüning apparently did not anticipate strong opposition from Hitler or Hugenberg. An earlier approach, the previous August, had, it is true, been unsuccessful; both Hitler and Hugenberg had then refused to support Hindenburg's reelection, even though Brüning seems to have suggested to them that he was willing to give up the chancellorship once he had attained a reparations settlement. Meanwhile, however, Schleicher's negotiations with the Nazi leaders had made some progress, according to his reports, and Hitler had even promised in writing that "my 107 men in the Reichstag are going to support the constitu-

[13] There existed precedents for Brüning's plan in the extension of Ebert's term of office in 1920 and 1922, but even so the project ran counter to the wording and the spirit of Art. 41 of the Weimar Constitution. Even among Brüning's strongest supporters there were serious misgivings about the constitutional propriety of his proposal. *Frankfurter Zeitung*, Reich ed., Jan. 9, 1932; Braun, *Von Weimar*, p. 371. Brüning might have argued, however, (and perhaps did) that a violation of the constitution was justifiable in order to shield the state against Hitler rather than surrender it to him by a rigid adherence to legality. Cf. Eschenburg, "Rolle der Persönlichkeit," p. 6.

[14] Meissner, *Staatssekretär*, p. 215; Braun to Severing, Jan. 19, 1932, Severing Papers/1932 I; Braun, *Von Weimar*, p. 371; *Frankfurter Zeitung*, Reich ed., Jan. 9, 12, 1932.

tional amendment about the extension of the President's term of office." (This promise may have been prompted by a desire to neutralize the recent embarrassing discovery in Hesse of local preparations for a violent coup.) And once Brüning had gotten Hitler's consent, Hugenberg could not possibly withhold his. Brüning's confidence was indeed such that he made plans to convene the Reichstag within a week after his talks with both men. He wished to have the necessary legislation enacted before the Reparations Conference met at Lausanne. He chose this particular time also to state publicly that any resumption of reparations payments was out of the question. His hope was that this move would help to break down the resistance of the "National Opposition" and that its support, in turn, would impress the Western Powers with the nationwide backing that his policies enjoyed.[15]

Hitler, then, was the first to be consulted. Early in January he had talks with Groener, Brüning, and Schleicher. He neither accepted nor rejected Brüning's proposal, but asked for time to consider it. Those who negotiated with him got the impression that he was not unwilling to support Brüning's plan. He did make it clear, however, that if he were to accept that plan, his cooperation could be had at a price only. There were three demands he seems to have made throughout these negotiations: the government was to recognize the "legality" of the Nazi Party and remove all restrictions imposed on party members and party activities; the Prussian Landtag elections were to be held at the proper time in the spring (there were rumors that they would be postponed to keep Prussia's Socialist-Center government in power); the Reichstag, finally, would at once be dissolved so that a newly elected, more representative parliament could enact the extension of Hindenburg's term. The first two demands presented no problem. According to Goebbels, Brüning was willing to acknowledge the legal character of the party, and Groener shortly afterwards repealed the order which barred Nazis from service in the Reichswehr and the navy. Nor had there been any plan to postpone the Prussian elections, and an official statement to that effect was published in the press. But the demand for immediate new Reichstag elections Brüning could not accept. It would have

15 Meissner, *Staatssekretär*, p. 216; Brüning, "Ein Brief," p. 5; Josef Becker, "Brüning, Kaas und das Problem einer Regierungsbeteiligung der NSDAP 1930-32," *Historische Zeitschrift*, CIVC (1963), 89-90; Vogelsang, *Reichswehr*, pp. 125-26; Hitler, in Pünder, *Reichskanzlei*, entry of June 7, 1932, p. 135; *Sozialdemokratische Partei-Korrespondenz*, No. 1, Jan. 1932, pp. 7-9; *Frankfurter Zeitung*, Reich ed., Jan. 10, 1932.

cost him the votes of the Social Democrats which he needed, it would have jeopardized his reparations and disarmament negotiations, and it would have ended his hope of avoiding a national election campaign during those perilous days. Possibly Hindenburg too would have rejected such an arrangement as incompatible with his dignity and the prestige of his office.[16]

If Hitler seemed willing to support Brüning's plan on certain conditions, Hugenberg made it clear that he would have nothing to do with it. He would not lend his hand, he declared, to any enterprise in which the Social Democrats participated, nor was he willing to take any step that could be interpreted as an expression of confidence in Brüning. Hugenberg succeeded in convincing Hitler that they would have nothing to gain from a parliamentary extension of Hindenburg's presidency. His suggestion was to reject Brüning's plan, but to make Hindenburg their candidate in a popular election, provided he were willing to dismiss Brüning and his cabinet and appoint at once a "national" government of their choosing. New Reichstag and Prussian Landtag elections were then to follow. Hitler agreed, and both president and chancellor were told that Nazis and German Nationals were unable, on both political and constitutional grounds, to support Brüning's plan; the possibility of supporting Hindenburg on their own terms, however, in the popular election was left open.[17]

The plans for an extension of Hindenburg's term thus had to be dropped, and he could stay in office only if he were willing to run in an election. Sensitive to any rebuff, he was disappointed and offended by the failure of Brüning's plan, but to the chancellor's relief, he declared himself ready to stand as a candidate. He insisted, however, that he would have to be the candidate, not of one party, but of the great majority of the people. Apart from the Communists, he must have no serious opponent since he would not want to get involved in a fight. His reelection, in other words, had to be assured in advance.

For this again the support of the right was required. Negotiations with Nazis and German Nationals continued, and Captain

<hr />

[16] Wheeler-Bennett, *Wooden Titan*, p. 361; Caro and Oehme, *Schleichers Aufstieg*, p. 222; Braun, *Von Weimar*, p. 371; *Frankfurter Zeitung*, Reich ed., Jan. 8, 11, 1932.

[17] Memoranda by Pünder, Jan. 1932, *RKz.*, R 43 I/583; Westarp to Hiller, Jan. 14, 1932, Westarp Papers; Josef Goebbels, *Vom Kaiserhof zur Reichskanzlei: Eine historische Darstellung in Tagebuchblättern* (Munich, 1940), entries of Jan. 6-12, 1932, pp. 19-24; Hugenberg to Hitler, Mar. 20, 1932, Matthias and Morsey, *Ende der Parteien*, pp. 627-28; Groener to Gleich, Jan. 24, 1932, Groener-Geyer, *General Groener*, p. 286; Dingeldey to *Amtsgericht* Berlin-Mitte, Dec. 15, 1932, reprinted in Vogelsang, *Reichswehr*, pp. 440-42.

Hermann Göring, Hitler's liaison man in Berlin who as a much decorated flying ace of World War I fame could count on a friendly reception by Hindenburg was a frequent caller at the Presidential Palace during the following weeks. But while Hitler and Hugenberg agreed that Brüning would have to go if they were to support Hindenburg, they could not agree on the composition of the new government they intended to form. Hitler demanded the chancellorship for himself and the Reichswehr and interior ministries for two of his party friends. German Nationals and *Stahlhelm* would have to make do with economics, finance, and labor. Neither Hugenberg nor Seldte were willing to surrender all major positions of power and they refused to accept these terms. The *Stahlhelm* insisted, moreover, on assurances that its organization would remain intact in case Hitler should become president. Since its members kept clashing with Nazi stormtroopers and its ranks were constantly raided by Nazi recruiters, it was concerned about its fate under Hitler, and its leaders became even more concerned when Hitler was evasive and refused to commit himself. Even if *Stahlhelm* and German Nationals had agreed to Hitler's demands, Hindenburg would have rejected them. While he was willing to part with Brüning, he was not prepared to make Hitler chancellor or let him take over the Reichswehr. The "Harzburg Front" thus was unable to present a government that might have replaced that of Brüning. Yet to Hindenburg, the rightist leaders insisted that only Brüning's presence in the chancellery kept them from supporting the president's renomination; if Brüning were to resign, Hindenburg would have the immediate support of the right in his quest for reelection.[18]

After two weeks had passed in desultory soundings and arguments, Brüning decided on a showdown, for unless he had the

[18] *Frankfurter Zeitung*, Reich ed., Jan. 12–13, 1932; Meissner, *Staatssekretär*, pp. 216–17; Stampfer, *Vierzehn Jahre*, pp. 612–13; Hugenberg to Hitler, Mar. 20, 1932, Matthias and Morsey, *Ende der Parteien*, p. 628; Westarp to Hiller, Jan. 14, 1932, Westarp Papers; Schleicher to Reichswehr commanders, Jan. 11, 1932, *Vierteljahrshefte*, II (1954), 415. Part of the difficulty in reconstructing the sequence of events results from the chronological confusion of Meissner's account. A careful comparison of his version with that of the *Frankfurter Zeitung*, Hugenberg's letter to Hitler, and Hindenburg's letter to Berg, Feb. 25, 1932, *Vierteljahrshefte*, VIII (1960), 79, makes it clear that the talks which Meissner reports to have had with Hitler and Göring were not concerned with the parliamentary extension of Hindenburg's term. They were held after this plan had been rejected and the nomination of Hindenburg as the candidate of the right in the popular election was being considered. Meissner, in fact, was absent from Berlin during the negotiations about the parliamentary extension; cf. *Frankfurter Zeitung, ibid.* The same applies to Hindenburg's letter of Jan. 28, 1932 which Meissner mentions.

president's backing, he could not proceed with his own plans. Pünder was sent to Meissner to find out what Hindenburg thought of the allegation that he, Brüning, was the sole obstacle to Hindenburg's renomination. Meissner's answer seemed reassuring: he was certain that Hindenburg was as devoted as ever to the chancellor. It was true, however, that a good many people were trying to influence the president against Brüning, and it might be tactically wise for him to offer his resignation. The president could then say, in case of new attacks on the chancellor, that the latter had offered to leave office, but that he, Hindenburg, had rejected his offer. In any event he was convinced that the president would not want to part with Brüning.[19]

A clearcut decision became the more urgent in Brüning's judgment as a day or so later news arrived at the chancellery that the Nazis were getting ready to nominate a candidate of their own. Presumably this would be Hitler, and Meissner soon confirmed this assumption. Göring, he reported, had told Oskar von Hindenburg that Hitler would indeed be the candidate of the Nazis. While some of Brüning's associates felt that under the circumstances an offer of resignation was no longer required, Brüning apparently wished to remove whatever doubts Hindenburg still might harbor. His fear was that unless the president agreed to his candidacy before the entire right was committed to Hitler, he might decide not to run at all.

His concern about the president's attitude proved unfounded. While Hindenburg would actually have been ready, as he wrote later, to drop Brüning had Hitler and Hugenberg formed an acceptable government, he now wanted Brüning to stay. When Groener saw him on January 27, he was willing to run again if this was the wish of the nation, and definitely rejected all thoughts of "buying" his reelection with the resignation of Brüning. Later that day Brüning himself called on the president and Hindenburg reiterated his readiness to seek a second term if the nation wanted to have him again. Nevertheless Brüning proposed to resign if this would facilitate matters. As he told Pünder immediately afterwards, Hindenburg dismissed his offer with tears in his eyes: "My dear old friend, you must not do this to me." They did discuss the possibility of a cabinet change after the Prussian Landtag elections, but the chancellor came away from the audience convinced that the president did not want to secure his election at the price of the cabinet's resignation.[20]

19 Memorandum by Pünder, Jan. 29, 1932, *RKz.*, R 43 I/583.
20 *Ibid.*; Hindenburg to Berg, Feb. 25, 1932, *Vierteljahrshefte*, VIII (1960), 79.

Actually Brüning's withdrawal could no longer have helped Hindenburg, and thus the marshal could readily say that he would not buy his election. Brüning's departure would have cost him the vote of the Socialists, but would not have gained him that of the Nazis since he would not accept Hitler's terms. He could not hope to win the election, however, without the support of either the Nazis or Socialists. If he did not understand this himself, Schleicher doubtless explained it to him. The general's role during those days still remains to be clarified, but the available evidence suggests that Schleicher gave Brüning his full support. Without Brüning's help, the general knew, Hindenburg's reelection would be gravely endangered. Whatever doubts Schleicher had about Brüning's effectiveness he decided to shelve until Hindenburg had been reelected.[21]

If Hindenburg was prepared to forego the support of Hitler and Hugenberg, he was not ready, however, to bypass the veterans organizations. He wanted to see at least his old soldiers aligned on his side. The *Stahlhelm* and *Kyffhäuser League,* the two leading ones, had been willing at first to support him even if the Nazis and German Nationals would not; but under pressure from Hugenberg the *Stahlhelm* began to waver. Given Hindenburg's ties to the *Stahlhelm,* the prospect of its defection greatly disturbed him, and special efforts were made to obtain the *Stahlhelm's* endorsement. The middle parties, Westarp's People's Conservatives, the People's Party, and the State Party, were urged to postpone any public announcement on the marshal's behalf. They had wanted to nominate Hindenburg as soon as Hitler and Hugenberg had rejected the parliamentary extension of his term, but Brüning warned them not to turn this into a matter of "party politics" lest they deter the non-Nazi "patriotic associations" from sponsoring Hindenburg's reelection. They agreed to wait, yet their self-effacement was in vain. The discussions with the *Stahlhelm* made no progress because the *Stahlhelm* itself injected "party politics" into them; it drew Hugenberg into the negotiations who, unyielding as ever, asked for Brüning's and Groener's removal as the price of his support.[22]

Time was now of the essence, however, if Hindenburg were to

---

21 Bracher, *Auflösung,* p. 457; Eschenburg, "Rolle der Persönlichkeit," p. 16; Vogelsang, *Reichswehr,* pp. 154–55.

22 Confidential memorandum on Stahlhelm by *Kyffhäuser League,* Apr. 18, 1932, Nazi Party *Hauptarchiv*/931; Schmidt-Hannover, "Vertrauliches Rundschreiben," June 1932, Schmidt-Hannover Papers; also memorandum by Pünder, Feb. 1932, in Pünder, *Reichskanzlei,* p. 112, n. 277; Westarp to Hiller, Jan. 14, 1932, Westarp Papers; *Frankfurter Zeitung,* Reich ed., Jan. 15, 1932.

capture any part of the rightist vote. Yet he still wished to wait for the *Stahlhelm's* decision before he would make up his own mind. In his talks with Groener and Brüning, however, he had not insisted on the *Stahlhelm's* support as a sine qua non, and the two men decided, with Schleicher's and Meissner's approval, to turn elsewhere to launch his candidacy. Other groups had meanwhile been forming to work for his nomination. They included conservatives, liberals, and also some Socialists, but in deference to the president's wishes, care had been taken to divest their support of all partisan taint. As "independent personalities" they wanted to call on the nation to make Hindenburg its candidate. The movement was headed by Berlin's Lord Mayor Heinrich Sahm and was supported by prominent individuals of all ranks and strata of German society. Sahm too had been asked by the chancellor to delay any action in the hope that the *Stahlhelm* and *Kyffhäuser League* could still be persuaded to join forces with him, but now he was told not to wait any longer and to start his campaign. On February 1, Sahm's committee published an appeal in which it called on the country to sign petitions urging Hindenburg to make himself available as the people's candidate. Tailored to Hindenburg's preferences, the appeal was pointedly apolitical; it had far more to say on Hindenburg's military accomplishments than on the years of his presidency: "Around this name there shines the glory of Tannenberg and the undying memory of the German Army of the World War which for four years protected the soil of our homeland and carried Germany's arms victoriously to far-away lands. Hindenburg—this is a life of duty in the service of the Fatherland from the proclamation of the German Emperor in 1871 to the presidency of the Republic. Hindenburg—this means the defeat of the party spirit, the symbol of the national community, the road to freedom . . ."

If the wording of the appeal pleased Hindenburg, some of its sponsors did not. Along with conservative politicians and businessmen and a number of nonpolitical professional men and artists, there were listed among the signers several prominent liberals and labor union leaders and even some Socialists (though right-wing ones), among them Gustav Noske, the one-time Reichswehr minister, and Karl Höltermann, the head of the *Reichsbanner*.[23] Hindenburg's first reaction seems to have been

[23]Memorandum by Pünder, Jan. 29, 1932, *RKz.*, R 43 I/583; Heinrich Sahm, "Erinnerungen," reprinted in Vogelsang, *Reichswehr*, p. 435; Schulthess, Feb. 1, 1932, pp. 21–22; *Berliner Tageblatt*, No. 53, Feb. 1, 1932.

one of anger, and some of his confidants apparently urged him not to associate himself with the Sahm committee. Dingeldey wrote to a party colleague on the basis of information obtained from a "military friend" that "the Old Gentleman and his son and his military advisers are all agreed that he must under no circumstances put his historical name at the disposal of a front that is set up like the Sahm committee."[24]

On February 6 Brüning saw him again. It was essential, he urged, that the question of the president's candidacy be settled as soon as possible. Many plans would have to be shelved until the situation had been clarified. Would the president make his decision by the end of the following week? Hindenburg was evasive. He could understand Brüning's position, he replied, and he hoped to make up his mind by then, but he could make no definite promise. Once more Brüning offered to resign since it was more important to reelect the president and avoid a "radical socialist" president, as he added for Hindenburg's benefit, than to keep the present government in office. Hindenburg brushed off the suggestion with an emphatic wave of his arm: he was not going to bow to the terms and conditions of any political parties.[25]

Two days later the negotiations with Hugenberg were broken off. Some of the *Stahlhelm* leaders were not certain, however, that the German National chieftain had exhausted all possibilities of reaching an understanding with Hindenburg. There were further discussions with Hindenburg, but pressure from the German Nationals and from the *Stahlhelm's* own district leaders increased, and on February 14, a leadership meeting of the *Stahlhelm* announced that it would support a Hindenburg candidacy only "if there were concrete evidence of a forthcoming change of course." Meissner was told that same evening that an unconditional support of Hindenburg was out of the question. But if the *Stahlhelm* had hoped that the president would now make concessions, it was mistaken. Hindenburg had made up his mind to accept the nomination with or without the *Stahlhelm's* support.[26]

Those who endorsed the marshal's candidacy had not been idle meanwhile. Sahm's appeal had had an excellent reception; within less than two weeks over three million voters had entered their

24 Dingeldey to Kalle, Feb. 5, 1932, Dingeldey Papers/34; Groener to Gleich, Jan. 24, 1932, Groener-Geyer, *General Groener*, pp. 288–89.
25 Memorandum by Pünder, Feb. 6, 1932, *RKz.*, R 43 I/583.
26 Memorandum by Schmidt-Hannover, June 1932, Schmidt-Hannover Papers; memorandum by *Kyffhäuser League*, Apr. 18, 1932, Nazi Party *Hauptarchiv*/931; Sahm, "Erinnerungen," in Vogelsang, *Reichswehr*, pp. 436–37.

names on petitions urging the renomination of Hindenburg. At the same time Westarp, Berg, and other friends and associates had tried to obtain conservative support for his candidacy and had gathered several hundred signatures. (They also suffered many a rebuff. Even old wartime comrades like Mackensen refused to align themselves with the president on the grounds that he would not break with the left, and Berg aroused such bitter opposition among his fellow aristocrats that he felt compelled to resign from his post as president of the German Aristocrats League.)[27]

Sahm's three million signatures from all walks of life, the rightist support which Westarp did gather, and the support of the *Kyffhäuser League* which was finally secured proved decisive,[28] and Hindenburg agreed to be a candidate. No doubt his acceptance was partly dictated by his sense of duty urging him not to give up his office at this critical moment, but, as always, he was also concerned with his public image. To abandon the field to the "Bohemian corporal" without a struggle would leave a blot on his historical record. After serious consideration, he told Brüning, he had come to the conclusion that he would have to protect his own name too; he could not assume the responsibility for arbitrarily leaving his post in these difficult times.[29]

His heart, however, was heavy with sorrow, for he knew that by accepting the support of the left he would arouse the indignation of many of his closest associates. Only a day before he had had another letter from Mackensen warning him not to accept the aid of the Socialists. Mackensen assured him at the same time that "Field Marshal von Hindenburg" would get the vote of all of his comrades "if the compass of his re-election points to the right."[30] This was in effect what the *Stahlhelm* had been saying.

But perhaps these critics could still be convinced that he actually was their man. Since he was announcing his candidacy without bowing to any conditions, he felt he could now make a conciliatory gesture. Having told Brüning of his decision, he brought up the question of replacing Groener with a permanent minister of the interior. As a suitable candidate he suggested an old German National friend, Oskar von Osten-Warnitz. Except

[27] Schulthess, Feb. 13, 1932, p. 25; Mackensen to Westarp, Feb. 18, 1932, Westarp Papers; on Berg, see Erich Matthias, "Hindenburg zwischen den Fronten," *Vierteljahrshefte für Zeitgeschichte*, VIII (1960), 78 n. 1.

[28] Its president was forced, however, to warn Hindenburg that a part of its membership would not follow its leaders and would cast its vote for Hitler. *Kyffhäuser* leaflet, Nazi Party *Hauptarchiv*/930. The public endorsement of Hindenburg by the *Kyffhäuser* leadership led to a serious crisis in the League. *Ibid.*/930–31.

[29] Memorandum by Pünder, Feb. 15, 1932, *RKz.*, R 43 I/583; Vogelsang, *Reichswehr*, p. 152; Eschenburg, "Rolle der Persönlichkeit," p. 16.

[30] Mackensen to Hindenburg, Feb. 13, 1932, copy in Nazi Party *Hauptarchiv*/930.

for his political affiliations, Osten had no special qualifications to recommend him. But he was a landowner of some substance, and Hindenburg may have hoped that he might help shield him from the persistent importunities of his fellow agrarians. Brüning received the proposal with evident coolness since he was not greatly impressed by Osten, an elderly man in his seventies. His own choice was Carl Goerdeler, the lord mayor of Leipzig, who was to acquire tragic fame later on as leader of the anti-Nazi resistance. Goerdeler had recently been appointed price commissioner to enforce the government's price-cutting program and Brüning knew him as an effective and energetic administrator of conservative background who could be expected to take strong measures against the Nazis when that day would come. But above all, he wished to avoid offending Groener who had been his loyal collaborator throughout these difficult days. He did not like to make any changes just then, he replied, when the Reichstag was about to meet to set the date for the presidential elections. A change might be feasible after the Reichstag session, but it would have to be approached with great caution. Hindenburg gave his reluctant consent, but he was doubtless unhappy.[31]

If the cabinet could not be reshuffled, there were other ways, though, to show where his sympathies lay. He arranged to make his first public announcement on his candidacy to General von Horn, the *Kyffhäuser* president. This done, he waited another day before he formally accepted the candidacy profferred to him by the Sahm committee. His brief acceptance speech was carefully worded: he emphasized that he considered himself the trustee of the nation and would not feel under any obligation to those who were going to vote for him. Few paid any attention to his statement. He had said the same thing in 1925, and it seemed in any event the appropriate thing to say. The full meaning of his words was lost on all but his closest entourage.[32]

✍

Once Hindenburg had committed himself, Hitler and Hugenberg acted too. Up to the last moment Hugenberg had tried to persuade Hitler to preserve the unity of the "National Opposition." After the negotiations with Hindenburg had broken down, he had once more hurried to Munich. He had pleaded with Hitler to modify the conditions under which he would second the president's candidacy. He knew how reluctant Hindenburg was to run against the "national" right, and he felt certain that

31 Memorandum by Pünder, Feb. 15, 1932, *RKz.*, R 43 I/583.
32 *Berliner Tageblatt*, No. 77, Feb. 15, 1932; Schulthess, Feb. 16, 1932, p. 25.

the marshal might yet be their candidate if Hitler scaled down his demands. By that time, however, Hitler had decided to run himself. Stateless as yet, he was merely biding his time until he was sure he could qualify as a candidate. Brunswick's Nazi minister of the interior was hard at work to obtain an appointment for him as professor of "organic sociology and politics" at Brunswick's School of Technology; as a civil service appointment, it would, according to German law, automatically bestow citizenship rights upon Hitler and thus make him eligible for the presidency. Hugenberg warned him that the *Stahlhelm* and German Nationals would never vote for him, but Hitler was not impressed. In that case, he coolly replied, they had better find candidates of their own. He felt confident that many if not most *Stahlhelmers* and German Nationals would vote for him rather than for such rival contenders.

Hugenberg was aware of this danger, but his fear of Hitler's ambitions was greater than his misgivings, and he refused to give in. He was certain, moreover, that Hitler could not win over Hindenburg and wished to spare himself the humiliation of a defeat at Hitler's side. He was all the more anxious to avoid such a setback because time, in his judgment, was working against the "National Opposition." Unless it gained soon access to the seats of power, it might be barred permanently from them. There were indications of an impending economic improvement, and there was reason too to believe that Brüning was about to score a success in the field of reparations and armament negotiations. In that case his position might become altogether impregnable. But such considerations were lost on Hitler; the Nazi leader was so firmly convinced of the doom of the existing regime that he brusquely brushed them aside. "The Fuehrer had a talk with Hugenberg," Goebbels noted that day in his diary. "He does not mince his words. The reactionaries are trying to fool us. They won't get anywhere; never yet has that which belongs to the past won out over the future. It may seem that way sometimes, but in the end youth always turns out to be right."[33]

Unable to come to terms with Hitler, Hugenberg decided to run himself as a candidate; but the *Stahlhelm* informed him that it was nominating a candidate of its own, and he decided to back the latter.[34]

[33] Hugenberg to Hitler, Mar. 20, 1932, Matthias and Morsey, *Ende der Parteien*, pp. 628–29; Goebbels, *Vom Kaiserhof*, entries of Feb. 2, 4, 1932, pp. 36, 29; Morsey, "Braunschweigischer Regierungsrat," *Vierteljahrshefte*, VIII (1960), 429–32.

[34] Schmidt-Hannover, "Confidential Memorandum," June 1932, Schmidt-Hannover Papers.

The *Stahlhelm's* choice was its second-in-command, Theodor Duesterberg. A staff officer of proven ability in World War I, Duesterberg had found his career cut short by the loss of the war. Unable and unwilling to accept the democratic republic, he had lent his organizing ability to the *Stahlhelm* and in 1926 had been elected its co-leader together with the volatile and emotional Seldte. A man of few words, stiff and factual, every inch the professional soldier, Duesterberg was no spellbinder; in fact, he had little to recommend him to the great mass of the voters. But as a candidate of the Hugenberg-*Stahlhelm* group, he served his purpose. His military past, his record as a *Stahlhelm* leader, his prominent position in the camp of the "National Opposition," were assets in the eyes of those to whom he was to appeal. Moreover, his function was merely to gather enough votes so that neither Hitler nor Hindenburg would obtain a majority. The *Stahlhelm* and German Nationals would then be in a position to influence the second election by throwing their vote behind a more acceptable candidate.[35]

Before Duesterberg's candidacy was announced, Hugenberg made one last attempt to persuade Hitler to agree to a common candidate of the "National Opposition." The Fuehrer was in Berlin, and Hugenberg called on him at the Hotel Kaiserhof where Hitler stayed during his visits to the capital. This time he brought up two new names for the nomination—Albert Vögler, the Ruhr industrialist, and Prince Oskar of Prussia, the second son of the ex-Emperor.[36] Vögler's nomination was to serve notice that the National Socialists were supporters of the capitalist system; the Prince's candidacy in turn was to commit them to the eventual restoration of the monarchy. But it was meant also to embarrass Hindenburg who, it was hoped, would refuse to run against a son of his Emperor.

Both names were singularly ill-chosen. To the Nazi mind they symbolized those forces of "social reaction" with which Hitler might work temporarily to further his ends, but which at heart he opposed as relentlessly as "Marxists" and Jews. "Curious how little Hugenberg knows about the mind of the people," Goebbels

[35] Borchmeyer, *Hugenbergs Ringen*, I, 19; Bullock, *Hitler*, p. 176; *Frankfurter Zeitung*, Reich ed., Jan. 15, 24, 1932; Schulthess, Feb. 13, 1932, p. 25; Theodor Duesterberg, *Der Stahlhelm und Hitler* (Wolfenbüttel and Hanover, 1949), p. 34.

[36] William II had let Oskar join Hugenberg's German National People's Party, evidently in order to maintain close ties with this monarchist party. Yet to be in touch also with Hitler, he had permitted his son August William to join the Nazis. Klaus W. Jonas, *The Life of Crown Prince William* (Pittsburgh, 1961), pp. 171–72; Prince August William of Prussia to König, Sept. 15, 1932 (copy), *RKz.*, R 43 I/2684; *Frankfurter Zeitung*, Reich ed., Apr. 10, 1932.

commented, "The German National Party is and will always re-main the organization of all reactionary forces."[37]

Since the talk with Hugenberg had made it clear that German Nationals and the *Stahlhelm* would go their separate ways, it seemed imperative that Hitler announce his candidacy before they had a chance to come forward with their own nominee. Yet he still had not gotten his German citizenship; opposition to the professional appointment had been so strong that that plan had to be dropped. Efforts had meanwhile been made to arrange his assignment as an attaché to Brunswick's Berlin legation, and on February 22, just a day after his meeting with Hugenberg, he learned that this appointment was now assured. With his citizen-ship in sight, he decided to move. Goebbels was instructed to proclaim his candidacy that very evening at a Nazi mass meeting in the Berlin Sports Palace. It was the kind of assignment the propaganda chief loved, and with his flair for the dramatic, he made the most of his opportunity. After raging for more than an hour against the iniquities of the republic, the Brüning regime, and the Social Democrats, whipping his audience into a frenzy, he solemnly announced that the Fuehrer would be the party's candidate in the presidential election. And having made his announcement, he promised the jubilant crowd that he would be not only its candidate, but also its president.[38]

The announcement of Duesterberg's candidacy followed im-mediately on that of Hitler. The Communists had nominated their leader Ernst Thälmann in January; he had also been their candidate in 1925.[39]

Hindenburg followed these developments with a heavy heart. For Hitler and Duesterberg were appealing to those sectors of

[37] Hugenberg to Hitler, Mar. 20, 1932, Matthias and Morsey, *Ende der Parteien*, p. 629; Goebbels, *Vom Kaiserhof*, entry of Feb. 21, 1932, p. 49.

[38] It was rumored at the time that the announcement had not been authorized by Hitler and that Goebbels, by making it, had forced the candidacy on Hitler against the latter's will. Krebs, *Gestalten*, pp. 153, 167, 191–92. The rumor was widely believed since it confirmed the picture of Hitler which most non-Nazi outsiders had formed at that time—that of a vacillating, irresolute man who was the prisoner of his entourage. Actually there is not the slightest indication that Hitler was not all along in full control of developments.

[39] *Frankfurter Zeitung*, Jan. 1932, *passim*. Technically, there was a fifth candidate, Gustav Winter, a self-taught economist who ran on a platform promising the revaluation of prewar 1,000-mark banknotes that would put them on a par with the current reichsmark currency. He was unable to campaign actively, however, since he was serving a fifteen-months jail term for fraud committed in connection with his revaluation scheme. Nevertheless he received 11,000 votes in the election. He did not run in the second campaign. *New York Times*, Mar. 1, 6, 1932; *Statistisches Jahrbuch für das Deutsche Reich, 1932*, p. 547.

the electorate that should have been his supporters. That the *Stahlhelm* was turning against him after he had so often held his protecting hand over it was a particularly hard blow. Others followed in rapid succession. The *Landbund,* for which he had tried to do so much, declined to support him since it could not "elect the President arm in arm with the antipeasant Social Democrats." The League of Patriotic Societies withheld its endorsement on the grounds that he had signed the Young Plan. And there were indications, soon to be confirmed, that the ex-Crown Prince and other members of the Imperial family would likewise decide not to cast their vote for him. To counteract these trends, Hindenburg pleaded with Oldenburg-Januschau to ask Hugenberg and the German National Party to stop spreading the falsehood that he was the nominee of the left, but Oldenburg remained noncommittal.[40]

In his deep concern Hindenburg decided to explain his position once more to some of his friends and acquaintances. In a long letter to Berg he defended his candidacy and the circumstances under which he accepted it.[41] He also asked Berg to inform his closer acquaintances discreetly of what had really happened; copies of the major part of the letter were sent at the same time to several other conservative leaders.

The letter throws much light on Hindenburg's views and policies and on his political plans for the future. Denying sharply that he was the candidate of the left and running against "the national Germany," he insisted that it was not his fault if the Brüning government had not been replaced by a rightist one. Despite his high personal regard for the chancellor he had been ready to part with him and to appoint a cabinet of the right if this had been feasible. He described the negotiations that had taken place and come to an end because of the inability of Hitler and Hugenberg to reach an agreement. "You may see from this that the allegation that I am opposed to a rightist government is entirely false. I did not put any obstacle in the path of such a development, nor did Chancellor Brüning, it was *merely the disunity of the right,* its inability to agree even on the main points. It is most regrettable that the right—torn as it is—is being led into

[40] Groener to Gleich, Jan. 24, 1932, Groener-Geyer, *General Groener,* p. 286; *Landbund* statement, in Buchta, *Junker,* p. 26; Schulthess, Feb. 13, 17, 1932, pp. 25, 26; Hindenburg to Oldenburg-Januschau, Feb. 17, 22, 1932, in Vogelsang, *Reichswehr,* pp. 442–44.

[41] According to information which Dingeldey received at the time, the letter was drafted by Hindenburg himself and not, as was customary, by Meissner. Dingeldey to Kalle, Mar. 10, 1932, Dingeldey Papers/34.

insignificance and self-destruction by leaders one-sidedly concerned with their party political ambitions. Whether and when this state of affairs will change no one can tell." Yet to assure his intimates that he shared their political views, he added, significantly: "Despite all these setbacks I shall not give up my efforts to further a healthy development toward the right. I hope that it will be possible, after the Prussian elections which *must* take place at the lastest in May, to resume the negotiations about the formation of a government of national concentration." Brüning's position thus was as precarious as ever, and in the light of this letter his dismissal, some three months later, appears much less surprising than it seemed to the contemporary observer. It also shows how sadly mistaken those were who believed that they were supporting Brüning when they chose Hindenburg as their candidate.

In his anxiety to minimize his support from the left, Hindenburg insisted that the bulk of his voters stood politically right of center. "In the rightist press and in meetings people are being stirred up against me with the claim that I have accepted my candidacy one-sidedly from the left or a 'black-red coalition.' This allegation is an outright lie! The candidacy was offered to me by the parties between Center and German Nationals [there followed a detailed list], which were later joined by the Center and the Bavarian People's Party . . . To them must be added a number of groups and organizations such as the Young German Order, the Association of Christian Labor Unions, the Evangelical [Christian-Social] People's Service, the Christian Peasants Associations, the German Veterans League *"Kyffhäuser,"* universities and similar institutions of higher learning, and others. These parties and organizations embrace a very large part of those voters who called me in 1925 to the high office of Reich President." The 3.5 million signers of the Sahm committee's appeal had further convinced him that there was a widespread desire, regardless of party affiliations, to see him remain at his post. If the Social Democrats were asking their followers to vote for him, there was nothing he could do about this; any attempt to repel these voters "would also run counter to my goal of uniting the German people in the great questions of politics."

In a concluding paragraph he confided to Berg how badly let down he felt by the *Stahlhelm.* "From a sense of loyalty which I feel towards my old comrades-in-arms I kept my hand over the Stahlhelm from the first days of my Presidency. I refused to give up my honorary membership in the Stahlhelm after this was

276

suggested to me by the Government for political reasons, and through the years I maintained friendly and personal relations with the Stahlhelm and its leaders. In fact, if someone else had been elected President in 1925, I feel certain after all the experiences I have had in the last seven years that the Stahlhelm would long have been dissolved." And then he told how, as a matter of course, he had come to its rescue after it had been suppressed in the Rhineland and in Westphalia. "I cannot follow the Stahlhelm leaders who maintain in their public statements that they still are loyal to me. Yet they oppose me in the election and emphasize their opposition by presenting, together with the German National People's Party, their second-in-command as a rival candidate who claims to represent the black-white-and-red idea— against me, of all people. You can understand that I feel very bitter about the Stahlhelm's attitude towards me. This is not my idea of loyalty."[42]

∽

At the very time at which the letter was being written, Hindenburg was the focal point of a furious debate. The Reichstag had been called into session to set the date for the presidental election(s)—a task assigned to it by the constitution. The short four-day meeting proved a revealing barometer of the nation's views of the marshal. Each party sought to justify its stand toward him, and his name thus was drawn directly into the discussion. No one apologized for this departure from custom; the fact was accepted that he had become a legitimate topic of parliamentary debate. Nor was his name mentioned with that reverent awe that reflected the veneration in which he had always been held. To almost all speakers he was now plain "Hindenburg" or *"der Reichspräsident"*; only Westarp and Brüning continued to refer to him as *"der Herr Reichspräsident."*

The Nazis seized on the opportunity to express their abiding contempt for him. "It is a grave mistake for the President to declare that he may not abandon his post in accordance with his own wishes," Goebbels charged. "He has been put in his post for seven years, and when the seven years are up, he leaves his post not in accordance with his own wishes, but as a matter of duty. If he wishes to get our vote again, then he must accept the fact that the nation will want to examine the policies for which he is responsible and to which he has lent his name. And if these

---

[42] Hindenburg to Berg, Feb. 25, 1932, *Vierteljahrshefte,* VIII (1960), 78–82; also editorial comment by Matthias, *ibid.,* pp. 76–78; Bracher, *Auflösung,* pp. 452–54.

policies do not stand such a test, he must expect that the nation will refuse to vote for him." Having said that, Goebbels gave free rein to his peculiar gift for melifluous invective and lunged into a more direct attack:

"I protest against the charge which has been levelled against the National Socialist movement that it has abandoned Hindenburg. No, Hindenburg has abandoned the case of his one-time voters. We entrusted him with the highest office of the Republic in the belief that at least in basic questions he would adopt the policies which the national Germany considered vital. He has done the very opposite. He has unequivocally sided with the middle, he has sided as openly with the Social Democrats."

Having prepared the ground, he hurled his most defiant blow at the marshal:

"We National Socialists have a saying which has never failed to prove true: Tell me who praises you, and I tell you who you are! Praised by the asphalt press, praised by the party of the deserters—"

He was not allowed to finish that sentence and was excluded from that day's session when he refused to withdraw the remark. But the incredible had happened—the nation's hero had been publicly associated with treacherous deserters. When Goebbels appeared at the Sports Palace that evening to address an overflow Nazi audience, he received a hero's welcome.[43]

Whatever else may be thought of Goebbels' aspersions, they were above all an example of the complete confusion of facts and fronts that could be perpetrated with some hope of success. To be sure, to associate Hindenburg with deserters was so inane a charge that Goebbels himself had second thoughts about it and tried to explain it away; but the very fact that he voiced it at all is proof that he expected it to make sense to a great many Germans. The assertion that the Social Democrats were the "party of the deserters" was just as brazen a piece of demogoguery and was rejected at once by one Socialist spokesman with the pointed reminder that his Reichstag delegation included a larger percentage of veterans than did that of the Nazis. But such factual arguments carried no weight with his frenzied foes.

Equally untrue was Goebbels' claim that the National Socialists

43 Goebbels and Strasser, Feb. 23, 1932, *Verhandlungen*, Vol. 446, pp. 2250. 2253–54, Goebbels, Feb. 25, 1932, *ibid.*, pp. 2346–47; *Vom Kaiserhof*, entry of Feb. 23, 1932, p. 51.

had entrusted Hindenburg with the presidency in the hope that he would pursue at least a basically "national" policy. The party was much too small and discredited in 1925 to play a decisive role in the nomination or election of Hindenburg; aside from that, it had accepted his candidacy only with great misgivings. Its spokesman on the Loebell committee had resisted his nomination until the last moment, for the party had little respect for the marshal. (This was also true of the present leaders of the German National People's Party. Hugenberg and his associates had opposed Hindenburg's candidacy as vigorously in 1925 as they did now.)[44]

But there was something equally unreal about the voices which were raised in support of Hindenburg. Some of the old feelings for the nation's hero echoed through the speeches of those who had supported him also in 1925—Count Westarp, now the spokesman of the People's Conservatives; Friedrich Baltrusch, a German National in 1925 and now one of the leaders of the *Jungdeutscher Orden;* the speakers of the Christian-Social People's Service; the *Landvolk;* and other splinter groups that had broken away from the German Nationals. Yet these men spoke for groups doomed to impotence now because of their numerical smallness. Their references, moreover, to the "victor of Tannenberg" and to Field Marshal von Hindenburg as a symbol of German unity had a decidedly hollow ring. For it was clear that the "Hindenburg concept," as one contemporary writer called it, was no longer strong enough, if it ever had been, to unite the nation beyond all partisan differences.[45]

While People's Conservatives, *Landvolk,* and other conservative groups could back Hindenburg without ideological qualms, the Social Democrats found it most difficult to explain their support of his candidacy. The Nazis kept pointing to what they had said in 1925, while the Communists thundered against the political and social betrayal that was implied in their backing of Hindenburg. In their embarrassment the Socialists did not insist on speaking first as they had a right to as the largest party, but waited until the second day of the debate. When Breitscheid, their spokesman, did take his turn, he was careful to explain that ideologically his party was still poles apart from the president, but that it had changed its opinion of him in one vital respect:

44 Goebbels, *ibid.,* p. 52; Fritz Baltrusch, "Wer war 1925 für Hindenburg?" *Kölnische Volkszeitung,* No. 45, Feb. 14, 1932.

45 Baltrusch, Feb. 23, 1932, Westarp and Simpfendörfer, Feb. 24, 1932, *Verhandlungen,* Vol. 446, pp. 2261–62, 2299, 2303; Metzsch, *Hindenburg,* p. 32.

while it had earlier feared that he might lend his hand to unconstitutional ventures, it was now convinced that he never would. If it supported Hindenburg, it did so solely because his continued presence in the presidency was the only effective guarantee that the Weimar Constitution would be preserved and that Germany would not fall victim to a Nazi dictatorship.[46]

The "Alice-in-Wonderland" mood which pervaded the entire debate culminated in the speeches made by Deputy Bolz, the Centrist spokesman, and his party friend Brüning who addressed the session as chancellor. Bolz too faced the task of explaining away earlier statements made by his party about Hindenburg's advanced age and his lack of political understanding, but he could do so more easily than his Socialist colleague. Nor did he face the Socialists' social and ideological difficulties in justifying the Center's support of the president. Yet without realizing it, it was he, the chancellor's colleague, who passed in effect the most damning verdict on Hindenburg. Describing the negotiations with the Nazis and German Nationals on Hindenburg's candidacy, Bolz made much of the fact that the right had always insisted, in earlier times, on the nonpartisan status of Hindenburg's office and had wished to make him even more independent of parties and parliament than he already was:

"Yet today the selection of the nominee is made dependent on party political commitments. Today the candidate is expected to repudiate the past and to agree in advance to a new, future system; to prove his good faith, Hindenburg is asked to send the Government to the devil. On these terms [the right] would have been ready to settle for Hindenburg as its candidate. A Hindenburg tainted with such a lack of character would have been acceptable, but they rejected a free Hindenburg responsible only to his people and to his conscience!"

Bolz of course did not know that Hindenburg had been prepared to dispense with Brüning in order to come to terms with the right. For Brüning had kept his difficulties with the president a secret even from his own party, and he had taken only the party leader, Monsignor Kaas, into his confidence.

The chancellor's own speech was of course as little indicative of the worsening relations between him and the president. On the contrary, in his anxiety to secure Hindenburg's reelection, Brüning painted a picture of him that bore little resemblance to the fickle old man with whom he was dealing. He acquitted him-

<hr />

[46] Breitscheid, Feb. 24, 1932, *Verhandlungen*, Vol. 446, pp. 2271, 2279.

self so well of his task that he, usually so cool and restrained, spoke the only moving words on behalf of Hindenburg when he urged his audience to vote for his reelection:

"If during the last two years I was able to keep up my hope to cope with all difficulties, I could do so, not only due to my faith in a higher Power, but also due to the fact that I was permitted to serve a man like Herr Reich President von Hindenburg. Anyone who has had the good fortune of serving this man will understand that I—and with me, I believe, the majority of the German people—will do everything to make certain that this man will continue to determine the fortunes of Germany. Don't think that any of you can measure up to a historical figure such as he is, and don't forget one thing: it will depend on the reelection of the Herr Reich President whether the world is to believe that true reverence, a sense of history and of tradition, and the ability to acknowledge human greatness are still alive in Germany."[47]

With all speeches made, the Reichstag agreed to the election dates of March 13 and April 10, as proposed by the government. It dismissed a no-confidence motion against the cabinet by the slim margin of 24 votes; the German People's Party and *Landvolk* supported the motion, explaining that their support of Hindenburg did not imply approval of Brüning.[48] The motions against Groener and Dietrich were also rejected. On February 26, the Reichstag adjourned once more *sine diem*.

With the setting of the election dates one of the last campaign technicalities had been settled. As it happened, Hitler cleared at that very same moment the legal hurdle that had barred him from running for the presidency. On February 25, he was formally appointed a government councillor (*Regierungsrat*) by Brunswick and assigned to its Berlin legation, and on the following day he took his oath of office. The appointment was obviously not made in good faith—he set foot in the legation only once, for the swearing-in ceremony—but neither the Reich government nor any other agency or party challenged this illegal arrangement. It seemed wiser to defeat him in open battle rather than by a technical argument.[49]

✑

[47] Bolz, Feb. 24, 1932, *ibid.*, p. 2281; Brüning, Feb. 25, 1932, *ibid.*, p. 2333; same, "Ein Brief," p. 8.

[48] Dingeldey and Döbrich, Feb. 25, 1932, *Verhandlungen*, Vol. 446, pp. 2362, 2371; Dingeldey to Rademacher, Feb. 29, 1932, Dingeldey Papers/38.

[49] Goebbels, *Vom Kaiserhof,* entry of Feb. 25, 1932, p. 53; Morsey, "Braunschweigischer Regierungsrat," pp. 440–48. Hitler's appointment proved expensive for Brunswick's taxpayers; for reasons of economy the Brunswick government had

With only two weeks left until election day, the campaign got under way at once. Sahm's Hindenburg committee meanwhile had undergone some significant changes. Sahm himself had resigned since, as he claimed, the nonpartisan character of the committee had been jeopardized by the support of the government parties and its activities hampered by the interference of the government and the "house of Hindenburg," that is, Meissner and Oskar von Hindenburg. The membership list of the national committee was purged of all left-wingers and provincial committees went even further. The head of the Hanoverian committee reported that it would drop not only the names of all Socialist and State Party officials in the province, but also those of two members of the German People's Party who had on occasion run afoul of the right. Yet these efforts to make itself acceptable to rightist voters were only moderately successful. As one confidant reported to Schleicher, the feeling was widespread in rural areas that "you cannot vote for a man for whom Scheidemann speaks at election meetings." Perhaps as effective was a whispering campaign alleging that Hindenburg's son, Oskar, and State Secretary Meissner were dues-paying members of the Social Democratic Party, and that the president's daughters were leaders of the Socialist Students League. (One daughter was in her fifties, the other in her late forties at the time). Another rumor had it that Hindenburg had agreed to his candidacy at the insistence of his family since without his presidential salary he would not be able to keep Neudeck; and still another rumor claimed that Oskar had become a Catholic. The Hindenburg committee spent a great deal of time refuting these stories which were widely believed. Even someone as familiar with the Hindenburgs as the ex-Crown Prince seems to have been impressed by them, and Schleicher had to explain in all seriousness to the Prince's aide that Oskar von Hindenburg was no registered member of the Social Democratic Party, if for no other reason than the fact that as an active officer he was not allowed to belong to any political party.[50]

---

planned to close its Berlin legation on March 31, 1932, but this plan had now to be given up, and the legation remained open. *Ibid.*, p. 433.

[50] Sahm, in Vogelsang, *Reichswehr*, pp. 438–39; *Dt. Tageszeitung*, No. 64, Mar. 5, 1932; letter to Schwertfeger, Feb. 26, 1932, Schwertfeger Papers/111/255; letter to Schleicher, Mar. 10, 1932, Schleicher Papers/24/18; letter to *Kyffhäuser* League, Feb. 11, 1932, Nazi Party *Hauptarchiv*/930; *Frankfurter Zeitung*, Reich ed., Mar. 2, 7, 1932; circulars of *Hauptgeschäftsstelle* of Hindenburg Committees, Mar. 1932, and of Bavarian Hindenburg Committee, Schwertfeger Papers/111/255, 257; Schleicher to Müldner von Mülnheim, Mar. 11, 1932, Schleicher Papers/32/111.

With the Hindenburg camp seriously split from the start, this rumor campaign served to perpetuate the existing divisions. Any cooperative effort by all of the marshal's supporters was out of the question. The meetings which the Hindenburg committee arranged all catered to his right-wing supporters: the German People's Party, the group around Westarp, and like-minded parties and organizations. When Leipzig's local committee wanted to ask Finance Minister Dietrich to address a campaign meeting, the People's, Economic, and other bourgeois parties threatened to withdraw from the committee. The chairman reported to Dietrich, "There was a real palace revolution. If we had not given in, the committee would have broken up . . . . [These people] are determined to overthrow Brüning's Government and do not want to give any cabinet member a chance to make propaganda in Leipzig for the cabinet as well as for Hindenburg. [They] would have broken away also if the Chancellor himself had wanted to speak in Leipzig." The Socialists, Center, and State Party all arranged their separate meetings.[51]

By stressing their differences, the Hindenburg forces played directly into the hands of their opponents. The latter gleefully derided the claim that Hindenburg, unlike Hitler, Thälmann, and Duesterberg, was the candidate of the united nation, and they could contrast the unity of their own followings with the disarray of the Hindenburg camp. Hindenburg's backers appeared indeed as a badly divided conglomeration of parties and groups, each endorsing the president for its own particular reasons. While Westarp was trying to prove that he was as much of an anti-Socialist and an antiparliamentarian as any Nazi or German National, the Socialists, for their part, urged their followers to vote for Hindenburg as the only remaining bulwark of parliament and democracy. And if Westarp praised Hindenburg as the hero of Tannenberg, the Socialists assured their audiences that it was not his military but his constitutional record that mattered. His conservatism now became an asset in Socialist eyes. "The very fact that he is not only the guarantor of the Constitution, but also the conservative leader," wrote a contributor to the *Sozialistische Monatshefte*, "assures us that the Republic will be safeguarded." However sincerely all of his supporters worked for his reelection, it was clear that the tenuous tie that held them together expressed nothing more than their opposition to Hitler.[52]

[51] *Frankfurter Zeitung*, Mar. 1932, *passim;* letter to Dietrich, Mar. 5, 1932, Dietrich Papers/226/137.
[52] Westarp, *Hindenburg und seine Wähler von 1925* (pamphlet, Berlin, 1932);

Nor did Hindenburg himself attempt to establish a measure of unity among his supporters. Quite apart from the fact that he refused to establish closer rapport with Center and Socialists, he was unwilling as a matter of principle and unable physically to embark on an active campaign. To reassure the country on the state of his health, he reviewed the Berlin Guard Regiment on the Moabit parade grounds. Movie cameras recorded the event for the newsreels so that the nation could see for itself that he was as sturdy as ever. Perhaps this was as effective an appeal to the voters as any campaign speech. A *New York Times* correspondent found it a "stirring" picture when the old marshal, "a veritable mountain of a man whose black and gold spiked helmet towered a full head above even the tall and slimmer figures of his gray-green clad staff," gravely saluted the troops as they were goose-stepping by his review stand.

Only twice did he enter directly into the campaign. He allowed a short film to be made of him reading the speech with which he had accepted his candidacy, and on March 10, three days before the election, he broadcast an address to the voters over the radio. This latter appeal reiterated the arguments he had used in his letter to Berg, and while he was somewhat more careful in his language, he made it abundantly clear that he was not the candidate of the left or a "black-red coalition." The first request for his candidacy, he pointed out proudly, had reached him from right-wing groups. He had consented to his nomination only after he had convinced himself that a great many Germans, regardless of party affiliations, wished him to remain in his office. And he was offering himself as a candidate merely in order to prevent the election of a radical of either the right or the left— an event which would expose the Fatherland to grave risks. "I cannot believe," he concluded, "that Germany is to be plunged into domestic feuds and civil war. I recall to you the spirit of 1914 and the frontline attitude which was concerned with the man and not with his social status or his party. . . . I will not give up the hope that Germany will come together again in new unity." There was no mention in the statement about any plans for the future.[53]

It was the chancellor who more than any other individual fought for Hindenburg's reelection. He spent the entire last week before the election addressing overflow audiences in all parts of Germany

Walther Pahl, in *Sozialistische Monatshefte*, LXXV (1932), pp. 229; *Sozialdemokratische Partei-Korrespondenz*, No. 2, Feb. 1932, pp. 91-92.

[53] *New York Times*, Mar. 5, 1932; *Frankfurter Zeitung*, Reich ed., Mar. 4, 1932; Hindenburg's address, in Schulthess, Mar. 10, 1932, pp. 55-57.

from the Rhineland to East Prussia, from the North Sea to Bavaria. Once more this unemotional skeptic moved his audiences with exultant eulogies of Hindenburg's wisdom and perception. He called him a man sent by God to the German people:

"Who has had the good fortune, like me, to talk frequently with the President must say from deep conviction: I would like to find the man who has that same knowledge of life, that same ability to judge character and personality, who has the same keen ability to get quickly at the heart of things and to express them in a few sentences of classical simplicity. . . . Only someone like Hindenburg who has the kind of mind to reduce the confusion of events and the immense complexity of all difficulties to a clear and simple denominator, only such a man is able, in a situation, at a time, at which a nation faces a chaotic chasm . . . , to reach those decisions and persevere in them which alone can save that nation."

There was also the inevitable reference to Tannenberg and to the decisive role Hindenburg had played there (which touched off a new deluge of protests from Ludendorff and his adherents). Kaas eagerly seconded the chancellor. "[Hindenburg's] victory will be Germany's victory," he proclaimed, and in voting for him, the country was electing the worthiest man "whom a German mother has born for this time of crisis." Exalting the president into a mystical hero symbol, he dismissed every other candidate as a "negation of the German demand for unity."

That Brüning would paint so unreal a picture of Hindenburg is a measure of his anxiety to assure the latter's election. Much more was at stake, as he knew, than the completion of his own plans and policies. In fact, he could not even be certain that he would see them bear fruit if Hindenburg were reelected. Yet this did no longer matter since the fight was now turning on more fundamental issues. The question was simply, in the words of the *Berliner Tageblatt,* whether culture would win over anticulture and brain over brawn. Of this he had new confirmation each day in the viciousness with which the campaign was fought by the Nazis, in their calumnies and distortions, in the unending street fights and beerhall clashes, and in the open and silent terror with which they harassed their opponents.

Aware of the stakes, the Socialists too were lavish in praise of Hindenburg. Otto Braun explained in *Vorwärts* that he would vote for him since he saw in him the embodiment of calmness and steadiness, of manly loyalty and a deep sense of duty that was untiringly devoted to the entire nation. Whatever separated him from the president, Braun assured his readers in another appeal for Hindenburg's reelection, he had got to know him "as a man of his word, as a man of noble intentions and mature judgment." But Braun's focus was on the past, as all campaigning for Hindenburg was; he deserved to be president because of past accomplishments rather than because he held out hopes for the future.[54]

In praising Hindenburg in these terms his supporters suggested that he would preserve rather than change, and unwittingly they depicted him thus as a symbol of the unhappy present rather than that of a better future. On this fundamental weakness the Nazis trained the full force of their propaganda artillery. In doing so they could also divert the voters' attention from their main problem of strategy—checking rightist extremists in the hope of attracting the moderate right (just as the Hindenburg committee was trying to play down its leftist support to win over that same group). This was no mean task. Bitterness toward Hindenburg, that seeming protector of the hated republic, had constantly grown in the Nazi Party and had been eagerly nurtured by its speakers and newspapers. Early campaign posters pictured Hindenburg as the candidate of the Jews; one, for example, showed in its upper part the faces of a number of prominent Jews and the caption, in Hebrew-like script: "We are voting for Hindenburg!" and in the lower part a number of Nazis, selected for their Teutonic looks, with the caption (in Gothic script): "We Are Voting for Hitler!" And when the *Münchener Illustrierte Presse*, an industry-financed weekly of conservative leanings, published a picture of Hindenburg during those weeks, it was deluged by bitter protests for showing that "vicious traitor Hindenburg," thus disclosing its true Jewish-Bolshevik nature. Die-hard Nazis approved of such actions, but they were bound to repel those "bourgeois" voters whose support would mean the difference between victory and defeat. Party speakers and publicists were instructed therefore to aim their attacks not against Hindenburg himself, but against the "bourgeois-Social Democratic system" which he represented. "This system is to be fought with all available means while the person of y [*sic*] is to be mentioned only incidentally." But the main emphasis was to be put on the fact that Hitler, unlike Hindenburg, was the man of the future. "Adolf Hitler is our last hope," became the official propaganda slogan, and it was reiterated day after day in editorials and speeches. Thus Goebbels wrote in his *Angriff:*

[54] Brüning, *ibid.*, Mar. 10, 11, 1932, pp. 57–59; Kaas quotation in Matthias and Morsey, *Ende der Parteien,* p. 303; Braun to Kautsky, Feb. 19, 1932, in *Vierteljahrs-*

"In the desperate misery of the postwar years a new political faith has come to life. It is founded on a glowing, dedicated idealism. . . . This is the work of Adolf Hitler! In him the masses see their last hope, and to millions his name has become the shining symbol of Germany's will to freedom. . . . Those who wish that everything remain as it is in Germany simply yield to despair. We can't blame them for giving their vote to the representative of the existing system. We, however, want to see everything changed in Germany. Those who do not want class struggle and fratricide, those who are looking for a way out of the errors and the confusion of our time cast their vote for Adolf Hitler. He embodies the awakening young German idealism, he is the spokesman of national activism, he is the exponent of a dawning social and economic revival. Therefore we call on you: Give power to Adolf Hitler so that the German people will once more secure the right to live. For freedom and bread!" [55]

In organizing the campaign propaganda, Goebbels proved himself an accomplished master. The country was flooded with posters and leaflets, many of them dropped from airplanes; some 50,000 gramophone records with Nazi messages were mailed to known opponents, and there was a back-breaking schedule of speeches. Between March 1 and 11 Hitler and Goebbels made at least one major speech each day, and on most days they spoke two or three times. Unable to get to a meeting in Hamburg on time, Goebbels addressed the audience by telephone from the train; even so the crowd waited patiently until he finally came in person at midnight. Meetings at which Hitler was scheduled to speak were filled to capacity many hours before he appeared, although only few were able to see him in the huge halls used for his meetings. The meetings themselves were carefully built up into colorful ceremonies with flag-draped halls, flower-laden lecterns, singing, and band music. Masses of stormtroopers lined walls and passageways, not so much to guard against hecklers—they had long been frightened into silence—but to impart to the gathering a kind of martial atmosphere impressing audiences with the Nazis' soldierly discipline and dedication.

Ever new rumors and innuendoes were, moreover, circu-

hefte, VIII (1960), 83–84; Berliner Tageblatt, No. 123, Mar. 12, 1932; also Dt. Volkswirt, Mar. 4, 1932, p. 731.
55 Heiden, Führer, pp. 446–47; on Münchener Illustrierte Presse, Aretin, Krone, pp. 65, 70–71; circular of Reichspropagandaleitung, Nazi Party Records/176/318177; Goebbels, "Wir Wählen Adolf Hitler," in Josef Goebbels, Wetterleuchten: Aufsätze aus der Kampfzeit (Munich, 1939), pp. 269–70; New York Times, Mar. 7, 1932.

lated to unnerve the opposition. Besides those picturing Hindenburg as the victim of Jews and Socialists, there was a constantly recurring one that he had died. In East Prussia on which the Nazis focused their special attention, the story was spread that if Hindenburg were reelected the Poles were sure to invade the province. These tales were not without effect; despite Neudeck and Tannenberg, Hitler got a larger vote in East Prussia than in most other election districts.[56]

The two other candidates, Thälmann and Duesterberg, faced a curiously similar task. Neither one had any hope of winning the election, but their ability to bring some pressure to bear on political developments depended on their success in drawing votes away from the Hindenburg camp—Thälmann, by appealing to the Social Democrats, Duesterberg, by addressing himself to the conservative bourgeoisie. Ironically their individual success depended as much on the other's effectiveness as it did on their own. Thälmann's ability to draw large numbers of Socialists away from Hindenburg would reduce the margin between Hindenburg and Hitler and thus give the Duesterberg block a better chance of having some influence in the selection of the candidate for the second election. A large-scale migration of moderate conservatives into Duesterberg's camp, on the other hand, could conceivably lead to a withdrawal of Hindenburg from the second contest and thus open the way for the selection of a left-wing candidate.

Thälmann's campaign presented no special problems. It moved in its traditional channels and turned on the Socialists as its primary target. At the same time it kept hammering away at the claim that a vote for Hindenburg was a vote for Hitler, a prediction that came tragically true due in large part to the Communist refusal to join forces with the Socialists and other democratic forces in their struggle against the Nazis.

Duesterberg faced a more delicate task. His candidacy was to block the election of both Hitler and Hindenburg; he had therefore to keep the decision open until the second election by preventing either from getting a majority in the first. At the same time he was to gather as many votes as he could since the ability of the *Stahlhelm* and German Nationals to help choose the right's final candidate would depend on the size of his following. The Duesterberg spokesmen thus kept telling their audiences why they ought not to support either man—Hitler would simply establish a Nazi

[56] Goebbels, *Vom Kaiserhof,* entries of Feb. 29–Mar. 11, 1932, pp. 54–61; Hitler schedule, in *Publizistik,* IV (1959), 115; Rumbold to Simon, Mar. 16, 1932, *BDFP.,* ii, III, 103–08; *Frankfurter Zeitung,* Mar. 17, 1932.

party dictatorship, while Hindenburg was too closely identified with the existing political system. But there were complications. Since they had in their own ranks many a Nazi sympathizer, they had to tone down their attacks against Hitler; attempts to appeal to the Protestant voters by denouncing the Fuehrer as "Roman" by religion and character aroused so much bitterness that they were quickly discouraged. Hindenburg's honorary membership in the *Stahlhelm* also created problems; to bridge this difficulty, the opposition to his reelection was justified on the grounds that the *Stahlhelm* and German Nationals respected the marshal too much to see him abused by traitors and interest peddlers. Even so, some *Stahlhelmers* insisted on actively campaigning for Hindenburg, and some of them were promptly expelled. But the greatest difficulty of the Duesterberg forces stemmed from the fact that they were engaged in a holding operation and had no positive goal. It took someone of Hugenberg's single-minded persistence to blandly ignore this problem; in one of his few public appearances he urged his audience to vote for Duesterberg. "As for what is going to happen afterwards," he cheerfully added, "kindly leave that to me." [57]

Hugenberg was merely franker than Hitler and Hindenburg when he admonished the voters not to ask any questions. The *carte blanche* on which he openly insisted, the others demanded implicitly. On their actual plans, all candidates were purposely vague.

Hitler had never been one to take his audiences into his confidence; as always his speeches were journeys into the realm of history, philosophy, and biology rather than talks on specific problems. Their impact lay in the forcefulness with which he presented his views and in the feeling he gave to his listeners that he was lifting them up to a higher idealist plane. As they hung on his words, they felt they were sharing in an exalting experience and were being absorbed into the unending historical process. Thus Hitler expounded to them in one of his speeches:

"From blood, authority of personality, and a fighting spirit springs that value which alone entitles a people to look around with glad hope and which is the indispensable basis of the life which men desire. Once this has been established, we will also have secured what the political parties are trying to get for us: prosperity, individual happiness, family life, etc. First we must regain honor, then freedom, and out of these will emerge happiness, prosperity,

[57] Duesterberg campaign leaflet, Munich Coll./29; circular of Stahlhelm *Bundesamt*, Feb. 25, 1932, *Nazi Party Records*/90/103305, also *ibid./116/passim; Frankfurter Zeitung*, Reich ed., Mar. 6–8, 1932; memorandum of Schack, n.d., Westarp Papers; *Tagebuch*, Mar. 5, 1932, pp. 349–50.

life: in a word, we will recapture these conditions which we Germans perhaps saw dimly before the First World War, when men can live once more with joy in their hearts because life has a meaning again and a purpose, because the close of life is no longer in itself the end, since there will be an endless chain of generations to follow: man will know that what we create will not sink into Orcus but will be passed on to his children and to his children's children."

In the face of such world historical vistas it no longer mattered that he never told them what he proposed to do, and they could cheer him and shout their approval when he announced: "When someone comes along and asks our program, my answer is, I have been preaching my program for thirteen years. The program is very simple and clear: Germany must be freed of the poison of democracy and internationalism." And if the program was vague, they were exhorted nevertheless that it was their mission and their responsibility to carry it out:

"I believe in the capacity, talents, and resources of my people. Only one thing is necessary to liberate these powers—a union of national forces. . . . In the German people we now see a new will being forged like steel—a new unity and determination. Hundreds of thousands in Pomerania, Bavaria, the Rhineland and everywhere are ready and anxious to make any sacrifice to save this people which has been the victim of the present system."

Exalted into makers of history, his listeners refused to worry about his unwillingness to tell them how he would ban the specter of unemployment. They believed Goebbels when he told them that "when a man has the strength and the gift to transform a small sect of seven individuals into a movement of millions . . . , he will also find the way towards a new unity of the entire nation— a unity which will overcome the terrible political, ideological, and social conflicts which today divide and devour our people." [58]

If Hitler was vague as to what he proposed to do, so were Hindenburg and those who spoke for him. The marshal insisted in all of his statements that he felt himself under no obligation to any party and that he retained full freedom as to what he would do in the future. He carefully refrained from associating Brüning with his policies, and the latter of course was in no position to be more explicit. While Hindenburg's supporters expected him to safe-

[58] Norman H. Baynes, ed., *Hitler's Speeches* (New York, 1942), I, 190; Goebbels, *Wetterleuchten*, p. 270.

guard the Weimar Constitution, the more perceptive ones knew that his reelection meant a leap into the dark. "Hindenburg," mused the *Frankfurter Zeitung*, "can't tell us what he is going to do in the future, what measures he will take if there is a further aggravation of our situation or a political relaxation, whom he is going to appoint as Chancellor if a change should become necessary. He cannot tell us, but in his case we need not know, for we have the experience of the last seven years to go by, and the pledge of the Old Gentleman that he will not deprive us of our constitutional rights." Yet the same editorial admitted that Hindenburg would have to be watched "carefully and cautiously" to prevent the emergence of "groups of privileged personalities who are able, at the decisive moment, to exert a dangerous influence." [59]

The claim that the marshal would safeguard the constitution was not without ambiguity either. There was widespread agreement that political reality had moved far away from the premises of the Weimar Constitution and that that document was in need of substantial amendment if it was not replaced by a new constitution altogether. The *Frankfurter Zeitung*, while vouching for Hindenburg's abiding respect for constitutional rights, granted at the same time that the Weimar Republic was in the process of being transformed, and welcomed the fact that the country had gotten away from the nefarious regime of parties. The question might have been raised which constitutional rights Hindenburg should be expected to safeguard, but this issue was never touched upon in the campaign. All that could be said, the *Frankfurter Zeitung* stated, was that the Reich president was to be looked upon as the trustee of the nation. The substance of his mandate seemed of little import in view of the fact that this was above all a struggle between a civilized way of life and barbarian brutality. [60]

On March 13 Hindenburg polled 18,650,730 votes, an impressive plurality and just 345,323 votes short of a majority. Center and Social Democrats voted for him in good discipline: of the 17 districts in which he obtained majorities, 14 were Catholic strongholds while 8 had large working-class constituencies. Ten other districts in which he received large pluralities were also Centrist and Socialist bailiwicks. Hitler received 11,339,285 votes, and pluralities in only 3 districts. Thälmann got 4,983,197 votes, and Duesterberg 2,558,000. A sigh of relief ran through the Hindenburg camp; Hindenburg's plurality was such that his reelection in the second election seemed assured. "Hitler had staked his political

[59] Rudolf Kircher, in *Frankfurter Zeitung*, Reich ed., Mar. 2, 1932.
[60] *Ibid.; Berliner Tageblatt*, No. 123, Mar. 12, 1932.

existence on March 13," rejoiced the *Deutscher Volkswirt,* "The National Socialists would like to forget this fact. It is too late, the game is over, the decision has been made." [61] There was, on the other hand, deep disappointment in the ranks of the Nazis; carried away by Goebbels' persuasive propaganda, they had taken for granted the victory of their Fuehrer.[62]

Hindenburg himself found little cause for jubilation in the outcome of the election. He was shocked to discover that one-half of the electorate no longer had any confidence in him. That many of his one-time supporters would reject him, he had of course known, but there were also some new and unexpected repudiations. He received one of his smaller pluralities in his home province, East Prussia, despite all the help he had given it, and in Tannenberg and the Masurian lake district, the sites of his greatest military victories, Hitler was able to poll more votes than he. He suffered a similar setback in Dietramszell where he went for a few weeks hunting each fall; Hitler defeated him there 228 : 157. No matter how large the margin of his plurality, these disavowals were painful experiences. One of Hugenberg's papers, *Der Montag,* came close to expressing his innermost feelings when it gleefully headlined its election story:

Hindenburg Defeated by a Narrow Margin
Remained 168,453 Votes Short of Absolute Majority.[63]

A second look at the election returns gave rise to some serious soul-searching among his supporters. Between September 1930 and March 1932, in just one-and-a-half years, the parties voting for Hindenburg had lost 12.3 per cent of the vote while the Nazi vote had increased by 11.9 per cent. The Nazis, moreover, presented themselves as a unified force—at least in the sense that personal rivalries and ideological divergences were held in check by Hitler's unchallenged authority. Hindenburg's plurality, on the other hand, was based on the support of the most divergent elements. Nor was it clear how many of his supporters were prepared to con-

---

[61] *Dt. Volkswirt,* Mar. 18, 1932, p. 812.

[62] In fact, as investigations of the Prussian police revealed, preparations had been made by the Nazis to seize power forcibly had Hitler won the election. Stormtroop units had been alerted, plans had been drawn up to get control of arms depots of the Reichswehr, to detain administrative and police officials in the rural districts, and to take over local telephone and telegraph services. Severing, *Lebensweg,* II, 328–29; *Frankfurter Zeitung,* Reich ed., Apr. 4, 6, 1932.

[63] Returns in *New York Times,* Apr. 9, 1932; Dietramszell returns in Bullock, *Hitler,* p. 180; East Prussian figures in *Völkischer Beobachter,* No. 103, Apr. 12, 1932; *Der Montag,* No. 11, Mar. 14, 1932. The correct number of votes by which Hindenburg failed to get a majority was 345,323.

tinue to fight against Hitler beyond the presidential elections. Many who had been drawn to the polls by the historical name of the marshal were likely to lapse back into political indifference and would stay on the sidelines in future contests; others opposed to Brüning and his policies could be expected to vote the Nazi ticket in the forthcoming parliamentary elections. Finally there were the divisions within the Hindenburg camp that even the campaign could not bridge; they pointed up the ambiguity of the victory, for they blocked the adoption of a positive program by the Hindenburg forces and restricted their efforts to barring Hitler from the presidency. "The election has proven that Hindenburg and the System are not identical," wrote the right-wing *Deutsche Tageszeitung,* which had supported the president, in a post-election editorial, "The equation Hindenburg-Brüning is wrong." And the *Tägliche Rundschau,* another pro-Hindenburg organ, close to the Christian-Social People's Service, wondered how many of those who supported Hindenburg did so from patriotism: "What matters to us is to see the Presidential office gain in dignity, rigid nonpartisanship, national import with the re-election of Hindenburg. . . . We shall not permit it to become the plaything of party groups which did not hesitate to carve up the state for the benefit of their followers and never showed the re-quired ruthlessness and determination towards the unending de-mands from abroad in the decisive foreign political questions." To which the *Sozialistische Monatshefte* replied that the 8.5 million Social Democrats who had cast their vote for Hindenburg "want peace, they want work, they want to be freed from that terrible pressure that has been weighing on them for months and years now. They have a right to clear *political leadership.* They would indignantly reject any attempt to misuse their loyal collaboration for a nationalist all-or-nothing policy." And it added the warning that a continued policy of emergency decrees might well drive many of them into the arms of the Communists.

Sober reflection thus led to the conclusion that other deci-sive battles were still to come. These would be the second presi-dential contest in which Hitler would have to be dealt a worse defeat even than in the first, and the diet elections in Prussia, Bavaria, Württemberg, and a number of smaller states, scheduled for April 24. The latter would have to be fought without the bene-fit of Hindenburg's name on strictly partisan lines; a foretaste of what this might mean was provided in Mecklenburg-Strelitz. There diet elections were held simultaneously with the presidential election on March 13, and thousands of Hindenburg voters cast their ballot for the Nazis and German Nationals in the local contest.[64]

With this diagnosis the National Socialists agreed. They knew that Hitler could not possibly win the presidential election, and they decided therefore to use the second campaign as a jumping-off place for the diet elections. By gaining additional votes during the second presidential contest, their party would appear to be irresistible. On the crest of this wave, it would be swept to victory in the state elections and thus by roundabout ways bring Hitler to power.[65]

◈

The second campaign did not get under way until early in April. To spare the country the tensions of a prolonged contest, the government had proclaimed a political truce to last until Easter Sunday, April 3. While all political meetings were banned until then, the time was used by both camps to prepare for the coming battle. Each had its own problems to deal with. While the Nazis had to fight defeatism in their ranks, the Hindenburg forces had to guard against being overconfident. With Hindenburg's reelection assured, there was the danger that many of his supporters might stay away from the polls. If their number was large enough, they might even throw the victory into Hitler's lap, or more likely reduce Hindenburg's margin so much as to render his victory meaningless. Thus everywhere new slogans were being coined, new posters drawn, new leaflets printed. Goebbels also devised the ingenious plan of having Hitler campaign by airplane. Not only would the Fuehrer be able to cover more territory during the one week of campaigning before the second election (on April 10), but use of a plane would also point up the contrast between the resourcefulness of the Nazis who went along with the times, and their unimaginative opponents who continued in their antiquated slow-moving ways. The Hindenburg committee, capitalizing on Hindenburg's photogenic appearance, produced a new movie, *The Life and Deeds of Our Hindenburg*, to be shown in every movie theater during the campaign week. The Iron Front, a protective formation recruited from labor unions, workers clubs,

---

[64] Dt. Tageszeitung, No. 74, Mar. 15, 1932; Tägliche Rundschau, quoted in Tat, XXIV (1932), 6–7; Sozialistische Monatshefte, LXXV (1932), 301–02 (italics in original); also Berliner Tageblatt, No. 179, Apr. 15, 1932, and Dt. Allgemeine Zeitung, quoted in Dt. Tageszeitung, No. 75, Mar. 16, 1932.

[65] Goebbels, Vom Kaiserhof, entries of Mar. 14–15, Apr. 8, 11, 1932, pp. 63–64, 77, 78.

and the Social Democratic party, arranged 10,000 meetings for each day of that week.[66]

Duesterberg of course refrained from running in the second campaign. Nor was Hugenberg in a position to insist on a candidate who was more to his liking. Undaunted, he suggested that in return for new Reichstag elections, Hindenburg be considered elected, but the proposal was ignored by both Hitler and Hindenburg. Hopelessly outmaneuvered, Hugenberg finally told his followers to vote for whomever they wished. "This is the moment," he wrote Hitler, "when the national interest . . . requires that the differences of opinion between us be made public. It is to be a clear manifestation of these differences if we [German Nationals] stand at ease in this pointless second Presidential election." Duesterberg on his part appealed to his voters to vote for Hindenburg. The Nazis hit back by disclosing that one of his grandfathers had been of Jewish descent.[67]

A few days later an attempt was made to proclaim the candidacy of the ex-Crown Prince. The plan was worked out by a few third-string Nazis and *Stahlhelmers* in the hope that both Hitler and Hindenburg would withdraw from the contest. Hitler could thus be saved from defeat and Hindenburg from his republican-Socialist entanglements. The Crown Prince himself was interested, and so allegedly was Hitler who was said to be ready to drop out of the race if Hindenburg would do the same. The plan was stillborn, for the ex-Kaiser refused to approve it, and the Crown Prince would not defy his father's wishes. In the election, the Crown Prince voted for Hitler.[68]

The brief campaign, when it got under way, was as vigorous as the first one. The Nazis sought to capture the 2.5 million Duesterberg votes. Hitler, Goebbels, Göring, and a host of other Nazi speakers crisscrossed the country, creating an impression of ubiquituousness that reached into the remotest hamlet. During the week of April 3 to 9, Hitler, on his first *Deutschlandflug,* spoke before mass audiences in no less than twenty German cities: Dresden, Leipzig, Chemnitz, Plauen, Berlin, Potsdam, Lauenburg, Elbing, Königsberg, Würzburg, Nürnberg, Regensburg, Frankfurt am Main, Darmstadt, Düsseldorf, Essen, Münster, Schwenningen, Stuttgart, and Munich. Goebbels, according to his diary, had as

[66] *Ibid.,* entry of Mar. 18, 1932, p. 67; *New York Times,* Apr. 8, 1932; *Frankfurter Zeitung,* Reich ed., Apr. 9, 1932.

[67] *Dt. Allgemeine Zeitung,* Mar. 20, 1932; Hugenberg to Hitler, Mar. 20, 1932; Matthias and Morsey, *Ende der Parteien,* p. 629; Duesterberg, *Stahlhelm,* pp. 34–35.

[68] Bracher, *Auflösung,* pp. 476–77; Jonas, *Crown Prince William,* pp. 172–76.

crowded a schedule. On the eve of election day he spoke first to a mass meeting in the Berlin Sports Palace, then raced by car to Stettin, some 150 miles to the north, where around midnight he launched into a last venemous attack against the "System" before an overflow crowd of 12,000 people. Under this relentless barrage, flagging spirits revived and during the last part of the week the enthusiasm of the Nazi audiences was as boisterous as ever.[69]

Brüning, Dietrich, Westarp, and the "associated" forces of the Social Democrats worked almost as furiously. Yet while the Nazi forces managed to present a picture of youthful vigor, bursting with ideas and stratagems, the tactics of the president's camp lacked sparkle and novelty. The audiences were as large as before, but the campaign relied on its traditional, reasoned appeals rather than on exciting new spectacles. Nor did the Hindenburg forces, after their victory, seize the initiative and carry the attack to the enemy. As in the first campaign, they remained largely on the defensive. Even if they had wished to be more aggressive, Hindenburg's ambiguous attitude and their own heterogeneous makeup left them no choice. Brüning, moreover, refused as before to take the electorate into his confidence concerning his plans and hopes for the future. "As long as our people do not have enough to eat," Nazi campaigners kept telling their audiences, "there *must* be work available for people who want to produce food. As long as our people walk around in shreds, work *must* be available in textile plants. As long as our people vegetate in dark holes, there *must* be work to build new and better housing. *There cannot be a lack of work as long as the misery of the German people is crying to heaven.*" But when in reply, Finance Minister Dietrich suggested in one of his speeches that public work projects were being prepared by the government, there was at once an official denial of any such plans although they were indeed being drafted. Evidently the chancellor was concerned that any premature publicity might impair his claim that Germany was no longer in a position to pay reparations. (A tentative budget for 1932–33, on the other hand, published during these days with an eye on the election, no longer made any provision for reparation payments.)[70]

[69] Itinerary in Bernhard Schwertfeger, *Rätsel um Deutschland: 1933 bis 1945* (Heidelberg, 1947), p. 111; Goebbels, *Vom Kaiserhof*, entries of Apr. 4–9, 1932, pp. 75–77; *New York Times*, Apr. 5, 11, 1932.

[70] *Nazi Party Records*/176/318220 (italics in original); discussion of works projects, in cab. mtg., Apr. 12, 1932, RKz./1709/789756–74; also in Gerhard Ritter, *Carl Goerdeler und die deutsche Widerstandsbewegung* (Stuttgart, 1955), pp. 48–49; denial in *Frankfurter Zeitung*, Reich ed., Apr. 7, 1932; budget in *New York Times*, Apr. 6, 1932.

There were other factors that favored the Nazis. Hitler was tirelessly traveling across the country while Hindenburg stayed at home and did not speak once during the second campaign—a constant reminder of the difference in their age and endurance. Many stories were spread by the Nazis to drive home this point: Hindenburg was gravely ill, he would withdraw his candidacy; he slept every morning until eleven, he could barely sign a few papers; at noon, two chaplains, handpicked by Brüning, were guiding his hand when he wrote. Other rumors had it that all pensions and salaries were to be cut after his election; pensions for the disabled and unemployment relief would be abolished; and businesses would be taxed 20 per cent of their capital.[71]

There were also some untoward incidents that caused the Hindenburg camp some embarrassment. One concerned a clumsy attempt to manipulate the voting at Dietramszell. A Munich newspaperman had gone to the village before the first election to gather material for a story on Hindenburg's popularity. To his dismay he discovered that Hindenburg was anything but popular there; he had never had any contact with the local population, nor had he ever contributed a penny to alleviate the lot of the village poor. (A perceptive observer might have noticed some time earlier that all was not well: a newsreel on Hindenburg's life, compiled on his eightieth anniversary, showed him in Dietramszell with a village delegation greeting him with a noticeable lack of enthusiasm.) To improve matters for the second election, the journalist donated 400 reichsmark to be distributed to the needy on behalf of a "Hindenburg friend." His hope was that this might help to swing Dietramszell's vote to the president. The money was distributed in 5-mark amounts for which each recipient had to sign a receipt. On some of these receipts the source of the gift was erroneously designated as *"Hindenburg-Spende"* rather than *"Hindenburg-Freund-Spende."* Hitler's *Völkischer Beobachter* published a picture of one of the misworded receipts and raised the alarm that the *"Hindenburg-Spende,"* established for the benefit of war invalids, war widows and orphans, and aged veterans, was being misused to buy votes for Hindenburg. The story was spread assiduously and was apparently widely believed. (The rescue action failed to accomplish its purpose; in the second election Hitler won Dietramszell again by a wide margin, 230 to 179.)[72]

[71] Materials in *RKz.*, R 43 I/586.

[72] Rabe to Dietrich, Mar. 7, 1932, Dietrich/226/177–78; Zahn to Wiedemann, Mar. 18, 1932, *RKz.*, R 43 I/583; Jaud (mayor of Dietramszell) to Karstedt, Apr. 9, 1932 (copy), *BdRPr.*, R 54/298; also additional materials in *RKz.*, R 43 I/583; *Völkischer Beobachter*, No. 91, Mar. 31, 1932, No. 103, Apr. 12, 1932.

The disunity among Hindenburg's supporters was even more obvious than during the first campaign. His rightist supporters, worried about the forthcoming diet elections, became more outspoken now in their opposition to the Center and Socialists. "[Hindenburg's statement] that he is accepting the election without strings or commitments," Westarp announced, ". . . is directed above all against the Social Democrats." In the same vein, one of Westarp's associates urged his fellow Protestants to accept the Center's support "as a stroke of good luck, for on the basis of the returns of March 13 the Center is unfortunately still holding the key position" on the political stage. Brüning was made to feel this hostility when he was scheduled to speak at Königsberg on the eve of the election: the place and date had been carefully chosen to bring the campaign to a climax in Hindenburg's home province. But the chairman of the local Hindenburg committee was not pleased with this plan. In Königsberg, he informed the chancellor, the Hindenburg committee was composed only of rightists and was catering only to rightists so as not to give the opposition any ammunition to use against them. If Brüning were to speak, some of the committee members would refuse to sponsor such a meeting. His conclusion was blunt: "From a Brüning meeting we could expect . . . only disadvantages for the success of our efforts." He was not even certain that a Centrist meeting with Brüning would be advisable. However, the People's Party hastened to assure the chancellor that many of its members would welcome his appearance, and in the end he spoke as a "private individual" under the auspices of the Hindenburg committee.[73]

The election returns clearly reflected these facts: Hindenburg received 19.4 million votes, 700,000 more than on March 13; Hitler captured 2 million additional votes, bringing his vote up to a total of 13.4 million; Thälmann's votes dropped to a hopeless 3.7 million.[74] Hindenburg's majority of 53 per cent as against Hitler's 36.8 per cent was impressive; it was obvious too that the Nazi movement was still gaining ground.

The lack of unity among Hindenburg's followers makes it dif-

[73] Westarp, Dryander, and Rademacher, *Hindenburg und seine Wähler von 1925: Zum zweiten Wahlgang* (pamphlet, Berlin, 1932), pp. 11–12, 14; letters to Brüning, Mar. 24, 26, 1932, *RKz.*, R 43 I/586.

[74] There is some evidence that not a few Communists voted for Hitler in the second election in the belief that Communism stood to gain from the increasing unrest caused by the further growth of Nazism. In some parts of the country Communist agitators were even reported to have passed the word among their followers to vote for Hitler. *Frankfurter Zeitung*, Reich ed., Apr. 12, 1932; *Dt. Volkswirt*, Apr. 15, 1932, p. 935; Rumbold to Simon, Apr. 13, 1932, *DBFP.*, ii, iii, 111; Milatz, in Matthias and Morsey, *Ende der Parteien*, p. 764.

ficult to determine what mandate he received from the voters. The only definite fact emerging from his reelection was their opposition to a Nazi dictatorship. On the other hand, while Socialists, left-wing Centrists, and liberals were opposed to Nazis entering the government, millions of others did favor their entry under adequate safeguards. Hindenburg, moreover, had insisted that he would make his decisions independently of his electors. Many may have hoped that the door would stay open for the survival of Weimar democracy, if only in a modified form, but they had clearly no claim on its preservation. All they could expect, on the basis of the marshal's record and statements, was a policy that would shield the country from violent upheavals and a lawless dictatorship. Nothing more was implied in Hindenburg's pledge that he would always respect the constitution—no promise in any event to work actively for its defense and improvement. Yet much of what the marshal had sanctioned had been of dubious constitutionality, and he had been far more concerned with the technicalities of the constitution than with its spirit. He had viewed it primarily as a procedural code, not as a safeguard of parliamentary democracy—he clung to the constitutional forms, one liberal editor wrote, while the substance was being eroded.[75]

That this could happen was due as much to the weakness of those who still believed in constitutional legality as it was caused by Hindenburg's acquiescence. The demoralization of the republican camp was sadly attested in its inability to elect anyone more effective than this octogenarian who did not believe in the democratic republic and who was incapable, both mentally and physically, of coping with the immense tasks that were placed upon him.

The crisis, however, was not merely a constitutional one. If there was any doubt on that score, the two election campaigns had demonstrated that the nation's social and moral foundations were in grave peril. To save them, a firmer hand was required than the faltering one of the marshal who, as so often before, contented himself with urging the nation to unite for its common welfare: "Forget your quarrels and close ranks! Again, as I did when I assumed office seven years ago, I am asking the entire German people to work with me. We must concentrate our strength if we are to cope with the confusion and misery of the times. Only if we stand together, will we be strong enough to master our fate. Forward therefore in unity and with God!"[76]

[75] Baynes, *Hitler's Speeches*, I, 188; Stolper, in *Dt. Volkswirt*, June 3, 1932, p. 1179.
[76] Hindenburg, in Schulthess, Apr. 10, 1932, p. 66.

It was not a message apt to inspire a nation which increasingly came to believe that the spreading disintegration was the inescapable prelude to a better future and ought not to be stopped. "The road is leading straight into chaos," the widely read and respected *Tat* editorialized at that time, "and since there is no escape, we must accept this process of disintegration; it is also a purging process for it destroys old and rotten positions." Or, as that journal put it on another occasion: "We can master this disintegration by recognizing and supporting it—by consciously organizing the collapse." Less sanguine observers agreed that the time was past for mere adjustments if it had ever existed. "Such sharp, deep and justified contrasts as those existing within the state itself and between state and nation," wrote one of Hindenburg's wartime associates during those days, "can no longer be settled amicably; they must be decided in an open contest. The Hindenburg concept is no longer adequate to reconcile one Germany with the other. . . . As venerable a representative of the Reich as Hindenburg is, his mere presence is not sufficient to rescue the Reich." [77]

[77] *Tat*, XXIII (1931–32), 553, 940; Metzsch, *Hindenburg*, pp. 32, 69.

CHAPTER 9

THE DISMISSAL OF BRÜNING

HE brittleness of Brüning's success became painfully evident on the very morning following Hindenburg's reelection. That morning the chancellor called on the president to convey his congratulations. His reception was far from cordial. The marshal was not gratified by his victory since it had been bought with the defection of so many of his old friends and associates. He knew, moreover, that the government wished him to take a step from which he had long shied away—the dissolution of the Nazi stormtroopers (S.A.) and the Nazi elite guards (S.S.) as a threat to the state. His son Oskar had warned him that very morning against starting his second-term with a measure bound to arouse the right; sensing new troubles ahead of him, the president was resentful that Brüning would not spare him such difficulties. He felt that he had a claim on the chancellor's gratitude, for it was at his urging that he had accepted the presidency for another seven years. Brüning, he felt, ought at least to consider his sensibilities.

The chancellor proffered the cabinet's resignation that morning, but what was intended as a conventional courtesy became a matter of serious discussion. The president insisted that after the Prussian elections some changes would have to be made in the government and collaboration with the Socialists brought to an end. Brüning was able to obtain his consent to the proscription of the S.A. and S.S., yet the chancellor came away from the meeting wondering whether he still had the president's confidence. The official communiqué on the audience could but confirm his misgivings: reporting that the chancellor had submitted the cabinet's resignation according to custom on the president's reelection,[1] it stated cryptically that the president had requested Brüning "to withdraw this resignation."

How short-lived a victory the chancellor had won, he learned that same afternoon. Only a few hours after Hindenburg had agreed to the suppression of S.A. and S.S., Brüning was informed

---

[1] Custom did not actually require him to do so. When Hindenburg had been elected for the first time in 1925, the Luther cabinet, then in office, decided that it need not, on constitutional or any other grounds, resign or offer its resignation, and consequently did neither. Luther, *Politiker*, p. 334.

that the president had changed his mind and would not sign the dissolution decree. Prompted by Schleicher, Oskar von Hindenburg had been urging his father to withdraw his approval, and Hindenburg, tired and worried, had bowed to his pleas.[2]

Until recently Oskar von Hindenburg had played an inconspicuous role among his father's advisers. As the president's military aide he served as liaison man between Hindenburg and the army, but his functions had been mostly routine since Groener and Schleicher had ready access to the president. Occasionally he was asked to bring some proposal to his father's attention, but to the great disappointment of plotters like Class, he refused to assist them in their intrigues. Indolent and without political interest, he preferred to confine himself to his duties as the president's adjutant. He knew, moreover, that any intervention on his part was likely to be unsuccessful, for his father insisted on a strict departmentalization of duties in his official family. Nor would Oskar have dared to ignore these wishes; he meant it when he kept signing his letters, "your obedient son."[3]

A gradual change in Oskar's status seems to have set in, however, some time in 1931. Two factors apparently accounted for it —Hindenburg's physical decline which increased his dependence on his son, and his growing sense of estrangement from those circles to which he felt closest by background and inclination. As he came to identify his personal and political problems, he tended to turn more frequently to his son to unburden himself of his worries. Oskar shared his distress at this growing isolation, and when Schleicher, his long-time friend, began to suggest that this need not be, Oskar sided with him against Brüning. He did so to ease the life of his father who was visibly suffering from this estrangement, but he was also concerned with his own position. There would be a time when he would no longer be living in the protective shadow of his father, and he feared that then he and his family might find themselves social outcasts, shunned by those who had once been their friends. It was as the son, the bearer of the name of Hindenburg and of the family tradition, that he began to caution his father against Brüning and the latter's collaboration with the Center and Socialists. To these arguments the president proved increasingly susceptible. Not surprisingly it was

[2] Pünder, *Reichskanzlei*, entry of Apr. 11, 1932; Vogelsang, *Reichswehr*, pp. 185–86; communiqué in *Frankfurter Zeitung*, Apr. 12, 1932.

[3] Groener to Schnee, Nov. 13, 1932, *Dt. Rundschau*, LXXVII (1951), 793; Carlowitz, in *Vierteljahrshefte*, I (1953), 271; Schwerin-Krosigk, *Es geschah*, p. 141; Oskar von Hindenburg to his father, July 12, 1929, *BdRPr.*, R 54/319; personal information.

Oskar who first warned him against lending his name to the suppression of the S.A. and S.S.[4]

∽

The plan to dissolve the Nazi organizations had been virtually forced on the Reich by some of the state governments. The latter had become highly dissatisfied with the Brüning cabinet's dilatory tactics against the Nazis. And when evidence was found after the first presidential election that the Nazis had made preparations to seize power forcibly in the event of Hitler's victory, Prussia, Bavaria, Württemberg, Saxony, and some of the smaller states threatened to suppress the S.A. and S.S. on their own unless the Reich took some action. Faced with this ultimatum, Groener decided that the prestige of the Reich president and government required his intervention. This was not an easy decision for him, for it vitiated his long cherished plan of integrating the S.A. and S.S. into a Reich-supervised organization designed to strengthen the country's military potential. After delays of many months the time finally seemed ripe for this step after Hindenburg's reelection. Yet Groener felt the more justified in proscribing the Nazi formations as police raids had just uncovered some alarming Nazi directives. These instructions ordered stormtroopers in the East German provinces not to take part in the country's defense in case of a Polish attack, but instead to seize power internally. That these orders were sanctioned by Hitler himself, the Fuehrer proudly confirmed in one of his speeches. As he bluntly explained, he could not expect his men to come to the defense of the corrupt "system" that was now in power.

The suppression of the S.A. and S.S. was bound to affect the army's defense plans since it counted on assistance from these units in case of a Polish invasion. Thus before taking action, Groener consulted the leaders of the armed forces. Schleicher and Hammerstein agreed at once to the step; Admiral Raeder, the Navy chief, wondered whether for the sake of justice it was not advisable to dissolve the *Reichsbanner* too, but Schleicher replied that this was out of the question. Schleicher expressed his wholehearted agreement on at least one other occasion that same afternoon.

On the following day, however, Schleicher told Groener that he had changed his mind. He proposed to place the onus for the proscription on Hitler by imposing upon him certain demands

4 Groener to Schnee, *loc. cit.*; same to Gleich, Apr. 25, 1932, Groener-Geyer, *General Groener*, p. 311; Ott, ZS./270.

concerning the S.A. and S.S. Should he fail to comply with these conditions, there would then be full justification for dissolving his Brown Shirts. Exactly what caused Schleicher to change his mind is not clear. Some of his subordinates have since testified that he had always opposed the forcible suppression of the Nazis, and he had of course tried for some time to effect a rapprochement with them. In the face of the evidence of the Nazis' treasonous activities he apparently gave up this hope, only to reconsider when he learned that the ban of S.A. and S.S. would be strongly resented by the Reichswehr's junior officers since many of them were in deep sympathy with the Nazis. The compromise that he now proposed was meant to prove to the doubters that suppression was a last resort to which the Nazis had forced the government by their intractability. Possibly he hoped also, on second thought, to gain time for further negotiations which might now fare better with the suppression of S.A. and S.S. threatening in the background. In any event Schleicher seemed to be driven by frenzied anxieties; Groener had the impression that he was close to a nervous collapse and that at times he was almost out of his mind.

That same afternoon Groener called on Hindenburg in order to submit his plans to the president. Dutifully he also reported on Schleicher's alternative plan, but Hindenburg dismissed it as impractical and expressed himself in full agreement with Groener. Nor did Meissner voice any objections.[5]

Brüning had been away from Berlin during those days, on the last leg of his speech-making campaign on Hindenburg's behalf. Efforts to keep him informed of Groener's plans had apparently failed; according to his recollections, he learned about the proposed dissolution only on his return to the capital the morning of election day, April 10. He questioned the timeliness of the move, so shortly before the state diet elections where the Nazis could be expected to make the most of the suppression, but felt that preparations had gone too far at this point to be recalled. Since foreign diplomats had undoubtedly learned of the plans,[6] a cancellation would have a disastrous effect on the forthcoming disarmament talks at Geneva. For these reasons the chancellor decided to consent to the move.

When Brüning met with his principal advisers in the evening

[5] Groener, "Chronologische Darstellung der Vorkommnisse, die zu meinem Rücktritt als Reichswehr- und Reichsinnenminister geführt haben," Oct. 1932, in Vogelsang, *Reichswehr,* pp. 449–51; Pünder, "Niederschrift über die Besprechungen in der Reichskanzlei über das Verbot der S.A.," Groener Papers/25/231.

[6] The *New York Times* reported on the proposed measures as early as April 6, 1932.

304

of April 10, most of them sided with Groener. Meissner, however, was now inclined to support Schleicher. The president, he reported, was fully in favor of taking steps against the Nazis, but was wondering whether a sharp and clearly timed ultimatum of, say, a week might not be preferable to an outright suppression of their special formations. He added that Hindenburg was greatly concerned about the attacks he would have to endure after their dissolution. Schleicher seconded the suggestion and explained at some length why this procedure would prove more embarrassing to Hitler. An outright suppression would place the Nazis in the role of martyrs, this would be different if the blame for the suppression could be shifted to the Fuehrer. Moreover, Groener could write the letter giving the ultimatum, sparing the president too much involvement. The minister of justice, on the other hand, voiced legal objections to Schleicher's plans. Brüning, still in favor of Groener's proposal, decided to call on the president the next day to obtain his consent to the immediate proscription.

The meeting with Hindenburg on the following morning has been described. A few hours later Hindenburg had his change of heart and wished to see the decree postponed until after the Prussian elections. Oskar von Hindenburg, it developed, had conferred that same morning with Schleicher about the suppression of the S.A. He had been greatly disturbed by the plan, as Schleicher told Groener, but he, Schleicher, had refused to be drawn into a discussion of the measure on the grounds that he had nothing to do with it. Schleicher's ostensible dissociation from so vital a step was sufficient to convince Oskar that his father ought not to approve it, and he rushed back to the Palace to so advise him. At a luncheon that same day Meissner could already inform an aide of Groener that the president had made up his mind not to sign the S.A. decree.

The younger Hindenburg readily admitted his intervention when Groener tried to find out on the following morning why he had cautioned his father against the government's plans. In great excitement, Oskar complained that it was asking too much of his father to have him sign another emergency decree just after he had been reelected; it was bound to provoke new mud-slinging attacks on the part of the right. The fate of the S.A. was a matter of utter indifference to him, he hastened to add, but the government should take no action until after the Prussian elections. Groener noted that Oskar had no substantive objections against the decree, but since he seemed too upset to discuss the matter, the minister did not attempt to reason with him.

Before calling once more on the president, Brüning and Groener consulted with Braun and Severing. Could the proscription, they wondered, be postponed until after the Prussian elections? The two Prussian ministers rejected any delay and warned that they would disband the Nazi formations in their state at once if the Reich government would not act. Chancellor and minister then went to see Hindenburg. Like Oskar, Groener noted, the president had no objections to the measure as such; what worried him most was that he was asked to intercede against one particular group just after he had pledged himself publicly to deal impartially with all Germans. The ministers argued that equal treatment did not extend to the toleration of illegal activities, but the argument did not impress him. Could one not wait at least until after the Prussian elections, he wondered. Brüning, anxious not to place too heavy a strain on their tenuous relationship, was willing to delay until then; but Groener, in view of the attitude of the Prussian government, insisted that the dissolution must be enacted at once. He would have to resign should Hindenburg refuse them his signature. Brüning now felt compelled to warn Hindenburg that if Groener resigned, he would have to leave too. He did not make this threat lightly, for he knew how much the marshal resented such pressure. But when Groener offered to take full responsibility before public and parliament, Hindenburg gave his grudging consent, "for reasons of state," as the minutes of the conference explicitly stated.

The decree was promulgated the next day, and a day later S.A. and S.S. quarters and offices throughout the country were closed by the police. There was virtually no resistance, except in Breslau where unemployed stormtroopers tried to fight their expulsion; but it was obvious that the Nazis had been forewarned and had hidden weapons and incriminating documents before the police appeared. Lack of open resistance, moreover, did not mean acceptance of the suppression. Organizationally the S.A. and S.S. continued to exist in the guise of "anti-Communist leagues," sport clubs, or new party units. Yet their unwillingness to defy the decree openly served to convince the president, the army, and the bulk of their sympathizers that they were law-abiding groups that had been subjected to a grave injustice.[7]

While outwardly the measure touched off no major disturb-

[7] Groener, "Chronologische Darstellung," Vogelsang, *Reichswehr*, pp. 451–54; Pünder, "Niederschrift," Groener Papers/25/231; Hindenburg and Meissner, "Niederschrift," in Vogelsang, *Reichswehr*, pp. 460–61; Brüning, cab. mtg., Apr. 13, 1932, *RKz.*/1709/789794–95. On Nazi evasion of proscription, Zörgiebel to Police Commissioner, Hagen, May 28, 1932, *Nazi Party Records*/90/103278.

ances, behind the scenes it led to a serious crisis. There was the expected flood of protests deluging the Presidential Palace, and the Reichswehr ministry too received a great many complaints from its commanders as Schleicher told Groener with evident satisfaction. The president who dreaded this sort of uproar was badly upset by the furor, and the complaints were indeed calculated to cause him serious concern. There were intimations that the ban was a payoff to the left for services rendered in the presidential elections. Many of the critics suggested also that it exposed the Reichswehr to charges of partisanship since any action of Groener as minister of the interior reflected on the army as well. What worried Hindenburg too was the fact that a number of generals on active duty were highly critical of the step; in his anguish he failed to perceive the grave breach of discipline these men were committing in complaining to him and bypassing their immediate superiors. Since a repeal of the decree was out of the question, he decided to put himself in the right with his critics by demonstrating his impartiality. This he proposed to do by demanding the dissolution of the *Reichsbanner* (though not of the *Stahlhelm*). General von Hammerstein, the army chief, was asked to submit documentary material that would justify such a measure—an improper procedure on Hindenburg's part, since as a purely political matter the request should have gone to Groener as the responsible minister.

Provided with what little material Hammerstein was able to gather, Hindenburg sent Groener a letter in which he requested him to determine whether other groups similar to the S.A. and S.S. should not also be banned. In its tenor the letter was intentionally unfriendly, pointedly asking Groener to explore this question as seriously as he, Hindenburg, had examined Groener's demand that the Nazi formations be dissolved. As a further deliberate slight the letter was made available to the press before it could have reached Groener. Once again the president was desperately anxious to assure his old friends that at heart he was still on their side.

Groener was facing a difficult situation. He chose to ignore Hindenburg's calculated discourtesies, and he also ignored the disloyalty and insubordination of Schleicher and Hammerstein. Had he asked Hindenburg for their dismissal, he would have embittered the marshal and destroyed all chances of further collaboration. Yet if he were forced to relinquish his office, the entire Brüning cabinet would most likely collapse, on the very eve of the crucial Prussian elections and the resumption of the reparations and disarmament talks at Geneva. Groener was certain that only Brüning could rescue the country, and he was determined to help him remain in office, even at the price of the humiliations to which he himself was being subjected. On the other hand, he could not fulfill the president's wish and dissolve the *Reichsbanner.* The material which had been submitted to him was too flimsy to justify its suppression—the more so as the *Reichsbanner,* to preclude such a move, had just then dissolved its so-called protective formations (*Schutzformationen*), a semimilitary body of retired police officers set up to protect Socialist meetings against Nazi and Communist disturbances. To meet the president halfway, however, the cabinet decided to propose a decree that would place all existing paramilitary organizations under the direct control of the state. Since such a step would affect the *Stahlhelm,* the president's protégé, a further gesture of conciliation seemed imperative: the new decree was to provide also for the dissolution of the Communist League of the Godless. Hindenburg had long asked for its ban, but the government had never felt that the legal grounds to suppress it existed. To please him, it now overcame its legal scruples—a reversal that was not lost on him. He signed the decree but felt that it hardly alleviated the injustice that in his judgment had been committed against the Nazi formations. That the latter were under orders not to defend their country against a foreign attack, but to foment trouble at home in such an event, did not seem to concern him.[8]

℗

Hindenburg's doubts about the wisdom of the proscription were reenforced by the outcome of the state diet elections on April 24. In each one of them the Nazis scored gains over the first presidential election. They could also boast a relative improvement of their position over the results of the second presidential contest; in spite of a 5 per cent decrease in voter participation (from 86 to 81 per cent of the electorate), they suffered a loss of less than 2 per cent of the votes. Except in Bavaria they emerged as the largest party in each one of the new diets.[9] Those rightist parties, on the other hand, that had supported Hindenburg's

---

[8] Groener, "Chronologische Darstellung," Vogelsang, *Reichswehr,* pp. 454–56; Hindenburg and Meissner, "Niederschrift," *ibid.,* p. 461; Hammerstein to Reichswehr commanders, May 21, 1932, *Vierteljahrshefte,* II (1934), 423–24; proposed cabinet measures, in cab. mtg., May 3, 1932, *RKz./*1709/789872–73; Groener to Gleich, Apr. 25, 1932, Groener-Geyer, *General Groener,* pp. 310–11.

[9] Statistics, in *Gesellschaft,* IX (1932), i, 473.

reelection lost heavily, and there was some evidence that the dissolution of the stormtroopers which they considered an unfair and unwise move had helped to drive many voters into Hitler's camp.[10]

At the same time the elections demonstrated anew the dilemma of those who still saw in Hindenburg the sole hope for a political and moral recovery. Some who had worked for Hindenburg's reelection had hoped to utilize the political momentum which had been generated by the campaign. They had thought of maintaining a "Hindenburg Front," and there was even talk of establishing a "Hindenburg newspaper" to publicize his opinions and policies. But the marshal's refusal to associate himself with any such efforts doomed them at once. As a result, the old cleavages and divisions reappeared; the leaders of this new movement refused to have any dealings with the left-liberal bourgeoisie, let alone with the Social Democrats; even among themselves such splinter groups as the German People's Party, the Economic Party, the Christian-Social People's Service, and the Landvolk, were unable to agree on a common course of action. Proceeding individually, they all tried to present themselves to the electorate as the supporters of "Hindenburg policies"; these were not specified, but seemed strongly reminiscent of those of the Nazis. Some of them got financial aid from funds collected for, but not used in, the presidential campaigns. But these efforts proved entirely futile; with the exception of the People's Party which was reduced from 40 to 7 seats in the new Prussian diet, and the Christian Socialists who obtained 4 seats, the "Hindenburg parties" lost their voters to the National Socialists.[11]

The German National People's Party shared the fate of all other bourgeois parties. Like them, it suffered heavy losses and returned to the Prussian diet with less than half of its former representation (in some of the other diets its decline was even more marked). In a desperate attempt to stave off defeat, Hugenberg had tried to enlist some radicals of National Bolshevik persuasion as candidates on his party's ticket. With their support he hoped to inject into his campaign that dynamism which alone could cope with the ruthless energies of the Nazis. But the National Bolsheviks did not care to collaborate with this spokesman

[10] Schmid to Schleicher, Apr. 18, 1932, Schleicher Papers/24/19; *Dt. Tageszeitung*, Apr. 16, 1932.

[11] Plans for Hindenburg Front, in *Frankfurter Zeitung*, Reich ed., May 23, 25, 27, 1933; Richthofen to Westarp, Mar. 19, 1932, Westarp to Richthofen, Mar. 22, 1932, Westarp Papers; *Dt. Tageszeitung*, Apr. 14–16, 23, 1932; campaign leaflets, in Munich Coll./28.

of industrial capitalism who had so suddenly discovered an interest in them.[12]

While the elections brought the Nazis new gains, their over-all outcome was, in the words of the *Deutsche Tageszeitung,* "negative in every respect." They destroyed the existing majority coalitions—partly bourgeois, partly bourgeois-socialist—that had governed these states, but they did not give the parties of the "Harzburg Front" a majority either. In the face of the existing political divisions it seemed unlikely that any governments based on parliamentary majorities could be formed in Prussia, Bavaria, or Württemberg. The immediate prospect was that the existing governments would have to continue in office as caretaker governments. But there was talk also of the possibility that the Reich president might have to intercede and on the basis of Article 48 appoint Reich commissioners to take over state governmental functions.[13]

More than ever, it was clear, the center of political gravity was to be found in the Reich and, more specifically, in the Reich president. The future course of developments depended on what he would decide or, more precisely, on what he would be prevailed upon to decide.

Pressures to have him replace the Brüning government continued relentlessly. They were not without effect. "Every effort is being made to remove me," Groener wrote to a friend after the Prussian elections, "unfortunately Brüning too has a black mark in the President's book. Hindenburg has discovered his conservative heart and wishes for a more rightist government than Brüning's. But he has not yet found a new chancellor. . . ."

Among those working most actively against Brüning were Schleicher and Oskar von Hindenburg; Meissner seems to have contented himself with the role of a bystander waiting to see what the future would bring. Oskar was greatly perturbed by the consistent intimations that his father was playing into the hands of the Socialists. Nor had he forgotten the campaign rumors that he himself was a Social Democrat, and he was anxious to purge himself of this taint.[14] Schleicher's plan of removing Brüning appealed

---

[12] Ernst Niekisch, *Gewagtes Leben* (Cologne-Berlin, 1958), p. 206.

[13] *Dt. Tageszeitung,* Apr. 26, 1932; Rumbold to Simon, Apr. 27, 1932, *DBFP.,* ii, III, 130; Westarp to Richthofen, Mar. 22, 1932, Westarp Papers.

[14] He was furious therefore when a representative of a republican organization, Severing's State Secretary Wilhelm Abegg, approached him to help set up a joint front against Hitler by acting as a go-between between the *Reichsbanner* and those rightist organizations which had supported his father's reelection. As his caller later reported, Oskar completely lost control of himself, and fuming with rage, showed the proponent the door. Hermann Schützinger, "Die 'Machtergreifung,'" *Deutsche Rundschau,* LXX (1947), 99.

to him, and he was glad to serve as the general's spokesman and pass on his views. Schleicher, in turn, found Oskar a useful ally; Oskar was constantly with the president, he knew his father's habits and moods, and could best judge when and how to approach him in political matters. Thus the two men worked closely together and through Oskar, the president was steadily kept informed on Schleicher's views and activities.[15]

These centered, as before, on a rapprochement with the Nazis. Since Brüning's main failing in Schleicher's eyes was his inability to reach an understanding with Hitler, Schleicher kept trying to come to terms with the Fuehrer. Immediately after the stormtroops had been dissolved, he let Hitler know that he had been opposed to this step and engaged in new talks with a number of Nazi spokesmen. His hope was to establish a non-Nazi government of the right that Hitler would tolerate and into which some Nazis could later be invited. Schleicher was confident that by that time the new government would be so firmly established that the Nazis would have to join it on his terms rather than theirs and would never get full control of it. In return for their toleration of that government, the dissolution of the S.A. and S.S. would be repealed, new Reichstag elections would be held, and they would have full freedom in their propaganda activities during the election campaign.

Schleicher's plan was a measure of his supreme self-confidence. Where Brüning had failed, he would quickly succeed. His finesse had disarmed so many opponents, it would triumph as readily over the Nazis as it had over the Socialists. Brüning lacked flexibility, he confided to Meissner, it had always been the special task of the Center to form coalitions with either the right or the left; if it had been possible for the Christian Center to collaborate with the atheist Socialists, it ought to be no more difficult for it to come to terms with the Nazis. He never understood the totally different nature of he Nazi movement and saw it as simply another political party, though more unpredictable and dynamic than most. Essentially the Nazis were little children, he assured Finance Minister Dietrich, one must take them by their hand and guide them. Resourceful in tactical deals and devices, in roundabout ways and manipulations, he was sure he could do this.[16]

The talks between General von Schleicher and Hitler's emissaries proceeded well enough to culminate on April 28 in a meeting between Schleicher and Hitler; according to Goebbels' diary, it went

15 Eschenburg, "Rolle der Persönlichkeit," pp. 22–23.
16 Meissner, *Staatssekretär*, pp. 224–25; personal information.

smoothly. On May 8, the two men met again, and this time Meissner and Oskar von Hindenburg also attended. This second conclave produced an oral agreement in which Hitler appeared to accept Schleicher's terms. At least the general now felt assured of the Nazis' benevolent neutrality, and armed with what he thought a firm pledge on their part, he hoped to induce Hindenburg to appoint a more capable chancellor. If we can believe Goebbels, Brüning was to be replaced within the next few days and the Reichstag dissolved immediately upon his departure.[17]

Brüning was once more able, however, to ward off Schleicher's intrigues. That he could do so was due perhaps more to Hindenburg's habitual reluctance to take action than to the force of his arguments, for they could hardly have sounded convincing to the president. The chancellor had just come back empty-handed from the Disarmament Conference at Geneva; while Ramsay MacDonald, the British prime minister, and Secretary of State Henry Stimson had been ready to accept his proposals for some concessions—a reduction of the term of service for part of the Reichswehr and a substantial decrease of the existing land armaments—French Premier Tardieu had kept neither of two appointments that had been arranged with him, evidently because the forthcoming elections in France made it impossible for him to enter into any commitments. Again the diplomatic success he so desperately needed had eluded the chancellor.

His position thus was more precarious than ever. On the very day of his return from Geneva, his enemies scored another success. After discussions with Schleicher, Warmbold, the minister of economics, submitted his resignation. He professed himself unable to accept an increase of the turnover tax and a shortening of the working day, as proposed by the government; it was obvious, however, that the basic reason for the departure of this lone spokesman for industry in the cabinet was that Brüning was losing ground among his remaining industrial backers.

That same day Hindenburg, obviously prodded by Schleicher, advised the chancellor that he wished to discuss the political situation with the various party leaders and asked whether Brüning had any objections. The chancellor pointed out that such talks would be interpreted everywhere as a move directed against him —they would undermine his position so seriously that they might lead to the downfall of the cabinet. In a personal talk with

17 Edgar von Schmidt-Pauli, *Hitlers Kampf um die Macht* (Berlin, 1933), pp. 38–39; Walther Schotte, Die Regierung Papen-Schleicher-Gayl (Leipzig, 1932), p. 14; Goebbels, *Vom Kaiserhof*, entries of April, May 1932, *passim*.

the marshal on May 9, he repeated his warnings; any overt gesture against him would gravely weaken his position in the disarmament discussions to be resumed at Geneva on May 17 and in the reparations negotiations scheduled for mid-June in Lausanne. There was no reason why the president should not consult with the party leaders, but he urged him to wait for a more opportune moment, after the Prussian diet had met on May 24. Hindenburg hesitated to commit himself. Only the day before Schleicher had reached his agreement with Hitler, and a talk with the latter as well as talks with the other party leaders had been considered for the following days. But Brüning would not give in. He would have to resign, he warned, if the president consulted with the party leaders before the opening of the Prussian diet. Hindenburg finally yielded, but he doubtless resented Brüning's concern with his own position and his apparent unwillingness to consider the marshal's prestige and authority.

As the conversation turned to the political situation, the president again brought up the need of shifting the center of political gravity further towards the right. This time Brüning agreed that the Nazis ought to be taken into the Prussian government. Convinced of the need for their participation, the chancellor asked the president to issue a formal appeal to the party leaders—from Nazis to Centrists—and urge them with the full weight of his authority to work in good faith toward the formation of a new government. Brüning also conceded that in the interest of a close cooperation between the Reich and Prussia, some Nazis would have to be appointed to the Reich government too, but only after the conclusion of the Lausanne Conference so as not to endanger the reparations negotiations.[18]

Although he survived this latest attack, Brüning did not emerge unscathed. Unable to remove him, his opponents managed to strike down one of his allies: the faithful Groener fell victim to a concerted assault on him in the Reichstag.

The Reichstag session had started off rather quietly. There were indications that the Nazis were on their best behavior to prove to the president that they could assume the responsibilities of government. On the second day, however, when Groener tried to defend the dissolution of the stormtroopers, they reverted to their customary obstructionist tactics and started to interrupt him. Groener, no impressive speaker even under the best of circum-

18 Deist, "Brüning," *Vierteljahrshefte*, v (1957), 257–59; Warmbold, in Schulthess, May 6, 1932, p. 70; Westarp, in *Vierteljahrshefte*, i (1953), 283; Hindenburg and Meissner, "Niederschrift," Vogelsang, *Reichswehr*, pp. 461–62.

stances, allowed himself to be drawn into personal exchanges with some of his hecklers and gave a poor account of himself. Schleicher decided to strike and announced that Groener would have to resign in the interest of the army; if Groener remained, he himself and all the generals in the Reichswehr ministry would hand in their own resignations. Hindenburg who had considered Groener a liability since the proscription of the Nazi formations sided with Schleicher, but Brüning wished to retain Groener as minister of the interior lest his departure be viewed as a disavowal of the stormtroop decree. There followed some frantic conferences to patch up the crisis. Unprepared yet for a change in the chancellery, Hindenburg contented himself in the end with Groener's resignation as Reichswehr minister. But he wished it to be understood that his decision was not final and that he would ponder the matter during his forthcoming stay at Neudeck. Brüning, on his part, tried to placate the president by offering only a perfunctory defense of the S.A. decree when he addressed the Reichstag during that ill-fated session.[19]

The chancellor emerged from the session with a slim majority of 27 votes. He had gained a breathing spell, but he was not allowed to forget how precarious his position was. Wisely he sought to win over Schleicher by offering him the post of Reichswehr minister, but the general proved a slippery negotiator. While he seemed willing to enter the cabinet, he warned against rushing matters; yet a tentative agreement was apparently reached between the two men. Nevertheless Berlin was buzzing with rumors that Schleicher was unwilling to work with Brüning and that he was waiting to join a new government soon to be formed. Schleicher dismissed these stories as wholly unfounded; he was entirely at Brüning's disposal, he assured Pünder, and merely objected to undue haste. He would, however, do anything *der Herr Reichskanzler* demanded, "for Brüning is the only one who can master the situation in Germany in the foreseeable future." Whether he was untruthful or vacillating again, three days later he no longer wished to be considered a candidate: "For all practical purposes Schleicher has turned us down," Pünder wrote sadly in his diary, "apparently wants to save himself for future appointments." Brüning was also unable to find another economics minister to take Warmbold's place; several soundings he made drew

[19] Groener, "Chronologische Darstellung," Vogelsang, *Reichswehr*, pp. 456–57; Hindenburg and Meissner, "Niederschrift," *ibid.*, pp. 462–63; Westarp, "Zu Brünings Rücktritt," June 1, 1932, *Vierteljahrshefte*, I (1953), 282; Mellenthin, ZS./105; Carlowitz, ZS./218.

negative responses. His failure to reconstitute his cabinet was the more perturbing as it could but confirm Hindenburg's view that the Brüning government lacked popular backing.[20]

But the chancellor still hoped to weather the crisis. He felt certain that the reparation and disarmament problems were about to be settled in Germany's favor.[21] He was the more confident as the elections in France had produced a leftist majority. It was more likely to make concessions to Germany than the conservative-nationalist forces that had held power till then. Domestically, too, the situation looked a little more promising. There were indications of an economic improvement; he thought he could risk inaugurating the long-planned public works program as soon as the reparation debts had been cancelled, and such a program would help to speed economic recovery. Outwardly, there was indeed no suggestion that the chancellor and his ministerial colleagues had any doubts about their political future. They met almost daily during the following weeks to complete work on the budget and public works plans: road and canal building projects, land reclamation schemes, a comprehensive program of modernization for the railways, and an ambitious land resettlement program.[22]

∽

It was the planned land resettlement program that contributed to the cabinet's downfall two weeks later. In addition to sponsoring small-scale gardening in suburban communities, it provided for the breakup of those large estates that repeated governmental aid had not been able to put back on a paying basis. These bankrupt estates were to be carved up into small farms and turned over to unemployed settlers. Altogether it was hoped, quite unrealistically, that up to 600,000 people or 10 per cent of all the unemployed could be provided with land; unemployment would be reduced substantially, hopelessly languishing estates would be transformed into profit-making small farms, and the thinly settled areas of rural eastern Germany would benefit from a substantial influx of new settlers.

Land reform was not new. It had been discussed during the early days of the first Brüning government, but its implementa-

20 Pünder, *Reichskanzlei*, entries of May 10–11, 1932, pp. 120–22; Holtzendorff, in *Vierteljahrshefte*, I (1953), 272–73.

21 Cab. mtg., May 2, 1932, *RKz.*/1709/789752–54.

22 Eyck, *Weimarer Republik*, II, 466–67; Ritter, *Goerdeler*, pp. 48–49; cab. mtg., May 20, 1932, *RKz.*/1709/789966–74; Wheeler-Bennett, *Wooden Titan*, p. 388; Meinecke, *Dt. Katastrophe*, p. 99.

tion had been postponed for political and financial reasons. Meanwhile repeated government subsidies had failed to rehabilitate a great number of the larger estates, and the resettlement project had been revived. Since money would now be made available to buy them up and finance their partition into small farms, the cabinet decided to act and the necessary decree was being prepared. Finance Minister Dietrich announced the plan to the Reichstag in May.[23]

Greatly perturbed by this prospect, the landowners quickly struck back. They managed to get draft copies of the decree and railing against its purposes and provisions dispatched furious protests to Hindenburg. Since the program had been discussed for some time by the cabinet, Meissner had doubtless reported to him on the plan, but at first he showed no concern. Most likely he did not grasp its significance until the complaints aroused his attention. He was shocked to hear it denounced as an attempt to socialize German agriculture and to deprive some of Prussia's oldest families of the land that had been theirs for many generations. His old admirer Baron von Gayl warned him, moreover, that such expropriations might well undermine the will of the population to defend its soil against foreign attack, and this, as he added, was also a source of serious alarm to the military authorities.[24]

Evidently these warnings were part of a renewed effort to convince Hindenburg that Brüning's dismissal must be delayed no longer. "The whole thing will lead to a dictatorship which we shall claim of course for a man of the right," Oldenburg-Januschau predicted confidently. The protests also struck a sensitive chord in Oskar von Hindenburg, who had accompanied his father to Neudeck. Oskar reacted sharply to the charge that Brüning's government promoted "state socialism," and he feared this might again reflect on him and his father. Schleicher, moreover, was in constant communication with him and kept him informed of the army's growing uneasiness and the insistence of the eastern commanders that for military reasons a firm understanding should be reached with the Nazis. On visits to neighboring estates and

[23] Brüning, cab. mtgs., Apr. 16, May 7, 1930, RKz./1705/783349. 783532; Dietrich and Treviranus, Jan. 25, 1932, 1709/789160–63; Stegerwald and Dietrich, Feb. 5, 1932, 1709/789178–79, May 20, 1932, 1709/789969–72, 789988–790002; Dietrich, May 9, 1932, Verhandlungen, Vol. 446, p. 2473; Schlange-Schöningen, Am Tage Danach, p. 70.

[24] Letters of protest to Hindenburg, in Buchta, Junker, pp. 136–39; Gayl to Hindenburg, May 24, 1932, Meissner to Gayl, May 26, 1932, Vierteljahrshefte, I (1953), 276–77; Hindenburg and Meissner, "Niederschrift," Vogelsang, Reichswehr, p. 463; Bracher, Auflösung, pp. 511–17.

nearby garrisons, Oskar encountered the same pessimistic mood about Brüning's handling of the country's political and economic problems.

Schleicher meanwhile kept the president informed of his continuing talks with the Nazis. These were reaching the point where the actual composition of the new government was being discussed. On May 24, Goebbels noted in his diary that Franz von Papen was to be the new chancellor and Neurath his foreign minister. To undermine Brüning's position more effectively the news was allowed to leak out; the French Ambassador knew about the proposed appointment of Papen several days before the latter had been approached or before Hindenburg had approved it. At Neudeck, at the same time, Oskar von Hindenburg was talking of the need for a government in which noblemen would play a prominent role.[25]

At that very moment Meissner was on his way to Neudeck to acquaint the president with the new budgetary and economic proposals which the government had meanwhile completed. For their enactment, by another presidential decree, the government needed Hindenburg's signature, and Brüning had offered to come himself to explain the proposed measures. Knowing Hindenburg's growing reluctance to sign any further decrees, he thought it doubly important that the president understand fully the need and significance of his new program. In the peace of Neudeck, with the marshal relaxed and well rested, there would be an opportunity also to discuss once more the chancellor's over-all policies, and his long-range plans for the future. He had been able so many times to bring the president back to his side in such talks that he was hopeful that he could do so again. But Hindenburg declined to see Brüning, perhaps because he dreaded the latter's involved explanations, or possibly simply because he wanted to have his peace. During his two weeks' stay, he saw none of his friends except Count Brünneck who could be expected not to ply him with angry complaints. Meissner's call was to be merely informational, the chancellor was told; no decision would be made until Hindenburg came back to Berlin and had spoken with Brüning.

How well Meissner discussed the decree with Hindenburg will never be known. Steering a cautious course between Schleicher and Brüning, he had not commited himself fully to either man,

25 Westarp, "Zu Brünings Rücktritt," *Vierteljahrshefte,* I (1953), 284; Oldenburg-Januschau to Gayl, May 21, 1932, *ibid.,* pp. 277–78; Meissner, *Staatssekretär,* p. 227; Bracher, *Auflösung,* pp. 520–21; Oskar von Hindenburg, in Pünder, *Reichskanzlei,* entry of May 29, 1932, p. 127.

but was waiting for Hindenburg's decision. He had attended one of the Schleicher-Hitler talks and seems to have voiced no objections to the impropriety of the arrangements made behind Brüning's back. He was also responsible for at least one of the letters of protest against the resettlement decree that Hindenburg received; when Baron von Gayl telephoned to express his misgivings, Meissner asked him to sum up his views in a letter that he would take with him to Neudeck. Yet as long as Hindenburg hesitated to part with the chancellor, Meissner sought also to remain on good terms with Brüning and kept him informed of the president's mood and of Oskar's ascendancy. As the president's man, Meissner was likely to stress those points of the program that were of particular interest or concern to the president. Hindenburg, too, unable to follow any long explanations, focused his attention on these particular points relating to the reduction of payments to disabled war veterans and the breakup of the hopelessly encumbered estates. These at least were the only items that the marshal remembered a few days later. The decrease in the pension payments had troubled him for some time; as for the proposed agrarian reforms, he told Meissner that he had been besieged by agricultural circles not to approve them in their proposed form. Convinced of their unfairness, he would have to insist on a more equitable treatment of the estate owners and their creditors in the land reform program. He also demanded the elimination of the proposed reduction of veterans pensions since he, the "Reich President and Field Marshal General," could not take the responsibility for so unjust a measure.

The talk veered farther away from its supposedly informational nature when Meissner brought up the question of the government's future. Brüning, he reported, did not want to assume the blame for another unpopular decree if he were to be dropped a few weeks later. Hindenburg replied that he wished to keep working with him, but Groener would have to go. If he were to give Groener a permanent appointment as minister of the interior, he would be expressing his confidence in him, and this he could not do after the bad mistake Groener had made in suppressing the Nazi formations. His discussion with Meissner suggests that he did not intend to part with Brüning. Meissner was to ask him in fact to form a new government of the right after Lausanne. The Nazis would be excluded from it, but to assure their support he wished them to enter the new Prussian cabinet. And in an obvious effort to bring pressure to bear on Brüning, Meissner was also to warn him that the president would not make any new appointments to

318

THE DISMISSAL OF BRÜNING

fill the vacancies in the existing cabinet. Its days, he wished to make clear, were numbered, and it would in any event be replaced by a more acceptable one after Lausanne.

Upon his return to Berlin, Meissner had two long talks with the chancellor. Brüning felt little encouraged. He knew of Schleicher's cabals and had also learned that the general had hand-picked Herr von Papen as the next chancellor. He asked Meissner pointblank whether the president was really willing to retain him and his cabinet until after Lausanne. Was Hindenburg not getting ready for an immediate change under the pressure of military and other influences? He would have to insist on frankness when next he would see the president. As he told Treviranus that same day, he would not submit to any more pressures by the Reichswehr or Schleicher.

Brüning's fears were well founded. The indefatigable Schleicher was indeed hard at work to have the president deal him the *coup de grâce*. Through Oskar, and possibly personally on a hurried visit to Neudeck that Schleicher allegedly made at that time, he kept warning the marshal that the chancellor was losing ground rapidly and his cabinet could be expected to fall very soon. He also reported that he had found the right successor in Papen. As a Centrist with monarchist leanings, he would end the chancellor's unholy alliance with the Socialists. Since Papen was also acceptable to the Nazis, his cabinet would rest on a stable majority, and there would be no need for any more presidential decrees. But weaving his intricate net of intrigues, Schleicher strove also to keep on good terms with the chancellor. More than once he let Brüning know through the credulous Pünder that he considered him indispensable. He was confident that the chancellor would swallow his blandishments and be taken entirely by surprise when Hindenburg asked for his resignation.[26]

Thus tension was mounting as the day of the president's return to Berlin approached. A seemingly minor occurrence on the eve of his arrival hastened the final crisis. After his visit to Neudeck, Meissner had informed Stegerwald, the labor minister, and Schlange-Schöningen, the eastern aid commissioner, as the two cabinet members most directly concerned, of the amendments which Hindenburg wished to see made in the resettlement decree.

26 Hindenburg and Meissner, "Niederschrift," *loc. cit.,* pp. 463–64; Meissner, *Staatssekretär,* pp. 223–24, 226, 230–31; Brüning, "Ein Brief," pp. 8–9; Gayl memorandum, n.d., Gayl Papers, unnumbered folder; Pünder, *Reichskanzlei,* entry of May 26–29, 1932, pp. 126–28; Westarp, "Zum Rücktritt Brünings," *loc. cit.,* p. 282; Eschenburg, "Rolle der Persönlichkeit," p. 25.

Contrary to custom, both ministers explained their dissenting views to Hindenburg in writing rather than call on him and defend their plans personally, and both rejected the presidential suggestions. Schlange, moreover, who had long been resentful of the president's attitude toward the cabinet, chose to write him a somewhat brusque letter and to dryly offer his resignation should he no longer enjoy the president's confidence. Always a stickler for etiquette, Hindenburg frowned on this "rather unusual procedure of a young minister." But he was even more shocked to discover that he could be denied his wishes so bluntly.[27]

Thus he was in a somber mood when he received Brüning on May 29, just after he had read Schlange's and Stegerwald's letters. The chancellor reported to him on conditions at home and abroad; frustrated and bitter, he abandoned his usual reserve and gave free vent to his feelings. He complained about the intolerable intrigues of irresponsible interlopers and especially of the military. If he were to continue as chancellor, this would have to come to an end. He also requested a public expression of Hindenburg's confidence and asked that new appointments be made to the vacant cabinet posts. Makeshift arrangements would not allow him sufficient authority to enact the new budget and represent Germany effectively at Lausanne. He did not take up the question of Groener's dismissal or the marshal's objections to his projected decrees, but he seems to have been prepared to drop Groener if Hindenburg were to insist.

Hindenburg's answer had been prepared in advance, and he read it off from a sheet of paper: he would sign no more decrees proposed by this cabinet, and he would make no further ministerial appointments to it. It had been so badly discredited, he added, that some of its members would doubtless be forced out of office and some of the government's decrees repealed at the next Reichstag session. Hence his refusal to sign any new ones.

For Brüning to ask the Reichstag to pass his proposals was out of the question. Even if he should find the needed majority, the Nazis and Communists could so delay their enactment that government would come to a standstill. Yet Brüning needed quick action on two proposals at least—the budget and a bill transferring the Prussian police and judiciary to the Reich should the Nazis get control of the Prussian government as the result of the recent elections. If Hindenburg did not approve these measures, he could not continue office.

[27] Meissner, *Staatssekretär*, p. 226; Schlange-Schöningen, *Am Tage Danach*, pp. 70–73.

By now Hindenburg was laboring under great strain. "I must turn right at long last," he argued with tears in his eyes, "the newspapers and the whole nation demand it. But you have always refused to do so." This Brüning denied, pointing to the preparations for a government of the right under Goerdeler in Prussia and to his repeated discussions with Hitler and other rightists. Yet Hindenburg would not accept this; "the others" were telling a different story. Brüning still had his full confidence, he assured him, but the present cabinet was not getting anywhere, and the best possible solution might indeed be an entirely new one in which Brüning would, however, retain the foreign ministry. The chancellor rejected the offer since it would put him in an impossible position both at home and abroad. Nor could he reconcile it, as he pointedly added, with his concept of loyalty towards the president's voters. He suggested that the discussion be continued the next day, and Hindenburg agreed. "You can then bring me the cabinet's resignation," he suggested off-handedly.[28]

Meeting with his ministerial colleagues the next morning, Brüning proposed that the cabinet hand in its resignation. All agreed and approved the curt letter to Hindenburg which the chancellor had drafted. There was bitter resentment at the way in which the president had treated the government; Groener, in Schlange's words, "blew up" and swore that he would tell the country the whole sordid story and not hesitate to name names. Brüning pleaded with him not to do this, and he implored him in words which must have had a sadly familiar ring to the general: "I beg you, don't. In spite of all Hindenburg is the only rallying point the country still has."

To some extent this was doubtless still true, and it is to Brüning's great credit that he could see this in spite of his disenchantment. But Brüning may also have hoped that the breach with Hindenburg was perhaps not yet irrevocable. Hindenburg had

---

28 Hindenburg and Meissner, "Niederschrift," *loc. cit.*, pp. 464–65; Pünder, *Reichskanzlei*, entry of May 29, 1932, pp. 127–29; Meissner, *Staatssekretär*, pp. 226–27; Brüning, "Ein Brief," p. 9. There exists no authentic record of the talk between Hindenburg and Brüning; for unexplained reasons Meissner did not sit in on it, and thus no notes were taken. The above account is based on the existing records, all of them either second-hand or written down long after the event, one of them probably edited for political reasons, and several contradicting each other. The testimony of the two participants, moreover, may have been affected by the fact that both were angered and disappointed, and Hindenburg, who seemed fatigued, found it difficult to concentrate on the discussion. The present summary, based on a careful collation of the existing sources, can therefore be no more than an approximation of what transpired, but it probably does reconstruct accurately the gist of the talk.

changed his mind so often; was it not possible that he would do so again? Earlier that morning Meissner had called and reported that the president was greatly disturbed about losing Brüning; he would have preferred to make the turn to the right with him. Brüning also wished to select his successor; if his advice were to carry any weight with the president, he had to refrain from all criticism of Hindenburg. His candidate for the chancellorship was Goerdeler, for he was convinced of Papen's utter inadequacy.

At noon Brüning called on the president to submit the cabinet's resignation. Hindenburg seemed apologetic and explained once more why he had to turn to the right: the time for emergency decrees was past, the country did not want any more. But if he had thought of offering Brüning the chancellorship in a new government of the right, he must have again changed his mind, for he made no such suggestion. Nor did he repeat his request that Brüning take over the foreign ministry in the new cabinet. He did, however, agree to see Goerdeler and discuss the crisis with him.[29]

Shortly afterwards Hindenburg seems to have had another change of mind. After Brüning's departure he received Luther, the president of the Reichsbank, who had come to discuss the financial outlook. The meeting had been intended to buttress Brüning's position, but events had moved faster meanwhile. Luther painted a dark picture of the country's finances and warned that the budget could not be balanced nor the new programs adopted unless the president approved the proposed economies. Hindenburg was impressed by Luther's report. He had not known how serious things were, he explained, and was willing to sign a decree cutting or cancelling *all* pensions and providing for other savings. This included the pensions of war invalids, widows, and orphans, which he would not let the government reduce only a few days before. Brüning was consulted at once but was unwilling to submit a decree that would provide only a partial solution and would place the burden for all the unpopular measures upon himself.

Whether a more positive approach on his part might have led

[29] Cab. mtg., May 30, 1932, *RKz.*/1709/790069–72; Groener and Brüning remarks in Schlange-Schöningen, *Am Tage Danach*, p. 73; Pünder, *Reichskanzlei*, entry of May 30, 1932, pp. 129–30. In a letter written in 1947, fifteen years after the event ("Ein Brief," pp. 10–11), Brüning has given an entirely different account of what transpired at his last meeting with Hindenburg, but he obviously confused dates and events in this belated report. It has been refuted in part by Deist, "Brüning," pp. 269–72. Whether Brüning saw Hindenburg once more on May 31, the day on which he was received by the president according to his 1947 report, still remains

to his reappointment is hard to say, but throughout the following days many who called on the president found the marshal bewildered and helpless, and men like Goerdeler who were known to favor Brüning's reappointment were not allowed to see him until after Papen had become chancellor. When Brüning called on the president a few days later to take his official leave, Hindenburg seemed rather worried. "We have now the kind of government that I always wanted," he confided, "but once more I have been misled. This chancellor [Papen] is not going to do the job. I am not yet too old to see this. You should have remained, and everything would have been all right."[30]

ꙮ

The dismissal of Brüning was one of the critical turning points in the history of the Weimar Republic. That it was a tragic mistake need hardly be added; its tragedy was the greater as there existed no pressing necessity for a change at the time, but this of course was not evident to many of the main actors. Since the human element played such a decisive role in this fateful development, an inquiry into the personal attitudes of the chief participants may be useful.

Hindenburg, the central figure, has been charged with a violation of the elementary rules of loyalty. Only six weeks earlier he had been reelected with the votes of those who had been supporting the Brüning government and with the untiring, dedicated help of the chancellor himself. Now he was dropping Brüning and turning away from his voters.

This viewpoint hardly does justice to Hindenburg. He had announced when standing for reelection that he did not feel under any obligation to those who voted for him; his public statements, the makeup of his campaign committee, in fact, his whole attitude had made it clear that his sympathies still belonged to the right. Nor did his republican voters elect him because they expected him to be guided by their views and wishes, but rather because they thought that he alone possessed the prestige to deny Hitler the presidency. All they expected him to do was to safeguard the constitution and shield them against a denial of their civil and legal rights. "The Reich President," wrote the Socialist *Vorwärts,*

---

to be clarified. He has left unanswered two inquiries on this point. The *Deutsche Zentralarchiv* in Potsdam has informed me that it has found no materials in its files of the *Büro des Reichspräsidenten* which would throw light on this question.

[30] Memorandum by Pünder, May 30, 1932, *RKz.,* R 43 I/1309; Ritter, *Goerdeler,* pp. 53–54; Brüning, "Ein Brief," p. 11.

"has by no means assumed the obligation to form only Governments of center and left when he let himself be elected by center and left; but he has assumed the obligation to protect the constitutional rights of the Opposition."[31] This Hindenburg was determined to do; indeed, the basic reason for his dismissal of Brüning was his belief, carefully nurtured by his entourage, that the chancellor could not cope with the Nazi movement and must be replaced by someone able to tame it if the country were not to be plunged into civil war. However mistaken his action was, it was not an act of disloyalty.

Brüning's dismissal, however, was engineered by backstairs intrigues that were possible only because Hindenburg tacitly tolerated them. He may not have thought Schleicher's endeavors objectionable since they were presented to him as imperative in the interest of the Reichswehr; as a military man, moreover, he had always had alternates ready for any command post, and he had never fully accepted the fact that political practices differed from those of the army. But it is not even certain that he realized what was happening; tired and weak, he probably had no clear picture of the scope of Schleicher's activities nor may he have had the strength to withstand his son's arguments any longer. More than ever he lived in a world of his own and viewed political and economic realities with weary detachment. It was the price his voters were paying for their failure to find a more competent spokesman than this weak and apathetic octogenarian.

In sharp contrast to the hesitant, diffident Hindenburg, Schleicher, impatient and confident of his political flair, was given to bustling activity. He was acting in good faith in the sense that he was concerned about the continuing growth and radicalism of the Nazis and believed that Brüning was helpless to cope with them. He was haunted by fears of a Nazi rising that might lead to a serious conflict of loyalties within the army and might also touch off a Polish invasion. In addition, he was anxious to take the army out of the political firing line into which the unending crises had drawn it. If it was improper for him as a military man to act as a policy maker, no one in authority had pointed this out to him, and some did in fact encourage him in his activities. Given the weakness of the government and the presence of a fellow soldier at the head of the state, such a development was almost inevitable; Schleicher himself could assume his key role all the more easily

---

[31] Severing, *Lebensweg*, II, 337; Schiffer, *Liberalismus*, pp. 56, 238; *Vorwärts*, May 31, 1932, morn. ed.; *Sozialdemokratische Partei-Korrespondenz*, No. 6–7, June-July 1932, pp. 312–18.

because he was certain that no one could play it better than he.

Whatever the impropriety of his actions, they might perhaps have been pardonable had he been justified in his self-estimation. But Schleicher's gravest mistake was that he greatly misjudged his political talents. Relying on hasty improvisations and short-range maneuvers, hurriedly shifting from one scheme to another, he was lacking in vision and substantive plans. Such methods worked as long as he dealt with opponents who were no match for his tactical ingenuity, but they failed, when he did meet his match in Hitler and his lieutenants—unprepared for their cynicism, he mistook their vague assent to his plans as a binding commitment. In return, he deliberately undermined the cohesion of the governmental apparatus, he encouraged disloyalty and insubordination, and injected on the highest level of government an atmosphere of backstairs maneuvers to which in the end he was to fall victim himself.

While Schleicher could claim that he was acting on behalf of the army, Oskar von Hindenburg, according to the testimony of all observers, was mainly concerned with protecting himself and his father. That he lacked the political insight to grasp the significance of Brüning's departure merely underlines the tragedy of the chancellor's fall.

The agrarians too were motivated primarily by their self-interest when they raised the 'specter of agrarian Bolshevism, but their role in effecting Brüning's dismissal was of only secondary importance. So, apparently, was Meissner's who was reverting increasingly to the role of legal adviser, as Oskar was gaining in influence. Mindful of his weakened position, he preferred to remain in the background, prepared to work with the victor.[32]

Of the main protagonists in this drama, Brüning alone played a role that commands respect. Throughout these weeks of crisis he worked tirelessly at his various tasks. His hopes were fixed on the reparations and disarmament issues in which he expected to score some early successes. So certain was he indeed of their decisive effect that he was little concerned with the political climate at home. If Schleicher was a tactician without a strategic concept, Brüning was a strategist inclined to neglect his tactics. Convinced of the correctness of his course, he left his opponents an almost free hand both in the national arena and in their efforts to turn the president against him. This, to be sure, was not entirely or

---

[32] Eschenburg, "Rolle der Persönlichkeit," pp. 23, 27; Holtzendorff and Noeldechen, in *Vierteljahrshefte*, I (1953), 267, 274; Carlowitz, ZS./218; Brüning on Schleicher, in *Frankfurter Hefte*, XI (1956), 120.

even primarily a matter of his own choice. As long as he had hopes of enlisting Hitler's support for Hindenburg's reelection, he had to refrain from arousing the nation to the terror, the lawlessness, and the moral corruption that the Nazis were inflicting on the country. Nor did he have a free hand after these hopes had been squashed, given Hindenburg's (and Schleicher's) attitude towards the "national" movement and his dependence on the support of the president. But he might at least have answered the lies that were being spread about him and his ministerial colleagues. Instead he prided himself on ignoring such tales; what mattered, he kept telling the country, was above all to keep calm.

In staking his political future on a success in the reparations and armaments issues, Brüning relied on the country's understanding and insight. He expected it to accept a success in diplomacy as a vindication of his domestic policies. Yet with this assumption he discounted not only the anxieties of people who above all needed jobs and economic security, but also the relentless determination of Hitler and Hugenberg to drive him from office, and the emotional frenzy of their followers. By his refusal, moreover, to engage in polemics, he enabled his opposition to establish itself so firmly politically that its position could in any event no longer be undermined by a foreign political victory. His successor, Papen, was to learn this to his distress a few weeks later.

Brüning was similarly unrealistic in his dealings with Hindenburg. Granted that to check Schleicher's (and Oskar's) interference by complaints, however cautious, to Hindenburg would have been exceedingly difficult, he nevertheless might have tried to protect himself against the general's machinations by asking that the marshal consult such trusted advisers as Westarp who might have presented his case more effectively than he could himself. Brüning needed such advocates all the more urgently as he had never been able to establish full rapport with the president. Nor does he seem to have understood the workings of Hindenburg's mind. Little concerned with the marshal's emotions, he never grasped fully Hindenburg's anxiety to protect his personal standing with his peers as well as the nation. Relying on the president's oft-proven commonsense, he underestimated his susceptibility to public opinion, a trait that age had in no way dulled. In consequence he seems to have been convinced almost to the last moment that, however reluctantly, Hindenburg would follow his lead.

When he realized that he had been mistaken, his disenchantment was such that he made but a half-hearted attempt to resist his dismissal. Thus he did not insist on a visit to Neudeck to counteract the intrigues of Schleicher and others against him. As Pünder repeatedly noted in his diary, Brüning approached the decisive talk with the president worn out and discouraged, and one wonders how strongly he pleaded his case when he set forth his views. Nor did the cabinet encourage him to fight against his dismissal after his first talk with Hindenburg. Whether from anger, despair, or disillusionment, his colleagues agreed "at once," as the minutes state, that they would have to resign.

Brüning was right, on the other hand, not to appeal to the Reichstag, for he could not expect any help from that quarter. Once it was known that he no longer had the backing of Hindenburg, those small parties of the right that had so far helped him to secure his precarious majorities—the Economic Party, the Christian-Social People's Service, and a few other splinter groups —would undoubtedly have abandoned him, for they had always insisted that in voting for him they were not so much backing him as the president. His political fortunes thus rested entirely on Hindenburg's continued confidence, and he was helpless once that was withdrawn. The *Tat* observed aptly, "Brüning's downfall became inevitable after the character of the Chancellor was found to be lacking in vitality and imagination to cope with the conflicting forces in present-day Germany. From this weakness of Brüning's personality everything else follows. The Chancellor lacked the strength to create a following of his own which could have carried and supported him." Or as Theodor Eschenburg put it thirty years later: "He was a nonpolitical politician, he stood above parties, groups, and movements, single-mindedly determined to cope with the crisis by the proper technical measures. That there can be no such nonpolitical politician, no matter on how high an intellectual plane or of how strict an ethical attitude, the tragic figure of Brüning attests."[33]

[33] Bracher, *Auflösung*, pp. 508–10; Pünder, *Reichskanzlei*, entries of May 26, 28, 29, 1932, pp. 126–27; cab. mtg., May 30, 1932, *RKz.*/1709/790070; Zehrer in *Tat*, xxiv (1932), 194; Eschenburg, "Rolle der Persönlichkeit," pp. 27–29.

CHAPTER 10

THE PAPEN ERA

HE new government was formed with the same speed that characterized the formation of the Brüning cabinet two years earlier. Two days after Brüning's resignation, on June 1, an official communiqué announced the appointment of Franz von Papen as chancellor; Gayl became minister of the interior; Schleicher, Reichswehr minister; Warmbold, minister of economics; Baron Magnus von Braun, minister of agriculture; and Baron Paul von Eltz-Rübenach, minister of postal services and transportation. On the following day Neurath took over the foreign ministry; the Bavarian minister of justice, Dr. Franz Gürtner, accepted the justice portfolio; and the budget expert in the finance ministry, Count Lutz Schwerin von Krosigk, took charge of that ministry. Schleicher had done his spadework well.

Nevertheless Hindenburg had not been completely convinced of Papen's qualifications and had spent some time with Meissner and Schleicher considering other possible chancellors: Westarp, Gayl, Goerdeler, and his old friend Count Brünneck. But Schleicher prevailed, and Papen was chosen as the man best equipped to come to terms with the Nazis. From the marshal's viewpoint he had some commendable attributes: he was a member of the land-owning Westphalian aristocracy, he had been a general staff officer in the old Prussian army, he was a "national-minded" conservative, and, though a Centrist, he had come out in support of Hindenburg rather than Marx in 1925. He had recently called on the Center to help draw the Nazis into responsible cooperation with the government—just as his party had worked with the Socialists earlier—and at the same time he had urged the Center to help set up a new conservative bloc out of the remnants of the liberal parties. Papen had written that such a bloc "alone can restore our health and help us master the party political chaos into which Weimar democracy has plunged us with its artificial mechanics." These thoughts echoed Hindenburg's own hopes, and thus he agreed with Schleicher that Papen, as an experienced conservative of military decisiveness, would know how to handle the Nazis and also retain the respect and support of the Center Party.

Yet before any final decision was made, the president insisted on receiving the party leaders. Such consultations were to him no mere courtesies in accordance with traditional practices; he thought them essential to shield him against any charges of unconstitutional actions. At the same time they were to assure him that he had no alternative but to appoint a nonparty government as Schleicher proposed it. However confident the general was, Hindenburg still wondered and worried, and more than one of his visitors came away with the feeling that he felt deeply troubled by the new task which had been imposed on him.[1]

His first caller in the afternoon of May 30, a few hours after Brüning's resignation, was Löbe, the Reichstag president. Meissner had asked him, "since this was the customary procedure," to discuss with the president the question of a new government, but had clearly implied that he considered this talk an empty formality. For now that the die was cast, the state secretary wanted to lighten his master's burden and hold him to his decision in favor of Papen. If Hindenburg should again change his mind, there was bound to be further confusion and difficulties. Meissner thus tried to act as a buffer in the talks with the party leaders, guiding the conversation, answering questions, keeping critics away or trying to cut them short. Hindenburg listened in silence, uneasy and careworn, his thoughts apparently wandering. Occasionally he would mutter a few apologetic words.

When Löbe called on the president, he thus found himself talking with Meissner. Meissner was full of confidence; a rightist government would now be formed; the Nazis would definitely tolerate it; the Reichstag would not be dissolved. Only once did the president intervene. When Löbe wondered whether the departure of Brüning would not have serious effects abroad, Hindenburg ventured the hope that Brüning might still be persuaded to stay on as foreign minister.

Löbe was followed by the two Socialist leaders Breitscheid and Wels. The conversation ran along the same lines and was carried on in the same manner as that with the Reichstag president. Hindenburg spoke up once again when the talk turned to a point on which he felt strongly. Breitscheid had stressed the necessity of observing the constitution when the new government would be formed; the president interjected at once that his past ought to be assurance enough that he would never act unconstitutionally.

---

[1] Meissner, *Staatssekretär*, pp. 230–31; same, affidavit, Nov. 28, 1945, I.M.T., *Trial of Major War Criminals before the International Military Tribunal* (Nürnberg, 1947–49), XXXII, 153; Papen, in *Ring*, Apr. 15, 1932, quoted in Schotte, *Regierung Papen*, p. 27; Görlitz, *Hindenburg*, p. 373.

His next visitors that afternoon were Hitler and Göring. They assured him that they were prepared to support any government that would rest on a strong "national" foundation. Such a foundation, however, they left no doubt, could only be created by a repeal of the decree prohibiting the S.A. and S.S. and the granting of new elections. According to Goebbels' diary, Hindenburg assured them that both demands would be met, but the official minutes of the meeting do not record such a promise.

On the following morning Hindenburg saw two representatives of the Center. Monsignor Kaas suggested that he appoint a government of the right; Nazis and German Nationals should be compelled at long last to take on responsibility. Yet while they ought to be forced to face up to Germany's problems, the Center would have to oppose such a government in the Reichstag. Informed of Hindenburg's plans for a presidential cabinet without Nazis, Kaas would commit the Center to no more than a wait-and-see attitude. No Centrist would enter that government, and Brüning's participation thus was out of the question.

The Center leaders were followed by two German National spokesmen. They expressed their readiness to cooperate with a government of the right, but Hugenberg, mindful of his disappointments with Hitler, wondered how long Hitler would support such a government. There followed talks with the heads of the smaller parties; they too failed to produce any new proposals. Westarp, speaking for the People's Conservatives, once more impressed upon Hindenburg the risks of the course on which he was now embarked. Not only would the Social Democrats whom Brüning had curbed tend to become more radical again, new elections would also eliminate 100 deputies of the smaller moderate parties who had helped to provide a buffer between the right and the left. Nor would the new government do better than Brüning's had; it would be much weaker, in fact, since its life would depend on the uncertain toleration of the Nazis. To have some assurance of their continued support, Westarp counseled that they be invited into the new cabinet.

Meissner made light of Westarp's warnings, but Hindenburg listened attentively, and more than once he nodded approvingly. When his old confidant took his leave, he abandoned his cautious reserve. He was in a terrible position, he confessed, whom was he going to appoint as chancellor? Westarp had the impression that the tired old man was turning to him in the forlorn hope that he might have some better solution, but the Count remained silent; he could not suggest his own appointment after he had been considered (as he knew) and evidently been rejected. Any such offer, he wrote later, would have come too late anyway "since everything had been arranged already."[2]

If the conferences with the party leaders proved anything, it was their inability, or unwillingness, to propose an alternative to Schleicher's plans. The Social Democrats worried about the rights of the Reichstag, but they conceded the right to the president to keep his own counsel in choosing the new government. They knew they were helpless and openly said so. "Aufhäuser," states an account of their deliberations,

"asked for a new program of action. Tarnow made some grave comments on the economic situation. Thus we debated back and forth for a while. No decisions were made for we had nothing to say any more. The only result was the announcement of a proclamation against the new Government which the party leaders were to publish in the press the next day."[3]

The Center was less fatalistic than the Socialists, but had no solution to offer either. Kaas merely stressed in his talk with the president that the time had come for a shift to the right; there was no room any more for "interim solutions." Hugenberg welcomed Hindenburg's plans, and Hitler was not yet ready to show his hand. Significantly even Centrists and Socialists do not seem to have asked about the policies of the new government—substantive questions played even less of a role in this crisis than at the time of Brüning's appointment. What mattered was to let "the others" assume the burdens of government in the hope that the consequences would not be too damaging.

⁓

While Hindenburg worried about the constitutional niceties before appointing Papen as chancellor, he made no attempt to inquire further into the latter's qualifications. Evidently he was satisfied with what little he himself knew about him and what Schleicher in addition had told him. Papen's name was not brought up in the talks with the party leaders, and these talks took up so much of his time and strength that he could hardly have consulted anyone else between the time of Brüning's resignation on May 30 and his invitation to Papen the following day to accept his appointment as chancellor. Possible critics of Papen, more-

[2] Memorandum (by Meissner), May 31, 1932, in Vogelsang, *Reichswehr*, pp. 458–59; Keil, *Erlebnisse*, II, 445–47; Görlitz, *Hindenburg*, pp. 373–74; Westarp, in *Vierteljahrshefte*, I (1953), 297; Pünder, *Reichskanzlei*, entry of May 31, 1932, pp. 131–33; Goebbels, *Vom Kaiserhof*, entry of May 30, 1932, p. 104.

[3] Keil, *Erlebnisse*, II, 448.

over, were purposely kept away from him. Goerdeler who tried to see him was told that the president was not well enough to receive him, and if Brüning did see him once more on May 31, his call was arranged so that he could talk to him only for a few minutes. (When Goerdeler was received a day or two later, he stated his reservations about Papen's chances of success. Meissner attempted to cut him short, but Hindenburg insisted on hearing him out.)[4]

There was good reason to be dubious about Papen's political talents. Domestically, he had at best played a peripheral role in the Center Party and was unlikely therefore to influence its decisions. Diplomatically, he could be expected to be *persona non grata* in Washington; as German military attaché he had been involved there in a number of sabotage acts in World War I and had been expelled in 1916. This was a grave liability at a time when the good will of the United States was indispensable to Germany if she was to obtain a satisfactory reparations and armaments settlement. Above all, however, Papen was a man without political flair, dabbling in various social and cultural activities; a man, in the words of the French ambassador, whom neither his friends nor his enemies took very seriously. What recommended him to Schleicher was his social poise and his conservative-military bent, both traits that were bound to appeal to Hindenburg. He was also endowed with a good dose of dash and daring that would not be discouraged by the adversities of the political crisis. If he had none of the qualities of true statesmanship, the general was not concerned, for he intended to direct the government from behind the scenes. When an acquaintance warned him that Papen did not have much of a head, the general replied smilingly: "He need not have, but he'll make a fine hat!" "No chancellor," notes the historian Karl Dietrich Bracher, "was ever chosen more frivolously."[5]

How subordinate a role Schleicher planned to assign to Papen, the circumstances of his selection make clear. Rumors that he had been picked as Brüning's successor circulated in Berlin as early as May 23, a week before Brüning's resignation, and Goebbels notes his selection in his diary on May 24. Yet Papen states in his memoirs that he did not learn about his prospective appointment until May 28 when he returned to Berlin after a ten-day absence and answered a summons from Schleicher.[6] By that time Schlei-

[4] Ritter, *Goerdeler*, pp. 56, 450 n. 26; Brüning, "Ein Brief," pp. 10–11.

[5] Braun, *Von Ostpreussen*, p. 257; Zechlin, *Pressechef*, pp. 124–25; Bracher, *Auflösung*, p. 519 n. 179, 531.

[6] Papen seems to have known, however, that Schleicher was thinking of him as a possible successor to Brüning. Cf. Papen, *Wahrheit*, pp. 276–77.

cher had also decided upon most of the other members of the new cabinet.

Their initial talk was characteristic of the curiously personal way in which the new government was to be formed. After a review of the political situation, Schleicher asked Papen whether he would be willing to become chancellor. Papen declined, but Schleicher replied that he had mentioned his name to Hindenburg and that the "Old Gentleman" was very anxious to have him. When Papen demurred, Schleicher took him by his arm and playing upon their old friendship tried a more personal tack: "You must do me and Hindenburg this favor. There is too much at stake. I can't find anyone who could do a better job . . . I have already compiled a cabinet of experts which I am sure you will like." In the face of this appeal Papen relented and asked for some time to make up his mind.

He consulted with a friend who, as it happened, had doubts about Papen's qualifications and suggested that he decline Schleicher's offer. But Schleicher insisted that "Hindenburg expects as a matter of loyalty that you will not desert him in this crisis," and Papen reconsidered once more. Since he could not hope for a Reichstag majority without the support of the Center, however, he wished to consult Monsignor Kaas before making a final decision.

Kaas pleaded with Papen to decline the appointment. The party would find it intolerable to see a Centrist take Brüning's place. Apparently Papen agreed, for the prelate came away from their meeting confident that Papen would not accept the chancellorship.

After his talk with Kaas, Papen called on the president. Hindenburg, he recalls, received him with fatherly affection. "Well, my dear Papen, are you going to help me in this difficult situation?" Papen tried to explain why to his great regret he could not, but Hindenburg was not impressed. Rising heavily from his chair, he took his visitor's hands. "How can you desert an old man who once more has taken on the responsibility for the Reich despite the weight of his years—now that he asks you to take on a task on which depends the Reich's future? I expect of your sense of duty that you will not decline my call." He did not care, he continued, whether the Center would disapprove or even oppose him; at long last he wished to see around him men who were independent of parties and would act according to their best judgment to help their country out of its troubles. And with raised voice he added: "You have been a soldier and did your duty in the war. In Prussia we know only obedience when the Fatherland calls!"

Confronted with this appeal to his loyalty and obedience, Papen writes, he gave in. Were there not higher duties than party discipline? He took the proffered hand of the marshal. And Schleicher who had stood by in the next room rushed in to congratulate him on his decision.[7]

Thus, throughout the story of Papen's appointment, there runs a thread of appeals to old friendships and personal favors. Schleicher had begun by asking for his help as an act of friendship; Hindenburg had similarly insisted that he assist him in his difficulties, and he had all but identified his own cares with those of the country. Brüning, he argued, wished to keep governing with "those emergency decrees"; he did not understand "that I can't forbid the armed formations of the Nazis only"; but above all: "Into what situation has he brought me! Now I have been re-elected by the left while the right, my own people, put up that private first-class against me." When Papen accepted the appointment, he did so as the "Lieutenant Colonel" taking orders from his "Field Marshal" rather than as a political leader reaching a considered agreement with the head of the state.

Other ministers were won over by Hindenburg in similar ways, and Gayl whom the president himself had selected as minister of the interior said so quite frankly. He had serious misgivings about the understandings between Schleicher and the Nazis, and was wondering also about the permanence of the shift to the right. Hindenburg sought to reassure him on both points; he would ask for written commitments from Hitler, and as for the duration of the course to the right, "you know me. If I have issued an order, I stick to it. I have ordered the turn to the right, and you know I'll stay with it." And then came the inevitable appeal to the soldier's duty: "I have no one else, you are not going to desert your old commander-in-chief." Gayl accepted, but as he wrote in his memoirs, "I had the feeling to be committed against my better judgment. I did not accept from conviction, but obeyed an order, after an appeal to my soldierly duty." In a similar vein Neurath was asked to take over the foreign ministry in fulfillment of a promise he had once made to Hindenburg, and Count Schwerin von Krosigk likewise entered the cabinet only upon the personal

[7] *Ibid.*, pp. 182–90; Pechel, in *Dt. Rundschau*, LXXVIII (1952), 1232; Kaas to Papen, June 3, 1932, in Georg Schreiber, *Brüning-Hitler-Schleicher: Das Zentrum in der Opposition* (Cologne, 1932), p. 20.

appeal of the marshal. Eltz-Rübenach, in turn, was a personal friend of Papen.

The nonchalant, almost cynical way in which the government was brought together is perhaps best illustrated by the account which Baron von Braun has given us of his appointment. Schleicher who had had no quarrel with Brüning's agrarian policies and had agreed with him on the need to expropriate and resettle the bankrupt estates, wished to make sure, however, that the new cabinet would not be attacked by the agrarians—always a serious concern to Hindenburg. He had therefore asked that inveterate foe of Brüning, Count Kalckreuth, the president of the *Landbund,* to select the minister of agriculture for the new cabinet. Baron von Braun was Kalckreuth's choice. As Braun recalls, the Count came to him late in May and told him that the fall of Brüning was imminent, that Papen would form a new government, and that both Papen and the *Landbund* wished him to become minister of agriculture. "If I wished to be in on this [*"Falls ich mitmachen wolle"*], I ought to go to Papen . . . in the afternoon." Braun did. "Papen received me with his characteristic charm and these words so characteristic of him: 'Dear Braun, would you like to form with me a cabinet of gentlemen and take over the Ministry of Agriculture?' " Braun accepted. "I had known Papen for a long time . . . I considered him a gentleman—then as I do today."

The new cabinet was held together not only by its social homogeneity, but also by the close socio-military relationship that linked it to Hindenburg. "When we were taking our oath," Braun wrote later, "we had the feeling that the President felt happy and contented among his new cabinet members. . . . Papen, Gayl, Eltz, and I had belonged to Potsdam guard regiments, Schleicher had been in the same regiment as the Hindenburgs, father and son, Gürtner was a Bavarian artillery man, Neurath had been with the Württembergian Olga dragoons, Krosigk with the Pommeranian dragoons." As Bracher puts it, officers were rallying here around their general.[8]

Politically the cabinet was equally homogeneous. Guided by Hindenburg's and his own preferences, Schleicher had assembled a government that was nonparty in the narrowly technical sense that it was not tied to any party directly. But since its members all shared the same outlook—monarchist, antidemocratic, entrepreneurial—it was far more partisan than Brüning's had been;

[8] Papen, *Wahrheit,* pp. 189–90, 183; Gayl memorandum, n.d., Gayl Papers, unnumbered folder; Braun, *Von Ostpreussen,* pp. 208, 228; Bracher, *Auflösung,* pp. 531–34.

that cabinet had tended toward the right but could not completely ignore the concerns of its Social Democratic supporters. Brüning's government, it has rightly been said, represented the "state above the parties," Papen's, the "rightist state above the parties."[9]

Due to its one-sided alignment with Hindenburg's special social and political concerns, the new cabinet had only a very small popular basis. Brüning could at least count on the backing of millions of Centrists and Social Democrats, and while they were not sufficient to provide a majority in the Reichstag, their support had some useful psychological value. The Papen government, on the other hand, owed its existence solely to Hindenburg's backing—a factor that was the more serious since he was unlikely to throw his authority more openly into the scales to support it than he had done before. Papen's government was not, as has sometimes been claimed, made up of Junkers; only three of its members, Gayl, Braun, and Schwerin-Krosigk, could be classed as such. But the strong preponderance of aristocrats was bound to anger a nation that in large part scorned the nobility as a class and was disdainful of all monarchist aspirations. To most Germans the Papen regime seemed a retreat to an outdated past to which they refused to return. If for no other reason, the Nazis could not tolerate Papen for long and still retain the respect of their followers. But these facts Schleicher, so sensitive as a rule to such matters, preferred to ignore; even the criticisms of friendly organs such as the *Tat* do not seem to have shaken his confidence in his own judgment.[10]

How poor a judge he was in reality, Schleicher was soon to discover. His talks with Hitler in which he thought he had bought the Fuehrer's forbearance, turned out to have been equivocal arrangements. Hitler refused to consider as binding what Schleicher had thought was a pledge to support Papen's cabinet. When Papen tried to obtain a written commitment, a Nazi statement advised him that the attitude of the Nazi Party would depend on that of the government. Papen's main task, he was sharply reminded, was to dissolve the Reichstag, arrange for new elections, and restore full freedom for organizations, propaganda, and demonstrations for the "unbelievably harassed National Socialist movement." There was no concrete assurance, however, that such measures would earn him the support of the party.[11]

[9] Besson, *Württemberg*, p. 364.

[10] Goebbels, in *Angriff*, June 2, 1932, reprinted in *Wetterleuchten*, p. 313; same, *Vom Kaiserhof*, entry of June 23, 1932, p. 116; *Tat*, XXIV (1932), p. 309; Meissner and Wilde, *Machtergreifung*, pp. 74, 77.

[11] Brüning, "Ein Brief," p. 13; Stampfer, *Vierzehn Jahre*, p. 622; Goebbels, *Vom*

One after the other, all these concessions were made. The Reichstag was dissolved on June 4, and on June 14, a second decree repealed the proscription of the S.A. and S.S. and lifted or modified other restrictions. Yet although the cabinet met promptly the Nazis' demands, Goebbels, on June 6, wrote a pointed polemic against the chancellor, and on June 14, the day of the readmission of the S.A. and S.S., he launched another bitter attack against him.[12]

Only on one point did the government go its own way. To the Nazis' dismay it postponed the elections to the last permissible day, July 31. It wished to gain time to impress the nation with its constructive achievements. "The Government is making no promises," its first official announcement declared, "It is going to act and wants to be judged by its actions." By a series of rapid successes it hoped to outflank the Nazis. Given the short time the cabinet had, its plans were overly sanguine, but apparently they did not seem so to most of the ministers.[13]

In foreign policy, thanks to the spadework of Brüning, Papen succeeded in settling the burdensome reparations problem. At the Lausanne Conference, in June and July, all reparations debts were forgiven except for a final lump sum of 3 billion marks ($715,000,000), which no one actually expected to be paid. Papen failed to secure any further concessions, however, such as a repudiation of the "war-guilt clause," or the right to rearm. The intransigent right thus dismissed the Lausanne agreement as another defeat while the Center gave Brüning credit for what was accomplished. Only the Socialists seemed appreciative, but the chancellor cared little for their approval. It could not make up for the sneers of the Nazis and the blind hatred of Goebbels' hoodlums who pelted him with rotten eggs and tomatoes when he returned to Berlin.[14]

If Papen accomplished little in foreign affairs, he was entirely unsuccessful domestically. The readmission of the Nazi formations, far from promoting internal peace, led to increased clashes between right and left. Hardly a day passed which did not witness

---

Kaiserhof, entry of June 2, 1932, p. 105; Nazi Party statement, in Bracher, *Auflösung,* p. 546.

[12] Goebbels, *Vom Kaiserhof,* entries of June 6, 14, 1932, pp. 108, 111.

[13] Schleicher, in cab. mtg., June 2, 1932, *RKz.*/1709/790075–76; Ritter, *Goerdeler,* p. 449 n. 22; Meissner, affidavit of Nov. 28, 1945, I.M.T., *Trial,* XXXII, 147.

[14] Schleicher, in cab. mtg., July 11, 1932, *RKz.*/1710/790369–70; Mierendorff, in *Sozialistische Monatshefte,* LXXV (1932), 658; Goebbels, *Vom Kaiserhof,* entry of July 8, 1932, p. 125; Meissner and Wilde, *Machtergreifung,* p. 89; Hugenberg to Papen, July 23, 1932, copy in *RKz.*/1710/790473.

a half-dozen street battles and large numbers of casualties; 99 lives were lost in these encounters during the first month after the repeal of the S.A. decree. Papen aroused much bitterness also with the financial decrees he issued. They were largely those prepared by Brüning—amended, however, so as to be acceptable to Hindenburg and his insatiable agrarian friends. They were supplemented by others that reduced the tax burden on industrial enterprises to stimulate expanded production, yet slashed even further the meager relief and insurance payments to those out of work. But Papen made enemies also among that other important sector of Brüning's supporters—the various state governments.

The South German states had been greatly alarmed by the fall of Brüning. They opposed the readmission of the S.A. and S.S. lest they plunge the country into new disorders. They worried also about the rumored replacement of Prussia's caretaker government by a Reich commissioner. Unable themselves to form majority governments, Bavaria, Württemberg, and Baden had similar make-shift arrangements; if they allowed Prussia to be administered by the Reich, they feared that the same fate might also befall them, and their states might be reduced to provinces ruled from Berlin. Deeply concerned, the heads of the three states decided to undertake a joint demarche in Berlin. But they did not content themselves with a protest to Papen, and asked to be received by the president too. Hindenburg, they feared, was not being fully informed of Papen's intentions and should be acquainted firsthand with their views and anxieties.[15]

The discussion with the Reich president was no more reassuring than that with the chancellor. Papen was present and guided the conversation on Hindenburg's part, while the latter quietly listened. The South Germans had marshalled their arguments with great care to make an impression on Hindenburg. Held, the Bavarian minister-president, warned that an intervention in the internal affairs of Prussia was likely to be unconstitutional while the repeal of the anti-S.A. decree would impair the authority of the president. For all practical purposes it would mean a legalization of Nazi terrorism and might even lead to civil war. Held's colleagues also foresaw grave dangers to the strength and stability of the state should the S.A. and S.S. be readmitted again.

Papen, addressing himself as much to the president as to the South Germans, denied any plan of intervening in Prussia. There was no intention to appoint a Reich commissioner for that state; such an appointment would be justifiable only as an *ultima ratio*

[15] Besson, *Württemberg*, pp. 275–76.

if vital interests of the Fatherland were at stake. As for the repeal of the S.A.'s dissolution, this was simply a matter of restoring equality before the law; if there were any danger of civil war, all paramilitary organizations would at once be outlawed. To check their activities they would also be placed under the supervision of the Reich minister of the interior.

But Held was not satisfied. Speaking again to Hindenburg rather than to Papen, he warned that among the millions of Nazi voters there doubtless were many Communists. More important, those who had cast their ballot for Hindenburg's reelection had done so to be protected from the S.A. and S.S. These forces could not be suppressed once the country was threatened with civil war. Any party army, he reiterated, helped to destroy the authority of the state; all such organizations should be outlawed. In the end Hindenburg spoke up himself. He confirmed that there was no plan to appoint "at this time" a Reich commissioner for Prussia. Press reports to the contrary were exaggerations or outright inventions similar to many published in the papers. And having this chance to unburden himself of what upset him much more, he complained to his visitors: "The press has claimed, for example, that political talks and negotiations took place at Neudeck when I was there; I can assure you that I saw there only one single visitor, my neighbor Count Brünneck. Nor is it right, as has been alleged, that my son has a decisive political influence on me."

Reverting to the problems at hand, he insisted that he was greatly concerned with South Germany. "I have always tried to support the bridge across the Main River;[16] I urge you not to destroy it, for unity is the foundation of our power, and only power can secure our rights for us." He then turned to a discussion of the S.A. decree, recalling his misgiving about the timeliness of the decree right after his reelection and his subsequent efforts to obtain equal treatment for all such organizations. If he readmitted the Nazi formations, he did so because they would now be more closely controlled by the government; but, he added, "no matter how much remains to be clarified, the National Socialist movement, and its youth in particular, are inspired by strong national feelings." Should he prove wrong in his expectations, the decree would of course be repealed. And the states had also the right, within their own jurisdiction, to take all required police measures.

[16] The Main River has been considered the dividing line between Northern and Southern Germany since Bismarck, after the Prusso-Austrian War of 1866, incorporated all states north of the Main River in the North German Confederation.

339

Yet Held was not reassured, and the discussion ended on a note of asperity. The president need not worry, he replied somewhat acidly, that the Main bridge might be destroyed by the South, but it might well be destroyed by wrong policies of the Reich. As ever conciliatory, Hindenburg assured him again that the Reich had no such intention. But he could not help adding that the South was too easily inclined to blame all misfortunes on the North: "yet I'd like to remind you that when Munich had a Soviet government [in 1919], it was Prussian troops which restored order."[17]

The South German ministers departed doubtful that anything had been accomplished. But Hindenburg had taken notice of what they had said. When he signed the decree rescinding the ban on the Brown Shirts, he advised Gayl in a covering letter, intended for publication, that the repeal was based on his expectation that the political struggle would be fought peaceably in the future. Should he be mistaken, he would intervene against any new acts of violence with all means at his disposal. Hindenburg also insisted, when a second decree made further concessions, that an official statement make clear that the Reich had no wish of tampering with the police powers of the states.[18]

As the South Germans were quick to discover, such statements had little significance, and a postmortem on their talk with the president did nothing to allay their concern. Both Held and his Badensian colleague, Dr. Schmitt, had explicitly stated that they would again outlaw the S.A. and S.S. in their states, should the Reich repeal their proscription, but of this the minutes said nothing. It was in reply to these statements, they maintained, that Hindenburg had assured them that they could take whatever measures they wished within their own jurisdiction. Meissner claimed that this was a misunderstanding; they could merely deal with individual situations, but could not resort to a general ban. If they did, the president would demand the repeal of such measures. Confronted with this exegesis, the South Germans could not but wonder how far Hindenburg was still the master in his own house, and how reliable a support of the state and the constitution he still provided.[19]

The decree legalizing the Nazi formations was issued a few days later. Bavaria and Baden forbade at once all outdoor meetings and the wearing of political uniforms. Württemberg con-

[17] Minutes of meeting, reprinted in Besson, *Württemberg*, pp. 401–05, and Vogelsang, *Reichswehr*, pp. 466–70.

[18] Meissner, *Staatssekretär*, p. 234; same, in cab. mtg., June 25, 1932, *RKz.*/1710/790280–01.

[19] Besson, *Württemberg*, pp. 280–82; also Vogelsang, *Reichswehr*, pp. 215, 217.

tented itself with the prohibition of open-air demonstrations. These steps interfered of course with the plans of the Reich to achieve a *modus vivendi* with Hitler. Schleicher, who clung to his hopes for such an *entente*, demanded that the new restrictions should at once be removed. For once he felt no compunction in involving the army and was even ready to resort to a state of emergency to force the South German states into line. The latter proved adamant and would not yield to Berlin. In the end Papen got a new presidential decree; superseding all state regulations, it sanctioned the wearing of private uniforms and the holding of open-air meetings. "The fears which have been expressed about these rights are exaggerated," Gayl asserted in an official statement, "the Reich Government has no reason at this time to take any special measures." The fact that the number of clashes had trebled since the S.A. and S.S. had been readmitted was blandly discounted. As Gayl put it, "It was to be expected that during the transition period there would be occasional difficulties until the public had gotten used to the changed situation." Whatever disturbances there had been, moreover, had all been Communist-inspired. And placing responsibility where he claimed it belonged, Gayl cavalierly concluded that it was up to the states to maintain order; they had ample power to do so.[20]

∽

While the South German states were wrangling with Papen, Prussia tried hard to collaborate. The Prussian government readmitted the S.A. and S.S. and permitted the wearing of uniforms and the holding of open-air demonstrations. Though politically much farther removed from the Papen regime than its South German counterparts, it made every effort to comply with the Reich's requests.[21]

Papen on his part showed no such spirit of accomodation. He announced that Prussia would no longer be represented at meetings of the Reich cabinet, but would be invited only if a matter of special concern to her would be discussed. Collaboration was to be distant and formal; rather than call on their Prussian colleagues, as had been the custom, the newly appointed Reich ministers decided to leave their visiting cards. The Reich government also tried to embarrass Prussia financially by withholding a pay-

[20] Cab. mtgs., June 18, 21, 25, 1932, *RKz.*/1710/790237–40, 790250–51, 790277–82; Gayl, in Schulthess, June 29, 1932, pp. 115–16.

[21] Weissmann, in *ibid.*, June 9, 1932, p. 105; Gayl, in cab. mtgs., June 21, 25, 1932, *RKz.*/1710/790250–51, 790277–78; Besson, *Württemberg*, pp. 289–91; Severing, *Lebensweg*, II, 339.

ment of 100 million marks due her on the grounds that no funds were available. But the Prussian government would not strike back. Within a week after Papen's appointment rumors were rife in Berlin that the chancellor was looking for a pretext to remove the Braun-Severing cabinet, and the latter did not wish to provide him with one.[22]

Papen was indeed determined to take over the Prussian government. This last major foothold of Social Democracy was a symbol of the detested Weimar Republic and was blocking the way to the authoritarian state he hoped to establish. German Nationals and German People's Party had long been demanding the absorption of Prussia into the Reich, and the Reichswehr too was in favor of the prewar arrangement by which the power resources of the Reich and Prussia were concentrated in the same hands. Thus, by removing the caretaker cabinet of Centrists and Socialists, Papen hoped to improve his popular standing; but he also expected to strengthen his bargaining position vis-à-vis Hitler once he controlled the Prussian police.[23] The main problem was to find legal grounds for the step that would satisfy the South Germans and above all put Hindenburg's mind at rest. As much as the president could be expected to welcome a step that would restore the Reich-Prussian relationship of the days of the Empire, he would have to be fully assured that the move was entirely constitutional before he would give his consent.[24]

The only charge that seemed usable turned on Prussia's alleged inability to deal with the Communist threat. Reports had been coming in about the formation of "socialist action groups" under Communist auspices, and much was made of an attempt of Severing's State Secretary Abegg to induce the Communist Party to stop its terroristic activities which were not only illegal but also senseless, and to join a proposed anti-Nazi front. Surprisingly Abegg failed to inform Severing of his negotiations, perhaps because he felt they were futile. Even more surprising, however, was the attitude of the Reich cabinet; rather than take up this matter with Severing, it seized on it to support its charge that Prussia was coddling the Communists. Yet this, as it knew, was not true, for Severing fought them as hard as he could. If he was uncoopera-

---

[22] Cab. mtg., June 2, 1932, *RKz./*1709/790077; Pünder, *Reichskanzlei*, entry of June 7, 1932, pp. 136–37 and n. 331; Bolz, in mtg. of Wuerttemberg cabinet, June 10, 1932, Besson, *Württemberg*, p. 398.

[23] Bracher, *Auflösung*, pp. 569–73; Scholz, Jan. 20, 1925, *Verhandlungen*, Vol. 384, p. 125; Schleicher to Scholz, Jan. 22, 1925, Schleicher Papers/69/93; Ott, *ZS./* 279; Carlowitz, *ZS./*218; Brüning, "Ein Brief," p. 9.

[24] Ott, Carlowitz, *ZS./*279, 218; Ott to Papen, jr., Dec. 12, 1949, copy in *ZS./*279.

tive, it was in his treatment of the Nazis; he insisted on dealing with their offenses as strictly as with Communist breaches of law. His intransigence on this point seemed a major reason why the Reich government had not been successful in improving its relations with Hitler.[25]

The Nazis, in fact, were becoming increasingly critical of the Reich government. Complaining about their harassment by Severing, they clamored for an intervention in Prussia as evidence of the government's good faith and "national reliability." So did Papen's German National backers. Yet what made such an action even more urgent in Papen's and Schleicher's judgment was the unfavorable domestic reaction to the Lausanne settlement. With the Reichstag elections drawing nearer, they felt they must take some step to improve their prestige, and the removal of the Prussian government seemed the most promising move.[26]

On July 11, three days after Papen's return from Lausanne, the cabinet considered the matter. Gayl, who had earlier conceded that the Prussian government was dealing effectively with the Communists, now claimed that it was not. It was essential therefore that the Reich take over the Prussian police. Papen agreed, charging that Prussia had sabotaged all policies of the Reich. How unconvincing these arguments were, the ensuing debate demonstrated. With one exception, Labor Minister Schäffer, everyone agreed to the intervention, but stressed at the same time the need for a valid reason. Knowing Hindenburg's scruples, Meissner too voiced his concern on this point.

He returned to it the following day at another cabinet session. It had been customary on other occasions, he noted, to present state governments with an ultimatum, and the Reich had resorted to intervention only in cases of wilful obstructions on the part of a state. It was imperative to have a strong case should the matter reach the *Staatsgerichtshof*. But Schleicher and Gayl, anxious for speedy action, insisted that this procedure could not be applied here. Gayl then reported on the negotiations between Abegg and the Communists "concerning a union (*Zusammenschluss*) of the Social Democratic and Communist Parties." After some further

---

[25] Bracher, *Auflösung*, pp. 578–80; Meissner and Wilde, *Machtergreifung*, p. 279 n. 71; Gayl, in cab. mtg., June 25, July 11, 1932, *RKz.*/1710/790278–79; Abegg to Severing, Aug. 4, 1932, cited in Vogelsang, *Reichswehr*, p. 237; Joachim Petzold, "Der Staatsstreich vom 20. Juli 1932 in Preussen," *Zeitschrift für Geschichtswissenschaft*, IV (1956), 1179; Severing, *Lebensweg*, II, 340–41.

[26] Petzold, "Staatsstreich,", pp. 1151–56; Goebbels, in *Angriff*, June 11, 1932, *Wetterleuchten*, p. 309; Bracher, *Auflösung*, pp. 578, 581; cab. mtg., July 11, 1932, *RKz.*/1710/790365, 790369–71, 790377–82.

exchanges the cabinet agreed to the drafting of a decree installing the chancellor as Reich commissioner for Prussia. The date was set for July 20.

New difficulties developed the following day. Max Peters, a retired Prussian state secretary, selected to take charge of the strategic ministry of the interior which controlled the police, would not accept the appointment; in his view conditions in Prussian did not warrant as yet the removal of the Prussian government. Worse, Severing issued a decree calling for strictest police measures against anyone found in illegal possession of arms and for the prohibition of all political demonstrations for which no adequate police protection could be provided. The decree demonstrated so clearly the determination of the Prussian government to maintain law and order that the Reich cabinet decided that action against Prussia would have to wait until the effect of the statement could be determined.[27]

Meanwhile Papen and Gayl scurried to Neudeck to obtain Hindenburg's signature on the decree, with the date for the action left open. Their reception was warm and cordial. When Papen offered to resign because of the poor domestic reception of the Lausanne settlement, the president would not hear of it. He asked the chancellor to convey to the cabinet his thanks for its work—something he had not done since the early days of the Brüning government.

Nevertheless he examined the Prussian decree with great care. He had not forgotten the warnings of the South German ministers, and he was seriously worried that he might be impeached before the *Staatsgerichtshof*. He sensed that conditions in Prussia were not as clearcut as Papen and Gayl would have him believe, and Meissner seems to have warned him of the dubious legality of the move. As the state secretary testified at the Nürnberg Trial, Hindenburg was very reluctant at first to approve the decree, but in the end Papen won out. There is no indication, however, that Hindenburg felt any twinges of conscience about charging with a flagrant dereliction of duty the very men who only a few months before had worked hard for his reelection. Sentimentally the marshal welcomed this partial return to Imperial days when the chancellor also had headed the Prussian government.[28]

A new reason for intervention in Prussia was found earlier than

[27] *Ibid.*, also cab. mtgs., July 12, 13, 1932, 790386–88, 390396–97; Severing, II, 344; Vogelsang, *Reichswehr*, pp. 242–43.
[28] Papen, in cab. mtg., July 16, 1932, *RKz.*/1710/790404; Meissner and Wilde, *Machtergreifung*, pp. 91–92; verdict of Denazification Board against Papen, Feb. 24, 1947, copy in Meissner Document Book, I, 63, I.M.T., War Crimes Case No. 11; Meissner letter, quoted in Besson, *Württemberg*, p. 297.

had been expected. On Sunday, July 17, Nazis and Communists clashed in a street battle in the North German city of Altona near Hamburg. There were 81 casualties including 17 deaths. The carnage was ultimately the responsibility of the Papen cabinet; by permitting propaganda marches in uniform it had rendered the task of the police authorities increasingly difficult. Its one-sided favoritism for the Nazis, moreover, had caused local police officials to treat them with greater leniency too. The Nazi parade through Altona's working class districts that touched off the massacre of July 17 had been permitted by the local police chief, a Social Democrat, only because he assumed that had he forbidden the march, his decision would have been overruled by the Berlin authorities.[29]

Three days later, on July 20, the Prussian government was removed by Papen on the grounds, manifestly untrue, as Schleicher himself later boasted,[30] that it was no longer able to maintain law and order. There was no resistance; after some formal protests Severing and his ministerial colleagues left their offices. (Braun, worn out and ill, was absent on leave.) The next day the Prussian government, in what seemed like a sadly anticlimactic move, filed a formal complaint with the *Staatsgerichtshof* and asked that court to declare the Reich's intervention unlawful.

The question has long been debated whether the Prussian government could and should have fought back. There is no evidence that it could have done so with any hope of success. Except in isolated local instances, preparations for armed resistance were virtually nonexistent, while Papen had at its disposal not only the Reichwehr but the *Stahlhelm* and Nazi formations as well. Nor could there be full reliance on the Prussian police. Parts of that force were wavering in their loyalty, either from sympathy with the right or as a matter of self-protection. Moreover, since Hindenburg had proclaimed a state of emergency in Prussia and the Prussian police had been placed under army orders, many otherwise loyal officers would have refused to obey orders issued by Severing. Again, it has been suggested that no matter how hopeless the odds, there ought to have been an attempt to resist for the sake of a demonstration. It would have salvaged republican self-respect and might have prevented the disastrous events that were soon to follow. Whether or not it would have achieved this is highly uncertain, and it might well have been that resistance would have precipitated the Nazis' seizure of power. Was it wise

29 Severing, *Lebensweg*, II, 345–46.
30 Schleicher, in Pünder, *Reichskanzlei*, entry of Oct. 8, 1932, p. 149.

to rise against Papen and Hindenburg who were opposed to giving Hitler full power and did not seem likely to do just that only six months later?

But the very suggestion is unhistorical. The decision to remain passive was not made on July 20, 1932, or on one of the preceding days; it had been made over many years. The Center Party was both ideologically and organizationally entirely unprepared for such a fight, and the Socialist leaders whose party might have become the nucleus for armed resistance had consistently discouraged all preparations for a violent conflict.[31] If, then, at the news of the forthcoming coup the Socialist leaders decided, some days before Papen acted, that they could and would not resist him, they merely confirmed a long-held position. "I have been a democrat for forty years, and I am not going to become a condottiere now," Braun replied to his secretary when he was told that the masses expected him to become the center of the anti-Papen resistance. As Julius Leber, one of the younger of the Socialist leaders, commented later, "these men [Braun and Severing] could not act any differently than they did."[32]

Braun was not even certain, as his statement makes clear, that resistance was legally justifiable and his misgivings were shared by other Socialist leaders. For this reason too, they agreed in advance that they would resort only to a judicial complaint and would not, whatever might happen, "abandon the legal foundations of the Constitution." The phrasing of the decision was meant not merely to mask their weakness—it expressed also a haunting feeling that Papen's coup was perhaps not illegal in an ultimate sense. Given the returns of the *Landtag* elections, one deputy wrote in the *Sozialistische Monatshefte,* the action was not entirely incompatible with the spirit of the constitution, a viewpoint that Severing notes in his memoirs he found of special interest at the time. This was what Braun, too, believed—apart from its hopelessness, resistance was impermissible since it would have defied the popular will no matter how badly misguided. They surrendered to it as they had surrendered to Hindenburg in the presidential election

[31] That the Communists were not prepared for armed resistance would seem to follow from a recent East German study on Papen's coup which passes over this question in silence. Petzold, "Staatsstreich," pp. 1179–82.

[32] Severing, *Lebensweg,* II, 352–59; Stampfer, *Vierzehn Jahre,* pp. 631, 632; Bracher, *Auflösung,* pp. 597–600; Brecht, "Weimarer Republik," pp. 300–04; Erich Matthias, "Der Untergang der alten Sozialdemokratie," *Vierteljahrshefte für Zeitgeschichte,* IV (1956), 251–56; Braun, quoted in Hermann von Lindheim, "Zu Papens Staatsstreich vom 20. Juli 1932," *Geschichte in Wissenschaft und Unterricht,* XI (1960), 162; Leber, *Ein Mann,* pp. 239–42.

—for lack of a realistic alternative. As Braun and Grzesinski later admitted, they would not have known what to fight for had they wanted to take up the struggle.[33]

✌

If the Socialist leaders felt that they had no mandate to strike back at Papen, they were hopeful, however, that Papen's coup would turn the antirepublican tide. They seem to have thought that it would open the eyes of many to the dangers of a dictatorship, and they expected to emerge with new strength from the forthcoming Reichstag elections.[34]

Once again they sadly misread the signs of the times—popular disgust with the parliamentary system was steadily growing. Fully aware of this trend, the Nazis made the Center and Socialists the main target of their campaign. Similarly, while at first they refrained from direct attacks on the Papen government and the president, they suggested that both had ties with the left. The Papen government was not appointed by the National Socialists, but by the Reich president, Hitler maintained, adding that it was the Center and Socialists who had reelected the latter. This theme was reiterated at thousands of meetings and coupled increasingly with bitter attacks on Hindenburg who had tolerated the misdeeds of Centrists and Social Democrats during the last seven years.[35]

While the main issue of the campaign was of course the future of the Papen government, the latter was in a singularly unfavorable position to present its case to the country. There had been some new attempts to found a "Hindenburg Party" under men like Jarres and Eckener to provide the government with a mouthpiece and its supporters with a means to express their approval. Yet again these efforts had failed, partly because vested interests and personal rivalries kept interfering, but chiefly because Hindenburg's support could not be enlisted and Papen too did not wish to be burdened with the stigma of a party affiliation.[36] The gov-

[33] Mierendorff, in *Sozialistische Monatshefte*, LXXVI (1932), 656; Severing, *Lebensweg*, II, 347, 359; on Braun, Matthias, in Matthias and Morsey, *Ende der Parteien*, p. 144; Grzesinski, quoted in *ibid.*, pp. 225–26.

[34] Stampfer, *Vierzehn Jahre*, pp. 631–32; Wilhelm Hoegner, *Der schwierige Aussenseiter: Erinnerungen eines Abgeordneten, Emigranten und Ministerpräsidenten* (Munich, 1959), p. 63; Severing, *Lebensweg*, II, 357; Matthias, "Untergang," p. 253; Kircher, in *Frankfurter Zeitung*, Reich ed., July 24, 1932.

[35] Deputy Hinkel, quoted in *Völkischer Beobachter*, July 28, 1932, repr. in *Gesch. in Wiss. und Unterricht*, X (1959), 223; Hitler, speech of July 27, 1932, *ibid.*, p. 224; Nazi Party leaflet, in *Nazi Party Records*/164/302349.

[36] Hecker to Dingeldey and Papen, June 8, 1932, Dingeldey Papers/60; *Tagebuch*, June 18, 1932, p. 927; Papen, *Wahrheit*, p. 238; Ritter, *Goerdeler*, p. 58.

ernment thus could be backed only indirectly by a vote for the German National or German People's Party, the groups closest to the cabinet in their political and socio-economic position. Neither choice was attractive to those who did not in any event support these parties. Hugenberg's stubbornness was repellent to many who liked Papen's greater adroitness, while Dingeldey's People's Party seemed doomed to become a miniscule splinter party. Schleicher, however, more realistic than Papen, appreciated the political value of any gains the two parties might score and contributed to their campaign chests from funds made available by his industrial friends. But this assistance could not stop their decline: the German Nationals lost almost 300,000 votes in the elections and the People's Party over a million. With Nazis, Center, Socialists, and Communists aligned against it, the government thus was clearly disavowed by the country. Apart from this fact the returns produced no conclusive decision.[37]

The Nazis scored only minor gains over the second presidential election, getting but 37.4 per cent of the vote. Unable to take over the government by themselves, they required at least the support of the Center, which they distrusted as much as the Center distrusted them, in order to form a majority government. Their only other chance lay in coming to terms with Papen and Schleicher, and last but not least with Hindenburg. After the extravagant hopes they had aroused, these were disappointing prospects, and Goebbels' postelectoral entries in his diary reflect his keen disenchantment.[38] The democratic parties, on the other hand, had obtained only 35 per cent of the seats, and a moderate coalition cabinet was thus equally out of the question. Theoretically there existed one other possibility: a coalition of Nazis and Communists who together held 52 per cent of all seats. While a positive collaboration between them seemed academic, they could be expected, however, to block any solution in which neither one had a voice.

The elections, then, settled nothing, but their inconclusiveness enabled Papen to claim that since he was not identified with any party or parties, he could ignore the returns and stay in office. In saying this, he of course expressed Hindenburg's views who was determined to retain him as chancellor. Papen also announced that he would make the enactment of some constitutional reforms a major concern of his cabinet.[39]

[37] Görlitz, *Hindenburg*, pp. 386–87; Schleicher Papers/17,iv/56, 58, 60, 68–69.
[38] Goebbels, *Vom Kaiserhof*, entries of July 31-Aug. 2, 1932, pp. 135–37.
[39] Papen, in Schulthess, Aug. 1, 1932, p. 136.

Yet no matter how contemptuous president and chancellor felt of the party and the parliamentary system, as long as the Weimar Constitution remained in force Hindenburg's backing was not sufficient for the government's continued existence; the chancellor still needed the Reichstag's support. If he wanted to secure a majority, however, the Nazis would have to back him, and to obtain their vote, some Nazis might have to be taken into the cabinet.[40] To explore Hitler's intention thus became the most urgent task. If a new government had been formed, this would have been the prerogative of the president; since only a reorganization of the incumbent cabinet was being considered, Hindenburg left it to Papen and Schleicher to sound out the Fuehrer.

Of the two, Schleicher was on better terms with the Nazis, and he initiated the talks. The general approached his task with his habitual confidence. He was all the more certain of his success as he had learned that Hitler's associates wished him to join the cabinet; under such pressure, Hitler could be expected to be satisfied with the post of vice-chancellor in a reorganized Papen government. Schleicher was shocked therefore when he learned on August 3 that Hitler would demand the chancellorship in the forthcoming negotiations. What bothered him most was his fear that Hindenburg would not agree to such an arrangement. If younger men were prepared to ignore the Nazis' excesses, the president was not. He still distrusted the unrestrained Hitler and had an instinctive feeling that the Fuehrer's plans went far beyond those of the usual politician. He could be expected to balk, therefore, at appointing him chancellor, and Schleicher's hope of taming the Nazis within the government would come to nothing. Yet Schleicher was firmly convinced that they could not be dealt with effectively in any other way. A new terror campaign was spreading just then across the country, skillfully timed to support Hitler's claims. Beginning with a carnage at Königsberg on election night, it accounted for a series of political murders, as well as incendiary raids on Center and Socialist headquarters, on banks and department stores, and the homes of political opponents. During the few days since the elections, some 25 people had been killed in street clashes, 5 police officers had lost their lives, and more than a score had been wounded. Nazi participation in the government, Schleicher reasoned, might lead to a break between the Nazi ministers and the S.A. and S.S. The ministers would be anxious to dissociate themselves from the unruly stormtroopers and would

40 Lersner to Schröder, Aug. 2, 1932, *Records of Private Austrian, Dutch, and German Enterprises: 1917–1946*/101/3476720; Vogelsang, *Reichswehr*, pp. 255–56.

try to curb them; this would be the best way of handling them and would also spare the Reichswehr from fighting them. That he could so completely misjudge the spirit and structure of the Nazi movement is the more surprising as only a few days before Göring and Röhm had told his aide, Colonel von Bredow, that the storm-troops had a right to wreak vengeance on "Marxism," that they had been trained for years for this day of revenge, and that they, Röhm and Göring, would not even allow the Fuehrer to deprive them of it.[41]

Two days later the general met with Hitler somewhere in Mecklenburg, determined to "talk him out of his plans." But Hitler would not give in. He could not, he argued, accept a subordinate post in which his prestige might be used up in a background role. Not only did he insist on being made chancellor, he also asked for the post of Prussian minister-president for himself and demanded the Reich and Prussian ministries of the interior, justice, agriculture, and aviation, and a newly to be created ministry of education and propaganda for other National Socialists. The Reichstag would have to be asked to pass an enabling act providing the new government with all the powers it needed; should it refuse to enact it, it would again be dissolved. Schleicher suggested that if he, Hitler, could not accept anything less than the chancellorship, he might delegate a lieutenant to assume the post of vice-chancellor. Hitler's reply was that such an arrangement would never do; in keeping with the Nazis' *Führerprinzip*, his men would have to consult him on all important decisions, and such a procedure, awkward and slow, would all but paralyze the government. That this suggested an undisguised party regime, Schleicher would not see—he thought that the point had merit. If he were to draw the Nazis into governmental responsibility, as he felt he must, he concluded that he would have to concede the chancellorship to Hitler and the ministry of the interior to his second-in-command, Gregor Strasser. There would have to be adequate safeguards of course: all other key ministries would be given to experts to preclude "undesirable experiments." But on these terms he was prepared to let Hitler head the new government.

There was still that one hurdle, however, that had to be cleared;

---

[41] Thilo Vogelsang, "Zur Politik Schleichers gegenüber der NSDAP 1932," *Vierteljahrshefte für Zeitgeschichte*, VI (1956), 91; also Vogelsang, *Reichswehr*, p. 256; Schleicher on splitting Nazis, cab. mtg., Aug. 10, 1932, *Vierteljahrshefte*, VI (1958), 97; Göring-Röhm visit, memorandum by Bredow, July 26, 1932, Vogelsang, *Reichswehr*, pp. 475–76.

Hindenburg had now to be persuaded to accept Hitler as chancellor. Whether Schleicher warned Hitler that this would be a difficult task is not clear; in his self-certain way he may have left Hitler with the impression that the "Old Gentleman" would readily take his advice. Yet he knew he had no such assurance.

Schleicher at once set to work to win the president over, either on a hurried visit to Neudeck or through phone calls to Oskar (the evidence is not clear). But for once his persuasive charm failed to work—Hindenburg rejected his plan out of hand. "I am told you want to hand me over to the Nazis," he growled indignantly, and with a decisiveness unusual for him, he let the general know that it was his "unshakable" will not to entrust Hitler with the chancellorship. He would not even appoint him if Hitler were able, by some pact with the Center, to obtain a majority in the Reichstag, but would rather resign. Schleicher assured him that he would never turn over all power to Hitler, but Hindenburg was not satisfied. His faith in his long-time confidant had suffered a shock from which it would never recover.[42]

Schleicher of course had no choice but to submit to the president; he was still convinced, however, that the Nazis could be controlled only if they were taken into the government. If this could be accomplished only with Hitler as chancellor, Hitler ought not to be barred for good from the chancellery. Papen, it seems, shared Schleicher's views. Both men were evasive when the question came up in the cabinet, and Papen refused to commit himself when Gayl wished the record to show that a Nazi as head of the government could never be tolerated.[43]

On August 10, Hindenburg returned to the capital. Papen reported to him on Hitler's demand for a presidential cabinet led by the Fuehrer. He offered to resign so as not to stand in the way of such a solution if the president wished to adopt it. Hindenburg would not hear of losing the chancellor; Hitler had broken his promises concerning the Papen government and could not be trusted; besides he lacked all governmental and administrative experience and could not even control his own party.[44]

---

[42] *Ibid.*, pp. 256–58; memorandum by Bredow, Aug. 15, 1932, *Vierteljahrshefte,* VI (1958), 100; Schleicher to *Vossische Zeitung,* Jan. 30, 1934 (draft), *ibid.,* p. 89. On question of Schleicher's visit to Neudeck, see Vogelsang, *Reichswehr,* p. 260 n. 1214; Hindenburg's remark, *ibid.*

[43] Papen, *Wahrheit,* pp. 222–24; same, memorandum of Nov. 12, 1957, in *Vierteljahrshefte,* VI (1958), 108–10; same, cab. mtg., Aug. 10, 1932, *ibid.,* pp. 93–94; Bredow, in *ibid.,* p. 100; Schleicher to Körner, Aug. 5, 1933, *ibid.,* pp. 88–89; *Frankfurter Zeitung,* Reich ed., Aug. 11, 1932.

[44] Papen, in cab. mtgs., Aug. 9, 1932, *RKz.*/1710/790520, Aug. 10, 1932, *loc. cit.,* pp. 93–94; Goebbels, *Vom Kaiserhof,* entry of Aug. 10, 1932, pp. 141–42; Wilhelm

For Papen, Schleicher, and their associates these were trying days. While the Nazi terror spread unabated, millions of Germans were clamoring for Hitler's appointment, and among them were many close to the government. Industrialists from the Ruhr were especially anxious to see him installed as chancellor since he seemed the only one able to restore order and strong enough at the same time to do away with the democratic-parliamentary system. More alarming, the Nazis were known to have mobilized large numbers of Brown Shirts around Berlin. The purpose apparently was, not to stage a march on the capital in emulation of Mussolini's March on Rome ten years earlier, but to frighten the government into yielding to Hitler's demands. The cabinet appears to have understood this, but it had to be prepared for the worst—the more so as it could not be certain that Hitler would be able to control his men. The police guarding Berlin's government quarter were equipped with heavy carbines, and extra units were held in readiness to rush to their aid should the Brown Shirts move on the capital. And as Schleicher did not fail to warn Hitler, the Reichswehr too was alerted to deal with a possible rising.[45]

Fortified by Hindenburg's stand, Papen and Schleicher arranged to confer with the Fuehrer. The latter had learned meanwhile that he could not expect to become chancellor. For a time he seems to have wondered whether he should come to Berlin at all, but in the end he decided to call on Papen and Schleicher, fearful perhaps that his failure to face the two men might place them in a stronger position.

The outcome of the talks seemed clearly predictable, but they produced an unexpected climax. At noon, on August 13, Hitler called on Schleicher and immediately afterwards on Papen; both men told him that the president was not willing to let him have more than the vice-chancellorship. His talk with Schleicher was short; he berated the general for having broken his promise and walked out abruptly. The conference with Papen lasted for over an hour. Told that he could not be chancellor, he launched into a bitter attack on the government, charging that it dealt much too leniently with the old system. As a result, Hitler complained, the Marxist parties had gained some 3 million votes (a purely fictitious figure since the Communists, the sole "Marxist" beneficiaries of the elections, had gained only 700,000 votes and this "Marx-

Hoegner, *Die verratene Republik* (Munich, 1958), pp. 317–19; *Frankfurter Zeitung*, Reich ed., Aug. 10–11, 1932; letter to Strasser, Sept. 20, 1932, *Nazi Party Records/* 1/11444; Vogelsang, *Reichswehr*, pp. 262–63.

45 Holtzendorff, *ZS./248*; Vogelsang, *Reichswehr*, pp. 262–63.

ist" gain in turn was offset by the Socialists' loss of 600,000). The "system" parties would have to be destroyed by fire and sword, and one ought not to shy away from bloodshed—this was the lesson of history. He had made it the task of his life to wipe out the Marxist parties. He would have to insist therefore on taking over himself the leadership of the government; he could govern only according to his own methods. Hitler then referred to the example of Italy. The King of Italy did not offer Mussolini the vice-chancellorship after the March on Rome, but gave him full power. When Papen reminded him of his earlier assurance that he would tolerate his government beyond the elections, Hitler replied that toleration was no longer an issue, there was only one thing that mattered: the taking over of power by the National Socialists.

Papen, deeply perturbed, tried to calm him as best he could. He had offered him the vice-chancellorship actually without authorization, for an appointment to that post had not yet been sanctioned by Hindenburg. He felt he should make this offer, however, to draw Hitler into the government, and he expected that the president would agree to such an arrangement. Now he went further. He assured Hitler that he was prepared to vacate the chancellorship once Hitler had proven himself in the vice-chancellor's post. After what Hitler had just revealed about his intentions, the offer seems hard to believe, but Papen may have been confident that Hitler would not pass that test. Hitler, according to Goebbels, appears to have thought so, and he rejected this new proposal too. Nor was he any more willing now to delegate some of his subleaders.

Since no agreement seemed possible, Hitler wished to break off the talks right then and there. There did not seem any point in his calling on Hindenburg, he did not wish to get involved in an argument with the president. But Papen could not afford to bear the onus of having barred Hitler from power, and he insisted that the final decision must rest with the president. The nation, he stated, would not understand it if he, Hitler, did not see the president in this hour of crisis. Reluctantly Hitler agreed to call on the marshal at the latter's convenience.

He drove to Goebbels' apartment in one of Berlin's western suburbs, an angry and frustrated man. At three o'clock a call came from the chancellery from Planck, Papen's state secretary. Hitler wanted to know whether the president had made up his mind not to appoint him chancellor. In that case there was no point in his calling on him. Planck was evasive: the president wished to talk to him first. Was there perhaps still some hope? In any case Hitler could not refuse this summons, and accompanied by Frick and Röhm, the chief of staff of the S.A., he set out for the Presidential Palace.

He had chosen his escort with special care. He took Röhm, a notorious pervert, though the marshal was known to detest him. But what looked like a sign of defiance was done as a necessity: the S.A. chief was to see for himself that the president would crush any effort to seize power forcibly. Thousands of stormtroopers were waiting for the signal to strike; to restrain them and yet retain their allegiance, Hitler needed the full support of their leader. Röhm, he was certain, could not fail to be impressed by the awesome personality of the old marshal, just as he himself always was, and would bow to the president's will. Frick, on the other hand, belonged to that element of the party that was counseling caution and opposed the Brown Shirts' brutal excesses.

The meeting with Hindenburg lasted for just over twenty minutes. Throughout the tenor was courteous, nor did Hindenburg remain standing, as rumor had it, so as not to offer seats to his callers.[46] The president opened the conference by stating that he was willing to have the Nazi Party take part in the government; in fact, he would welcome such participation. Was Hitler willing to enter the Papen government? Hitler replied that such an arrangement was out of the question. He could not possibly join an existing government. As the leader of the largest party, he would have to demand the formation of a new cabinet of which he would be the head. This, Hindenburg ruled out. He could not "before God, his conscience, and the Fatherland" assume the responsibility for turning over all power to one party. There was, Hitler insisted, no other possibility. "You are going into opposition, then?" the president asked. "I have no other choice," was the answer.

Hindenburg had been prepared for it. Talking now "marshal" to "corporal," he expressed his regret that Hitler could not work with Papen's "national" government although, as he pointedly added, he had earlier pledged his support. He had no doubt, he went on, that Hitler was acting from patriotism, but he urged him to fight a chivalrous fight. He would not tolerate any terrorist acts, "as members of the S.A. had unfortunately committed them too." Perhaps he did, as Meissner asserted at the Nürnberg Trials, chide Hitler for the crimes of his Brown Shirts, but the minutes convey

[46] Pünder, *Reichskanzlei,* entry of Aug. 18, 1932, p. 141.

the impression that his criticisms were made in regret rather than anger. And with a typical conciliatory gesture he concluded: "We are both old fellow soldiers and want to remain so since our paths may be crossing again. Thus I want to extend my hand to you as a fellow soldier."

In Hindenburg's presence Hitler had been calm and restrained. As always he had felt ill at ease when he confronted the marshal. But as soon as the door of the president's study had closed behind him and the chancellor, he recovered his self-assurance. He berated the hapless Papen for having exposed him to this shameful humiliation. Developments could only lead to the solution that he had proposed, but the delay might have to be paid for with the overthrow of the president; he, for one, would not want to take the responsibility for what might now follow. Papen retorted meekly that had he taken the vice-chancellorship, he might have been chancellor in a very short time.[47]

Returning to Goebbels' home, Hitler closeted himself with his advisers to plot his next steps. But for once his opponents were quicker than he. Into the consultations burst the news that the government had already issued a communiqué on his talk with the president showing him in a very bad light. It reported that Hindenburg had refused to turn over all power to him since Hitler wanted to use it one-sidedly; it told of the president charging him with breaking his promise to support the Papen government; it concluded that Hindenburg had admonished him to fight the government with chivalrous methods and that he had urged him to keep in mind his responsibility to nation and Fatherland. A countercommuniqué was drafted at once, but too late to catch up with the government's bulletin. The latter was broadcast by radio, published in extras, and posted in public places and caused a sensation. The feeling was widespread that the country had lived through a historic hour; did it herald perhaps the turn of the tide?

Hitler still had to deal with another chore. His S.A. commanders had been called together to be told that victory again had eluded them and there was nothing to do now but to wait for a better time to seize power. It was not an easy task to convince these men that they would have to accept defeat. According to reports which Papen received, 90 per cent of those present demanded immediate

47 Meissner memorandum, Aug. 13, 1932, Nazi memorandum, Aug. 13, 1932, RKz./ R 43 I/1309; Goebbels, *Vom Kaiserhof,* entries of Aug. 11–13, 1932, pp. 142–46; Papen, *Wahrheit,* pp. 222–24; same, cab. mtg., Aug. 15, 1932, RKz./1710/790543–46.

action. But Hitler, assisted by Röhm, convinced them that armed action was futile. The gathering disbanded, faced with the task of explaining away this stinging setback that the Nazi Party had suffered less than two weeks after its most recent electoral victory.[48]

Hitler was not the only protagonist in this crisis whom the events of the day left distraught. Schleicher was no less shaken than he that evening. He was still anxious to see the Nazis enter the government and wished to avoid an irreparable break. He had tried to reach Hitler after his audience with Hindenburg to assure him that all was not lost yet. To his dismay his feeler was brusquely rebuffed and he was given to understand that Hitler no longer trusted him. A friend who saw him that evening found him pale and upset, unable to speak coherently; later he took to muttering to himself until finally his speech became intelligible: "The decision was right, one could not have given all power to Adolf Hitler." Eventually the mood passed, and Schleicher became again his caustic and witty self. But for a time he had seemed a very frightened man.[49]

Of the main actors in the events of that day only Hindenburg seemed completely unmoved. As soon as Hitler had left him, he ordered his son to arrange for their return trip to Neudeck. The city was full of rumors that afternoon about an imminent Nazi rising. Oskar von Hindenburg was warned that it might not be safe for the president to drive to the station; others feared that his train might be blown up by a rebellious S.A. But Oskar refused to pass on these warnings to his father who he knew would have ignored them. That evening, satisfied that he had done his duty, the president departed as scheduled.[50]

The bulk of next day's editorials hailed him once more as the nation's hero. If his name had been mentioned at all in recent weeks, the reference had been critical, if not slighting. Even on Constitution Day, a few days before, reports had merely mentioned the fact that he had attended the traditional ceremony in the Reichstag. But on August 14, the marshal made headlines once more, editorials paid tribute again to his tireless sense of duty, his leadership qualities, and his role on the political stage. The *Deutsche Allgemeine Zeitung* which had been in favor of giving governmental responsibility to Hitler now pictured the

[48] Goebbels, *Vom Kaiserhof*, entry of Aug. 13, 1932, p. 146; Papen, in cab. mtg., Aug. 15, 1932, *RKz.*/1710/790946.

[49] Goebbels, *loc. cit.;* Rheinbaben on Schleicher, quoted in *Vierteljahrshefte*, VI (1958), p. 99 n. 29.

[50] Görlitz, *Hindenburg*, p. 382; Aretin, *Krone*, pp. 139–40.

president as "the man who approaches his tasks with the nerves of Tannenberg." The *Berliner Tageblatt,* consistently critical of him since the dismissal of Brüning, praised him again as the "guardian of the Constitution." A wave of relief seemed to be spreading across the country, and those who had supported his reelection felt gratified that their faith had not been unjustified.[51]

ॐ

Hindenburg had not come to Berlin for the purpose of meeting with Hitler. The trip had been planned weeks before as another manifestation of that formalist legalism with which the marshal looked on the constitution. Anxious to demonstrate his abiding respect for that document, he had announced in mid-June that he would interrupt his stay at Neudeck to attend the traditional Reichstag ceremony on August 11, Constitution Day. As planned, then, he had returned to the capital for that occasion.[52] This time the event resembled a wake rather than an anniversary celebration. The president sat with Siegfried von Kardorff, one of the vice-presidents of the Reichstag, since neither Paul Löbe, the Social Democratic president of the parliament, nor his deputy, Thomas Esser, a Centrist, would serve as his escort. On his left sat Schleicher as the representative of the government. The main address was delivered by Gayl. After dwelling on the flaws of the Weimar Constitution, he proceeded to outline some of the constitutional reforms which the government was considering: a revision of the suffrage system, the elimination of splinter parties, the establishment of an upper chamber, a permanent end to the dualism between Reich and Prussia. Papen added a few concluding words and called for cheers, not, as was customary, for the German republic, but for the German Reich. In the words of the *Bayerische Staatszeitung,* the whole event was essentially a leave-taking from the Weimar Constitution.

In this tenor the meeting reflected, of course, a widely held attitude. There were few now who wished to retain the constitution as it was. Even among the republic's supporters, agreement was general that basic reforms were needed. And by its indifference toward the day, now greater than ever before, the nation further attested its lack of faith in the ideas of Weimar.[53] But formally

51 Press comments in *Zeitspiegel,* Aug. 13, 27, 1932; *Frankfurter Zeitung,* Reich ed., Aug. 14, 1932.

52 Meissner, in cab. mtg., June 18, 1932, *RKz.*/1710/790235.

53 Gayl, in Schulthess, Aug. 11, 1932, p. 139; *Frankfurter Zeitung,* Reich ed., Aug. 12, 1932; *Bayerische Staatszeitung,* Aug. 12, 1932, quoted in *Zeitspiegel,* Aug. 27, 1932. Proposals for constitutional changes: Schäffer, in Schwend, *Bayern,* p. 460;

the constitution was still the law of the land, and much as he might have wished to, Papen could not ignore it. There existed the possibility, though admittedly a rather remote one, that Nazis and Centrists might form a coalition and command a majority in the Reichstag. Above all, Papen was certain to face a no-confidence motion as soon as the Reichstag assembled. Plans thus had to be made to meet both eventualities.

On August 15, two days after Hitler's call on the president, Papen met with his cabinet. He reported on what had occurred and professed to be satisfied with the outcome. It had been out of the question to deliver the state without checks to the Nazis; on the other hand, Hitler, so used to being the all-powerful leader of his party, would hardly have tolerated any restrictions. "By the same token," the minutes report him as saying, "[Hitler] would in the long run have made himself independent of the Wehrmacht." Once chancellor, Papen seemed to suggest, Hitler could not be restrained even if the Reichswehr were left in non-Nazi hands—a statement of some interest in the light of the course that Papen would later pursue.

Yet Papen was under no illusion that relations between the Nazis and the government had been settled for good. In view of the strength of the movement, he maintained, it was still necessary to associate it more closely with the state.[54] Meanwhile every effort would have to be made to anchor the government more securely among the people. Neither Lausanne nor the Prussian coup had produced the hoped for support; obviously popular backing could be won only by economic accomplishments, especially by a successful attack on the unemployment problem. What was needed then was "action, action, action." The cabinet agreed with him;

Koch-Weser to Gessler, Mar. 26, 1932, Gessler, *Reichswehrpolitik*, p. 504; Fraenkel, in *Gesellschaft*, IX (1932), ii, 194–209; Kirchheimer, in *ibid.*, pp. 486–500.

[54] Apparently this remark was reported to Hindenburg, for he had one of his aides call the chancellery the next day to find out whether any new negotiations were under way with the Nazis and whether any concrete offer had been made to them. He did not wish any new negotiations to be started, he let it be known, unless he were informed and could make a decision. Evidently he was fearful of another arrangement in which Hitler might once more be conceded the chancellorship; encouraged by the popular acclaim his stand on August 13 had evoked, he was determined for once to keep control of the situation. Planck replied that neither side was inclined to embark on new talks or had made any move. Should any negotiations be initiated, the president would at once be informed. Half an hour later Hindenburg's aide called back to report that the president had been highly gratified to learn how things stood. Memorandum by Planck, Aug. 19, 1932, *RKz.*, R. 43 I/1309.

economic measures would have to receive top priority, and action was of the utmost importance.[55]

Papen wasted no time. On August 28, in a speech at a meeting of farmers in Münster, he presented his plans to the nation. He proposed some additional public works projects, largely prepared by Brüning; an extension of the voluntary labor service that had recently been established, based on plans worked out by his predecessor; and a large-scale program of repair and maintenance work that was to be stimulated by the granting of tax credits. Employers would likewise be given tax credits for hiring additional workers. To provide further incentives for increasing employment, Papen also proposed another reduction of wages. For the rest, he promised a series of constitutional and administrative reforms to enable the nation to develop its potentialities. He concluded by explaining how he proposed to implement these plans:

"Our work . . . can be done only by an authoritarian and independent government deeply aware of its duties toward God and nation. From this conviction I consider it my duty to keep partisan influences from disturbing my work. Only he can cope with great tasks in the service of the nation who considers himself the servant of the entire people and not that of a class or a party. . . . The Constitution provides in the Reich President a focus unaffected by the plan of the parties—a focus in which the uniform and independent conduct of government business is securely anchored. From this power, at once authoritarian and democratic, embodied in the person of Reich President von Hindenburg, the Government derives the authority and the mandate for its actions. . . . I appeal to the nation: Think only of Germany." [56]

A day later Papen, Schleicher, and Gayl journeyed to Neudeck to submit their plans to the president. Once again Hindenburg proved a tower of strength, perhaps because for once his East Prussian neighbors approved of the government he had appointed. If Meissner's minutes are an accurate record of what transpired, he seemed well informed and knew his own mind. There were none of the customary platitudes or equivocations. He approved Papen's economic program urging him merely to assure an even distribution of the new burdens. Clearly he did not grasp that Papen's one-sided catering to business and agriculture precluded an equitable allotment. He also agreed with the chancellor that a Nazi-Center coalition, should it materialize, would not accom-

[55] Cab. mtg., Aug. 15, 1932, *RKz.*/1710/790546–53.
[56] Schulthess, Aug. 28, 1932, pp. 144–49.

plish anything, and he brushed aside a Centrist statement, forwarded through Meissner, that the Center was conducting its
negotiations with the Nazis in the hope of forming a government
based on a clear majority in the Reichstag and willing to work
with the parliament in accordance with the intent of the constitution. He could not believe that a working majority could be
found in the Reichstag, and he would not have any dealings with
a pseudo-majority. Once it was clear that there was no majority
willing to work with him, he would dissolve the Reichstag again.

After the question of the fate of the Reichstag had been settled,
there arose the much touchier one of what was then to be done.
Was another election to be held within 60 days as the constitution
demanded? Any delay beyond the 60-day period could technically
be considered a violation of the constitution, Papen conceded,
but the country was faced with an emergency situation (*staatlicher
Notstand*) that would justify a postponement. It was the president's
duty to protect the people from harm; much harm would come from
new elections held at a time when they were bound to provoke
new acts of murder and terrorism. Papen thought there was no need
to reach a decision as yet, but the matter should be thought over.

Gayl seconded him, certain that the nation would approve a
postponement of the elections under existing conditions. People
and press, he claimed, did not even expect new elections. It all
boiled down to the question "as to whether we wished to do what
was needed for Germany or whether we would allow the wording
of the Constitution to keep us from doing it. As long as it can be
established that an emergency exists, one should feel free in good
conscience to disregard [Article 25]. . . ." "If," Papen summed up,
"Field Marshal General and Reich President von Hindenburg
who has upheld the Constitution so conscientiously decides in the
case of a special emergency to deviate just once from the Constitution, the German people will surely accept this."

To these arguments Hindenburg seems to have yielded with
unusual readiness. He could reconcile it with his conscience, he
stated, in order to protect the German people from harm, to
interpret Article 25 in the sense that new elections should be
postponed until a later time because of the special circumstances.
He then signed a decree dissolving the Reichstag, with the date
and reason to be filled in later. Papen also obtained his signature
on another decree placing the Prussian police under the jurisdiction of the Reich minister of the interior should Nazis and Center
succeed in forming a coalition in Prussia.[57]

[57] Minutes of Neudeck Conference, Aug. 30, 1932, Schleicher Papers/17,iv/115–23.

Confident now that the president would back them to the limit of his authority, the ministers returned to Berlin. There, at the very time at which they had been meeting with Hindenburg, the Reichstag had been convened to elect its officers. The negotiations between Nazis and Center had not produced a governmental coalition, but they had led to a last-minute arrangement to make possible the election of a Reichstag presidium. On the basis of this agreement Göring was elected president, while the three vice-presidential posts were filled with a representative each of the Center, the German Nationals, and the Bavarian People's Party. The Social Democrats, the second largest party, were entitled to the first vice-presidency, according to custom, but their claim was ignored. Göring concluded the opening session with a statement in which he pointed to the election of the Reichstag presidium as proof that the Reichstag was able to work constructively. There was no reason therefore to dissolve the Reichstag again. To make this clear to the president, he would ask him to receive the newly elected presidium at once rather than, as was customary, at his convenience.[58]

During the following days each side worked to improve its position. On September 4, Papen's economic decree was published, but since the new program attacking the problem of unemployment from the production end could offer immediate relief, if at all, only to business and property owners, almost all the parties denounced it and so did the labor unions. But to Papen's great disappointment, the direct beneficiaries were not satisfied either. Employers organizations warned against "limitless" public works projects, and the *Landbund*, as usual, rejected the decree on the grounds that it failed to do justice to agricultural needs.[59]

Meanwhile the talks between Nazis and Centrists continued; both sides approached the discussions with great reservations and little is known of what was proposed. If the Center was willing to negotiate with the Nazis at all, it was not only because it wished them to assume political responsibility under proper safeguards. Significantly, its leaders were perhaps as much concerned with shielding Hindenburg—the one element of stability still existing. As Brüning has pointed out, many Centrists were fearful that he might be forced from office as the result of unconstitutional steps he might take to keep the unpopular Papen in office.[60] It is doubt-

58 Morsey, in Matthias and Morsey, *Ende der Parteien*, pp. 316–20; Göring, Aug. 30, 1932, *Verhandlungen*, Vol. 454, p. 10.

59 Bracher, *Auflösung*, p. 625; Heiden, *Fuehrer*, p. 487; *Sozialistische Monatshefte*, LXXVI (1932), 851; Schulthess, Aug. 30, 1932, p. 151.

60 Vogelsang, *Reichswehr*, pp. 270, 273, 276.

ful, however, that an agreement could have been reached between the two parties even if there had been more time; the dissolution of the Reichstag in any case brought the talks to an abrupt end.

The Reichstag presidium had meanwhile been awaiting the president's pleasure, but no call came from Neudeck. It was not until he returned to Berlin that Hindenburg received the newly elected officials. The meeting was not a success. Göring asserted that a large majority of the Reichstag believed that the Reichstag was able to function and ought not to be dissolved. The two vice-presidents from the Center and the Bavarian People's Party agreed, but their German National colleague objected that the *Reichstagspräsident* had no right to make political statements on behalf of the Reichstag. The German Nationals, he added, welcomed the president's efforts to set up a government immune from party maneuvers and they would not interfere with his plans. They were certain, moreover, that large parts of the German people shared their views.

The gentlemen did not seem to agree, Hindenburg noted, and then he read off a statement which Meissner had drafted. He saw no reason to dismiss the government simply because this was the wish of some parties; he approved of its actions which were inspired by strong patriotism and would retain it even in the face of a no-confidence vote. To a suggestion that he consult with the party leaders before he made a final decision, he gave a noncommittal reply.[61]

On September 12, the Reichstag convened again. The opposition had been unable to agree on an alternative government; a last-minute proposal of the Center for a non-Nazi (Schleicher?) as chancellor had been rejected by Hitler. The session was one of the shortest in that parliament's troubled history. The agenda called for a policy statement by Papen, but the Communists moved that the Reichstag vote at once on a repeal of the latest emergency decree and on their no-confidence motion. The request was meant to be nothing more than an empty gesture; a last-minute change of the agenda was possible only if adopted unanimously, and the German Nationals had announced, when the agenda had been accepted, that they would reject any change in the order of business. Yet to everyone's surprise they now voiced no objection. Hugenberg knew that the government was empowered to dissolve the Reichstag and had decided to force through the dissolution at

[61] Minutes of conference of Hindenburg and Reichstag Presidium, Sept. 9, 1932, Schleicher Papers/17,iv/136–40; Meissner to Planck, n.d. (Sept. 8, 1932?), *RKz.*/R 43 1/1309; Goebbels, *Vom Kaiserhof*, entry of Sept. 12, 1932, p. 162.

once lest Nazis and Center reach a last-minute agreement over his head.

Meant to assist the government, Hugenberg's scheme almost led to its downfall. Papen had not been informed of the change in plans and he was thus as little prepared for it as was anyone else outside the German National delegation. He had been certain that there would be no action that day on the no-confidence motion and had not brought with him the dissolution decree; without it, he might now have to stand by while the Reichstag voted him out of office. He was saved by the Nazis who asked for a half-hour adjournment to consult with Hitler about the stand they should take. This gave the chancellor time to send for the dissolution document. Hitler in the meantime instructed his men to vote in support of both motions.

When the session resumed, the chancellor held the traditional red dispatch case containing the dissolution decree in his hands. But Göring ignored his request to be recognized and called for a vote on the motions. This was a clear violation of the Reichstag's rules which gave the chancellor the right to be heard before any vote was taken. Papen rose and approached Göring, but the *Reichstagspräsident* still pretended he did not see him. Red with anger, Papen tossed the decree on Göring's desk and walked out with his ministerial colleagues. Legally the Reichstag was now dissolved, but Göring allowed the vote to continue. Even if it had no legal effect, it was a significant demonstration. Of 559 votes, 512 supported the no-confidence motion; only 42 votes were cast for the government while five of the deputies abstained.[62]

There followed a heated exchange between Hindenburg, Göring, and Papen on the legality of the dissolution, but in the end Göring had to accept the inevitable. Once more Hindenburg stood fully behind his chancellor, ready to proclaim a state of emergency to bar the Reichstag from reconvening by force of arms if necessary. Yet if the dissolution could not be attacked on technical grounds, it was vulnerable on substantive ones. The decree justified the dissolution on the grounds that the Reichstag would ask for the repeal of the presidential decree of September 4; to ask for such a repeal was one of the Reichstag's prerogatives and to use this request as a reason for dissolving that body clearly ran counter to the intent of the constitution. While this point was raised by the Center Party, no one attempted to press it. Each party for

[62] Vogelsang, *Reichswehr*, pp. 276–77; Reichstag session, Sept. 12, 1932, *Verhandlungen*, Vol. 454, pp. 13–15, 21; Eyck, *Weimarer Republik*, II, 527–28; Goebbels, *Vom Kaiserhof*, entry of Sept. 12, 1932, p. 162.

reasons of its own welcomed the dissolution and constitutional subtleties were not to be allowed to stand in the way.[63]

Given this indifference, an immediate referendum on the government's constitutional reforms would have seemed to be Papen's next move, but the chancellor's hands were tied. There was no indication that the country was prepared to accept the specific reforms he proposed, and there was no time left to campaign for their acceptance. Nor would it have been technically possible to complete the involved referendum procedure within the allotted 60-day period within which new Reichstag elections had to be held. Again the question arose whether the elections should not be postponed. Clearly the government could not hope to secure a majority under the present electoral system. Gayl and apparently Schleicher, forever shifting his stand, favored such a postponement; but most of the ministers, including the chancellor, believed the time premature for a breach of the constitution. For Papen this was a sharp change from the position he had taken before, but he had come to understand that he would have to have more support before he could attempt such a coup. He had also learned that the Nazis were considering the impeachment of Hindenburg in case of a postponement of the elections, and while no impeachment was possible if there was no Reichstag to vote on it, the president should not be subjected to the indignity even of a threat of this nature. The cabinet decided to hold new elections, and the date was set for the last possible day, November 6.[64]

The Nazis, determined to discredit Hindenburg, also explored other avenues of a presidential impeachment. Similarly the question was raised whether the government was not legally vulnerable in Prussia; to obstruct its work, a resolution supported by Nazis and Communists in the Prussian *Landtag* directed all Prussian officials to ignore the instructions of the Reich-appointed commissioners. Hitler knew that he could come to power only with Hindenburg's consent, and since the president refused to appoint him chancellor, he was casting about for some way of extorting this approval.[65]

While these maneuvers worried the president and the government, they caused the Nazis some headaches too. Pro-Hitler busi-

---

[63] Poetzsch-Heffter, in *Jahrb. d. öff. Rechts,* XXI (1933–34), 68–72; Meissner, in cab. mtg., Sept. 12, 1932, 4:30 p.m., *RKz./*1710/790730–31; Schulthess, Sept. 13, 1932, p. 164.

[64] Cab. mtg., Sept. 14, 1932, *RKz./*1710/790745–52; Schwend, *Bayern,* pp. 487–89; *Dt. Führer-Briefe,* Aug. 26, 1932, *Nazi Party Records/*1/11344.

[65] Reinhardt and Göring, in *Nationalsozialistische Monatshefte,* III (1932), 443, 445–46; Brüning, "Ein Brief," pp. 13–14.

ness circles were beginning to wonder whether he really was their man. They had welcomed him as the foe of parliamentary government, and had been shocked to discover that he would negotiate with the Center. His threat to impeach Hindenburg, suggesting the will to uphold the constitution, appeared to confirm their misgivings and his professed anti-Communism also seemed open to question. Goebbels' denunciations of the Papen cabinet as a "reactionary barons clique" and Strasser's recurrent attacks on exploitation by employers sounded suspiciously like Marxist class struggle doctrine. Nor did Nazi collaboration with the Communists, as in the Prussian *Landtag*, go unnoticed. In their alarm many businessmen pleaded with Hitler to make his peace with the government since his quarrel with Papen could benefit only the "Marxists," but others decided to leave him and switched their support to the chancellor.[66]

But if Hitler was losing ground, the government was not gaining enough to consolidate its position. Economic recovery was lagging behind expectations, agricultural measures met with the furious objections of the intractable agrarian organizations, and labor's resentment of the government's social policies touched off continuous waves of strikes. The government remained as anxious as ever therefore to reach some understanding with Hitler although there were continuous reminders of what manner of man he was. Only recently Hitler had openly sided with five stormtroopers who had dragged a Polish miner from his bed in the little Upper Silesian village of Potempa and had literally trampled him to death; he had denounced the death sentence imposed on them as a "monstrous blood verdict," and publicly pledged his honor to fight for their immediate release. In a National Socialist Germany, he had stated a few days later, five Germans would never be convicted because of one Pole, and Alfred Rosenberg, the "party philosopher," had raged in the *Völkischer Beobachter* against the equation of man and man that was undermining the "most elementary instinct of a nation for its self-preservation." In this verdict, "according to bourgeois justice, one Communist, and a Polish one at that, equals five Germans, veterans. . . . For National Socialism soul does not equal soul, or man, man; it knows no 'law as such,' for its goal is the strong German man, it is com-

66 *Dt. Führer-Briefe,* Aug. 26, 1932, *loc. cit.;* letter to Strasser, Sept. 20, 1932, *Nazi Party Records*/1/11436–45; Lehmann to Stellbrecht, Sept. 15, 1932, *ibid./* 11534–38; memorandum by Alvensleben, Aug. 31, 1932, Schleicher Papers/17,iv/27; Harbou to Schleicher, Sept. 16, 1932, *ibid.*/5/81; Hermann Rauschning, *Men of Chaos,* (New York, 1942), pp. 218–21.

mitted to protect this German, and law and society, politics and business, have to adapt themselves to this objective."

But this callous defiance of law and of human rights did not weaken the chancellor's hope of coming to terms with Hitler. Like Schleicher he seems to have felt that he could handle the Fuehrer once he had brought him into the government. One gathers that Hitler's moral and legal cynicism merely seemed proof to him of an inferior intellect with which men of a higher social and educational background would know how to deal. Various middlemen moved back and forth between Berlin and Munich to let Hitler know that Papen, as well as Schleicher, still hoped to see him enter the cabinet in the not too distant future. They also took care to tone down all official statements critical of the Nazis lest they impair these efforts. "From all sides attempts are being made to bring us and the Government together," Goebbels noted resentfully, "Thank God, the Fuehrer won't play." As before, Hitler insisted on his appointment as chancellor.[67]

Hitler decided, however, not to antagonize needlessly either business or government. Party speakers were asked to drop any slogans reminiscent of Marxist terminology in their attacks on the government and they were warned not to give the impression of defending the parliamentary system in assailing the dissolution of the Reichstag. Nor should they accuse the Papen regime of holding office illegally; rather they ought to point out that it was not using its powers wisely and show how much more a Hitler government could do for Germany. These orders were promptly followed. When on October 2, Hindenburg celebrated his eighty-fifth birthday, Nazi editorials took notice of the event with noticeable restraint. Goebbels' *Angriff* had never thought much of the president, but now it contented itself with expressing the hope that the marshal would find the way to the "new Germany." Yet some days later Hitler once more asked for full powers in a public address and ignoring his own directives, ridiculed the Reich government as an antiquated noblemen's clique. Papen, in an answering speech, rejected his totalitarian demands, but in the same breath paid tribute to the "great and meritorious National Socialist movement."[68]

---

[67] Papen, in cab. mtg., Oct. 7, 1932, *RKz./*1711/790954–55; Goebbels, *Vom Kaiserhof,* entries of Sept. 24, Oct. 1, 7, 10, 1932, pp. 169, 173, 174, 176, 178; Severing, *Lebensweg,* II, 366; Papen to Schröder, Oct. 1, 1932, *Records of Private Enterprises/* 101/3476721; Alvensleben to Hitler, Sept. 21, 1932, *Nazi Party Records/*1/11335–36; Lehmann to Stellbrecht, Sept. 15, 1932, *ibid./*11540–41; Paul Kluke, "Der Fall Potempa," *Vierteljahrshefte für Zeitgeschichte,* v (1957), 278–97.

[68] Memorandum by Hess, n.d., *Nazi Party Records/*1/11427–32; *Angriff,* Oct. 1,

As always, Hindenburg's anniversary provided a reliable barometer of the national mood. Like the Nazis, most other parties and groups paid homage to him in a roundabout way; indeed, the tenor of the occasion stood in marked contrast to the festivities five years before, on the president's eightieth birthday. The government, to be sure, extolled him in panegyrics as ecstatic as ever. "I believe," Papen observed, "that Providence has sent us a man in Hindenburg as we need him in this most difficult emergency. Miracles do still occur in the history of our people." But except for the Hugenberg press, now once more fully behind Hindenburg, most bourgeois papers would not conceal their concern over his recent actions and future plans. "Today Hindenburg constitutes the essential foundation of our state," wrote the Centrist *Germania*, "and we have the wish and the hope that he will defend it as the guardian of the people and of its rights and guide it wisely and safely through the present crisis." "Our faith in Hindenburg's allegiance to the Constitution, in his political integrity and selflessness," the *Bayerische Kurier* tried to reassure its readers, "must not be shaken by anyone or anything." And the *Vossische Zeitung* voiced its misgivings with similar circumspection: "In awe of his achievements, respectful even of their inevitable limitations, we are greeting today . . . the grand old man of the German people." Despite all disappointments, however, the bourgeois press still clung to the marshal as the one last anchor in the political storms.

The most melancholy comment was made by the Socialist *Vorwärts,* which six months earlier had been Hindenburg's loyal supporter in the presidential campaign: "Half a year ago the German Social Democrats cast their ballot for him to ward off grave political dangers. If they cannot wholeheartedly join in [today's] celebrations, their aloofness is due to the many events which have taken place between that election and this anniversary. . . . This may be hard, but for the sake of truth it must be said that our political opposition which we have never concealed and which we have carried on in chivalrous form against our aged head of state has been reenforced by many human disappointments. These disappointments keep us from entering the circle of the celebrants."[69]

1932, quoted in *Zeitspiegel*, Oct. 8, 1932; Goebbels, *Vom Kaiserhof,* Sept. 30, 1932, p. 172; Lersner to Schröder, Oct. 8, 1932, *Records of German Enterprises*/101/3476727.

[69] *Germania,* Oct. 2, 1932, and other editorials and statements, in *Zeitspiegel,* Oct. 8, 1932; *Vorwärts,* in Schulthess, Oct. 2, 1932, p. 172.

Their disappointments had been many indeed. To Brüning's dismissal and the Prussian coup, there had been added a succession of slights and embarrassments. Nevertheless the Socialists had been careful to abide by all regulations decreed by the government. Some of their leaders had even persuaded themselves that any alternative to Papen's government would be a change for the worse, and therefore wished Papen to stay. Yet the latter persisted in his hostility toward them, and some of his colleagues thought that they differed very little from the Communists. What made this impasse even more frustrating was the knowledge that Papen's antagonism was not entirely a matter of choice. Even if he had wished to, he could not have sought a rapprochement with the Socialists if he was not to lose whatever support he had elsewhere. The fact was that so deep a chasm had opened between them and the moderate right that it precluded any collaboration.[70]

Late in October, however, the Socialists scored something of a moral victory over the Reich government. On October 27, the *Staatsgerichtshof* rendered its verdict in the case of Prussia *vs.* the Reich. The court rejected the claim of the Reich that the Prussian government had been derelict in its duties. It justified, on the other hand, the Reich's temporary intervention in Prussia since law and order had been in grave danger. At the same time it felt that a Reich-appointed commissioner could assume only certain specified functions of the Prussian ministers and the latter could not be removed altogether. The Braun-Severing government thus was partly restored to office; yet as a result, Prussia had two governments and new trouble was bound to result. The court was not unaware of the problems its verdict created, but the judges were faced with a delicate task. While they were convinced that the Reich had overstepped its rights, they also wished to safeguard as far as they could the authority of Hindenburg and the Reich government.[71]

The desire to spare the president was shared by all parties to the dispute. The chief Prussian spokesman, Dr. Brecht, made it clear at the outset that his government did not wish to attack the person of the president. The Prussian ministers, he stressed, were convinced of the president's determination to observe the constitution. They had made every effort to ensure his reelection, and they still looked on him with the deep respect he could claim as

[70] Social Democrats' interest in retaining Papen, Keil, *Erlebnisse*, II, 456; also Lersner to Schröder, Aug. 2, 1932, *Records of Private Enterprises*/101/3476720; Gayl and Gürtner on Socialists, cab. mtg., Aug. 10, 1932, *Vierteljahrshefte*, VI (1958), 95, 97.

[71] *Preussen contra Reich vor dem Staatsgerichtshof* (Berlin, 1933), pp. 511–17.

the head of the Reich. And shifting the blame to where he felt it belonged, Brecht charged that it was the president's advisers who by misinforming him and suggesting to him a misleading interpretation of the constitution had been the ones responsible for the violation of the constitution. Similarly the presiding judge was anxious to keep Hindenburg's *name* out of the proceedings. When one of the Prussian spokesmen referred to the fact that it was he, not the Prussian government, who had issued the decree proscribing the S.A. and S.S., and that any charge of one-sided discrimination against the Nazis in Prussia was thus directed against Hindenburg, the court president rebuked him for having brought Hindenburg's name into the discussion. It would have been sufficient to state that the Reich government had proposed this measure to him.[72]

Given this determination to shield the authority of the president, a full reinstatement of the Prussian government was clearly out of the question. Even the Prussian ministers did not expect the complete reversal of Papen's coup, for they made it known that they were mainly concerned with purging themselves of the charges that they had been derelict in their duties and in their loyalty towards the Reich. As much as Hindenburg had disappointed their hopes, they knew that the survival of any measure of constitutional government depended on the preservation of his authority. So did the bulk of the press. Papers which considered the verdict a defeat of the Reich thought it a setback for Papen rather than Hindenburg. Those, on the other hand, which hailed it as a victory of the Reich called it a vindication of the president and barely mentioned the chancellor.[73]

As it was, the Prussian government's faith in the president was ill rewarded. A few days after the court had spoken, Otto Braun called on Hindenburg to take up with him some difficulties which had arisen between Reich and Prussia over the interpretation of the decision. Papen had proceeded immediately to reorganize the Prussian administration in clear defiance of the court's conclusion that he could take only provisional measures, but Braun received no help from the president. Papen who took part in the conference acted as Hindenburg's spokesman and parried all questions that Braun tried to raise. Hindenburg himself merely made a brief statement that the Reich could be governed properly only if Reich and Prussia pursued the same policies and the power resources of both were united; for the rest he muttered a few

[72] *Ibid.*, pp. 8, 10, 236, 295–96.
[73] Braun, *Von Weimar*, pp. 414–15; press comments, in *Zeitspiegel*, Nov. 5, 1932.

vague exhortations about the loyal fulfillment of the verdict. To Braun he seemed ill at ease; the minister-president had come to reproach him for having consented to measures which were incompatible with the judgment, but his bitterness turned to compassion for this helpless old man who, as he saw it, was being abused by his entourage.[74]

Altogether the marshal seems to have been a man very different from the one who had vigorously held off Hitler two months before and who had later been willing to suspend the constitution and proclaim a state of emergency. In the isolation of Neudeck things might have looked simple and promising under Papen's stewardship, but in Berlin he could no longer escape from the deepening crisis, and the difficulties that Papen kept facing were weighing heavily on him.

Braun was not to see Hindenburg again although friction continued undiminished between the two Prussian governments. Hindenburg, the guardian of the constitution, refused to deal with Prussia's recurrent complaints and passed them all on to Papen. And when Papen asked for additional powers, he readily complied with his wishes.[75] The Braun-Severing cabinet thus was quickly reduced to fighting pinprick battles against its all-powerful rival. Soon, however, even its supporters lost interest in its plight, for some weeks later the country was plunged into another national crisis. This latest emergency was brought on by the inconclusive Reichstag elections of November 6.

[74] Memorandum by Meissner, Oct. 29, 1932, *RKz.*, R 43 I/2281; Braun, *Von Weimar*, pp. 415–18.
[75] *Ibid.*, pp. 418–20.

CHAPTER 11

FROM PAPEN TO SCHLEICHER

HE Reichstag elections of November 6 were the fifth major contest to take place that year. The country was emotionally exhausted, its passions spent. The sluggish campaign lacked drive and enthusiasm; the posters were uninspired; the speeches routine. Even the Nazis could no longer muster their old fighting spirit and attendance at meetings was markedly smaller. Except for the Communists, all the parties were clearly on the defensive. Moreover, the issues were blurred as they had been in July. Most non-Nazis opposed a Hitler dictatorship—the Communists alone seemed prepared to accept this as a preliminary to their own seizure of power—but disagreed on any alternative course to pursue. Hugenberg's German Nationals wished Papen to stay in power; the Center spoke vaguely of an emergency coalition (*Notgemeinschaft*) including the Nazis; and the Socialists dreamed of somehow returning to the parliamentary ways of Weimar democracy.

Added to the lack of reality in these plans was the inability of Papen's supporters to cast their ballot directly for him. Again there was no "Presidential Party" for which they could vote, although many more now sided with him than in July. As the *Deutscher Volkswirt* suggested, they might best have shown their approval by abstaining from voting, thus backing the government's claim that it was tied to no parties. But unless very large numbers of voters stayed away from the polls, the government was not likely to benefit from this course, and there was no time to organize such a boycott. Once more voting for Papen meant voting for Hugenberg since efforts to remove him as party leader had been unsuccessful; or possibly voting for the German People's Party, "the only party," as it proudly proclaimed, "which has stood by Hindenburg through all political shifts and changes."[1]

Aware of the German Nationals' key position, the Nazis made them the prime target of their election campaign. They knew

[1] Stolper, in *Dt. Volkswirt*, Nov. 11, 1932, p. 167; "Sinnlose Wahlen," *ibid.*, Sept. 16, 1932, p. 1656; materials in *RKz.*, R 43 I/1008; memorandum on board meeting of German National People's Party, Oct. 6, 1932, *Nazi Party Records*/1/11362; Kroeger to Schleicher, Oct. 10, 1932, Schleicher Papers/17,iv/159–60; German People's Party, in *Dt. Gesch.-Kal.*, 1932, A, 307.

that they were facing a critical struggle. In recent communal elections they had suffered marked setbacks; even in rural strongholds like Oldenburg and East Prussia their losses had ranged up to 60 per cent, and in each case the gainers had been the bourgeois parties. Since Socialist losses had accrued to the Communists, it was unlikely that new votes could be found on the left; the only hope therefore lay in drawing voters away from the German Nationals. If this could be done, Papen would likewise be disavowed and Hitler's bargaining power improved correspondingly.

Yet this strategy was not without problems, for the Nazis were also committed to oppose "bourgeois reaction," a stand that might frighten away the very voters they hoped to convert. The Nazis' election propaganda thus followed a double track: Göring was outspoken in his disdain of the "Philistine bourgeois"; Strasser presented the party as the champion of private property. Others, while thundering against "Marxist" greed, warned that Papen's decrees were driving the country into Moscow's arms. And while all of them pictured Nazism as the last bulwark against Bolshevism, the party also worked hand in hand with the Communists in fomenting a series of strikes. The most sensational of these joint efforts was a strike of Berlin's transport workers that tied up life in the capital in early November. Worried businessmen were told ominously that in this way alone the Nazis could hope to restrain the masses. And the somber warning was added that the party could not do so much longer unless Hitler were made chancellor.[2]

The decline of the party could not be brought to a halt by such tactics; on November 6, the Nazis lost 2 million votes and 34 seats in the Reichstag. Voter participation had been remarkably high (80.6 per cent as against 84.1 per cent in July), and abstentions thus could account for no more than a fraction of these losses. The setback was due in large part to the fears that Nazi radicalism and terrorism had aroused, but Hitler's failure to enter the government also had hurt him, since many who had voted for him in July felt that he was frittering away the fruits of his victories. ("It is the height of presumption," a party announcement retorted, "if small minds which don't have the slightest idea of politics feel qualified to pass judgment on the greatest political leader of present-day Germany.") Most of them, if they voted again, turned

---

[2] Hess memorandum on election propaganda, n.d., *Nazi Party Records*/1/ 11427–32; Goebbels, *Vom Kaiserhof*, entries of Oct.-Nov. 1932, *passim;* same, *Wetterleuchten,* pp. 334–39; Strasser and Göring, quoted in *Gesellschaft,* IX (1932), ii, 401 n. 5.

to Hugenberg, but those of a more radical bent of mind threw their support to the Communists. Together with a large number of disillusioned Socialists, they helped to increase the vote of the Communists by 700,000 to almost 6 million.

The increase in the vote cast for the German Nationals (almost 800,000) and the minor gains of the People's Party (225,000) were proof that Papen was gaining ground. Yet in parliamentary terms the chancellor's position was still as untenable as before. Between them the German Nationals and People's Party controled only 63 seats, a number that could possibly be increased to 97 should the remnants of the small bourgeois parties and the Bavarian People's Party come to Papen's aid. Against them, however, were ranged 487 opponents eagerly waiting to drive him from office.

Even though the opposition was numerically still overwhelming, it was politically weaker. Nazis and Center no longer had a majority, and they would need the support of the German Nationals to form a majority government. Yet the latter were known to oppose what they denounced as a return to parliamentary chaos, and were pleading with Hindenburg to retain Papen's cabinet, with Hugenberg as economics minister and General Joachim von Stülpnagel as a replacement for Schleicher, now suspected of opportunism. If the government had been hoping to show that no coalition could supersede it, the election returns had provided that proof. As for Hindenburg, he drew from this fact the welcome conclusion that Papen should remain at his post.[3]

When the cabinet reconvened on November 9, it quickly agreed that it ought not to resign. No alternative government seemed in sight and it was therefore its duty to stay in office. That no majority government could be formed would have to be demonstrated, however, by talks with the parties. Schleicher, ever anxious to prove to both country and army that all had been done to come to terms with the Nazis, proposed a series of negotiations: first, between the chancellor and the parties, and after their failure, between the president and the parties. The decision, he stated, rested solely with Hitler. Hitler, however, still asked for the chancellorship, and recent exchanges of Schleicher with Gregor Strasser had shown that none of the Fuehrer's lieutenants would challenge his stand. Thus there would be no working

[3] Announcement by *Gaupropagandaleitung* Schleswig-Holstein, Election Circular No. 3, Oct. 20, 1932, *Nazi Party Records*/164/302865; on German Nationals, Decker, in *Gesellschaft*, IX (1932), ii, p. 467.

majority in the new Reichstag, and once this was clearly established, it ought not even to meet. Most cabinet members agreed on the need for discussions since all legal paths must be explored before one resorted to suspending the constitution. Some concern was also expressed that unless the Nazis were given a share in the government, its younger element might switch to the Communists, a fear zealously encouraged just then by Goebbels and other Nazi writers and speakers.[4]

During the following days invitations went out to the party leaders for consultations. The outcome was wholly negative. The Social Democrats refused to call on the chancellor, the assailant of the Braun-Severing government. Triumphant over Hitler's electoral setback, they were certain that Papen rather than Hitler was now their major opponent. Since he had been defeated twice at the polls, he had forfeited the right to negotiate and ought to resign at once. Who was to take his place, they did not say; they contented themselves with attacking the chancellor, confident that whatever might happen, Hindenburg would not appoint Hitler.[5]

The Center was equally determined to force Papen out of the chancellery. Kaas and Joos warned the chancellor that the country was drifting into a revolutionary situation not unlike 1918. Kaas saw as the only solution a government based on a solid majority in the Reichstag. Given adequate safeguards, he thought that even a government headed by Hitler that enjoyed broad popular support was preferable to a presidential government led by the unpopular Papen. Unlike the Center the Bavarian People's Party was willing to support Papen, but since he could not find adequate backing, it too felt he ought to resign. Only the German Nationals and the German People's Party stood fully behind him.[6]

All depended of course on the attitude of the Nazis. Hitler, however, refused, as did his Socialist foes, to enter into direct negotiations with Papen. Still haunted by the memory of the ill-fated August 13, the Nazi chieftain did not want to see the hopes of his followers raised by new talks with the chancellor. They would be disappointed again, he asserted, since his demand for the chancellorship was certain to be rejected. On the other hand, he

[4] Cab. mtg., Nov. 9, 1932, *RKz.*/1711/791161–71; Goebbels, *Wetterleuchten*, articles of Nov. 7, 17, 1932, pp. 339, 344.

[5] *Sozialdemokratische Partei-Korrespondenz*, No. 10–12, Oct.-Dec. 1932, p. 520; Keil, *Erlebnisse*, II, 468–70, Stampfer, *Vierzehn Jahre*, p. 655; Schwertfeger, *Rätsel*, pp. 179–80.

[6] Papen, *Wahrheit*, pp. 239–41; excerpt of minutes of Papen-Center talk, Nov. 16, 1932, in *Z. f. GeschWiss.*, VI (1958), 544 n.6; Schwend, in Matthias and Morsey, *Ende der Parteien*, p. 475; Hugenberg, in I.M.T., *Trial*, XL, 575.

was unwilling, in spite of all setbacks, to accept a subordinate role in a Papen-led cabinet; with his party declining, the danger was now even greater that as second man in the government he would soon disappear into the background. Nor did he wish to be outmaneuvered once more in the war of communiqués as had happened on August 13. He demanded that all further discussions must be in writing and ought to be published. And with an eye on prospective readers (among them the president) he warned Papen that there could be no fruitful exchange of views unless he, Papen, were prepared to assume the responsibility for his actions. To blame the failure of the August 13 talks on the eighty-five year old president and thus drag him into this controversy was not only unfair, but also a violation of that sacred relationship between head of state and minister by which the latter protects his "sovereign" in all political matters.[7]

Having dutifully approached the parties, Papen reconvened his cabinet on November 17. He saw his next move clearly laid out: the government would have to resign, he advised his colleagues, since a government of "national concentration" could not be formed under him; though the president wished them to stay in office, they ought to relinquish their posts. The president must have a completely free hand when he tried now to gather all "national" forces. Should he fail and call them again, the cabinet ought to be ready, of course, to serve him once more.

The majority of the cabinet agreed with Papen. Its enemies, Schleicher argued, must not be given the chance to challenge the president's efforts as an insincere *"coup de théatre."* If the president should not succeed, the cabinet ought to be ready indeed for further service. In that case, he concluded, the president's mandate ought to state clearly that the government would have the right to resort to "ultimate measures."[8]

That same afternoon Papen submitted the cabinet's resignation to the president. Was it really worthwhile to talk to the party leaders, Hindenburg wondered; he was not willing to work with any but a presidential government. Papen explained that the attempt would have to be made, if for no other reason than to prove a parliamentary majority did not exist. Once this had been established, he pointed out, a new presidential cabinet could act with much greater authority.[9]

[7] Papen to Hitler, Nov. 13, 1932, Hitler to Papen, Nov. 16, 1932, *Jahrb. d. öff. Rechts*, XXI (1933–34), 163–66; Goebbels, *Vom Kaiserhof*, entries of Nov. 9, 12, 1932, pp. 199, 202.

[8] Cab. mtg., Nov. 17, 1932, *RKz.*/1711/791173–80.

[9] Papen, *Wahrheit*, p. 241.

Thus Hindenburg had to submit again to the ordeal of receiving the party leaders. Altogether five were invited: the heads of the German National Party, the Center, the German People's and the Bavarian People's Party, and above all, of course, Hitler. Since the Social Democrats had refused to see Papen, their refusal was used as a welcome excuse not to extend an invitation to them, and the Socialists would not ask for an audience to make their views known. Talks with the other bourgeois parties, reduced now to minuscule splinter groups, were bypassed as pointless. And the Communists, having their own unacceptable terms, had never been brought into any such consultations. To conduct such discussions had never been easy for Hindenburg, but it was now an almost impossible task. Meissner wrote down word for word the questions he must put to his callers and the statements he was to make after they had had their say. His final response was purposely vague: he could not say anything definite yet, but would first have to talk to the other party spokesmen and might then call them back either singly or jointly. Yet on two points the prepared answer was unequivocal: "At this time I limit myself to the statement that I shall under no circumstances turn over the government to the parties again, nor am I willing to appoint a government formed by the parties and dominated by them. I also am very anxious to keep intact the union of Reich and Prussia."

As expected, the talks produced no solutions. Again the party leaders could offer no constructive advice. Hugenberg, Kaas, Dingeldey, and Schäffer all agreed on the need to retain an authoritarian government and on the continued emasculation of the Reichstag; they also approved of a concentration of all "national forces" as the soundest foundation for such a government. All of them likewise agreed that the Nazis ought to be taken into the government, but except for Kaas, they had reservations about Hitler's appointment as chancellor. Hugenberg who had had the most painful experiences with Hitler had the strongest misgivings. "I have not found much willingness on Hitler's part to honor commitments," he warned, "his way of handling political matters would make it very difficult to entrust him with the political leadership, I would have the most serious objections." All of them conceded, however, that the choice of the chancellor was the prerogative of the president, and once he had made his decision, they would accept it. No one said so, but they all suggested implicitly that the day of the parties as shapers of policy belonged to the past.

Kaas' greater willingness to accept Hitler as chancellor stemmed from his fear that a Papen-led dictatorship without any popular backing would plunge the country into civil war. "We are facing a terrible winter," he warned the president, "twelve million Germans oppose the Government on the right and thirteen-and-a-half millions on the left. The goal of a national concentration including the National Socialists thus is a necessity." He urged the initiation of calm, thorough, and serious negotiations with them since the problems involved could not possibly be settled in hasty get-togethers; this was the general wish in all parts of the country, among farmers as well as in business circles. Nor should discussions be broken off just because of something said by one side or the other; such difficulties would have to be straightened out in talks of the party leaders. "The need for a positive result is so great that I would consider it a disaster if these negotiations were carried on merely as a formality and if they were broken off the moment the Nazis rejected them. . . . We shall support the President whenever demands are being made which he feels he cannot accept; but we also ask the President to make whatever concessions he can make without sacrificing basic convictions." If the negotiations should fail, the German people must be able to see that the responsibility did not lie with the leadership of the Reich.

The prelate suggested that Hindenburg choose a man he trusted to negotiate, preferably one who was not a candidate for the chancellorship. He believed that an agreement on the most pressing issues, something of an "agreement of faith" (*"Treue-Pakt"*), could be reached by three or four fearless party leaders. To issue emergency decrees and dissolve the Reichstag again was no longer enough to see the country through this winter; what was needed was a cabinet that derived its authority from the president, but was also supported, at least for a time, by a majority in the Reichstag.[10]

Behind Kaas' urgency lay also the haunting fear that the decline of the Nazis would redound to the Communists' benefit. The election returns that had given the Communist Party 100 seats in the Reichstag had come as a sharp shock to many. Isolated and without influential friends, the Communists presented much less of a threat than the Nazis, but their sweeping challenge of the existing order aroused apprehensions that allowed Nazism to appear as the lesser evil. The Nazis, moreover, skillfully nursed

10 Protocols of talks in *Z.f.GeschWiss.*, vi (1958), 545–50, 552–53; Papen, in cab. mtg., Nov. 17, 1932, *RKz.*/1711/791175.

these fears and somberly warned that their electoral setbacks were perhaps not a cause for rejoicing for their bourgeois opponents. Thus Goebbels wrote in his *Angriff:*

"We are entering a winter which lets us expect the worst and the very worst. Overnight the one hundred Bolsheviks in the Reichstag may double in number as a result of the economic depression and the limitless misery in which the majority of the German people finds itself. The hopeless desperation in which the masses are vegetating allows for even the most absurd possibility to come true. As a rule the responsible circles do not take our warnings very seriously; but if words carry no conviction, the facts are speaking an unmistakable language." [11]

Many leaders in banking and industry thought these warnings well founded. If they had been disenchanted with Hitler after the Brown Shirts' terroristic excesses and his talks with the Center that summer, the Communist gains on November 6 frightened them back into his camp. "Should we let the Nazis break their back," one of them summed up a widely held attitude, "and have the whole tide of the masses come flowing back on us? That would be the end!" "When on November 6," another business leader testified at the Nürnberg Trials, "the National Socialist Party suffered its first setback and appeared to have passed its peak, its support by Germany's heavy industry became a matter of special urgency." The *Deutscher Volkswirt,* widely read in banking and industrial circles, warned that any attempt to channel the Nazi movement into normal governmental procedures was bound to end in disaster, "not because of its program, which is nonexistent, but because of its specific spiritual and moral structure." What kind of a chancellor would a man be, the journal asked, who staked his personal honor on the fate of the Potempa murderers and who had recently saved two bomb throwers from the penitentiary by appointing them deputies in the Reichstag? (Two Nazi deputies had been asked to resign to make room for these convicts.) There could be no understanding with someone who defied the most elementary moral commands, whatever his pledges to act legally. Such warnings, however, were disregarded. Businessmen saw no reason why they should shun Hitler since the government was dealing with him and a churchman like Kaas was willing to work with him. Terrified at the prospect of a Bolshevized Germany, or even a Socialist one, they renewed their demand that Hitler be given the chancellorship.

[11] Editorial of Nov. 17, 1932, *Wetterleuchten,* p. 344.

One of Hitler's business advisers, Wilhelm Keppler, took matters in hand. With the help of Dr. Hjalmar Schacht, the former Reichsbank president, and a prominent Rhenish banker, Baron von Schröder, he initiated a concerted effort to prevail upon Hindenburg that he drop his objections. A letter was drafted, and some fifty prominent industrialists, bankers, shipowners, and agrarians were asked to sign copies which would be presented to the president. Hitler's appointment, the letter asserted, would help stabilize conditions, for "we recognize in the national movement . . . the promise of a new era. By ending the class struggle it is going to create the indispensable foundation for a new rise of the German economy." It added helpfully that Hitler's appointment would also eliminate "those flaws and blemishes which attach inevitably to any mass movement" and would have an inspiring effect on the millions of people who still stood aside. Although a number who were approached declined to sign, the final list was impressive, including many prominent Germans in business and agriculture. A few leading industrialists who had been invited did not sign, but stated that they approved the petition. The letters were handed to Meissner on the very day Hindenburg was to see Hitler.[12]

Marshal and Fuehrer met on the morning of November 19. Hitler's arrival was carefully staged; thousands of Nazis, hurriedly drummed together by Goebbels, hailed him with thunderous cheers as he drove the short distance from the "Kaiserhof" to the president's office. But if Hindenburg heard this rousing reception, he was not impressed with it. His mind was made up and in spite of the wishes of others, he would not appoint Hitler to head a presidential cabinet as the man of his special confidence.

At Hitler's request Hindenburg received him first by himself. To forego the protective presence of Meissner must have placed an additional strain on the marshal, but he was anxious to be as accommodating as possible. Hitler on his part, however, was disappointed if he hoped to be more persuasive in the absence of

12 Thyssen, in Rauschning, Men of Chaos, p. 221; Schröder, in Georges Castellan, "Von Schleicher, von Papen et l'avènement de Hitler," Cahiers d'histoire de la guerre, I (1949), 34–35; Stolper, in Dt. Volkswirt, Nov. 25, 1932, p. 228; a list of signers printed in Z.f.GeschWiss., IV (1956), 366–69; Schröder, in George W. F. Hallgarten, Hitler, Reichswehr und Industrie: Zur Geschichte der Jahre 1918–1933 (Frankfurt/M., 1955), p. 116. See also Meissner, Staatssekretär, p. 264. Papen who was consulted approved of the petition, made some suggestions as to how it could best be presented, and, according to one caller, seemed not averse to the idea of a cabinet which Hitler would head and in which he, in order to reassure Hindenburg, would assume the vice-chancellorship. Keppler to Schröder, Nov. 13, 1932, Records of Private Enterprises/101/3476741–42.

Meissner. In accordance with his prepared text, Hindenburg praised the national pride and idealism that Hitler had been arousing, but then he seems to have drifted off this subject, as Hitler later recalled it. Complaining about the offensive behavior of Nazi youngsters, Hindenburg brought up a haunting experience on the Tannenberg battlefield when they had shouted at him, "Awake, awake!" "Well, I am not asleep!" he grumbled. Hitler assured him that he had misunderstood or been misinformed. What he had heard was "Germany, awake!," the Nazis' famed battle cry, and no one had meant to offend him. The talk ended inconclusively; as the minutes record, it turned "essentially" on a restatement of their respective positions.

When Meissner joined them, they reiterated their views. Hindenburg urged Hitler once more to join a nonpartisan cabinet in which a number of portfolios would be assigned to him, while Hitler insisted that he could join a cabinet only if he were placed at its head. "I do not plan to fill all ministerial posts with National Socialists," he assured the president, "but the political leadership must be in one hand, for I am risking not only my own name, but also my movement." And playing on the widespread fear of a Communist threat, he gravely cautioned the marshal: "If this movement perishes, Germany would be in the greatest danger, for she would then be faced with 18 million Marxists, among them perhaps 14 to 15 million Communists. In the interest of the Fatherland my movement must be preserved, and this means that I must have the leadership." A nonparty government, backed by the state's power, might be able to govern for a little while longer, "but this would not last long; by February a new revolution would break out, and Germany would cease to be a power factor in world politics."

If the Nazis were the bitter enemies of the Communists, why, then, Hindenburg wanted to know, had they participated in the Berlin transportation strike? "People are very bittter," Hitler explained, seizing this opening to drive home his point: "If I had tried to restrain my people, the strike would have taken place nonetheless, but I would have lost my following among the workers; this would not have been in Germany's interest." And once more he warned that his appointment alone could shield the country against its Bolshevization.

But if politicians and businessmen could be impressed with this argument, Hindenburg could not. His distrust of Hitler was undiminished. Still, since Nazism was a "national movement," it was important to win him over. Hindenburg now tried that personal approach which had been effective so often before: "I can only repeat my request: Give me your help. I do appreciate the great idea which inspires you and your movement, and I would like to see you and your movement join the Government. I don't doubt the sincerity of your intentions, but I cannot accept a party government."

Would Hitler get in touch with the other parties? Not unless he received the mandate of forming a government; the decision was up to the president. But if he received such a mandate, he thought he could reach an agreement about a program and the personal makeup of the cabinet. His government would also be able to obtain an enabling act from the Reichstag to take what measures were needed. No one but he, he was certain, would get such an enabling act. It would solve all difficulties.

Even the prospect of having to sign no further decrees failed to sway Hindenburg: he would think about all these questions, and then they would talk about them again. Once more he appealed to Hitler's soldierly sense of duty, and for a moment he even forgot the deep chasm separating marshal and private first-class and spoke of the "old comradeship-in-arms which brought us together in the war. Meet me half-way in this matter so that we can work together."[13]

Two days later he saw the Nazi leader once more. Neither the warnings of Hitler nor the pleas for the latter's appointment which kept pouring into his office had changed his mind. Nor was Hitler willing to make any concessions. Hindenburg restated his views: since Hitler was a party leader, he could not head a presidential cabinet which could be led only by someone who was not affiliated with any party and enjoyed his special confidence. He therefore asked Hitler to ascertain within the next three days whether he would be able to secure a parliamentary majority which would support a government of which he would be the chancellor.

The pressures to which Hindenburg was being subjected thus had not been entirely without effect. While in August he had refused to appoint Hitler chancellor even if Nazis and Center should form a majority government, he now suggested that Hitler find out whether he could find a majority which would support him as chancellor. What induced him to change his mind is not

13 Goebbels, *Vom Kaiserhof*, entry of Nov. 19, 1932, pp. 205–06; Meissner and Wilde, *Machtergreifung*, p. 113; Hindenburg-Hitler talk, Nov. 19, 1932, *Z.f.Gesch-Wiss.*, VI (1958), 550–51, 557; Harry Picker, *Hitlers Tischgespräche in Führer-Hauptquartier, 1941–1944* (Munich, 1951), p. 410.

certain; he appears to have bowed to the argument, now constantly heard, that it was "undemocratic" to withhold the chancellorship from the head of the largest party. With its unspoken charges of unconstitutionality, the argument may have impressed him even though it was specious and insincere. To bar the professed foe of democracy from gaining power was clearly not undemocratic, nor had those who claimed that it was ever voiced that concern in the case of the Social Democrats. But given the trend of events, Hindenburg was no longer willing to defy the popular will in the unlikely case that Hitler should find a majority in the Reichstag.

To establish their respective positions beyond doubt and misrepresentation, Hitler and Hindenburg exchanged prepared memoranda. Hindenburg's was merely a summary of his views, but Hitler's, with an eye on public opinion, somberly warned that the alternative to an ineffective use of "his" movement was "Bolshevik chaos." It wondered also whether the president was not returning to the old parliamentary methods—a course of which the people should be informed and against which he, Hitler, could only warn.

While he saw little chance of forming a coalition, Hitler now asked about the conditions a majority government would have to fulfill. He was handed a statement stipulating the president's terms: All parties concerned would have to agree on an economic program (to preclude any socialist ventures); the old dualism between Reich and Prussia must not be restored, nor were any of the other states to be granted any special concessions in case of a Reich reform; Hindenburg would retain his emergency powers under Article 48. As for the personal makeup of the new cabinet, he reserved the right of approving all ministers, and he would select himself the foreign and Reichswehr ministers, in accordance with his constitutional rights as the international representative of the Reich and the commander-in-chief of the army.

Hitler promised to give a written reply that same afternoon. Again, Hindenburg made a determined effort to end this discussion on a friendly note. "How this entire matter and the negotiations will end, only God knows," he observed, "we don't know. But I want to stress one thing: however our talks may end, my door will always be open to you."[14]

There followed over the next three days an exchange of letters

14 Meissner, *Staatssekretär*, p. 264; minutes of Hindenburg-Hitler talk, Nov. 21, 1932, Schleicher Papers/25/27–33; Goebbels, *Vom Kaiserhof*, entry of Nov. 20, 1932, pp. 206–07; Heiden, *Fuehrer*, pp. 497–98.

between Hitler and Meissner in which both sides justified once more their respective positions. Meissner again stressed the fact that the president had no confidence in Hitler's nonpartisanship and feared that a presidential cabinet led by him would turn into a party dictatorship. When Hitler, in reply, pointed out that Brüning too had been a party leader and yet had been permitted to head a presidential cabinet, the answer was that Brüning had first formed a parliamentary government and had become the head of a presidential government only after he had earned the full confidence of the president. Once Hitler had gained Hindenburg's confidence, Meissner suggested, he too might be entrusted with the leadership of a presidential government, but he made clear that this day was not yet.

In a lengthy answer Hitler rejected the president's terms as unrealistic and unconstitutional and once more asked for a formal mandate to form a new government. Once he had such a mandate, he promised quick action and speedy solutions. Within 48 hours he would submit a short program outlining the domestic and foreign measures he intended to take. After the president had approved it, he would within 24 hours present a cabinet list; included in it would be Schleicher as Reichswehr minister and Neurath as foreign minister; several others of the present cabinet members would also be slated for reappointment. As chancellor he would act in accordance with the constitution; all he was asking was to be given those special powers which even parliamentary chancellors had held in times of crisis. "I promise," the letter ended, "that I shall sacrifice myself for the rescue of our Fatherland. To that end I myself as well as my movement shall make every possible effort."

But Hindenburg remained unconvinced. He could not, Meissner wrote back, assume the responsibility for giving *plein pouvoir* to the head of a party which kept stressing its totalitarian ambitions and had opposed not only him personally but also the political and economic measures he had thought necessary. "Under these circumstances," Meissner concluded, "the President must fear that a Presidential cabinet led by you would turn into a party dictatorship and the divisions splitting the German people would become even deeper. He would not wish to burden his oath and his conscience with the responsibility for such a crisis."

Hitler had the last word: in a final letter he denied all responsibility for the failure of the discussions. The present cabinet was no constructive force, he repeated, and he would never put the movement he had built at the disposal of any but the interests of the German people. He insisted that he too had a conscience and responsibilities: "I feel responsible to my consicence, to the honor of the movement led by me and to the millions of Germans who have been plunged into growing misery by the political experiments of the last few months."[15]

༄

While Hindenburg was engaged in his talks with the party leaders, Schleicher was also trying his hand at solving the crisis. The general was far more concerned about the existing impasse than was Papen. What haunted him was as always the perils he saw looming ahead for the army. Without a substantial popular following the government was compelled to lean on the Reichswehr to redress the sagging balance of power. The danger was growing that it would have to call on the army to uphold its authority, and the army was almost certain to be drawn into the political struggle should the Reichstag be closed and new elections postponed. While Schleicher had pledged the Reichswehr's support in that case, he was still hopeful he might spare it this odious task.

Casting about for a solution, Schleicher had started to toy with the thought of taking over the chancellorship himself. It was not a prospect he found attractive—he would have preferred to stay in the wings. But Papen, given his lack of support, was unlikely to steer clear of a forcible showdown. Schleicher, however, had many contacts, and in circles that were hostile to Papen. Center and unions, which hated Papen, might be prepared to accept him as chancellor, and even Hitler, still fuming at Papen for the ignominy of August 13, might be willing to work with the general.

All depended of course on Hitler's reaction, and he would have to be sounded out first. In earlier days Schleicher would at once have approached him and would have told Hindenburg afterwards what he had done. But he no longer dared show such independence. The working relationship between him and the marshal had suffered from the day when he had urged him to make Hitler chancellor. Hindenburg had lost faith in his counsel, and Papen had taken his place as the closest adviser. Nor could Schleicher count Oskar von Hindenburg his friend any longer— their long-time association had ended abruptly when a caustic remark he had made about Oskar had promptly been reported

15 Meissner-Hitler correspondence, Nov. 21–24, 1932, *Jahrb. d.öff. Rechts,* xxi (1933–34), 168–73; Meissner and Wilde, *Machtergreifung,* p. 119.

to the president's son. Yet as Reichswehr minister, Schleicher still had access to the president and he managed to get Hindenburg's grudging permission for a talk of his own with the Nazi Fuehrer.

Once more the general was to discover that he had under-estimated Hitler's acuity. Determined to become chancellor him-self, Hitler had no greater interest in a Schleicher-led government than in one led by Papen or anyone else, and neither the pleas of his restive lieutenants nor the increasing defections of his rank-and-file followers could shake his resolve. He told Schleicher at once that he would oppose him as chancellor and would have to insist on new Reichstag elections.

Hitler's hostility was compounded by Hindenburg's disappro-bation. When Schleicher reported back to the president, he was sharply rebuked for having brought up "prematurely" the ques-tion of his own chancellorship. Still anxious to reappoint Papen, Hindenburg felt himself being pushed into decisions that he was not prepared to make.

If Hindenburg considered a Schleicher-led cabinet a very re-mote possibility, Meissner apparently did not. He worked closely with Schleicher throughout these days, sent him the minutes of Hindenburg's talks with the party leaders, and let him read and revise the letters he was writing to Hitler in Hindenburg's name. Schleicher, in turn, seems to have helped to guide the president's moves with Meissner's assistance. On the day after Schleicher had talked to Hitler, Hindenburg called Kaas back to inquire whether the prelate still saw any way of concluding that "agree-ment of faith" he had proposed on his earlier visit. The invitation, so contrary to the marshal's real intentions, bears clearly the imprint of the general's direct or indirect influence. Schleicher had always insisted on exhausting the last legal chance, no matter how hopeless, before resorting to force, and the invitation to Kaas was just such a futile last attempt. Kaas could also be trusted to warn once again against the reappointment of Papen.[16]

Kaas thought that the matter had never been fully explored, but after one day of intensive soundings, he had to admit defeat. Dingeldey and Schäffer were willing to help, he reported, while Hugenberg still opposed a majority government. Hitler had pro-fessed to approve of Kaas' plan in principle, but had withheld his support on the grounds that any arrangement between them

16 Holtzendorff affidavit, Oct. 22, 1946, ZS./248; Bussche-Ippenburg to Hammer-stein, 1953, in *Frankfurter Hefte*, XI (1956), 119; Schleicher, in cab. mtg., Nov. 25, 1932, *RKz./1711/791208–09*; Vogelsang, "Schleicher und NSDAP," *Vierteljahrshefte*, VI (1958), 104–05; Meissner testimony, I.M.T., Case No. 11, transcript, p. 4477.

would be ignored in "influential places." Kaas complained with some bitterness that his task had been rendered more difficult by ill-advised statements of high officials suggesting that the president's mandate to him had not been meant seriously. Worst of all, someone else (obviously Schleicher) had been trying at the same time to find a basis for a new presidential cabinet. This working at cross-purposes had greatly impaired the success of his consultations.

Hindenburg wanted to know what he ought to do now. Whatever he did, Kaas replied, he ought not to reappoint Papen. His reappointment could cause serious trouble. A presidential government under a different chancellor might have a chance; it would be considered as something new, important from a psychological viewpoint. It ought to be formed completely anew and should be more representative of the people. Such a cabinet, he believed, might open up new possibilities for the future.

But Hindenburg clung to Papen. What actually was the Center's objection to him? Papen did not know enough about financial and economic problems, Kaas answered evasively, but not untruthfully, since the recent wage cuts had caused more bitterness among the mass of the people than any other of his emergency measures. Here Kaas was treading on dangerous ground. Hindenburg had come to identify himself so closely with Papen's program that he took Kaas' criticism to be directed at him as well. He wanted to know if he himself perhaps was an obstacle to a solution of the present crisis: "I am ready to leave any time, if I don't have the confidence at home or abroad which I must have. I don't want to force myself on the country; for this I am too proud."

Greatly perturbed by this outburst, Kaas hastened to reassure him: "I can understand the President's bitterness. But I am speaking from deepest conviction when I say: On the day on which you, *Herr Präsident*, leave us, the last hope for unity and collaboration would be gone. If there is something which stands above parties and keeps us united, it is your personality. I implore you in deepest respect, do not let this thought cross the threshold of this house." Yet Hindenburg was not satisfied, "In one hand they show me a carrot," he growled, "in the other a stick."

The talk turned to the question of the Center's support of another presidential cabinet. But again Kaas was evasive; he knew what he did *not* want, but was vague as to what he *did* want. The most important step was to form a new government—Center and other parties would then reexamine their attitude. It need not necessarily have a majority in the Reichstag, but must have wider support in the country than Papen. Perhaps it could get the Reichstag to adjourn for a while; one might thus get through the present crisis without a showdown. But Hindenburg, unimpressed, wished to hold on to Papen. "I am getting into an ever more difficult position," he complained, "They want to take away the man in whom I have confidence and force another Chancellor upon me." Once more Kaas assured him that it was the president's prerogative to choose the chancellor, leaving the president even more bewildered and lonely.[17]

While Kaas was having his talk with the president, the cabinet met in the chancellery to consider the situation. Schleicher reported on his talk with Hitler. His participation, he concluded, would have added real strength to the government; no one else could provide it. Another chancellor, someone so far uncommitted, might at first enjoy some support, but would not retain it for long. The Center wanted someone acceptable to all parties from the German Nationals to the Social Democrats. Naturally there was no such person. He thought that nothing was to be gained by a change of chancellors. Eltz and Gürtner agreed with him.

Others, however, felt distinctly uneasy at the prospect of seeing Papen remain in office. Baron von Braun who had been opposed all along to his reappointment wondered whether it might not drive 20 to 30 thousand stormtroopers into the streets in Berlin; he was also concerned about touching off a general strike. Schwerin-Krosigk foresaw trouble with the younger elements in the "national" camp who were sharply opposed to the cabinet; the government might have to call out the army against them. Others voiced similar concerns, but Schleicher tried to allay their misgivings. Since Hindenburg was determined not to give Hitler the chancellorship, there was nothing for the government to do but consider all contingencies and then take appropriate action. Papen, he repeated, ought to remain chancellor. He ruled himself out on the grounds that the chancellor ought not to be the Reichswehr minister too. Should a state of emergency be proclaimed, public attention would inevitably turn to the Reichswehr minister as the one who controlled all executive powers and the chancellor would cease to be in the firing line. This would ease the pressure on Papen which he agreed had been heavy.

Schleicher also had some reassuring words on the stand of the Reichswehr: it could be relied upon in every respect and had

17 Hindenburg-Kaas talks, Nov. 24-25, 1932, *Z.f.GeschWiss.*, VI (1958), 553-56.

lost its enthusiasm for Hitler. As for its technical readiness, all questions concerning a state of military emergency were being threshed out once more at the Reichswehr ministry. No one need worry that anything could go wrong. There was no need even for reenforcing the Reichswehr with other formations;[18] they would not improve the apparatus.

Papen, reluctant to plead his own case, had remained silent throughout the discussion. Now, at the end, he spoke up. The president, he stated once more, would not appoint Hitler as head of a presidential cabinet. But if Hindenburg were to recall the cabinet, he would doubtless insist on certain conditions. The cabinet would have to work even harder at providing work and bread, especially if the Reichstag were closed. During a state of emergency he would consider himself more than ever the guardian of the constitution and would not permit any constitutional reforms—a pledge that pleased Schleicher and others who wished to spare the cabinet the additional burden of constitutional changes that lacked popular backing. Papen concluded that he thought it the cabinet's duty to serve again should the president call on it, a sentiment to which no one objected.[19]

Several days passed, however, and no such call came. As much as Hindenburg wished to reappoint Papen, the widespread opposition to him had not failed to impress him. While still unwilling to part with "his" chancellor, he decided to delay his decision. Exploring alternatives, Meissner suggested Goerdeler. Goerdeler's name was also brought up by a German National emissary who submitted a ready-made cabinet list, headed by the lord mayor of Leipzig, with Brüning as foreign minister, Hugenberg in charge of the economics portfolios in both the Reich and Prussia, and trusted conservatives in control of interior and the Reichswehr. Hindenburg was not interested, but Brüning's name, mentioned already by Kaas, struck a responsive chord. His counsel might indeed be of help. To receive him officially, however, might lead to new controversies, and so Meissner called quietly on the former chancellor. But Hindenburg found Brüning's advice no more to his liking: he too was convinced that

---

[18] In the minutes Schleicher is quoted as speaking of the possible use of "formations of the s.a.," but this must obviously be a mistake since a military emergency, if it were proclaimed, would be directed primarily against the s.a. Schleicher undoubtedly spoke (or meant to speak) of the *Stahlhelm* which supported the Papen government. See also *Stahlhelm* memorandum of Sept. 16, 1932, on collaboration between *Stahlhelm* and Reichswehr, *Nazi Party Records*/1/11349–51.

[19] Cab. mtg., Nov. 25, 1932, *RKz.*/1711/791208–17; Braun, *Von Ostpreussen*, p. 256; Meissner and Wilde, *Machtergreifung*, p. 107.

Papen could not master the crisis; Schleicher must take his place as head of a coalition extending from the Social Democrats to the moderate right.

Though Meissner agreed, Hindenburg could not bring himself to accept this solution. Would Hitler perhaps heed a final appeal to soldierly duty and enter a Papen-led government? Once more he asked him to call on him, but Hitler, knowing that Hindenburg's rather than his terms were the order of business, curtly declined the marshal's request. He could do so the more confidently as the recurrent pleas for his collaboration convinced him of the weakness of his opponents' position and strengthened his faith that victory would soon be his.[20]

On the evening of December 1, Hindenburg met with Papen and Schleicher. Two weeks had passed since the cabinet's resignation, and a decision had to be reached since the new Reichstag was scheduled to meet on December 6. As always, when he was faced with a crisis, the president was listless and tired. The exact course of the meeting is hard to trace since the two existing accounts, Meissner's official protocol and Papen's recollections, conflict on essential points. Of the two, Papen's record seems more reliable than the contemporary one; while his report is not free from inaccuracies, Meissner's is blurred and incongruous.

Hindenburg first turned to Papen and asked for his views. The chancellor summed up the problems that had arisen over Hitler's failure to enter his cabinet or form a majority coalition. Under the circumstances a change of government was neither possible nor desirable, and he proposed that his cabinet be reappointed. The Reichstag probably would not support it; in that case the parliament would have to be suspended for a short time. This, he granted, would constitute a breach of the constitution, but the gravity of the situation would justify it. Papen assured Hindenburg that he knew how the president felt about the sacredness of his oath, but Bismark too had advised King William I of Prussia to ignore the constitution when he was battling the Prussian House of Delegates. He would not impose any constitutional changes on the country; such proposals would be submitted to a referendum or a newly elected national assembly. And once the proposed reform had been accepted, all legislative functions would revert at once to the parliament.[21]

20 Meissner, *Staatssekretär*, p. 247; Meissner and Wilde, *Machtergreifung*, p. 120; Brüning, "Ein Brief," p. 14; Schmidt-Hannover, *Umdenken*, pp. 315–16; Rumbold to Simon, Dec. 7, 1932, *DBFP.*, ii,IV, 94–97; Hitler to Meissner, Nov. 30, 1932, copy in Schleicher Papers/25/83.

21 Meissner memorandum, Dec. 2, 1932, on conferences with Hindenburg, Dec. 1

After Papen had concluded, Schleicher spoke. The general had been living through trying days since he last had met with the chancellor. The Reichwehr's preparedness of which he had spoken so confidently at the cabinet meeting had meanwhile been found to be sadly inadequate. At the suggestion of one of his staff members, Lieutenant Colonel Ott, a war game had been arranged at the ministry on November 25–26 to test the army's ability to cope with a general strike and/or armed risings. The results were disheartening. In the event of Nazi-Communist collaboration, an obvious possibility since the recent transportation strike in Berlin, the Reichswehr, it was discovered, would be unable to discharge all its tasks. Local forces, moreover, such as a specially organized Technical Emergency Service (*Technische Nothilfe*), police, and home guard units, were believed so demoralized and infiltrated by Nazis that they could not be counted on in a showdown with Hitler. And there was that ever dreaded danger of a Polish move against East Prussia whose defense the Nazis could easily block. Consultations with field commanders had confirmed the conclusion that the crisis ought to be solved without involving the army.

Confronted with Ott's report, Schleicher decided that the reappointment of Papen was out of the question. Yet surprisingly he failed to notify both Papen and Hindenburg of his conclusion. Why Schleicher kept his own counsel we can only guess: he may have been playing for time hoping meanwhile to find another solution. He spent the last days of November in a depserate search for such an alternative. Doubtless he was also reluctant to admit to the president that the Reichswehr was no longer able to safeguard domestic order. Knowing the marshal's aversion to forcible measures, he may have believed that once he had found a way out that would be both legal and nonviolent, Hindenburg, in his relief, would be inclined to take a less serious view of the army's shortcomings. And by keeping the news from the chancellor, he most likely thought he could outmaneuver Papen more quickly.

For a solution the general turned to a plan widely discussed for some time and in which he himself had taken a growing interest—a Nazi-Center-labor coalition. Since August he had explored such a possibility in informal talks with Gregor Strasser who as head of the Nazi Party bureaucracy was in close touch with

and 2, 1932, in *Vierteljahrshefte*, vi (1958), 105–07; Papen, *Wahrheit*, pp. 243–50; Meissner and Wilde, *Machtergreifung*, pp. 121–30; Ott, in I.M.T., Case No. 11, transcript, 10178.

the rank-and-file and was convinced that the party must enter the government if it was to retain its followers. Schleicher had also maintained his contacts with Center, labor unions, and *Reichsbanner* in the hope of eventually creating a front from the Nazis to the Socialists that would back a government willing to introduce comprehensive social reforms and vast public works projects. The *Tat* which had urged such a plan for some time hailed it as an auspicious fusion of the "spiritual Prussianism" of army and unions against the materialist trinity of large land-owners, heavy industry, and bank capital. To a nation by now overwhelmingly anticapitalist, the joining of soldiers and workers was expected to have a special appeal.[22]

Under the pressure of the deepening crisis, Schleicher had intensified his soundings, and the results were encouraging. He was given to understand that Gregor Strasser had stayed with Hitler out of loyalty only, but was now ready to go his own way if Hitler's demand for the chancellorship should again be rejected. Talks with two Socialist union spokesmen, Theodor Leipart and Wilhelm Eggert, suggested that an understanding with these groups could be reached, and a talk with a Catholic union leader, Bernard Otte, seemed promising too. Only Breitscheid, the Social Democratic chieftain, declined his approaches, but Schleicher, recalling the Socialists' passive acceptance of the Prussian coup, saw no cause for concern in their attitude. He was also in touch with Günther Gereke, the originator of a public works program that had been presented to Hindenburg. A close friend of Oskar von Hindenburg, Gereke had been able to interest both father and son in his plans, and Hindenburg's recent demands for more active efforts to fight unemployment had been partly inspired by Gereke's program. Thus, though he had no commitment from anyone, Schleicher was hopeful he could forge these groups into a working alliance. They would provide a majority in the Reichstag for any government willing to make their hopes its concern.[23]

Nevertheless when Hindenburg's call came, the general was still in the midst of his preparations. Worst of all, he had not yet found the right man to head the new government, for he himself preferred to stay in the background. Frantically searching for an available candidate, he had approached Schacht, Bracht,

[22] Meissner and Wilde, *Machtergreifung*, p 93; Bracher, *Auflösung*, p. 623; Vogelsang, *Reichswehr*, pp. 267–69; Zehrer, in *Tat*, XXII (1930), 510–11, XXIV (1932), 118–20; 386–93, 447–49, 630–34; Schwerin-Krosigk, *Es geschah*, p. 120.

[23] On Schleicher talks, Schulthess, Nov. 30, 1932, p. 214; Hoegner, *Aussenseiter*, p. 73; *Sozialdemokratische Partei-Korrespondenz*, No. 1, Jan.-Feb. 1933, p. 11; Schleicher, in cab. mtg., Nov. 18, 1932, *RKz.*/1711/791197–98.

a member of the new Prussian government, and even Meissner, but all declined his invitation. He had also that same day dispatched Colonel Ott to Hitler, hoping that Hitler might finally be willing to enter a government with Schleicher as chancellor. Restlessness was increasing among Hitler's lieutenants; Frick, the head of the Nazi Reichstag delegation, he had learned, was siding with Strasser, and Göring too seemed to be wavering since it was he who suggested that the general get in touch with the Fuehrer.[24]

These were all assumptions, however, and some of Schleicher's uncertainty showed in his words when his turn came to speak to the president. His customary aplomb was lacking; in contrast to his usual self-confidence he spoke of hopes rather than certainties. He saw a "possibility" to spare the marshal the need of violating his oath, he "thought" that the Nazis might change their mind; his "plan" was to find with their help a majority including all bourgeois parties as well as the Socialists. This majority would support a government headed by him with Strasser and some of his men joining him. There was, however, no mention of the inability of the army to back Papen's plan.

Papen doubted that the Nazi Party, sworn to allegiance to Hitler personally, could be as easily split as Schleicher assumed. His main objection, however, was that Schleicher proposed a return to the old parliamentary methods that the president wished to abandon. A parliamentary majority would never permit the basic reforms they had been asked to effect. Schleicher's plan might provide some temporary relief, but in the long run its value was dubious.

There followed a brief discussion of the merits of the two plans. Schleicher, unable to be more specific, proposed that no decision be made until developments in the Nazi camp had been clarified. But Hindenburg, completely exhausted by then, did not wish to wait any longer; his mind was made up to accept Papen's plan which he preferred in any event. Rising to indicate that the meeting was ended, he asked Papen to form a new government prepared to discharge the tasks he had outlined. Schleicher, taken aback, kept silent; military discipline precluded in any event that he reply after the marshal had closed the discussion. But silence did not mean submission. When Papen tried to enlist his assist-

---

[24] Hjalmar H. G. Schacht, *Confessions of the old Wizard: The Autobiography of Hjalmar Horace Greeley Schacht* (Cambridge, 1956), p. 273; Meissner and Wilde, *Machtergreifung*, pp. 120–21; Carlowitz, *ZS./218*; Holtzendorff, *ZS./248*; Goebbels, *Vom Kaiserhof*, entries of Nov. 27-Dec. 1, 1932, pp. 211–14.

ance after the meeting broke up, the general hurriedly went on his way, warning him curtly that he was headed for trouble.

On his return home Schleicher received a call from Ott. The colonel reported that his mission had failed. Hitler who had monopolized the three-hour long conversation had rejected all collaboration with a Schleicher-led government. When Ott left, Göring had caught up with him. He might be able to change Hitler's mind, he suggested, if he, Göring, were appointed Prussian minister-president and Reich minister of aviation. All restrictions on Nazi activities would moreover have to be lifted, he reiterated his July request, and stormtroopers must have full freedom to fight the "Marxists." (Goebbels in his diary called this a demand for "clear streets" [Strasse frei] and the right to self-defense.) Ott could only reply that the Reichswehr would never abet such plans of unrestrained terror.[25]

Caught between Hitler's unyielding opposition and Hindenburg's willingness to risk a showdown, Schleicher once more weighed the dangers of an armed conflict. To have full clarity on the army's stand, he himself now called the commanders of the seven army districts. He told them of Hindenburg's decision and inquired once more about the prospects of coping with unrest and strikes in case of a state of emergency. All seven generals advised against such a step and maintained that their forces were not adequate to meet all emergencies. There was nothing to do now but to inform the president of the dangers entailed in the reappointment of Papen.

Papen was not idle that evening either. Alarmed by Schleicher's hostility, he called to the chancellery the two cabinet members to whom he felt closest—Gürtner and Eltz. Both were ready to assist him in his new task, and they agreed that the course he proposed was justified by the existing emergency. But Schleicher, they added, had been warning most cabinet members that Papen's reappointment would mean civil war. The Reichswehr would be faced with a task which was not its job and which it could not fulfill. In view of Schleicher's apprehensions, the two men doubted that Papen could count on the solid support of the cabinet.[26]

Through Schwerin-Krosigk, who shared Schleicher's misgivings, the chancellor had known of the opposition existing in the

[25] Meissner memorandum, Dec. 2, 1932, *Vierteljahrshefte*, VI (1958), 105–07; Ott, affidavit of Jan. 12, 1949 (copy), ZS./259; Goebbels, *Vom Kaiserhof*, entry of Dec. 1, 1932, p. 213.
[26] Papen, *Wahrheit*, p. 246.

cabinet against his remaining in office. Wishing for clarity, he decided to confront his opponents and despite the late hour summoned a cabinet meeting on the following morning. There he learned that most of the ministers did indeed disapprove of his reappointment: Schleicher warned against any hasty decisions; Neurath opposed him outright; Krosigk refused to serve in a new Papen cabinet that was bound to arouse bitter hostility and thus impede the beginnings of economic recovery. Schleicher would have to become chancellor, Krosigk insisted, and except for Eltz-Rübenach, all ministers agreed with his views. Meissner doubted that Hindenburg would be willing to change his decision, but now Gürtner raised the question concerning the Reichwehr's ability to cope with all eventualities.

Ott was called in to report to the cabinet: he gave assurances that all possible preparations had been made to enforce a state of emergency. Discussing the war game, however, he pointed out that difficulties such as sabotage and passive resistance could not be resolved by force of arms; according to notes he had prepared for the meeting, he believed that in case of a general strike neither the Technical Emergency Service nor the police could guarantee the essential services, especially food supplies. There would also be the problem of countering the argument that police and army were being called out, not to maintain peace and order, but to defend the interests of a small upper class against the entire nation.

No one seems to have questioned Ott's pessimistic conclusions, perhaps because Schleicher explained that the point of the war game was to consider the worst possible contingency, not necessarily one that would actually materialize. Ott's report was most likely accepted, however, because most of the cabinet members were unwilling in any event to follow Papen.[27]

Papen closed the meeting without further discussion and hurried to Hindenburg. Even though his closest collaborators had abandoned him and the Reichswehr was clearly unwilling to follow his lead, he was not yet ready to give up. Whether from obstinacy or from loyalty to the president, he did not offer to return his mandate, but asked Hindenburg whether he still wished him to carry it out. In that case another Reichswehr minister would have to be appointed (apparently he had an available candidate in General von Stülpnagel who had earlier been the

[27] Ott's report, according to "Vortragsnotiz," Dec. 2, 1932, reprinted in Vogelsang, *Reichswehr*, pp. 484–85; see also *ibid.*, pp. 333–34 as against Papen, *Wahrheit*, pp. 247–49, and *Vierteljahrshefte*, II (1954), 427 n. 110.

choice of the German Nationals). He did not share Schleicher's fears, he explained, that a state of emergency would lead to a general strike and civil war, although there might be some local clashes. He was confident, however, that the great majority of the German people could be made to realize that he was only concerned with securing them bread and work and the restoration of a functioning democracy. He could be wrong, he conceded, and if the president did not wish to take the course he proposed, he ought to accept Schleicher's earlier suggestion and make the general chancellor.

If Hindenburg had been willing to side with Papen the day before, he was not the man to simply ignore the army's concern and the fear of domestic unrest. Much as he disliked parting with Papen, he felt that he had no choice. "You'll consider me a cad, my dear Papen," he said in a tired, tortured tone, "if I change my mind now. But I am too old to take now, at the end of my life, the responsibility for a civil war. We'll have to let Herr von Schleicher try his luck in God's name." Two tears rolled down his pale cheeks as he shook hands with Papen.

He went to great lengths to show Papen how much he regretted his departure. That same day he sent him his picture under which he had written the words of the old soldiers song: *"Ich hatt' einen Kameraden!"* And on the following day he wrote him a letter in which he expressed once more his personal sense of bereavement at seeing Papen leave office. "My trust in you and my respect for your person and for your work remain undiminished," he assured him, thanking him once more for his dedication and his readiness to assume responsibilities, for his selfless patriotism and his noble character. Always cool and detached, he had never found words of such warmth for any other departing chancellor.[28]

Shortly after Papen had left, Schleicher was called and Hindenburg asked him to form a new cabinet and carry out his proposed program. Schleicher was still reluctant to assume the chancellorship; again he would have preferred to stay in the background. "I am the last horse in your stable," he warned, "and ought to be kept in reserve." But Hindenburg insisted on his appointment—since Schleicher had forced him to part with Papen, he was the one to take Papen's place, and he was in any event the only available candidate. Should Schleicher refuse, he threatened, he himself would resign. As always, this ultimate weapon in his personal arsenal had the desired effect, and Schleicher accepted the mandate.

[28] Papen, *Wahrheit*, pp. 250–51; Meissner and Wilde, *Machtergeifung*, p. 129.

Nevertheless, Hindenburg was profoundly unhappy. Bitter over the loss of Papen, he had been even more shocked to discover that the army no longer stood fully behind him. Perhaps he remembered that earlier in the year his press aide Zechlin had warned him that he could not be certain the Reichswehr would fight the Nazis if ordered to do so. Was this not what had actually happened? He was furious to learn of Schleicher's consultations with the army commanders after he, Hindenburg, had accepted Papen's proposals. The generals' disapprobation seemed to him a political judgment, beyond the range of the military and impinging on his presidential prerogatives. To him its meaning was unmistakable: he had ordered the army to stand by and help Papen, and the army, in essence, had refused to obey that order. Even among soldiers his authority no longer seemed sacrosanct.[29]

His anger was the more bitter because, weary and helpless, he felt he had to submit to the army's decision. As its spokesman Schleicher, *persona non grata* already for other reasons, became the prime target of this resentment. Thus the general embarked on his chancellorship without that most essential prerequisite— the full support and confidence of the president. When Ott congratulated him on his appointment, the new chancellor, conscious of the precariousness of his position, answered with a wan smile: *"Morituri te salutant!"*[30]

[29] Zechlin, *Pressechef,* pp. 123–24; Holtzendorff, ZS./248; Papen, *Wahrheit,* p. 279; same, ZS./354; Braun, *Von Ostpreussen,* p. 258; Meissner and Wilde, *Machtergreifung,* pp. 129–30.
[30] *Ibid.,* p. 130.

CHAPTER 12

THE SCHLEICHER INTERLUDE

T the very moment that Schleicher was glumly pondering his political prospects, Hindenburg made a decision which, indeed, was to prove fatal to the new chancellor. If the president could no longer have Papen as chancellor, he wished to retain him at least as his personal adviser. With this confidant at his side, he would be able to protect himself against any further surprises of Schleicher's. Papen would see through Schleicher's maneuvers, he would keep the unpredictable general from surrendering to the political parties, and he would know what to think of any deals that Schleicher might make with the Nazis.

Hindenburg's decision came as a shock to the chancellor. He had wished Papen to leave Berlin and had offered him the ambassadorship to France to have him out of the way. Though he thought little of Papen's political talents, he knew his presence in Berlin, near the president, would render his own relations with Hindenburg even more difficult. As the news of Papen's new role became common knowledge, the authority of his office would be seriously weakened.

Outwardly, however, everything went well at first. In less than 24 hours Schleicher had formed his new cabinet, a record performance in the history of the Weimar Republic. With two exceptions he retained all of Papen's collaborators: Gayl, always opposed to his cautious tactics, departed and was succeeded by Bracht; and as a gesture of conciliation to labor, Labor Minister Schäffer was replaced by Friedrich Syrup, the president of the Reich Unemployment Insurance Office, who had more enlightened social and economic views than his predecessor. Gereke was put in charge of the government's public works program.

On other fronts too the clouds were beginning to lift. In the Reichstag, Schleicher could count on somewhat greater support than Papen: the moderate parties, including the Center, were willing to work with him; the German Nationals, though cooler to him than to Papen, also accepted him; and while nothing had changed on the left as yet, the outlook was not without promise. The Communists of course declared war on him right away, and the Socialists too turned against him. To them, he was still Papen's

397

accomplice in the coup against Prussia, a view they thought was borne out by his readiness to retain most of Papen's colleagues. Secure in their faith that the Nazi tide had been turned, they saw the need of the hour in a firm ideological stand. Yet whatever the views of the leaders, attitudes among Socialists were becoming more fluid.[1]

The unions in particular gave Schleicher a friendly reception. There were no specific commitments on anyone's part, but as the *Deutscher Volkswirt* expressed it, soundings seemed to create a different atmosphere, and this in itself was an achievement during this period of continuous tension. The *Volkswirt* confidently foresaw that "an election campaign under Schleicher would have a different flavor than under Papen. It would put any unconditional opposition more strongly in the wrong than under Papen and would render the Nazis' chances of success even more questionable."[2]

Ultimately Schleicher's future would of course turn on the attitude of the Nazis, and here the outlook seemed especially bright. Two days after he had been appointed, the Nazis suffered another sharp setback in Thuringia's communal elections. Schleicher reacted to it in characteristic manner. "Hitler's demand for the chancellorship is justified, according to the rules of the parliamentary game," he told one of his aides, "but if the President refuses to go along, this is his constitutional right which I cannot ignore." He would stay on until one of them would "come down with his price." He thought the moment propitious to resume his efforts for an understanding with Hitler after the Nazi defeat in Thuringia. But Hitler, sensing the chancellor's weakness, would not lower his terms, and for a while he even seems to have toyed with the thought of increasing them. Yet given the Thuringian debacle, he could not face another election and had to keep Schleicher from dissolving the Reichstag again. In return for an amnesty for political offenders and the repeal of Papen's most onerous economic decrees, he consented to support a motion for the Reichstag's adjournment.[3]

If Schleicher hesitated to challenge Hitler, his reluctance was reenforced by the fact that Strasser was unable to sway his Fuehrer. Immediately after the chancellor had formed his new cabinet, he

[1] *Sozialdemokratische Partei-Korrespondenz*, No. 1, Jan.-Feb. 1933, p. 11; Severing, *Lebensweg*, II, 376–77; Schiffrin, *Gesellschaft*, IX (1932), ii, 484; Hilferding, in *ibid*, x (1933), 3.

[2] *Dt. Volkswirt*, Dec. 2, 1932, p. 252; also Schleicher, in cab. mtg., Dec. 3, 1932, *RKz.*/1711/191245.

[3] Holtzendorff, *ZS.*/248; Goebbels, *Vom Kaiserhof*, entry of Dec. 6, 1932, p. 216.

and Strasser had met once again at the general's home. Goebbels claims in his diary that Schleicher offered Strasser the vice-chancellorship in his cabinet and the post of minister-president in Prussia, while Strasser in turn pledged himself to run on a separate ticket in the next Reichstag election. That Schleicher proposed such a deal is possible, but Strasser undoubtedly did not commit himself as Goebbels alleges. As critical as Strasser was of Hitler's intransigence, he lacked the toughness and independence to go his own way. Nor was Schleicher intent at this point on splitting the Nazi Party. Throughout these days Strasser, in agreement with Schleicher, kept looking for ways to bring the chancellor and Hitler together. Aware of the spreading despair in all ranks of the Nazi Party, he considered their collaboration essential for the movement's survival. At a meeting of party leaders on December 5, he pleaded with Hitler to take his advice, and Frick and a few others seconded him. But Hitler refused to listen to Strasser. The discussion was bitter and heated; Schleicher, Strasser warned, would dissolve the Reichstag if the Nazis would not support him, but Hitler, backed by Göring and Goebbels, would merely agree to a temporary adjournment. Two days later, on December 7, Hitler and Strasser confronted each other once more. Hitler charged his second-in-command with disloyalty and attempts to cheat him out of the chancellorship and the leadership of the party; Strasser retorted that he had always been loyal and was solely concerned with the interests of the party. On his return to his hotel, he sat down, deeply hurt and frustrated, and in a long letter warned Hitler again that his tactics were suicidal. In this mood of disgusted despair, he quite spontaneously, it would seem, resigned all his offices (though not his membership) in the Nazi Party. Having done so, he decided to forget his political troubles and took off with his family for the sunshine of Italy.

Had Strasser been ready to fight on (as he never was), he might have, with Schleicher's financial assistance, dealt Hitler a serious blow. With an empty party treasury, mutiny rampant among the Brown Shirts, and party officials longing for government jobs, Hitler was at that moment most vulnerable. But when Strasser vanished without a fight, his potential supporters felt helpless. Hitler grasped quickly, after the first shock had passed, that Strasser lacked the drive and ambition to build up a rival party. His confidence recovered, he rallied his lieutenants behind him by sentimental appeals and brutal threats, and through a radical overhauling of the party machinery gained still greater powers.

Strasser's following in the party was not alone in feeling itself

399

deserted. Schleicher, too, saw his best hopes collapse when Strasser simply withdrew. With his plans thus frustrated, all the chancellor could do was to play for time. But since Hitler was as anxious as he to avoid a showdown, Schleicher could weather the opening session of the new Reichstag without even having to make an appearance.[4]

The Reichstag had been convened on December 6, while the Strasser crisis was approaching its climax. The chairman was General Karl Litzmann, an 82-year old Nazi deputy, who had fought under Hindenburg in 1914. In his opening address Litzmann launched a furious attack on the president for having failed to appoint Hitler to the chancellorship. He gave vent to his indignation by casting aspersions on the marshal's military achievements; just 18 years before, Litzmann fulminated, his division had saved the day for the German forces in the battle of Lodz by a breakthrough on the Russian front: "Herr von Hindenburg became Field Marshal General as a result, and he admitted himself that he owed his marshal's baton to us, the Third Guards Infantry Division. Today," Litzmann warned bitterly, "more is at stake for him than just the marshal's baton. What is at stake is that history may not condemn him for having led our despairing people into the arms of the Bolsheviks although the savior was right at hand." The official protocol records strong applause by the Nazis and laughter among the Communists. No one apparently felt impelled to come to the marshal's defense, and the belated somewhat half-hearted protest of a German National deputy on the following day only served to underline the decline of Hindenburg's prestige.[5]

With similar disrespect, the Reichstag dealt with the first item on its agenda—a Nazi-sponsored bill to designate the president of the Supreme Court (*Reichsgericht*) as the deputy of the Reich president in case of the latter's incapacitation and as his interim successor in the event of his death. Even a year before, few deputies would have dared airing these contingencies as casually as was done now, nor would the parties have shown such nonchalance in

4 *Ibid.*, entries, of Dec. 5–12, 1932, pp. 215–24; Vogelsang, *Reichswehr*, pp. 340–42; Heiden, *Fuehrer*, pp. 504–08; Krebs, *Gestalten*, pp. 189–92; Schleicher, in cab. mtg., Dec. 7, 1932, *RKz.*/1711/791258.

5 Litzmann, Dec. 6, 1932, *Verhandlungen*, Vol. 455, p. 2; Freytagh-Loringhoven, Dec. 7, 1932, *ibid.*, pp. 26–27. During the election campaign one Nazi *Gauleiter* had gone even farther than Litzmann and had declared at a mass meeting: "Herr von Hindenburg, we have long lost our faith in you. Today we see in you the Field Marshal who lost the war." *Attacke*, supplement to *Isartal Zeitung*, Oct. 29, 1932, Nazi Party *Hauptarchiv*/837.

maneuvering for position as they now did to be ready for such an eventuality.

The Nazis did not officially explain their proposal, and some mystery surrounds the reasons behind it. The idea may not have been theirs originally but was possibly suggested to them by Schleicher. As Count Schwerin von Krosigk confided to the British ambassador, the chancellor proposed the motion to them, supposedly in their own interest. Hindenburg's main objection to Hitler's appointment as chancellor, Schleicher's argument ran, stemmed from his fear that if anything were to happen to him while Hitler was chancellor, the Nazi Fuehrer, according to present law, would assume his functions and would be the virtual dictator of Germany until a new presidential election. If the Supreme Court president rather than the chancellor were to take the president's place, Hindenburg might be persuaded to accept Hitler or any other Nazi as chancellor. This explanation accords with Schleicher's attempts to come to terms with the Nazi leader; it was also suggested by Breitscheid, the Socialists' spokesman, in the Reichstag debate.

While such considerations may have had some influence on the attitude of the Nazis, the latter were more concerned with keeping Schleicher from assuming the president's powers. This was the explanation supplied by the *Völkischer Beobachter,* and in view of the existing impasse the danger of Schleicher taking over Hindenburg's functions must have seemed more imminent to Hitler than the chance that he might be appointed as chancellor.

The bill became law with the votes of all parties except the Communists and the German Nationals. The former objected to the proposal on the grounds that the president of the Supreme Court was but the foremost exponent of a class-conscious judiciary utterly unfair to the workers and so closely allied with the Nazis that the next president of the Court would undoubtedly be a Nazi. The Communists, their speaker announced, would not lend their hand to helping the Nazis into power in this roundabout way. He concluded with a savage outburst against Hindenburg, "the representative of the fascist dictatorship, the direct representative of German monopoly capital and large estate owners; . . . [whose name is synonymous with] the program of the most shameless exploitation of the working people!" Once again the official protocol does not record any protest on behalf of the president.

The German Nationals rejected the bill for very different reasons of course. They distrusted the incumbent *Reichsgerichtspräsident,* for he had presided at the trial that had voided in part

401

Papen's coup against Prussia. Beyond that, they preferred an entirely different arrangement of the presidential succession. They moved that the president be granted the right to designate a deputy in case of his incapacitation and a temporary successor in the event of his death. Their hope of course was that under such an arrangement Hindenburg would nominate a member of the Imperial family, thus paving the way for a monarchist restoration. Even if their bill had been adopted contrary to all expectations, Hindenburg would not have been likely to comply with their wish, given his attitude on the monarchist issue.[6]

Turning to present needs, the Reichstag repealed those sections of Papen's economic decrees that allowed employers to lower wages if they employed additional workers. These provisions had aroused so much unrest and bitterness that Papen had already thought of revoking them. Schleicher also accepted an amnesty law that went farther than he would have wished in order to get the support of the Nazis and Social Democrats. And despite strong objections from business and his own finance ministry, he went along on a special emergency aid program (*Winterhilfe*) on which the Reichstag insisted. In return, motions for a no-confidence vote and for his appearance in person were voted down with the help of the Nazis, and the latter also accepted a sine die adjournment after a three-day session.[7]

But these were merely matters of tactics designed to tide Hitler over his financial and organizational troubles. Nazi hostility to Schleicher continued unchanged, as became evident immediately after the Reichstag's adjournment. A day later, the chancellor could announce to the nation that the Geneva Disarmament Conference had accepted the principle of full German equality in the forthcoming negotiations. The Nazi press sneered at this final fulfillment of a long-voiced demand, and Goebbels' *Angriff* took Schleicher to task for walking into an Allied trap.[8]

Yet Schleicher who had staked his political future on an *entente* with the Nazis would not turn his back on them. As he kept telling his callers, from the Socialist Otto Braun to the British ambassador, he was still very anxious to cooperate with the "nationally valuable" elements in the Nazi Party. Army commanders were

[6] *Verhandlungen*, pp. 23–30; Rumbold to Simon, Dec. 7, 1932, *DBFP.*, ii, iv, 91; Schleicher to Reichswehr commanders, Dec. 13, 1932, *Vierteljahrshefte*, ii (1954), 428; *Völkischer Beobachter*, Dec. 9, 1932, in *Zeitspiegel*, Dec. 17, 1932, p. 378.

[7] Bracher, *Auflösung*, pp. 679–81; Schäffer, in cab. mtg., Nov. 17, 25, 1932, Schleicher, in same, Dec. 3, 7, 1932, *RKz.*/1711/791181–82, 791219, 791246–47, 791256–58; *Dt. Volkswirt*, Dec. 2, 1932, p. 252.

[8] Eyck, *Weimarer Republik*, ii, 561.

also assured that a destruction of the Nazi Party was not in the interest of the state. He approached Göring who had made no secret of his interest in a government job. Göring had his eyes on the Prussian minister-presidency, but he also seems to have asked for the Prussian ministry of the interior which controlled the Prussian police. The negotiations came to a sudden end, however, when Göring called on Hindenburg and learned that the president would not consent to any arrangement suggesting a restoration of the former Reich-Prussian dualism.[9]

But as usual the president would make no positive effort to strengthen the hand of the chancellor. Schleicher thus had to try on his own to find a popular following, and on December 15, he presented himself to the nation in a radio address. Free from interference by hecklers and critics, he discussed his plans at some length. There was something for everyone in his program: assurances to the Weimar parties that he would not change the constitution; a pledge to the right to insist on a speedy implementation of Germany's military equality; public works projects to create employment for industrial labor; rural workers were to receive farmland in the east; business was promised a continuation of the economic policies inaugurated by the Papen cabinet; and agriculture was to have even greater protection from foreign competition. While governmental aid was proffered to the nation's economy in some areas, in others it might be withdrawn. Major enterprises which had received direct state subsidies would either have to submit to governmental management principles, especially in the matter of salaries, or be asked to return the aid they had received. Schleicher professed himself "enough of a heretic to confess that I am neither a supporter of capitalism nor of socialism. For me concepts such as 'private or planned economy' have lost their terror, simply because these concepts do not and cannot be upheld in absolute purity in our economic life. For this reason I feel that one ought to do for the economy what is reasonable at a given moment and will in all probability produce the best results for people and country, and not break each other's heads for the sake of a dogma."

And turning to the National Socialists, he tried to convince them that he was doing what they wished to accomplish—creating

[9] Braun, *Von Weimar,* p. 438; Rumbold to Simon, Dec. 21, 1932, *DBFP.,* ii, iv, 384; Schleicher to Reichswehr commanders, Dec. 13, 1932, *loc. cit.,* 428; on Göring's ambitions, Cerruti to Italian Foreign Ministry, Dec. 9, 1932, copy in Schleicher Papers/ 17,v/7; Meissner memorandum on Hindenburg's conference with Göring, Dec. 12, 1932, *RKz.,* R 43 I/2281.

a true national community based on social justice and the comradeship of the trenches. He was above all concerned with achieving social justice, he assured them, he was a "social general." There had never been anything more social than the army of universal compulsory military service, in which rich and poor, officer and enlisted man stood together. In the astounding deeds of the World War they all had displayed a comradeship and a sense of community such as history had not known before. This community he wished to recreate, and to achieve it he invited the collaboration of all who would help. Denying all dictatorial ambitions, he concluded that even an authoritarian government could not completely bypass the parliament and that determination and courage alone would not be sufficient; what was also needed was sympathy with the hopes and needs of the people.[10]

The speech, vague and inconsistent in parts, gained Schleicher few new friends, but cost him the support of some groups that he could ill afford to lose. Those of his proposals that were meant to impress the Nazis and Socialists aroused the ire of businessmen and agrarians. The businessmen resented his bow to the Reichstag and above all his dissociation from the free-enterprise system, and the agrarians stormed against the revival of Brüning's settlement plans. Suspicious of him in any event because of his dealings with labor, some of the most important of these groups angrily moved away from him.[11]

They had more reason than they knew to be concerned about Schleicher's intentions. Among the alternative policies he was contemplating should he not come to terms with the Nazis was an attempt to center his popular support on the Social Democrats. Supported by them as well as the unions and the moderate bourgeoisie, he considered dissolving the Reichstag and postponing new elections, outlawing the Nazi Party and its paramilitary formations, fusing *Reichsbanner* and *Stahlhelm* into one unit, and merging all unions into one labor organization. In return two Social Democrats or union leaders were to be taken into his cabinet.

The plan was a typical product of Schleicher's volatile mind. It was also, if he meant to go through with it, a program of desperation. That Hindenburg would be prepared to agree to so sharp a political turn was not likely, but Schleicher had an answer

---

[10] Schulthess, Dec. 15, 1932, pp. 223–31.
[11] Hans-Joachim Schoeps, "Das letzte Vierteljahr," *Geschichte in Wissenschaft und Unterricht*, VII (1956), 465; Goebbels, in *Angriff*, Dec. 21, 1932, *Wetterleuchten*, pp. 352–55; Bussche-Ippenburg, ZS./217; Anon., in *Ring*, Jan. 6, 1933, pp. 4–5.

to this too. He hoped to persuade the marshal after removing Oskar von Hindenburg, his most dangerous foe, from the president's entourage; the younger Hindenburg, promoted to major general, was to be given a field command in East Prussia. Again it is doubtful that the president, so dependent now on his son, would have agreed to dispense with his services. But he never had to make that decision. The whole plan collapsed since the Social Democrats, still deeply distrustful of Schleicher, refused to go along with the chancellor.[12]

If Hindenburg's passivity encouraged Schleicher to toy with all sorts of plans, it also led Papen as the president's special confidant to try his hand at ending the political impasse and once more seek an understanding with Hitler. An opportunity presented itself on the day after Schleicher's radio address when the *Herrenklub,* a gathering of the country's social elite, held its annual banquet, with Papen its guest of honor. After dinner the ex-chancellor spoke briefly to the group. He had considered it a main objective of his administration, he noted, to incorporate the "great National Socialist freedom movement" into a "national concentration," and this, he continued, must be the aim of any other government too. He warned the Nazis not to look upon their movement as an end in itself and to realize that they could not raise slander and lies to political principles. The road to power, he insisted, is one of truth and faith in the unchangeable rules of the Christian world view. "No one," he repeated, "could have longed more strongly for the union of all national forces and no one worked more earnestly and more sincerely for that goal than I did. How much farther ahead would we be now if on the evening of the 13th of August we could have said to the German people: We are marching together—against all opposition at home and abroad."

Turning to Schleicher, he paid him a few conventional compliments, and he suggested that politics required a certain amount of flexibility. But he warned him not to lose sight of such positive goals as the incorporation of the National Socialists into the government, the maintenance of an authoritarian government by appropriate constitutional reforms, and the revival of the private economy. "I expect" Papen added, "that regardless of all tactical maneuvers which may at the moment be needed, the Government will keep in mind the objectives which I have just outlined." He concluded with the hope that "we shall never tire of fighting, with

[12] Bracher, *Auflösung,* pp. 684–85; information from Rudolf Rothe, a Social Democratic party functionary.

the help of the old Ally up above and that of Hindenburg for a new Reich in a new age." [13]

Formally Papen spoke as a private citizen, but in the eyes of his audience he was more than just that. This gathering of politicians, high officials, social and business leaders, well informed on what went on in the Wilhelmstrasse, knew that Papen, though out of office, continued to act as a confidential adviser to the president. Papen himself had carefully passed the word that he enjoyed the special confidence of the "old Gentleman" to whom he was still "my Chancellor." Anything he said was taken therefore, rightly or wrongly, as reflecting the views of the president.

What struck Papen's listeners was his emphatic plea to the Nazis to see a friend and helper in him since he was anxious to see them participate in the government. Papen has since claimed that he wished to help Schleicher, but both substance and tenor of his talk convey a rather different impression, nor did his audience understand his remarks in this sense. Many, in fact, were dismayed that Papen was offering his hand to Hitler at the very moment Schleicher was apparently trying to split Hitler's movement. They viewed Papen's speech therefore as an open attack on the chancellor. "This is a stab in Schleicher's back," one of those present protested to the chairman of the meeting, "This offer to the Nazis to enter the Government is bound to provide them with new momentum. They know that Papen is Hindenburg's confidant."

That this reaction was not farfetched is confirmed by other developments that same evening. Among those who approached Papen after his speech was Baron von Schröder, the Cologne banker and one of the initiators a month earlier of the petition to Hindenburg to appoint Hitler to the chancellorship. His co-sponsors of that petition, Keppler and Schacht, had recently told him that Schleicher no longer had the full confidence of the president and that Hindenburg might be persuaded therefore to replace him with Hitler. Papen, both felt, would be the ideal middleman since he was the most trusted adviser of the "Old Gentleman." Schröder and Papen agreed on the need for coming to terms with the Nazis; who was the first to suggest a direct exchange of views between Papen and Hitler is a matter of controversy. It does not matter; obviously there was an immediate meeting of minds. Beyond this, Papen states in his memoirs, nothing specific was said, but Keppler whom Schröder informed of his

[13] *Ring,* Dec. 27, 1932, pp. 894–96.

talk told a different story when he reported to Hitler on the Papen-Schröder exchange. Papen, according to this account, complained to Schröder about Schleicher's intrigues which had kept inter-fering with Hitler's negotiations with Hindenburg and had led to Papen's own resignation. Yet Schleicher's position was now very weak, since the "Old Gentleman" had come to dislike him be-cause of his methods while Papen still enjoyed his full confidence. Keppler concluded hopefully: "Papen wishes to have a confiden-tial talk with you in order to inform you about the previous developments and discuss with you some possible future action." This, to be sure, was a second-hand report, but it was corroborated by Schröder at the Nürnberg Trial.[14]

While his adversaries were plotting Schleicher's removal, the chancellor busied himself to consolidate his position. His first effort was to establish contact with Strasser whom he finally traced to Rome. Schleicher's fertile mind had evolved a new plan to neutralize Hitler. A Social National Party was to be founded with Strasser its head which could be expected to draw large numbers of Nazis away from their Fuehrer. Well financed out of the secret funds of the Reichswehr, it would have a special attraction to Nazi Party officials whose livelihood was endangered by Hitler's financial plight. But to Schleicher's great disappointment Strasser would not return to Berlin at once. Strasser, in fact, was having second thoughts on his break with Hitler and was putting out feelers to him in hope of a reconciliation.[15]

Yet if Schleicher was unsuccessful behind the scenes, out-wardly he seemed in control of the situation. Some of the restric-tions imposed by Papen on political activities were lifted on the grounds that conditions were sufficiently stabilized to allow the parties greater freedom of action. The special aid program de-manded by the Reichstag was inaugurated and coal and foodstuffs offered to the needy at reduced prices. With the help of the Nazis, Schleicher also defeated a Socialist-Communist effort to recall the parliament before Christmas. When the British am-bassador called on him during these days, he professed to be

---

[14] Papen, *Wahrheit*, pp. 138, 251–54; same, *ZS./354*; memorandum of Nov. 12, 1957, *Vierteljahrshefte*, VI (1958), 113; Ewald von Kleist-Schmenzin, "Die letzte Mög-lichkeit: Zur Ernennung Hitlers zum Reichskanzler am 30. Januar 1933," *Politische Studien*, X (1959), 89; Theodor Eschenburg, "Franz von Papen," *Vierteljahrshefte für Zeitgeschichte*, I (1953), 163–64; affidavit of Schröder, Dec. 5, 1945, I.M.T., Case No. 5, Prosecution Document-Book, No. XIV-A; Keppler to Hitler, Dec. 19, 1932, in Vogelsang, *Reichswehr*, pp. 485–86; same to Schröder, Dec. 26, 1932, Jan. 21 (?), 1933, *Vierteljahrshefte*, VI (1958), 86–87.

[15] Meissner and Wilde, *Machtergreifung*, pp. 144, 149–50.

confident that the political crisis had passed its peak. Even the Nazis were quieting down, he assured the envoy. There was a group in the party, he claimed, which was ready now to support him, but Hitler's attitude was as unpredictable as ever. If he had the Nazis' support, his government would rest on a broad basis. "He disclaimed any hostility to that party," Rumbold reported, "and said that he would regret the collapse of the Hitler movement. Such a collapse would have positive dangers. His aim was to harness the movement in the service of the state." As for the Social Democrats, he still thought he would reach an understanding with them, and if not, their opposition might also prove useful.[16]

Such confidence did not seem entirely unjustified. Even though Hitler had coped with the Strasser crisis, he was beset by unending difficulties. "There is much trouble and unpleasantness in the party," Goebbels confided to his diary on December 21, "this is always the result of internal crises. . . . The monetary calamity continues. . . ." And on the following day: "We must reduce salaries in the district, otherwise we can't manage financially." But there were not financial worries alone; party discipline was rapidly deteriorating in many parts of the country despite Hitler's efforts to tighten it. Stormtroopers mutinied against their leaders; in Franconia the bulk of the S.A. broke away from Munich and established a separate "free corps." In several towns stormtroop barracks were turned into hideouts of organized gangs of thieves and robbers; among the gang leaders was one of the Bavarian *Gauleiters*. Even Hitler's own bodyguard was infected by this demoralization, as Schleicher learned through his spies in the party.[17]

The president, too, succumbed to this aura of confidence. In his isolation, the events of the outside world reached him only carefully screened, and he learned nothing of course of the intrigues and counterintrigues which were being woven and into which each camp hoped ultimately to draw him. The overriding fact to him was the political truce agreed upon by all parties for the Christmas season. "Christmas was never so peaceful before," he told the chancellor with unusual warmth, "I have to thank you for that, my dear young friend." The *Frankfurter Zeitung* agreed: "We know today that the cart is not hopelessly stuck in the mud. . . . We see in [the Chancellor] a statesman cautiously feel-

---

16 Schulthess, Dec. 18–21, 1932, pp. 231–32; Rumbold to Simon, Dec. 21, 1932, *DBFP.*, ii, iv, 383–84.

17 Goebbels, *Vom Kaiserhof*, entries of Dec. 21–23, 1932, pp. 227–29; Heiden,

ing the pulse of the nation and averse to any adventures—a man willing to help revive the democratic organism of the Weimar state as far as this depends on him." Leipart, the leader of the Socialist unions, likewise paid tribute to him as a man trying to help the working class by giving it jobs.

Encouraged by these developments, the chancellor was even ready for a showdown with the Reichstag. The Nazi Party, he felt certain, was so rapidly losing ground that it could not afford a dissolution of the Reichstag and would have to support him. Sure of his own strength, he had Planck announce to the Reichstag's council of elders on January 4 that he was ready to face the parliament at any time, but would have to insist in that case on a vote on the pending no-confidence motions. The council set the date for a new meeting for January 24, with its Nazi members abstaining from voting.

Like so many of the general's plans, though shrewdly conceived, this latest one also overlooked an essential factor. Schleicher did not foresee that influencial forces might be so averse to the prospect of a reviving democracy that they would redouble their efforts to reach an understanding with Hitler. Yet this was what was happening. The Papen-Schröder exchange of mid-December was followed by negotiations for a meeting of Papen and Hitler, and on December 29, while the left was glorying in the Nazis' decline, Goebbels happily noted in his diary: "There is a possibility that the Fuehrer may have a talk with Papen in a few days. A new chance is opening up."[18]

∽

The day before Goebbels jotted down these words, preparations for that meeting had in fact been completed. The two men were to meet at Schröder's house in Cologne on January 4. The arrangement was shrouded in deepest secrecy, and Hitler came to the meeting in true cloak-and-dagger style, in a borrowed car and by a circuitous route. But all precautions proved ineffective; a member of Hitler's own bodyguard had been bribed by Hans Zehrer, the editor of the *Tat* and more recently also of the Berlin daily, *Tägliche Rundschau*, to keep him informed of the Fuehrer's

---

Fuehrer, pp. 516–17; Hoegner, *Verratene Republik*, pp. 333–34; Brüning, "Ein Brief," p. 14; letter to Zur Muhlen, Jan. 26, 1950, Borcke-Stargordt Papers, ii, 127.

[18] Hindenburg, quoted in Wheeler-Bennett, *Nemesis*, p. 270; *Frankfurter Zeitung*, Reich ed., Jan. 1, 1933; Leipart, in Schulthess, Dec. 31, 1932, pp. 232–33; Goebbels, *Vom Kaiserhof*, entry of Dec. 29, 1932, p. 231.

movements, and through this contact Zehrer (and Schleicher) knew of the rendezvous as soon as it got under way.

There exist several versions of what transpired, but the two most specific ones, Papen's and Schröder's, agree on one significant point. Hitler opened the conversation by pouring abuse on Papen for having upheld the punishment of the Potempa defendants. Papen reports in his memoirs that he dismissed Hitler's charges as beside the point while Schröder recalls that the ex-chancellor disclaimed all responsibility for the fact that the convicted men were not pardoned. Whatever he said, once more he chose to ignore Hitler's contempt of human rights and of law and lawful procedures. Rather than shy away from seeking an understanding with one so disdainful of moral and legal commitments, Papen persisted in his endeavors to reach an agreement with him. Undaunted, he suggested to Hitler the formation of a duumvirate of Schleicher and Hitler (as he maintains) or of himself and Hitler (as Schröder, more plausibly, states) that would head a new cabinet of Nazis, German Nationals, and nonparty conservatives.

Hitler proved as uncompromising as ever. If Papen had expected him to be readier now to play a subordinate or coordinate role in a new coalition government, he found himself disappointed. As before, Hitler insisted that he would have to be the sole head of any government in which he took part. He would be willing to take some of Papen's supporters into such a government, provided they severed all party ties and agreed with him on general policies, and he mentioned specifically the elimination from public life of Social Democrats, Communists, and Jews.

Exactly what specific understandings, if any, the two men arrived at is not clear from the available evidence. But both of them came away from the meeting confident that they had accomplished something. Hitler, as he recalled later, viewed Papen's proposals as attempts, on Hindenburg's behalf, to sound him out on his attitude. Papen's suggestion of a duumvirate also left him with the impression that the president was weakening in his opposition to him and might in the end appoint him head of a presidential government. His confidence grew when Papen told him that Schleicher had as yet no dissolution decree. Papen may well have added, moreover, that given Hindenburg's distrust of Schleicher, he was not certain to get one. The specter of new elections suddenly seemed less menacing. "If this coup succeeds," Goebbels rejoiced in his diary, "we are not far from getting power." His hopes were raised further by a marked improvement

410

of the party's financial difficuties a few days after the meeting. Some industrialists, anxious to prevent the party's disintegration, were coming to the aid of the Nazi exchequer.[19]

Papen too appeared to be satisfied with the results of the conference. True, its immediate repercussions proved a source of some embarrassment to him. Aware that the meeting had not remained secret, he tried to head off any trouble with Schleicher by sending him an immediate report. But the chancellor, suspecting the worst, had mobilized Berlin's press, and headlines on January 5 pictured the meeting as a conspiracy aimed at the government.

Schleicher also scurried to Hindenburg to complain about Papen's activities. Furious at the ex-chancellor's meddling, he asked that the president no longer receive him. His indignation seemed little warranted, for he himself had often committed the same offense. The marshal had been as little informed about Papen's movements as had the chancellor, but he was either unable to appreciate the significance of the Papen-Hitler conclave or so used to such backstairs activities, thanks to Schleicher, that he was little impressed and would make no promises. When Papen requested to see him on his return to Berlin, he received him at once and accepted his explanations.[20]

Except for this initial mishap, however, Papen felt that the meeting was fruitful. He appears to have persuaded himself that Hitler had grown more tractable. Yet the Nazi leader had not scaled down his terms below his November demands; he still insisted on his appointment as chancellor and on his right to determine alone the policies he would pursue. Encouraged nevertheless, Papen met with German National spokesmen in Düsseldorf and discussed with them the formation of a new "front of national unity." Moving on to Dortmund, he had talks there with leading industrialists. Some of them had supported Hitler's chancellorship in November; worried now about Schleicher's plans, they welcomed the prospect of a rapprochement with the Nazi chieftain.[21]

On January 9, the ex-chancellor was back in Berlin. His first

[19] Papen, *Wahrheit*, pp. 255–57; Schröder, in *Nazi Conspiracy*, ii, 922–24; Picker, *Hitlers Tischgespräche*, p. 428; Meissner, *Staatssekretär*, p. 261; Meissner and Wilde, *Machtergreifung*, pp. 154–55; Bracher, *Auflösung*, pp. 692–94; Goebbels, *Vom Kaiserhof*, Jan. 5–9, 1932, pp. 235–38.

[20] Papen, *Wahrheit*, pp. 259–61; Bracher, *Auflösung*, pp. 694–95; Meissner, *Staatssekretär*, pp. 261–62; Schulthess, Jan. 7, 1933, p. 7; Hallgarten, *Hitler*, p. 116.

[21] Papen, *Wahrheit*, pp. 260–61; Eschenburg, "Franz von Papen," p. 164; Meissner, *Staatssekretär*, pp. 261–62; same, testimony, I.M.T., Case No. 11, transcript, p. 4489.

call was on Schleicher with whom, he claims in his memoirs, he cleared up all misunderstandings. Papen went next to the president and found his old protector only too willing to accept his reassuring explanations. Papen fails to state in his memoirs what exactly he said to Hindenburg; Meissner learned later from Hindenburg that Papen had found Hitler much less demanding at Cologne than before. He no longer insisted on getting all power, but was prepared to participate in a coalition government with the right. Papen even believed that the Center Party would be willing to support such a government so that it could count on a parliamentary majority. Of Hitler's terms there seems to have been no mention, for Hindenburg, evidently under the impression that the Fuehrer might now accept Papen as chancellor, authorized Papen to keep in touch with the Nazi leader. These contacts, informal and purely exploratory, would be pursued in strict secrecy, and the president asked Meissner not to reveal anything to the chancellor.[22]

By authorizing continued contacts with Hitler, Hindenburg was thwarting Schleicher's renewed attempts to break up the Nazi Party. The chancellor's efforts were entering just then a critical phase. Hitler had rejected Strasser's approaches, and Schleicher had once more offered Strasser the vice-chancellorship. This time Strasser, to the great concern of his party, seemed ready to accept. On January 4, the day when Papen and Hitler met in Cologne, Strasser had called on the president. The meeting seems to have been a success; Hindenburg was impressed with Strasser's disciplined calm, so different from the tense awkward ways of Hitler. "This fellow cuts a much better figure than Hitler," he later told Schleicher, "that's an entirely different matter. I like Strasser much better."

Schleicher felt greatly encouraged. The president seemed to be coming over to his side again. He even urged Schleicher, as the latter wrote later, not to waste any time on negotiations and dissolve the Reichstag immediately. But the chancellor preferred to wait, ever hopeful that he could find a majority that would grant him at least a breathing spell of some months.[23]

Did Hindenburg realize that he was guilty of a grave disloyalty when a few days later he permitted Papen, behind Schleicher's back, to pursue his rapprochement with Hitler? Had Papen con-

---

[22] Zechlin, *Pressechef*, pp. 121–22; Papen, *Wahrheit*, pp. 261–62; Meissner and Wilde, *Machtergreifung*, p. 158.

[23] *Ibid.*, pp. 150–52; Goebbels, *Vom Kaiserhof*, entries of Dec. 28–29, 1932, Jan. 3, 12, 1933, pp. 230–31, 233, 240; Meissner, *Staatssekretär*, pp. 251–52; Schleicher to *Vossische Zeitung*, Jan. 30, 1934, *Vierteljahrshefte*, VI (1958), 90.

vinced him that Schleicher could not succeed and that he must look for another solution? Or was he simply preparing two alternate strategies, in the familiar way of the general staff, hoping that one of them would prove effective? There had been no final commitment to Schleicher's solution, nor did Papen get more than an informal mandate. Again, Hindenburg may simply have waited for events to take care of themselves. All this must remain speculation, but there can be no doubt that he was fully aware of what he was doing. Even though he was no longer capable of any prolonged concentration and may have dozed off during lengthy conferences, he could well follow short and concise reports, according to the unanimous testimony of his close aides. Thus, if he did not grasp all the implications of Papen's activities, he must have understood a good deal, to judge by his instructions to Meissner not to disclose Papen's plans to the chancellor. He was at least partly responsible then for becoming ever deeper entangled in the intricate web of intrigues being spun around him while he was feeling his way in weary bewilderment.[24]

Hindenburg was not permitted to remain passive for long. On January 11, his office received an urgent call from the *Landbund*, requesting an immediate audience with the president. Its board of directors had just met, and its concern was such "that a conference with the president was absolutely imperative to allay the fears of the *Landbund* and the agricultural population represented by it." Ever accessible to the agrarians, Hindenburg ignored the peremptory tone of the request and received a delegation a half-hour later. His callers painted a dark picture of agriculture's desperate plight: the farmers were facing ruin, they were in a rebellious mood, they were being driven into the arms of the Communists. Reacting with unusual speed, Hindenburg summoned Schleicher and the ministers most directly concerned to a conference with the *Landbund*. Such was the importance he attached to this meeting that he himself took the chair. "Gentlemen," he warned in his opening statement, "I want to tell you that we are not going to leave here until this matter has been straightened out, and if it takes until five in the morning."

The *Landbund* spokesmen reiterated their complaints. The government had remained completely inactive; the chancellor had made many promises, but had not kept them. Grim stories were

24 On Hindenburg's good physical and mental condition, see Meissner, *Staatssekretär*, p. 214; information from Dr. Doehle; additional personal information. See also Hoegner, *Aussenseiter*, p. 66, and Alexander Rüstow, *Ortsbestimmung der Gegenwart: Eine universalgeschichtliche Kulturkritik* (Erlenbach-Zurich, 1950–57), III, 687 n. 114.

413

told of the plight of the farmers in all parts of the country. One of the speakers, with an eye on the president, hinted that the latter's wishes were being ignored. There were renewed warnings that the farmers were turning to Communism and the national substance was being frittered away. Schleicher's resettlement plans were sharply attacked: if Junkers as well as farmers were being abandoned, the country would be gravely endangered. To save them, the *Landbund* asked for a three-to-six month suspension of all foreclosures.

Schleicher in reply pointed out what had been accomplished during the five weeks of his chancellorship and what further aid was being prepared. But the farmers did not exist in a vacuum, he cautioned, and the other sectors of the economy had also rights that he could not ignore. To simply suspend all foreclosures would ruin tradesmen and others and was therefore out of the question. Baron von Braun, the *Landbund*'s own choice as minister of agriculture, and Warmbold, the economics minister, seconded him, but the men from the *Landbund* would not give in. Hindenburg, as ever inclined to side with them, grew impatient. According to one of the participants, he brought down his fist on the table and lapsing into his old habits, told the chancellor: "I request, Chancellor von Schleicher, and as an old soldier you know that a request is simply the polite form of an order, that the cabinet meet tonight to work out the necessary laws and submit them to me tomorrow morning for my signature." Something of the president's irritation echoes also through the official minutes which state that Hindenburg "requested" Schleicher to report to him the next day on the result of the deliberations. But the marshal would not have been himself, had he allowed the meeting to end on this note. After his outburst, Hindenburg adjourned the meeting with the characteristic remark: "And now, let's shake hands all around."

Nevertheless, from the *Landbund*'s viewpoint the meeting had served its purpose. Not only could further help be expected at once for the farmer—a few days later the government did tighten the antiforeclosure laws—but the conference also sharpened the tension between the president and the chancellor.

This result even an unpleasant epilogue could not undo. As the meeting broke up, some of the evening papers were handed into the conference room. On their front pages they featured an official statement of the *Landbund* that had been turned over to the press before the two meetings with the president and the chancellor. The statement asserted that the plight of German agriculture had

414

reached dimensions under the present administration "that would have seemed inconceivable even under a purely Marxist government." Reiterating the familiar complaints, it concluded by calling on every farmer to stand ready for an "ultimate effort in the struggle for his very survival that is being forced upon him." During the meeting Hindenburg had rejected charges that the Schleicher government was doing nothing to help agriculture. Angered by this new display of demagogy, he let it be known that he would not have received the *Landbund* leaders, had he known to what unfair tactics they would resort. Schleicher, on his part, broke off all official relations with the *Landbund* and refused to engage in further negotiations with it.[25]

If the incident failed to restore him in the marshal's good graces, one reason was that the agrarians did not depend on the *Landbund* for their access to the president. Hindenburg's old East Prussian neighbors could always be counted upon to serve as lines of communication, and through them a steady stream of complaints about Schleicher's resettlement plans and price policies continued to pour into the Presidential Palace. One of the most outspoken of these critics was the irrepressible Oldenburg-Januschau.

To the agrarians' concerns about Schleicher's program another was added during those days. The budget committee of the Reichstag was probing again into the administration of the Eastern Aid Program, and the press reported that the investigation had uncovered huge misappropriations of assistance funds. Beneficiaries, the stories ran, had used subsidies to pay gambling debts, buy race horses, vacation on the Riviera, or maintain mistresses. Some members of the oldest Prussian aristocracy appeared to be involved, and there were even reports that relatives of the president had benefited from these irregularities. In several of these cases Hindenburg allegedly had endorsed applications for aid.

The investigation was initiated with the help of the Nazis. Presumably they hoped to embarrass Hindenburg and his landowning friends and thus make the president more amenable to Hitler's chancellorship. The press campaign, however, was led by Hans Zehrer's *Tägliche Rundschau*, supposedly Schleicher's mouthpiece. Collaboration between Schleicher and Zehrer was actually much less close than was widely believed, and Schleicher

25 Minutes of Hindenburg-Landbund conference of Jan. 11, 1933, in Graf Henning von Borcke-Stargordt, *Der ostdeutsche Landbau zwischen Fortschritt, Krise und Politik: Ein Beitrag zur Agrar- und Zeitgeschichte* (Würzburg, 1957), pp. 176–80; Sybel to Borcke, Feb. 2, 1951, copy in Borcke-Stargordt Papers, II, 124–25; Schulthess, Jan. 11, 1933, pp. 11–14; Buchta, *Junker*, pp. 153–55; also *Völkischer Beobachter*, North German ed., No. 13, Jan. 13, 1933; Stampfer, *Vierzehn Jahre*, p. 665.

had cut off all subsidies to the *Rundschau* some time before. Whatever the facts, his enemies hastened to suggest to the president that the chancellor was master-minding the "Eastern Aid scandal" or at least doing nothing to quiet it down.[26]

To compound Schleicher's troubles, Strasser had a new change of heart. He had not yet accepted the vice-chancellorship, nor would he take the ministry of labor which Schleicher had also offered him, hopeful that he would secure the support of the rightist unions. By now Strasser was clearly afraid to assume an active role against Hitler; as he confided to Meissner, he would not dare to defy the Fuehrer after the threats he had been receiving. In fact, he still hoped against hope that Hitler might take him back into the fold, and he called on him twice in mid-January. But Hitler proved unforgiving and when Strasser tried to see him again a few days later he was not received. By then diet elections had been held in the little state of Lippe where the Nazis recouped some of their losses. Buoyed with success, Hitler now announced publicly that he had broken with Strasser, and threatened to "break the necks of all party defeatists."[27]

In the complex maneuvers following Schleicher's new troubles, the almost forgotten Hugenberg moved to the foreground once more. He too was aware that time was working against him—the approaching economic upswing was likely to lead the country back into democratic-parliamentarian paths. "With increasing business activity throughout the world," he announced, "everything will turn out well for Germany if those in power pursue a clear-cut authoritarian course, treat Hitler with icy aloofness, and carry out those remedial economic measures which we keep proposing to them every day." No time was to be lost if the country's economy was to be overhauled according to his ideas, and he was prepared therefore even to work with Schleicher. Taking advantage of the chancellor's clash with the *Landbund,* he offered to pacify agriculture if the chancellor would give him the portfolios of economics and agriculture. To his great disappointment Schleicher rejected the offer. Schleicher still hoped to form a coalition revolving around Center and unions and did not wish to jeopardize these negotiations by an alliance with this protagonist of reaction.

[26] Schulthess, Jan. 11, 16, 19, 1933, pp. 12, 20, 23; Braun, *Von Weimar,* p. 439; Stampfer, *Vierzehn Jahre,* p. 665; Severing, *Lebensweg,* II, 377; Meissner and Wilde, *Machtergeifung,* pp. 74–78; Hoegner, *Verratene Republik,* pp. 335–36; Papen, *Wahrheit,* p. 268.

[27] Meissner, *Staatssekretär,* pp. 253–54; same, in I.M.T., Case No. 11, transcript, p. 4485; Meissner and Wilde, *Machtergreifung,* pp. 167–68; Schulthess, Jan. 12, 17, 1933, pp. 15, 21; Goebbels, *Vom Kaiserhof,* entries of Jan. 19–20, 1933, pp. 244–45.

Hugenberg now turned to Hindenburg. He seems to have argued that Schleicher's ineptness made it imperative for Nazis and German Nationals to get together if the country were to be saved from catastrophe. Like Papen he held out hopes for a coalition with Hitler backed by a Reichstag majority. But Hindenburg, if we follow a blurred account based on the recollections of Meissner, seems to have been unwilling to give Hitler the chancellorship on these terms although in November he had been prepared to do so. "You can be assured, my young friend," Meissner recalls the president telling the 67-year old Hugenberg, "that Hitler is not getting all power from me."[28]

On January 16, Hugenberg met with the Nazi leader to explore a possible collaboration should Schleicher be forced to resign. Hugenberg found Hitler as unyielding as ever. Filled with new confidence by the Lippe elections, Hitler now held out also for the Prussian ministry of the interior. Hugenberg was prepared to accept him as chancellor, but he would not consent to Nazi control of the Prussian police. The discussion grew acrimonious, and the meeting broke up in mutual recriminations.[29]

Since Hugenberg did not return to Schleicher, however, the chancellor gained nothing from this contretemps. Nor did his talks with the left move ahead. Otto Braun offered help if he were reinstated as Prussian minister-president with full power, but Schleicher thought the proposal unfeasible. Hindenburg, he was certain, would never agree to the restoration of a separate Prussian government, nor was he likely to suspend the Reichstag, as Braun demanded. Other approaches to the Social Democrats were equally unrewarding. By this time the chancellor, worried and ill, was moving in all directions. While he had told Braun, correctly, that Hindenburg was unlikely to close the Reichstag, he tried to persuade the Socialist leaders to tolerate its suspension. Not only were his feelers rejected, but under pressure from the Socialist party chiefs, the union leaders, affiliated with them, also withdrew their offer of collaboration.[30]

⌖

Of these concerns the chancellor said nothing when he met with the cabinet on January 16. The question was simply, he reported,

[28] Meissner and Wilde, *Machtergreifung*, pp. 164–65; Schmidt-Hannover, *Umdenken*, pp. 317, 322; Papen, *Wahrheit*, Schulthess, Jan. 13–14, 1933, pp. 18–19; Hugenberg, quoted in Schmidt-Hannover, *Umdenken*, p. 317; Hindenburg, quoted in Meissner and Wilde, *Machtergreifung*, pp. 164–65.

[29] Borchmeyer, *Hugenbergs Ringen*, I, 25; Schmidt-Hannover, *Umdenken*, p. 322; Goebbels, *Vom Kaiserhof*, entry of Jan. 17, 1933, pp. 243–44.

[30] Meissner and Wilde, *Machtergreifung*, pp. 164, 166; Braun, *Von Weimar*, pp.

whether it would be possible to get the Nazis to work with the government, either directly by active collaboration or indirectly by toleration, or if they would rather fight. He himself hoped for an early showdown. If the Reichstag should soon reassemble and place a no-confidence motion on the agenda, he would at once hand it a dissolution decree. A new election campaign would have to be fought on a broader basis than the last one. On the other hand, business and parts of labor objected to early elections, and he himself was beginning to wonder whether it would not be better to postpone new elections until fall.

Continuing, he spoke of Strasser's appointment to a cabinet post as a distinct possibility, he professed confidence that Hugenberg could be won over to support him, and that a parliamentary basis extending from Strasser to the Center could be found for the government. All would of course depend on Hitler's next move. Schleicher did not think that Hitler was seriously counting on becoming chancellor; he was said to have asked for the post of Reichswehr minister although he must know that the president would never entrust the army to him. If his ministerial colleagues did not share Schleicher's confidence, no one said so outright. Some wondered whether, in case the elections would be postponed, the economic recovery would have advanced sufficiently by fall to risk new elections. Others worried whether or not it would be wise to announce at once the exact date of the fall elections. But no one questioned Schleicher's analysis of the over-all situation. An air of unreality hung over the entire discussion.[31]

One recent development was passed over completely. The day before the cabinet meeting, the diet elections in Lippe had taken place. During the preceding two weeks, tiny Lippe, one of the last remnants of German *Kleinstaaterei,* nestling between the foothills of the Teutoburg Forest and the Weser valley, with an electorate of less than 100,000 voters, had been a center of frantic political activity. Obviously Hitler's bargaining position would be greatly improved if he could demonstrate that the Nazis' recent setbacks had come to an end and that they had lost none of their irresistibility. During the first two weeks of January the party had blanketed this minuscule state with election meetings. Hitler addressed eighteen meetings during the twelve days between January 3 and 14; Goebbels, Göring, and other top echelon leaders spoke two

---

437–38; Noske, *Erlebtes,* pp. 310–11; unsigned memorandum, May 14, 1948, Severing Papers/1932 I.

[31] Cab. mtg., Jan. 16, 1933, *RKz./*1711/791447–53.

and three times an evening, often in remote hamlets and villages. Their efforts were not in vain. The Nazis received 38,800 votes in the election as compared to the 33,000 they had gotten on November 6, and their press exulted that the legend of their decline had been disavowed by these returns.

Actually there could be some doubt whether such optimism was justified. While the Nazis had scored substantial gains over the results of the last Reichstag election, the returns still were far below those of the July election when 42,300 votes had been cast for the party. There was also the question how representative the results really were. Obviously the Nazis could never match on a national scale the effort they had made in this small state. As a Protestant-rural area, moreover, it was especially receptive to the Nazi appeal. Goebbels seized on the returns with his usual skill, and the country accepted his interpretation that this new "victory" forecast Hitler's imminent seizure of power.

If one accepts the assertion, however, that the outcome reflected a new nationwide rise of Nazism, the Social Democrats could point to their new resurgence with much greater justification. In this nonindustrial region they had scored gains almost equal to those of the Nazis. Computed on a national scale, their success indicated even more substantial advances. They had moreover drawn their new votes from the Communists, suggesting that they were the most effective shield against Bolshevism. There was also the fact which should have given pause to Papen and Hugenberg that the Nazis had made their gains at the expense of the German Nationals who lost almost 40 per cent of the votes they had obtained in November; Lippe, moreover, was Hugenberg's home state. If their own followers proved so fickle, what chance would they have of curbing Hitler effectively in a coalition?[32]

All these factors were lost on Schleicher who might have used them to his advantage. Papen, on his part, took the returns more seriously, but only because he accepted the Nazi analysis. On January 10, he apparently had had another meeting with Hitler, late at night, at the suburban home of Joachim von Ribbentrop, then the well-to-do owner of an import and export business, who was later to gain notoriety as Hitler's foreign minister.[33] Politically ambitious, Ribbentrop had recently joined the Nazi Party and had

[32] Goebbels, *Vom Kaiserhof*, entries of Jan. 9-15, 1933, pp. 237-42; Bracher, *Auflösung*, pp. 701-03; Milatz, in Matthias and Morsey, *Ende der Parteien*, pp. 788-89; Schulthess, Jan. 15, 1933, p. 20.

[33] Papen (*Wahrheit*, p. 261) does not recall meeting Hitler on January 10, but the detailed recollections of Frau von Ribbentrop and her contemporary diary appear to bear out her claim that such a meeting took place; Joachim von Ribbentrop,

proven useful as liaison man between Hitler and Papen on some earlier occasions. To his dismay Papen learned that Hitler as before insisted on the chancellorship in any government in which he was to participate. When Papen reminded him that Hindenburg would not accede to this demand, Hitler refused to meet for any further discussions until after the Lippe elections, hopeful that he would then face Papen (and Hindenburg) in a stronger position. Papen, who understood this of course, foresaw new difficulties in the event of a Nazi success. His concern is clearly reflected in the postelectoral comments he jotted down in his diary: "The result is a surprisingly large gain of the Nazis and as surprising a setback of the right which loses one-third of its votes. . . . Like a by-election in England or Congressional elections in the United States in non-Presidential election years express clearly the thinking of the electorate at the time, the same applies here. The result is increased tension throughout the country." [34]

These comparisons with the unrepresentative Lippe elections were as inaccurate as they were misleading, and they merely weakened Papen's bargaining strength. He found his worst fears confirmed when he met Hitler again three days after the elections. Heartened by his latest success, Hitler again was unyielding on the chancellorship question. Hindenburg would never accept him as chancellor, Papen complained, even his influence was not such that he could persuade him to change his mind. The discussion ended inconclusively.

Neither side was interested in divulging this fact, however, and Goebbels' propaganda machine assiduously spread the news that the meeting had led to a far-reaching rapprochement toward a Nazi-conservative government. The plan, it was rumored, was to replace the Schleicher cabinet with one formed from the Harzburg groups under National Socialist leadership. Papen would take over the foreign ministry. By this "systematic campaign of attrition" Goebbels hoped to wear down the hated von Schleicher.

At the last moment, before Hitler and Papen separated, their host Ribbentrop suggested that a talk between Hitler and Oskar von Hindenburg might be helpful. Of his father's advisers Oskar was known to be the one most strongly opposed to Hitler's appointment. If his resistance could be overcome, the "Old Gentleman" too might change his mind. [35]

Zwischen London und Moskau: Erinnerungen und letzte Aufzeichnungen (Leoni, 1953), entries of Jan. 10, 18, 1933, pp. 38–39; also Bracher, *Auflösung*, pp. 707–08.
[34] Papen, *Wahrheit*, p. 263; Ribbentrop, *London und Moskau*, p. 38.
[35] *Ibid.*, entry of Jan. 18, 1933, p. 39; Schulthess, Jan. 18, 1933, p. 21; Goebbels,

The next three days, January 19 to 21, were filled with a new round of talks and discussions. Ribbentrop called on Papen to take up his suggestion of a meeting between Hitler and Oskar von Hindenburg. Papen promised to talk to the colonel. Ribbentrop brought also some new proposals: impressed by Hindenburg's firmness, Hitler was prepared to scale down his demands. While he would have to insist on the chancellorship, he was willing to allow most of the cabinet posts to go to non-Nazis. Only two of his party friends would enter the government—one would become the minister of the interior while another was to have cabinet rank as commissioner of a newly created department of aviation. He also laid claim for himself to the post of Reich commissioner of Prussia.

These proposals were far less generous than appeared on the surface. As Reich commissioner of Prussia, Hitler would be in control of the Prussian police, while the Nazi commissioner of aviation was to build up a military air force. Its potentialities, Göring, the candidate for the post, suggested when he openly boasted that with its help he would "unhinge" the entire Reichswehr. The ministry of the interior had limited powers, but Hitler planned to expand them by new decrees as soon as he was chancellor. Some of the pitfalls inherent in these proposals were hard to perceive, but others Papen should have foreseen; obsessed with his plan to form an alliance with Hitler, however, he accepted the Fuehrer's new terms as a basis for further negotiations. And since the Nazi leader would not settle for anything less than the chancellorship, Papen decided that it should be conceded to him. If he took counsel with any friends or associates, his memoirs do not mention the fact. Apparently he felt entirely capable of carrying on these talks on his own.

Indeed, Papen seems to have looked upon a coalition with Hitler as something of a personal challenge. Beyond any feelings of vindictiveness, fear of Communism, or aversion to parliamentarianism, Papen had come to see the success of his efforts as the ultimate test of his statesmanship. Where no one else had succeeded, he would bring Hitler into the government and channel his energies and those of his movement into disciplined and constructive collaboration. He and his conservative fellow ministers would of course emerge as the dominant figures in the new cabinet, thanks to their greater experience and sense of responsibility and,

---

Vom Kaiserhof, entry of Jan. 18, 1933, p. 244; same, "Schleichers Bilanz," in *Wetterleuchten,* pp. 358–60.

above all, their numerical superiority which would enable them to vote down any reckless proposals. There was something of the horseman's daring in the approach with which this one-time gentleman rider was taking the hurdles that blocked his path; whatever misgivings he himself may have had concerning Hitler as chancellor, they were now dismissed. In his singleminded determination he had propelled himself onto a course from which he could no longer turn away.

To gain another ally, he talked to Meissner. Meissner's reply was noncommittal; he did not think that the president would ever agree to any new government of which Papen was not the chancellor. Soon afterwards Papen saw Hindenburg. They talked under four eyes; later the president called in both Meissner and Oskar. Once more Papen explained Hitler's offer. He felt that Hitler could rightly insist on the chancellorship; he was after all the head of the largest party and he was furthermore asking for only two additional cabinet posts. He, Papen, would be satisfied with the vice-chancellorship. This time Meissner agreed. He could not suggest any better solution; above all, he was satisfied that it was in accord with the constitution.[36] There would have to be safeguards of course against any possible abuses of power by the Nazis, and the middle parties such as Center and Bavarian People's Party would have to enter the government too. Papen counted off the safeguards with which Hitler would be surrounded: the constitutional rights of the president; his position as commander-in-chief of the Reichswehr; the rights of Reichstag and Reichsrat. And according to Hitler's latest proposal, the bourgeois cabinet members would outnumber the Nazis, and thus could always outvote them. Finally Hitler had promised expressly to respect the rights of the president, the Reichstag, and the press. The great advantage of this solution was that by getting the Nazis to participate in the government, you would wean them away from their revolutionary ideas and put an end to their demagogic tactics.

It all sounded reassuring enough, but Hindenburg was not convinced. It is doubtful that he understood how weak the safeguards were in which Papen put so much trust: he himself, the

---

[36] The charge that Meissner was blackmailed into supporting the appointment of Hitler to avoid the baring of some allegedly dubious financial dealings has never been proven and was dismissed as entirely without basis by the Nürnberg War Crimes Tribunal. His belief that Hitler's appointment was "legal" was consistent with the positivist interpretation of the constitution which he had always followed. His attitude also reflected his constant concern with Hindenburg whom he wished to relieve of the onerous burdens that developments had imposed upon him.

aged and feeble president, who had always evaded showdowns; the Reichswehr which had only recently questioned his orders and dreaded a clash with the Nazis; the Reichstag and Reichsrat which lacked popular backing and, as Papen himself had proven, could easily be defied; and the pledges of Hitler whose concept of honor did not include the keeping of promises. More likely it was simply his instinctive aversion to Hitler that sustained his misgivings; he did not, however, ask Papen to break off negotiations on the ground that he would not make Hitler chancellor. He wanted to think matters over, he answered evasively. Only Oskar von Hindenburg's position remained unchanged, and he kept warning his father against Papen's plan.[37]

Evidently Oskar would have to be won over first before the president could be converted. Like his father's, Oskar's opposition to Hitler seems to have been emotional rather than rational, with an element of social snobism entering into it. Hitler, in his forceful persuasive way, might dispel his misgivings. Papen had become friendly with Oskar during the days of his chancellorship, and between friends he now urged the colonel to call on Hitler who was anxious to see him. But Oskar, fearful of any involvement, was reluctant to go. In the end, so as not to offend the Nazi leader, as he later explained, Oskar agreed to meet with him. But he insisted that Meissner as his father's official political adviser also take part in the talk. Hindenburg gave his approval; as he told Papen, it might be well to find out what Hitler's intentions were now that Schleicher seemed unable to cope with the situation.

This meeting too took place in deep secrecy. On the appointed evening, Oskar and Meissner first went to the opera and showed themselves to the public during the intermission. Shortly after the beginning of the final act they slipped away and by taxi made their way to the Ribbentrop villa. There they found Papen, Hitler, and a number of top Nazi leaders waiting for them. After a few moments of awkward small talk Hitler got up and asked Oskar to come with him to an adjoining room. The colonel, submitting to Hitler's commanding way, followed him without asking Meissner to join him.

We know little of what was said during this *tête-à-tête* which lasted for more than an hour. According to Oskar, Hitler did most of the talking and seems to have used all the familiar argu-

---

[37] Papen, *Wahrheit*, pp. 263–65, 271–72; Meissner, I.M.T., Case No. 11, transcript, pp. 4489–94; Göring's boast, in Holtzendorff, ZS./248; Göring, in I.M.T., *Trial*, ix, 248–49.

ments to change Oskar's mind: only he could save Germany from Communism; only he would be an effective chancellor; no government could survive without his support since he could always find a majority to drive it from office. Hitler may also have revived the threat of impeachment proceedings against the president, a danger which seems to have been very much on Hindenburg's mind during those days. Most likely, however, it was simply his masterful way of marshaling his arguments which won Oskar over. Whatever the reason, on their way home Meissner found Oskar preoccupied with what he had heard. After a long silence the colonel observed that he too had come to believe that Hitler ought to be given the chancellorship. Meissner, of course, had felt so before, and a talk with Göring, while he was waiting for Oskar, had confirmed him in this opinion. Göring had confirmed Papen's report of Hitler's proposals. He had also promised once more respect for the Weimar Constitution and loyal cooperation with the other "national" parties. There had even been a hint that Hitler might be able to fulfill the president's dearest wish and restore the monarchy.[38]

Hitler scored one other triumph that evening. When Meissner and Oskar left, Papen had stayed behind. Sensing a change in Hindenburg's attitude, he now promised Hitler that he would insist on the Fuehrer's chancellorship and not accept it himself. Hitler appeared unconvinced, for Papen, according to Ribbentrop's diary, proposed to withdraw from the negotiations if Hitler mistrusted him.

Somehow peace was restored again, and the next morning, Papen presented himself to the president. If Hindenburg had seemed to be weakening in his opposition to Hitler at their last meeting, he now was as unwilling as ever to accept him as chancellor. The instinctive aversion to Hitler, the old fears of his ultimate goals would not die down. Papen tried his persuasive best to convince him of the advantages of Hitler's offer, but Hindenburg would not listen. When Papen saw Ribbentrop later that day, he had to admit that he had failed to accomplish anything. Possibly at his suggestion Schacht was proposed to Hitler as a compromise candidate for the chancellorship, and some of Hitler's lieutenants, anxious to get at the government's fleshpots, seem to have welcomed this solution.

---

[38] Meissner and Wilde, *Machtergreifung*, pp. 161–64; Meissner, in I.M.T., *Trial*, XXXII, 152; same, Case No. 11, transcript, p. 4494; Papen, *Wahrheit*, pp. 265–66. It has been claimed that Hitler in his talk with Oskar von Hindenburg threatened to disclose some Eastern Aid scandals in which the latter allegedly was involved; cf. Bullock, *Hitler*, pp. 223–24. Oskar was found innocent of all such charges in his denazification proceedings.

But Hitler would not hear of it. To all appearances the negotiations had reached a hopeless impasse.[39]

∽

At this very moment a new chain of developments was set into motion by another turn of events. On the day on which Papen reported to Hindenburg on his latest talk with the Fuehrer, the president also received the chancellor. Despite all the precautionary measures which Meissner and Oskar had taken, Schleicher had learned of their visit to the Ribbentrop villa. With Oskar drawn into the negotiations with Hitler, Schleicher knew that he had to act swiftly if he was to remain in control of the situation. Time was pressing also since the Reischstag was to reconvene, after another postponement, on January 31; with Nazis, Socialists, and, of course, Communists, opposed to him, he was certain to face a hostile majority. To add to his troubles, the German Nationals too had turned against him on the grounds that "the present Government was suspect of liquidating the authoritarian idea which the President had established with the appointment of the Papen cabinet, and of steering German politics into those backwaters which it seemed to have left with the emergence of the national movement." The resolution was not to be published for another three days in the hope that the chancellor might mend his ways. It was clear that only a suspension of the Reichstag would satisfy the Hugenberg group.

The confrontation with Hindenburg was a painful experience. Schleicher had to admit that his attempts to split the Nazi Party had failed. There was no other way out now but to return to Papen's proposal of last December. The Reichstag must be dissolved and new elections postponed until conditions had become stable again. To suppress any possible Nazi resistance, he asked for emergency powers. As could be expected, Hindenburg balked at this plan conjuring the horrors of civil war. Had not Schleicher himself said a few weeks earlier that the Reichswehr would not be able to cope with a Nazi rising? Schleicher replied that the situation was different now. The Nazi party was substantially weaker than it had been in early December and the Lippe success had been greatly exaggerated. The Strasser crisis was still far from settled; Hitler's readiness to grant far-reaching concessions showed how worried he actually was. Unless he could soon offer something concrete to his stormtroopers, they would turn to the Com-

[39] Ribbentrop, *London und Moskau*, entries of Jan. 19–23, 1933, p. 39.

munists. It was this fear that had frightened so many into supporting Hitler as the only protection against Communism. Schleicher
was convinced that the Communists would not rise, nor would
there be a general strike, which had been his main concern in
December, since the labor unions would now support him. In case
of a showdown he was in a stronger position than Papen since he
was in charge of both political and military power. Thanks to the
advances made in the disarmament discussions, he could also re-
enforce the Reichswehr with volunteers without fear of objections
from the Western Powers, and with such reenforcements the
Reichswehr could easily deal with the Nazi formations.

But Hindenburg was not impressed. He was unable to see any
difference between Schleicher's position and that of Papen and
doubted that Schleicher's tactics would work. He would think
about the dissolution of the Reichstag, but for the time being he
would not postpone new elections beyond the appointed time since
everybody would hold a postponement against him as a violation
of the constitution. Clearly he found the Nazi threats of impeach-
ing him deeply disturbing. If he should ever take such a step, he
added, the party leaders would have to be asked whether they
acknowledged the existence of a state emergency, and thus could
not accuse him of violating the constitution. He was certainly
not ready to appoint Hitler as chancellor, he observed, since the
forces around Hitler had not even reached an agreement among
themselves. But this can hardly have seemed reassuring to Schleicher.[40]

The news of Schleicher's proposal quickly leaked out. Reaction
was swift and revealing. Center and Social Democrats vied with
each other in denouncing the plan as a crime. Otto Braun,
oblivious of his own somewhat similar scheme, denounced it as
"open high treason." Still unaware of the gravity of the crisis, the
republican forces determinedly closed their eyes to the probable
consequences of Schleicher's dismissal. Since Hindenburg would
not give him the needed powers in any event, Schleicher issued a
statement on January 24 denying that he had any intention of
violating the constitution. It helped to placate the Center, but infuriated the German Nationals who at once made public their
break with him.

For Hitler and Papen the German National move came as a

---

[40] On German Nationals, Schmidt-Hannover, *Umdenken*, pp. 323–24; on Hinden-
burg-Schleicher conference, unsigned memorandum, Jan. 28, 1933, in Vogelsang,
Reichswehr, p. 490; also Meissner, *Staatssekretär*, pp. 253–54; Meissner and Wilde,
Machtergreifung, pp. 166–68.

godsend. If Hugenberg could now be persuaded to join them, Hindenburg might be persuaded more easily to accept Hitler as chancellor. That afternoon Papen met with Frick, Göring, and Ribbentrop: "Decision to form a national front to support Papen's position with old Hindenburg," Ribbentrop's diary states. The turning point now seemed in sight. The next afternoon Oskar von Hindenburg came to tea with the Ribbentrops. "It appears," the host later noted, "that a Hitler chancellorship under the auspices of a new national front is not entirely hopeless." Before his father would make up his mind, Oskar promised to have another talk with von Ribbentrop.

No time was lost in approaching the *Stahlhelm* and German Nationals. Seldte, volatile and impulsive, was quickly persuaded to join; Duesterberg who had had his disheartening experiences with the Nazis opposed all collaboration. Hugenberg stood halfway between them—not completely opposed, but still most reluctant to ally himself with the slippery Fuehrer.

All efforts to change Hindenburg's mind remained unsuccessful, however. Although he no longer dismissed out of hand the appointment of Hitler, Papen was still the man of his choice. His callers were all assured that he would not make Hitler chancellor. Should Schleicher have to resign, Papen would take his place. With the stubbornness of old age, secluded and lonesome, he could not perceive that Papen would command still less support than Schleicher.[41]

Hindenburg now had less hesitation to part with Schleicher since the general had become dispensable as Reichswehr minister and a possible substitute had been found in General Werner von Blomberg, thus removing one of the president's main concerns. As commanding general in East Prussia, Blomberg had been a frequent caller at Neudeck; he had the pleasant manners and the natural charm that counted so much with Hindenburg, and the marshal had taken a liking to him. One of the few generals who sympathized with the Nazis, he had been called to the president's attention by Hitler's entourage, and sometime during these weeks Hindenburg sought his advice behind Schleicher's back. Consulted on the use of the army against the Nazis, Blomberg warned strongly against it. With Nazi sympathies widespread among officers and men he predicted certain defeat for the Reichswehr in a struggle against the S.A. and S.S. Blomberg felt that the best solution

41 Schmidt-Hannover, *Umdenken*, pp. 323–24; Duesterberg, *Stahlhelm*, p. 39; Ribbentrop, *London und Moskau*, entries of Jan. 24–26, 1933, pp. 39–40; Kleist-Schmenzin, "Letzte Möglichkeit," p. 89.

would be the appointment of Hitler as chancellor; he was confident that the army would welcome a Hitler-led government.[42]

The cabals and maneuvers of the following days are difficult to unravel. Much of the available documentation consists of statements uttered or written long after the event, with names and dates confused and recollections often fragmentary and self-contradictory. Yet whether or not wholly accurate, the sources all convey something of the tense conspirational atmosphere in which the main participants moved. Except for Hitler, they were all caught up in the momentum of their own machinations, and they were all drawn towards Hitler as moths are drawn to a flame in which they will ultimately perish. In their midst, sensing vaguely the struggle that was raging around him, stood the lonely old marshal, trying not to let himself be carried away by the tide of events, but lacking the strength and a realistic alternative to compel a change of direction.

Schleicher, unaware of Blomberg's emergence, still thought of himself as the Reichswehr's sole spokesman. As such, he was certain he would be a key factor in any new government, no matter who led it. His first move, after his audience with Hindenburg, was to have Hammerstein call on Hitler to inform him that the Reichswehr "could under no circumstances approve his chancellorship." The step was as futile as it was unwise. Hitler knew better and saw to it that Hindenburg was at once informed of Hammerstein's warning. When the latter called on the president the next morning, he was greeted grimly: the marshal would not stand for any of his generals interfering in politics; "if the generals won't obey, I'll dismiss all of them." Hammerstein reassured him that the Reichswehr was fully loyal to him, and Hindenburg became friendlier again.

But Hammerstein was not prepared to drop the matter of Schleicher's succession. He had come specifically to warn Hindenburg against dismissing Schleicher and appointing either Hitler

---

[42] Meissner, *Staatssekretär*, pp. 255–56, 264–66; Schmidt-Hannover, *Umdenken*, pp. 330–31; Bussche-Ippenburg, *ZS./217*; Brüning, "Ein Brief," p. 18. The exact time and circumstances of Blomberg's visit still remain to be clarified. It is probable that Blomberg saw Hindenburg during his Christmas leave in Berlin; Bracher, *Auflösung*, p. 713 n. 115; Schmidt-Hannover, *Umdenken*, p. 331. If Hindenburg summoned him secretly from Geneva some time in January, as Meissner reports, it is doubtful that Schleicher would not have heard of it. Blomberg himself does not mention any contact with Hindenburg prior to his appointment in his memoirs and is altogether very vague about his activities during this entire period. Cf. *Miscell. German Records*, Pt. III/185. See also Vogelsang, *Reichswehr*, p. 375, who, following Meissner, assumes that the Hindenburg-Blomberg talk took place during the last week of January.

or Papen as his successor. Like Schleicher, however, he was by now more concerned about Papen's candidacy than about Hitler's. Given Papen's unpopularity, he worried about the difficulties the army might face should it have to come to the aid of a Papen-Hugenberg cabinet. Perhaps Hindenburg was too tired to follow Hammerstein's arguments, perhaps he wished to ignore them. He still wanted Papen rather than Hitler as chancellor, and passing over Hammerstein's objections to Papen, he merely replied: "You don't believe I am going to make this Austrian corporal Chancellor." [43]

While Schleicher and Hammerstein kept worrying about Papen's candidacy, Papen was working harder than ever to secure Hitler's chancellorship. As he saw it, the main obstacle to a Hitler-led government was now not so much the president as Hugenberg and the German Nationals whom Hindenburg would want to see represented in such a cabinet. Hugenberg, however, who had a much clearer conception of the risks involved than did Papen, had his own terms on which he insisted: if he participated at all, he wished to have his economic program adopted, and he asked for the economic and agricultural portfolios in both Reich and Prussia. He also made clear that he would not consent to the Nazis taking over the Prussian police. Finally, he opposed a new dissolution of the Reichstag which Hitler also demanded. For he knew that with Hitler as chancellor the Nazis would gain greatly in strength, and as Lippe had taught, the German Nationals would be among the chief losers.

But Hitler was not easy to deal with either and Hugenberg's objections enraged him. Convinced that he was Germany's man of destiny, he was certain that fate would in any event soon place him at the head of the government. Should he bother therefore with small minds who failed to see this? He was ready to break off the negotiations and leave Berlin.

[43] Goebbels, *Vom Kaiserhof*, entry of Jan. 27, 1933, p. 259; Picker, *Hitlers Tischgespräche*, pp. 429–30. The Hindenburg-Hammerstein exchange is based on the three accounts of Hammerstein, Bussche-Ippenburg who also was present, and Meissner. All of them are fragmentary and marred by obvious inaccuracies; Hammerstein, memorandum of Jan. 29, 1935, in Bracher, *Auflösung*, p. 733; Bussche-Ippenburg, in *Frankfurter Hefte*, XI (1956), 125–26; Meissner, *Staatssekretär*, pp. 267–68. See also Kuntzen, in *Frankfurter Hefte*, XI (1956), 165; Schüddekopf, *Heer und Republik*, p. 356 n. 911. As for the exact date of the meeting, Hammerstein's account which is the one written closest to the event fixes it on January 27; Bussche-Ippenburg sets it for January 27 in Hermann Foertsch, *Schuld und Verhängnis: Die Fritsch-Krise im Frühjahr 1938 als Wendepunkt in der Geschichte der nationalsozialistischen Zeit* (Stuttgart, 1951), p. 26, and for January 26, in *Frankfurter Hefte*, *loc. cit.* See also the somewhat different account in Vogelsang, *Reichswehr*, pp. 378–79.

Lacking his sense of destiny, his entourage worked hard to induce him to stay; his lieutenants feared that by leaving he might pass up his last chance of gaining power. Ribbentrop suggested that Hitler present his case directly to Hindenburg, but Hitler thought little of the proposal. What could he possibly tell the "Old Gentleman" he had not said before? Nor did he wish to encourage false hopes, as doubtless he would, if his followers learned that he was going to call on the president. In the end he agreed that a meeting with Hindenburg might be arranged as a last resort, but he doubted that it would help. The old marshal, he knew, was one of the few people who had remained immune to his personal spell which had won over so many other doubters.

It was then decided that Hitler would meet first with Hugenberg and later that same day with Papen. Göring would contact Meissner and take Hitler's case through Meissner to Hindenburg. This latter meeting turned out to be highly encouraging. Once more Göring assured the state secretary that Hitler as chancellor would respect the rights of president, Reichstag, and Reichswehr, that he was anxious to shield the army from politics, and that he did not demand more than two cabinet seats for his party friends. To his happy surprise Göring discovered that he was proselytizing among the converted. While Hindenburg had not yet reached a final decision, Meissner assumed that Papen had convinced him of the merits of a Hitler-led government. Such a government, Meissner thought, would be formed in the next few days.

Fortified by this knowledge, Göring joined Hitler at the meeting with Hugenberg and his party friend Schmidt-Hannover, but this conference went badly. The German Nationals were little impressed with Göring's triumphant announcement that Papen was committed to Hitler's candidacy and that the *Stahlhelm* too had accepted Hitler's claim to the chancellorship. The Nazis insisted that their demands concerning cabinet posts, the Prussian police, and the Reichstag be met. The meeting ended in a fierce row. Hitler was beside himself with rage—again he wanted to break off all negotiations at once and leave immediately for Munich. "I have never seen Hitler in such a state," Ribbentrop noted morosely. Would the efforts of the last few weeks all be wasted? And with Hindenburg apparently ready to accept Hitler, was success to elude them again when it seemed in their grasp? Göring and Ribbentrop tried to calm Hitler and to assure him that nothing was lost. He was in the end persuaded to stay within easy reach if he insisted on leaving Berlin. Ribbentrop would talk matters over with Papen since Hitler refused to see him.

430

While tempers flared and nerves were snapping, nothing could faze the indefatigable Papen. The Hugenberg trouble, he assured Ribbentrop, was a minor matter; he himself remained firmly convinced of the necessity to make Hitler chancellor. Schleicher would lead the country back into Marxism, while another presidential cabinet could not provide a clear-cut solution either. "Papen is now convinced," Ribbentrop noted, "that he must insist on Hitler's chancellorship under all circumstances and that he ought not to hold himself in reserve for Hindenburg as a last resort. To my mind this conclusion of Papen's is the turning point in the matter." [44]

There was one final development that evening which sealed Schleicher's fate. The Reichstag's council of elders met once more to reconsider its decision to convene a plenary session on the thirty-first. On the twentieth the Nazis, uncertain of the future, had favored a new postponement of all plenary sessions, but now that they had been told that Hindenburg was considering Hitler's appointment as Schleicher's successor, they were anxious to remove the chancellor by a no-confidence vote. And if Hindenburg should make Papen chancellor, the latter, lacking any mass support, could be more easily dealt with than Schleicher. The decision to reconvene the Reichstag on the thirty-first was upheld with their support. [45]

On the morning of January 28, Papen was again received by the president. Once more he explained why a Papen-Hugenberg cabinet was unrealizable. A government headed by Hitler and checked by adequate safeguards was the only possible solution.

The president seemed to be wavering. Pressures on him had been mounting continuously. The unceasing flood of letters, telegrams, and petitions urging Hitler's appointment had deluged him for many months now. Blomberg had declared Hitler acceptable to the army, and so, for that matter, had Hammerstein. Even as impeccable a conservative as Oldenburg-Januschau had recently told him that he saw nothing objectionable in a Hitler-led government. And when Hindenburg had objected to the "uncouth and violent ways of the Nazis," Oldenburg had in his "jovial way," according to Meissner, told his old friend that he did not

---

[44] Papen, *Wahrheit*, pp. 267–69; Ribbentrop, *London und Moskau*, entry of Jan. 27, 1933, pp. 40–41; Goebbels, *Vom Kaiserhof*, entry of Jan. 27, 1933, p. 249; Schmidt-Hannover, *Umdenken*, pp. 332–33; Picker, *Hitlers Tischgespräche*, p. 429; Borchmeyer, *Hugenbergs Ringen*, I, 25–26; Göring, in I.M.T., *Trial*, IX, 248–49; Meissner, I.M.T., Case No. 11, transcript, p. 4597.

[45] Schulthess, Jan. 27, 1933, p. 28.

anticipate any difficulties in handling these young people "who were after all quite attractive." Oldenburg's assurances seemed to be borne out by Göring's legality pledge, reported to him that same morning by Meissner. Whatever might be said against Hitler, the "Czech corporal," Göring was a much decorated officer and air ace who had been awarded even the coveted *Pour le Mérite,* and the word of such a man carried great weight with the marshal. So of course did the counsel of the ever present Oskar, now fully on Papen's side, in those private father-and-son talks in which the father unburdened himself of his worries. And was it not his duty, as his advisers had discreetly suggested, to bring Hitler into the government while he could still be surrounded by effective controls under his, Hindenburg's, authority? Would not after his death a new presidential election throw all power to Hitler without such restraints?

True to form Hindenburg eschewed any commitment, but Papen could sense a change. When Ribbentrop called on him later that morning, Papen greeted him excitedly with the question: "Where is Hitler?" If he had left, he would have to be recalled at once, for there had been a shift in Hindenburg's attitude. He felt, Papen reported happily, that the "Old Gentleman" might now accept Hitler as chancellor. The overjoyed Ribbentrop hurried away to look for the Fuehrer.[46]

At that very moment the hapless Schleicher was meeting with his ministers. Since he was to face the Reichstag in three days, the cabinet had to decide on its course of action. Schleicher stated that he could go before the Reichstag only if he were armed with a dissolution decree. He doubted that the president would grant him one since he wished to avoid a showdown. There was nothing left, then, but to resign since he had not been able to gather a parliamentary majority. According to his information, however, another presidential cabinet would be formed, with Papen and Hugenberg its guiding spirits. Such a government would never receive any mass support and might well plunge the country into a grave crisis. He proposed to warn the president against Papen's appointment, and the cabinet voiced its agreement. Schwerin-

---

[46] Meissner, *Staatssekretär,* pp. 263–66, 272–73; Schmidt-Hannover, *Umdenken,* p. 324; Ribbentrop, *London und Moskau,* entry of Jan. 28, 1933, p. 41. Papen's call on Hindenburg is mentioned only in *ibid.* But Ribbentrop's detailed and consistent diary entries for this period appear more reliable than Papen's notations which are vague and incomplete. Papen himself states that he did not see Hindenburg that day until after the latter had received Schleicher; *Wahrheit,* p. 267. Schleicher's account of his conference with Hindenburg that day also lends credence to Ribbentrop's version of the day's developments; cab. mtg., Jan. 28, 1933, *RKz./*1711/791595.

Krosigk and Neurath offered to call on the president to add their own warnings to those of the chancellor.

The meeting was temporarily adjourned, and Schleicher went to see Hindenburg. His visit was short; in less than half an hour he was back with the cabinet. He had told the marshal of his misgivings and related to him Neurath's and Schwerin's offer to present their views. If the president did not wish to dissolve the Reichstag, he considered a Hitler-led government as the only possible alternative. Hindenburg seems to have paid little attention to what the chancellor was saying. The government had not been able to secure a majority, he growled, but he was hopeful of forming one now that would carry out his ideas. He would accept the cabinet's resignation; his mind was made up, and any further consultations would not make his task any easier. "Whether what I am going to do now is right, my dear Schleicher," the latter quoted him later, "I don't know; but I shall know it soon when I am up there," and he pointed towards the ceiling. Obviously the two men had been talking about different things: while Schleicher was pleading with him not to appoint Papen, Hindenburg was worrying about the appointment of Hitler.

This misunderstanding may also account for the confidence Schleicher and his entourage displayed in regard to the general's political future. Planck, his faithful aide, stated that same day that the general would be back in the chancellor's seat within two months; he would merely let the "Old Gentleman" struggle on by himself for a little while now. And in order to show how fully convinced he was of an early return to his post, Schleicher commissioned a leading economist to draw up a memorandum on the nationalization of the coal and steel industries by April 1.[47]

After Schleicher's departure, Papen was called back to the president, and in the presence of Meissner and Oskar the situation was once more thoroughly canvassed. Halfheartedly Hindenburg again brought up Papen's appointment, but it was obvious that he himself was no longer considering it seriously. All three men vowed that Hitler's chancellorship was the only constitutional solution and that with the safeguards devised he could be restrained. "It is my unpleasant duty then to appoint this fellow Hitler as Chancellor?" he sighed, carefully shifting the burden of the decision to his advisers. Papen was instructed to explore the

[47] Unsigned memorandum on Hindenburg-Schleicher conference, Jan. 28, 1933, in Vogelsang, *Reichswehr*, pp. 490–91; also *ibid.*, pp. 382–83; cab. mtg., Jan. 28, 1933, *RKz.*/1711/791595–97; Hindenburg's remark in Görlitz, *Hindenburg*, p. 401; Schleicher's confidence, in Eschenburg, "Franz von Papen," p. 163 n. 34.

possibility of a Hitler-led government "within the framework of the Constitution and in agreement with the Reichstag."

This qualified mandate, had he taken it seriously, would have barred Hitler's chancellorship from the outset, but Papen would not be held back. He plunged into a new round of conferences in pursuit of his mission. Hugenberg, informed of the president's wishes, voiced his earlier apprehensions. Nevertheless since Hindenburg was willing to bear with Hitler and the *Stahlhelm* was ready to enter a Hitler-led cabinet, the German National chieftain feared that he might be outflanked by the course of events. When Papen assured him that adequate safeguards would be built into the new cabinet, he promised his collaboration. As before, he insisted, however, on obtaining both the Reich and Prussian ministries of economics and agriculture in order to block any economic adventures.[48]

The negotiations with Hitler's spokesmen turned primarily on the allocation of the Prussian portfolios. Hitler still asked for the post of Reich commissioner of Prussia, which both Papen and Schleicher had held as chancellor, but Hindenburg wanted Papen to take over that post. Hitler also refused to look for a parliamentary majority in the existing Reichstag and insisted on new elections.

Since Papen's mandate called for a government acceptable to the Reichstag, he should either have insisted on a Reichstag majority or should have returned his mandate. As it was, he did neither. That same afternoon Center and Bavarian People's Party tried to inject themselves into the discussions, but Papen, knowing that Hitler would not collaborate with them, rejected their offer contrary to the marshal's instructions. When he reported back to the president later that evening, he pictured Hitler as moderate rather than intransigent. That the Fuehrer wished to be Prussian commissioner, he apparently did not mention, but much was made of his willingness to retain Neurath, Schwerin-Krosigk, Gürtner, and Eltz in their respective capacities. Both men failed to perceive why he had no objections to these nonpolitical civil servants. Hindenburg, perhaps, could not be expected to see

[48] Papen, *Wahrheit*, pp. 269–70; Meissner and Wilde, *Machtergreifung*, p. 177 (with Hindenburg's question). Shortly before, an alternate plan had been submitted to Papen and Hugenberg by some conservative friends. It proposed a cabinet headed by Papen, composed largely of nonpolitical experts, with Hugenberg in charge of all economic ministries and his party friend Ewald von Kleist-Schmenzin, a Pomeranian landowner, as minister of the interior. Kleist-Schmenzin, a house guest of Papen, urged his host to recommend this solution to Hindenburg. Papen,

through his reasoning, but Papen who took so much pride in the safeguards he had devised, never seems to have wondered either whether these technical experts could hold their own against Hitler's ruthless aggressiveness. Nor did it ever occur to him that Hitler who had moved the center of political gravity from parliament and conference room to the street might refuse to let himself be outvoted in orderly cabinet meetings.

Papen showed a similar insouciance in the choice of a Reichswehr minister, presumably the most critical of all appointments. Schleicher was no longer considered; an editorial in that morning's *Tägliche Rundschau*, supposedly inspired by him, had cautioned the president against a Papen-Hugenberg government that might try to hush up the Eastern Aid scandals and lead to his own overthrow, and the president had deeply resented this latest affront. Evidently Papen had not until then discussed this vital appointment with Hindenburg. He now proposed General Baron von Fritsch, an old friend of his and a capable soldier, whom Hindenburg knew only slightly. Hindenburg himself thought of Blomberg whom Papen in turn hardly knew. The president praised him "as a nonpolitical passionate soldier with pleasant manners." As a delegate to the Disarmament Conference he had moreover shown that he had the *savoir faire* a minister required. Papen agreed that Blomberg's qualifications, as described by the president, would make him a suitable Reichswehr minister; if he was a nonpolitical soldier, he reasoned, he would reject any Nazi intrusions into the army.

Papen made no attempt to make certain of Blomberg's qualifications. Obviously he did not dare question Hindenburg's judgment in a military matter although he ought to have wondered how good a judge the aged marshal still was. But Papen was also driven on by the fear that time was working against him and that any delay might deny him his final success. In this hasty, offhand manner, the man who was to be in charge of the main counterweight against Hitler was chosen. As it happened, Blomberg was one of the generals least likely to fight Hitler—on the other hand, it is hard to think of one who would actually have offered resistance. Indeed, the concept of the Reichswehr as a curb on Hitler was altogether a dubious one. If the army had been

---

however, dismissed the proposal as completely impractical unless an agreement with Hitler should prove impossible. Hugenberg's first reaction seems to have been favorable, but with Papen unwilling to consider the plan, he too rejected it as unfeasible. Cf. Kleist-Schmenzin, "Letzte Möglichkeit," pp. 90–92.

unwilling to check him while he was out of power, it was not likely to fight him once he was chancellor.[49]

Some months before Papen himself had voiced such doubts, but they played no role now in his thinking. They did so the less because he does not seem to have given much thought to the possibility of a conflict arising between Nazis and non-Nazis in the new government. Not only did he fail to concern himself with the political expertise and personal toughness of his ministerial colleagues, he also sidestepped consistently the question of new elections after Hitler's appointment. Although this was one of the major issues dividing Nazis and German Nationals, he thought it a minor question that ought to be settled after the cabinet had been formed. Nor does he seem to have mentioned to Hindenburg that this issue existed. In fact, he appears to have conveyed the impression to the president that a Hitler-led government would have a majority in the Reichstag. Throughout he seems to have felt, despite his experiences to the contrary, that he was dealing with men with whom collaboration would present no serious problem.

At the conclusion of their discussion Hindenburg asked Papen formally to assume the post of vice-chancellor, and Papen, as he puts it, felt that he ought not to disappoint the confidence of the president, and declared himself ready to take that post should the projected government under Hitler materialize. As a further safeguard against any surprises, it was also agreed that Papen would always be present when Hitler reported to the president.[50]

The following morning Hitler and Göring called on Papen for a final discussion. Hitler agreed to let Papen take the top post in Prussia if Göring were given the ministry of the interior, but he still insisted on new elections and the passage, by the next Reichstag, of a comprehensive Enabling Act. Papen promised to take up his requests with the president.

Hitler's demands apparently did not worry him, nor does he seem to have wondered how he could curb Göring's power, removed, as he, Papen, would be from the direct control of the Prussian police. He was equally unconcerned when he learned

[49] Whether Schleicher would have used his emergency powers in a forcible showdown had they been granted to him is also doubtful. He was not distinguished by strong nerves. On the other hand, it is also unlikely that the Nazis would have risen against him.

[50] Papen, *Wahrheit*, pp. 269–71, 289, 291; Schwend, *Bayern*, 504–05; Bracher, *Auflösung*, p. 721 n. 157. In case an agreement with Hitler should not prove possible, preparations were meanwhile made for a Papen-Hugenberg cabinet by Papen and his associates so that, if need be, it could be set up "within an hour." (Papen) Cf. Vogelsang, *Reichswehr*, pp. 385–87.

that morning that Dr. Wilhelm Frick had been selected by Hitler as Reich minister of the interior. Frick had gained notoriety in 1930 as Thuringian minister of the interior when he attempted to Nazify the Thuringian police and introduced racist-chauvinist prayers in Thuringia's schools. Nevertheless Papen considered him "an older official and moderate man who at one time had led the Thuringian Government with circumspection."

That same morning Papen also conferred with Hugenberg, Dingeldey, and the two *Stahlhelm* leaders, Seldte and Duester-berg. Hugenberg was now reconciled to Hitler's chancellorship, provided there would be no new elections. He was gratified to learn that Hindenburg was anxious to have him take over all the economic ministries—at long last the marshal was asking for his collaboration. Papen, moreover, hinted that should he refuse, Hitler might form a government with the Center. If he was to retain some measure of influence, he had to accept the president's invitation. In control of all economic ministries he thought he would have enough leverage to make his presence felt in the cabinet. When Duesterberg demurred and warned against Hitler's own dynamism and that of his fanaticized mass movement, Hugen-berg pointed out confidently that nothing could go wrong since Hitler was being checkmated by Hindenburg as president and commander-in-chief of the army, Papen as vice-chancellor, himself as the economic leader, and Seldte as minister of labor. Both Dingeldey and Seldte agreed. Seldte's participation, it was noted, would ensure the support of the *Stahlhelm* and thus provide a counterweight to the Brown Shirts. That large numbers of *Stahl-helmers* had voted for Hitler in all recent elections, no one seems to have mentioned.

After the meeting Papen and Hugenberg were once more be-sieged by conservative friends who warned them again not to court certain disaster by allowing Hitler to head the new govern-ment. When they found both men committed, they urged them to insist on a dissolution of the Reichstag without new elections. Hitler, they hoped, would find this demand unacceptable and refuse to take over the government on such terms. But neither Papen nor Hugenberg, each for his own reasons, would consider this counsel of desperation.

In the early afternoon Papen reported to the president that an agreement had been reached among all participants and that preparations had been completed for the formation of the new government. This time he also brought up Hitler's demand for new elections. He explained that a Hitler-led government was so basic a change that the agreement of the electorate should be obtained; Hitler, moreover, had promised that these would be the last elections. Again there was apparently no mention of the opposite view held by Hugenberg. Hindenburg, in Meissner's words, voiced no objections, but his subsequent attitude raises the question whether his silence meant assent or inability to grasp the issue. The presentation of the new cabinet to the president and the swearing-in ceremony were set for 11 o'clock the next morning.

When Göring called on him later that afternoon, Papen reported happily that everything had been arranged with the president. But while Hindenburg now was ready to dissolve the Reichstag, Hugenberg's opposition, he had to admit, had not yet been overcome. He dismissed this as of minor importance. "Let's not talk about new elections," he suggested to Göring, "that makes it only more difficult to set up the government." Göring agreed and hurried off to report to his Fuehrer that at long last the door to the Reich chancellery stood open to him. He found him at Goebbels' apartment, over coffee and cake. Goebbels himself has described the scene in his own dramatized style:

"This is certainly Göring's finest hour. . . . This upright soldier with a child's heart . . . is standing before his Fuehrer to bring him the happiest message of his life. For a long time we do not say anything, and then we rise and shake hands.

"A wordless oath to the Fuehrer: All shall remain as before! The world shall find us a glowing example of loyalty to the Fuehrer and of the noblest comradeship which can link men together.

"This shall be a pledge! . . .

"The great hour has come!"[51]

But the Nazi leaders were not to rejoice for long. Into their

[51] Papen, *Wahrheit*, pp. 271–73, Ribbentrop, *London und Moskau*, entry of Jan. 29, 1933, p. 42; Schmidt-Hannover, *Umdenken*, pp. 334–36; Borchmeyer, *Hugenbergs Ringen*, I, 26; Duesterberg, *Stahlhelm*, pp. 38–39; Kleist-Schmenzin, "Letzte Möglichkeit," pp. 91–92; Meissner, *Staatssekretär*, pp. 268–69; on Frick, Bracher, *Auflösung*, p. 360 n. 100; Goebbels, *Vom Kaiserhof*, entry of Jan. 29, 1933, pp. 250–51. Hindenburg's attitude throughout that day disproves the claim that he remained doubtful whether he ought to appoint Hitler as chancellor. Several conservative friends saw him that afternoon and urged him not to appoint Hitler. True to his penchant for sidestepping arguments by answering evasively, he may have been noncommittal. There is no positive evidence to support Brüning's assertion that "he was wavering in his decision until a few hours before Hitler's appointment." Brüning, in *Deutsche Zeitung*, May 28, 1952. According to Kunrat von Hammerstein, Hindenburg also told his press aide, when the latter reported to him on the morning of January 29, that he would appoint Papen as chancellor; Hammerstein, in *Frankfurter Hefte*, xi (1956), 128. One wonders, however, whether the date is correct since January 29 was a Sunday and Hindenburg was not likely to receive routine reports on a Sunday. Vogelsang, *Reichswehr*, pp. 391–92, believes that Hindenburg

celebrations burst the news that Schleicher had mobilized the Potsdam garrison; it was now on its way to the capital to bar Hitler from taking over the government. The report was wholly unfounded, and there is no need to speculate on who may have launched it and why. In the fetid atmosphere of intrigue and conspiracy that hung over Berlin during those days, it was widely believed and made sense above all to the Hitler camp. Schleicher had earlier that day made a last desperate effort to inject himself into the negotiations. Still fearful that a Papen-Hugenberg government had not yet been ruled out, he had sent Hammerstein to Hitler and had proposed to him an alliance between the Reichswehr and Nazis: together they would form a new government with Hitler as chancellor and Schleicher as Reichswehr minister. Hitler's answer had been evasive since he knew, unlike Schleicher and Hammerstein, that Papen's reappointment was no longer likely. Was Schleicher, who might meanwhile have learned that he was not to be retained as Reichswehr minister, trying to stay on in that post by armed force? Hitler issued orders to the Berlin stormtroops to hold themselves in readiness for emergency duty. Nazi connections with the Berlin police force were so close by this time that he could also notify a senior officer of the approaching trouble and suggest that he too alert his men. Hindenburg, informed by Papen of Schleicher's alleged plans, refused to believe that one of his generals would rise against him, the marshal. But he agreed that Schleicher would best be replaced as quickly as possible as Reichswehr minister. At Papen's suggestion he decided to swear in Blomberg (who had been called back from Geneva) ahead of the rest of the cabinet as soon as he reached Berlin. Oskar was ordered to meet him at the station the next morning and bring him at once to the president.[52]

When Blomberg arrived at Berlin's "Anhalter Bahnhof" in the early morning hours of January 30, he was greeted, not only by Oskar von Hindenburg, but also by Hammerstein's chief military aide. The latter had been sent to the station by Schleicher and Hammerstein who had learned of his impending return. The

---

did not reach a final decision on January 29 since Schwerin-Krosigk and Neurath were not notified until the following morning that a new government was to be formed with Hitler as chancellor and that they were to be sworn in at 11 o'clock. The delay, it would seem, was due to the fact that both men had already agreed to serve in such a government so that their notification was considered a mere technicality. See also p. 443 in the text.

[52] *Ibid.*; Picker, *Hitlers Tischgespräche*, pp. 430–31; Papen, *Wahrheit*, pp. 273–74; Meissner, *Staatssekretär*, p. 268; Meissner and Wilde, *Machtergreifung*, pp. 183–84; Hammerstein memorandum in Bracher, *Auflösung*, pp. 733–34; Kuntzen, ZS./889.

generals were still worrying about the formation of a Papen-Hugenberg government and they wanted to talk to Blomberg before he saw Hindenburg, hopeful that he might dissuade the "Old Gentleman" from making this grave mistake. Blomberg decided to go with Oskar von Hindenburg, since orders from the president, the commander-in-chief, took precedence over those of Hammerstein. He was at once received by the president and sworn in as Reichswehr minister. This done, no one seemed to remember the reason for this hurried procedure. Warned not to go to the Reichswehr ministry lest he be put under arrest there, Blomberg was left whiling away his time in the park behind the President's Palace.[53]

Papen too had risen early that morning. While Blomberg was being rushed to the president, he met once more with Hugenberg, Seldte, and Duesterberg. His great fear was that his precarious arrangements might collapse at the last moment due to Hugenberg's continued misgivings. He knew how strong the opposition was in the German National camp to a Hitler-led cabinet (that very morning Duesterberg and Schmidt-Hannover had pleaded with Seldte not to join such a government), he knew of the approaches to Hindenburg the day before by conservative circles, and he knew above all that Hitler and Hugenberg had not yet agreed on new elections. As he had feared, Hugenberg once more raised serious objections to a cabinet under Hitler. Papen, exasperated, now warned excitedly: "If the new government has not been formed by 11 o'clock, the Reichswehr is going to march. Schleicher and Hammerstein may establish a military dictatorship." When asked about the source of this information, he shouted impatiently: "From Hindenburg, Jr." Duesterberg and Schmidt-Hannover hastened over to Oskar von Hindenburg for further information, but the colonel, excited and nervous, was vague in his answers. Apparently the putsch rumors had been revived in the night when Meissner had been aroused from his sleep with the warning that Schleicher was going to arrest him and both the Hindenburgs. No one thought of dispatching an armed force to Reichswehr headquarters to thwart any imminent rising. It is difficult to believe therefore that Papen really feared a last-minute attempt by Schleicher and Hammerstein to defeat his plans, and the vagueness with which he treats this episode in his

---

[53] Hammerstein memorandum, *loc. cit.;* Kunrat von Hammerstein, "Schleicher, Hammerstein und die Machtübernahme 1933," *Frankfurter Hefte,* IX (1956), pp. 169 n.19, 171–72.

memoirs suggests that he was simply making a desperate effort to overcome Hugenberg's reservations.

Hugenberg seemed to relent, and at the appointed hour he joined the other prospective members of the new cabinet in Meissner's office. While they were waiting to be taken to Hindenburg, the question of new elections was brought up again. Hitler complained anew that he had been deprived of the post of Reich commissioner of Prussia that should be rightfully his. In return, he ought at least to be granted new Reichstag elections. Hugenberg objected heatedly on the grounds that elections had been held only a few weeks before, and a bitter argument followed. Once more the new government seemed endangered, for if Hugenberg were to withdraw now, Hindenburg might well refuse to appoint Hitler as chancellor. Sensing the danger, Hitler walked over to Hugenberg with outstretched hand: *"Herr Geheimrat,* I give you my solemn word of honor that I shall never part with any of the men who are present here no matter how the elections turn out." But Hugenberg was not impressed since he had been the victim of Hitler's broken promises too often to trust him now. Nor did he oppose new elections simply as a reinsurance against future dismissal. What he feared was that they would produce a Nazi majority and thus give Hitler full freedom of action.

Papen, impatient and anxious, found Hugenberg's worries unreasonable. Once more he saw his tenuous pact with the irate Hitler jeopardized. To his relief, Seldte and the three "experts," demonstrating at once their inefficacy as "safeguards," sided with him, but Hugenberg would not yield. At this moment Meissner, watch in hand, appeared in the door: "Gentlemen, it is five minutes past the appointed time. The President likes punctuality." Papen was frantic. *"Herr Geheimrat,"* he pleaded, "do you want to risk the national unity which has finally been achieved after so many difficult negotiations? You cannot possibly doubt the solemn word of honor of a German man!" But Hugenberg knew what was at stake, and the bitter debate continued.

Meissner had meanwhile been called back to Hindenburg's study. The president resented being kept waiting. "Let them make up their mind," he growled, "whether or not they want to form a government. There has been time enough for discussions." The state secretary rushed back to his office where the dispute still raged unabated. "The President requests you not to keep him waiting any longer," he warned. "It is now 11:15. The Old Gentleman may retire at any moment!"

There were new pleas, new arguments and counterarguments.

Hitler promised to contact at once the Center and Bavarian People's Party to secure as broad a foundation as possible for the new government. But to Hugenberg, who distrusted both parties, this was no inducement. In the end he decided to leave the decision to Hindenburg, perhaps because he assumed that the president would not want to dissolve the Reichstag again.

Twenty minutes late, the group hurried over to the presidential reception room. Hindenburg did not inquire why they were late. Nor did he address them and outline their task for them. It is unlikely that Meissner had not prepared a brief speech for him —infuriated by the delay, he may have wished to show his displeasure by omitting the customary amenities. After they had been sworn in, Hitler, unexpectedly, spoke up. He pledged himself solemnly to observe the constitution and respect the rights of the president. He would find a majority, he promised, and thus relieve Hindenburg of the burden of signing emergency decrees, he would deal with the economic crisis and would, above all, unite the strife-torn nation into a genuine national community.

Hindenburg still would not say anthing. As if he wished to wash his hands of the whole matter,[54] he dismissed them with one brief sentence: "And now, gentlemen, forward with God!"[55]

လ

There was something darkly symbolic in Hindenburg's failure to set forth the tasks that awaited the new cabinet. The fact was that at no point during the lengthy negotiations had the government's program been discussed. This in itself was perhaps nothing new; questions of policy had played a subordinate role in the formation of the Brüning cabinet and had been considered hardly at all when Papen and Schleicher were appointed. But these governments had been made up of men who shared common values and goals which provided some basis for their collaboration.

Such a foundation was lacking now. Nevertheless no effort was

[54] This may well have been the case. Hitler was the only chancellor to whom Hindenburg did not personally offer that post. Papen's role during those days recalls that of Groener during the winter of 1918–19 when Hindenburg kept carefully out of the negotiations with Ebert. Presumably he would have let the hapless Papen bear the sole responsibility in case Hitler's appointment should have proven ineffective. Conversely, true to himself, he made no effort to share the credit for the appointment with Papen when during the following months he himself was hailed as the man who had forged all "national" forces into a new union for the salvation of the Reich.

[55] Papen, *Wahrheit*, pp. 275–76; Schmidt-Hannover, *Umdenken*, pp. 337–38; Bracher, *Auflösung*, p. 721 n.161; Duesterberg, *Stahlhelm*, pp. 39–41; Meissner, *Staatssekretär*, pp. 269–70; Meissner and Wilde, *Machtergreifung*, pp. 188–91; Borchmeyer, *Hugenbergs Ringen*, I, 26, 28–29.

made to find any common denominators beyond the negative ones of "anti-Marxism" and antiparliamentarianism. The preliminary negotiations turned solely on posts and power, with each side trying to outwit the other. As part of these maneuvers the appointment of the nonpolitical "experts" was viewed as a mere technicality; if Schwerin-Krosigk's experience was representative, they had merely been sounded out as to their willingness to retain their posts either in a Hitler-Papen cabinet or a Papen-Hugenberg cabinet. As the finance minister testified at his trial in Nürnberg, he received a call from the president's office on January 30 to "report" to the president at 11 o'clock that morning. "There I met other members of the Schleicher Government who had received the same summons. Meissner told us Hindenburg would form a cabinet under Hitler that same morning and wished us to keep our posts in this cabinet. Then we were taken to a room where Hitler and all other members of the future cabinet were assembled to take the oath. There I saw Hitler for the first time." Schwerin barely had time to ask the chancellor-to-be whether he would be allowed to pursue an orderly financial policy to which Hitler gave him a reassuring reply.[56]

If Papen had neglected to discuss with Hitler what policies the new government would pursue, his failure to do so was not accidental. He saw no need to take up substantive questions that were likely to complicate matters further since he expected to have the decisive say in any event. For he was certain that he had finally brought off what no one else had accomplished—he had "engaged" Hitler to work for him and his conservative friends. "In two months we'll have pushed Hitler into a corner so hard he'll be squeaking," he assured his friend Kleist-Schmenzin.[57]

Most Germans may not have been quite so certain, but the news of Hitler's appointment was received with remarkable calm by the majority of his opponents. The liberal bourgeois press, the *Berliner Tageblatt* and the *Frankfurter Zeitung*, commented on it matter-of-factly, and their editorials do not indicate that they were conscious of the imminence of revolutionary changes. Outwardly of course the conservative element seemed to predominate in the new cabinet: the three Nazis, Hitler, Göring, and Frick, were outnumbered by the non-Nazis, Papen, Hugenberg, Seldte, Neurath, Schwerin von Krosigk, Eltz-Rübenach, and the nondescript

[56] Papen, *Wahrheit*, p. 298; Stolper, in *Dt. Volkswirt*, Feb. 3, 1933, p. 565; Neurath, in I.M.T., *Trial*, XVI, 607–09; Schwerin-Krosigk, in Vogelsang, *Reichswehr*, p. 386, and I.M.T., Case No. 11, transcript, p. 22886.

[57] Kleist-Schmenzin, "Letzte Möglichkeit," p. 92; also Schwerin-Krosigk, *Es geschah*, p. 147.

Blomberg. Gereke was retained as commissioner of public works, and Gürtner, after some delay, as minister of justice. "The makeup of the cabinet shows that Herr Hitler had to accept significant conditions," the *Frankfurter Zeitung* commented on January 31, and on February 2 it noted that "it has become all too evident that the Government revolves around Hugenberg, not the Chancellor." Nor did the Center press betray any sign of serious alarm. "The Center Party," wrote *Germania,* "assumes an attitude of ice-cold detachment toward this cabinet which was formed without its knowledge and collaboration. . . . It bears not the least responsibility for the developments which are getting under way now." *Der Deutsche,* the organ of the Catholic labor unions, agreed with the *Frankfurter Zeitung* that the policies of the new government would be determined by Papen and Hugenberg.

The Social Democrats' *Vorwärts* announced that the politically enlightened masses would "coldbloodedly" watch developments and hold themselves in readiness for decisive action as soon as that moment should come. *Vorwärts* was not just whistling in the dark. Many Socialist leaders were confident that Hitler would never receive the required two-thirds majority to change the constitution. While they were reconciled to a period of persecution on the model of Bismarck's anti-Socialist legislation with curbs on their freedoms of press and assembly, they looked upon these difficulties as merely a passing episode from which party and labor unions would emerge stronger than ever before. "On the whole," the British ambassador noted, "the press has taken the appointment of Herr Hitler to the chancellorship with almost philosophic calm," and he added that "the populace took the news phlegmatically."[58] Only a week before the Weimar parties had furiously protested against Schleicher's intention of suspending the constitution, but they saw nothing objectionable in Hitler's chancellorship because all constitutional niceties had been observed.

The view that the Weimar Republic was a political neuter equally open to all parties and ideologies had come full circle. Even staunch republicans accepted the view, irrespective of the intent of the constitution, that the assumption of power by Hitler, the irreconcilable foe of that constitution, was legal.[59] Those who

[58] In a similar vein the *New York Times* reported on January 31 that Hitler "was maneuvered into heading a coalition Government of National Socialists and Nationalists by Lt. Col. Franz von Papen, former Chancellor. . . . The composition of the Cabinet leaves Herr Hitler no scope for the gratification of any dictatorial ambition." And a day later it noted that "it is generally felt that the Government is Colonel von Papen's show."

[59] Nazi jurists were frank to state later that Hitler's "appointment was 'legal' only

felt uneasy at the thought of Hitler in charge of the government consoled themselves with the thought that it was just as well, in the words of the *Deutsche Allgemeine Zeitung,* to take the plunge and get it over. The feeling was widespread that Hitler's appointment had become inevitable in any event.[60]

Besides, there was always that imperturbable guardian of the constitution, the venerable president. True, there were rumors that not all was well with him any longer and that he was showing increasing signs of senility. A story made the rounds after January 30, telling how he was watching the Brown Shirts parading along the Wilhelmstrasse and, turning to Meissner, exclaimed in great surprise: "I had not realized, Ludendorff, that we had taken so many Russian prisoners." But the bulk of the press still suggested a very different picture and hailed him as the country's faithful custodian holding as always his shielding hand over the nation. "With gratitude we think in this hour of the President whose determined action has put . . . an end to these weeks of chaos," one editorial exulted, and Hugenberg's *Berliner Lokal-Anzeiger* wrote on January 31 that "the decisive credit for this impressive solution of one of the gravest crises within forty-eight hours belongs to the aged President." And somewhat cryptically it added: "History is going to inscribe in its records Hindenburg's decision of January 30, 1933 . . . as the President's greatest, whatever its outcome, just as it will always praise that of Tannenberg as the greatest of the strategist Hindenburg." The ambiguity of this statement reflected Hugenberg's continued misgivings. That same day, while the *Frankfurter Zeitung* described him as the center of the new government, he confided to his party friend Goerdeler: "Yesterday I committed the worst folly of my life: I became the ally of the greatest demagogue in world history."

Papers, on the other hand, that were critical of Hitler's appointment, if they brought up Hindenburg's name at all, blamed the decision on his advisers or on "unscrupulous elements" who had maneuvered him into it. There were but few dissenting voices, such as that of the *Tägliche Rundschau* which could not forgive

---

in a formal literal sense, but no one is going to claim that it was compatible with the true meaning of the Weimar Constitution to place its sworn enemy at the head of the Reich." Ernst Rudolf Huber, *Verfassungsrecht des Grossdeutschen Reichs,* quoted in Bracher, *Auflösung,* p. 731.

60 Press reaction, in *Zeitspiegel,* Feb. 5, 1933, pp. 38–39; *Frankfurter Zeitung,* Reich ed., Jan. 31-Feb. 2, 1933; Schoeps, "Letztes Vierteljahr," pp. 470–71; Matthias, in Matthias and Morsey, *Ende der Parteien,* p. 339; same, "Untergang," p. 266; Noske, *Erlebtes,* p. 311; Rumbold to Simon, Feb. 1, 1933, *DBFP.,* ii, IV, 401–04.

him Schleicher's dismissal and found it a disservice to Hindenburg to look for the culprits among his advisers. "In the last analysis," it staunchly maintained, "the President makes his decisions according to his own best judgment; he is responsible for them."

In the face of this worshipful image, as always carefully nurtured even by those who knew so much better, a believing nation remained confident that the old Hero of Tannenberg had lost none of his powers and would somehow be able to keep Hitler in check.[61]

[61] Editorials, in *Zeitspiegel*, Feb. 5, 1933, pp. 55–56; Hugenberg, in Ritter, *Goerdeler*, p. 60.

CHAPTER 13

SURRENDER

O N the evening of January 30, 1933 a torchlight parade
of jubilant stormtroopers and *Stahlhelmers* marched
through Berlin's government quarter to the Wilhelmstrasse to pay homage to the president and the
chancellor. The Brown Shirts vastly outnumbered
the men of the *Stahlhelm* who had been included only at the insistence of Hindenburg, ever their faithful protector. With new
zest the S.A. men sang their familiar fighting songs in which much
was said of struggle and death and little of life and happiness, and
their "Heil Hitler" shouts took on a fresh vigor. They were certain that the day had witnessed not merely the formation of
another "national" government of predominantly conservative
leanings, as Hindenburg, Papen, and Seldte believed. In their
eyes it had ushered in a new era in which Hitler would control
the government just as he was controlling his party. Their whole
attitude reflected this confidence. Nazi newspapers were still careful to hail Hindenburg as the day's hero who by his "generous
decision" had called Hitler to the Reich chancellery, and Goebbels
dutifully concluded a brief address to the marching men with a
"Heil" for both Hindenburg and Hitler. But the Brown Shirts
knew better. Papen, watching the marchers from the background,
felt the first twinges of uneasiness: "As the paraders approach the
window at which . . . the old President stands, one hears shouts,
jubilant but restrained and respectful. About a hundred meters
away Hitler stands on the small balcony of the new chancellery.
When they see him the masses burst into frenzied applause that
spreads across the vast Wilhelmsplatz like a tornado. . . . When I
compared how these masses which viewed themselves as the representatives of a new era marched with restrained joy by Hindenburg, the symbol of the past, and how they saluted the Messiah of
their hopes with the fervor of revolutionaries, I had the feeling of
listening to a fanfare announcing a period of radical changes."[1]

Papen, however, was now the prisoner of his commitments. That
same afternoon the new cabinet had met and had taken up the

---

[1] Papen, *Wahrheit*, p. 297; Goebbels, *Vom Kaiserhof*, entry of Jan. 30, 1933,
pp. 253–54; Renondeau (French military attaché), quoted in Castellan, "Von Schleicher," p. 30.

question of new elections. Hugenberg again had opposed them and had proposed the proscription of the Communist Party to secure a majority in the existing Reichstag. Almost all of the other non-Nazis who spoke up in the ensuing discussion, Seldte, Neurath, Schwerin-Krosigk, and Gereke, sided with Hitler, fearful lest a ban of the Communists would lead to serious internal difficulties and possibly even to a general strike. Papen, who thought that the Reichstag might provide a majority, wished to delay the decision. But the next day he readily sided with Hitler despite the uneasiness he had felt the previous evening. He accepted Hitler's assertion that the support of the Center was uncertain, and he himself proposed that the forthcoming elections be announced as the last ones, thus barring any possibility of rectifying at some later date an outcome that might be unfavorable from the conservative viewpoint. And when Hitler and he presented themselves to the president to obtain his signature for the dissolution decree, Papen helped persuade the hesitant Hindenburg to accept the proposal. Nor did he intervene when someone observed that the entire cabinet approved of the dissolution, except for Hugenberg who objected for "partisan reasons." This last remark proved decisive for Hindenburg; incensed over these "never ending party political considerations," he set his name under the dissolution decree.[2]

Papen proved to be no more effective as a check on Nazi ambitions during the following days. On February 2 Frick presented to the cabinet the draft of a decree "for the protection of the German people"; it provided far-reaching controls over political meetings and open-air demonstrations, and checks on the press and other publications. More important, complaints against the application of the decree had to be lodged with the police authorities and, as a last administrative control, with the Reich minister of the interior—Frick himself—before there could be an appeal to the courts. This meant that any immediate remedy rested, in Prussia at least, with Nazi police commissioners, for Göring was hard at work there replacing "unreliable" police officials with trusted S.A. leaders. Again Papen had no objection; his one contribution to the discussion of the decree was to demand the introduction of a stiff fine for political slander.

[2] Cab. mtgs., Jan. 30, 1933, I.M.T., *Trial*, xxv, 373–76, Jan. 31, 1933, *Documents on German Foreign Policy* (hereafter cited as *DGFP.*), Ser. C, I, 5–8, respectively; Picker, *Hitlers Tischgespräche*, p. 431; Erich Kordt, *Nicht aus den Akten: Die Wilhelmstrasse in Frieden und Krieg: Erlebnisse, Begegnungen und Eindrücke 1928–1945* (Stuttgart, 1950), pp. 109–10; Meissner and Wilde, *Machtergreifung*, pp. 198–99, 296, n. 9.

None of Papen's non-Nazi colleagues in the cabinet seemed perturbed either by this measure that, for all practical purposes, empowered the Nazis to neutralize rival parties and leaders, and to dominate public opinion. They also accepted a decree that in spite of the *Staatsgerichtshof* decision transferred all remaining functions of the Braun-Severing government to Papen and his collaborators. In this case Meissner and Hugenberg, along with Papen, helped to devise "legal" ways by which the old Prussian government could be eliminated and the Prussian *Landtag* dissolved. Perhaps they expected to strengthen von Papen's hand, but since Papen first used his newly acquired powers to sanction the dissolution of the *Landtag*, the Nazis were again the actual beneficiaries.[3]

Except for Hugenberg, the main concern of the non-Nazi ministers was to establish friendly relations with the new chancellor in the interest of a good working relationship. This they felt could be done easily since the first measures that Hitler proposed seemed directed only against Socialists and Communists. Blomberg, moreover, had been won over by Hitler's pledge that the Reichswehr would not be called upon to enforce these measures; in consequence he thought them of no concern to the "nonpolitical" army. Most of the non-Nazi ministers also looked on the Nazi movement with that ambivalent mixture of sympathy and dislike which was characteristic of the attitude of the aristocracy and bourgeoisie towards Nazism from Hindenburg down. Eltz-Rübenach, a devout Catholic, Papen recalls, soon became an admirer of Hitler, and Hitler later praised Seldte and Neurath as ready supporters in the cabinet.[4]

Hindenburg did not prove any more effective as a safeguard against Hitler's ambitions. His resistance to the dissolution of the Reichstag was overcome quickly, and he signed the two decrees of February 4 and 6 without hesitation. Otto Braun sent him a warning, "in the interest of the authority of the state, the *Staatsgerichtshof,* and the concept of government by law," not to sign the Prussian decree since it could not be based on Article 48, nor

[3] Bracher, in Bracher, Sauer, Schulz, *Nationalsozialistische Machtergreifung,* p. 55; Papen, in cab. mtg., Feb. 2, 1933, *DGFP.,* C, I, 17; Jan. 31, 1933, *ibid.,* 7–8; Feb. 3, 1933, *RKz.,* R 43 I/1459.

[4] Papen, *Wahrheit,* p. 327; Picker, *Hitlers Tischgespräche,* p. 431; Hugenberg, Hitler, and Blomberg, in cab. mtg., Jan. 30, 1933, I.M.T., *Trial,* xxv, 374–75; Blomberg and Hitler to Reichswehr commanders, Feb. 3, 1933, *Vierteljahrshefte,* II (1954), 433, 435; Sauer, in Bracher, Sauer, Schulz, *Nationalsozialistische Machtergreifung,* pp. 715–17. On Eltz, see also Morsey, in Matthias and Morsey, *Ende der Parteien,* p. 352.

could it be justified on the grounds of a state emergency (*Staats-notstand*). But Meissner was able to remove whatever scruples Hindenburg may have had, and so he accepted the decree which blandly stated that "due to the attitude of the *Land* Preussen toward the verdict of the *Staatsgerichtshof* of October 25, 1932, much confusion has been created in public life which endangers the public order."[5]

Hindenburg was no more receptive to other complaints. On February 1, 1933, Hitler broadcast an "Appeal to the German People" (approved by the cabinet) in which he described the preceding fourteen years as a period of continued decay and disintegration. "Fourteen years of Marxism have ruined Germany . . . . The heritage which we assume is terrifying." Protests to the president against this distortion of the historical facts were passed on without comment to Hitler. Hindenburg did not object to this deprecation of the republican era during which he himself played such a significant role on the political stage; just as he had let others take the blame for the defeat of 1918, he now dissociated himself from the failings of the Weimar Republic.

Other complaints which were increasing in numbers with the tightening Nazi repression, he either disregarded or passed on to the chancellor. Hitler on his part felt free to ignore them since the president did not seem to attach much importance to them. One wonders how many complaints Hindenburg actually saw; most likely he gave Meissner blanket instructions to forward them directly to the chancellery or the ministry concerned, except in special cases. On rare occasions he would himself take up a complaint. Once he gently rebuked Hitler when a teachers' association complained that the chancellor had held up to public contempt the Weimar Republic's first president, Friedrich Ebert. Hitler had said in a speech that he had never heard that Ebert and Scheidemann had been good soldiers in battle, and Hindenburg had Meissner reply:

"In answer to your letter . . . the President has asked me to refer you to the remarks he made in his address when he took office on May 12, 1925, and which read as follows: 'It is not my task to describe and evaluate the work of my predecessor who so suddenly passed away. This, Chancellor Luther has done. His accomplishments in restoring peace and order in Germany after the collapse are undeniable. This even his political opponents

[5] Braun to Hindenburg, Feb. 5, 1933, Hindenburg to Braun, Feb. 6, 1933, in Braun, *Von Weimar*, pp. 442–43.

will always acknowledge. He always sought to serve the German people faithfully.' "[6]

He allowed the letter to be published, but this cold impersonal tribute to Ebert gave little comfort to the republicans, nor can it have caused Hitler any serious concern.

Obviously Hindenburg was not willing to play the part as the guardian of constitutional rights that had been assigned to him in Papen's system of checks and balances. He had long hesitated to appoint Hitler as chancellor, but once he had done it, he seems to have felt he had "done his duty" and relapsed into his customary passivity. Perhaps, as has been suggested by Bernhard Schwertfeger, the military historian, who knew him well as a staff officer in World War I and as a fellow Hanoverian, there was an element of sullenness in this attitude, not uncommon in old age. Papen, after all, had been the one who had kept pressing for Hitler's appointment; let him and his colleagues take care now of any problems that might arise. As for himself, Hindenburg was willing to adjust to the new reality as he had adjusted to other changes. Papen regrets in his memoirs that he did not ask sooner for the president's intervention to deal with the abuses of the Nazi *Gauleiter* and the excesses of the S.A. and S.S.; he did not do so, he explains, in the hope that Hitler in time would modify his goals and his methods. Nonetheless he writes at the same time that Hindenburg was neither willing nor able, due to his age, to cast his authority into the scales, and one must conclude that he also refrained from calling for the president's help because he sensed that it would not be given.

Hitler, moreover, knew how to ingratiate himself with the president. Skillfully marshalling his arguments, drawing apt parallels to military situations, the chancellor exerted his dialectical talents on Hindenburg and overcame his distrust as he had disarmed many another opponent by the forcefulness and seeming logic of his reasoning. He agreed with him on the need to curb some of his "overzealous" subordinates and promised immediate measures to prevent further abuses. He also assured the president that he wished to restore the monarchy once Germany had recovered her full sovereignty. Hitler always approached the marshal with the deferential respect the latter considered his due—to please Hindenburg he even adopted a regular working schedule,

6 Hitler's "Appeal," in Schulthess, Feb. 1, 1933, pp. 34–37; protests to Hindenburg, in *RKz.*, R 43 I/1263, 1281; Besson, *Württemberg*, pp. 335–36; Meissner to Dt. Republikanischer Lehrerbund, Mar. 1, 1933, *Frankfurter Zeitung*, Reich ed., Mar. 4, 1933.

appearing at his office at 10 o'clock in the morning (an unduly early hour for one who normally turned night into day) and maintaining a fairly regular office routine.[7] Soon he gained Hindenburg's confidence, and some weeks later the arrangement was dropped by which Papen was to be present whenever Hitler called on the president.

Hindenburg's entourage encouraged this rapprochement. Meissner explained away constitutional objections to Hitler's decrees, and he and Oskar barred callers such as the Socialist leaders who might have proved troublesome. Hitler also replaced Hindenburg's press aide with one of his own men, Walter Funk, an old family friend of the Hindenburgs. In his daily reports to the president, Funk gave enthusiastic accounts of Hitler's activities, and since Hindenburg liked and trusted Funk, these reports did not fail to impress him.[8]

Not all critics and complainants could be ignored, however. Among these latter, the Bavarian government was one of the most persistent. Shocked by the arbitrary removal of the old Prussian government, it kept warning against the appointment of a Reich commissioner in Bavaria. Hindenburg had to write to Minister-President Held that there was no intention of dispatching a commissioner to Bavaria. The Bavarians, however, recalling the president's statements about Prussia some months before, did not feel reassured, and on February 17 Hindenburg was forced to receive Schäffer, the head of the Bavarian People's Party and a member of the Bavarian government. The meeting was unsatisfactory for both participants: Hindenburg had to listen to warnings that the Reich was pursuing a dangerous course, and Schäffer came away with the impression that the president was becoming increasingly the captive of Hitler and was unlikely to intervene any longer in political matters. He drew what comfort he could from Hindenburg's renewed promise, at the conclusion of the discussion, that he would never send a commissioner to Bavaria.

Since it was doubtful whether the president was still the master of his decisions, Bavarians began looking for other ways of forestalling Berlin's intervention. One possible solution seemed to present itself in monarchist restoration plans that had been

[7] Yet true to form, Hitler would revert to his old irregular habits whenever the president left Berlin. Cf. Otto Dietrich, *12 Jahre mit Hitler* (Munich, 1955), pp. 41, 249.

[8] Schwertfeger, *Rätsel*, pp. 223–24, 226–27; Papen, *Wahrheit*, pp. 291–92, 295; Picker, *Hitlers Tischgespräche*, pp. 431–32; Meissner, *Staatssekretär*, pp. 322–23; Funk, in I.M.T., *Trial*, XIII, 92, 137; also on Funk, Schmidt-Hannover, *Umdenken*, p. 331.

revived during the Papen regime—they assumed a new significance now that Hitler was chancellor. Perhaps a Reich intervention could be prevented by the proclamation of Crown Prince
Rupprecht as a special commissioner general who would supersede the Bavarian government and eventually convert Bavaria
into a monarchy. Schäffer favored the plan and so did some of
Bavaria's Socialist leaders. The Crown Prince was willing to take
the post if it were offered to him by the Bavarian government;
but the government hesitated to give its consent, partly for constitutional reasons and partly because it doubted that the Reichswehr would tolerate the move.

The answer to this last question was quickly given. Two confidants of the Crown Prince had gone to Berlin late in February
to sound out the president and to assure him that Rupprecht
would do nothing to endanger the unity of the Reich. The hope
was that the president and his conservative advisers would order
the army to lend its support. On February 24 one of the envoys,
Prince Oettingen-Wallerstein, was received by Hindenburg.
Oettingen tried to enlist the president's monarchist sympathies,
and explained that with the help of a monarch Hitler could be
kept from establishing a centralized totalitarian state. Hindenburg,
who had been forewarned of the plan, rejected it out of hand and
warned Oettingen to drop it at once lest he be tried for high
treason. Obviously the president could not be counted upon to
provide any help. The Reichswehr command on its part made
clear its position when it sent two high-ranking officers to Munich
a few days later to take over its Bavarian contingent should the
local commander try to assist the monarchists.[9]

ɷ

With all other safeguards neutralized within weeks, if not days,
there remained only the Reichstag as a possible counterweight
against Hitler. Or so it seemed. Actually Hitler was determined
to stay in power regardless of the outcome of the elections, and to
selected groups he would say so quite frankly. He told a group of
industrialists on February 20, "We are facing the last election.
Whatever the results, there can be no turning back, even if the
coming election is inconclusive. One way or another, if the election is indecisive, the decision must be brought about in some
other way."

9 Schwend, *Bayern*, pp. 509–10; same, in Matthias and Morsey, *Ende der Parteien*,
p. 482; Aretin, *Krone*, pp. 144–50; Meissner, *Staatssekretär*, p. 315; Sauer, in Bracher,
Sauer, Schulz, *Nationalsozialistische Machtergreifung*, pp. 712, 722–23.

Meanwhile Hitler did everything to ensure a "legal" victory. Once more Goebbels displayed his remarkable propagandistic talents and mapped out a campaign that took the Fuehrer and other top party speakers to every corner of the country. Appealing to the nation's need for faith, he gave meetings something of a religious flavor, with church bells ringing and Hitler ending at least one of his speeches with a solemn "Amen." Nazi speakers also were careful to stress that the new government owed its appointment to the confidence of President Hindenburg, skillfully using his name, not only to prove the legitimacy of the government, but to suggest also that its policies had the marshal's blessing. Underlining the value of his approval, speakers who only a short time before had assailed Hindenburg as a senile, incompetent bumbler, as the man who had lost the war, as the tool of Marxists and Jesuits, now hailed him as a towering heroic figure —the faithful, indefatigable trustee of his people and the field marshal of the unbeaten German armies.

Full advantage was taken of the radio; all major Nazi and German National Party speeches were broadcast and loudspeakers were set up in streets and public squares. This time money also was plentiful since industrial circles contributed at least 3 million marks—as much as a matter of self-protection as of political sympathies. And there were above all the power resources of the state. On February 17 Göring instructed the Prussian police, now thoroughly Nazified, to take a cooperative attitude toward Brown Shirts and *Stahlhelmers* in case of clashes and to support them against their opponents. He vowed to protect any officers who in the fulfillment of their duties made use of their firearms, whatever the consequences.[10] Some days later he recruited some 50,000 stormtroopers and *Stahlhelmers* into an auxiliary police force equipped with pistols and rubber truncheons, thus giving his men the "freedom of the streets" for which they had clamored for so long. The opposition, harassed and obstructed, was being subjected to a reign of terror; even Brüning was prevented from speaking on one occasion, and Stegerwald was brutally beaten on

---

[10] When Adenauer in his capaciy as president of the Prussian *Staatsrat* wished to protest to Hindenburg against Göring's "firearms" instructions, Papen intervened and arranged a meeting between Adenauer and Göring. According to press service reports, Adenauer received a satisfactory interpretation of the decree from Göring and thought it no longer necessary to ask for an appointment with the president. *Vossische Zeitung*, No. 97, Feb. 26, 1933. One wonders why Papen wished to prevent Adenauer's appeal to the president. Did he consider it pointless? Did he wish to conceal from the president how helpless he was in controlling the course of events? Or how badly he had misjudged the Nazis?

another. All in all, in those states in which the Nazis controlled the police, the opposition parties could no longer wage an effective campaign.[11]

The anti-Nazis nonetheless kept fighting as best they could. Given the preponderance of power and money which the Nazis enjoyed, their only chance of defeating Hitler lay in joining all forces against him. For such a coordinated effort, however, the groups in question, from the Center to the Communists, were not prepared either politically or psychologically. Nor was there any collaboration on a more limited scale: the Socialists and Communists had a few desultory talks that ended inconclusively; neither the Center nor Socialists would consider any joint effort; nor did the Center seek a rapprochement with other bourgeois parties. Except for some purely technical electoral arrangements, the bourgeois parties remained as divided as ever.

In no case, of course, could an all-inclusive bourgeois bloc have been established. As a governmental party the German National Party could not and would not join forces with the Center or Bavarian People's Party which were strongly opposed to the new government. Papen therefore made an attempt to create a new grouping in which non-Nazi conservatives could be gathered; it would provide a political mass basis for the non-Nazi ministers and permit them to press their "Christian-conservative" views more forcefully in the cabinet. The effort failed. What emerged as a new *Kampffront Schwarz-Weiss-Rot*, nominally a coalition of German Nationals, *Stahlhelm,* and other conservative elements, turned out to be simply the German National People's Party under a different name. Hugenberg's insistence on a predominance of German National candidates prevented the creation of something new.[12]

In one respect only did the *Kampffront* differ from the German National Party—in its open identification with Hindenburg. If earlier the German Nationals had claimed to be the "party of Hindenburg," they had done so half apologetically for having drawn the president's name into the political arena; this time, however, Hindenburg's name became an official plank of the *Kampffront's* platform, and the Prussian branch of the *Front,* in the simultaneous *Landtag* campaign in that state, adopted as its

11 Hitler, quoted in I.M.T., *Trial* xxxv, 46; Bracher, in Bracher, Sauer, Schulz, *Nationalsozialistische Machtergreifung,* pp. 59–74, 88–93; Schulz, in *ibid.,* p. 430; Hoegner, *Verratene Republik,* pp. 344–45.

12 Papen, *Wahrheit,* pp. 298–99; Hiller von Gaertringen, in Matthias and Morsey, *Ende der Parteien,* pp. 581–83; Bracher, in Bracher, Sauer, Schulz, *Nationalsozialistische Machtergreifung,* pp. 344–45.

official slogan, "With Hindenburg for a national Prussia." Seldte proudly announced at a press reception at which he discussed the purposes of the *Kampffront* that this was done with the president's express approval, adding with pointed off-handedness that Hitler too had been informed in advance. Evidently Papen had been able to persuade Hindenburg that the *Kampffront* was no ordinary political party, but a movement designed to preserve those Christian-monarchist-conservative principles that Hindenburg himself had always upheld.

To the *Kampffront* the Hindenburg name was of course a prime asset. It was the one name that Hitler's name did not outshine completely. The president, moreover, could be presented as an authority towering above the Nazis and their Fuehrer. As Papen proclaimed: "We must combine the two principles of democracy and aristocracy. We need men who are masters because they can serve, who do not engage in demonstrative actions, but radiate dignity. The only man of whom all of us can say that he has these qualities is our Reich President." Linked closely to him, the *Kampffront* could hope to establish itself as an instrument of the president, designed to help him accomplish the arduous task of curbing the Nazis' ambitions. To indicate Hindenburg's focal role, Hugenberg and other German National speakers always referred to the government as the "Hindenburg Government of National Concentration." "To fight with Hindenburg for a new Germany—this is the meaning of March 5 [the day of the elections]," one German National poster announced, and another urged voters to support the *Kampffront* in its struggle "for a new Germany with Hindenburg under the black-white-and-red flag." But not all members of the *Kampffront* considered Hindenburg a name to conjure with. *Stahlhelm* leaders used it but sparingly in their speeches and manifestos. They worried, on second thought, that any strong emphasis on Hindenburg might antagonize the large contingent of Nazi sympathizers in the ranks of their organization.[13]

Other parties too drew the president's name openly into their campaigns. The German People's Party, which had always prided itself on being the one party that had never deserted Hindenburg, urged voters to "help us keep up the fight for a national Germany with Hindenburg under black-white-and-red." Its speeches and posters differed little from those of the *Kampffront;* indeed, had it

[13] Seldte and Hugenberg, in Schulthess, Feb. 10, 1933, p. 45; Papen, in *Frankfurter Zeitung*, Reich ed., Feb. 23, 1933; German National materials, in Munich Coll./32, and *Zeitspiegel*, Mar. 5, 1933; Stahlhelm, *ibid.*; Papen, *Wahrheit*, p. 299.

not been for Hugenberg's intransigence, the party would have been willing to join the *Kampffront*. Outside of it, it considered itself a third "column" of a "Christian-national bloc" in which the forces of "national determination" were joined "with coolheadedness and economic rationality."[14]

The German National Party and the German People's Party invoked Hindenburg's name to legitimize themselves as the executors of the president's wishes. The Catholic parties, on the other hand, drew him into the campaign in anxious appeals to protect them against the lawlessness and terrorism of the National Socialists. The Bavarian People's Party was the more aggressive; since Bavaria still had a non-Nazi government, the party felt strong enough to defy Hitler openly. Its main concern was that Berlin would replace the Bavarian government with a Reich commissioner. Recent interventions in Lübeck, Hesse, and Saxony had increased these fears. For this reason Schäffer and Held made the most of Hindenburg's pledge that no commissioner would be sent to Bavaria. Should one be appointed nevertheless, they announced, such a move would defy the will of the president and hence be unlawful. Under the circumstances, the Bavarian government would feel justified in arresting a commissioner as soon as he would set foot on Bavarian soil. Frick reacted with furious counterthreats, and Hitler responded with some veiled warnings against those "who are threatening us with a new *Mainlinie*"; newspaper accounts reported shouts of "Hang them, Hang them" at this point of his speech. Papen, who was the *Kampffront's* top candidate in Bavaria, sought to mediate and wrote Held a letter assuring him that the president's statements were as valid as ever. Seizing on this latest pledge, Schäffer announced at a Center meeting in Frankfurt on February 27: "Since forty-eight hours I have a written assurance which was sent to me at the request and in the name of the Reich President that no acts of violence are being contemplated against Bavaria either by him or by the Government which he has appointed, should this state make use of its rights and jurisdiction within the framework of the Constitution."

Did he and Held actually believe that Hindenburg could and would protect Bavaria against Hitler? They had no illusions about the weakness and the passivity of the president and yet they were not simply pretending when they tried to reassure their followers by using the magic name Hindenburg. "Despite all experiences

---

14 *Zeitspiegel*, Mar. 5, 1933; Matthias and Morsey, *Ende der Parteien*, p. 588 n. 18.

to the contrary and despite their awareness of his personal limitations and those of his office," notes Karl Schwend, a witness to these events, "they still had some hope that Hindenburg would stand by his repeated declarations that he was not planning an . . . intervention in Bavaria. . . . Curiously enough, some last confidence-inspiring quality still attached to the old man and to the institution which he personified. And behind him stood the sphinx-like Reichswehr which Hitler, it seemed, had not yet brought entirely under his control."[15]

Such a last residue of faith in the marshal-president was also characteristic of the Center's campaign. Kaas attacked the "manipulators operating back of the Presidential Palace" who were using Hindenburg as a front for their activities. Brüning, in his speeches, kept appealing to the president to safeguard freedom and law. Again these appeals were no empty gestures. His frustrating experiences with Hindenburg notwithstanding, Brüning was still hopeful that the president would take action against the Nazi excesses. His faith was sadly misplaced. Hindenburg could not be moved, and to protests against the Nazis' brutalities Meissner's answer invariably was that the complaints had been forwarded to the chancellor or the minister of the interior. (Even subsequent events did not disillusion Brüning entirely: fourteen years later he wrote of Hindenburg, "Old as he was, he was not inclined to act incisively or decisively. He did not wish to enter history . . . as the initiator of a civil war." Yet even then Brüning still felt justified in having counted on Hindenburg to curb Hitler with the help of the Reichswehr.)[16]

As for the Social Democrats, they could not invoke Hindenburg's name as freely as did the bourgeois parties, but they too clung to the belief that Hindenburg would not tolerate the destruction of the constitutional order. "You may be convinced," Breitscheid assured his party colleagues after Hitler's appointment, "that the President's custodians in the cabinet were appointed or retained . . . to restrain and check Herr Adolf Hitler, the man who wishes to rule alone." Even some weeks later the Socialists had not yet given up hope that Hindenburg and Papen could be brought to intervene against the terrorism to which their party was being subjected. On February 25 *Vorwärts* still com-

15 Schwend, *Bayern*, pp. 509–11; same, in Matthias and Morsey, *Ende der Parteien*, pp. 480–81; Hitler, in Schulthess, Feb. 24, 1933, Schäffer, *ibid.*, Feb. 27, 1933, pp. 49, 50.

16 Kaas and Brüning, quoted in Matthias and Morsey, *Ende der Parteien*, pp. 351–52; Brüning, "Ein Brief," pp. 3, 20; Besson, *Württemberg*, pp. 335–36; 347–48, esp. n. 1.

mented, "The President has the right to appoint and to *dismiss* Chancellors, the right to dismiss is not at all dead."

This mystic faith in Hindenburg survived even the wholesale consignment of Socialist leaders to concentration camps, the dismissal of Socialist government officials, the destruction of the unions, and the forcible dissolution of the party in June of that year. Three days after that event, one of the exiled leaders stated at a press conference in Prague: "The Reichswehr is a sphinx. It is still considered a reliable instrument in the hand of the President, and Hindenburg's future intentions are an impenetrable secret . . ."[17]

How little this faith was justified was plainly evident since that fateful day, late in February, when the Reichstag building went up in flames. The question of who set it afire need not be explored here since historically the answer is of secondary importance. What matters is the political use the Nazis made of the fire. Despite all efforts to frighten and paralyze the opposition parties, there was still no assurance that the government would obtain a majority in the elections. The fire, Hitler was certain, would change all this; he no longer doubted, he told the cabinet, that the government would capture 51 per cent of the vote. He was not prepared, however, to stake his hopes solely on the fright of the German people and proposed a "ruthless settling of accounts" with the Comunist Party which "must not be made dependent on legal considerations." He had therefore requested the preparation of an urgently needed decree for the protection of the nation against the Communist danger.

Frick then read to the cabinet the draft of the decree. It suspended most constitutional liberties and authorized the Reich minister of the interior to take over a state government temporarily if public order were not adequately maintained. No one objected to the first part, though its provisions could be applied against anyone and no legal recourse was granted against abuses; nor did anyone question the need for such far-reaching measures. But Papen, who had pledged the president's word that there would be no intervention in Bavaria, warned that the second article would embitter the South German states—it would be better to arrange with them the steps to be taken. Hitler objected that some government might not take the required action. In the end a minor modification was adopted, authorizing intervention *insofar as* a state was not taking the needed measures. That after-

[17] Social Democratic materials, quoted in Matthias and Morsey, *Ende der Parteien*, pp. 160–61, 164 n. 11 and 14.

noon the cabinet met once more to discuss the final text of the decree. Once more Papen brought up the question of intervention in state affairs and asked that the right to decide on such a move be reserved to the president. But this Hitler refused, and since Meissner kept silent, all Papen could obtain was a change requiring that the decision rest with the government rather than the minister of the interior.

Hindenburg signed the decree that same evening. Although it put an end "for the time being" to most civil liberties without legal safeguards and authorized searches and confiscations of property beyond the established limits, the president accepted the decree without hesitation. Hitler justified it as a weapon needed to crush the Communists, and neither Papen nor Meissner voiced any objections. In view of their silence it is doubtful Hindenburg realized that he was giving Hitler the particular right that he himself had always wished to withhold from him—to "legally" terrorize the country and deal with his opponents as he pleased. Nor did Hindenburg object to yielding his right to decide on state intervention although he had always carefully watched his presidential prerogatives. Hitler on his part used the president's name to conceal the fact that he was perpetuating his rule—while the decree was supposed to be a temporary emergency measure, it remained in force to the last day of the Nazi regime.[18]

∽

The German voters did not give Hitler a majority on March 5 despite the harassment, repression, and outright terror that all anti-Nazi forces were suffering. The Nazis, gaining 5.5 million votes, received 43.9 per cent of the vote, an increase of over 30 per cent over the November returns, but a conspicuous setback in terms of their expectations. In view of the methods to which they had resorted, the popular vote against them was impressive.

The setback of the *Kampffront Schwarz-Weiss-Rot* was even more striking, comparatively speaking. While it obtained a small numerical gain of 200,000 over the November vote of the German Nationals, its relative share dropped from 8.3 to 8 per cent. Hindenburg's name had not been the hoped for asset; large numbers of *Stahlhelmers,* as Papen sadly noted, continued to vote for the Fuehrer rather than President Hindenburg. Of the few

18 Cab. mtgs., Feb. 28, 1933, 11 A.M., *DGFP.,* C, I, 88–90; Feb. 28, 1933, 4:15 p.m., *RKz.,* 43 1/1459; also Göring, in cab. mtg., Mar. 2, 1933, *DGFP.,* C, I, 95; Papen, *Wahrheit,* p. 304; Meissner, *Staatssekretär,* pp. 281–82; Bracher, in Bracher, Sauer, Schulz, pp. 82–88.

electoral districts in which the Nazis won a majority, Hindenburg's home province of East Prussia was the one in which they
gained the largest majority (56.5 per cent), while the *Kampffront*
suffered its sharpest drop there (from 14.4 to 11.3 per cent). The
German People's Party, the other "Hindenburg party," suffered
setbacks both absolutely and relatively. It lost 230,000 votes, that
is, one-third of its November vote, and its relative share dropped
from 1.9 to 1.1 per cent.

The losses of the Center and Bavarian People's Party, on the
other hand, were moderate (from 11.9 to 11.7 and from 3.1 to 2.7
per cent), and the Center even managed to gain 200,000 votes over
the last returns. The Social Democrats held their own numerically, but lost 10 per cent of the total vote; given the difficulties
the party had faced throughout the campaign, this was a remarkable accomplishment. The Communists lost 1,100,000 votes, or
almost 20 per cent; even they did not suffer a crushing defeat.[19]

These figures were misleading, however, inasmuch as they no
longer reflected the true distribution of power. Even if Hitler
obtained only 43.9 per cent of the vote (or 44.5 per cent of the
seats in the Reichstag), he was already strong enough to stay in
office regardless of the election returns. Together with the votes
of the *Kampffront,* moreover, the government commanded a
majority in the Reichstag which, for appearance's sake, Hitler
did welcome. He could do this the more readily because the
Kampffront was too weak to act as a restraining influence on the
cabinet. Not surprisingly the Nazi press immediately hailed the
March 5 election as solely a Nazi victory.

The opposition parties seized at once on the existence of the
government majority and in veiled appeals to the president urged
a return to constitutional government. An emergency no longer
existed, wrote *Germania,* and the basis had been created for a
parliamentary government: "The word and the oath of Reich
President von Hindenburg must be a guarantee in this hour . . .
that the Government pursue its policies within the framework of
the Constitution." The Social Democratic press service too pointed
out that there now existed the possibility of governing strictly
in accordance with the constitution, and reminded the government of its own oath and that of the president.

But these were futile arguments. So was Seldte's opposite one
that the authority of the government was based, "not on mass and
majority, but above all on the authority of the Reich President,

---

[19] Election returns in *Frankfurter Zeitung,* Reich ed., Mar. 7, 1933, and Matthias
and Morsey, *Ende der Parteien,* pp. 792–93; Papen, *Wahrheit,* p. 299.

Field Marshal von Hindenburg." Seldte's reminder was not impressive since so many of his own *Stahlhelmers* had voted for Hitler rather than Hindenburg.[20]

How completely unfounded were hopes based on Hindenburg was clearly demonstrated by the president's attitude during the next few days. On March 7 the Bavarian envoy to the Reich government, Franz Sperr, passed on to Munich the advice Meissner had given not to oppose a Nazi demand for new *Landtag* elections in Bavaria; this was the only way, Sperr was told, to avoid a Reich intervention. Yet when Sperr, who had just been appointed to his post, called on Hindenburg the next day to present his credentials, Hindenburg observed resentfully that he thought it almost insulting that Munich kept doubting his word: Bavaria had no reason to be concerned and no intervention was planned. Of course she would have to draw certain conclusions from the Reichstag elections, he added vaguely, but "for God's sake no new elections." Hitler, whom Sperr saw next, also denied any intention to interfere in Bavaria, but warned that pressure from below might become so strong that he would have to intervene.

That "pressure" began to make itself felt the morning of March 9. Munich's stormtroopers organized a march on the government to ask for its resignation. The Bavarian government telegraphed a protest to Hindenburg, who in turn called in Hitler. The chancellor described the Munich developments as an internal Bavarian problem in which the Reich government ought not to intervene; it was up to the Bavarian cabinet to restore order and reorganize itself. Hindenburg accepted these explanations and throughout the day Sperr, who kept getting calls from his government about the growing seriousness of the situation, was being assured by the Presidential Palace (as well as by the Reich chancellery) that there was no plan to appoint a Reich commissioner in Bavaria.

The appointment of a Reich commissioner to Bavaria was made late that evening. On the following morning, Held protested once more to Hindenburg; he asked for a repeal of the measure, denouncing it as unjustified on both legal and substantive grounds. Meissner was sent to Hitler who explained that the intervention had become necessary to prevent bloodshed. Once again Hindenburg contented himself with the chancellor's answer. Held was informed that the "Reich Government had acted within its own competence," and was asked not to call on the president since any

[20] *Germania* and *Sozialdemokratischer Pressedienst,* in *Zeitspiegel,* Mar. 19, 1933; Seldte, in *Nazi Party Records*/90/103293.

complaints he might have ought to be addressed to the chancellor. Hindenburg remained equally passive when a day later the same fate befell Württemberg.[21]

Legally there was indeed little he could have done to help Bavaria since he had signed away his pertinent presidential rights in the decree of February 28. But the arbitrariness with which Hitler had personally usurped these powers although they had been turned over, not to him, but to the Reich government ought to have warned the president not to relinquish any of his remaining prerogatives. Yet the very opposite happened. On March 15, the cabinet discussed the Enabling Act by which the newly elected Reichstag was to transfer its law-making powers to the Reich government. The act would have to be worded in such a way, Frick announced, that the government would have the right to disregard any provision of the constitution. Hugenberg asked whether the president would have any part in the legislation that would be enacted on the basis of the Enabling Act. Meissner hastened to reply that it would not be necessary to concern the president with these matters since he would not ask for the right to have his say on them. As an afterthought he added that it might perhaps be desirable to draw on the authority of the president in cases of special significance, but the suggestion clearly was made in order to help the government rather than provide a check on it. As the state secretary testified at his postwar trial at Nürnberg, Hindenburg had always objected to assuming the responsibility for unpopular emergency decrees and was glad therefore to be relieved of this burden by the Enabling Act; he did not wish to serve, Meissner quoted him, as a "signature machine" or as a "cover" for Hitler. Hindenburg not only accepted but welcomed this further curtailment of his authority and readily surrendered his right to examine and promulgate laws. Neither Papen nor anyone else seems to have tried to dissuade him from abandoning this vital presidential duty that was now more important than ever, although the whole concept of "taming" Hitler was based on Hindenburg's active participation. Thus, Hindenburg offhandedly gave up his much vaunted role as the guardian of the constitution and of lawful and civilized government.[22]

Even he must have realized what was at stake. At the time the government was also considering a decree of execution for those

21 Schwend, *Bayern*, pp. 533–40; Meissner, *Staatssekretär*, pp. 315–16; Besson, *Württemberg*, pp. 347–48.
22 Meissner, in I.M.T., Case No. 11, transcript, p. 4514; Hugenberg and Meissner, in cab. mtg., Mar. 15, 1933, I.M.T., *Trial*, xxxi, 407.

convicted of having set fire to the Reichstag. For once Hindenburg rebelled: he would not sign a decree retroactively stiffening
a criminal penalty in violation of all traditional concepts of law
and justice. Meissner informed the cabinet of Hindenburg's opposition at a cabinet meeting on March 7, but Hitler kept pressing
for the decree, and a week later the question came up again.
Again Meissner reported that the president was strongly opposed
to the introduction of the death penalty for the arsonists; the
state secretary suggested that the government might enact such a
measure later on the basis of the Enabling Act. It is hard to believe that Meissner had not discussed this proposal with Hindenburg; obviously the Enabling Act would again relieve the president of unpleasant responsibilities, for he did not feel strong
enough to oppose the death penalty forever.[23]

By then Hindenburg probably sensed that Hitler had a way of
getting the things he wanted—even in matters the marshal had
always felt strongly about he had to give in to the Fuehrer. Immediately after the elections, Nazi stalwarts had begun to hoist swastika
flags on public buildings and a few days later Hitler asked Hindenburg to sign a decree substituting the swastika for black-red-
and-gold as the national flag of the country. Papen, as he states in
his memoirs, opposed the proposal; he wished to see black-white-
and-red restored as the national colors, and Hindenburg sided
with him at first. But in the end he accepted a compromise by
which black-white-and-red and the swastika were to be hoisted
jointly as the official Reich colors. This arrangement, eliminating
black-red-and-gold by a simple decree that was not even based on
Article 48, was of course unconstitutional.[24]

It was not only old age and Hindenburg's natural lethargy that
account for this ready surrender of all his powers; his health was
beginning to fail and preoccupied him now more than ever as did
the thought of his death. When Duesterberg called on him one
Sunday in mid-March, he talked at length of the arrangements he
had made for his burial at Neudeck. Later he turned to the subject of politics, but as usual the talk revolved around trivialities,
the use of the old *Garnisonkirche* in Potsdam for the opening
ceremony of the new Reichstag, and the replacement of the old
Prussian "Hurrah" with the ubiquitous "Heil Hitler." Hindenburg gave Duesterberg the impression that his rights were being
infringed upon against his will, and when Duesterberg explained

---

[23] Meissner, in cab. mtg., Mar. 7, 1933, *DGFP.*, C, I, 118, Mar. 15, 1933, I.M.T.,
Trial, XXXI, 408–09.
[24] Papen, *Wahrheit*, pp. 323–24.

that he was trying to preserve the integrity of the *Stahlhelm,* the President nodded approvingly and muttered some words of agreement. Duesterberg came away with the feeling that the "Old Gentleman" was one last bastion the Nazis had not yet taken.[25]

༺

Watching the colorful opening of the new Reichstag in Potsdam's garrison church, the uninitiated observer would have agreed with this view. Resplendent in his field marshal's uniform, Hindenburg seemed the center of everything. The unpretentious old army church in which Frederick the Great and his father, the "Soldier King" Frederick William I, lay buried provided a fitting setting for the evocation of that Prussian-Protestant spirit of which the president seemed the perfect embodiment. Out of respect to him some seats had been set aside for the Imperial family, and as a special tribute to the marshal one chair was left vacant in honor of the ex-Emperor. Making his way to his own seat, Hindenburg bowed deeply and raised his marshal's baton as he passed the Imperial box.

The president opened the ceremony with the reading of a brief address, "In the Reichstag elections of March 5 our people has backed with a clear majority the Government called into office by my confidence and has provided it with the constitutional basis for its work." The tasks that awaited it were many and difficult, and he hoped that the members of the new Reichstag would support the government and do everything to assist it in its hard work. He invoked the spirit of the "old Prussia which in awe of God became great through dutiful labor, unshakable courage, and dedicated patriotism. . . . May the old spirit of this celebrated site inspire our present-day generation, may it deliver us from selfishness and party quarrels and rally us in national self-realization and spiritual revival for the benefit of a united, free, and proud Germany!"

Hitler spoke after Hindenburg. He surveyed the sad legacy he had taken over and outlined what he hoped to accomplish. His words were addressed as much to the president as they were to the general audience, as if he wished to demonstrate his subordination to Hindenburg: "In a unique rising the German people has restored its national honor in just a few weeks, and thanks to your understanding, *Herr Reichspräsident,* it has joined together the symbols of old greatness and youthful vigor." And he ended with a special tribute to the marshal:

25 Duesterberg, *Stahlhelm,* pp. 47–48.

"In our midst we see an aged head. We rise before you, *Herr Generalfeldmarschall.* Three times you fought on the field of honor for the existence and future of our people. As a lieutenant in the armies of the King [of Prussia] for German unity, in the armies of the old Emperor for the glorious establishment of the Reich, in the greatest war of all times as our Field Marshal for the survival of our Reich and for the freedom of our people. You witnessed the creation of the Reich, you saw yourself the achievements of the great Chancellor, the wondrous rise of our people, and led us in those great times which fate allowed us to witness and fight through. Today, *Herr Generalfeldmarschall,* Providence lets you be the custodian of the new rise of our people. Your astounding life symbolizes to all of us the indestructible vigor of the German nation. Germany's youth thanks you today, and so do we all. We consider it a blessing to have your consent to the work of the German rising. May this vigor inspire also this newly inaugurated representation of our people. May Providence give us the courage and perseverance which we sense in this place so sacred to every German, as we strive for the freedom and greatness of our people, at the grave of its greatest king."

Hindenburg then descended slowly to the crypt behind the altar, followed by his son and another adjutant who laid down wreaths at the tombs of the two Prussian kings. The marshal remained standing in thought before the two graves while the sound of cannon shots reverberated in the awed silence. When he emerged from the vault, Hitler accompanied him to the door, where he reviewed a parade of Reichswehr, police, Brown Shirts, and *Stahlhelm* contingents. "I had the impression," the British ambassador noted, "that the old Field Marshal could no longer be described as the 'President of the Republic,' but rather as a *'Reichsverweser'* or 'Regent.' "[26]

The main business of the new Reichstag was the enactment of the Enabling Act. Since it "amended" the Weimar Constitution, Hitler, ever anxious to observe the niceties of constitutional procedures, needed a qualified majority for the bill's passage. According to Article 76 of the Weimar Constitution, two-thirds of all deputies had to be present at the time of the voting, and of these, two-thirds had to approve. The matter was discussed with cynical frankness in the cabinet: Göring noted that the Communist deputies were all in jail and thus could not vote; some of the Socialists could be jailed on charges of conspiring with the

26 Schulthess, Mar. 21, 1933, pp. 60–64; Rumbold to Simon, Mar. 21, 1933, *DBFP.,* ii, IV, 425.

Communists and others could be expelled on some pretext during the deliberations; the Socialists might even abstain from voting, and to make certain that a quorum would be present, the rules ought to be changed to deprive deputies who left to avoid voting of both travel passes and salary. At a later cabinet session Frick suggested that those absent without excuse ought to be counted as present.

Actually it was not so much the attitude of the Socialists as that of the Center that was of real importance. With the various procedural changes and forcible measures proposed by Göring and Frick a two-thirds majority could of course be secured even if the Center opposed the bill; but as Hitler confided to the cabinet, the support of the Center would improve the government's standing abroad. Centrist approval would also have its beneficial effect at home.[27] A few days before the decisive Reichstag session, Hitler and Frick therefore entered into talks with the Center, seemingly ready to concede some checks on the powers which the Enabling Act was to confer on the government. The rights of the president and of Reichstag and Reichsrat, they falsely promised, would not be infringed, and they professed to be willing to set up a small body of consultants that would be informed of the measures the government planned to enact. That evening the text of the bill was published: the government was given the right to pass laws that could deviate from the constitution; these laws would be signed and promulgated by the chancellor. The Reichstag in addition would be excluded from the ratification of foreign treaties. One provision stated that the rights of the president were not to be changed—actually they would be greatly reduced since he would not examine the laws passed on the strength of the Enabling Act.

As the Center well knew, under existing conditions the effectiveness of any governmental concessions would depend on the future status of the Reich president. In a second meeting with Hitler, the Center spokesmen asked for the inclusion in the Enabling Act of a provision granting the president the right to sign and promulgate laws or giving him a new right of veto. They made other demands (concerning the consultants, relations between church and state, state and school, and so forth), but the discussion turned primarily on the future position of Hindenburg. Hitler refused to include in the act the presidential rights they requested, but he assured them that he would enact laws of far-

---

[27] Cab. mtgs., Mar. 7, 1933, *DGFP.*, C, I, 118, Mar. 20, 1933, I.M.T., *Trial*, xxxi, 411–12.

reaching importance only after consultation with the president. He accepted virtually all of the other demands of the Center and promised to repeat these assurances in the statement he would make to the Reichstag. The Center was to submit its demands in writing, and he in turn would give it a copy of his statement before the Reichstag convened.

The Center leaders immediately compiled the required list. Convinced that any insistence on additional rights for the president would be futile, they contented themselves with asking that the government, in taking measures based on the Enabling Act, would not only respect the rights of the president, but would, "as a matter of course," proceed only "in that trusting collaboration and agreement with the supreme representative of the law which is the indispensable foundation of the confidence of the great majority of our people in this time of change and new beginnings."

But in discussions with the Reichstag delegation the following morning the Center leaders admitted that they no longer placed much hope in the president. He had resigned himself to accepting the Act, Kaas reported, apparently unaware of the fact that it was not a matter of resignation, but of ready acceptance. Brüning too expressed his deep disappointment about Hindenburg's passivity; he had urged Hindenburg's reelection, the ex-chancellor noted bitterly, on the express grounds that Hindenburg was the guardian and trustee of the constitution. Now the constitution was gravely threatened, largely because Hindenburg had resigned himself to its emasculation. Brüning concluded that he could hardly vote for the law.

Since Hitler had not yet sent his statement, the delegation adjourned without a decision. In the afternoon the chancellor spoke to the Reichstag; his speech contained all the guarantees requested by the Center though some of them were worded ambiguously. The chancellor added that Hindenburg's status and rights remained unchanged and that it would be the foremost task of the government to achieve an "inner agreement with his will."

The Kroll Opera House in Berlin, where the Reichstag was forced by the fire to meet, resembled an armed camp with stormtroopers patrolling the hallways and aisles. The fear that dissenters would be manhandled or hauled off to jail or to concentration camps hung heavily over the session and had its effect on the attitude of the Centrists. A faint hope persisted, however, that something might yet be salvaged if the delegation supported the Enabling Act. When Kaas asked for a straw vote during the adjournment, a large majority favored acceptance of the Enabling Act.

Brüning was still among those who voted "no." Once more he urged his colleagues to side with him: it would be better to perish honorably than to support a policy that would destroy the Center in any event. He was convinced that Hitler's promises were worthless, and again he made clear that he felt morally responsible to those who had voted for Hindenburg in response to his pleas and whom he was now asked to abandon by supporting the Enabling Act: "I appealed to millions to elect the Reich President, I have a responsibility to these millions who voted for the President to save the Reich—what is going to happen to these millions? The Majority Socialists voted for the President at my urging." But in the end he submitted to the will of the majority and voted "aye" on the act. It was passed by 441 votes against the 94 votes of the Socialists who courageously chose to oppose it.[28]

Among those who failed to understand the true significance of the Center's surrender was Hindenburg—he commended Kaas for having generously lent his support to Hitler. Later, learning of some Centrists' misgivings, he sent the leaders a letter in which he tried to dispel their anxieties, "I wish to assure you that the Chancellor has expressed his willingness, even without formal constitutional obligations, to take measures based on the Enabling Act only after consultations with me. I shall always try to remain in close touch with him and, faithful to my oath, 'do justice to all men.'" The letter, vague though it was, revived old hopes. Despite the many disappointments he had had, Brüning for one seems to have hoped once more that the president might still be induced to intervene against Hitler.[29]

He was soon to be disillusioned again. Equipped with the unlimited powers of the Enabling Act, Hitler proceeded to overhaul the political, social, and economic structure of the country. The independence of the states was abolished by the appointment of *Reichsstatthalter* and the regrouping of the state diets in accordance with the election returns of March 5. In Prussia, Hitler himself assumed the post of *Statthalter*, replacing Papen, who readily resigned as Reich commissioner. Hindenburg also accepted this change without objections. A law, aiming at the "restoration of the professional bureaucracy," eliminated "non-Aryans" and those who were considered "nationally unreliable" from their posts. Hindenburg obtained exemptions for Jewish war

28 Materials in *Vierteljahrshefte*, IV (1956), 302–07, IX (1961), 195–210; Morsey, in Matthias and Morsey, *Ende der Parteien*, pp. 353–67, 429–32, 434–35; Bracher, in Bracher, Sauer, Schulz, *Nationalsozialistische Machtergreifung*, pp. 159–68.

29 Morsey, in Matthias and Morsey, *Ende der Parteien*, pp. 366–67; Hindenburg letter, in Wheeler-Bennett, *Wooden Titan*, p. 449; Brüning, "Ein Brief," p. 18.

veterans, but he did not challenge the basic injustice of the law. Similarly he accepted the destruction of the labor unions, the "coordination" of other professional organizations, and the gradual strangling and final abolition of the political parties.

The fact is that he had made his peace with Hitler. The practice of having Papen attend his conferences with Hitler had gradually been abandoned, and in April he told the vice-chancellor that he would rather see Hitler alone so as not to hurt the chancellor's feelings. On Hitler's birthday, April 20, he sent him a telegram expressing his sincere appreciation of the "great patriotic work which you have achieved" and conveying his "comradely greetings." By this time the *Stahlhelm* was already under heavy fire as a haven for "Reds," and many of its leaders had been arrested and entire units dissolved. The Protestant Church was being harassed, state commissioners took over the functions of local church councils, and a Nazi-controlled "German Christian" movement challenged the integrity of the existing church authorities and asked for a church that "would share the destiny of its people and the perils of its historical life." On April 26 Duesterberg was relieved of his post and the *Stahlhelm* subordinated to Hitler; Hindenburg, who only a week before had asked Seldte to maintain an independent organization, voiced no objection to this capitulation. With similar equanimity he accepted the explanation of Duesterberg's departure "for reasons of health," and contented himself with sending the colonel a letter in which he thanked him for having preserved, in difficult times, "patriotism and soldierly virtues." Nor does he seem to have been unduly perturbed when Schleicher called on him to tell him of the inhuman conditions that prevailed in the concentration camps. On May 1, which Hitler proclaimed a "Day of National Labor" as a challenge to the traditional Marxist "May Day," Hindenburg gave his open support to the Fuehrer by speaking at the opening ceremony.[30]

With the marshal obviously unconcerned about the harassment of his immediate supporters, Hitler intensified his campaign against the right. German National leaders were manhandled and arrested, others were dismissed from public and semipublic offices, and meetings terrorized or broken up by stormtroopers. There were also increasing demands by agrarian and other organizations, obviously centrally directed, for Hugenberg's dismissal from the government. When a group of German National deputies called

[30] Papen, *Wahrheit*, p. 295; Picker, *Hitlers Tischgespräche*, p. 410; Duesterberg, *Stahlhelm*, pp. 54, 60; Hiller von Gaertringen, in Matthias and Morsey, *Ende der Parteien*, p. 600; Görlitz, *Hindenburg*, p. 415.

on Hitler to protest against these occurrences, they were treated to a harangue in which Hitler threatened "to turn over Berlin to the S.A. for three days and nights if they persisted in their opposition."

Early in June the marshal departed for Neudeck, leaving the German Nationals to their fate. In the latter part of June the party's offices and meetinghalls were closed by the police, and once more there were brutal beatings and wholesale arrests. Written protests to Hindenburg proved futile. As a last resort Hugenburg, the hapless party chief, sent Hergt, his old party colleague, to Neudeck to ascertain whether he could count on any assistance from the president. Hugenberg was also encountering personal difficulties in the cabinet which, admittedly, were partly of his own making, and had to have Hindenburg's backing if he were to remain in the cabinet. Hergt was never received by the president. He had a two-hour talk with Oskar von Hindenburg in which he complained about Hindenburg's inactivity and asked for his intervention in support of Hugenberg, who, as he stressed, represented Hindenburg's original voters in the Reich government—hardly a compelling argument in view of Hugenberg's attitude during the last few years. Hergt found little understanding for Hugenberg's plight; in fact, Colonel von Hindenburg seemed favorably impressed with the accomplishments of the Nazis and suggested that the president would favor an adjustment on Hugenberg's part to the course of the government.

Obviously no help could be expected from Hindenburg. Hugenberg resigned from the cabinet two days later and on the same day the German National leaders decided to dissolve their party. The Social Democrats had been suppressed a week before; the State Party, German People's Party, Christian Socialists, Bavarian People's Party, and Center disbanded during the following week.

Hindenburg's inactivity on this as on other occasions has frequently been blamed on the narrow-mindedness and/or the Nazi sympathies of his son. Nothing in the available evidence supports this assumption. Whatever Oskar von Hindenburg did, he appears to have acted, if not on his father's express instructions, in accordance with his views and wishes. Frau Meissner complained to the British ambassador at that time that when she or her husband tried to point out to the president some of the darker aspects of the Hitler regime, he suggested to them that they mind their own business and keep quiet. When the British ambassador called on the president a few days after the resignation of Hugenberg and the dissolution of the German National Party, Hindenburg seemed entirely unperturbed by these developments.[31] On rare occasions the president would still voice objections on some matter on which he felt strongly. He held up the appointment of the Nazi *Gauleiter* of Mecklenburg as *Reichsstatthalter* and insisted on an investigation of charges that the man was involved in the slaying of a rival stormtrooper leader. He protested against the refusal of the government, on technical grounds, to confirm the election of the distinguished, but independent-minded pastor Friedrich von Bodelschwingh as Reich bishop of the Lutheran Church. On another occasion he objected to the use of the Berlin castle for the opening ceremony of a newly appointed Prussian *Staatsrat* on the grounds that the Emperor might take offense. But even in these cases he contented himself with some minor concessions. He appointed the Mecklenburg *Gauleiter* as *Reichsstatthalter* although the investigation did not give the latter a clean bill of health. He failed to obtain Bodelschwingh's installation and settled for some modifications of the official Nazi position towards church matters. Nor did he intervene, despite many appeals, when new church elections were clearly manipulated by the Nazis. And he remained silent when Göring convened the *Staatsrat* in one of the Hohenzollern's castles in Potsdam rather than in Berlin.

How much he might have done to check Hitler is a matter of conjecture of course, but it is evident that Hitler, whether from awe of the marshal or from fear of political repercussions, did not ignore his objections if they were made with sufficient vigor. Yet as so often before, Hindenburg refused to involve himself in troublesome controversies, and the decline of his physical strength served to reenforce his natural lethargy. Thus he also tolerated the replacement of a *Stahlhelm* honor guard at Neudeck by a stormtrooper detachment and submitted to controls on his callers which earned Neudeck the name of Germany's smallest concentration camp. Count Brünneck, who saw him occasionally during the summer, felt that the old man was anxious to maintain harmonious relations with Hitler and was trying to persuade himself that Hitler was reciprocating the feeling and loyally fulfilling his promises. Even Brüning came to the reluctant conclusion that

[31] Bracher, in Bracher, Sauer, Schulz, *Nationalsozialistische Machtergreifung*, pp. 208–13; Schmidt-Hannover, *Umdenken*, pp. 353–54; materials in Borchmeyer, *Hugenbergs Ringen*, I, 78–80; Hiller von Gaertringen, in *op. cit.*, pp. 606–16; Anton Ritthaler, "Eine Etappe auf Hitlers Weg zur ungeteilten Macht: Hugenbergs Rücktritt als Reichsminister," *Vierteljahrshefte*, VIII (1960), 193–219, esp. 199–200 (Hergt); Rumbold to Simon, June 30, 1933, *DBFP.*, ii, v, 387–88.

he could no longer count on Hindenburg to oppose Hitler openly and call out the Reichswehr to put an end to the Nazi terror.[32]

The quiet of those summer days was interrupted but once. On August 27, the anniversary of the Battle of Tannenberg, the marshal attended a ceremony at the Tannenberg Memorial at which he was presented with two large properties, one of them once part of the Hindenburg family estate, the other a forest, the Preussenwald, that was given to him as Bismarck had been given the Sachsenwald in 1871 in recognition of his achievements. Hindenburg seems to have been reluctant at first to accept these gifts, and his acceptance speech omitted the customary tribute to the new spirit and the achievements of the Hitler regime, as if to stress that his support could not be bought by any such gifts. Having paid tribute to those who gave their life at Tannenberg, he expressed his "respect, loyalty, and gratitude to my Emperor, King, and Lord whose confidence and command once brought me here." And he concluded with the old soldier's cry which once had been thundering across this battlefield: "Germany, hurrah! hurrah! hurrah!" [33]

✍

With his health failing, Hindenburg stayed longer than usual at Neudeck that year. When he returned to Berlin in mid-October, he was once more, for a brief moment, drawn into the political arena. France, alarmed by the German resurgence, wished to delay the implementation of the agreement, reached the previous December, that had established the "principle" of Germany's full equality in armaments. Hitler, who had long wished to break off the negotiations, decided to withdraw from the Geneva Disarmament Conference and the League of Nations. For both these steps he thought it advisable, however, to invoke the prestige of the president. The chancellor also wished to dissolve the Reichstag

---

[32] Meissner, *Staatssekretär*, pp. 323–24; Bracher, in *op. cit.*, pp. 333–34; Meissner to Göring, July 21, 1933, *B.d.RPr.*, R 54/272; Schulthess, Sept. 15, 1933, p. 209; "concentration camp," in Severing, *Lebensweg*, II, 404; Brünneck, in Borcke-Stargordt Papers; Brüning, quoted in Gordon to Phillips, June 23, 1933, *Papers Relating to Foreign Relations of the United States* (hereafter cited as "*U.S. For. Relations,*"), 1933, II, 234–35.

[33] Schulthess, Aug. 27, 1933, pp. 196–97. Like Neudeck, the new holdings were exempted from taxes. In addition, Hitler and Göring promised orally to contribute 400,000 marks each from Reich and Prussian funds for the rehabilitation of the property. When no payments had been made after three weeks, Hindenburg had Meissner ask for a written confirmation of the promise and for payment of the amount "as soon as possible." Memorandum by Wienstein, Sept. 18, 1933, *RKz.*, R 43 I/581.

and arrange a plebiscite on the two moves in order to demonstrate by the returns that his policies enjoyed the support of the nation, and for the dissolution decree he needed Hindenburg's signature. Taking Papen and Neurath with him, Hitler explained his plans to the president. According to Meissner, Hindenburg wondered about the wisdom of leaving the League and Hitler replied that the move was required to affirm Germany's full equality. Moreover, the withdrawal would be effective only after two years, according to the League Covenant, so that there would be ample time for the other Powers to reconsider their position and by proper concessions enable Germany to remain in the League. Both Papen and Neurath agreed, and Hindenburg gave his approval. When the cabinet was called together to be informed, Hitler could announce that the Reich president was in full agreement with him.[34]

Hitler even succeeded in enlisting Hindenburg's help in the plebiscite campaign. On the eve of the plebiscite and the Reichstag elections, on November 11, 1933, the president broadcast an appeal to the nation. Taking full credit for the decisions that had been made, he said, in part:

"I and the Reich Government, united in the wish to lead Germany out of the strife and impotence of the postwar years, have called on the German people to decide for itself and to announce to the world whether it wants to approve and to identify itself with the policies which we have inaugurated. . . . Thanks to the courageous, determined, and vigorous leadership of Chancellor Hitler and his associates, appointed by me last January 30, Germany has again found herself and regained the strength to take the road which national honor and her future are prescribing for her."

The speech continued in this vein, assuring both Germany and the world that the withdrawal was not meant to obstruct efforts to achieve peace and disarmament, but that true understanding could be achieved only on the basis of full equality. It concluded with an appeal to "you, *deutsche Volksgenossen*" (a favorite Nazi phrase that had never been part of his vocabulary) to demonstrate tomorrow "your national honor and your identification with the Reich Government. Speak up with me and the Chancellor for the principle of equality and for peace with honor and show to the world that we have recovered German unity and with God's help shall preserve it." When the plebiscite produced a 95.1 per

[34] Cab. mtg., Oct. 13, 1933, *DGFP.*, C, I, 924–26; Meissner, *Staatssekretär*, pp. 347–48.

cent majority approving the foreign policy of the government and the Reichstag election a vote of 92.2 per cent of all ballots cast for the Nazi Party, the only party running in the election, Hindenburg, according to the official communiqué, "conveys his deeply felt gratitude to the Chancellor for having attained the political unity of the German people, and expresses the confident hope that on this foundation endeavors at home and abroad can be continued for the benefit of the Fatherland and the German people." These statements were issued not merely for public consumption, but evidently expressed the marshal's true feelings. Observers who had occasion to see Hindenburg and Hitler together at that time noted that the president treated the chancellor with special benevolence.[35]

Even a rather serious contretemps could not affect this relationship. Towards the end of 1933, Hammerstein, almost totally isolated and on bad terms with Hindenburg and Blomberg, submitted his resignation. Hitler and Blomberg wished Major General Walther von Reichenau, Blomberg's chief aide and a devoted National Socialist, to succeed Hammerstein as chief of the army command. Hindenburg thought Reichenau too young for the post; he distrusted him too because of his political interests that might lead him to draw the Reichswehr into politics. At the same time he resented Hitler's intrusion into a domain that he considered solely his own, and he became furious when Blomberg tried to compel him to appoint Reichenau by threatening to resign. This he considered rank insubordination. Hitler, anxious not to annoy the marshal, gave in, and General von Fritsch, earlier Papen's candidate for the post of Reichswehr minister, received the appointment.[36]

Effective resistance thus was still possible, but after having taken a stand on this particular issue, Hindenburg relapsed into his customary lethargy and agreed to steps that largely undid what he had wished to achieve. While he had objected to Hitler's interference in his domain as commander-in-chief, he gave up at that very time a substantial part of his military authority, accepting a law and signing an executive order by which members of the armed forces no longer swore to obey the Reich president and their superiors, but rather affirmed their willingness, "as obedient

[35] Schulthess, Nov. 11–12, 1933, pp. 241–43; Erich von Manstein, *Aus einem Soldatenleben 1887–1939* (Bonn, 1958), p. 212; Funk, in Schulenburg, *Welt um Hindenburg*, p. 194.

[36] Friedrich Hossbach, in *Jahrbuch der Albertus-Universität zu Königsberg/Pr.*, VIII (1958), 223 n. 63; Papen, *Wahrheit*, pp. 324–25.

soldiers," to sacrifice their life in the fulfillment of their military duties. In February 1934 Hindenburg signed another order affixing the insignia of the Nazi Party to the uniforms of the army and navy—a decision wholly at variance with his recent objections to Reichenau's appointment as chief of the army command on the grounds that he was likely to involve the Reichswehr in politics.[37]

Hitler on his part treated the president with special consideration. Except for the Reichenau case, he carefully refrained from openly interfering in matters of military appointments, and he observed the same restraint in regard to the personnel policies of the foreign office. He could do this the more easily as he had willing collaborators in Blomberg and Neurath and through them could exert a decisive influence on both military and foreign policy. He also professed to be willing to fulfill Hindenburg's greatest wish, the restoration of the monarchy. Even before he came to power, he had suggested as much to the president; as chancellor he kept assuring the marshal that eventually he hoped to restore the Hohenzollerns to their throne. He warned, however, against any precipitous action—the time was not ripe yet, for Germany would have to regain first her full sovereignty and equality if the monarchy was to be more than a mere shadow. Hindenburg, taking Hitler at his word, agreed with this view. Organizations and individuals who urged him to take steps now to restore the monarchy were invariably cautioned to bide their time. He wrote to his old friend Cramon that he did not think foreign powers would passively stand by for his sake while the monarchy was being restored. If the plan failed, it would have to be shelved for a long time or even abandoned forever: "To say this is very difficult for me, but I believe that I . . . can thus serve my Imperial Lord better than by blindly agreeing to your plan."[38]

But the question of restoring the monarchy could not be put to rest. It gained in importance as a monarchist restoration became the only conceivable alternative to a Nazi dictatorship. It was also obvious that, if possible at all, it could be achieved only while Hindenburg was still alive or immediately after his death. When it became clear therefore that the president would not have much longer to live, monarchist circles intensified their endeavors. Toward the end of 1933, after feelers by such spokesmen as Cramon

37 Hossbach, in *op. cit.*, pp. 218, 222; Schulthess, Feb. 21, 1934, p. 73.

38 Hans-Günther Seraphim, *Das politische Tagebuch Alfred Rosenbergs aus den Jahren 1934–35 und 1939–40* (Göttingen, Berlin, Frankfurt/M., 1956), pp. 18, 20; Meissner, *Staatssekretär*, pp. 322–23; Hindenburg to Cramon, Oct. 23, 1933, in *Neue Zeitung*, Mar. 19, 1949; Görlitz, *Hindenburg*, p. 416.

had been unsuccessful, the ex-Kaiser himself wrote to Hindenburg, suggesting that the time had come to complete the rehabilitation of Germany by restoring the monarchy.

Hitler had several times stated publicly that an immediate restoration of the monarchy was out of the question, but out of respect for Hindenburg he had not directly interfered with the monarchist movement. With Hindenburg's death approaching, he decided, however, that he could not afford to stand by any longer. After public warnings by Nazi subleaders had failed to intimidate the monarchists, orders were issued to break up all gatherings celebrating the Emperor's 75th birthday on January 27, 1934. On January 30, the anniversary of Hitler's appointment as chancellor, Hitler warned in a speech to the Reichstag that the National Socialist Party was only concerned with the vital needs of the nation and could not accept "past dynastic interests . . . as an ever lasting obligation of the German people." Three days later all monarchist organizations were dissolved by Frick.[39]

The monarchists were not yet ready to drop their plans. With any public agitation excluded, they could hope to achieve their goal only through an approach to Hitler and Hindenburg. Even if Hitler was opposed to an immediate monarchist restoration, his further remark in his Reichstag address that the question of the *"final* form of the German state" was not a matter for discussion "today" seemed to suggest that his mind was not entirely closed to the eventual reestablishment of the monarchy.

Papen took up the matter with Hitler in March 1934 and tried to persuade him that even from his, Hitler's, viewpoint a monarchy would have certain advantages, permitting him to remain the National Socialist leader instead of being forced as formal head of the state to be wholly nonpartisan. This argument can hardly have impressed Hitler, but he professed to be interested in the return of a Hohenzollern to the throne. Again Hitler stressed that Germany would have to recover her full sovereignty before a monarch could ascend the throne with any hope of retaining it, but he was willing to discuss candidates, and he promised Papen to appoint the man of his choice to a post in the chancellery so that he might learn something about governmental affairs. Evidently he was anxious to please Hindenburg during the few remaining months of his life.

Hopefully Papen hurried to Hindenburg and urged him to draw up a "Political Testament" recommending the restoration of

[39] Heiden, *Fuehrer,* p. 735; Sauer, in Bracher, Sauer, Schulz, *Nationalsozialistische Machtergreifung,* pp. 910–11; Hitler, in Schulthess, Jan. 30, 1934, p. 39.

the monarchy in case of his death or incapacitation. At the marshal's request Papen prepared such a document. After pondering the matter for several weeks, Hindenburg decided not to press the demand for the monarchy. He divided Papen's document into two separate parts: one, a "political testament" addressed to the German people, a sort of *compte rendu* of his presidency; the other, a personal letter to the chancellor recommending to Hitler the return of the monarchy. He had no wish to become the subject of controversy either in life or death. The "political testament" was published a few days after Hindenburg's death, but the letter was not. Yet it cannot be said that Hitler, in keeping it secret, went counter to Hindenburg's wishes. Oskar von Hindenburg testified after World War II that his father had left it to Hitler to determine the opportune moment for its publication.[40]

Hindenburg's desire for peace was now greater than ever. He sensed that all was not well under Hitler, and he complained to Papen about the state of affairs and wrote worried letters to Brünneck about the plight of the Protestant Church. But publicly he went out of his way to show his esteem for the chancellor. On Hitler's birthday he sent him a message of congratulations "in faithful comradeship and with cordial greetings." And when he reviewed the Berlin garrison on Memorial Day, he ostentatiously honored Hitler, who was standing behind him, by motioning him to his side.[41]

On June 4, 1934, he departed as usual for Neudeck. By then he was suffering from a bladder ailment which, according to all indications, would lead to his death within less than three months. The affliction was painful at times, but he still led his regular life and attended to his official duties. But what little strength he had left was gradually ebbing away.

In mid-June Papen made his now famous speech to the students of Marburg in which he warned against the lawlessness and radi-

---

40 Papen, *Wahrheit*, pp. 369–72; Oskar von Hindenburg, in *Neue Zeitung*, Feb. 12, 1949; also Braun, *Von Ostpreussen*, p. 265. While Hindenburg was prepared to yield to Hitler in such matters of fundamental concern and accepted the fact that he was bypassed in almost all others, he held on jealously to some very minor prerogatives. At one cabinet meeting in May 1934 Göring raised the question whether the Maltese and St. John's Crosses ought still to be awarded. He had his doubts since the St. John's Cross, for one, was awarded only to noblemen. For months Meissner had attended cabinet meetings without saying a word, but now he spoke up and insisted that any decision on this matter be postponed; he would have to take it up first with the president. Cab. mtg., May 15, 1934, *RKz.*, R 43 I/1469.

41 Papen, *Wahrheit*, p. 344; Hindenburg to Brünneck, May 4, 1934, in Lucas, *Hindenburg*, p. 132; same to Hitler, Apr. 19, 1934, Schulthess, Apr. 20, 1934, p. 109; see also Lucas, *Hindenburg*, p. 129.

calism of the Nazi regime. As an open challenge to Hitler his remarks caused a sensation, but they did not arouse Hindenburg. Funk, the old friend of the family, was immediately dispatched to Neudeck to tell him that Papen, in making the speech, had been guilty of a severe breach of discipline and would resign from the government. Possibly Hindenburg was too feeble to grasp the full implications of Papen's move; he accepted Funk's explanation and, according to the latter's testimony, only remarked: "If he does not maintain discipline, he must be prepared to take the consequences." The old faith in Hindenburg's fortitude still persisted, however, and it was widely believed at the time that he sent Papen a telegram congratulating him on this courageous action. Papen made some belated efforts to go to Neudeck, but the president's entourage, most likely instructed or intimidated by Hitler, declined to arrange a meeting.[42]

Papen was most anxious to meet with the president since he had learned through various channels that a revolt of the stormtroopers was in the making. Röhm, their chief, had long hoped to merge his units into the Reichswehr and to take over the post of Reichswehr minister; he was said to be ready now to enforce these claims. Since Papen was unable to call on the president, one of his associates tried to reach Hindenburg through Oskar von Hindenburg to get the marshal to proclaim a state of emergency and call out the army, but Oskar refused to pass on the appeal to his father. Whether Hindenburg would have acted had he been reached seems doubtful, however. The day before, Fritsch and another general had called on him on official business and had found him in very poor health and clearly declining mentally: most of the time he kept reminiscing about the wars of 1866 and 1870.[43]

Similarly Hindenburg received with relative calm the news of the suppression of the alleged Röhm Putsch of June 30, 1934. His immediate reaction was to complain to Meissner: "For months I have told the Chancellor to get rid of this immoral and dangerous Röhm and lock him up; unfortunately he did not listen to me; now it again cost much blood." According to Funk, who was with him at that time, he also observed: "Who wants to make history like Hitler must be prepared to let guilty blood flow and not be soft." His attitude changed, however, when he learned a day later

42 Meissner, *Staatssekretär*, p. 375; Funk, in I.M.T., *Trial*, XIII, 137–38; Dodd to Hull, June 26, 1934, *U.S. For. Relations*, 1934, II, 228; Heiden, *Fuehrer*, p. 752; Papen, *Wahrheit*, pp. 350–51; affidavit by Schaffgotsch, in I.M.T., *Trial*, XL, 559.
43 Sauer, in *op. cit.*, p. 959; on Hindenburg-Fritsch talk, Mellenthin, ZS./105.

that Schleicher and his wife were among those who had been killed. Deeply upset, he asked for an immediate investigation and refused to accept Hitler's and Göring's explanation that the general and his wife had been shot while resisting arrest on charges of conspiracy with Röhm and treasonous contacts with other countries. Yet when Hitler suggested the next day that the president send him a telegram stating that Röhm and his associates were guilty of treason and that Hitler had crushed their conspiracy in defense of the state, he followed this suggestion—after checking with Blomberg, who readily confirmed the accuracy of Hitler's and Göring's accounts.[44]

His acceptance of this version of the Röhm Putsch may have been due in part to the fact that he was unable to contact Papen; he did send a telegram to his trusted confidant as soon as he learned of the Putsch, but Papen was himself under house arrest and never received the message. Papen in turn was equally unsuccessful in his attempts to reach Hindenburg after he had regained his freedom since Hindenburg's aides refused to arrange a visit on the grounds that the marshal's health did not permit it. This allegation was later disavowed by the testimony of Hindenburg's personal physician and disproved by the fact that the president received other official callers during that time. Possibly his entourage felt that Hindenburg could have changed nothing and that a talk with Papen would have meant a needless emotional strain at a time when his strength was quickly declining. Even without Papen's version of the Putsch he seems to have been gravely shocked by what he learned subsequently about the events of June 30. He felt, however, according to Meissner, that the lawless excesses committed on that day were not Hitler's fault, but that of criminal elements over which the chancellor had lost control. He urged Hitler, through Meissner, to rid himself of the culprits and subject them to the strictest punishment.[45]

On July 25 he learned of the Nazi rising in Austria and of the

---

[44] Meissner, *Staatssekretär*, pp. 368–69; Hindenburg to Funk, quoted in Hans Frank, *Im Angesicht des Galgens* (Munich, 1953), p. 144. Meissner states in his memoirs that a draft of the proposed telegram was submitted to him by Funk and that he toned it down somewhat before passing it on to Neudeck by telephone. Yet the published version, apparently the original one, was considerably stronger than Meissner's. Whereas the state secretary wished Hindenburg merely to convey his "thanks," in the published telegram Hindenburg expressed "my deeply felt thanks and my sincere appreciation." Meissner, *Staatssekretär*, p. 369; Schulthess, June 30, 1934, p. 168.

[45] Braun, *Von Ostpreussen*, p. 265; Papen, *Wahrheit*, pp. 355–56, 361–62; Schaffgotsch, in I.M.T., *Trial*, XL, 559–60; Görlitz, *Hindenburg*, p. 424; Meissner, *Staatssekretär*, pp. 375–76.

murder of Chancellor Dollfuss. His physical condition declined rapidly from the shock over these new acts of violence, and he no longer could leave his bed. The end was imminent. He did have the final gratification of receiving a special "get well" message from the ex-Emperor and his last thoughts, according to his son, centered on "his Kaiser." When Hitler rushed to his bedside on August 1, the marshal was already near death.[46]

Hindenburg died on August 2, 1934. His wish had been to be buried at Neudeck, but Hitler insisted on a state funeral in the Tannenberg Memorial. There, on August 7, he was laid to rest in an impressively staged military ceremony. (His wife's remains also were brought from Neudeck to Tannenberg.) As the text for his funeral sermon he himself had chosen the passage from the Revelation of St. John, 2:10 "Be thou faithful unto death, and I will give thee a crown of life"—a selection which must have caused many a bitter thought. After the Lutheran army bishop had spoken, Hitler addressed the mourners. He described the marshal's military achievements in glowing terms from the days of the wars of German unification through World War I:

"A mystical power emanated from the name of the Field Marshal General who with his armies beat down in Russia the then largest military power in the world. And when—too late, alas—the Emperor called him to the command of all armies in the field, he was able, with his ingenious collaborators, not only to check the most serious crisis for the time being, but to arouse German resistance to unheard of victories for another two years. Historically the tragic end of this greatest conflict cannot be held against the military leader, but only against the politicians!"

He came, "historically," closer to the truth when he continued:

"It is one of the wondrous turns of an unfathomable wise fate that under the Presidency of this first soldier and servant of our people we could work for the rise of our German people until he himself finally opened the door to Germany's rejuvenation. In his name the alliance was concluded which merged the dynamic power of this rising with the finest minds of the past. As Reich President the Field Marshal became the Lord Protector of the National Socialist Revolution and of the rebirth of our people...."[47]

[46] Braun, *Von Ostpreussen*, pp. 265–66; Meissner, *Staatssekretär*, p. 376.

[47] Hindenburg's selection of bible text, cab. mtg., Aug. 2, 1934, 8 p.m., *RKz.*, R 43 1/146; Hitler, in Schulthess, Aug. 7, 1934, pp. 200–01.

The grief of the nation over the death of the field marshal-president was genuine. In spite of his age, in spite of his utter passivity during the last year, and above all, in spite of the many bitter disappointments he had caused those who had seen in him a last impregnable bulwark against the brutalities and excesses of the Nazis, faith in him as an ultimate check on Hitler had never wholly died. Now that he was gone, there was an uneasy feeling that the last link with the old traditional order had disappeared and that the nation was now completely at Hitler's mercy. "Everywhere little groups formed to discuss the event and its possible consequences," noted the Berlin correspondent of the *New York Times,* "on every face grief was mingled with anxiety."

This uneasiness found its cautious expression in efforts to conjure up once more the image of the marshal as the symbol of justice and loyalty, cautiously hinting the direction in which the country should move. "The hard times and tests which the German people will face," observed the editor of the *Deutsche Rundschau,* "it will have to meet with unity and discipline in Hindenburg's spirit and in accord with his counsel." Or, as the *Frankfurter Zeitung* put it more directly,

"The sense of right, the iron will to demand and do justice— these qualities every German has sensed in the life and actions of the old Marshal. We shall cherish them as the most precious part of his bequest. It encompasses a tradition which the Germans must not and shall not lose." [48]

෴

On August 1 the Reich government had passed a law merging the functions and prerogatives of the president with those of the chancellor on Hindenburg's death. In a letter to Frick, on the following day, Hitler abolished the title of Reich president (too reminiscent of the defunct republic) on the grounds that "the greatness of the deceased has endowed that title . . . with a unique significance." He, Hitler, wished to be addressed officially as "Fuehrer and Reich Chancellor." He also decreed that the transfer of the presidential functions to him be sanctioned expressly by the German people in a "free and secret" plebiscite. The date was set for August 19.

The plebiscite campaign, unopposed of course, was uneventful. On August 15 Hindenburg's "Political Testament" was published

[48] *New York Times,* Aug. 3, 1934; R[udolf] P[echel], in *Dt. Rundschau,* Sept. 1934, p. 129; *Frankfurter Zeitung,* Reich ed., Aug. 5, 1934.

in which the marshal had words of high praise for "my Chancellor Adolf Hitler and his movement" although he did add that much remained to be done and that he hoped that the national rise and unification be followed now by "an act of reconciliation embracing the entire German Fatherland." On the eve of the plebiscite Oskar von Hindenburg, yielding to mounting pressures, broadcast a radio appeal to the country:

"The late Reich President and Field Marshal General . . . having concluded his compact with Adolf Hitler on January 30 of last year and having confirmed it during that sacred hour in the *Garnisonkirche* at Potsdam on March 21, always supported Adolf Hitler and approved all important decisions of [Hitler's] Government. . . . My father himself saw in Adolf Hitler his direct successor as head of the German state, and I am acting in accordance with my father's wishes when I call on all German men and women to vote for the transfer of my father's office to the Fuehrer and Chancellor." [49]

In saying this, Oskar von Hindenburg clearly expressed his father's views. The elder Hindenburg had never evisaged an immediate restoration of the monarchy, and his son was not untruthful, as has often been charged, when he stated that the marshal had seen in Hitler his direct successor, leaving open the question of a subsequent permanent settlement of the succession problem.[50]

The plebiscite produced the expected overwhelming majority (90 per cent of the vote) in support of the new arrangement. Of the 35 electoral districts, Hindenburg's home province, East Prussia, recorded the largest majority with 95.9 per cent.

[49] *Ibid.*, Aug. 19, 1934.

[50] In this connection some significance has been read into the fact that Oskar von Hindenburg was shortly afterwards promoted to the rank of major general; William L. Shirer, *The Rise and Fall of the Third Reich* (paperback ed., Greenwich, 1962), p. 315 n. There was nothing unusual about this, however. Oskar's promotion was awarded to him upon his resignation from the army; it was customary to confer the next higher rank on an officer at the time of his retirement.

POSTSCRIPT

INDENBURG'S tomb remained at Tannenberg for just ten years. In the fall of 1944, on Hitler's personal orders, the coffins of the marshal-president and his wife were removed from the Memorial to keep them from falling into the hands of the Russians. After an Odyssey extending over more than a year the marshal and Frau von Hindenburg were reburied in the St. Elizabeth Church in Marburg in 1946.

Few Germans know this today. A visitor to Marburg, inquiring about Hindenburg's grave, will find that many of the townspeople are unaware of its existence. So are most of the tourists inspecting the church, according to its custodian. Veterans organizations still come to pay homage, but to the bulk of the nation Field Marshal von Hindenburg, Reich president of the Weimar Republic, is little more than a name now. With his military and political repute in decline, Hindenburg has become almost solely the historian's concern. His evanescence seems fittingly symbolized by the brief inscription engraved on his tombstone; it does not give his full name and dates, let alone his titles and offices, but simply reads:

Paul von Hindenburg

1847–1934 [1]

[1] Personal experiences, and information from a Marburg resident.

BIBLIOGRAPHY

Unpublished Sources
  Bundesarchiv
    a) Governmental and Party Records
      Büro des Reichspräsidenten
      Reichskanzlei
      Deutsche Volkspartei (German People's Party)
    b) Personal Papers
      Bauer, Col. Max, cit. by vol.
      Bülow, Fürst Bernhard von, cit. by vol. and page
      Dingeldey, Eduard, cit. by vol.
      Foerster, Maj. Gen. Wolfgang
      Gayl, Freiherr Wilhelm von, cit. by vol.
      Gothein, Georg, cit. by vol. and page
      Hoffmann, Maj. Gen. Max, cit. by vol.
      Koch-Weser, Erich, cit. by vol. and page
      Saemisch, Dr. Moritz, cit. by vol.
      Schleicher, Gen. Kurt von, cit. by vol. and page
      Schwertfeger, Maj. Gen. Bernhard, cit. by vol.
      Wegener, Dr. Leo, cit. by vol.
      Wild von Hohenborn, Gen. Adolf, cit. by vol.
    c) Militärarchiv
      Stülpnagel, Gen. Joachim von, 75 Jahre meines Lebens (Selbst-
        verlag, als MS. gedruckt, Oberaudorf, Obb., 1960)
  Columbia University
    Stresemann, Dr. Gustav (microfilm), cit. by vol., roll, and frame
  Hoover Institute and Library
    Duke Collection, cit. by envelope
    Munich Collection, cit. by folder
    Seeckt, Col. Gen. Hans von (microfilm), cit. by roll and page
    War Crimes Trials, Nürnberg, Cases No. 5 and 11. (mimeo-
      graphed)
  Institut für Zeitgeschichte
    Borcke-Stargordt, Graf Henning von
    Groener, Gen. Wilhelm (microfilm), cit. by roll and item
    Zeugenschrifttum (letters, statements, affidavits by various per-
      sons), cit. by folder
  Institute of Social History
    Braun, Otto
    Grzesinski, Albert
  Ohio State University
    Miscellaneous German Records (microfilm), Parts I and III, cit.
      by roll and frame

485

National Socialist German Labor Party (microfilm), cit. by roll and frame

Protocols of cabinet meetings, Reich Chancellery, cit. by roll and frame

Records of Private Austrian, Dutch, and German Enterprises, 1917–1946 (microfilm), cit. by roll and frame

Social Democratic Party, archives
Severing, Carl, cit. by year
Stadtarchiv Köln
Marx, Wilhelm, cit. by folder
U.S. Document Center, Berlin
National Socialist German Labor Party, *Hauptarchiv,* cit. by folder
In Private Hands
Marx, Wilhelm
Schmidt-Hannover, Otto
Westarp, Graf Kuno von

Books

Abernon, Viscount Edgar Vincent d', *An Ambassador of Peace: Pages from the Diary of Viscount d' Abernon* (London, 1929–30)

Alter, Junius, *Nationalisten: Deutschlands nationales Führertum der Nachkriegszeit* (Leipzig, 1930)

Amtliche Urkunden zur Vorgeschichte des Waffenstillstandes 1918, Auswärtiges Amt und Reichsministerium des Innern, eds. (Berlin, 1924)

Aretin, Erwin von, *Krone und Ketten: Erinnerungen eines bayerischen Edelmannes,* Karl Buchheim and Karl Otmar von Aretin, eds. (Munich, 1955)

Bachem, Karl, *Vorgeschichte, Geschichte und Politik der deutschen Zentrumspartei* (Cologne, 1927–1931)

Bauer, Oberst [Max], *Der grosse Krieg in Feld und Heimat: Erinnerungen und Betrachtungen* (Tübingen, 1921)

Baynes, Norman H., ed., *The Speeches of Adolf Hitler, 1922–1939* (New York, 1942)

Beck, Ludwig, *Studien,* Hans Speidel, ed. (Stuttgart, 1955)

Beer, Rüdiger Robert, *Brüning* (Berlin, 1931)

Bennett, Edward W., *Germany and the Diplomacy of the Financial Crisis, 1931* (Cambridge, 1962)

Bernhard, Ludwig, *Der Hugenberg-Konzern: Psychologie und Technik einer Grossorganisation der Presse* (Berlin, 1928)

Bernhardi, Friedrich von, *Denkwürdigkeiten aus meinem Leben* (Berlin, 1927)

Berthold, Lothar, and Helmut Neef, *Militarismus und Opportunismus gegen die Novemberrevolution: Das Bündnis der rechten SPD-Führung mit der Obersten Heeresleitung, November und Dezember 1918* ([East] Berlin, 1958)

Besson, Waldemar, *Württemberg und die deutsche Staatskrise, 1928–1933: Eine Studie zur Auflösung der Weimarer Republik* (Stuttgart, 1959)

Bethmann Hollweg, Th[eobald] von, *Betrachtungen zum Weltkrieg* (Berlin, 1920–21)

Boetticher, Friedrich von, *Schlieffen* (Göttingen, 1957)

Bonn, Moritz Julius, *So macht man Geschichte* (Munich, 1953)

Borchmeyer, Dr., *Hugenbergs Ringen in deutschen Schicksalsstunden* (Detmold, 1951)

Borcke-Stargordt, Graf Henning von, *Der ostdeutsche Landbau Zwischen Fortschritt, Krise und Politik: Ein Beitrag zur Agrar- und Zeitgeschichte* (Würzburg, 1957)

Bracher, Karl Dietrich, *Die Auflösung der Weimarer Republik: Eine Studie zum Problem des Machtverfalls in der Demokratie* (Stuttgart and Düsseldorf, 1955)

———, Wolfgang Sauer, Gerhard Schulz, *Die nationalsozialistische Machtergreifung: Studien zur Errichtung des totalitären Herrschaftssystems in Deutschland 1933/34* (Cologne and Opladen, 1960)

Braun, Magnus Freiherr von, *Von Ostpreussen bis Texas* (Stollhamm [Oldb.], 1955)

Braun, Otto, *Von Weimar zu Hitler* (New York, 1940)

Breucker, Wilhelm, *Die Tragik Ludendorffs* (Stollhamm [Oldb.], 1953)

Buchheim, Karl, *Geschichte der christlichen Parteien in Deutschland* (Munich, 1955)

Buchta, Bruno, *Die Junker und die Weimarer Republik: Charakter und Bedeutung der Osthilfe in den Jahren 1928–1933* ([East] Berlin, 1959)

Bülow, Furst Bernhard von, *Denkwürdigkeiten;* ed. by Franz von Stockhammern (Berlin, 1930–31)

Bullock, Alan, *Hitler: A Study in Tyranny* (New York, 1953)

Bund zur Erneuerung des Reiches, *Die Rechte des Deutschen Reichspräsidenten nach der Reichsverfassung* (Berlin, 1930)

Caro, Kurt, and Walter Oehme, *Schleichers Aufstieg* (Berlin, 1933)

Choltitz, Dietrich von, *Soldat unter Soldaten* (Zurich, 1951)

Craig, Gordon A., *The Politics of the Prussian Army: 1640–1945* (New York and Oxford, 1955)

Curtius, Julius, *Sechs Jahre Minister der deutschen Republik* (Heidelberg, 1948)

Delbrück, Hans, *Vor und nach dem Weltkriege* (Berlin, 1926)

Dietrich, Otto, *12 Jahre mit Hitler* (Munich, 1955)

Documents on British Foreign Policy, 1919–1939, E. L. Woodward and Rohan Butler, eds., Ser. II

Documents on German Foreign Policy, 1918–1945, Paul R. Sweet et al., eds., Ser. C

Drucker, Peter F., *The End of Economic Man* (New York, 1939)

Duesterberg, Theodor, *Der Stahlhelm und Hitler* (Wolfenbüttel and Hanover, 1949)

Egelhaaf, Gotthold, *Politische Jahresübersichten, 1925–1933*

Elze, Walter, *Tannenberg* (Breslau, 1928)

Endres, Fritz, ed., *Hindenburg: Briefe, Reden, Berichte* (Munich, 1934)

Ernst, Fritz, *Aus dem Nachlass des Generals Walter Reinhardt* (Stuttgart, 1958)

Erzberger, Matthias, *Erlebnisse im Weltkrieg* (Stuttgart and Berlin, 1920)

Eyck, Erich, *Geschichte der Weimarer Republik* (Erlenbach/ Zurich and Stuttgart, 1954–56)

Faber du Faur, Moriz von, *Macht und Ohnmacht: Erinnerungen eines alten Offiziers* (Stuttgart, 1953)

Fischer, Fritz, *Griff nach der Weltmacht: Die Kriegszielpolitik des kaiserlichen Deutschlands* (Düsseldorf, 1961)

Flechtheim, Ossip K., *Die Kommunistische Partei Deutschlands in der Weimarer Republik* (Offenbach/M., 1948)

Foertsch, Herrmann, *Schuld und Verhängnis: Die Fritsch-Krise im Frühjahr 1938 als Wendepunkt in der Geschichte der nationalsozialistischen Zeit* (Stuttgart, 1951)

Foreign Relations of the United States, Papers Relating to, edited by U. S. Department of State, 1932–33

Frank, Hans, *Im Angesicht des Galgens* (Munich, 1953)

Freytagh-Loringhoven, Axel Freiherr von, *Die deutschnationale Volkspartei* (Berlin, 1931)

Gengler, Ludwig F., *Die deutschen Monarchisten 1919–1925* (Erlangen, 1932)

Gessler, Otto, *Reichswehrpolitik in der Weimarer Zeit,* Kurt Sendtner, ed. (Stuttgart, 1958)

Goebbels, Josef, *Vom Kaiserhof zur Reichskanzlei: Eine historische Darstellung in Tagebuchblättern* (Munich, 1940)

——, *Wetterleuchten: Aufsätze aus der Kampfzeit* (Munich, 1939)

Goebbels Spricht: Reden aus Kampf und Sieg (Oldenburg, 1933)

Görlitz, Walter, *Hindenburg: Ein Lebensbild* (Bonn, 1953)

Gordon, Harold J., *The Reichswehr and the German Republic: 1919–1926* (Princeton, 1957)

Groener, Wilhelm, *Lebenserinnerungen: Jugend, Generalstab, Weltkrieg,* ed. by Friedrich Freiherr Hiller von Gaertringen (Göttingen, 1957)

Groener-Geyer, Dorothea, *General Groener: Soldat und Staatsmann* (Frankfurt/M., 1955)

Gründel, E. Günther, *Die Sendung der jungen Generation: Versuch einer umfassenden revolutionären Sinndeutung der Krise* (Munich, 1932)

Grzesinski, Albert C., *Inside Germany* (New York, 1939)

Haeften, Hans von, *Hindenburg und Ludendorff als Feldherren* (Berlin, 1937)

Hallgarten, George W. F., *Hitler, Reichswehr und Industrie: Zur Geschichte der Jahre 1918–1933* (Frankfurt/M., 1955)

Heiden, Konrad, *Der Fuehrer: Hitler's Rise to Power* (Boston, 1944)

Heilfron, Eduard, ed., *Die deutsche Nationalversammlung im Jahre 1919 und 1920* (Berlin, n.d.)

Heinz, Friedrich Wilhelm, *Die Nation greift an: Geschichte und Kritik des soldatischen Nationalismus* (Berlin, 1932)

Hertzman, Lewis, "The German National People's Party (DNVP.): 1918–1924," PhD. thesis, Harvard, 1954

Heydebreck, Peter von, *Wir Wehr-Wölfe: Erinnerungen eines Freikorps-Führers* (Leipzig, 1931)

Hiller, Kurt, *Köpfe und Tröpfe* (Hamburg and Stuttgart, 1950)

Hindenburg, Bernhard, *Paul von Hindenburg: Ein Lebensbild* (Berlin, 1915)

————, Gert von, *Paul von Hindenburg: Vom Kadetten zum Reichspräsidenten* (Leipzig, 1932)

————, Generalfeldmarschall [Paul] von, *Aus meinem Leben*, (Leipzig, 1920)

Hitler, Adolf, *Mein Kampf* (New York, 1941)

Hoegner, Wilhelm, *Der schwierige Aussenseiter: Erinnerungen, eines Abgeordneten, Emigranten und Ministerpräsidenten* (Munich, 1959)

————, *Die verratene Republik: Geschichte der deutschen Gegenrevolution* (Munich, 1958)

Hoffmann, Max, *Die Aufzeichnungen des Generalmajors Max Hoffmann*, ed. by Karl Friedrich Nowak (Berlin, 1929)

Horkenbach, Cuno, *Das Deutsche Reich von 1918 bis heute* (Berlin, 1932)

Hugenberg, Alfred, *Streiflichter aus Vergangenheit und Gegenwart* (Berlin, 1927)

International Military Tribunal, *Trial of Major War Criminals before the International Military Tribunal* (Nürnberg, 1947–49)

Jonas, Klaus W., *The Life of Crown Prince William* (Pittsburgh, 1961)

Jünger, Ernst, *Der Arbeiter: Herrschaft und Gestalt* (Hamburg, 1932)

Kaufmann, Walter H., *Monarchism in the Weimar Republic* (New York, 1953)

Keil, Wilhelm, *Erlebnisse eines Sozialdemokraten* (Stuttgart, 1947–48)

Kessler, Harry Graf, *Tagebücher 1918–1937* (Frankfurt/M., 1961)

Kleinau, Wilhelm, *Soldaten der Nation: Die geschichtliche Sendung des Stahlhelms* (Berlin, 1933)

Kordt, Erich, *Nicht aus den Akten: Die Wilhelmstrasse in Frieden und Krieg: Erlebnisse, Begegnungen und Eindrücke 1928–1945* (Stuttgart, 1950)

Krebs, Albert, *Tendenzen und Gestalten der NSDAP: Erinnerungen aus der Frühzeit der Partei* (Stuttgart, 1959)

Kruck, Alfred, *Geschichte des alldeutschen Verbandes: 1890–1939* (Wiesbaden, 1954)

Kühlmann, Richard von, *Erinnerungen* (Heidelberg, 1948)

Leber, Julius, *Ein Mann geht seinen Weg: Schriften, Reden und Briefe* (Berlin and Frankfurt/M., 1952)

Liebe, Werner, *Die DeutschnationaleVolkspartei 1918–1924* (Düsseldorf, 1950)

Litzmann, Karl, *Lebenserinnerungen* (Berlin, 1927–28)

Loebell, [Friedrich Wilhelm] von, ed., *Hindenburg: Was er uns Deutschen ist* (Berlin, 1927)

Lucas, Friedrich J., *Hindenburg als Reichspräsident.* Bonner Historische Forschungen, vol. XIV (Bonn, 1959)

Ludendorff, Erich, *Vom Feldherrn zum Weltrevolutionär und Wegbereiter Deutscher Volksschöpfung: Meine Lebenserinnerugen von 1919 bis 1925* (Munich, 1940); vol. II, *Von 1926 bis 1933* (Stuttgart, 1951)

———, *Meine Kriegserinnerungen 1914–1918* (Berlin, 1919)

Lüttwitz, Walther Freiherr von, *Im Kampf gegen die November-Revolution* (Berlin, 1934)

Luther, Hans, *Politiker ohne Partei* (Stuttgart, 1960)

Maercker, Georg, *Vom Kaiserheer zur Reichswehr* (Leipzig, 1921)

Mann, Rudolf, *Mit Ehrhardt durch Deutschland* (Berlin, 1921)

Manstein, Erich von, *Aus einem Soldatenleben 1887–1939* (Bonn, 1958)

Matthias, Erich, and Rudolf Morsey, eds., *Das Ende der Parteien 1933* (Düsseldorf, 1960)

Max von Baden, Prinz, *Erinnerungen und Dokumente* (Stuttgart, 1927)

Meinecke, Friedrich, *Die deutsche Katastrophe: Betrachtungen und Erinnerungen* (Wiesbaden, 1947)

———, *Strassburg, Freiburg, Berlin: 1901–1919* (Stuttgart, 1949)

Meissner, Hans Otto, and Harry Wilde, *Die Machtergreifung: Ein Bericht über die Technik des nationalsozialistischen Staatsstreichs* (Stuttgart, 1958)

———, Otto, *Staatssekretär unter Ebert-Hindenburg-Hitler: Der Schicksalsweg des deutschen Volkes von 1918–1945, wie ich ihn erlebte* (Hamburg, 1951)

Merton, Richard, *Erinnernwertes aus meinem Leben, das über das Persönliche herausgeht* (Frankfurt/M., 1955)

Metzsch, Horst von, *Hindenburg* (Leipzig, 1932)

Miller, Max, *Eugen Bolz: Staatsmann und Bekenner* (Stuttgart, 1951)

Morrow, Jan F. D., *The Peace Settlement in the German-Polish Borderlands* (Oxford and London, 1936)

Müller, Georg Alexander von, *Regierte der Kaiser? Kriegstagebücher, Aufzeichnungen und Briefe des Chefs des Marine-Kabinetts Admiral G. A. von Müller*, Walter Görlitz, ed. (Göttingen, 1959)

Nazi Conspiracy, see Office of U.S. Chief Counsel

Niekiesch, Ernst, *Gewagtes Leben* (Cologne-Berlin, 1958)

Niemann, Alfred, *Hindenburg: Ein Lebensbild* (Berlin, 1926)

——, *Revolution von oben, Umsturz von unten* (Berlin, 1928)

Noske, Gustav, *Erlebtes aus Aufstieg und Niedergang einer Demokratie* (Offenbach/M., 1947)

——, *Von Kiel bis Kapp: Zur Geschichte der deutschen Revolution* (Berlin, 1920)

Office of U.S. Chief Counsel for Prosecution of Axis Criminality, *Nazi Conspiracy and Aggression* (Washington, 1948)

Official German Documents Relating to the World War (New York, 1923)

Olden, Rudolf, *Hindenburg oder der Geist der preussischen Armee* (Paris, 1935)

Oldenburg-Januschau, Elard von, *Erinnerungen* (Berlin, 1936)

Papen, Franz von, *Der Wahrheit eine Gasse* (Munich, 1952)

Picker, Harry, *Hitlers Tischgespräche im Führer-Hauptquartier, 1941–1944*, Gerhard Ritter, ed. (Munich, 1951)

Prange, Gordon, W., ed., *Hitler's Words* (Washington, 1944)

Preller, Ludwig, *Sozialpolitik in der Weimarer Republik* (Stuttgart, 1949)

Preuss, Hugo, *Deutschlands Republikanische Reichsverfassung* (Berlin, 1923)

——, *Staat, Recht und Freiheit: Aus 40 Jahren deutscher Politik und Geschichte* (Tübingen, 1926)

Preussen contra Reich vor dem Staatsgerichtshof. Stenogrammbericht der Verhandlungen vor dem Staatsgerichtshof in Leipzig vom 10. bis 14. und 17. Oktober 1932 (Berlin, 1933)

Pünder, Hermann, *Politik in der Reichskanzlei: Aufzeichnungen aus den Jahren 1929–1932*, Thilo Vogelsang, ed. (Stuttgart, 1961)

Rabenau, Friedrich von, *Seeckt: Aus seinem Leben, 1918–1936* (Leipzig, 1940)

Rassow, Peter, ed., *Deutsche Geschichte im Überblick: Ein Handbuch* (Stuttgart, 1953)

Rauschning, Hermann, *Men of Chaos* (New York, 1942)

Rheinbaben, Werner Freiherr von, *Viermal Deutschland: Aus dem Erleben eines Seemanns, Diplomaten, Politikers 1895–1954* (Berlin, 1954)

Ribbentrop, Joachim von, *Zwischen London und Moskau: Erinnerungen und letzte Aufzeichnungen* (Leoni, 1953)

Ritter, Gerhard, *Carl Goerdeler und die deutsche Widerstandsbewegung* (Stuttgart, 1955)

———, *Europa und die deutsche Frage* (Munich, 1948)

Röhm, Ernst, *Die Geschichte eines Hochverräters* (Munich, 1928)

Roos, Hans, *Polen und Europa: Studien zur deutschen Aussenpolitik: 1931–1939* (Tübingen, 1957)

Rosenberg, Arthur, *Geschichte der deutschen Republik* (Karlsbad, 1935)

Rossbach, Gerhard, *Mein Weg durch die Zeit: Erinnerungen und Bekenntnisse* (Weilburg/Lahn, 1950)

Rüstow, Otto, *Ortsbestimmung der Gegenwart: Eine universalgeschichtliche Kulturkritik* (Erlenbach/Zurich, 1950–57)

Salomon, Ernst von, ed., *Das Buch vom deutschen Freikorpskämpfer* (Berlin, 1938)

Schemann, Ludwig, *Wolfgang Kapp und das Märzunternehmen vom Jahre 1920* (Munich and Berlin, 1937)

Scheringer, Richard, *Das grosse Los unter Soldaten, Bauern und Rebellen* (Hamburg, 1959)

Schiffer, Eugen, *Ein Leben für den Liberalismus* (Berlin-Grunewald, 1951)

Schlange-Schöningen, Hans, *Am Tage Danach* (Hamburg, 1946)

Schmidt-Hannover, Otto, *Umdenken oder Anarchie: Männer-Schicksale-Lehren* (Göttingen, 1959)

Schmidt-Pauli, Edgar von, *Hitlers Kampf um die Macht* (Berlin, 1933)

Schmitt, Carl, *Der Hüter der Verfassung* (Tübingen, 1931)

———, *Positionen und Begriffe im Kampf mit Weimar-Genf-Versailles: 1923–1939* (Hamburg, 1940)

———, *Verfassungsrechtliche Aufsätze aus den Jahren 1921–1954* (Berlin, 1958)

Schotte, Walther, *Die Regierung Papen-Schleicher-Gayl* (Leipzig, 1932)

Schreiber, Georg, *Brüning-Hitler-Schleicher: Das Zentrum in der Opposition* (Cologne, 1932)

Schüddekopf, Otto-Ernst, *Das Heer und die Republik: Quellen zur Politik des Reichswehrführung 1918 bis 1933* (Hanover and Frankfurt/M., 1955)

Schulenburg, Dieter von der, *Welt um Hindenburg: Hundert Gespräche mit Berufenen* (Berlin, 1935)

Schultze-Pfaelzer, Gerhard, *Hindenburg* (Leipzig and Zurich, 1930)

———, *Wie Hindenburg Reichspräsident wurde* (Berlin, 1925)

Schwend, Karl, *Bayern zwischen Monarchie und Diktatur* (Munich, 1954)

Schwerin von Krosigk, Lutz Graf, *Es geschah in Deutschland: Menschenbilder unseres Jahrhunderts* (Tübingen and Stuttgart, 1951)

Schwertfeger, Bernhard, *Kaiser und Kabinettschef: Nach eigenen Aufzeichnungen und dem Briefwechsel des Wirklichen Geheimen Rates Rudolf von Valentini* (Oldenburg, 1930)

——, *Rätsel um Deutschland: 1933 bis 1945* (Heidelberg, 1947)

Seraphim, Hans-Günther, *Das politische Tagebuch Alfred Rosenbergs aus den Jahren 1934–35 und 1939–40* (Göttingen, Berlin, Frankfurt/M., 1956)

Severing, Carl, *Mein Lebensweg* (Cologne, 1950)

Shirer, William L., *The Rise and Fall of the Third Reich: A History of Nazi Germany* (Greenwich, 1962)

Sozialdemokratischer Parteitag Magdeburg, 1929, *Protokoll* (Berlin, 1929)

Spartakus, *German Communists* (London, 1944)

Spengler, Oswald, *DerMensch und die Technik: Beitrag zu einer Philosophie des Lebens* (Munich, 1931)

Stadtler, Eduard, *Bahn frei für Hugenberg* (Berlin, 1930)

Stahlhelm, Der, *Stahlhelm-Handbuch*, Heinrich Hildebrandt and Walter Kettner, eds., 3rd and 4th eds. (Berlin, 1929 and 1931)

Stampfer, Friedrich, *Die vierzehn Jahre der ersten deutschen Republik* (Hamburg, 1953)

Stenographische Berichte der Verhandlungen des Deutschen Reichstages (Berlin, 1871–1944)

Stockhausen, Max von, *Sechs Jahre Reichskanzlei: Von Rapallo bis Locarno*, Walter Görlitz, ed. (Bonn, 1954)

Thaer, Albrecht von, *Generalstabsdienst an der Front und in der O.H.L.: Aus den Briefen und Tagebuchaufzeichnungen 1915–1919*, Siegfried A. Kaehler and Helmuth K. G. Rönnefarth, eds. (Göttingen, 1958)

Timm, Helga, *Die deutsche Sozialdemokratie und der Bruch der Grossen Koalition im März 1930* (Düsseldorf, 1953)

Tirpitz, Alfred von, *Erinnerungen* (Leipzig, 1919)

Troeltsch, Ernst, *Spektator-Briefe* (Tübingen, 1924)

U. S. Foreign Relations, see *Foreign Relations of the United States*

Urkunden der Obersten Heersleitung über ihre Tätigkeit 1916/18, Erich Ludendorff, ed. (Berlin, 1920)

Ursachen des deutschen Zusammenbruchs, Die, Das Werk des Untersuchungsausschusses, Ser. iv, vols. *i-iii* (Berlin, 1925)

Verhandlungen des Deutschen Reichstags, Stenographische Berichte der, 1925–33

Vogelsang, Thilo, *Reichswehr, Staat und NSDAP: Beiträge zur deutschen Geschichte 1930–1932* (Stuttgart, 1962)

Volkmann, E[rich] O[tto], *Revolution über Deutschland* (Oldenburg, 1930)

Wahrmund, Dr., *Gericht über Hugenberg* (Dillingen, 1932)

Waite, Robert G. L., *Vanguard of Nazism: The Free Corps Movement in Postwar Germany: 1918–1923* (Cambridge, 1952)

Weber, Marianne, *Max Weber: Ein Lebensbild* (Tübingen, 1926)

Weiss, Max, ed., *Der nationale Wille: Werden und Wirken der Deutschnationalen Volkspartei 1918–1928* (Leipzig, 1928)

Westarp, Kuno Graf von, *Das Ende der Monarchie am 9. November 1918*, ed. by Werner Conze (Stollhamm [Oldbg.] and Berlin, 1952)

Wheeler-Bennett, John W., *The Nemesis of Power: The German Army in Politics: 1918–1945* (New York and London, 1953)

———, *Wooden Titan: Hindenburg in Twenty Years of German History* (New York, 1936)

Widenmann, Wilhelm, *Marine-Attaché an der kaiserlich-deutschen Botschaft in London 1907–1912* (Göttingen, 1952)

Wilhelm II., Kaiser, *Ereignisse und Gestalten aus den Jahren 1878–1918* (Leipzig and Berlin, 1922)

Zechlin, Walter, *Pressechef bei Ebert, Hindenburg und Kopf* (Hanover, 1956)

ARTICLES

(only those cited more than once are listed)

Brecht, Arnold, "Die Auflösung der Weimarer Republik und die politische Wissenchaft," *Zeitschrift für Politik*, n.s., II (1955), 291–308.

Brüning, Heinrich, "Ein Brief," *Deutsche Rundschau*, LXX (1947), 1–22.

Castellan, Georges, "Von Schleicher, Von Papen et l'avènement de Hitler," *Cahiers d'histoire de la guerre*, I (1949), 25–37.

Conze, Werner, "Die Krise des Parteienstaates in Deutschland 1929–30," *Historische Zeitschrift*, CLXXVIII (1954), 47–83.

———, "Zum Sturz Brünings," *Vierteljahrshefte für Zeitgeschichte*, I (1953), 261–88.

Craig, Gordon A., "Briefe Schleichers an Groener," *Welt als Geschichte*, XI (1951), 122–33.

Deist, Wilhelm, "Brüning, Herriot, und die Abrüstungsgespräche von Bessinge 1932," *Vierteljahrshefte für Zeitgeschichte*, V (1957), 265–72.

Dorpalen, Andreas, "Empress Auguste Victoria and the Fall of the German Monarchy," *American Historical Review*, LVIII (1952), 17–38.

———, "Hitler—Twelve Years After," *Review of Politics*, XIX (1957), 486–506.

Eschenburg, Theodor, "Die Rolle der Persönlichkeit in der Krise der Weimarer Republik: Hindenburg, Brüning, Groener, Schleicher," *Vierteljahrshefte für Zeitgeschichte*, IX (1961), 1–29.

———, "Franz von Papen," *ibid.*, I (1953), 153–69.

Hammerstein, Kunrat Freiherr von, "Schleicher, Hammerstein und die Machtübernahme 1933," *Frankfurter Hefte*, XI (1956), 117–28, 163–76.

Hossbach, Friedrich, "Die Entwicklung des Oberbefehls über das Heer in Brandenburg, Preussen und im Deutschen Reich von 1655–1945, Pt. II, 1918–1945," *Jahrbuch der Albertus-Universität zu Königsberg/Pr.*, VIII (1958), 194–280.

Kleist-Schmenzin, Ewald von, "Die letzte Möglichkeit: Zur Ernennung Hitlers zum Reichskanzler am 30. Januar 1933," *Politische Studien*, X (1959), 89–92.

Matthias, Erich, "Hindenburg zwischen den Fronten: Zur Vorgeschichte der Reichspräsidentenwahlen von 1932," *Vierteljahrshefte für Zeitgeschichte*, VIII (1960), 75–84.

———, "Der Untergang der alten Sozialdemokratie 1933," *ibid.*, IV (1956), 250–86.

Morsey, Rudolf, "Hitler als braunschweigischer Regierungsrat," *ibid.*, VIII (1960), 419–48.

Petzold, Joachim, "Der Staatsstreich vom 20. Juli 1932 in Preussen," *Zeitschrift für Geschichtswissenschaft*, IV (1956), 1146–86.

Schoeps, Hans-Joachim, "Das letzte Vierteljahr," *Geschichte in Wissenschaft und Unterricht*, VII (1956), 465–75.

Vogelsang, Thilo, "Neue Dokumente zur Geschichte der Reichswehr 1930–1933," *Vierteljahrshefte für Zeitgeschichte*, II (1954), 397–436.

———, "Zur Politik Schleichers gegenüber der NSDAP," *ibid.*, VI (1958), 86–118.

INDEX